Second Edition

Antique Trader™

AMERICAN & EUROPEAN

Art
Pottery

PRICE GUIDE

Edited by Kyle Husfloen

Published by
Antique Trader Books, A Division of

**krause
publications**

**700 E. State Street • Iola, WI 54990-0001
Telephone: 715/445-2214
Web: www.krause.com**

Please call or write for our free catalog of publications.
our toll-free number to place an order or obtain a free catalog is
800-258-0929 or please use our regular business telephone, 715-445-2214.

Library of Congress Catalog Number: 2001097825
ISBN: 0-87349-405-9

Introduction

For thirty years, The Antique Trader has been publishing an antiques and collectibles price guide, always striving to present the most comprehensive and detailed coverage of this booming field. Our annual *Antiques & Collectibles Price Guide* has become a mainstay of the antiques marketplace, and today, Antique Trader Books, a division of Krause Publications, has expanded its role by publishing a range of more specialized pricing guides. Beginning in 1994, we released three new volumes dealing in-depth with popular collecting fields, including ceramics, American pressed glass and bottles and, American and European decorative and art glass. New editions of these references recently have been published, and our line of price guides continues to expand with books now available on country Americana, toys, jewelry and advertising items, as well as a newly updated *American & European Furniture Price Guide*. The volume you hold is a completely revised and updated guide to the popular collecting field of art pottery, a sequel to our first volume released in 1995.

Art pottery is a unique and highly specialized segment of the ceramics collecting field that we feel deserves a collecting and pricing guide of its own. What sets "art pottery" apart from all other collectible earthenwares, utilitarian pottery and porcelain is that pieces were originally crafted as works of art with no purpose other than to please the eye and gratify the senses, much as a fine painting might. In fact, fine hand-painting is one hallmark of some of the finest examples of art pottery; the pottery piece actually became a canvas for artistic expression.

The art pottery movement originally had its origins in Europe, especially in France, and its first presentation to the American public was made at the 1876 Centennial Exhibition in Philadelphia. It was here that American ceramists caught their first glimpse of the new and exciting wares being produced in France, as well as the exotic and unique ceramic wares from the Far East, most notably Japan. Within a few short years, the American art pottery movement was well established with the Rookwood Pottery in Cincinnati, Ohio, leading the way.

By the turn of the 20th century another cross-current of art was having a great affect on the American art pottery movement. The English Arts & Crafts and Aesthetic movements brought about a shift from the fussier forms and decorating of late Victorian art pottery to simpler, more naturalistic shapes and glazes. Firms such as Grueby and Teco offered simple, bold designs highlighted by rich glazes that were meant to complement the quiet restrained interiors of early 20th century Art & Crafts homes. The "Mission Oak" style in furniture was enhanced by a broad range of decorative accessories besides art pottery, and it remained a popular trend into the 1920s. It was the Great Depression of the 1930s that really sounded the death knell of art pottery. Labor and production costs had grown tremendously and made it difficult for more expensive handmade wares to compete with a flood of cheap, mass-produced ceramics from Europe and Japan. Only the well-heeled could afford "art for art's sake," and the majority of the American buying public was satisfied with bright and cheap pottery available at the local five-and-dime.

For the next thirty years, art pottery, as a collecting field, was practically non-existent. Only a handful of collectors were much interested in the finest examples of Rookwood and a few others. Finally, in the late 1960s, the market began to revive, thanks in part to the publication of important new reference books such as *The Book of Rookwood Pottery* by Herbert Peck (1968) and Lucile Henzke's *American Art Pottery* (1970). Today, more than thirty years later, the collecting of American and European art pottery is an important segment of the antiques marketplace with prime examples selling for many thousands of dollars. You might say *The Antique Trader Price Guide* and the art pottery market have grown up together. Today we're proud to present you with our expanded guide, a tribute to this exciting and diverse collecting field.

We have designed this volume to serve as more than just a guide to pricing. It is also a useful reference to art pottery collecting. We begin with an indepth history of the American art pottery movement written by noted Arts & Crafts and art pottery auctioneer/dealer, Don Treadway of Cincinnati, Ohio. We've followed this with a series of sketches highlighting typical shapes you will encounter in art pottery such as pitchers, bowls, and vases. Each pricing category we list begins with a brief introduction to that company's history, as well as a sketch of the mark or marks they may have used on their products. At the conclusion of our price listings we include a "Glossary of Terms" and several helpful Appendices.

We have drawn our prices, descriptions and illustrations from a number of sources, including all the major firms that specialize in the sale of fine art pottery, as well as from several authorities in specific lines of pottery. Our sincere thanks to them for their cooperation and assistance with this project.

It is hoped that all our readers will find the *American & European Art Pottery Price Guide, 2nd Edition,* a useful and easy-to-use guide to a fascinating and beautiful world of collecting. We're always interested in your comments and suggestions, and we make every effort to respond personally, so let us hear from you.

Kyle Husfloen, Editor

Photography Credits

Photographers who have contributed to this volume include:

Stanley L. Baker, Minneapolis, Minnesota; Donna Bruun, Galena, Illinois; Susan N. Cox, El Cajon, California; Susan Eberman, Bedford, Indiana; and Robert G. Jason-Ickes, Olympia, Washington.

For other photographs, artwork, data or permission to photograph in their shops, we sincerely express appreciation to the following auctioneers, galleries, museums, individuals and shops:

Christie's, New York, New York; Cincinnati Art Galleries, Cincinnati, Ohio; A Collector's Passion Shop, Olympia, Washington; DeFina Auctions, Austenburg, Ohio; William Doyle Galleries, New York, New York; DuMouchelles, Detroit, Michigan; John Fontaine Auction, Pittsfield, Massachusetts; Garth's Auctions, Inc., Delaware, Ohio; Green Valley Auctions, Mt. Crawford, Virginia; Jackson's Auctions, Cedar Falls, Iowa; Dave Rago, Lambertville, New Jersey; Skinner, Inc., Bolton, Massachusetts; Sotheby's, New York, New York; Temples Antiques, Eden Prairie, Minnesota; and The Don Treadway Gallery, Cincinnati, Ohio.

On The Cover: Left - A handsome Grueby Pottery vase with unusual narcissus decoration; Right - A Rookwood Standard glass ewer with silver overlay.

Special Contributors

Clarice Cliff -

Carole A. Berk
4918 Fairmont Ave.
Bethesda, MD 20814
(800) 382-2413 or (301) 656-0355
Fax: (301) 652-5859
e-mail: cab@caroleberk.com
http:.//www.caroleberk.com

Cowen -

Tim & Jamie Saloff
e-mail: tgsaloff@erie.net
http://www.erie.net/~jlsaloff

Frankoma -

Susan N. Cox
800 Murray Dr.
El Cajon, CA 92020
e-mail: antiqfever@aol.com

Gonder -

James & Carol Boshears
917 Hurl Dr.
Pittsburgh, PA 15236-3636
(412) 655-1380
e-mail: gondernut@aol.com

Owens -

Frank Hahn
P.O. Box 934
Lima, OH 45802-0934
(419) 225-3816 or (419) 222-3816
Fax: (419) 227-3816
e-mail: ggb@wcoil.com

Teplitz-Amphora -

Les & Irene Cohen
P.O. Box 17001
Pittsburgh, PA 15325-0001
(412) 793-0222 or (412) 795-3030
Fax: (412) 793-0222
e-mail: www.am4ah@hotbot.com

Torquay -

J. Wucherer
Transitions of Wales, Ltd.
P.O. Box 1441
Brookfield, WI 53008

The Evolution of the American Art Pottery Movement

by Don Treadway

After the introduction of European art pottery at the 1876 Centennial Exposition in Philadelphia, American ceramists developed numerous styles of decoration. Designs from the Victorian era and Aesthetic Movement gave way to those of the Arts & Crafts period which blended with Art Nouveau and eventually evolved into a modern decoration. Artistic merit reached its peak at the turn of the century.

The Limoges style, Haviland's trademark and named because it came from Limoges, France, was very influential. Serving as a backdrop for floral and scenic painting, the smeared and blended background colors were often found on broad and narrow forms utilized like canvasses. This style of artwork was not original to the French potters as exemplified by the paintings of Corot and others. Cincinnati potters like McLaughlin, T. J. Wheatley and numerous artists at Rookwood were the main proponents of this style in the United States. The New Jersey ceramic artist Charles Volkmar was the East Coast's principle purveyor of the Limoges style.

The pottery of William Grueby of Boston followed a distinctly different route than those influenced by the Philadelphia display. Grueby noted the work of French potters including Auguste Delaherche and Ernest Chaplet and by combining thrown forms with sculpted and applied work, offered the ultimate in Arts & Crafts pottery. Matt glazes, which he excelled at but didn't originate, covered most of his pots and his popular style was eventually copied by others.

The Northeast region of the United States had several pottery producers with a distinctive Arts & Crafts influence. Marblehead made primarily hand thrown and decorated ware often utilizing geometric and stylized designs with muted matt glazes. Single colored vases of various hues and shades were most common. Marblehead was in business for a short period of time but produced a consistent product

A fine example of Grueby Pottery, ca. 1900. They produced the best of Arts & Crafts ceramics.

A rare and important example of the Arts & Crafts ceramics produced by the Marblehead Pottery, ca. 1910.

A rare slip-decorated Marblehead vase.

that is quite popular today with Arts & Crafts collectors. The immediate area around Boston found several fine examples of Arts & Crafts ceramics in S.E.G., Paul Revere and Merrimac. All of these potteries are popular today but their work is in relatively short supply.

In the Midwest, Teco Pottery of Terra Cotta, Illinois was quite innovative in their production of pottery designed by architects. Radical new forms with organic, streamline and futuristic designs were covered mostly with matt glazes. The use of pierced bodies, cut-out and swirling applied handles was unlike anything American pottery companies had produced. As with Grueby, Teco made architectural work for outdoor and interior use and also found some of their designs to be imitated by others.

Teco Pottery, from the Chicago area, produced a wide range of architectural designs around the turn of the century. This paneled vase is especially rare.

A nice example of Newcomb College Pottery with their trademark Spanish moss and moonlight landscape, ca. 1915.

Further south in New Orleans, a school for women produced pottery with an Arts & Crafts flavor. Around 1895, Newcomb College offered painted and carved forms usually hand-thrown by men. Their earliest work was primarily covered with a clear high-glaze over locally inspired floral and landscape designs. Their trademark was a scene of moss-laden trees in front of a bright moon. Around 1910, Newcomb College began to almost exclusively produce matt glaze examples of these earlier designs. Production continued through the 1940s with the school eventually joining the established Tulane University located next door.

Combining bizarre forms with exceptional glazes, George Ohr created a pure American art form. These varied pieces date from around 1900.

George Ohr was another Southern ceramic artist who began his work in the 1880s. A true innovator with little or no influence from the European or Asian potters, Ohr produced wonderful pots of assorted size which blended wafer thin walls with original forms. His glazes were varied, from multicolored high gloss to one-color to volcanic textured matts, and covered shapes sometimes

A fine example of Art Nouveau design in American ceramics, this vase was created by the Van Briggle Pottery, ca. 1907.

simple, often tortured and almost always hand thrown. Ohr stopped making pots in 1909 and died in 1918 though over 6000 pieces of his work were kept in an attic until their dispersal in the 1970s.

At the turn of the century, Rookwood's Artus Van Briggle returned from his study abroad to introduce America's purest form of Art Nouveau ceramics. Before he left Cincinnati for this study, Artus had started to experiment with carved figures and floral subjects, a change from the Victorian style of portrait and floral painting found in Rookwood's Standard glaze examples. By the time he relocated to Colorado Springs to rehabilitate from a lung disorder, it became his main design approach. His carved forms were covered almost exclusively with matt glazes, the majority of which were single-colored. The period leading up to his death in 1904 found his ware to include the most supreme examples of Art Nouveau ceramics ever produced in this country. His work was also appreciated in Europe where he received numerous awards at international expositions. The Van Briggle Pottery continued production after Artus' death, making some of their finest examples of suspended glazes between 1907 and 1912. This was a matt glaze which seemed to have spots or groups of solid glaze suspended in a more translucent one. No American pottery could match Van Briggle's glazes at this time. After 1912, the company fell into the traps of commercialism, which sapped their creative efforts.

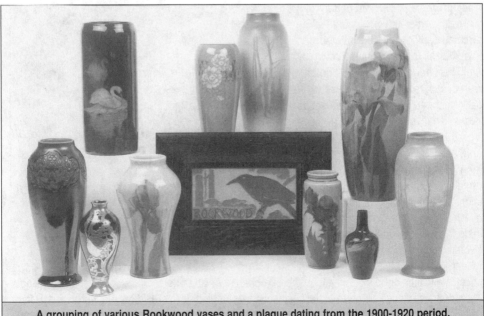

A grouping of various Rookwood vases and a plaque dating from the 1900-1920 period.

The most varied and successful ceramic of America's art pottery movement was Cincinnati's Rookwood Pottery. Beginning with the Limoges style seen at the Centennial, Rookwood employed different Victorian era and Aesthetic Movement influenced designs. These dark smeared glazes gave way to lighter bisque type finishes, heavily influenced by Japanese pottery. The 1890s found Rookwood experimenting with darker high glazes called "Standard Ware," which led to the accidental "Tiger Eye" glaze that won the award at the Paris Exposition in the late 1890s. Next, Rookwood began experimenting with translucent and tinted high glazes called "Iris," "Aerial Blue" and "Sea Green." These glazes covered examples

This vase featuring a combination of metal and pottery was executed for Rookwood by Kataro Shirayamadani around 1900.

Very rare early Roseville Rozane "Della Robbia" vase.

that ranged from Victorian to Aesthetic to Japonisme to Arts & Crafts or Art Nouveau design. Such variety was an attempt to remain economically successful; Rookwood strove to produce something for everyone. The turn of the century found Rookwood producing carved and painted matts though problems of production and expense created only limited success. The introduction of the Vellum glaze in the early 1900s made for a boost in sales and became Rookwood's new claim to fame. Floral and landscape designs in this glaze were perfected over the next 20-30 years. The result was a flawless union of clay and glaze and uncrazed pieces unlike anything else in the ceramic world. The 1920s through 1940s found Rookwood producing porcelains with a variety of glazes and subject matters. Modern designs were popular and were best portrayed by Jens Jensen and W. E. Hentschel. Also throughout the century, Rookwood produced a nationally successful line of garden and architectural pottery. The company closed and was moved to Mississippi in the late 1960s but never returned to the success they once enjoyed.

Two fine examples of Weller's fine Sicard line.

Cincinnati was the center of a good deal of pottery production prior to the turn of the century. Companies like Wheatley, Dallas, Cincinnati Art Pottery, Losanti, Coultry and Rettig-Valentien produced the Limoges and European Faience style of decoration until it fell out of vogue. Wheatley

A variety of American art pottery pieces, including Weller and Roseville.

continued by making gardenware and Arts & Crafts pots after designs by Teco and Grueby. Ohio was undoubtedly the largest pottery producing area with commercially successful companies like Roseville, Weller, Clewell and Cowan turning out quality work for many years. Roseville and Weller's early years saw innovative new designs that ran the gamut from Victorian to Art Nouveau to Arts & Crafts. Later, they both turned to mass-produced wares that kept them financially solvent. Clewell produced a unique pottery covered with copper that usually carried a colorful patina of orange, blue and green color. They utilized pottery shapes made by other companies and sometimes created inlaid or etched work. Cowan made some of this country's finest Art Deco pottery. The work of Cowan artist Viktor Schreckengost is very highly regarded and includes probably the best example of Art Pottery made in America, the "Jazz" bowl.

Art Pottery thrived on the West Coast as well, particularly in California. Arequipa, under the direction of Frederick Rhead, produced Arts & Crafts pots using the squeezebag decoration that made for a simple handcrafted design. Lured by a commission from Ellen Browning Scripps to paint California's wild flowers, Albert and Anna Valentien left Rookwood for San Diego where they later opened the Valentien Pottery. Their production of Arts & Crafts ceramics with sculptural designs and matt finishes turned out to be relatively unsuccessful. A Zanesville type of art pottery was produced by the Stockton Art Pottery, one of the earliest of California companies. Roblin Pottery was produced in the Bay area for a short period of time in the early 1900s. Frederick Rhead traveled from various companies throughout the United States but produced some of his best work in Santa Barbara at Rhead Pottery and was a gold medal winner at the San Diego Exposition of 1915.

The effects of depressions and world wars were reflected in the dissolution of numerous pottery companies in the United States. As expenses grew, commercialism crept into the workplace and stifled the artistic development so necessary for true art pottery lovers' discerning eye. Faience tiles, garden pottery and flower vases ruled the cash registers while artists starved and moved about the country. The 1940s through the 1960s saw a big decline in the production of art pottery though a new wave of artists was discovered and is finding success up to the present day.

Perhaps the purest example of Art Deco design in American ceramics is the "Jazz" bowl designed by Viktor Schreckengost for Cowan Pottery.

Looking back at the production of art pottery in the United States should give all collectors and appreciators of art an insight into the marvel of art pottery production around the turn of the century. With extremely limited experience and knowledge of ceramic production, this group of artists produced the finest objects imaginable. This is reason enough for the undying desirability of this work to modern day collectors. While not totally original in concept and design, this period of ceramics was indeed special.

About the Author

Don Treadway is co-owner of the Treadway Gallery Inc., Cincinnati, Ohio.

Treadway Gallery Inc. has been in business for over two decades and maintains an active gallery and auction business. Their specialties include: Arts & Crafts period furniture and decorative arts, American art pottery, American and European art glass, Tiffany, Handel and other quality lamps, 1950s/Modern furniture and decorative arts, Italian and Scandinavian glass.

Treadway Gallery Inc. holds several 20th Century auctions each year with the John Toomey Gallery of Oak Park, IL. In addition to these 20th Century auctions, the Treadway Gallery Inc. sells Rookwood and American art pottery at their annual "Important Rookwood Auction" in Cincinnati, and "Pottery Lovers Auction" in Zanesville, Ohio.

Don Treadway is a member of several national and international associations. These include: National Antique Dealers Association, American Art Pottery Association, International Society of Appraisers, and American Ceramic Arts Society.

TYPICAL ART POTTERY SHAPES
Bowls

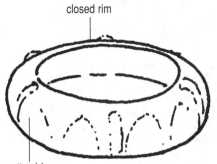

closed rim

squatty sides

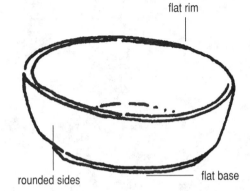

flat rim

rounded sides

flat base

Bowl
Squatty rounded sides with a wide closed rim.

Bowl
Wide flat base and short rounded sides with a flat rim.

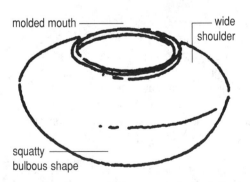

molded mouth

wide shoulder

squatty bulbous shape

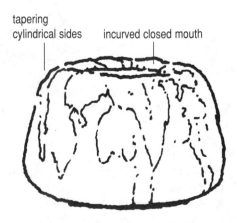

tapering cylindrical sides

incurved closed mouth

Bowl-vase
Squatty bulbous shape with a wide rounded shoulder and small molded mouth.

Bowl-vase
Deep slightly tapering cylindrical sides with incurved closed mouth.

TYPICAL ART POTTERY SHAPES
Ewers & Pitchers

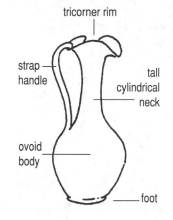

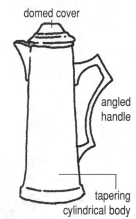

Ewer

Squatty bulbous base tapering to a flaring cylindrical neck with tricorner rim; long strap handle.

Ewer

Ovoid footed body tapering to a tall cylindrical neck with tricorner rim; long strap handle.

Pitcher

Tankard with domed cover; tall tapering cylindrical body; angled handle.

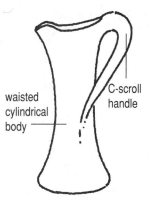

Pitcher

Squatty bulbous ovoid body tapering to a short cylindrical neck with pinched spout; C-scroll handle.

Pitcher

Tankard with swelled cylindrical body tapering to a slightly flaring rim with pinched spout; small C-form handle.

Pitcher

Tankard with waisted cylindrical body; long C-scroll handle.

TYPICAL ART POTTERY SHAPES
Vases

stick neck

spherical body

footring

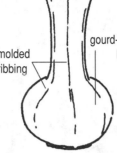

swelled rim

molded ribbing

gourd-form body

trumpet-form body

swelled foot

Vase

Bottle-form; spherical footed body tapering to a tall stick neck.

Vase

Gourd-form with swelled rim and bulbous base; molded ribbing up the sides.

Vase

Trumpet-form with swelled foot.

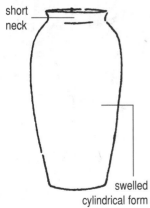

short neck

swelled cylindrical form

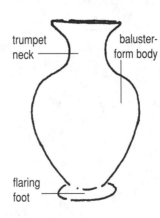

trumpet neck

baluster-form body

flaring foot

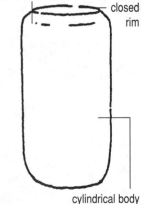

rounded shoulder

closed rim

cylindrical body

Vase

Swelled cylindrical form with short flaring neck.

Vase

Baluster-form body with trumpet neck and flaring foot.

Vase

Cylindrical body with rounded shoulder and base and 'closed' rim.

TYPICAL ART POTTERY SHAPES
Vases

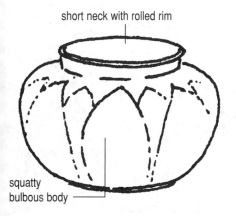

short neck with rolled rim

squatty
bulbous body

Vase
Squatty bulbous body with a short wide neck with rolled rim.

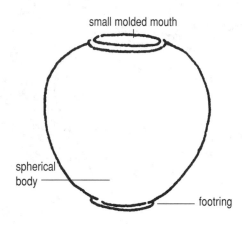

small molded mouth

spherical body

footring

Vase
Spherical body with small molded mouth and narrow footring.

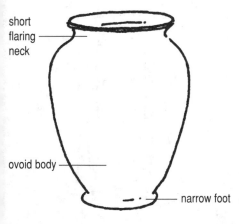

short flaring neck

ovoid body

narrow foot

Vase
Ovoid footed body with a short flaring neck.

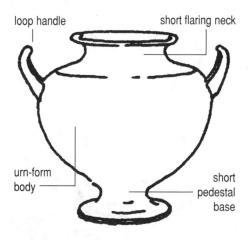

loop handle

short flaring neck

urn-form body

short pedestal base

Vase
Urn-form raised on a short pedestal base; short flaring neck and loop handles at the shoulder.

TYPICAL ART POTTERY SHAPES
Vases

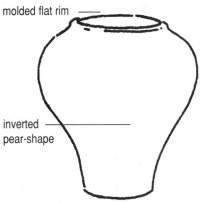

molded flat rim

inverted pear-shape

Vase

Inverted pear shape with molded flat rim.

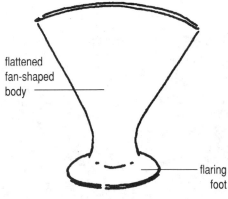

flattened fan-shaped body

flaring foot

Vase

Fan-shaped flattened body on a flaring foot.

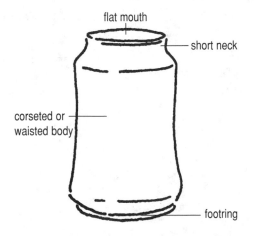

flat mouth

short neck

corseted or waisted body

footring

Vase

Corseted or waisted cylindrical body on a narrow footring; short tapering neck with flat mouth.

short neck

buttress handle

conical body

Vase

Conical body with flaring neck; four heavy buttress handles down the sides.

Arequipa

AP

Arequipa Marks

Dr. Philip King Brown established The Arequipa Sanitorium in Fairfax, California, in the early years of the 20th century. In 1911 he set up a pottery at the facility as therapy for his female tuberculosis patients since he had been impressed with the success of the similar Marblehead pottery in Massachusetts.

The first art director was the noted ceramics designer Frederick H. Rhead who had earlier been art director at the Roseville Pottery.

In 1913 the pottery was separated from the medical facility and incorporated as The Arequipa Potteries. Later that year Rhead and his wife, Agnes, one of the pottery instructors, left Arequipa and Albert L. Solon took over as the pottery director. The corporation was dissolved in 1915 and the pottery closed in 1918 although the sanitorium remained in operation until 1957.

Bowl, 6 1/2" d., 2 1/4" h., wide flat bottomed form w/squatty bulbous incurved sides w/a wide flat mouth, embossed w/eucalyptus branches under a dark matte green & blue glaze, stamped mark, incised "KH - 11" **$880**

Vase, 3 1/4" h., 3" d., miniature, simple wide ovoid form w/closed rim, decorated in squeeze-bag w/stylized leaves in a fine organic matte green w/small red circles, against a matte yellow ground, incised mark "?27 - Arequipa - California - 1912" (ILLUS. center with larger vases) **6,325**

Rare Miniature Arequipa Vase

Vase, 3 1/2" h., 2 1/2" d., miniature, simple ovoid body w/closed rim, decorated in squeezebag w/a rim band of holly leaves & red berries against a matte, mottled greenish blue ground, by Frederick Rhead, white & brown glaze mark (ILLUS.) **6,325**

Early Arequipa Vases

Variety of Arequipa Vases

Early Arequipa Squatty Vase

Vase, 4 1/4" h., 7" d., footed wide squatty bulbous form w/the wide shoulder tapering to a short flared neck, enamel-decorated w/a plant w/white berries against a semi-matte greyish blue ground, rare early mark, incised "AP - 1911" (ILLUS.) **660**

Vase, 4 3/4" h., 3 1/4" d., swelled cylindrical body w/a narrow rounded shoulder to the short, wide neck, smooth matte leathery dark green glaze, incised "3 - Arequipa - Cal." (ILLUS. right with 7" squeezebag vase) **358**

Vase, 6" h., 3 1/4" d., simple ovoid body w/wide incurved rim, decorated w/incised abstract leaves in a flowing, glossy dark blue against a turquoise ground, restoration to small inner rim chip, Frederick Rhead period, signed in ink "Arequipa California - 1912 - 463 - 4" (ILLUS. center with 7" squeezebag vase) **2,420**

Vase, 6 1/4" h., 5" d., bulbous shouldered ovoid body w/a wide flat rim, decorated in squeeze-bag w/stylized yellow flowers over large, bright green leaves w/blue veins, from the Frederick Rhead period, blue ink mark "Arequipa - California," ca. 1911-12, minute glaze nick on raised point (ILLUS. left with miniature vase) **9,350**

Vase, 7" h., 4" d., simple ovoid body decorated in squeeze-bag w/stylized leaves in brown on a matte feathered green ground, a dark green drip down from each leaf, fine glaze nicks on rim, Rhead period, ca. 1912, blue enamel mark (ILLUS. left with two other vases) **3,740**

Vase, 7 1/2" h., 4" d., bulbous base below tapering cylindrical sides, decorated in squeeze-bag w/a wreath of heart-shaped leaves under a fine leathery pea green matte glaze, Frederick Rhead period, marked in ink "Arequipa California 1913 - 2123 - 123" (ILLUS. right with miniature vase) **1,980**

Vase, 11" h., 6 1/4" d., baluster-form w/a short flaring neck, hand-cut w/large upright bell-shaped flowers around the sides & small daisy-like blossomheads around the neck, clear brown glossy glaze, die-stamped mark & "403-22 -WI" **770**

Boch Freres

Boch Freres Mark

The Belgian firm, founded in 1841 and still in production, first produced stoneware art pottery of mediocre quality, attempting to upgrade their wares through the years. In 1907, Charles Catteau became the art director of the pottery and slowly the influence of his work was absorbed by the artisans surrounding him. All through the 1920s wares were decorated in distinctive Art Deco designs and

Boch Freres Charger & Vases

are now eagerly sought along with the hand-thrown gourd-form vessels coated with earthtone glazes that were produced during the same time. Almost all Boch Freres pottery is marked, but the finest wares also carry the signature of Charles Catteau in addition to the pottery mark.

Box, cov., low rectangular form w/rounded corners, decorated w/crossed bands of stylized flowers in turquoise, sapphire blue, yellow & black on a crackled ivory ground, brass hinge & border, base w/circular stamp "Boch F La Louviere," brass stamped "France," ca. 1920s, 4 x 5 1/2", 1 1/2" h. **$288**

Charger, large round form w/flanged rim, decorated in the center w/a large grazing antelope, the border band w/round geometric devices, in sapphire blue, turquoise green & black on a crackled ivory ground, marked "D943 - Ch. Catteau - 22p C K," ca. 1920s, 14 1/2" d. (ILLUS. center) **1,150**

Inkstand, stoneware, white w/h.p. blue floral sprigs & bands, rectangular dished base w/rounded corners & serpentine sides centering a rectangular upright block fitted in the top w/an open inkwell & covered sander, 19th c., 8 3/4" l. **110**

Lamp base, bulbous ovoid body tapering to a short flared neck w/lamp fittings, inscribed w/stylized vines & fruits descending from the shoulder in shades of yellow, brown & blue against an oatmeal ground, glossy glaze, marked "Keramis - Made in Belgium," ca. 1928, crazing, 24 1/4" h. (ILLUS.) **316**

Vase, 7" h., bulbous ovoid body tapering sharply to a small neck, decorated w/a repeating floral design of yellow blossoms, bluish green leaves & burgundy berries on branches, on a sapphire blue ground, separated by bands of blue, green, orange & black, circular stamp mark "Boch F La Louvière," ca. 1920s (crazing) **920**

Vase, 8 1/2" h., ovoid body tapering to a tall slender & slightly tapering neck, decorated w/three stylized flowers & leaves in a basket w/double swag, repeated in three sections, divided by border of multiple ovals, in yellow, orange, sapphire blue & light blue on an ivory crackled ground, circular mark "Boch F La Louvière," Belgium, ca. 1920s **403**

Two Boch Freres Vases

Vase, 8 3/4" h., footed ovoid body w/the swelled shoulder tapering to a wide, short flared neck, decorated overall w/large stylized yellow blossoms & leafy vines in yellow, turquoise, sapphire blue, orange & pale green w/blue borders on a crackled ivory ground, partial stamp "Keramis - Made in Belgium - 31," ca. 1920s (ILLUS. right) **690**

Boch Freres Pottery Lamp Base

Vase, 8 3/4" h., low footring supporting a wide bulbous cylindrical body w/a wide rounded shoulder centering a thick molded rim band, decorated w/a wide center band featuring a continuous row of large upright stylized penguin-like birds in black against a yellow ground, black borders at the base & top, signed & stamped "Ch. Catteau - Keramis - Made in Belgium - Grès Keramis - 1059 C," ca. 1928-29......... **6,600**

Vase, 9" h., wide ovoid body w/a wide rounded shoulder centering a short cylidnrical neck, decorated w/a continous band of large grazing antelope in sapphire blue, turquoise, bluish green & black on a crackled ivory ground, marked "Boch F La Louvière - D943 - 13 - 1291," ca. 1925 (ILLUS. left with flower-decorated vase) **1,265**

Vase, 9 1/4" h., very wide bulbous ovoid body tapering to a short cylindrical neck, decorated w/symmetrical stylized floral reserve in sapphire blue, bluish green & orange on a crackled white ground, stamped "Keramis - Made in Belguim - D60 - R V Larouche Belge - 1293," ca. 1920s **805**

Vase, 9 1/2" h., bulbous ovoid body tapering to a tiny cylindrical neck, decorated w/a white central band painted w/large stylized black bears against a white band w/narrower brown upper & lower bands trimmed w/black banding & zigzag lines, signed & stamped "Ch. Catteau - D. 1487 - Keramis - Made in Belgium - Grès Keramis - 996 C" **5,100**

Vase, 10 1/2" h., flat-bottomed wide ovoid body w/a small cupped neck, decorated w/large brown & black flying bats against a greenish grey sky w/dark grey clouds, design 1378, signed & impressed "D. 1378 - Ch. Catteau - Keramis - Made in Belgium - Grès Keramis - 1053 C.," ca. 1929 (drilled) **3,840**

Boch Freres Vase with Sunbursts

Vase, 10 1/2" h., simple ovoid body tapering to a flat molded mouth, decorated w/four large repeating stylized swirled sunburst flowers in sections separated by a wavy line w/alternating oval dots, in turquoise, yellow & sapphire blue on an ivory crack-

led ground, turquoise border bands, stamped & signed "Boch F La Louvière - D889 - CT - K 899," ca. 1920s **575**

Vase, 10 1/2" h., simple ovoid form w/a footring & rim ring, decorated w/wide color vertical bands of stylized tulips & flowers w/leaves in yellow, sapphire blue, green & brown on an ivory crackled ground, sapphire blue bands, marked "Keramis - Made in Belgium - D2779 - 9 - 899," ca. 1920s **690**

Vase, 11" h., simple ovoid form tapering to a small flat mouth, decorated around the sides w/large black flamingos running the full length of the sides against a mottled yellowish green ground, signed & stamped "C.Catteau - D. 979 - Keramis - Made in Belgium - Grès Keramis - 987," ca. 1925 .... **9,000**

Vase, 11 1/8" h., ovoid body tapering slightly to a wide short neck w/molded rim, the upper portion decorated w/a wide band featuring large stylized oblong black & white bird-like creatures against a mottled dark grey ground, a wide lower band w/a lattice design in light brown & black, a narrow crosshatch band around the rim, signed & stamped "Ch. Catteau - D. 1025 - Keramis - Made in Belgium - 967 - Grès Keramis," ca. 1925 .... **10,200**

Vase, 12" h., large wide ovoid body tapering gently to a wide, short cylindrical neck, decorated w/stylized flowers & leaves in pinks, sapphire blue, yellow, brown & grey on a pale yellow ground, bordered w/a ring of small blossoms & leaves & sapphire blue bands, marked "Keramis - Made in Belgium - 2243 - 909," ca. 1920s (crazing) **805**

Vase, 12 1/8" h., wide ovoid body tapering to a short rolled neck, decorated w/a wide central band featuring a continuous design of large stylized black & white owls against a tan ground, white dash & solid thin bands above & below the center band, black bands around the top & base, signed & stamped "Ch. Catteau - D. 1060 - Keramis - Made in Belgium - Grès Keramis - 914 C," ca. 1925 .... **5,760**

Catteau-designed Boch Freres Vase

Vase, 12 1/4" h., ovoid body tapering slightly to a short, flaring molded neck, decorated w/a wide center band w/a continuous row of large white stylized bird-like creatures against a black ground w/thin brown lines, white upper & lower bands w/thin brown scalloped designs, signed & stamped "Ch. Catteau - D 1026 - Boch Frs. - La Louvière - Made in Belgium - Fabrication Belgique - Grès Keramis - 911 C," ca. 1925 (ILLUS.) **6,600**

Vase, 12 1/2" h., stoneware, tall simple ovoid form w/a thick short rolled neck, a wide central band decorated in black & cream w/a row of large stylized birds, the upper & lower bands in black w/cream fishscale designs, designed by Charles Catteau, signed "Ch. Catteau - D. 1026A" & incised "Gres Keramis" w/wolf mark & "Keramis - Made in Belgium," original retailer's sticker, ca. 1925 .... **3,300**

Boch Freres Antelope Vase

Vase, 13 1/2" h., wide ovoid body tapering to a wide cupped neck, decorated w/a wide central band of stylized antelope in dark blue & black grazing on blue & green grass at the bottom & w/leaves & geometric designs around the top, against a crackle-glazed white ground, signed & stamped "Ch. Catteau - Boch Frs. - La Louvière - Made in Belgium - Fabrication Belgique - 911," ca. 1924 (ILLUS.) **6,000**

Vase, 15 5/8" h., bulbous ovoid body w/short incurved cylindrical rim, decorated w/colorful repeating design of yellow, orange fruit w/brown leaves & light blue ribbon streamers on a white crackle glaze, the rim a darker blue decorated w/a band of orange fruit & brown leaves, marked w/Boch Freres, La Louviere ink stamp & "D 745 DK" & "951 K" **990**

Vase, 16" h., tall baluster-form w/a cylindrical short neck, decorated w/a wide band of gazelle in dark blue, purple & black among stylized foliage against a creamy white ground, the neck & lower body w/overall geometric ring designs in matching colors, designed by Charles Catteau, signed "Ch. Catteau - D. 943,"

stamped "Keramis - Made in Belgium - 24," inscribed "762" **3,300**

Vase, 19 1/4" h., large ovoid form w/a heavy rolled rim, the body painted w/large stylized exotic birds among large rounded blossoms & leafy branches w/berries in greenish yellow on a dark brown ground w/black base & rim bands, designed by Jules-Ernest Chaput, signec, ca. 1930 .... **12,000**

Large Boch Freres Floral Vase

Vase, 19 1/2" h., large, tall ovoid form tapering to a tiny neck w/deeply rolled rim, wide vertical bands of stylized creamy white blossom clusters & green scrolls alternating w/narrow creamy white zigzag stripes, stamped & signed "Ch. Catteau - D. 1003 - Boch Frs. - La Louvière - Made in Belgium - Frabication Belgique - Grès Keramis - 961 - V.," ca. 1925 (ILLUS.) **6,000**

Vases, 11 1/2" h., ovoid body tapering to a short cylindrical neck w/molded rim, decorated w/two large stylized standing birds w/extended wings among leafy vines, in sapphire blue, blue, bluish green & pale green on an ivory crackled ground, striped border bands, stamped "Keramis - Made in Belgium - D4507," ca. 1920s, pr. (ILLUS. left & right with charger) **920**

Clarice Cliff Designs

FANTASQUE
HANDPAINTED
Bizarre
by
Clarice Cliff
NEWPORT POTTERY
ENGLAND

Clarice Cliff Mark

Clarice Cliff was a designer for A. J. Wilkinson, Ltd., Royal Staffordshire Pottery, Burslem, England when they acquired the adjoining Newport Pottery Company whose warehouses were filled with undecorated bowls and vases. About 1925 her flair with the Art Deco style was incorporated into designs appropriately named "Bizarre" and "Fan-

tasque" and the warehouse stockpile was deco-
rated in vivid colors. These hand-painted
earthenwares, all bearing the printed signature of
designer Clarice Cliff, were produced until World
War II and are now finding enormous favor with col-
lectors.

Note: *Reproductions of the Clarice Cliff "Bizarre"*
marking have been appearing on the market
recently.

Bone dish, Tonquin patt., black......................... **$30**
Bowl, 5" d., Tonquin patt.. **5**
Bowl, 6 1/4" d., octagonal flanged rim on
the rounded body, Woodland patt., stylized landscape w/trees in orange, green,
black, blue, purple & yellow, marked............. **550**
Bowl, 6 1/2" d., 3" h., "Bizarre" ware, footed
deep slightly flaring sides, Crocus patt.,
the sides divided into two horizontal
bands of color w/a band of small crocus
blossoms along the upper half, in orange,
blue, purple & green, stamped mark............. **550**

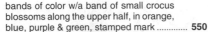

Caprice Pattern Bowl & Vase

Bowl, 8" d., "Bizarre" ware, Caprice patt.,
stylized landscape w/hills, arch & tall

trees in lavender, blue, yellow, green &
brown (ILLUS. left) **2,800**
Bowl, 8" d., 3 3/4" h., "Bizarre" ware, deep
gently rounded sides tapering to a footring, Original Bizarre patt., a wide band of
blocks & triangles around the upper half
in blue, orange, ivory & purple, purple
band around the bottom section, marked..... **650**
Bowl, 8" d., 4 1/4" h., "Bizarre" ware,
octagonal, h.p. w/Original Bizarre patt.,
large crudely painted bands of maroon,
dark orange & dark blue diamonds above
an ochre base band, ink mark..................... **1,100**
Bowl, 9" d., deep rounded sides, the upper
half w/a wide band in polychrome featuring large stylized cottages w/pointed orange roofs beneath arching trees, lime
green banding, marked................................. **800**
Bowl, 9 1/2" d., 4 1/2" h., orange, green &
blue h.p. poppies **600**
Butter dish, cov., "Bizarre" ware, Crocus
patt., a wide shallow base w/low, upright
sides fitted w/a shallow, flat-sided cover
w/a slightly domed top & flat button finial,
the top decorated w/purple, blue & orange blossoms on an ivory ground,
marked, 4" d., 2 3/4" h. **550**
Butter dish, cov., "Bizarre" ware, short wide
cylindrical body w/an inset cover w/large
button finial, Secrets patt., decorated w/a
stylized landscape in shades of green,
yellow & brown w/red-roofed houses on a
cream ground, marked, 4" d., 2 5/8" h.
(ILLUS. left) **550**
Candleholders, figural, modeled as a
kneeling woman w/her arms raised high
holding the candle socket modeled as a
basket of flowers, My Garden patt., orange dress & polychrome trim, marked,
7 1/4" h., facing pr. **575**

A Variety of Clarice Cliff Patterns

Various Clarice Cliff Items

Candleholders, Fantasque line, cylindrical form w/flared base & rim, Melon patt., decorated w/a band of overlapping fruit in predominantly orange glaze w/yellow, bluish green & brown outline, stamped on base "Hand Painted Fantasque by Clarice Cliff Wilkinson Ltd. England," ca. 1930, minor glaze nicks, two small firing cracks to inside rim of one, 3 1/4" h., pr. (ILLUS. bottom of previous page, front) **1,380**
Candlestick, loop-handled, Tonquin patt., red **30**

Clarice Cliff Figural Centerpiece

Centerpiece, "Bizarre" ware, model of a stylized Viking longboat, raised on trestle supports & w/a frog insert, glazed in orange, yellow, brown & black on a cream ground, printed factory marks, ca. 1925, restored, 15 3/4" l., 9 5/8" h., 2 pcs. (ILLUS.) **1,500**

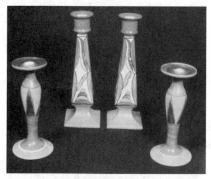

Two Pairs of Clarice Cliff Candlesticks

Candlesticks, slender baluster-form shaft above a disk foot & w/a wide flattened rim, painted w/bold geometric designs in blue, orange & green, Delecia Citrus patt., brightly painted fruits on a cream ground pr. (ILLUS. left & right).................... **2,500**
Candlesticks, squared pedestal foot supporting a tall square tapering shaft & cylindrical socket w/flared rim, decorated in bold geometric designs in orange, cream, green, blue & yellow, pr. (ILLUS. center) **2,900**

Rare Crest Pattern Charger

Delecia Citrus Cracker Jar & Vases

Charger, large round dished form, Crest patt., three large Japanese-style crests in gold, blue, rust red, black & green on a mottled green ground (ILLUS.) **12,000**

Coffee service: cov. coffeepot, creamer, open sugar bowl, five cake plates & six cups & saucers; Ravel patt., creamer & sugar w/pointed conical bodies supported by buttress legs, other serving pieces w/flaring cylindrical bodies, marked, coffeepot 6" h., the set **1,100**

Condiment set: two jars w/silver-plated lids & a small open bowl fitted in a silver-plated frame w/a looped center handle; each piece h.p. w/stylized red & blue flowers on an ivory ground, marked, tray 4 1/2 x 5", the set (small chip on one piece) **523**

Cracker jar, cov., "Bizarre" ware, Blue Chintz patt., stylized blue, green & pink blossom forms w/blue border band (ILLUS. center w/plate) **1,800**

Cracker jar, cov., "Bizarre" ware, bulbous barrel shape w/large side knobs to support the arched woven wicker bail handle, wide flat mouth w/a slightly domed cover centered by a large ball finial, Gayday patt., decorated w/a wide band of large stylized flowers in orange, rust, amethyst, blue & green above a lower band in orange on a cream ground, the cover w/an orange finial & yellow band, 5 7/8" d., 6 1/4" h. (ILLUS. right w/butter dish) **975**

Cracker jar, cov., "Bizarre" ware, squatty kettle-form w/side knobs supporting the swing bail handle, Delecia Citrus patt. (ILLUS. right) **1,400**

Cup, "Bizarre" ware, tall slightly tapering cylindrical form w/D-form handle, Chintz patt., painted in orange, brown & black, stamped factory mark & gilt Lawley's stamp, ca. 1932, 3 5/8" h. **460**

Cup & saucer, "Bizarre" ware, Autumn Crocus patt., Athens shape **300**

"Bizarre" Demitasse Set

Demitasse set: cov. coffeepot, six demitasse cups & saucers, creamer & open sugar bowl; "Bizarre" ware, Fantasque patt., decorated w/a stylized tree on one side, the other w/stylized hollyhocks, small chips to one saucer, 15 pcs. (ILLUS. of part) **3,200**

Demitasse set: cov. cylindrical coffeepot, creamer, open sugar bowl & six cylindrical demitasse cups & saucers; Honeyglaze, each body in deep orange, the angled handles in black & dark green, all marked, coffeepot 6" d., 6 1/4" h., the set (chip inside pot cover, minor flake on sugar bowl) **3,400**

Dinner service: four dinner plates, thirteen luncheon plates, fifteen soup bowls, eight fruit plates, seven appetizer plates, four dessert plates, seven cups & saucers, cov. sugar, creamer & serving bowl; Biarritz patt., the square plates w/deep rounded wells, the creamer & sugar w/upright flattened round shapes, each decorated w/concentric bands in black, maroon, taupe, gold & yellow on a cream ground, ca. 1929, marked, the set **1,150**

Dinner set: service for six w/8" d., 9" d. & 10" d. plates, three oval platters, two cov. serving dishes & one pitcher; "Bizarre" ware, stepped geometric border design in orange, blue & black against an ivory ground, all marked, the set **1,200**

Figures "Bizarre" ware, flat cut-outs, comprising two groups of musicians & two groups of dancing couples, all highly stylized & glazed in reddish orange, yellow, lime green, cream & black, printed factory marks, ca. 1925, 5 5/8 to 7" h., 4 pcs. . **29,000**

Gravy boat & underplate, Tonquin patt., black, 2 pcs.. **40**

Jam jar, cov., cylindrical body, Melon patt., decorated w/a band of overlapping fruit, predominantly orange w/yellow, blue & green w/brown outline, ca. 1930, restoration to rim & side, marked, 4" h. (ILLUS. top right w/candleholders) **690**

Jam pot, cov., Blue Firs patt., flat-sided round form on small log feet, domed cover w/flat round knob, stylized landscape w/trees, marked, 4 1/4" h. **900**

Canterberry Bells Pattern Jar

Jar, cov., "Bizarre" ware, a sharply tapering conical base supported on four squared buttress feet & w/a sharply inward tapering shoulder supporting the conical cover w/four small buttress tabs at the top, Canterberry Bells patt., mottled brown rim & shoulder over a stylized floral band in orange, shades of green, blue, amethyst & mottled yellow on a cream ground, 6" d., 8 1/8" h. (ILLUS.) **1,300**

Jardiniere, "Fantasque" line, Melon patt., Dover shape, deep cylindrical sides on three small tab feet, decorated w/Cubist-style fruits in orange, yellow, blue, green & amber against a cream ground, orange base & rim bands, marked, 6 1/4" d., 6 1/4" h. (minor inside paint wear) **1,900**

Lemonade set: 8" h. tankard pitcher & four cylindrical tumblers; each decorated in an abstract geometric pattern in orange, blue, purple, green & yellow, marked, the set... **1,100**

Pitcher, 5 1/8" h., "Fantasque" line, squared base w/flattened spherical sides, Autumn (Balloon Trees) patt. in blue, yellow, green, orange, black & purple, stamped on base "Registration Applied For Fantasque Hand Painted Bizarre by Clarice Cliff Newport Pottery England," ca. 1931, minor glaze bubbles & nicks (ILLUS. center right w/candleholders) **920**

Pitcher, 5 3/4" h., "Fantasque" line, Melon patt., wide conical body w/solid triangular handle, orange & thin black bands flanking a wide central band of stylized melons in yellow, blue, green & orange, marked, ca. 1930 (tiny glaze nicks at rim & base, faint scratch in lower orange band)... **875**

Pitcher, 6 3/8" h., "Fantasque" line, footed ovoid octagonal form w/large D-form handle, Alpine patt., decorated w/trees & house in shades of orange & black w/wide border bands, marked on the base, ca. 1930 (minor glaze flakes)........... **1,725**

Pitcher, 6 7/8" h., "Bizarre" ware, flaring cylindrical body w/a wide rim & wide arched spout opposite an angled handle, Secrets patt., decorated w/a stylized landscape in shades of green, yellow & brown w/a red-roofed house on a cream ground, stamped mark................................... **900**

Pitcher, 7" h., 6" d., jug-type, "Bizarre" ware, Lotus shape, Coral Firs patt., wide ovoid body w/a wide flat rim, heavy applied loop handle, decorated w/a wide landscape band in brown, orange, yellow, brown & grey on an ivory ground, marked **1,200**

Pitcher, 7" h., 7" d., "Bizarre" ware, tapering cylindrical body w/flat rim & wide pointed spout, flattened angled handle from rim to base, Sliced Fruit patt., wide band of abstract fruit in yellow, orange & red, stamped mark **1,800**

Pitcher, 7 1/2" h., 7 1/4" d., "Bizarre" ware, My Garden patt., bulbous base below a wide cylindrical body flaring slightly at the rim, an arched bumpy branch handle in mottled purple w/long sprigs of molded green leaves at the base on the all-black matte-glazed body, ink mark (small repaired chip on handle) **413**

Pitcher, 9 3/4" h., 7 3/4" d., jug-type, "Bizarre" ware, Isis shape, Summerhouse patt., decorated w/trees & gazebos in yellow, green, purple, red & blue against an ivory ground, marked.............................. **3,900**

Pitcher, 10" h., 7 1/2" d., "Bizarre" ware, ringed ovoid body tapering to a flat, round mouth, rounded C-form loop handle, Secrets patt., stylized landscape scene in yellow, green & blue, stamped mark... **1,400**

Pitcher, 10" h., 7 1/2" d., "Bizarre" ware, Viscaria patt., ringed ovoid body tapering to a flat rim w/pinched spout, heavy rounded C-form handle, large stylized blossoms in blue, yellow & brown, stamped mark **900**

Pitcher, 11 1/2" h., 8 3/4" d., "Bizarre" ware, wide ringed ovoid body tapering to a wide flat round mouth, rounded C-form handle, Area patt., wide central band of stylized florals in blue, red, yellow, purple, green & black, stamped mark **1,050**

Lotus Pitcher in Delecia Citrus Pattern

Pitcher, 12" h., "Bizarre" ware, Lotus shape, ringed ovoid body tapering to a wide cylindrical neck, heavy loop handle, Delecia Citrus patt., large stylized red, yellow & orange fruits around the top w/green leaves & streaky green on a cream ground (ILLUS.) **2,200**

Pitcher, 12" h., jug-type, "Bizarre" ware, Trees & House patt., ovoid w/molded narrow rings, decorated w/wide bands of orange & black flanking a wide central band w/green-roofed houses & black & orange trees, marked, ca. 1930 .... **1,265**

Lotus Pitcher with Sunrise Pattern

Pitcher, 12" h., jug-type w/ovoid body w/overall fine molded banding, Lotus shape, Sunrise patt., decorated in bright yellow & orange, marked (ILLUS.).............. **2,800**

Plate, 7 3/4" d., Broth patt., predominantly orange w/bubbles & orange, purple & blue cobwebs (few glaze scratches).............. **230**

Plate, 8" d., "Bizarre" ware, Blue Chintz patt., stylized blue, green & pink blossom forms w/blue border band (ILLUS. left) **600**

Plate, 8 3/4" d., "Bizarre" ware, Secrets patt., stylized central landscape scene w/banded borders in greens, yellow & orange, stamped mark (minor paint wear)....... **600**

Plate, 9" d., "Bizarre" ware, Blue Chintz patt., decorated w/stylized flowers in green, blue & pink against an ivory ground, marked... **650**

Blue Chintz Pattern Pieces

Plate, 9" d., "Fantasque" line, h.p. Melon patt., a wide band of stylized fruit in yellow, orange, red, blue & green w/an orange center circle & a narrow orange rim band, ink mark (minor wear) **775**

Plate, 9 3/4" d., "Bizarre" ware, Forest Glen patt., decorated in the center w/a landscape w/cottage in green, pale blue, orange, brown & black under a marbleized streaky sky in shades of red, brown & grey on a cream ground, impressed "10/35" (ILLUS. in center w/butter dish)........ **600**

Plate, 9 3/4" d., Forest Glen patt., a stylized cottage in a woodland scene in orange, ivory & green, die-stamped "Clarice Cliff - Newport Pottery - England"......................... **950**

Plate, 10" d., "Bizarre" ware, Pansies Delicia patt., decorated w/vivid blue, yellow & rose pansies w/yellow, rose & purple centers on pale & dark green leaves against a blue, green, cocoa, brown & yellow opaque drip glaze background, marked "Pansies - Bizarre by Clarice Cliff - Hand painted - England" & impressed "83" (minor wear) **121**

Plate, 10" d., "Fantasque" line, Autumn (Balloon Trees) patt. w/blue, yellow, green & purple trees & orange striped border bands, base stamped "Fantasque Hand Painted Bizarre by Clarice Cliff Newport Pottery England" (ILLUS. center left w/candleholders) **1,725**

Plate, 10 3/4" d., rounded w/four double-lobe protrusions around the sides, Sunrise patt., colorful center stylized sunrise design banded in orange & green, marked **900**

Plate, dinner, Tonquin patt., lavender................. **28**

Sauceboat & undertray, Tonquin patt., green, 2 pcs... **29**

Shaker, "Bizarre" ware, sharply pointed conical form, Trees and House (Alpine) patt., decorated w/orange & black borders & trees, green rooftop & grass, factory stamp on base, ca. 1930, 5 3/4" h. (minor glaze nicks, hairline in base) **1,380**

Sugar shaker, Autumn patt., sharply pointed conical form w/rows of small holes pierced around the top, decorated in pastel autumn colors, marked, 5 1/2" h. **1,200**

Sugar shaker, "Bizarre" ware, Bonjour shape, a flattened upright oval w/tiny feet across the base, Nasturium patt., stylized orange, red & yellow blossoms & pale green leaves, white at top & burnt orange at the bottom, ink mark, 1 3/4" w., 5" h. **550**

Sugar shaker, "Bizarre" ware, Crocus patt., sharply pointed conical form, decorated w/blue, purple & orange crocus flowers, marked, ca. 1930, 5 5/8" h. (chips on base) **460**

Sugar shaker, "Bizarre" ware, flattened egg-shaped body set on two tiny log-form feet, Crocus patt., banded body w/a central row of stylized crocus blossoms, in yellow, blue, orange & purple, stamped mark, 2 1/2" w., 5" h. **750**

Sugar shaker, "Bizarre" ware, small footring under slender tapering ovoid body w/rounded top, Viscaria patt., stylized blossom decoration in yellow, green & brown, stamped mark, 2 3/4" d., 4 3/4" h. **850**

Tea for two set: cov. small teapot, creamer, open sugar, two cups & saucers & two small plates; Banded patt., Bonjour shape, brown & green bands bordering the cream body, the set (ILLUS.) **1,800**

Teapot, cov., "Bizarre" ware, inverted conical form w/angled handle & spout, glazed in shades of orange, yellow & black, stamped mark on base, ca. 1932, 4 1/4" h. (minor glaze flakes, small spout chip) **2,185**

Tumbler, Sunray patt., conical form, polychrome decoration of a stylized sun, orange banding, marked, 3" h. **600**

Vase, 5 1/4" h., "Bizarre" ware, Shape No. 341, squatty bulbous chalice-form, Delecia Citrus patt., bright fruits on a creamy ground (ILLUS. left w/cracker jar) **900**

Vase, 6 1/4" h., 3 1/4" d., "Fantasque" line, Shape No. 196, Trees and House patt., a cylindrical body w/a widely flaring & rolled rim, decorated w/a wide central landscape band in black, orange & green against an ivory ground, marked **1,100**

Clarice Cliff "Fantasque" Vase

Vase, 7" h., 4 1/2" h., "Fantasque" ware, slightly tapering cylindrical body w/a closed rim & thick footring, decorated w/a stylized landscape in shades of blue, green, yellow & rose on an ivory ground, marked (ILLUS.) **770**

Vase, 7 1/2" h., 5 1/2" d., "Bizarre" ware, Inspiration patt., decorated in mottled blues, greens & purples, stamped mark **950**

Vase, 8" h., "Bizarre" ware, Isis shape, Caprice patt., stylized landscape w/hills, arch & tall trees in lavender, blue, yellow, green & brown (ILLUS. right w/bowl).......... **3,800**

Vase, 8" h., "Bizarre" ware, Nasturtium patt., footed ovoid body w/a flaring rolled rim, decorated w/vivid orange, red & yellow blossoms w/black, red, yellow & green leaves atop a mottled caramel & tan ground against a white background, marked "Nasturtium - Bizarre by Clarice Cliff - Hand painted - England" **900**

Vase, 8" h., "Bizarre" ware, Shape No. 358, bulbous ovoid lower body tapering to a heavily ringed tapering neck, Blue Chintz patt., stylized blue, green & pink blossom forms w/blue border band (ILLUS. right w/plate)... **2,800**

Vase, 8" h., "Bizarre" ware, Shape No. 362, ovoid upper body above a heavy ringed & waisted base, Delecia Citrus patt., brightly painted fruits on a cream ground (ILLUS. center w/cracker jar)...................... **1,200**

Banded Pattern Bonjour Shape Set

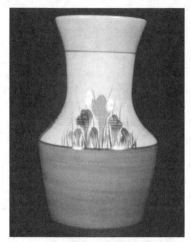

Crocus Pattern Vase

Vase, 8" h., "Bizarre" ware, Shape No. 386, swelled cylindrical base below the angled shoulder & tall gently flaring neck, Crocus patt., a yellow rim band & brown bottom section below a cluster of colorful crocus blossoms on a cream ground (ILLUS.) **1,500**

Vase, 9" h., 4 1/2" d., "Bizarre" ware, baluster-shaped w/a short, wide slightly flaring neck, decorated on the upper half w/a wide band of triangles alternating w/quadrilateral blocks in blue, yellow & purple on an orange ground, Shape No. 14D, marked **2,000-2,225**

Vase, 9" h., 4 3/4" d., "Bizarre" ware, baluster-shaped, Original Bizarre patt., a wide middle band of multicolored triangles flanked by a dark blue rim band & yellow & orange base bands, No. 264, ink mark (minor wear) **2,500**

Vase, 9 1/2" h., 6 1/2" d., "Bizarre" ware, Isis shape, ovoid body tapering to a wide, flat rim, decorated in the Melon patt., bold stylized abstract fruits in dark red, blue, orange, green & yellow around the middle flanked by wide dark orange bands, ink mark **3,200**

Vase, 10 7/8" h., "Bizarre" ware, My Garden patt., cylindrical form tapering to flared foot decorated w/h.p. relief-molded orange & yellow flowers & black leaves on golden mushroom ground, shape No. 664, Wilkinson, Ltd. **650**

Vase, 11 3/4" h., 10" d., "Bizarre" ware, Lotus shape, Geometric patt., urn-form, handled, decorated w/a wide maroon base band & wide green neck band flanking a wide central band of triangular devices in a row in cream, purple, blue, maroon & green, blue & cream rim bands & cream handles, marked **2,900**

Vase, 12 1/4" h., gently flaring conical body on a wide round foot, molded in bold relief w/green & yellow budgie birds on a leafy branch against a light blue shaded to cream ground **410**

Clarice Cliff Crocus Vase

Vases, 8" h., "Bizarre" ware, footed ovoid body w/flared rim, Crocus patt., orange, blue & purple crocuses, green, brown & yellow bands, small glaze chip, marked, pr. (ILLUS. of one) **690**

Clewell Wares

Clewell Wares Mark

Though Charles W. Clewell of Canton, Ohio, didn't operate a pottery, he is responsible for a category of fine art pottery through his development of a unique metal coating placed on pottery blanks obtained from Owens, Weller and others. By encasing objects in a thin metal shell, he produced copper- and bronze-finished ceramics. Later experiments led him to chemically treat the metal coating to attain the bluish green patinated effect associated with copper and bronze. Although he produced metal-coated pottery from 1902 until the mid-1950s, Clewell's production was quite limited for he felt no one else could competently recreate his artwork and, therefore, operated a small shop with little help.

Vase, 3 3/8" h., bulbous body w/short molded rim, brown patina on upper half w/crusty green patina below, marked "Clewell" (minor scuffs) **$252**

Vase, 4 5/8" h., bulbous ovoid shouldered body tapering to cylindrical neck w/flaring rim, green over brown patina, base incised "Clewell 466" (patina polished away in small spots about the shoulder) **224**

Vase, 5 1/4" h., 4 1/4" d., ovoid egg-shaped body w/a wide flat mouth, raised on three small peg feet, fine verdigris & bronze patina, incised "Clewell - 411-2-6" **550**

Vase, 5 1/2" h., 7 1/2" d., footed squatty bulbous body, the wide shoulder tapering to a cylindrical neck w/slightly flaring rim flanked by loop handles, rich deep orange to verdigris patina, etched mark **880**

A Variety of Copper-clad Clewell Vases

Vase, 5 1/2" h., 7" d., copper-clad, squatty bulbous body tapering to a short cylindrical neck w/slightly flaring rim, loop handles from center of body to rim, incised "Clewell - 408-2-6," normal wear to fine bronze to verdigris patina, tight lines in copper on shoulder (ILLUS. lower left).......... **788**

Small Clewell Vase

Vase, 6" h., simple ovoid body w/molded rim, original green, blue & orange patina, signed "Clewell 320-24" (ILLUS.)................ **2,200**

Vase, 6" h., 7" w., footed squatty bulbous oblong body tapering to a short flared neck w/integral handles from the rim to the shoulders, fine verdigris & bronze patina, incised "Clewell - 408-2-6".................. **1,540**

Vase, 6 1/4" h., 3 1/2" d., simple ovoid body w/molded rim, copper-clad w/fine verdigris to bronze patina, some patination flakes to rim, incised "Clewell - 321 - 24" (ILLUS. lower center) **619**

Small Slender Clewell Vase

Vase, 6 1/2" h., a wide round base tapering to a slender waisted body, deep red patina w/pale green patina band around the base, small glaze chips around base (ILLUS.)... **287**

Vase, 6 1/2" h., 4" d., simple ovoid form, fine verdigris & bronze patina, incised "Clewell - 32142"... **715**

Vase, 7" h., footed bulbous ovoid body w/a narrow shoulder & wide flaring rim, verdigris & dark bronze patina, incised "Clewell" **1,760**

Clewell Vase with Shiny Patina

Vase, 7" h., simple ovoid form tapering to a small flat mouth, overall shiny coppery patina, light scratches & wear, signed (ILLUS.) **374**

Clewell Vase with Original Patina

Vase, 7 1/4" h., round foot below the bulbous lower body tapering to tall trumpet-form sides, even dark bronze original patina, signed (ILLUS.) **287**

Vase, 7 1/2" h., 3 1/2" d., footed bulbous base w/trumpet form neck, copper-clad w/verdigris & bronze patina, incised "Clewell - 290-2-6" (ILLUS. upper left) **675**

Clewell Vase with Shaded Patina

Vase, 7 1/2" h., 3 1/2" d., ovoid body w/the rounded shoulder centering a small flaring neck, dark green verdigris shaded to

dark reddish bronze patina, incised "Clewell - 351 - 215" (ILLUS.) **1,725**

Clewell Vase with Dark Green Patina

Vase, 7 1/2" h., 3 3/4" d., ovoid body w/the rounded shoulder centering a small flaring neck, overall shaded dark green to lighter green verdigris patina, couple of small patina flakes near base, incised "Clewell - 351- 6" (ILLUS.) **920**

Clewell Vase No. 463

Vase, 8 1/2" h., broad-shouldered tapering ovoid body w/a small, short rolled neck, No. 463, some surface glaze flaws & flaking (ILLUS.) **431**

Ovoid Clewell Base

Vase, 8 1/2" h., 5" d., simple ovoid form tapering to a flat rim, deep reddish bronze & verdigris patina, pea-sized colored spot near base, incised "Clewell - 60-215" (ILLUS.) **978**

Vase, 9" h., 4 1/2" d., tall slender tapering urn-form body w/a flattened shoulder centering a short rolled neck flanked by small angled handles, bronze & verdigris patina, incised "C.W. Clewell - 520-220" (few patina chips on base) **1,125**

Rare Clewell Vase

Vase, 9" h., urn-shaped body w/flaring rim flanked by small angled handles from shoulder to rim, rich verdigris patina, etched mark (ILLUS.).................................... **1,210**

Unusual Clewell Vase

Vase, 9 1/2" h., 4" d., tapering cylindrical body raised on a flaring footed pedestal base, decorated w/embossed Egyptian designs under a rich brown patina, probably on an Owens Pottery blank, unmarked (ILLUS.).. **495**

Clewell Vase No. 305-6

Vase, 10" h., tall baluster-form body, fine bronzed patina, No. 305-6, signed (ILLUS.).. **862**
Vase, 11" h., 7 3/4" d., copper-clad wide slightly flaring cylindrical body w/a narrow angled shoulder to the wide closed rim, unusual striated gold, green & copper patina, minor ceramic loss inside rim, incised "Clewell" (ILLUS. far right) **1,392**
Vase, 11" h., simple tall ovoid body w/a rounded shoulder centered by a short

rolled neck, original orange to green to blue patina, incised "Clewell 272-2-6" **1,430**
Vase, 11 1/2" h., slender ovoid body w/a short flaring neck, original drippy orange, green & blue patina, signed "Clewell 302-2-6".. **1,430**
Vase, 11 1/4" h., 8" d., large slightly flaring cylindrical body w/a narrow angled shoulder to the wide closed rim, crisp verdigris & bronze patina, incised "Clewell - 485-215".. **1,650**
Vase, 11 1/4" h., 8 1/2" d., a large gently flaring cylindrical body w/a wide angled shoulder centering a low squatty neck, verdigris finish, signed **2,760**
Vase, 14 1/2" h., 6 1/4" d., tall baluster-form copper-clad body w/flared rim on the short cylindrical neck, bronze to verdigris patina, small flakes to verdigris & some splits to copper on neck, incised "Clewell - 378 - 26" (ILLUS. top center) **2,588**
Vase, 14 1/2" h., footed ovoid body tapering to a cylindrical neck w/flat rim, covered in a rich orange to green patina, etched mark.. **1,980**
Vase, 17" h., floor-type, shouldered ovoid body tapering to a short wide cylindrical neck, deep green patina, etched mark....... **1,540**
Vase, 17" h., wide bulbous ovoid body w/a narrow shoulder to the wide, short cylindrical neck w/flaring rim, original orange, brown, green & blue patina, signed "Clewell 460-26" **9,350**
Vase, 19" h., tall footed baluster-form body w/widely flared rim, original orange, green & blue patina, signed "Clewell 430-2-6"... **6,600**

Clifton Pottery

William A. Long, founder of the Lonhuda Pottery, joined Fred Tschirner, a chemist, to found the Clifton Art Pottery in Newark, New Jersey in 1905. Crystal Patina was their first art pottery line and featured a subdued pale green crystalline glaze later also made in shades of yellow and tan. In 1906 they introduced their Indian Ware line based on the pottery made by American Indians. Other lines which they produced include Tirrube and Robin's-egg Blue. Floor and wall tiles became the focus of the production after 1911 and by 1914 the firm's name had changed to Clifton Porcelain Tile Company, which better reflected their production.

Clifton Pottery Humidor

Humidor, cov., Indian Ware, cylindrical w/inset cover w/large knob handle, dark brown ground w/black stylized geometric designs, two chips at rim (ILLUS.) **$109**

Pitcher, 7" d., wide squatty bulbous body tapering to a wide slightly rolled rim w/low arched spout, D-form loop handle, cream ground incised & painted w/stylized geometric black flying birds **176**

Vase, 6" h., wide bulbous tapering ovoid body w/a small cylindrical neck w/flared rim, bold Greek key-style Native American designs in deep brick red outlined in cream against a black ground, incised mark **275**

Clifton Native American-style Vase

Vase, 9 1/2" h., Native American form vessel w/a wide squatty bulbous base centered by a wide cylindrical neck, incised & painted w/geometric designs in black, cream, tan & dark brown, incised mark (ILLUS.) **330**

Vase, 9 1/2" h., 4 1/2" d., ovoid form tapering to a short cylindrical neck, Crystal Pa-

tina, mottled creamy white & greenish yellow glaze, incised "Clifton - 158" **385**

Cowan

Cowan Marks

R. Guy Cowan opened his first pottery studio in 1912 in Lakewood, Ohio. The pottery operated almost continuously, with the exception of a break during the war, at various locations in the Cleveland area until it was forced to close in 1931 due to financial difficulties.

Many of this century's finest artists began with Cowan and its associate, the Cleveland School of Art. This fine art pottery, particularly the designer pieces, are highly sought after by collectors.

Many people are unaware that it was due to R. Guy Cowan's perseverance and tireless work that art pottery is today considered an art form and found in many art museums.

Ashtray, model of a ram, green, designed by Elizabeth Eckhardt, 5 1/4" l., 3 1/2" h. (ILLUS. lower left with ashtray/nut dish) **$250**

Cowan Ashtrays, Flower Frogs & Vase

Variety of Cowan Animal Pieces

Ashtray, three section base w/figural leaping gazelle & foliage on edge, Oriental Red glaze, designed by Waylande Gregory, 5 3/4" h. **400**

Ashtray/nut dish, model of a chick, green glaze, Shape No. 768, 3 1/2" h. (ILLUS. bottom center) **70**

Book end, model of a stylized horse, back legs raised in kicking position, black, designed by Waylande Gregory, Shape No. E-1, 9" h. (ILLUS. top center) **900**

Book ends, figural, model of a fish, Oriental Red glaze, Shape No. 863, 4 5/8" h., pr. **750**

Book ends, figural, a nude kneeling boy & nude kneeling girl, each on oblong bases, creamy white glaze, designed by Frank N. Wilcox, Shape No. 519, Marks 8 & 9, ca. 1925, 6 1/2" h., pr. (ILLUS. top right & lower left with horse book end) **610**

Book ends, figural, model of a unicorn, front legs raised on relief-molded foliage base, orange glaze, designed by Waylande Gregory, Shape No. 961, mark No. 8, 7" h., pr. (ILLUS. left) **800**

Book ends, figural, model of a ram, black, thick rectangular base w/slanted top, Shape No. E-3, designed by Waylande Gregory, 7 1/2" h., pr..................................... **2,500**

Book ends, figural, a little girl standing wearing a sunbonnet & full ruffled dress, on a thick rectangular base, ivory semi-matte glaze, Shape No. 521, impressed mark & "Z," ca. 1925, 4" w., 7 1/4" h., pr....... **550**

Bowl, miniature, 2" d., footed, flared body, Shape No. 514, mark No. 5, orange lustre **45**

Bowl, w/drip, 3 x 9 1/2", blue lustre finish, Shape No. 701-A... **80**

Bowl, 10" d., 2 1/2" h., Egyptian blue, Shape No. B-12 .... **75**

Bowl, 2 1/4 x 10 1/4", blue pearl finish **140**

Bowl, 3 x 10 x 11 1/2", leaf design, ivory & green, designed by Waylande Gregory **75**

Bowl, 3 x 9 1/4 x 12 1/4", copper crystal glaze, Shape No. B-785-A **150**

Bowl, 3 x 6 x 12 1/2" oblong, caramel w/light green glaze, Shape No. 683................ **50**

Bowl, 3 x 8 1/2 x 16 1/4", footed shallow form, flaring scalloped sides & rim, down-curved side handles, ivory exterior w/blue interior glaze, Shape No. 743-B **120**

Bowl-vase, green & gold, Shape No. B-4, 11"... **300**

Bust, "Colonial Head," stylized angular bust portrait w/long wavy hair, on a rectangular plinth, overall peach crackled glaze, by Waylande Gregory, circular mark, 7" w., 14" h. (ILLUS. at right) **3,656**

Buttons, decorated w/various zodiac designs, by Paul Bogatay, 50 pcs. **500**

Candelabrum, "Pavlova," porcelain, two-light, Art Deco style, a footed squatty tapering central dish issuing at each side a stylized hand holding an upturned cornucopia-form candle socket, the center fitted w/a figure of a nude female dancer standing on one leg w/her other leg raised, her torso arched over & holding a long swirled drapery, Special Ivory glaze, stamped mark, 10" l., 7" h. (chip under rim of one bobeche) **248**

Cowan Bust and Vases

Candleholders, Etruscan, Oriental Red
glaze, Shape No. S-6, 1 3/4" h., pr. **60**
Candleholders, footed, designed by R. G.
Cowan, ivory, Shape No. 811, 2 3/8" h.,
pr. **50**
Candleholders, blue lustre finish, Shape
No. 528, 3 1/2" h., pr. **35**
Candleholders, semi-circular wave design,
white glaze, Shape No. 751, 4 3/4" h., pr. **90**

Candlestick, flared base below twisted column, blossom-form cup, green & orange
drip glaze, Shape No. 625-A, 7 3/4" h.
(ILLUS. far right) **50**
Candlestick, figural, Byzantine figure
flanked by angels, golden yellow glaze,
designed by R.G. Cowan, 9 1/4" h.
(ILLUS. left) **350**

Various Cowan Pieces

Byzantine Angel Candlesticks

Candlestick, figural, Byzantine figure flanked by angels, salmon glaze, designed by R.G. Cowan, 9 1/4" h. (ILLUS. right).. **400**

Cowan Figural Nude Candlestick

Candlestick, two-light, large figural nude standing w/head tilted & holding a swirling drapery, flanked by blossom-form candle sockets supported by scrolled leaves at the base, matte ivory glaze, designed by R.G. Cowan, Shape No. 745, 7 1/2" w., 9 3/4" h. (ILLUS.)............. **1,000-1,300**

Candlestick/bud vase, tapering cylindrical shape w/flared foot & rim, blue lustre, Shape 530-A, 7 1/2" h....................................... **80**

Candlestick/bud vase, tapering cylindrical shape w/flared foot & rim, rainbow blue finish, Shape 530-A, 7 1/2" h. **50**

Candlesticks, curled form, royal blue, 1 1/2" h., pr. **45**

Candlesticks, figural grape handles, ivory glaze, 4" h., pr. **50**

Candlesticks, w/loop handle, green, Shape No. 781, 4" h., pr.. **40**

Candlesticks, figural sea horse w/flared base, green, Shape No. 716, 4 3/8" h., pr. **45**

Candlesticks, "The Girl Reserve," designed by R. G. Cowan, medium blue, Shape No. 671, 5 1/2" h., pr. **300**

Candlesticks, model of a marlin on waveform base, verde green, designed by Waylande Gregory, 8" h., pr. **2,000**

Schreckengost-designed Charger

Charger, round, decorated in the center w/a large stylized leaping horse & rider surrounded by smaller figures of stylized dogs, birds, horse & flowers w/greenery, glossy glaze w/multicolored animals in light shades of blue, yellow, gree & brown on an oatmeal-colored ground, green scallop inner border, designed by Viktor Schreckengost, ca. 1930s, crazing, 11 1/2" d. (ILLUS.) **978**

Charger, "Polo" plate, incised scene w/polo players & flowers under a blazing sun, covered in a rare glossy brown & cafe-au-lait glaze, designed by Victor Schreckengost, mark Nos. 8 & 9, Shape No. X-48, impressed "V.S. - Cowan," 11 1/4" d. (grinding chips to retaining ring).. **770**

Charger, wall plaque, yellow, 11 1/4" d............. **150**

Charger, octagonal, hand-decorated by Thelma Frazier Winter, 13 1/4" **1,800**

Cigarette/match holder, sea horse decoration, pink, No. 726, 3 1/2 x 4"....................... **65**

Clip dish, green, 3 1/4" d. (part of desk set, Shape PB-1).. **20**

Comport, footed, square, green & white glaze, Shape No. 951, 4 1/2" sq., 2 1/4" h. **40**

Console bowl, footed, low rounded sides w/incurved rim, orange lustre, Shape No. 567-B, 2 3/4 x 9 3/4" **45**

Console bowls, 3 3/4 x 4 1/2 x 11", two-handled, footed, widely flaring fluted sides, verde green, Shape No. 538, pr. **300**

Console set: 6 1/2 x 10 1/2 x 17" bowl & pr. of candleholders; footed bowl w/figural bird handles, lobed sides, designed by Alexander Blazys, Shape No. 729, mottled blue glaze, the set................................... **400**

Decanter w/stopper, figural King of Clubs, a seated robed & bearded man w/a large crown on his head & holding a scepter, black glaze w/gold, designed by Waylande Gregory, Shape E-4, 10" h. **1,000**

Decanter w/stopper, figural Queen of Hearts, seated figure holding scepter & wearing crown, Oriental Red glaze, designed by Waylande Gregory, Shape No. E-5, 10 1/2" h. (ILLUS. right)......... **800**

Desk set, w/paperclip dish, Oriental Red glaze, Shape PB-1, 2 1/2 x 5 1/2", the set..... **125**

Figurine, "Spanish Dancer," female, white, designed by Elizabeth Anderson, Shape No. 793, 8 1/2" h. (ILLUS. right).................. **900**

Figurine, "Spanish Dancer," male, white, designed by Elizabeth Anderson, Shape No. 793, 8 3/4" h. (ILLUS. left)................... **900**

Figurine, Russian peasant, "Tambourine Player," white crackle glaze, designed by Alexander Blazys, Shape No. 757-760, 9" h. (ILLUS.)................................. **1,000**

Figurine, "Nautch Dancer," female w/a flaring pleated skirt on rectangular base, semi-matte ivory glaze w/silver accents, incised "Waylande Gregory," impressed mark, 6 3/4 x 9 1/4", 17 3/4" h. **10,450**

Figurines, "Spanish Dancer," male & female figures h.p. in polychrome glazes, the male mark No. 9, Shape No. 794-D, 8 1/4" h. & the female mark No. 8, Shape No. 793-D, 8 1/2" h., designed by Elizabeth Anderson, impressed marks, pr. **2,530**

Flower frog, figure of a nude female, one leg kneeling on thick round base, head bent to one side & looking upward, one arm resting on knee of bent leg w/the other hand near her foot, ivory glaze, designed by Walter Sinz, 6" h. (ILLUS. left with Diver flower frog) **450**

Russian Tambourine Player Figurine

Cowan Figurines & Flower Frog

Cowan Female Form Flower Frogs

Flower frog, figural Art Deco style nude dancing lady in a curved pose, standing on one leg & trailing a long scarf, Ivory glaze, designed by Walter Sinz, Shape No. 698, 6 1/2" h. **275-325**

Flower frog, figural, Art Deco nude scarf dancer, No. 35, ivory glaze, signed, 7 1/4" h. **400**

Flower frog, figural, an Art Deco dancing nude lady leaning back w/one leg raised & the ends of a long scarf held in her out-stretched hands, overall white glaze, im-pressed mark, 7 1/2" h. **201**

Flower frog, "Diver," wave-form base w/tall wave supporting nude female figure, back arched & arms raised over head, ivory glaze, designed by R. G. Cowan, Shape No. 683, 8" h. (ILLUS. right above) **900**

Flower frog, model of a deer, designed by Waylande Gregory, ivory glaze, Shape No. F-905, 8 1/4" h. (ILLUS. right with unicorn book ends) **550**

Flower frog, model of a leaping stag, relief-molded ribbed leaves in center & around base, designed by Waylande Gregory, mark Nos. 8 & 9, Shape No. 905, 1929, 8 1/2" h. **413**

Flower frog, figural, "Awakening," an Art Deco lady draped in a flowing scarf stand-ing & leaning backward w/her arms bent & her hands touching her shoulders, on a flower-form pedestal base, ivory glaze, designed by R. G. Cowan, Shape No. F-8, impressed mark, 1930s, 9" h. **550-650**

Flower frog, figural Pan sitting on large toadstool, ivory glaze, designed by W. Gregory, Shape No. F-9, 9" h. (ILLUS. with ram ashtray) **1,100**

Cowan Figural Flower Frog

Flower frog, figural, "Swirl Dancer," Art Deco nude female dancer standing & leaning to the side, w/one hand on hip & the other holding a scarf which swirls about her, on a round lobed base w/flower holes, glossy white glaze, impressed mark, 4 1/4" d., 9 1/2" h. (ILLUS.) **1,100**

"Swirl Dancer" Flower Frog

Flower frog, figural, "Swirl Dancer," Art Deco nude female dancer standing & leaning to the side, w/one hand on hip & the other holding a scarf which swirls about her, on a round lobed base w/flower holes, ivory glaze, designed by R.G. Cowan, Shape No. 720, 10" h. (ILLUS.) **1,500**

Flower frog, "Wreath Girl," figure of a woman standing on a blossom-form base & holding up the long tails of her flowing skirt, ivory glaze, designed by R. G. Cowan, Shape No. 721, 10" h. (ILLUS. center with Diver flower frog) **900**

Flower frog, figural, modeled as a slender, leaping female dancer w/long flowing dress, curved backwards above open scrolls on a molded plinth base, ivory semi-matte glaze, stamped mark, 6 1/2" d., 10" h. (glazed-over very tight crazing line to base) **2,200**

Flower frog, fluted flower-form base centered by relief-molded stalk & leaves supporting the figure of a female nude standing w/one leg bent, knee raised, leaning backward w/one arm raised overhead & the other resting on a curved leaf, ivory glaze, designed by R. G. Cowan, Shape No. F-812-X, 10 1/2" h. (ILLUS. center with Spanish Dancers).................................... **900**

Flower frog, model of a reindeer, designed by Waylande Gregory, polychrome finish, Shape No. 903, 11" h. (ILLUS. center with unicorn book ends)............................... **1,000**

Flower frog, figural nude w/long flowing scarf, ivory, designed by R.G. Cowan, Shape No. 687, 11 3/4" h. (ILLUS.) **900**

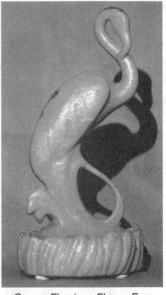

Cowan Flamingo Flower Frog

Flower frog, model of a flamingo, orange glaze, designed by Waylande Gregory, Shape No. D2-F, 11 3/4" h. (ILLUS.).......... **1,400**

Ginger jar, cov., orange lustre, Shape No. 583, 10" h.. **500**

Lamp, candlestick-form, a disk foot & spiral-twist standard w/a flaring molded socket fitted w/an electric bulb socket, overall marigold lustre glaze, impressed mark, 11" h. **52**

Lamp, w/fittings, moth decoration, blue, 13" h., overall 22" h. **350**

Lamp base, Art Deco style, angular, green, designed by Waylande Gregory, Shape No. 821, 8 3/8" h.. **195**

Cowan Lamp Base

Lamp base, round domed base below modernist teardrop-shaped body decorated w/nude female figure, ivory & brown glaze, designed by Waylande Gregory, 11" h. (ILLUS.).. **1,500**

Bird on Wave Model

Model of a bird on wave, Egyptian blue, designed by Alexander Blazys, Shape No. 749-A, 12" h. (ILLUS.) **1,500**
Model of a ram, Oriental Red glaze, designed by Edris Eckhart, 3 1/2" h. **240**
Model of elephant, standing on square plinth, head & trunk down, rich mottled Oriental Red glaze, designed by Marga-

ret Postgate, ca. 1930, faint impressed mark on plinth & paper label reading "X869 Elephant designed by M....et P....," 10 1/2" h. **4,620**
Pen base, maroon, Shape No. PB-2, 3 3/4"..... **100**
Pitcher, 8 3/4" h., foliage decoration................. **300**
Plaque, terradatol, designed by Alexander Blazys, Egyptian blue, Shape No. 739, 15 1/2" **1,000**
Strawberry jar w/saucer, Oriental Red glaze, designed by R.G. Cowan, Shape No. SJ-1, mark No. 8, 7 1/2" h., 2 pcs.......... **450**
Trivet, round, center portrait of young woman's face encircled by a floral border, white on blue ground, impressed mark & "Cowan," 6 5/8" d. (minor staining from usage).. **303**
Urn, Lakeware, blue, Shape V-102, 5 1/2" h. (ILLUS. left, bottom of page).......... **100**
Vase, 4" h., bulbous ovoid tapering to cylindrical neck, Jet Black glaze, Shape No. V-5 (ILLUS. center w/urn, bottom of page)... **300**
Vase, 4" h., waisted cylindrical body w/bulbous top & wide flaring rim, mottled orange glaze, Shape No. 630 (ILLUS. second from left w/No. 625-A candlestick) **80**
Vase, 4 1/4" h., mottled green, Shape No. V-54 .... **75**
Vase, 4 3/4" h., bulbous body w/horizontal ribbing, wide cylindrical neck, mottled turquoise glaze, Shape No. V-30........................ **80**
Vase, 4 3/4" h., waterfall, designed by Paul Bogatay, maroon, hand-decorated, Shape No. V-77 .... **700**
Vase, 4 3/4" h., wide tapering cylindrical body, mottled orange, brown & rust, Shape No. V-34 (ILLUS. second from right w/No. 625-A candlestick)........................ **80**

Cowan Lakeware Urn & Vases

Vase, 5" h., fan-shaped, designed by R.G. Cowan, golden yellow, Shape No. V-801 70

Vase, 5 1/2" h., footed wide semi-ovoid body w/flaring rim, dark bluish green, Shape 575-A, mark No. 4................................ 50

Vase, 5 1/2" h., orange lustre, Shape No. 608 40

Vase, 6 1/4" h., six-sided w/stepped neck, blue rainbow glaze, Shape No. 546................ 75

Vase, 6 1/4" h., 5 1/4" d., bulbous ovoid body tapering to a tiny molded mouth, decorated overall w/small stylized fish, seaweed & bubbles in light green sgraffito on an emerald green ground, small interior rim repair, circular mark & "Cowan" (ILLUS. center with bust)............................. 1,069

Vase, 6 1/2" h., footed, squatty bulbous base w/trumpet-form neck, flattened sides w/notched corners, green glaze, Shape No. V-649-A (ILLUS. right w/urn) 150

Vase, 6 1/2" h., wide bulbous body, yellow glaze, Shape V-91 650

Vase, cov., 6 1/2" h., wide bulbous body, blue glaze, Shape V-91 650

Vase, 6 5/8" h., bright yellow glaze, Shape No. 797.. 80

Vase, 6 3/4" h., footed bulbous ovoid body w/wide tapering cylindrical neck, Jet Black glaze, Shape V-25 500

Vase, 7" h., fan-shaped w/scalloped foot & domed base decorated w/relief-molded sea horse decoration, pink glaze, Shape No. 715-A.. 60

Vase, 7" h., footed bulbous base, the narrow shoulder tapering to tall wide cylindrical neck, Oriental Red glaze, Shape No. V-79 250

Vase, 7" h., Lakeware, bulbous base w/trumpet-form neck, Oriental Red glaze, Shape No. V-75 90

Vase, bud, 7" h., blue lustre glaze 75

Vase, 7 1/2" h., flared foot below paneled ovoid body, orange lustre glaze, Shape No. 691-A, mark No. 6 75

Vase, 7 1/2" h., tall slender ovoid body w/short cylindrical neck, orange lustre, Shape No. 552 (ILLUS. lower right w/ram ashtray) 90

Vase, 8" h., bulbous body tapering to cylindrical neck w/flaring rim, gold, Shape No. V-932 (ILLUS. far left w/No. 625-A candlestick) 200

Vase, 8" h., bulbous body tapering to cylindrical neck w/flaring rim, Feu Rouge (red) glaze, Shape No. V-932 550

Vase, 8" h., footed bulbous body w/trumpet-form neck, yellow shading to green drip glaze, Shape No. 627 (ILLUS. top center w/No. 625-A candlestick)................................ 250

Vase, 8" h., 8" d., wide bulbous body w/narrow molded rim, embossed w/a band of stylized leaves and covered in a Persian blue crackled glaze, Shape No. V-61, impressed mark... 880

Vase, 8 1/4" h., "Logan," footed, compressed bulbous base w/trumpet-form neck, flattened sides w/notched corners, decorative side handles, designed by R.G. Cowan, caramel glaze or Egyptian blue glaze, Shape No. 649-B, each 200

Vase, 8 1/2" h., bulbous ovoid form decorated w/relief-molded squirrel & foliage, designed by Waylande Gregory, green, Shape No. V-19 850

Vase, 8 1/2" h., Lakeware, cylindrical body w/slightly flared rim, turquoise glaze, Shape No. V-74 90

Vase, 8 1/2" h., matte greenish blue, Shape No. V-897.. 160

Vase, 8 3/4" h., Lakeware, green, Shape No. V-71... 100

Vase, 11 1/4" h., Chinese Bird patt., footed urn shape w/relief-molded birds at base, tan & brown crystalline glaze, impressed mark, Shape No. V-747 (small stilt pull on bottom not visible from side)......................... 880

Cowan Chinese Bird Vase

Vase, 11 1/4" h., Chinese Bird patt., footed urn shape w/relief-molded birds at base, green glaze, designed by R.G. Cowan, Shape No. V-747 (ILLUS.) 950

Vase, 11 1/2" h., 6 1/2" w., Chinese Bird patt., a fanned & lightly ribbed upper body above a large stylized exotic long-tailed bird at the bottom resting on an oblong scalloped foot, covered in in a Jade Green glaze, stamped mark 495

Vase, 11 3/4" h., blue lustre, Shape No. 691-C.. 250

Vase, 11 3/4" h., two-handled, flared foot below tall slender fluted ovoid body w/cylindrical neck, orange lustre, Shape No. 652-B, mark No. 8 300

Vase, 12 1/4" h., footed bulbous body tapering to wide cylindrical neck, green crystalline glaze, designed by Arthur E. Baggs, Shape No. V-47............................... 1,800

Tall Cowan Vase

Vase, 13" h., swelled cylindrical body w/a narrow shoulder to the short cylindrical wide neck covered in a lustered grey & yellow dripping glaze, mark No. 7, Shape No. 552, stamped ink mark (ILLUS.) 825

Vase, 11 1/4" h., 8" w., Chinese-style pillow form, each w/an oval paneled platform base supporting a large reclining molded phoenix bird below the large flattened, ribbed & fanned vase, crackled green glaze, small manufacturing bruise on base of one, circular mark, pr. (ILLUS. left with bust) 1,350

Vase, 13 1/2" h., baluster-form body w/flaring rim, light blue glaze, Shape No. 563 (ILLUS. left w/candlesticks)............................ 275

Wine cups, Oriental Red glaze, Shape No. X-17, 2 1/2" h., each.. 45

Dedham & Chelsea Keramic Art Works

Dedham & Chelsea Keramic Art Works Marks

This pottery was organized in 1866 by Alexander W. Robertson in Chelsea, Massachusetts, and became A. W. & H. Robertson in 1868. In 1872, the name was changed to Chelsea Keramic Art Works and in 1891 to Chelsea Pottery, U.S.A. About 1895, the pottery was moved to Dedham, Massachusetts, and was renamed Dedham Pottery. Production ceased in 1943. High-fired colored wares and crackle ware were specialties. The rabbit is said to have been the most popular decoration on crackle ware in blue.

Since 1977, the Potting Shed, Concord, Massachusetts, has produced quality reproductions of early Dedham wares. These pieces are carefully marked to avoid confusion with original examples.

Bowl, 4 1/2" d., Swan patt., blue registered stamp... **$460**

Dedham Turtle Pattern Bowl

Bowl, 7 1/2" d., 2 1/2" h., Turtle patt., flat rim, several small chips to edge, ink stamp mark (ILLUS.)...................................... 660

Large Dedham Rabbit Bowl

Bowl, 8" d., 3" h., footed wide & deep rounded form w/flat rim, Rabbit patt., blue ink stamp (ILLUS.)... 633

Bowl, 8" d., 3" h., footed wide rounded form, Rabbit patt., blue ink stamp (ILLUS. top row, far left, bottom of page) 506

Bowl, 8 1/4" square, 2 3/4" h., Swan patt., blue registered stamp 920

Variety of Dedham Crackleware Pieces

Bowl w/spoon, 5 3/8" d., 2 1/8" h., cereal, Rabbit patt., Chinese spoon w/rabbit decoration, both w/ink stamp mark, the set.. 413

Candlesticks, Elephant patt., blue stamp, initials "A.R.," 2" h., the pair 978

Centerpiece bowl, Rabbit patt., ink stamp mark, 3 x 12" (peppering to glaze)................ 523

Creamer, Elephant patt., blue registered stamp, 3" w., 3" h... 1,265

Cup & saucer, extra large coffee-size, Rabbit patt., blue ink stamp, 5" d., 3" h., the set (ILLUS. center, bottom row with bowl) 338

Cup & saucer, Grape patt., blue registered stamp, 6" d., 2 3/4" h...................................... 173

Cup & saucer, Owl patt., blue registered stamp, 6 1/4" d., 2 1/2" h. 1,955

Cup & saucer, Snow Tree patt., blue registered stamp, 6" d. 173

Cup & saucer, Rabbit patt., ink stamp mark, cup 2 1/4" h. 193

Cups & saucers, tea-size, Rabbit patt., blue ink stamp, saucer 6" d., set of 6 (ILLUS. bottom row, far left with bowl) 1,238

Dish, 7 1/4" d., Rabbit patt., star-shaped, blue registered stamp, two impressed rabbits.. 374

Dish, oyster shell-shaped, decorated w/a free-hand painted blue rabbit, blue ink stamp mark, 4 1/2" w. 193

Egg cup, Elephant patt., blue stamp, 3 1/2" d., 3" h... 1,380

Flower holder, standing bunny, hint of blue stamp, 4 1/4" d., 6 1/4" h. 1,150

glaze, by Hugh Robertson, incised "HCR - James Kelley," w/a rare catalog "American Decorative Tiles 1870-1930" which includes the piece, medallion 4 x 4 3/4"........ 844

Model of a boot, Swan patt., blue stamp, 4" w., 5" h... 1,093

Oyster dishes, modeled as an oyster half-shell w/a small molded blue-glazed pearl, ink stamp mark, 4 1/2" l., pr. 660

Paperweight, model of turtle, blue registered stamp, 2 1/4" w., 3 1/4" l. 1,035

Pitcher, 4 3/4" h., 6 1/4" d., Grape patt., blue registered stamp 259

Pitcher, 5" h., 5 1/4" d., "Night and Day" design, blue ink stamp (ILLUS. top row, far right with bowl) 619

Pitcher, 6" h., 6 1/4" w., Oak Block design, blue registered stamp 978

Pitcher, 6 1/4" h., 7" d., Rabbit patt., blue registered stamp...................................... 575

Pitcher, 7 3/4" h., tall rectangular tapering form w/a squared stepped rim spout & square loop handle, incised w/a Greek key border & geometric linear border at the rim, handle & base, glossy green glaze later painted w/birds & nest in a flowering tree, impressed Chelsea Keramic Art Works mark, ca. 1885..... 800-1,000

Dedham Plates

Plate, 6" d., Horse Chestnut patt. border, blue mark & one foreshortened rabbit, early 20th c. (ILLUS. right) 173

Plate, 6" d., Dolphin patt., blue registered stamp, two impressed rabbits, blue numbers.. 518

Plate, 6 1/4" d., Chick patt., blue stamp, one impressed rabbit 2,415

Plate, 6 1/4" d., Lily patt., central lily decoration w/"o" mark on stem, decorated by Maude Davenport, blue mark & one foreshortened rabbit, early 20th c. (ILLUS. left) 1,150

Plate, 6 1/2" d., strawberry raised design, signed Jacob 2,415

Plate, 7 1/2" d., Crab patt.................................... 575

Plate, 8 1/2" d., luncheon size, Crab patt.......... 374

Plate, 8 1/2" d., luncheon size, Day Lily patt., blue stamp...................................... 1,093

Plate, 8 1/2" d., luncheon size, Duck patt. 230

Unusual Chelsea Keramic Jar

Jar, cov., oval flattened 'pilgrim flask'-form, raised on four wide rounded tab feet, small scroll side handles, the flattened & domed cover w/a fanned finial, a molded oval side scene base on a printed image by L. Knauss showing a little girl feeding geese under a glossy dark teal blue glaze, the border, feet & cover in glossy green, modeled by Hugh Robertson, stamped Chelsea Keramic Art Works mark, 10 1/2" w., 9 1/4" h. (ILLUS.) 1,840

Medallion, oval, molded w/a scene of a trumpeting postboy riding a horse & viewed from behind, based on an image by J.E. Kelly, covered in a forest green

Plate, 8 1/2" d., luncheon size, Grape patt., blue ink stamp, bruise to table ring (ILLUS. bottom row, second from right with bowl) 141

Plate, 8 1/2" d., luncheon size, Lobster patt. (rim glaze imperfection) 345

Plate, 8 1/2" d., luncheon size, Turkey patt. (ILLUS. top row, second from right with Rabbit bowl 100-200

Plate, 8 3/4" d., Grouse patt., blue stamp, one impressed rabbit (glaze pitting to edge surface) 2,875

Plate, 10" d., Crab patt., blue stamp, one impressed rabbit 1,093

Plate, 10" d., dinner, Rabbit patt., decorated by Maude Davenport, ink stamp mark (small glaze nick on edge of rim) 303

Plate, 10" d., Dolphin patt., early mark 844

Plate, 10" d., Horse Chestnut patt. 86

Plate, 10 1/4" d., Cloverleaf patt., rim w/experimental greenish glaze on molded cloverleaf design, interior blue accent band w/circular greenish glazed dots, Chelsea Keramic Art Works cipher mark, ca. 1891 920

Plate, 12" d., Wolves & Owl patt., blue stamp (three tight hairlines, peppering) 2,300

Plates, 6" d., bread & butter size, Rabbit patt., restoration to small chip on rim of one, blue ink mark, set of 6 (ILLUS. bottom row, second from left with bowl) 619

Plates, 8 1/2" d., luncheon size, Horse Chestnut patt., blue ink mark, pr. (ILLUS. bottom row, far right with bowl) 309

Plates, 8 1/2" d., luncheon size, Rabbit patt., blue ink mark, short, tight line in one, set of 6 (ILLUS. top row, second from left with bowl)............................ 844

Platter, 12" d., round dished form w/wide flanged rim, Grape patt., marked 201

Platter, 13" oval, Dolphin patt., blue registered mark, one impressed rabbit 2,760

Teapot, Rabbit patt., blue registered stamp, 7" w., 5 1/2" h. 920

Toothpick holder, floral design, obscured blue stamp, 2 3/4" d., 2 3/4" h. 1,150

Tureen, cov., Rabbit patt., blue stamp, 11" w., 8" h. 2,645

Tureen, cov., Turkey patt., blue stamp, 9" d., 5 3/4" h... 2,300

Miniature Dedham Robertson Vase

Vase, 2 3/4" h., 2" d., miniature, simple ovoid form w/flat mouth, dripping oxblood, green & blue mottled glaze, by Hugh Robertson, short opposing firing lines in rim, Dedham mark (ILLUS.) 575

Vase, 5 3/4" h., terra cotta, classical urnform w/two applied leaf-form handles, ca. 1880, impressed Chelsea Keramic Art Works cipher (firing cracks to base & handles) 633

Vase, 6 1/4" h., Iris patt., cylindrical form, blue stamp, impressed "C.K.A.W." 1,840

Chelsea Keramic Bottle-form Vase

Vase, 6 1/2" h., 4" d., footed bottle-form, squatty bulbous body tapering to a tall cylindrical neck, unusual oxblood & slate grey glaze, stamped Chelsea Keramic Art Works mark (ILLUS.) 1,725

Azalea Pattern Tureen

Tureen, cov., Azalea patt., blue stamp, 9 1/2" d., 5 3/4" h. (ILLUS.) 920

Chelsea Keramic Pilgrim Vase

Dedham & Chelsea Keramic Vases

Vase, 6 3/4" h., 4" w., flattened upright rectangular flask-form w/rounded flat borders
& a small spout neck, embossed on the
side panel w/a scene of an elderly bearded pilgrim walking through a landscape,
panel w/a deep teal blue glossy glaze,
the border w/an olive green glossy glaze,
by H. Robertson, short, tight opposing
lines at the rim, small stilt pull chip on the
back, stamped "CKAW - HCR" (ILLUS.) **731**

Vase, 7 1/2" h., 5" d., wide baluster-form
w/short cylindrical neck, experimental example by Hugh Robertson, covered in a
superior mirrored oxblood dripping glaze,
incised "Dedham Pottery - HCR" (ILLUS.
left, top of page) **1,980**

Chelsea Keramic Pilgrim Flask Vase

Vase, 7 1/2" h., 6 1/4" w., flattened round
pilgrim flask-form on four peg feet, tapering to a short cylindrical neck, the sides
incised w/pine boughs & flowers under a
speckled amber glossy glaze, by George
Ferrety, stamped mark & artist-signed
(ILLUS.) **1,495**

Vase, 8" h., 3" d., slender tall ovoid form,
experimental fine mirrored oxblood
glaze, by Hugh Robertson, incised
Dedham Pottery mark **605**

Vase, 8 1/4" h., 3 1/2" d., slightly flaring cylindrical body w/a wide angled shoulder
tapering to a short cylindrical neck, fine
oxblood "orange peel" semi-matte glaze,
unsigned Chelsea Keramic Art Works
(ILLUS. center with experimental vase)..... **1,760**

Vase, 8 1/2" h., 5" d., tapering cylindrical
form, incised "Dedham Pottery," initialed
"B.W." **3,105**

Vase, 8 1/2" h., 5 1/4" h., Chinese bronze-
shaped, squared, tapering double-lobe
form embossed in the side panels w/flow-
ers or geometric designs resembling
decorated bronze, overall white crackled
glaze, Dedham rabbit ink stamp (ILLUS.
right with experimental vase, above)............. **550**

Vase, 8 1/2" h., 9 1/2" d., spherical form
w/extended raised rim & tapered base,
glossy mottled sea green glaze, modeled
by Hugh Robertson, incised "Dedham
Pottery 10.11.96 H.C.R. 3016B" (in-the-
making glaze chips near base)................... **2,070**

Fine Lustre Glazed Dedham Vase

Vase, 7 1/2" h., 4" d., ovoid body tapering to
a tall, wide cylindrical neck, fine experi-

mental lustered oxblood glaze, by Hugh Robertson, Dedham mark (ILLUS.) **4,313**

Large Chelsea Keramic Pillow Vase

Vase, 11" h., tall flattened ovoid pillow-form body on knob feet, tapering to a flared scalloped mouth, the sides embossed w/scrolls & overall flowers, butterflies & bees, mottled glossy green glaze, artist-signed, Chelsea Keramic Art Works mark (ILLUS.) **633**

Frankoma

Frankoma Mark

John Frank studied at the Chicago Art Institute and was fortunate to train under two noted ceramic artists: Mrs. Myrtle Merritt French and Dr. Charles F. Binns. When a Dr. Jacobsen asked Professor French to find someone to begin a new ceramic art department at the University, she highly recommended John Frank. That position enabled him to study and formulate various glazes. From these experiments he was able to create a beautiful rutile glaze that had been used only sparingly in the past.

When he founded Frankoma Potteries in 1933 Mr. Frank almost always used the rutile technique which helped to create beautiful glazes for his pottery.

With his family, Mr. Frank moved his operation from Norman, Oklahoma to Sapulpa, Oklahoma. He felt he had come home. The family and its company have remained in Sapulpa since that time.

Over the years Frankoma products have been marked in a variety of ways. The "pot and leopard" mark was used from 1935-1938 when a fire on November 11, 1938 destroyed everything including the mark.

A creamy looking clay known as "Ada" is highly collectible today but it was discontinued in 1953. Frankoma then began using the clay from Sapulpa which resulted in a red brick color.

In May 1970 John Frank was contacted by a writer and in response to his questions Mr. Frank

personally sent the writer the answers. There has been much controversy over the actual date when John Frank changed from Ada clay (which is more valuable) to Sapula clay. Below is a paragraph from John Frank's letter to the writer, signed by him, that explains the date. You can find the entire letter printed beginning on page 13 of the "Collectors Guide to Frankoma Pottery," Book II, by Susan N. Cox.   "...We have always used an Oklahoma clay as the base of all our pottery. The first clay came from Ada, and we used it until 1953 when we switched over to a local brick shale that we dig right here in Sapulpa. Using this as a base we add other earths and come up with what we call our Frankoma Pottery. Peculiar in itself, and it is not available anywhere else, nor is it used by any other pottery, it fires a brick red and we are able to temper it in the cooling so that all of our ware is guaranteed oven proof."

When Richard Bernstein purchased Frankoma in 1991 a new era began resulting in different products and glazes. True Frankoma collectors search for the products made before 1991 and certainly those made before 1953. Lucky ones can find pot and leopard-marked pieces and those marked "Frank Potteries."

Baker, Westwind patt., Model No. 6vs, Peach Glow glaze, 1 1/2 pt. **$24**

Book ends, Bucking Bronco, Model No. 423, Prairie Green glaze, 5 1/2" h., pr.......... **400**

Frankoma Leopard Book End

Book ends, model of leopard, Pompeian Bronze glaze, Model No. 431, 9" l., 5 1/2" h., pr. (ILLUS. of one).......................... **900**

Book ends, seated figure, Ivory glaze, Model No. 425, 1934-38, 5 3/4" h., pr. **1,000**

Ocelot Book Ends

Book ends, Walking Ocelot on a two-tiered oblong base, black high glaze, Model No. 424, signed on reverse of tiered base "Taylor" denoting designer Joseph Taylor, pot & leopard mark on bottom, 7" l., 3" h., pr. (ILLUS.)...................................... **1,015**

Bottle-vase, V-1, 1969, limited edition, 4,000 created, small black foot w/Prairie Green body, 15" h. **125**

Bottle-vase, V-7, limited edition, 3,500 created, Desert Gold glaze, body w/coffee glazed stopper & base, signed by Joniece Frank, 13" h. **100**

Bowl, 11" l., divided, Lazybones patt., Brown Satin glaze, Model No. 4qd 18

Brooch, four-leaf clover-shape, Desert Gold glaze, w/original card, 1 1/4" h. 40

Catalog, 1953, unnumbered sixteen pages, dated July 1, 1953, two versions for color cover, one w/photograph of Donna Frank or one w/photograph of Grace Lee Frank, each 45

Christmas card, figural fish tray, Woodland Moss glaze, marked, "1960 the Franks, Frankoma Christmas Frankoma," 4" l. 75

Christmas card, "Statue of Liberty Torch," White Sand glaze, created by Grace Lee Frank Smith for her & Dr. A. Milton Smith's friends, 1986, 3 1/2" l. 75

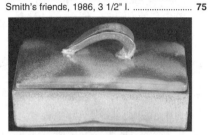

Bronze Green Cigarette Box

Cigarette box, cov., rectangular, cover w/single raised & hard-to-find curved leaf handle, Bronze Green glaze, Ada clay, marked "Frankoma," 4 x 6 3/4", 3 1/2" h. (ILLUS.) 150

Figure of Fan Dancer, seated, No. 113, Ivory glaze, Ada clay, 14" l., 9" h................... 800

Figure of farmer boy, wearing dark blue overalls, light blue short-sleeved shirt, black scarf tied around neck, yellow hair & ivory wide-brim hat w/only brim showing from front, black shoes, bisque arms, hands, face & neck, marked "Frankoma 702," 6 3/4" h. 125

Figure of gardener girl, holding pale green apron to form a basket in front of her, light blue dress w/short puffed sleeves & scooped neckline, long yellow hair w/dark blue bow on top, bisque face, neck, arms & hands, marked "Frankoma 701," 5 3/4" h. 125

Frankoma Indian Chief Figure

Figure of Indian Chief, No. 142, Desert Gold glaze, Ada clay, 7" h. (ILLUS.) 165

Mug, 1968, (Republican) elephant, white........... 80

Mug, 1970, (Republican) elephant 60

Mug, 1971, (Republican) elephant 55

Mug, 1973, (Republican) elephant 40

Mug, 1974, (Republican) elephant 30

Pitcher, Wagon Wheel patt., Model No. 94d, Prairie Green glaze, Ada clay, 2 qt........ 45

Plate, 8 1/2" d., Bicentennial Series, Limited Edition No. 1, "Provocations," eleven signers of the Declaration of Independence, White Sand glaze, 1972, mispelling of United States as "Staits"...................... 155

Plate, 7" d., Wildlife Series, Limited Edition No. 1, Bobwhite quail, Prairie Green glaze, 1,000 produced 125

Plate, 7 1/2" d., Easter 1972, "Jesus Is Not Here...He Is Risen," scene of Jesus' tomb... 20

Plate, 8 1/2" d., Bicentennial Series, Limited Edition No. 1, "Provocations," eleven signers of the Declaration of Independence, White Sand glaze, 1972 95

Plate, 8 1/2" d., Christmas 1968, "Flight into Egypt".. 45

Political chip, John Frank's profile on front surrounded by the words, "Honest, Fair, Capable," & at bottom "Elect John Frank Representative 1962," obverse w/outline of Oklahoma state w/"One Frank" inside it, around it "Oklahomans deserve outstanding leadership" & "For statesmanship vote Republican," unglazed red brick color, 1 3/4" d., 1/8" h...................... 25

Postcard, color photograph of Joniece Frank sitting w/various Frankoma products used to show the current Frankoma glazes, 5 1/2 x 6 1/2"............................... 10

Salt & pepper shakers, model of a Dutch shoe, Desert Gold glaze, Model No. 915h, ca. 1957-60, 4" l., pr............................... 50

Salt & pepper shakers, model of an elephant, Desert Gold glaze, No. 160h, produced in 1942 only, Ada clay, 3" h., pr. 135

John Frank Tournament Stein

Stein, footed, advertising-type, for John Frank Memorial Charity Gold Tournament, Blue, 150 created, 1973 (ILLUS.) 16

Teapot, cov., Wagon Wheel patt., Model No. 94j, Desert Gold glaze, Ada clay, 2 cup **35**

Trivet, Eagle sitting on branch, large wings fill up most of the trivet, Peach Glow glaze, Model No. 2tr, 6" sq. **65**

Trivet, Eagle, undated, Woodland Moss glaze, Model No. AETR, 6" d. **25**

Trivet, Lazybones patt., Model No. 4tr, produced in 1957 only, hard-to-find, 6" d. **65**

Trivet, Spanish Iron patt., created by Joniece Frank, Woodland Moss glaze, produced 1966-1989, 6" sq. **25**

Tumbler, juice, Plainsman patt., Model No. 51c, Autumn Yellow glaze, 6 oz. **7**

Vase, 3 1/2" h., round foot rising to bulbous body w/short neck & rolled lip, unusual high gloss deep blue, marked "Frank Potteries" **550**

Vase, 4" h., small foot rising to a flat, narrow body w/tab handle on each side, Ivory glaze, marked "Frankoma" **70**

Vase, 4" h., small foot rising to a flat, narrow body w/tab handle on each side, Ivory glaze, pot & leopard mark **155**

Vase, 6" h., square-shaped w/relief-molded flying goose, relief-molded reed decoration on reverse, No. 60B **35**

Vase, 7" h., Art Deco-style w/round foot w/panel on each side at base, rising to a plain, flat body w/stepped small elongated handles, Jade Green glaze, Model No. 41, pot & leopard mark **195**

Wall masks, bust of Oriental man, No. 135 & Oriental woman, No. 133, Jade Green glaze, pot & leopard mark, Ada clay, man 5 1/2" h., woman 4 3/4" h., pr. **385**

Fulper Pottery

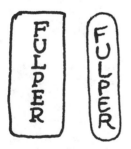

Fulper Marks

The Fulper Pottery was founded in Flemington, New Jersey, in 1805 and operated until 1935, although operations were curtailed in 1929 when its main plant was destroyed by fire. The name was changed in 1929 to Stangl Pottery, which continued in operation until July of 1978, when Pfaltzgraff, a division of Susquehanna Broadcasting Company of York, Pennsylvania, purchased the assets of the Stangl Pottery, including the name.

Book ends, figural, each molded as a large spread-winged eagle perched atop a large thick rectangular platform w/an embossed American shield at the front, Cucumber green matte Crystalline glaze,

rectangular ink stamp, 7 1/2" w., 9" h., pr. (restoration to beak & neck of one) **$1,069**

Book ends, figural, "Roman Mausoleum" model, bold classical doorway w/peaked roof over fan light above the door which stands ajar, sheer mottled ivory & white matte glaze w/clay showing through, rectangular ink mark, 5 1/2" w., 6" h., pr. (small chip & restoration to corner of one) **605**

Fulper Liberty Bell Book Ends

Book ends, model of the Liberty Bell in mounting, Verde Antique crystalline glaze, rectangular ink mark & paper label, 4" w., 7 1/4" h., pr. (ILLUS.) **690**

Book ends, square base w/figural Egyptian "Rameses" covered in a matte green glaze, ink marks, 8" h., 4" sq., pr. **770**

Bottle, footed bulbous base tapering to tall cylindrical neck w/flat rim, embossed salamander at base of neck, Cat's Eye flambé glaze, rectangular ink mark, 8" h., 4" d. **1,800**

Bowl, 10" d., 4" h., wide low cushion form w/the wide shoulder centered by a wide, low cylindrical neck, rich Flemington Green flambé glaze over a mustard yellow ground, rectangular ink mark **1,013**

Bowl, 10" d., 6" h., deep rounded sides, the slightly rounded shoulder tapering to a wide, flat molded mouth, decorated w/molded thistles & branches & covered in an ivory to Chinese blue flambé glaze, rectangular ink mark (rim chip & hairline) **523**

Bowl, 11 1/2" d., a small, low cylindrical foot supporting a wide wide rounded & cupped blossom-form bowl w/wide ribs around the exterior & a lightly scalloped & pointed rim, exterior w/multi-toned green crystalline glaze, pale yellow interior, incised vertical mark (minor flakes on foot) **231**

Bowl, 11 1/2" d., 6 1/2" h., footed, deep flaring sides, interior covered in Flemington green glaze, exterior in Famille Rose glaze, unmarked **825**

Bowl w/flower frog, 7 1/4" d., 5" h., "Vazbowl," a wide flat-bottomed compressed squatty form on tiny feet, a ringed shoulder w/a flattened rim, the center w/a tall waisted three-legged flower frog, Blue Wisteria & Mirrored Green glaze, rectangular ink mark, Pan-Pacific & original Fulper paper labels (ILLUS. left, top next page) **518**

Fulper Vaz-bowl and Small Vases

Bowl-vase, squatty bulbous body raised on three tiny feet, the wide shoulder tapering to a short cylindrical neck, smooth matte green glaze, professional chip restoration to two feet, mark obscured by glaze, 6 3/4" d., 3 1/2" h. **413**

Bulb bowl, shallow round body w/wide closed rim, glossy streaked brown, blue & green glaze interior, glossy & matte dark blue & rose exterior, early 20th c., faint vertical Fulper stamp, 9 1/4" d., 2 1/4" h. **144**

Candlesticks, flaring socket on a simple four-sided columnar standard above the flaring, stepped round foot, top w/a glossy ivory shading down to a streaked French blue flambé glaze, ink racetrack mark, 10 1/2" h., pr. **550**

Center bowl, figural, "Ibis" model, three stylized birds w/wings spread support the wide shallow bowl w/incurved sides, Flemington Green flambé exterior & brown flambé over mustard matte exterior, rectangular ink mark, 11" d., 5 3/4" h. **935**

Center bowl, wide flat bottom w/low incurved sides, embossed fish design covered in a green & Butterscotch flambé glaze, rectangular ink mark, 11" d., 3" h. ... **1,125**

Center bowl, Effigy-type, a wide flat-bottomed shallow bowl w/incurved sides raised on three crouching figures resting on a molded thick disk base, cat's-eye flambé, blue crystalline & speckled brown matte glaze, ink racetrack mark, 13" d., 4 1/2" h. **715**

Console bowl, a very wide shallow form w/rounded incurved sides, raised on three short peg legs, dark green crystalline matte glaze, stamped vertical mark, 10 1/2" d. (minor flakes) **523**

Doorstop, model of a cat, reclining animal facing viewer, tail curled along the body, creamy ground w/streaky brown cat's-eye flambé glaze, ink racetrack mark, 9" l., 6" h. **1,069**

Fulper Flagon

Flagon, footed bulbous ovoid body w/three ribbed bands & upright curved neck w/square cut-out above applied braided handle, Chinese blue flambé glaze, incised racetrack mark, 11" h., 7" d. (ILLUS.) **440**

Flower frog, figural, modeled as an Indian maiden seated in a canoe perched on a rocky outcrop, in green, mahogany, & brown matte glazes, unmarked, 7" l., 4" h. (small flat bottom chip, probably in the making) **520**

Flower frog, model of a medieval castle on grassy base, brown & green matte glaze, early ink mark, 5 x 5" (a few minor nicks to edges) **440**

Flower frog, figural, a penguin standing atop a large rocky outcrop base w/flower holes, the bird in cream, brown & blue matte glazes w/brown matte glaze on the base, rectangular ink mark, 7" h. **303**

Flower frog, figural, standing full figure Egyptian by John Kunzman, green & turquoise flambé glaze, rectangular ink stamp & "Made by John Kunzman, 1909," 7 1/2" h. (two small chips & bruise to base) **788**

Flower frog, figural, frog on lily pad, mirrored green & caramel flambé glaze, vertical inkstamp rectangle mark, 7" d. **220**

Incense burner, cov., wide squatty bulbous body on four tiny feet & w/four tiny squared buttresses around the shoulder, the low neck w/a domed, pierced cover, matte green crystalline glaze, rare, early, unmarked 5" d., 4" h. (bruise to lip interior, restoration to chip) **1,069**

Jug, inverted pear-shaped body w/flared foot, the wide shoulder w/short cylindrical neck & spout w/molded rims, loop handle from shoulder to rim, blue, green & ivory flambé glaze, one of three known, rectangular ink mark, 7" d., 9 3/4" h. (chip to base, mostly under foot) **2,588**

Rare Fulper Lamp Base & Shade

Lamp, table model, an 18" d. domical pottery shaded in Chinese blue flambe glaze w/bands of triangular & almond-shaped caramel slag glass segments flanking green slag eyebrow segments around the rim, raised on a matching pottery base w/a knopped standard & widely flaring squatty bulbous base, original porcelain sockets, invisible repair to shade,

rectangular ink & Vasecraft marks, 18" h. (ILLUS.) **10,350**

Fulper "Mushroom" Lamp

Lamp, table model, a wide low domed mushroom-shaped pottery shade, inset around the sides w/textured amber slag glass & iridescent green jewels, raised on a tall slender waisted cylindrical base w/a widely flaring foot, two electric sockets, grey & light blue flambé glaze over mirrored lustre gunmetal, base stamped w/vertical "FULPER" in a box, circular "VASECRAFT" stamp, also stamped "Patent Pending U.S. and Canada" & "6," shade stamped "17-17-8," unobtrusive crazing, 20 1/2" h., shade 17" d. (ILLUS.) **21,850**

Pipe holder, figural, modeled at the front w/a fox (?) lying on a snag log w/a large & smaller cylindrical upright log forming holders behind, match striker section to one side of the base, overall Mahogany glossy glaze, unmarked, 6 1/2" w., 3 1/4" h. (repair to fox ears & largest log) **900**

Urn, a small foot supporting a wide, deep urn-form body w/an angled shoulder tapering to a short flared neck, upright pierced square handles at the edge of the shoulder, fine frothy blue to Famille Rose flambé glaze, inked racetrack mark, 8" d., 9 1/2" h. **1,575**

Urn, small round pedestal foot supporting a large bulbous ovoid body w/a wide rounded shoulder to a short wide flat mouth flanked by small loop handles, fine ochre, mahogany & pale blue flambé glaze over textured body, raised racetrack mark, 9" d., 9" h. **935**

Urn, tall slender classical form w/wide shoulders & a short neck w/widely rolled rim, upright scroll-tipped handles from the shoulder to the rim, overall Mirror Black glaze on a "hammered" body, rectangular ink mark, 5 1/2" d., 11" h. **495**

Urn, Chinese-form, footed tapering bulbous ovoid body w/a tall cylindrical neck & flared rim, small squared loop shoulder handles, overall Mirror Black glaze over a "hammered" body, raised racetrack mark, 8" d., 11" h. (reglued handle tip) **1,045**

Urn, footed baluster-form, shoulder tapering to cylindrical neck w/molded rim, flanked by scrolled handles, covered in a glossy & matte Chinese blue flambé glaze, rectangular ink mark, 11 1/4" h., 5 3/4" d. **715**

Vase, 3" h., miniature, a squatty bulbous base w/an angled shoulder below the conical neck flanked by arched handles from the rim to shoulder, gunmetal crystalline glaze over a caramel crystalline flambé glaze, stamped vertical mark............. **220**

Vase, 3" h., squatty bulbous body tapering gently to a closed rim, overall dark purple & mottled blue matte glaze, vertical stamped mark... **176**

Fulper Miniature Vases

Vase, miniature, 3 1/2" h., 3" d., footed squatty bulbous base tapering to a rounded stepped neck w/molded rim, Copperdust crystalline glaze, ink racetrack mark (ILLUS. left).................................. **358**

Vase, 3 3/4" h., 6" d., low squatty bulbous lower body centering an upright short wide neck w/incurved mouth, fine green to Chinese Blue flambé glaze, rectangular Prang mark... **366**

Vase, 4" h., 5" d., nearly spherical melon-lobed form, green & Chinese Blue flambé glaze, ink racetrack mark (ILLUS. right with vaz-bowl)..................................... **633**

Vase, 4 1/2" h., swelled cylindrical body w/a sharply angled shoulder to the wide, short cylindrical neck, fine brown, blue & caramel drippy flambé glaze, stamped vertical mark **319**

Vase, 4 1/2" h., swelled cylindrical body w/an angled shoulder to a short, wide cylindrical neck, green over blue to red overall drip glaze, unmarked.......................... **176**

Vase, 4 1/2" h., 4 1/2" d., footed, lobed bell pepper-shaped, w/small closed mouth, blue over Famille Rose flambé glaze, rectangular ink mark **660**

Vase, miniature, 4 3/4" h., 3 1/4" d., bulbous ovoid body w/closed mouth, covered in a fine ivory to cat's-eye flambé glaze, ink racetrack mark (ILLUS. right, above)... **165**

Vase, 5" h., wide half-round lower body w/an angled center shoulder below the wide tapering neck w/flat rim, squared curled C-scroll handles from rim to shoulder, overall purple & blue mottled matte glaze, stamped vertical mark......................... **231**

Vase, 5" h., 7 1/4" d., a wide half-round lower body below a wide angled shoulder centered by a short, wide cylindrical neck, frothy Flemington Green flambé glaze, rectangular ink mark (ILLUS. center with vaz-bowl)... **431**

Vase, 5 1/4" h., 6 3/4" d., footed spherical body w/incurved rim, light blue to elephant's breath flambé glaze, ink racetrack mark **385**

Vase, 5 1/2" h., bulbous ovoid body tapering to a wide heavy molded rim, overall Copperdust glaze, embossed vertical mark... **319**

Vase, 5 1/2" h., 4 1/2" d., bulbous ovoid body tapering to a wide short flared rim, dark mirrored green & blue flambé glaze, raised mark... **330**

Vase, miniature, 5 3/4" h., 2 1/4" d., slender cylindrical form covered in cat's-eye flambé glaze, interior line does not go through, rectangular ink mark (ILLUS. center, previous column) **275**

Vase, 6" h., 9" d., squatty bulbous form, the wide shoulder tapering to molded rim, Mirrored Black flambé glaze, ink racetrack mark **619**

Fulper Vase with Wisteria Matte Glaze

Vase, 6" h., 9" d., wide footed squatty bulbous form w/a wide rounded shoulder centered by a small rolled neck, frothy Wisteria Matte glaze, minor grinding chip on base of footring, mark obscured by glaze (ILLUS.) **863**

Vase, 6 1/4" h., 3 1/4" d., footed squatty bulbous base tapering to a tall cylindrical body w/a bulbed neck w/a flat rim, Rose Famille glaze, experimental, squat rectangular ink mark & "121 - McConnell"........ **1,463**

Vase, 6 1/4" h., 8 1/2" d., footed spherical body w/short wide cylindrical neck, three loop handles, matte Wisteria glaze, incised racetrack mark.................................... **385**

Vase, 6 1/2" h., ovoid body w/an angled shoulder at the short, widely flaring neck, three flat pierced short handles from the rim to the shoulder, green to blue to charcoal semi-gloss drip glaze over a red matte ground, vertical stamp mark **253**

Vase, 6 1/2" h., 8" d., wide bulbous body w/angled shoulder handles, purple & blue crystalline glaze, impressed racetrack mark.. **275**

Vase, 6 3/4" h., ovoid body w/cream flambé over Wisteria glaze, raised vertical mark **303**

Vase, 6 3/4" h., 4'" d., footed cylindrical body w/rolled rim, incised vertical ribbed bands, covered w/a rich, flowing brown matte finish, impressed mark **3,080**

Vase, 7" h., a flaring pedestal base supporting a large spherical body tapering to a tiny flared neck, the upper body in cream shading to a striped cream, blue & green drip glaze & mottled blue pedestal, impressed mark **286**

Vase, 7" h., simple ovoid body w/heavy molded rim, blue, brown & gunmetal flambé glaze, embossed vertical mark **231**

Vase, 7" h., wide gently tapering cylindrical body w/a rounded bottom edge & closed flat rim, cat's-eye flambé glaze, impressed vertical mark (minor grinding chips to base) **248**

Fulper Vase with Frothy Blue Glaze

Vase, 7" h., 4 1/2" d., swelled cylindrical body w/a narrow angled shoulder & wide short rolled neck w/short buttress handles from rim to shoulder, lustered frothy turquoise glaze over a matte blue ground, obscured racetrack mark (ILLUS.) **978**

Vase, 7 1/4" h., 5" d., wide gently tapering cylindrical body w/a rounded bottom edge & closed flat rim, cat's-eye flambé glaze, ink racetrack mark **385**

Squatty Bulbous Fulper Vase

Vase, 7 1/4" h., 7 1/4" d., wide squatty bulbous form w/the wide rounded upper body centering a short, small molded neck, frothy Wistaria Matte glaze, mark obscurbed by glaze (ILLUS.) **978**

Vase, 7 1/2" h., baluster-form w/rolled neck rim, fine purple crystalline glaze over grey & salmon, stamped vertical mark **605**

Vase, 7 1/2" h., 5 1/2" d., bulbous ovoid body tapering to a short trumpet neck, overall frothy matte Wisteria glaze, ink racetrack mark **358**

Vase, 7 1/2" h., 5 1/2" d., gourd-form, bulbous ovoid shouldered body w/a short tapering cylindrical neck w/flared rim, curved integral handles from rim to shoulder, Leopard Skin crystalline glaze, ink racetrack mark **825**

Vase, 8" h., footed baluster-form w/a gently flaring neck, outswept & upturned loop shoulder handles, a creamy drip over a rust flambé glaze, stamped vertical mark **523**

Vase, 8" h., 6" d., baluster-form w/a wide flat molded mouth, covered in a frothy matte Cucumber glaze, incised racetrack mark **468**

Vase, 8" h., 6" d., bulbous nearly spherical body w/a short cylindrical closed neck flanked by angled handles w/small round openings from rim to shoulder, fine green crystalline glaze, vertical mark under glaze **440**

Vase, 8" h., 7" d., seven-sided gently tapering ovoid body, flowing matte olive flambé glaze, incised racetrack mark **495**

Vase, bud, 8 1/4" h., slender slightly tapering square form raised on a low angled square foot, glossy & matte Chinese blue flambé glaze, rectangular ink mark **275**

Vase, 8 1/2" h., squatty bulbous base w/tall tapering cylindrical neck, four buttressed handles, cat's-eye flambé glaze, ink racetrack mark **440**

Vase, 8 1/2" h., wide bulbous body w/short wide cylindrical neck flanked by four buttress handles to the shoulder rim, Wisteria matte glaze, raised racetrack mark (hairline to one handle) **1,100**

Vase, bud, 8 1/2" h., 3" d., slender baluster-form w/very slender trumpet neck, Leopard Skin crystalline glaze in shades of green, cream & brown, rectangular ink mark **1,430**

Vase, 8 1/2" h., 8 1/2" d., squatty bulbous body w/a wide shoulder attached to the short flaring neck w/four arched short handles, turquoise & Moss to Rose flambé glaze, raised racetrack mark **2,588**

Squatty Bulbous Fulper Vase

Vase, 8 3/4" h., 11" d., footed squatty wide bulbous body w/a wide shoulder centering a short flared neck, Mirror Black glaze, raised racetrack mark & perfect paper label (ILLUS.) **1,955**

Vase, 9" h., 2 1/2" d., very slender tall baluster-form w/a tiny flared neck, Butterscotch flambé glaze, inked racetrack mark **309**

Vase, 9 1/2" h., baluster-form, Leopard Skin crystalline glaze, incised racetrack mark **523**

Vase, 9 1/2" h., large bulbous nearly spherical body w/a short cylindrical neck & thick rim flanked by five small oval ring shoulder handles, overall streaky bluish green crystalline glaze, paper label (grinding flakes on base) **770**

Vase, 9 1/2" h., large ovoid body w/a narrow rounded shoulder centering a short, wide cylindrical neck w/closed rim flanked by pierced squared handles from the rim to the shoulder, green crystalline glaze, incised vertical mark.. **605**

Vase, 9 1/2" h., tapering wide foot supporting a wide slightly flaring cylindrical body flanked by low angled & ribbed buttress handles part way up the sides, a dark blue over caramel drippy glaze, impressed mark.. **550**

Vase, 9 1/2" h., 5" d., "Fool's Cap" tall corseted form, overall Flemington Green flambé glaze, rectangular inked mark **675**

Vase, 9 3/4" h., 6 1/2" d., bulbous baluster-form, fine Leopard's Skin pale green crystalline glaze, inked racetrack mark........ **675**

Vase, 10" h., compressed bulbous base tapering to tall cylindrical neck w/flat rim flanked by angular loop buttress handles, covered in fine Copperdust crystalline to green flambé glaze, raised racetrack mark **715**

Vase, 10" h., slender baluster-form w/flared rim, overall dark matte green glaze, incised oval vertical mark **489**

Vase, 10" h., wide baluster-form w/a wide cylindrical neck w/flaring rim, brown, blue & cream flambé glaze, incised vertical mark (drill hole in base) **320**

Vase, 10" h., 7 1/2" w., Pilgrim flask-form, an oval foot supporting an upright round flattened disk body tapering to a short cylindrical neck w/flared rim, S-scroll shoulder handles, fine curdled green, Mirror Black, blue & ivory flambé glaze, rectangular ink mark.. **1,045**

Vase, 10" h., 10" d., bulbous ovoid body w/the round shoulder centering a short cylindrical neck, overall Chinese Blue flambé glaze, raised racetrack mark (minor scratches near rim)................................. **1,913**

Vase, 10 1/2" h., footed wide bulbous body, the wide shoulder tapering to a short cylindrical neck, Mirror Black flambé glaze, raised racetrack mark **1,870**

Vase, 11" h., tall slender slightly waisted cylindrical body w/rectangular narrow buttress handles halfway down the sides, each w/a narrow rectangular opening, unusual blue & green flambé over red matte glaze, incised vertical mark.............. **1,100**

Vase, 12" h., large classic baluster-form body w/flaring rim covered in a Rouge flambé glaze, raised racetrack mark **715**

Vase, 12" h., large classic baluster-form body w/flaring rim, overall two-tone light green crystalline glaze, stamped vertical mark.. **440**

Vase, 12" h., raised & flared neck on a tall ovoid body, ochre rim & sparse cobalt blue crystals on a periwinkle blue ground, vertical black ink stamp mark, ca. 1915....... **633**

Vase, 12" h., 4 1/2" d., tall slender baluster-form body w/a rounded shoulder to the small flared neck, Butterscotch flambé glaze, inked racetrack mark........................... **619**

Vase, 12" h., 7" d., simple ovoid body tapering to wide cylindrical neck w/flaring rim, frothy Rouge Flambé glaze, raised racetrack mark **731**

Vase, 12" h., 7 1/2" d., tall baluster-form body w/heavy loop handles arching from the neck down to the shoulder & along the sides, fine Mirrored Green, Mahogany & Ivory flambé glaze, rectangular ink mark **1,350**

Vase, 12 1/2" h., bulbous ovoid body w/four shoulder handles, collared neck w/flat rim, Chinese blue flambé over Famille Rose glaze, vertical die-stamped race track mark (one handle reglued) **715**

Vase, 12 1/2" h., bulbous ovoid horizontally ribbed body tapering to a tall smooth flaring neck, small arched shoulder handles, cream flambé drip glaze over orange & brown w/a gunmetal crystalline glaze at the bottom, incised vertical mark **1,210**

Vase, 12 1/2" h., footed bulbous ovoid body w/short cylindrical neck w/molded rim, loop shoulder handle, Leopard Skin crystalline glaze, incised racetrack mark **2,530**

Rare & Early Tall Fulper Vase

Vase, 12 3/4" h., 5 1/4" d., Vasekraft, tall cylindrical lower body below four small buttress projections supporting a narrow flaring shoulder below the tapering cylindrical neck molded w/pointed panels, speckled cafe-au-lait glaze, long hairline from rim, few glaze chips on base, rare & early, rectangular ink mark (ILLUS.)........... **1,265**

Vase, 12 3/4" h., 7 3/4" d., bullet-shaped body w/two ring handles, covered in text-book Cucumber & Leopard Skin crystal-line glaze, ink racetrack mark **3,850**

Vase, 13" h., tall cylindrical form w/flat rim, overall relief-molded cattails & long slen-der leaves, covered in a Matte green & Leopard Skin crystalline glaze, the brown clay showing through, rectangular ink mark (restoration to lines from rim)............. **1,760**

Tall Fulper Vase with Cattails

Vase, 13" h., 4 3/4" d., tall slightly waisted cylindrical form, embossed w/tall cattails under a Cucumber Matte crystalline glaze, rectangular mark, shown in Paul Evans pottery book (ILLUS.)........................ **5,750**

Tall Trumpet-form Fulper Vase

Vase, 13" h., 5 1/2" d., low squatty bulbous base w/a wide shoulder to the tall trum-pet-form neck, overall Cat's Eye to blue flambé glaze, impressed racetrack mark, early (ILLUS.)` **1,955**

Vase, 13" h., 12" d., Roman Urn-form, a large bulbous ovoid body tapering to a short cylindrical neck & molded rim, the shoulder mounted w/four small C-scroll handles, Mirror Black crystalline glaze, incised racetrack mark (restoration to handles, tight lines in rim, several short scratches) **788**

Vase, 13 1/4" h., squatty bulbous base w/tall trumpet-form neck, gunmetal & Chinese blue flambé glaze, incised race-track mark & remnant of paper label **1,650**

Vase, 15" h., 8" d., tall classical urn-form, the angled shoulder mounted w/two up-right inwardly scrolled handles, Mirror Black to Copperdust Crystalline glaze, paper label & "MR" in red (glaze chip on one handle)... **1,575**

Vase, 16 1/4" h., tall slightly expanding cy-lindrical body w/short molded rim, cov-ered in a frothy Moss to Rose glaze, ink racetrack mark **1,540**

Vase, 17" h., tall swelled cylindrical body ta-pering slightly to a short cylindrical neck, Leopard Skin glaze w/large crystals in green &·tan, impressed vertical mark......... **2,530**

Vase, 17" h., 8" d., floor-type, tall swelled cylindrical form tapering to a short cylin-drical neck, Chinese blue & brown mirror flambé glaze, rectangular ink mark (drilled hole in bottom) **1,688**

Vase, 17 1/2'" h., 9" d., floor-type, tall balus-ter-form w/a short rolled neck, mirrored Flemington Green flambé glaze, incised racetrack mark (burst bubble near base)...... **495**

Wall pocket, spearpoint-form Pipes of Pan design w/a cluster of tapering tubes form-ing the upper body, Cucumber green matte glaze, rectangular ink mark, 4 3/4" w., 10 1/2" l. **450**

Vase, footed, wide bulbous base tapering to short wide cylindrical neck, large loop handles from mid section to rim, matte purple & blue glaze, black vertical Fulper in lozenge mark... **460**

Gallé Pottery

Gallé Pottery Mark

Fine pottery was made by Emile Gallé, the multi-talented French designer and artisan, who is also famous for his glass and furniture. The pottery is relatively scarce.

Gallé Lion Candlestick

Candlesticks, figural, in the form of a seated roaring lion wearing a crown that forms the socket, a large shield at the front decorated w/a thistle, other floral decoration, in grey, black & red on a light blue ground w/gilt trim, signed, late 19th c., repairs, 8" h., pr. (ILLUS. of one)............ **$575**

Dish, foliate-shaped bowl, the interior painted in naturalistic colors w/wild flowers in front of a shore landscape, gilded rim, base w/red stamp mark, late 19th c., 10 1/4" w. (restored).. **316**

Gallé Cat with Flowers & Stripes

Model of cat seated w/head turned facing the viewer, bulging eyes w/smiling expression, glazed in white & decorated w/pale lavender bands & reddish orange & green floral clusters, a painted neck chain w/a locket holding a dog portrait, minor chips to paws & one ear, ca. 1895, 12 3/8" h. (ILLUS.).. **5,700**

Gallé Pottery Seated Cat

Model of cat seated w/head turned facing the viewer, bulging eyes w/smiling expression, glazed in white & decorated w/scattered ringed dots & heart-like devices, signed, ca. 1890, 13" h. (ILLUS.)..... **3,600**

Rare Gallé Pottery Dog

Model of dog, seated Boston Terrier-like animal facing the viewer, open front legs, bulging eyes & angry expression, painted in white w/scattered ringed dots & heart-like devices, signed, ca. 1890, 12 5/8" h. (ILLUS.)`.. **6,000**

Gallé Owl

Model of owl, faience, molded in full relief, perched owl w/glass eyes, glazed in shades of grey & amber on russet base, inscribed (ILLUS.) **3,737**

Pitcher, 9" h., figural, a footed bulbous squatty body w/swirled rib surface centered by a tall cylindrical neck w/rim spout & looped branch handle opposite a swan's-neck spout w/a duck head finial, underglaze decorated on pansies trimmed w/gold, impressed "E (cross) G" & marked in red "E. Gallé Nancy deposé," glaze chip on top rim (ILLUS. center, bottom of page) **1,265**

Plaque, pierced to hang, round, decorated in the Limoges style w/a bucolic landscape featuring four cows, marked in black underglaze "E. Gallé - E (cross) G," 12 1/2" d. (ILLUS. left, below) **748**

Plaque, pierced to hang, oblong cartouche form w/a large shell at the top center & small shells at the center of each side, decorative border bands & the center w/a large stylized bird on a scrolling branch in

grey, amber & Delft blue in a tin glaze, inscribed "Gallé ---Nancy," 12 1/2 x 14" (ILLUS. right, below) **575**

Plates, 9" d., each enamel-decorated w/a variety of insects, fruits & vegetation, printed marks, late 19th c., set of 11 .... **1,495**

Tray, oval, painted underglaze w/a genre scene of a child at play w/a ram pull-toy & winged insect at each side, molded mark in lower left "E (cross) G," 19th c., 8 3/4 x 15 1/4" **633**

Wall pocket, figural, model of a large round tambourine painted on the front w/delicate wildflowers, a grasshopper & a French inscription, suspended at the top by a pointed pale blue ribbon & bow w/applied pine cone, signed "Emile Gallé - Déposé," late 19th c., 9 1/2" h. (minor flaws) **1,100**

Goldscheider

Goldscheider Marks

The Goldscheider firm, manufacturers of porcelain and faience in Austria between 1885 and the present, was founded by Freidrich Goldscheider and carried on by his widow. The firm came under the control of his sons, Walter and Marcell, in 1920. Fleeing their native Austria at the time of World War II, the Goldscheiders set up an operation in the United States. They were listed in the Trenton, New Jersey, City Directory from 1943 through 1950 and their main production seems to have been art pottery figurines.

Gallé Pottery Pieces

Goldscheider Bust of a Lady

Bust of a lady, stylized elongated head of a lady w/tightly curled brown hair & green close-fitting hat, wearing a green jacket w/lace collar & cuffs, her long hands together beside her cheek, stamped marks in black on base, Austria, ca. 1920s, crazing, 15 1/4" h. (ILLUS.) **$920**

Two Goldscheider Figures

Figure group, tall svelte Art Deco lady wearing a long flowered dress & wide-brimmed hat, one hand on her hip, the other holding her hat, striding beside her sleek wolfhound, printed & impressed marks, 15" h. (ILLUS. left) 575

Figure of ballerina, wearing a lace skirt, printed marks, 17" h. 862

Figure of dancer, the tall slender young lady w/long hair posed wearing a halter top & long flowered skirt which she holds out to the sides, on a plinth base, printed marks, 17 3/4" h. (ILLUS. right) 747

Figure of nude lady, an Art Deco style lady standing nude except for stockings & a floral-decorated drapery, wearing a high upswept hat, on a paneled plinth, impressed, printed & painted marks, 19" h.... **2,875**

Lamp base, finely detailed figure of a woman decorated in colors of green, yellow, purple & blue, on a bluish white ground & a black base, signed "Goldscheider,

Wien, Made in Austria, XXVII," 32" h. overall **1,610**

Plaque, molded in relief w/the head of a young woman, stamped mark, 12 1/4" h. **460**

Gonder

Lawton Gonder founded Gonder Ceramic Arts in Zanesville, Ohio in 1941 and it continued in operation until 1957.

The firm produced a higher priced and better quality of commercial art potteries than many firms of the time and employed Jamie Matchet and Chester Kirk, both of whom were outstanding ceramic designers. Several special glazes were developed during the company's history and Gonder even duplicated some museum pieces of Chinese ceramic. In 1955 the firm converted to the production of tile due to increased foreign competition and by 1957 their years of finest production were over

Increase price ranges as indicated for the following glaze colors: red flambé - 50 percent, antique gold crackle - 70 percent, turquoise Chinese crackle - 40 per cent, white Chinese crackle - 30 per cent.

Gonder Rectangular Ashtray

Ashtray, rectangular w/wavy wide edge, Chinese White Crackle glaze on edges & brown on interior, no mold number (ILLUS.) **$75-100**

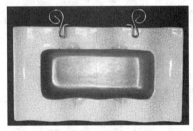

Ashtray with Trojan Horse Head

Ashtray, oblong w/model of Trojan horse head on rim, Mold No. 548, gunmetal glaze, 6 x 6 1/2" (ILLUS.) 25-50

Ashtray, square, Mold No. 805, 9 1/4" 20-40

Ashtray, "S" swirl design, Mold No. a 408, 2 1/2 x 10" 25-35

Ashtray, square, Mold No. 586 20-30

Bank, figural Sheriff, 8" h. 200-250

Basket, shell shape w/overhead handle,
Mold No. 674, 7 x 8"...................................... **25-50**
Basket, Mold No. L-19, 9 x 13"........................ **20-30**
Bell, figural "Sovereign Bonnet Lady," Mold
No. 800, 3 1/2" h... **50-75**
Beverage set: 8" h. pitcher & six 5" h.
mugs; LaGonda patt, Mold No. 917 &
909, the set.. **50-75**
Book end, model of horse, Mold No. 582,
10" h... **100-125**

Trojan Horse Head Book Ends

Book ends, model of Trojan horse head,
mottled green glaze, Mold No. 220,
7 1/2" h., pr. (ILLUS.) **100-150**
Bowl, 13" d., oak leaf design, Mold No. 591 .. **40-60**
Bowl, low, scalloped tulip shape, Mold No.
523... **35-50**
**Butter warmer, cover & candleholder
base,** Mold No. 996, 2 1/2 x 4 1/2", 3
pcs... **25-40**
Candleholders, model of dolphin, Mold No.
561, 2 1/4 x 5", pr. **40-60**

Shell-shaped Console Bowl

Console bowl, oblong shell-molded
w/pointed ends & starfish molded at the
sides, speckled brown on yellow glaze,
Mold No. 500 (ILLUS.) **100-125**
Console bowl, lobed incurved sides, Mold
E-12, 2 1/2 x 7" **5-15**
Console bowl, crescent moon shape, Mold
J-55, 5 x 12"... **15-30**
Console bowl, seashell shape, Mold No.
521, 7 x 12".. **25-40**
Console bowl, rectangular base, body
w/relief-molded center fan shape flanked
by cornucopia forms, Mold K-14,
7 1/2 x 12 1/2" **150-200**
Console bowl, model of banana, "Banana
Boat," Mold No. 557, 7 x 16" **40-55**
Console bowl, seashell design, Mold No.
505, 7 1/4 x 17 1/2" **50-65**
Console set: 5 x 12" bowl & pr. of 6 1/2" h.
candleholders; crescent moon shape,
Mold Nos. J-55 & J-56, the set **60-70**
Console set: 14" l. bowl & pr. of 5" h. can-
dleholders; shell shape, Mold Nos. 505 &
552, the set **100-125**
Console set: 16" l. bowl & pr. of candle-
holders; "Banana Boat" bowl, Mold Nos.
565 & 567, the set **75-100**
Cookie jar, Pirate, 8" h................................ **200-250**

Cookie jar, Mold No. P-24, 8 1/2" h............... **15-30**
Cookie jar, Sheriff, Mold No. 950,
12" h. **1,000-1,200**
Cornucopia-vase, ribbed, Mold No. 360,
7" h. **20-35**
Cornucopia-vase, square base, Mold E-5,
7" h. **15-30**
Cornucopia-vase, w/round handles, Mold
No. 380, 7" h. **20-35**
Cornucopia-vase, leaves at base, Mold
No. 691, 7 1/2" h... **50-75**
Cornucopia-vase, held by figural hand,
oval base, Mold No. 675, 7 1/2 x 8"......... **75-100**
Cornucopia-vase, ribbed, curled handles,
Mold No. 419, 8" h... **30-45**
Cornucopia-vase, shell form, Mold No. H-
84, 8" h.. **15-25**
Cornucopia-vase, square base, Mold No.
H-14, 9" h. **20-35**
Cornucopia-vase, w/leaf design, Mold No.
J-61, 9" h.. **50-60**
Cornucopia-vase, uneven double swirl de-
sign, Mold No. H-48, 4 x 9 3/4" **50-60**
Cornucopia-vase, on flat square base,
Mold No. J-66, 10" l.. **20-35**
Cornucopia-vase, double loop handle,
Mold J-69, 11" h... **50-65**
Dish, flat, dog bone shape, Mold No.,
2 x 11 1/2".. **25-50**

Gonder Slant-top Ewer

Ewer, bulbous base tapering to a tall slant-
ed top w/pointed spout & integral handle,
Mold 410, Chinese Turquoise Crackle
glaze (ILLUS.) **75-100**
Ewer, fluted, Mold No. E-60, 6" h. **5-15**
Ewer, "Z" handle, Mold No. E-65, 6 1/4" h. **10-20**
Ewer, Mold No. H-73, 8" h. **15-25**

Carafe-shaped Ewer

Ewer, w/stopper, carafe-shaped, gunmetal glaze, Mold No. 994, 8" (ILLUS.) **75-100**
Ewer, Mold H-33, 9" h.. 30-50
Ewer, scrolled handle, Mold No. H-606 & 606, 9" h.. 50-75
Ewer, Mold No. J-25, 8 x 11"........................... 50-75
Ewer, Mold No. M-9, 14" h............................... 50-75
Ewer, shell-shaped, Mold No. 508, 14" h. (no starfish)... **75-100**
Ewer, shell-shaped w/starfish on base, Mold No. 508, 14" h............................... 50-75
Figure group, pair of chair bearers w/chair, Mold No. 765, 12 1/2" **100-150**
Figure of Chinese peasant, kneeling & reaching forward, Mold No. 546, 4 1/2 x 6 1/2" 25-40
Figure of Chinese peasant, standing figure, Mold No. 545, 8" h............................. 15-30
Figure of coolie, kneeling & bending forward, Mold No. 547, 5" h............................. 15-30
Figure of Oriental male, Mold No. 773, 11" h.. 40-60
Figure of Oriental mandarin, Mold No. 755, 8 3/4" h. 50-75
Ginger jar, cov., square, 10" h.................. **100-150**
Ginger jar, cov., decorated w/Oriental dragon, pedestal base, Mold No. 533, 11" h., 3 pcs. **150-200**
Lamp, model of Foo dog, 8" h........................ 50-75
Lamp, cookie jar shape, Mold No. P-24, 8 1/2" h.. 20-40
Lamp, model of Trojan horse head, 8 1/2" h.. 20-35
Lamp, feather plume design, 10" h. 45-60
Lamp, model of Trojan horse head, Mold No. 540, 10" h. **75-100**
Lamp, driftwood design, 12" h........................ 25-50
Lamp, model of two horse heads, 12" h. 40-50
Lamp, Oriental dual figures on side, 16" h. **150-200**
Model of cat, seated "Imperial Cat," Mold No. 521, 12" h. **200-250**

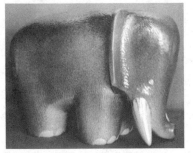

Gonder Model of an Elephant

Model of elephant, stylized standing animal w/greenish brown glaze & ivory trim, Mold 108 (ILLUS.) **400-500**
Model of panther, recumbent, Mold No. 217, 12" l... 30-50
Model of panther, standing, Mold No. 205, 12" h.. 30-50
Model of panther, recumbent, Mold No. 217, 15" l... **75-100**
Model of panther, recumbent, Mold No. 210, 19" l... **75-125**
Model of panther, standing, Mold No. 206, 19" h.. 40-60

Model of racing horse head, Mold No. 576, 13 1/2" l., 5 3/4" h. **100-150**
Models of geese, one looking down & one w/neck stretched upward, Mold Nos. B-14 & B-15, 3 1/2 & 5 1/2" h., pr. **25-40**
Mug, swirled wood finish, Mold No. 902, 5" h.. **15-30**
Pedestal base, Mold No. 533-B, 6" d. **25-50**
Pitcher, 6 1/2" h., squatty bulbous base, cylindrical neck w/flared rim, zigzag handle, Mold No. E-73 & E-373............................. **25-35**
Pitcher, 7" h., ruffled lip, Mold No. 1206 .... **25-50**
Pitcher, 5 x 8", ridged wood-tone glaze, Mold No. 901.. **50-75**
Pitcher, 9" h., plain lip, Mold 1205 .... **50-75**
Pitcher, 10" h., Mold No. 682...................... **50-75**

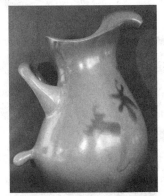

Gonder Two-handled Water Pitcher

Pitcher, 12 1/2" h., water, two-handled, tan glaze decorated w/black figures, Mold No. 104 (ILLUS.)..................................... **350-450**
Planter, w/hole, Mold No. 738, 2 3/4 x 4 1/4" (top to Mold No. 724)............. **5-15**
Planter, footed, square w/hole in base, Mold No. 706, 5" h................................... **10-20**
Planter, Mold No. 724, 4 x 5" (bottom to African violet planter No. 738)......................... **5-15**
Planter, bulbous body w/tab handles, decorated w/relief-molded flowers, Mold No. H-83, 5 1/2" h. **50-60**
Planter, model of swan, Mold No. E-44, 5 1/2" h.. **5-15**
Planter, figural Madonna, Mold E-303 & R-303, 4 x 6".. **5-15**
Planter, square flared form, Mold No. 733, 2 1/2 x 6 1/2" **15-30**
Planter, rectangular, Mold No. 701, 5 3/4 x 7 1/2" **15-30**
Planter, basket shape w/overhead handle, Mold H-39, 7 x 8"... **5-15**
Planter, model of swan, Mold No. J-31, 8 1/2" h.. **15-30**
Planter, figural, standing coolie figure, Mold No. 519, 9" h. **20-35**
Planter, model of wishing well, 6 1/2 x 9 1/4" **100-125**
Planter, model of Chinese sampan (junk), Mold No. 550, 10" l................................ **10-25**
Planter, figural nude w/deer, Mold No. 593, 9 1/2 x 14"... **250-300**
Planter, figural, Oriental water carriers, gold trim, 14" **200-250**

Planter, figural, Bali girl carrying basket on head, 14 1/2" h. **50-75**
Planter, model of large Chinese sampan (junk), Mold No. 520, 15" l. **25-40**
Planter, two-footed w/flared top, Mold No. 716 .... **25-40**
Planters, figural Bali man & Bali woman w/buckets, 14" h., pr. **60-80**
Plate, square, LaGonda patt. **10-20**

Divided Relish Dish

Relish dish, shallow, divided, six lobe-form sections, mottled yellow glaze, Mold No. 871, 11 x 18" (ILLUS.) **90-120**

Gonder La Gonda Pattern Teapot

Teapot, cov., upright rectangular form, LaGonda patt., creamy yellow glaze, Mold 914 (ILLUS.) **50-75**
Teapot, cov., Mold No. P-31, 6 1/2" h. **15-25**
Tray, pillow form, flat, Mold No. 544, 7 x 10" .. **40-60**
Tray, rectangular, flat, Mold No. 700 .... **20-35**
TV lamp, figural "Comedy & Tragedy Mask," Mold No. 519, 6 1/2 x 10" **75-100**
TV lamp, model of chanticleer rooster, 9 1/2 x 14" **40-60**
TV lamp, model of masted ship, 14" h. **15-25**

Gonder Oriental-style Vase

Vase, squared Oriental-style w/angular neck handles, pale green glaze, Mold 537 (ILLUS.) **50-75**
Vase, 5" h., cylindrical, Mold No. 710 .... **10-20**
Vase, 5 x 5" sq., flared, leaf decoration, Mold No. 384 .... **25-35**
Vase, 5 3/4" h., square pillow form, Mold No. 705 .... **10-20**
Vase, 6" h., bulbous base w/flared top, leaf decoration, Mold E-66 .... **10-20**
Vase, 6" h., fan shape w/relief-molded scroll design, Mold No. H-82 .... **25-35**
Vase, 6" h., footed, bulbous lobed base w/flaring square top, Mold E-71 .... **5-15**
Vase, 6" h., footed, squatty bulbous base, cylindrical neck w/flared rim, applied leaf decoration, Mold E-68 .... **15-30**
Vase, 6" h., waisted twisted form, Mold E-64 .... **5-10**
Vase, 5 x 6 1/4", rectangular, Mold No. 709 .. **10-25**
Vase, 6 1/2" h., bulbous base w/scalloped trumpet-form neck, Mold E-49 .... **10-25**
Vase, 6 1/2" h., footed bulbous base w/trumpet-form neck, leaf-shaped handles, Mold No. E-67 .... **15-25**
Vase, 6 1/2" h., hourglass shape w/large applied leaf, Mold E-70 .... **15-25**
Vase, 6 1/2" h., ribbed bulbous base w/cylindrical neck, angled handles, Mold No. E-48 .... **10-25**
Vase, 6 1/2" h., ribbed, swirl design, Mold No. 381 .... **20-35**
Vase, 6 1/2" h., seashell shape, Mold No. 216 .... **70-90**
Vase, 6 1/2" h., two-handled, draped inverted bell design, Mold No. 418 .... **40-55**
Vase, 6 1/2" h., urn shape w/leaf design, single handle, Mold No. H-80 .... **20-30**
Vase, 4 1/2 x 7", ovoid body w/flared top, shoulder handles, Mold E-1 .... **5-15**
Vase, 7" h., bottle form, Mold No. 1203 .... **30-50**
Vase, 7" h., pinched leaf design, Mold No. E-372 .... **15-30**
Vase, 6 1/2 x 7 1/4", scroll footed, Mold No. E-4 or 304 .... **10-25**
Vase, 4 1/2 x 7 1/2", footed, model of single flower, Mold No. #-3 .... **10-20**
Vase, 7 1/2" h., basketweave w/knothole design, Mold No. 867 .... **30-50**
Vase, 7 1/2" h., flared foot below inverted pear-shaped body, flaring lobed top, Mold No. E-6 .... **10-20**
Vase, 7 x 7 1/2", model of seashell w/two dolphins at base, Mold No. 558 .... **50-75**
Vase, 7 x 7 1/2", two-handled, bulbous base w/wide flaring neck, Mold H-42 .... **25-35**
Vase, 7 3/4" h., two-handled, Mold No. H-49 .. **40-60**
Vase, 6 x 8", model of starfish, Mold No. H-79 .... **15-25**
Vase, 7 1/4 x 8", cuspidor top, Mold No. 559 .... **200-250**
Vase, 8" h., flared bulb to square top, Oriental design, Mold No. 537 or 718 .... **50-75**
Vase, 8" h., flaring form w/relief-molded swans at base, Mold No. H-47 .... **15-25**
Vase, 8" h., flat, Lotus design, Mold No. 402 .. **20-30**
Vase, 8" h., two-handled, relief-molded fern decoration, Mold No. H-77 .... **15-30**
Vase, 5 x 8 1/2, rectangular, Mold No. H-74 .. **15-25**
Vase, 6 x 8 1/2", modified rectangle w/raised flowers, Mold No. 687 .... **50-75**

Vase, 7 x 8 1/2", flaring body w/one angled handle at rim, the other at base, Mold No. H-56 .... **15-30**

Vase, 7 x 8 1/2", leaf form w/flared rim, Mold No. H-86 .... **20-35**

Vase, 8 1/2" h., bottle form, Mold No. 1211 .... **75-100**

Vase, 8 1/2" h., flat leaf design, Mold No. H-78 .... **15-30**

Vase, 8 1/2" h., footed bulbous body w/flaring rim, triple loop handles, Mold No. H-75 .... **15-25**

Vase, 8 1/2" h., model of a stylized swan, Mold No. 511 .... **30-45**

Vase, 8 1/2" h., rectangular, decorated w/relief-molded crane, Mold No. H-76 .... **30-40**

Vase, 8 1/2" h., relief-molded double leaf form w/berries, Mold J-70 .... **35-50**

Vase, 8 1/2" h., six-fluted top w/raised leaf design, Mold H-11 .... **20-35**

Vase, 8 1/2" h., tapering pillow form, Mold No. 702 .... **35-50**

Vase, 8 1/2" h., triple leaf form, Mold No. H-67 .... **15-25**

Vase, 8 1/2" h., two-handled, flared foot below horizontal ribbed base & bulbous lobed top, Mold No. H-52 .... **15-30**

Vase, 4 1/4 x 8 3/4", fluted handle, Mold H-34 .... **15-30**

Vase, 6 1/2 x 9", model of stylized horse w/wings, Mold No. 553 .... **10-25**

Vase, 6 x 9", basketweave design w/flared top, Mold H-36 .... **40-50**

Vase, 6 x 9", flame shape, Mold No. H-69 ..... **25-40**

Vase, 6 x 9", tulip form, Mold No. H-68 .... **10-25**

Vase, 9" h., bottle form, Mold No. 1210 .... **25-50**

Vase, 9" h., footed, square double bulb form, Mold No. 607 & H-607 .... **75-100**

Vase, 9" h., footed, two-handled, bulbous base, squared top, Mold No. H-7 .... **15-30**

Vase, 9" h., lyre shape, Mold J-57 .... **50-75**

Vase, 9" h., shell form, three dolphins at base, Mold No. H-85 .... **15-25**

Vase, 9" h., squatty bulbous base, tapering cylindrical neck, twisted handles, Mold No. H-5 .... **25-35**

Vase, 9" h., tapering cylindrical form w/relief-molded peapod decoration, Mold No. H-87 .... **30-40**

Vase, 9" h., tieback drape design, Mold No. 605 & H-605 .... **40-60**

Vase, 9" h., two-handled fan vase, Mold H-10 .... **15-30**

Vase, 9 1/4" h., fan shape, Mold No. H-601 ... **25-40**

Vase, 9 1/4" h., footed leaf form w/open circle in center, Mold No. H-603 .... **25-35**

Vase, 9 1/2" h., model of fawn head, Mold No. 518 .... **75-100**

Vase, 9 1/2" h., two-handled, twisted baluster-form body, Mold No. H-62 .... **15-30**

Vase, 10" h., Art Deco free form design, Mold No. 636 .... **80-100**

Vase, 10" h., feather form, Mold No. 539 .... **50-75**

Vase, 10" h., hooked squares design, Mold No. 512 .... **75-100**

Vase, 10" h., model of Trojan horse head, Mold No. 540 .... **75-100**

Vase, 10" h., square form w/impressed flower design, Mold No. 688 .... **50-75**

Vase, 10" h., two-handled, flared footed w/bulbous base & square neck w/flaring rim, Mold No. H-604 .... **40-55**

Vase, 7 x 10", conical w/relief-molded leaves at base, Mold J-64 .... **40-50**

Vase, 7 x 10", model of a butterfly, Mold No. 523 .... **75-150**

Vase, 7 x 10", model of leaves on branch, Mold No. 683 .... **50-75**

Vase, 9 x 10", model of angel fish on waves, Mold No. 522 .... **75-125**

Vase, 6 x 10", model of swan, Mold No. 802 .. **25-50**

Vase, 10 1/4" h., zigzag & buttons design, Mold No. 517 .... **75-100**

Vase, 4 1/2 x 10 1/2, square form w/round top, Mold No. 534 .... **50-75**

Vase, 10 1/2 x 11", model of Pegasus, Mold No. 526 .... **175-250**

Vase, 11" h., flat form, model of swan, Mold No. 530 .... **100-125**

Vase, 8 1/2 x 11", flame design, Mold No. 510 .... **60-75**

Vase, 8 x 11", figural leaf design, Mold No. 504 .... **25-40**

Vase, 11 1/2" h., blades of grass design, Mold No. 861 .... **40-60**

Vase, 11 1/2" h., fan shape, relief-molded shell decoration, Mold No. J-60 .... **40-55**

Vase, 11 1/2" h., orchid design, Mold No. 513 .... **50-75**

Vase, 7 x 11 1/2", triple "S" design, Mold No. 594 .... **50-75**

Vase, 8 x 11 1/2", leaf swirl design, Mold No. 596 .... **50-75**

Vase, 11 3/4" h., swallow design, Mold K-25 .... **150-200**

Vase, 12" h., footed ovoid body w/small rim handles, decorated w/relief-molded flowers & leaves **50-75**

Vase, 12" h., swirl design w/two openings, Mold No. 862 .... **75-125**

Vase, 6 x 12", Chinese Imperial dragon handle, w/base, Mold No. 535, 2 pcs. ... **200-250**

Vase, 6 3/4 x 12 1/2", model of cactus, Mold No. K-26 or 826 .... **50-75**

Vase, 13" h., trellis w/flowers design, Mold No. 863 .... **50-75**

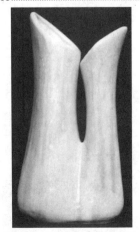

Double Cylindrical Form Vase

Vase, 6 1/2 x 13", double, tall slender cylin-
drical forms joined at triangular form
base, slanted rim, mottled green glaze,
Mold No. 868 (ILLUS.) **150-200**
Vase, 6 1/2 x 13", double, triangular, Mold
No. 368 .... **70-100**
Vase, 15 3/4" h., leaves & twigs design,
Mold No. 599 .... **100-150**

Gouda

Gouda Pottery Marks

*While tin-enameled earthenware has been made
in Gouda, Holland since the early 1600s, the productions of modern factories are attracting increasing collector attention. The art pottery of Gouda is
easily recognized by its brightly colored peasant-
style decoration with some types having achieved a
"cloisonné" effect. Pottery workshops located in, or
near, Gouda include Regina, Zenith, Plazuid,
Schoonhoven, Arnhem and others. Their wide
range of production included utilitarian wares, as
well as vases, miniatures and large outdoor garden
ornaments.*

Unusual Gouda Clock

Clock, wall-type, a large flattened disk centered by a small round dial w/Arabic numerals, the front decorated in dark blue
w/stylized irises & foliage in shades of
green, blue, mauve, rust & yellow, glossy
glaze, clock works marked "Junghans,"
crazing, clock not working, ca. 1900,
9" d. (ILLUS.) **$805**
Toothpick holder, floral decoration on
black ground, side medallion KLM logo
silhouette, 208 Zenith, Gouda Fleer,
1 3/4" h. **80**
Vase, 4" h., decorated w/glossy multicolor
florals on mottled grey ground, green interior, Royal Areo 2841 House mark **125**
Vase, 9" h., footed bulbous nearly spherical
body centered by a tall slender neck
w/flared rim, high slender loop handles
from rim to shoulder, decorated in rust &
moss & grass green w/stylized tulip blossoms & leaves swirling against a dark
green ground, glossy glaze, painted
marks **413**

Floral-Decorated Gouda Vase

Vase, 9" h., ovoid shouldered body w/a
slender swelled neck, decorated w/styl-
ized flowers & leaves in shades of dark
green, rust, brown, pale green & white,
matte glaze, signed "Made in Holland"
(ILLUS.) **176**
Vase, 11" h., shouldered ovoid body, deco-
rated w/butterflies & foliage, signed **1,092**
Vase, 12 1/2" h., tall baluster-form w/a short
small cylindrical neck, a black ground
decorated w/stylized florals in shades of
green, cobalt blue, mustard yellow, rust,
mauve & purple, glossy glaze, marked
"304 - Gouda - Holland - J.B." w/a house
(minor glaze imperfections) **575**
Vase, 12 1/2" h., 4 3/4" d., footed tall slen-
der tapering cylindrical form w/a short cylindrical neck, dark green ground decorated w/a standing profile portrait of a
Dutch peasant woman w/white cap,
green neckerchief & purple blouse, dark
blue apron & orange dress, marked
"#7052 RR Holland Gouda - #1852R"
(flake on bottom) **385**
Vase, 22" h., tall slender ovoid body, deco-
rated in colors w/an exotic bird & foliage,
signed **2,760**
Vases, 11 1/4" h., ovoid body tapering to a
flared rim, decorated w/geometric & stylized foliage designs in blue, yellow, orange & green on a mottled greyish green
ground, blue painted & impressed marks
(minor base chips) **518**

Grueby

GRUEBY

Grueby Pottery Mark

*Some fine art pottery was produced by the
Grueby Faience and Tile Company, established in
Boston in 1891. Choice pieces were created with
molded designs on a semi-porcelain body. The
ware is marked and often bears the initials of the
decorators. The pottery closed in 1907.*

Bowl, 4" d., low squatty bulbous form w/in-curved sides, incised w/short vertical leaves around the sides, dark green matte glaze, artist-initialed, impressed mark & partial paper label **$990**

Bowl, 4 3/4" d., 3 3/4" h., coupe-form, the deep half-round bowl raised on a low funnel foot, mottled matte green glaze w/glossy interior, impressed flower mark...... **495**

Bowl, 5 1/2" d., low wide form w/flaring rounded sides & a wide incurved rim, exterior w/dark blue matte glaze, impressed mark & two paper labels **935**

Bowl, 7" d., 3 1/2" h., deep flaring floriform five-lobed sides w/tooled buds on slender stems, fine curdled matte green glaze on exterior, glossy green interior glaze, circular pottery mark & "RE 339-2" .. **2,750**

Grueby Bowl with Square Rim

Bowl, 7 1/2" w., 3 1/2" h., deep rounded sides curving up to a wide square rim, tooled & applied overlapping pointed leaves around the exterior under a smooth speckled ochre matte glaze, glossy green interior glaze, by Wilhelmina Post, minute nick on edges of some leaves, small glaze miss on side, stamped mark (ILLUS.)................................ **2,300**

Bowl, 8" d., 2" h., wide shallow rounded flaring sides w/a closed rim, interior w/streaky light green glossy glaze, the exterior w/a dark green matte glaze, paper label, impressed mark (minute inside rim flake) **495**

Wide & Shallow Grueby Bowl

Bowl, 8" d., 2 1/2" h., wide flat bottom below low incurved sides & wide flat rim, speckled matte green glaze w/mineral deposits, glaze bubbles on side, signed (ILLUS.)... **575**

Rare Grueby Papyrus Bowl-vase

Bowl-vase, wide squatty bulbous form w/the wide shoulder centered by a short rolled neck, tooled & applied papyrus design under a fine oatmealed matte green glaze, by Wilhelmina Post, minor glaze flakes on base, 10" d., 5" h. (ILLUS.) **10,925**

Candlestick, tall slender corseted form w/flaring foot & bulbed neck below the flaring socket rim, tooled & applied leaves around the sides, leathery dark greenish blue matte glaze, paper label, 4" d., 8 1/2" h. **2,530**

Rare Grueby Covered Humidor

Humidor, cov., tapering cylindrical form w/waisted neck & fitted disk shape lid w/knob finial, decorated w/repeating floral band on rim, curdled matte sea-green glaze, impressed mark & incised "ER, 3 - 14," glaze bursts, 8" h. (ILLUS.) **1,093**

Grueby Jardiniere by W. Post

Jardiniere, slightly tapering ovoid form w/a wide & low rolled rim, tooled & applied up the sides w/long, wide leaves, frothy matte green glaze, by Wilhelmina Post, few minor glaze nicks, stamped mark, 10 1/2" d., 6" h. (ILLUS.) **5,175**

Large Grueby Jardiniere

Jardiniere, wide bulbous body w/a narrow rounded shoulder & wide, low rolled rim, molded w/continuous wide pointed leaves up the sides alternating w/blossoms on thin stems, green matte glaze, impressed mark, artist-signed, minor rim repair, 9" d. (ILLUS.) **2,310**

Paperweight, figural, oblong model of a large scarab beetle, matte bluish grey glaze, Grueby Faience stamped mark, 2 3/4 x 4" **563**

Paperweight, figural, oblong model of a large scarab beetle, matte greenish brown glaze, Grueby Faience stamped mark, 2 3/4 x 3 3/4" (small glaze flake on front) **731**

Paperweight, figural, oblong model of a scarab beetle, overall white curdled glaze, impressed pottery mark, 4" l., 2 3/4" h. **880**

Paperweight, figural, model of a scarab beetle, covered in a leathery mustard matte enamel, impressed "Grueby Faience Co. - Boston USA" & paper label, 3" l., 2" h. **770**

Tile, square, cuenca, sea gulls diving in high waves, browns, green & French blue enamels, unframed, unmarked, 4" sq. **770**

Fine Grueby Cuenca Tile

Tile, square, cuenca, decorated w/a three-masted ship & rolling waves against a blue sky, browns, ivory & French blue matte enamels, "MM" in glaze, unframed, 6" sq. (ILLUS.) **660**

Tile, square, depicting the cupid Eros in red bisque clay w/a matte mustard glaze background, unmarked, unframed, 6" sq. **330**

Tile, square, sculpted & painted design of tulips in blue & green w/green stems & leaves against darker green matte ground, unframed, 6" sq. (minor flakes) **990**

Tile, rectangular, sculpted candle & chamberstick in yellow, black & green against a darker green matte ground, unframed, 4 1/2 x 6" **2,860**

Vase, 3" h., miniature, bulbous ovoid body w/a thin shoulder centered by a flattened flaring neck, thick dark green matte glaze, impressed mark **1,045**

Vase, 3 3/4 x 4", footed squatty bulbous body w/flared rim, modeled w/stylized leaf design under a rich dark blue matte glaze, impressed pottery mark & "DS" **1,980**

Vase, 4 1/2" h., bulbous ovoid body w/a wide rounded shoulder centered by a short flaring neck w/flattened rim, the sides sculpted & applied w/wide vertical leaves, dark green matte glaze, impressed mark, artist-signed **1,210**

Vase, 4 1/2" h., 4 1/4" d., bulbous ovoid body w/a rounded shoulder centering a short rolled neck, crisply tooled & applied wide pointed leaves alternating w/yellow buds around the shoulder, leathery matte green glaze, no visible mark (minor touch-ups to edges, restoration to small rim chips) **5,225**

Vase, 5" h., 3 1/2" d., footed bulbous body w/slightly flaring rim, semi-matte leathery green glaze, impressed mark (small chips to rim) **880**

Squatty Bulbous Grueby Vase

Vase, 5" h., 5 1/2" d., footed wide squatty bulbous body w/a wide shoulder tapering to a short, wide flaring neck, tooled & applied w/wide arched & pointed leaves around the lower body alternating w/stems below large yellow blossoms around the rim, circular mark (ILLUS.) **12,650**

Vase, 5 1/2" h., 4" d., ovoid body w/a short flaring neck, incised vertical ridges, matte green enamel, impressed circular mark **1,540**

Vase, 6" h., 8 1/4" d., wide squatty tapering bulbous body, the wide shoulder centering a wide short cylindrical neck, wide applied pointed leaves alternating w/small buds around the shoulder, fine matte green glaze, impressed round pottery mark, by Florence Liley **5,500**

Grueby Vase with Crocus Buds

Vase, 6 1/4" h., 3 1/2" d., ovoid body w/wide flat rim, tooled & applied full-height leaves alternating w/large white crocus buds, matte French blue ground, stamped mark, two paper labels (ILLUS.) **19,800**

Vase, 6 1/4" h., 5" d., bulbous nearly spherical bottom below a wide cylindrical ringed neck, speckled bluish grey matte glaze, Grueby Pottery stamped mark (touch-up to rim nick) **900**

Vase, 6 3/4" h., 7 1/4" d., very wide ovoid body w/a closed rim, molded in low-relief w/tall wide leaves alternating w/slender stems w/tiny yellow & orange buds around the rim, leathery matte green glaze, circular mark & incised "RE," by Ruth Erickson **28,125**

Vase, 7" h., footed cylindrical body, the rounded shoulder tapering to flared rim, covered in a thick honey matte glaze, stamped pottery mark **1,870**

Vase, 7" h., 3" d., cylindrical body w/an inset footring & shoulder centered by a low rolled neck, thick oatmealy matte glaze, Grueby Faience stamp mark **956**

Grueby Vase with Leaves & Buds

Vase, 7" h., 5" d., narrow footring below bulbous ovoid body tapering to a short cylindrical neck, the sides tooled w/wide tapering leaves alternating w/thin stems topped by buds, oatmealy dark green matte glaze, partially obscured mark, remnant of paper label, touch-up to rim nick (ILLUS.) **2,760**

Vase, 7 1/4" h., 4 1/2" d., ovoid body tapering to a cylindrical neck w/flat rim, tooled w/a band of tall, wide leaves, matte green glaze, Grueby Faience stamped mark & "ERF," by Ellen Farmington (minor nick to one leaf edge)... **2,925**

Vase, 7 1/4" h., 4 3/4" d., simple ovoid form tapering to a flat rim, molded around the sides w/wide rounded leaves alternating w/stems & blossoms, buds reaching to the rim, leathery matte green glaze, stamped circular Faience mark w/"LEM" ... **2,813**

Vase, 7 1/4" h., 7 3/4" d., squatty bulbous body w/a wide shoulder centered by a wide cylindrical neck, tooled & applied around the body w/a band of large overlapping upright leaves, fine leathery matte green glaze, pottery stamp & "WP - 6- 8" (restoration to rim, touch-ups to leaf edges) **2,813**

Vase, 7 1/4"h., 10" d., squatty bulbous shouldered body w/a short flaring neck, the sides applied w/wide pointed overlapping leaves, pulled leathery matte green, circular stamp mark (touch-ups to minor flecks on leaf edges & invisible restoration to rim chip) **9,000**

Vase, 7 1/2" h., swelled cylindrical body w/a pentagonal rim, molded w/five alternating leaf & bud designs, matte green glaze, modeled by Gertrude Priest, signed, ca. 1905 (minor chips, restoration to chip at top of rim)............................. **1,955**

Vase, 7 1/2" h., 4" d., footed nearly spherical lower body tapering to a tall gently flaring neck, the base w/applied rounded leaves, rare celadon green semi-matte glaze, faintly impressed round mark........... **1,980**

Vase, 7 1/2" h., 4 1/2" d., ovoid body tapering to a wide cylindrical neck, the lower two-thirds of the body w/applied broad oblong leaves alternating w/slender stems w/buds around the rim, matte green glaze, circular stamp (small flecks to leaf edges).. **4,400**

Vase, 7 1/2" h., 8 1/2" d., wide bulbous ovoid body w/a deep rounded shoulder centered by a large cylindrical neck w/rolled rim, the body carved & applied w/a continuous band of wide, pointed overlapping leaves, two-tone green matte glaze, signed "W. Post," impressed mark (neatly restored drill hole in base)..... **2,860**

Vase, 7 3/4" h., 4" d., ovoid body w/floriform rim, applied broad leaves alternating w/flower buds, leathery matte green glaze, circular Faience mark **4,219**

Vase, 7 3/4" h., 4" d., slightly swelled cylindrical form w/a ruffled floriform rim, tooled & applied w/full-length broad pointed leaves, leathery matte green glaze, circular Faience mark...................... **2,640**

Vase, 8" h., squatty bulbous base w/shoulder tapering sharply to tall cylindrical neck w/slightly flaring rim, tooled & applied rounded leaves at the base, covered in matte green glaze, impressed circular "Faience" mark (touch-up to minor nicks at edges of leaves)............................ **2,860**

Vase, 8 1/4" h., 7 1/2" d., flat-bottomed spherical body w/horizontal ridges, tapering to a slender short trumpet neck w/flattened rim, overall matte green glaze, impressed Faience mark (rim chip restoration)... **3,850**

Vase, 8 3/4" h., 7" d., bulbous ovoid body w/a wide flat molded mouth, tooled slender matte green leaves against a mustard yellow ground, by Ruth Erickson, impressed pottery mark & "RE - 9 - 22 - 37" (stilt pulls on base)....................................... **5,500**

Vase, 9" h., slender waisted cylindrical form w/a small molded mouth, sculpted & applied vertical leaves under a thick suspended green matte glaze, signed by Ruth Erickson, impressed mark **2,640**

Vase, 9" h., tapering ridged cylindrical body, slightly rounded at the base, rich matte cucumber green glaze, impressed circular "Pottery" mark... **1,540**

Vase, 9" h., 3 1/2" d., cylindrical body slightly rounded at base & shoulder w/rolled rim, covered in a matte leathery bluish grey enamel, impressed mark (small chips to rim) **825**

Tall Waisted Grueby Vase with Buds

Vase, 9 1/2" h., 4 1/4" d., tall gently waisted cylindrical form rounded at the bottom & the shoulder, short, wide molded mouth, tooled & applied w/full-length rounded leaves alternating w/stems topped w/yellow buds, fine frothy matte green glaze, by Wilhelmina Post, circular mark & "WP - 322 - 11.20.5" (ILLUS.)............................ **6,900**

Grueby Bottle-form Vase

Vase, 9 1/2" h., 5 3/4" d., bottle-form, a wide bulbous base w/a wide flattened shoulder centering a tall cylindrical neck w/slightly flared rim, the base molded & applied w/an overlapping band of wide rounded leaves, fine organic matte green glaze, touch-up to edge & rim, stamped mark & "190" (ILLUS.)................................. **5,175**

Grueby Vase with Buds & Leaves

Vase, 9 7/8" h., 4 1/4" d., cylindrical body swollen at base, decorated w/matte yellow glazed buds on elongated stems alternating w/elongated leaf blades under matte green glaze, designed by Wilhelmina Post, impressed marks & incised artist's initials (ILLUS.)..................................... **4,888**

Rare Grueby Vase with Jonquils

Vase, 10" h., large bulbous ovoid body w/a wide shoulder & short flaring neck, unusual decoration w/three sets of sculpted & applied jonquils, the flowers in red, green & yellow on green leafy stems against a fine suspended green matte background, by Marie Seaman, impressed mark (ILLUS.)............................... **46,000**

Vase, 10 1/4" h., 8" d., footed wide ovoid body w/short flaring neck, molded w/wide leaves alternating w/buds, curdled matte green glaze, circular Grueby Faience stamp & "AL - 100" (four opposing hairlines, drilled hole at base, few minor glaze nicks to edges, glaze chip to base) .. **2,588**

Vase, 11" h., simple ovoid body w/a five-sided pinched & flared rim, the sides sculpted & applied w/tall pointed leaves divided by carved stems & tiny buds, overall dark green matte glaze, impressed mark (repaired chips)... **2,310**

Vase, 11" h., 5 1/4" d., tall ovoid body w/slightly flared & pinched rim, decorated w/relief-molded daffodils in profile in yellow, red & blue on long slender green leaves outlined in yellow, leathery matte green glaze, circular Grueby paper label & paper label from Geo. W. Benson Art Shop, Buffalo, incised "RE," by Ruth Erickson (small chip to inner rim, color run to one flower)....................................... **21,375**

Large Grueby Vase

Vase, 11 3/4" h., 8" d., wide cylindrical body w/round shoulder & short molded rim, decorated w/two tiers of overlapping leaf blades & alternating bud on stem, thin matte green glaze trailing & gathering at decoration edges & base, pale matte yellow glaze on buds, designed by Wilhelmina Post, No. 36, tight spider hairline in base, impressed marks & incised artist's initials (ILLUS.).. **5,750**

Very Rare Grueby "Kendrick" Vase

Vase, 12" h., 8" d., "Kendrick" design, tall gourd-form w/low incurved rim, sides & rim tooled w/long pointed leaves in a fine

pulled & leathery matte green glaze, chip to base, few small chips on leaftips, circular mark (ILLUS.).................................... **51,750**

Vase, 13 3/4" h., a narrow footring supporting the tall tapering & waisted cylindrical body, molded w/tall overlapping tapering leaves around the sides, some leaftips showing the clay body, heavy matte green glaze, faint round impressed mark, attributed to Ellen R. Farrington, ca. 1902.. **7,475**

Large Ovoid Grueby Vase

Vase, 13 3/4" h., 9" d., large bulbous ovoid body tapering to a cylindrical neck w/flat rim, tooled & applied around the lower half w/overlapping bands of broad rounded leaves below alternating blossoms & tall buds, fine leathery matte green glaze, circular "Faience" mark, w/letter from Grueby family member, through whose family it descended, restoration to inner rim chip (ILLUS.).. **8,625**

Vase, 16" h., 8 1/2" d., squatty bulbous base w/the shoulder tapering to very tall slender cylindrical neck w/flat rim, tooled & applied leaves on the base, leathery matte green glaze, spherical pottery mark, "133A" & paper label......................... **1,870**

Rare & Unusual Tall Grueby Vase

Vase, 17 1/2" h., 8 1/2" d., large bottle-form w/squatty bulbous base & tall slender cylindrical neck w/flaring rim, tooled & applied small quatrefoils around the rim, broad pointed leaves around the lower body, fine leathery green matte glaze, No. 133A, stamped mark & paper label (ILLUS.) **57,500**

Large Rare Grueby Vase

Vase, 20" h., bulbous ovoid body w/tapering neck, flat rim, decorated w/tooled & applied waterlily blossoms in yellow & red & large curled leaves under a rich thick matte green glaze, impressed circular mark, some color run (ILLUS.) **22,000**

Unusual Grueby Wall Pocket

Wall pocket, bulbous ovoid form w/flat arched backplate, the front tooled & applied w/broad ribbed, rounded overlapping leaves, leathery matte green glaze, enlarged hanging holes, unmarked, 5 3/4" w., 7" h. (ILLUS.) **1,840**

Grueby Wall Pocket with Leaves

Wall pocket, long ovoid body molded w/long pointed leaves up to the flared rim, w/a molded bulbed bottom tip, thick oatmealy matte green glaze, unmarked, 3 1/2" w., 8 1/2" l. (ILLUS.) **3,738**

Hampshire Pottery

Hampshire Marks

Hampshire Pottery was made in Keene, New Hampshire, where several potteries operated as far back as the late 18th century. The pottery now known as Hampshire Pottery was established by J. S. Taft shortly after 1870. Various types of wares, including Art Pottery, were produced through the years. Taft's brother-in-law, Cadmon Robertson, joined the firm in 1904 and was responsible for developing over 900 glaze formulas while in charge of all manufacturing. His death in 1914 created problems for the firm and Taft sold out to George Morton in 1916. Closed during part of World War I, the pottery was later reopened by Morton for a short time and manufactured white hotel china. From 1919 to 1921, mosaic floor tiles became the main production. All production ceased in 1923.

Low Hampshire Bowl in Mottled Blue

Bowl, 5 1/4" d., 2 1/4" h., wide flattened bottom below the squatty bulbous sides tapering to a wide flat mouth, the sides molded w/wide low arches alternating w/triple grooves, mottled dark blue matte glaze, two opposing rim cracks, signed (ILLUS.) **$288**

Hampshire Bowl with Trilliums

Bowl, 9" d., wide flat bottom below low incurved sides & a wide mouth, molded around the sides w/large stylized trillium blossoms, matte green glaze w/cream showing through, marked (ILLUS.) **460**

Hampshire Pottery Low Bowl

Bowl, 10" d., 3" h., a wide flat-bottomed round form w/low incurved sides molded w/a band of rounded lily pads alternating w/buds on stems, dark green matte glaze, signed, glaze miss on rim, tight line from rim (ILLUS.) **345**

Bowl-vase, low sides decorated w/repeating petals & leaves in low-relief, matte two-tone blue glaze highlighted w/strands of pale blue, impressed & incised marks, No.132, designed by Cadmon Robertson, 6" d., 3" h. **546**

Bowl-vase, squatty bulbous form w/a wide rounded & flattened shoulder centered by a low, wide mouth, molded w/wide leaves up around the sides, overall dark blue matte glaze, embossed mark, 6" d., 4" h. **550**

Bowl-vase, wide bulbous tapering form w/a wide rounded shoulder centering a short molded mouth, overall green matte glaze, embossed mark, 3 1/2" h. **308**

Hampshire Green Bowl-Vase

Bowl-vase, wide squatty bulbous form w/the wide shoulder centered by a low rolled rim, heavy matte green glaze, Model No. 136, inscribed mark, chip on glaze drip (ILLUS.) **258**

Bowl-vase, wide squatty bulbous base below sharply tapering incurved sides w/a wide, flat rim, the sides incised w/a wide band of linear & scrolled repeating design, mottled matte green glaze, ink stamp on base, ca. 1910, 4 1/2" d., 2 3/4" h. **690**

Chamberstick, deep tricorner base w/infolded sides centering a cylindrical socket w/flared rim, high loop handle at the back, dark green glossy glaze, impressed mark, 7" w., 3 1/2" h. **253**

Hampshire Pottery Chamberstick

Chamberstick, round dished base tapering to a cylindrical standard w/a wide rolled socket rim, a round loop handle near the base, mottled blue glaze, impressed mark, two chips, firing lines in base rim (ILLUS.) **115**

Hampshire Matte Green Ewer

Ewer, footed squatty bulbous lower body tapering to cylindrical sides w/a high arched spout opposite & high arched & looped handle, matte green glaze, 8" h. (ILLUS.) **431**

Ewer, wide squatty bulbous form w/the wide shoulder centered by a short slender neck w/a wide inwardly folded tricorner rim, round loop handle from back of rim to base of neck, shaded dark brown, green & gunmetal glossy glaze, impressed mark, 6" h. **143**

Hampshire Ewer

Ewer, the wide squatty bulbous footed base w/a wide shoulder tapering to a cylindrical neck flaring to a long arched spout & incurved tab attached to the top of the slender C-scroll handle, matte green glaze, impressed mark, 9 3/4" h. (ILLUS.) **440**

Inkwell, low cylindrical form, the flat top pierced w/pen holes centering the small round cap w/button finial, w/liner, smooth matte green glaze, impressed mark, 3 1/2 x 4" **385**

Lamp, table model, a wide squatty lobed bulbous base w/wide vertical ribs & a wide shoulder tapering up to a flat rim supporting a domed metal burner, shoulder & burner fitted w/a widely flaring conical leaded glass shade composed of a stylized geometric design of green slag glass & small bands of blue & red diamonds, pink blossoms & purple top segments, base w/impressed mark, overall 22" h.. **2,200**

Unusual Hampshire Lamp Base

Lamp base, a thick rounded flaring base molded w/pointed leaves & tapering to a slender standard molded w/buds on stems, matte green glaze, missing socket & wiring, 12" h. (ILLUS.).......................... **1,380**

Lamp base, a wide round cushion foot molded in relief w/five repeating tulips, a tall tapering slender shaft molded w/the

stems below a bulbed top w/the electric socket, matte green glaze, marked on the base, ca. 1910, 11" h. (wear to lamp fittings)... **920**

Lamp base, ovoid form, decorated w/alternating bud on stem & lotus leaves in relief under a dark matte blue glaze, raised on a carved Oriental-style wood base, green glass & brass finial, modeled by Cadmon Robertson, impressed "Hampshire Pottery 42" w/a Robertson cipher, ca. 1910, 19 1/4" h. (minor glaze bursts) **575**

Hampshire Lamp Base with Tulips

Lamp base, tall gently flaring cylindrical form w/rounded shoulder to a wide flat mouth, molded up the sides w/broad pointed tulip leaves alternating with blossoms around the rim, dark matte green glaze, signed, several burst bubbles, small grinding chip on base, w/patinated rim ring (ILLUS.) **1,150**

Lamp base, wide flared disk foot tapering to a tall slender trumpet-form body w/a wide rounded shoulder centered by the electric fittings, embossed w/twining lilypads around the sides, smooth olive green glaze, verdigris patina on the fittings, stamped "Hampshire Pottery - 0018," 7" d., 16" h. **1,013**

Hampshire Pottery Large Urn-Vase

Urn-vase, a bulbous base tapering to a tall slightly tapering cylindrical neck flanked by slender angled & pierced handles from high on the neck to the shoulder, embossed Greek Key design bands around the upper neck & the lower body, matte green glaze, light abrasion to the base, stamped "Hampshire Pottery - 88," 9" d., 15" h. (ILLUS.) **1,913**

Vase, 2 1/2" h., 5 1/2" d., squatty bulbous form tapering to a wide flat mouth, incised geometric design under a matte green glaze, marked on the base & w/the cipher of "M" as tribute to Cadmon Robertson's wife, Emoretta, early 20th c. **345**

Vase, 2 7/8" h., miniature, flattened square form w/inverted rim, brown over green curdled matte glaze, designed by Cadmon Robertson, impressed mark, artist's cipher & No. 149 on base (glaze burst at rim) **288**

Miniature Hampshire Vase

Vase, 3 1/2" h., miniature, bulbous ovoid body tapering to a small flat mouth, embossed around the sides w/large pointed upright leaves, matte brown glaze, marked (ILLUS.) **690**

Vase, 3 3/4" h., miniature, bulbous ovoid form tapering to a tiny mouth, the sides molded w/wide pointed & veined leaves up the sides, green & brown matte glaze, impressed mark, experimental glaze **715**

Vase, 4 1/4" h., simple ovoid form w/a rounded shoulder centering a short, small rolled neck, lightly molded arched panel-style leaves up the sides, mottled green matte glaze, impressed mark, experimental glaze **413**

Vase, 4 1/2" h., bulbous tapering ovoid form w/a very wide flat mouth, incised around the rim w/a wavy band of stylized leaves & blossoms, dark green matte glaze **605**

Hampshire Moss Green Vase

Vase, 4 1/2" h., wide ovoid body tapering to a wide, flat mouth, overall dark moss green matte glaze, raised mark (ILLUS.) **517**

Vase, 4 3/4" h., flat-bottomed ovoid body w/a rounded shoulder centered by a short rolled neck, light vertical panels covered w/an overall dark blue matte glaze, impressed mark **286**

Vase, 5" h., a flat-based wide bulbous ovoid body w/a rounded shoulder tapering to a wide trumpet neck, overall mottled multi-toned greyish blue matte glaze, impressed mark **605**

Vase, 5" h., 6" d., wide bulbous ovoid body w/wide closed rim, fine overall dark blue & green matte glaze, impressed mark **413**

Vase, 6" h., an oblong boat-shaped base w/pulled-out tapering end handles looping up & connecting asymmetrically to a slender cylindrical neck which tapers up from the lower body, green matte glaze, impressed mark **660**

Vase, 6" h., slightly flaring cylindrical form w/a rounded shoulder tapering slightly to a wide flat mouth, good green matte glaze, incised mark **385**

Vase, 6 1/4" h., 3 1/2" d., incised foliate design under a matte green glaze w/frothy white highlights, incised "Hampshire Pottery 52/2" **403**

Vase, 6 1/2" h., Arts & Crafts style shouldered cylindrical body w/flat rim, decorated w/relief-molded tulips & leaves, matte green glaze, impressed "Hampshire Pottery," "33" & M inside an O **605**

Vase, 6 3/4" h., 3 3/4" d., gently tapering cylindrical form w/a wide rounded shoulder centering a flat mouth, embossed around the shoulder w/broad stylized green leaves on a blue ground, incised mark **825**

Hampshire Handled Blue Vase

Vase, 7" h., a squatty bulbous bottom tapering sharply to a cylindrical body w/a narrow neck & molded small rim flanked by two small shoulder handles, matte blue glaze, impressed mark, clay bubbles on side of base (ILLUS.) **460**

Vase, 7" h., expanding cylinder w/rounded shoulder, relief-molded leaf decoration, thick feathered blue & white matte glaze, impressed "Hampshire Pottery" **660**

Vase, 7" h., simple ovoid form w/a wide flat mouth, the sides molded w/stylized three-petal blossoms above pairs of leaves atop tall slender stems down the sides, good medium green matte glaze, impressed mark **715**

Vase, 7" h., simple swelled cylindrical form w/a closed rim, fine slightly mottled dark blue matte glaze w/black highlights, impressed mark (hard-to-find hairline) **275**

Hampshire Vase with Lightning Decor

Vase, 7 1/2" h., wide gently swelled cylindrical form w/a closed rim, overall dark matte blue glaze w/bold crackled design, impressed mark **605**

Hampshire Vase with Molded Leaves

Vase, 7" h., wide ovoid body tapering to a wide flat mouth, the sides molded w/a band of wide pointed leaves alternating w/stems & buds, dark green matte glaze, impressed mark (ILLUS.) **1,092**

Vase, 7 1/2" h., elongated ovoid body w/an inverted rim, mottled matte green glaze, by Cadmon Robertson, impressed marks **575**

Vase, 7 1/2" h., simple ovoid form w/small loop handles at the center sides, a molded band at the base & rim, each issuing creamy white lightning-like bars all against a matte green ground, impressed mark (ILLUS.) **575**

Hampshire Vase with Wave Band

Ovoid & Tall Hampshire Vases

Vase, 7 3/4" h., slightly swelled cylindrical form tapering to a short flared neck, a narrow embossed band of repeating wave-like scrolls around the shoulder, dark green matte glaze, signed (ILLUS.) **575**

Vase, 8" h., wide ovoid body w/a wide low rolled rim, molded w/broad overlapping & slightly swirled leaves, unusual blue & green suspended matte glaze, impressed mark & paper label (ILLUS. right, bottom previous page) **1,495**

Vine-handled Hampshire Vase

Vase, 8 1/2" h., ovoid body tapering to a flaring neck, vine-form open handles on each side connecting to long molded spearpoint leaves down the sides, matte green glaze, signed, light line in one handle (ILLUS.) **748**

Vase, 9" h., wide ovoid form tapering to a wide, flat mouth, overall dark brown matte glaze, raised mark **605**

Vase, 9" h., 13" d., lobed circular body, matte green glaze, designed by Cadmon Robertson, impressed "Hampshire - M (in a circle) - 900," ca. 1908 (hairline) **863**

Vase, 9 1/2" h., squat body w/repeating stylized leaf design, extended neck w/flared rim, matte marbleized blue glaze, designed by Camdon Robertson, No. 124, impressed marks **978**

Tall Ovoid Hampshire Green Vase

Vase, 11" h., round dished foot w/a slender stem supporting a tall ovoid body w/a molded flat mouth, green matte glaze, impressed mark, small firing line, light crazing (ILLUS.) **460**

Vase, 12" h., a tall gently swelled cylindrical form w/a narrow rounded shoulder &

wide cylindrical neck w/flat rim, fine dark blue matte glaze, impressed mark **1,045**

Vase, 12" h., tall slender swelled cylindrical form w/a narrow shoulder to the short rolled neck, overall multi-toned blue matte glaze, impressed mark **990**

Very Large Blue Hampshire Vase

Vase, 12 1/4" h., 5" d., tall slender ovoid body tapering to a short rolled neck, very thick frothy blue & bluish green matte glaze, green spot on side, stamped mark (ILLUS.) **1,725**

Vase, 15" h., wide squatty bulbous base tapering to a tall & slightly tapering cylindrical neck flanked by long slender angled & pierced handles, a narrow geometrical dash band around the top of the neck & a wider matching band around the lower body, green matte glaze, impressed mark (ILLUS. left with broad ovoid blue vase) **2,070**

Jugtown Pottery

Jugtown Pottery Mark

This pottery was established by Jacques and Juliana Busbee in Jugtown, North Carolina, in the early 1920s in an attempt to revive the skills of the diminishing North Carolina potter's art as Prohibition ended the need for locally crafted stoneware whiskey jugs. During the early years, Juliana Busbee opened a shop in Greenwich Village in New York City to promote the North Carolina wares that her husband, Jacques, was designing and a local youth, Ben Owen, was producing under his direction. Owen continued to work with Busbee from 1922 until Busbee's death in 1947 at which time Juliana took over management of the pottery for the next decade until her illness (or mental fatigue) caused the pottery to be closed in 1958. At that time, Owen opened his own pottery a few miles away, marking his wares "Ben Owen - Master Potter." The pottery begun by the Busbees was reopened in 1960, under new management, and still operates today using the identical impressed mark of the early Jugtown pottery the Busbees managed from 1922 until 1958.

Bowl, 4 1/2" d., 1 1/2" h., a small raised footring supporting a wide rounded bowl w/a flat rim, Chinese blue glaze, impressed mark **$55**

Bowl, 7 1/4" d., 4 1/2" h., a footring supporting a deep rounded bowl w/slightly flared rim, Chinese blue glaze, circular stamp mark (three small glaze misses on interior) **825**

Pitcher, 10 1/2" h., redware, bulbous ovoid body tapering to a flared rim w/rim spout, small C-form shoulder handle, pumpkin orange glaze, impressed mark **303**

Jugtown Hexagonal Vase

Vase, 3 1/2" h., hexagonal body w/wide shoulder tapering to wide flat rim, semi-matte white glaze, impressed mark (ILLUS.) **248**

Vase, 3 1/2" h., simple ovoid body tapering to a small flat mouth, mottled & streaky glossy brown glaze, impressed mark **121**

Vase, 4" h., 3" d., simple ovoid form tapering to a small flat mouth, Chinese blue glaze w/mottled dark brown, circular mark **825**

Vase, 4 1/4" h., ovoid body w/closed rim, covered in a frothy semi-matte white glaze, impressed mark **165**

Vase, 5 1/4" h., 6 1/4" d., wide bulbous body w/a wide shoulder tapering to a short rolled neck, mottled turquoise, red & purple Chinese blue glaze, impressed circular mark **825**

Pear-shaped Jugtown Vase

Vase, 5 1/2" h., 4 1/2" d., pear-shaped body tapering to flat incurved rim, covered in a

flowing red & turquoise Chinese blue glaze, impressed circular mark (ILLUS.) **660**

Vase, 6" h., ovoid body tapering to a closed mouth, covered in rich Chinese blue glaze w/red veining, impressed mark **495**

Vase, 6 1/4" h., 7" d., bulbous body w/wide shoulder tapering to short neck w/flat rim, Chinese blue glaze, impressed circular mark **1,463**

Jugtown Vase with White Drippy Glaze

Vase, 6 1/2" h., 4 1/4" d., ovoid body tapering to a small flat mouth, dripping white semi-matte glaze over a brown clay body, circular stamp mark (ILLUS.) **495**

Egg-shaped Jugtown Vase

Vase, 7" h., ovoid egg-shaped body tapering to a flat mouth, embossed w/two medallions, mottled light blue glaze w/clay band showing around the base, bruise on rim, short firing line in base of neck, stamped mark (ILLUS.) **288**

Jugtown Chinese Translation Vase

Vase, 8" h., slightly ovoid body tapering to a wide flaring neck, unusual Chinese translation form in dark red & blue mottled glazes (ILLUS.) **698**

Longwy

This faience factory was established in 1798 in the town of Longwy, France and is noted for its enameled pottery which resembles cloisonné. Utilitarian wares were the first production here but by the 1870s an Oriental style art pottery that imitated "cloisonné" was created through the use of heavy enamels in relief. By 1912, a modern Art Deco style became part of Longwy's production and these wares, together with the Oriental style pieces, have made this art pottery popular with collectors today. As interest in Art Deco has soared in recent years, values of Longwy's modern style wares have risen sharply.

Longwy Floral Cup & Saucer

Cup & saucer, decorated w/overall vibrant colored stylized flowers, ink stamp marks, rim chips on both pieces, cup 2 1/4" h., the set (ILLUS.)............................... **$67**

Vase, 11 3/4" h., flared neck on a round flattened body raised on an oval foot, the exterior w/turquoise blue crackle glaze, base w/a green ink stamp mark "Primavera Longwy France," after 1913 .... **230**

Vase, 12 1/2" h., tapering ovoid body w/everted lip, molded w/a mythological ram & bird w/two female nudes amid a stylized landscape, covered in ivory, turquoise blue, cobalt blue, purple & black glaze, green printed mark "Primavera - Longwy - France," ca. 1925 .... **2,587**

Large Longwy Vase

Vase. 22" h., ten sided melon-form body w/stepped tapering neck & circular foot, molded w/stylized teal & pink berries on black vines reserved on a crackled ivory ground, sawtooth border at neck & cobalt glazed rim & foot, ca. 1925, printed "Societe Des Faienceries - Longwy - France" (ILLUS.)... **2,300**

Marblehead

Marblehead Mark

This pottery was organized in 1904 by Dr. Herbert J. Hall as a therapeutic aid to patients in a sanitarium he ran in Marblehead, Massachusetts. It was later separated from the sanitarium and directed by Arthur E. Baggs, a fine artist and designer, who bought out the factory in 1916 and operated it until its closing in 1936. Most wares were hand-thrown and decorated and carry the company mark of a stylized sailing vessel flanked by the letters "M" and "P."

Book ends, square upright slant-fronted form, the face incised w/panels enclosing a view of ships under full sail, a different view on each, midnight blue matte glaze, impressed mark & paper label, ca. 1916, 5 3/8" h., pr. (hairline) **$690**

Pink-glazed Marblehead Bowl

Bowl, a small round base below widely flaring slightly rounded sides w/a wide flat rim, speckled dark pink matte glazed exterior & lighter pink interior, unmarked, 8 3/4" d., 3" h. (ILLUS.)................................. **431**

Marblehead Two-color Bowl

Bowl, 2 1/2" h., wide squatty flaring form w/a wide tapered shoulder & a wide flat mouth, molded around the shoulder w/a triangular linear design, matte brown on a green ground, impressed mark, by Hannah Tutt, early 20th c. (ILLUS.)............ **1,725**

Bowl, 4 1/8" h., tapered spherical form, dark teal blue glaze, impressed mark, early 20th c. **173**

Bowl, 6" d., 3" h., tapering wide squatty bulbous form w/a short wide rolled neck, overall brick red metallic glaze, impressed mark.. **385**

Bowl, 6 1/4" d., 2 1/4" h., compressed bulbous incurved sides, smooth dark blue glaze w/light blue interior, impressed ship mark **220**

Marblehead Lotus Leaf Bowl

Bowl, 8 1/4" d., 3 1/4" h., a small footring supporting a deep rounded bowl w/molded overlapping lotus leaves below the widely flaring flattened rim, speckled blue glaze, lighter speckled blue interior, impressed mark, minute rim fleck (ILLUS.) **402**

Marblehead Squatty Bowl

Bowl, 8 3/4" d., 4" h., wide rounded incurved sides to a wide flat mouth, speckled matte brown glaze on exterior, celadon green & oxblood glossy interior glaze, stamped mark (ILLUS.)........................ **805**

Bowl-vase, miniature, a squatty bulbous form tapering to a flat rim, overall brown matte glaze, paper label, impressed mark, 3 1/2" d. (burst bubble on side) **198**

Bowl-Vase with Geometric Band

Bowl-vase, bulbous tapering form w/a wide flat mouth, carved around the top w/a geometric block design in dark brown against a matte green speckled ground, by Arthur Baggs, one-inch bruise, small rim hairline, illustrated in Paul Evans pottery book, marked, 5" d., 3 3/4" h. (ILLUS.).. **6,325**

Bowl-vase, wide bulbous body tapering slightly to a wide flat mouth covered in a smooth speckled brown glaze, impressed ship mark, 5 1/4" d., 2 3/4" h. **358**

Bowl-vase, a wide bulbous upper body w/wide closed rim, tapering sharply to a cylindrical base, overall lavender matte glaze, impressed mark, 5 1/2" d.................... **770**

Bowl-vase, deep slightly tapering cylindrical sides w/a closed rim, overall yellow matte glaze, impressed mark, 5 1/2" d., 3 1/2" h. **660**

Bowl-vase, wide gently flaring rounded cylindrical form w/a wide closed rim, matte green ground, incised w/a wide rim band in darker green of stylized blossoms w/twisted stems forms panels around the sides, marked & artist-initialed, ca. 1916, 6 1/2" d., 4 3/4" h. **6,900**

Bowl-vase, wide squatty spherical form tapering to a closed rim, fine speckled ochre matte glaze, impressed mark, 6 1/2" d., 5" h... **1,265**

Bowl-vase, deep wide cylindrical form w/wide flaring rim covered in matte mauve glaze, lavender interior, impressed ship mark, 7 1/2" d., 3 3/4" h. **385**

Flaring Marblehead Bowl-Vase

Bowl-vase, cylindrical waisted lower body below widely flaring sides w/a flat rim, yellow matte exterior & teal green matte interior, impressed mark, 8 1/2" d., 5" h. (ILLUS.).. **518**

Marblehead Squatty Humidor

Humidor, cov., squatty bulbous form w/incurved low sides & inset cover w/large knob handle, the cover painted w/a narrow ochre band of leaves, dark blue matte ground, stamped mark, 6" d., 4" h. (ILLUS.) **1,750**

Match safe, cov., octagonal, w/striker inside lid, covered in a fine smooth matte green glaze, impressed ship mark, 2 x 3" (glaze abrasion around rim) **385**

Marblehead Pitcher

Pitcher, 5" h., wide bulbous body w/arched spout & C-form handle, incised decoration of ship at sea, glossy blue glaze, impressed mark (ILLUS.) **330**

Pitcher, 5" h., 6" d., footed bulbous shouldered body w/a short neck w/pointed spout, loop handle, embossed around the neck w/waves, the sides w/rounded medallions around galleons under sail in blue, ochre & green, the waves & handle in blue & the background in cream, semimatte glaze, impressed ship mark **770**

Rare Marblehead Plate

Plate, 7 1/2" d., border decorated w/a frieze of camels and nomads in blue & yellow on white ground, impressed ship mark (ILLUS.) **1,045**

Tile, square, decorated w/a landscape of trees in dark green reflected in a lake, impressed ship mark & paper label, 4 1/4" sq. (small chip to front & back) **770**

Tile, square, depicting a cluster of trees in dark green under a blue overcast sky, impressed ship mark & paper label, 4 1/4" sq. **880**

Vase, 2 3/4" h., decorated in a teal blue matte glaze, black underglaze visible near rim, narrow mouth on a flared bulbous form, marked on base, ca. 1910 .... **374**

Vase, 3" h., 4" d., bulbous nearly spherical lower body w/a rounded shoulder centering a wide, swelled cylindrical neck w/closed rim, incised around the body w/four stylized geometric panels in dark olive brown against a green ground, marked, ca. 1908 (imperfection in the making) **1,265**

Vase, 3" h., 4 1/4" d., low squatty wide bulbous form tapering sharply to a rolled rim, ringed sides, smooth green & charcoal matte glaze, incised "winged M" mark **440**

Vase, 3 1/2" h., miniature, small wide bulbous ovoid body tapering to a short flared neck, matte greyish green ground w/a linear band at the rim connecting eight stylized trees around the sides in brown matte glaze w/round blue foliage, by Hannah Tutt, marked, ca. 1912 .... **6,900**

Vase, 3 1/2" h., miniature, small wide slightly tapering cylindrical form w/a closed rim, unusual very dark blue matte glaze, impressed mark **385**

Vase, 3 1/2" h., simple swelled cylindrical form w/a closed rim, overall unusual pink matte glaze, impressed mark **275**

Vase, 3 1/2" h., simple swelled cylindrical form w/a closed rim, overall dark blue matte glaze, impressed mark **286**

Vase, 3 1/2" h., 3 1/2" d., miniature, simple ovoid body tapering slightly to a wide flat mouth, speckled grey ground painted around the rim w/a stylized band of twotone greyish blue flying geese, stamped ship mark **1,688**

Vase, 3 5/8" h., short flared rim on a squat bulbous body, decorated w/repeating stylized trees, black trunks & blue leaves over a grey ground, impressed mark & initials of Hannah Tutt, ca. 1905 .... **2,415**

Miniature Blue Marblehead Vase

Vase, 3 3/4" h., miniature, swelled cylindrical form tapering slightly to a wide flat mouth, speckled matte blue glaze, impressed mark (ILLUS.) **460**

Vase, 4" h., 4" d., bulbous base tapering to a wide, short cylindrical neck, matte deep

blue ground w/incised rim band & stylized geometric border on neck in dark
green, by Arthur Baggs, factory mark &
artist-initialed **2,415**
Vase, 4" h., 5" d., wide ovoid body w/wide
flat mouth, matte blue exterior & light
blue interior, impressed ship mark **440**
Vase, 4 1/4" h., 4 3/4" d., bulbous ovoid
body w/a flat mouth, decorated around
the mouth w/red & purple stylized blossoms in a band on the semi-matte pink
ground, mark under glaze **880**

Unusual Marblehead Covered Vase

Vase, cov., 4 1/4" h., 4 3/4" d., wide
bulbous ovoid body tapering to a wide
flaring rim w/bobeche lid, covered in a
smooth matte grey glaze, paper label
(ILLUS.) **660**
Vase, 4 3/8" h., 3 7/8" d., a wide mouth on
a cylindrical body, green ground decorated w/a blue linear band at the rim w/eight
repeating stylized flowers w/multiple
trailing stems in two shades of matte
blue, by Hannah Tutt, marks & artist-
signed, ca. 1912 .... **4,888**
Vase, 4 3/4" h., swollen cylindrical form,
decorated around the rim w/repeating
raised flower & leaf design in faint blue,
red & tan on a speckled blue matte
ground, by Hannah Tutt, impressed mark
& artist's initials, early 20th c. **1,610**
Vase, 5" h., cylindrical w/rounded base &
shoulder w/a short rolled rim, medium
blue semi-gloss glaze, cipher & paper
label **259**
Vase, 5" h., small footring supporting a
widely flaring trumpet-form body, overall
brown matte glaze, impressed mark **550**

Dark Blue Marblehead Vase

Vase, 5" h., wide baluster-form w/a wide,
short flaring neck, overall dark matte blue
glaze, impressed mark (ILLUS.) **345**
Vase, 5" h., 3 1/4" d., swelled cylindrical
body w/a wide, flat rim, "watermelon rind"
glaze, slightly iridescent finish on a textured ground in rich green, stamped mark
& paper label, ca. 1908 .... **1,093**
Vase, 5 1/8" h., 3 1/4" d., a wide flat mouth
on a swelled tapering cylindrical body,
grey ground decorated w/a blue linear
rim band w/five repeating stylized flowers
w/trailing stems in three shades of matte
blue, by Hannah Tutt, marked & artist-
signed, ca. 1912 (rim hairlines) **1,150**
Vase, 5 1/4" h., 3 3/4" d., tapering ovoid
gourd-form w/a narrow shoulder to a
small flat mouth, incised w/four stylized
geometric panels in dark green, by Han-
nah Tutt, marked & artist-signed **19,550**
Vase, 5 1/2" d., a wide bulbous baluster-
form body w/the wide shoulder tapering
slightly to a wide flat mouth, dark blue
matte glaze, impressed mark (nearly in-
visible hairline at rim) **231**

Marblehead Vase with Grapevine

Vase, 5 1/2" h., a wide flat mouth on a gently tapering ovoid body, decorated w/a
band of blue & light green grapevines
around the top on a grey ground, chip in
base, impressed mark (ILLUS.) **1,380**

Marblehead Vase with Brown Glaze

Vase, 5 1/2" h., ovoid body tapering to a
widely flaring rim, brown speckled matte

glaze, impressed mark, small bruise on rim (ILLUS.) 575

Vase, 5 1/2" h., 5" d., short cylindrical bottom below widely flaring flat sides, dark blue matte exterior glaze, lighter blue interior, stamped ship mark & paper label 523

Small Marblehead Bud Vase

Vase, 6" h., bud-type, wide thick round flaring foot tapering to a tall, slender cylindrical body, overall deep rose glaze (ILLUS.) 345

Vase, 6" h., cylindrical, carved & painted around the rim w/alternating blue & brown dragonflies against the medium matte green ground, artist-signed "Hanna Tutt" & impressed mark (small base flake) 1,760

Vase, 6" h., wide ovoid body tapering to a short flared rim, matte ochre ground decorated w/five tall panels painted w/blueberries & leaves in matte green & matte blue, each panel framed in dark ochre matte glaze, by Hannah Tutt, marked & artist-signed 12,650

Vase, 6 1/4" h., 3 3/4" d., bulbous base below a wide cylindrical body w/flat rim, repeated design around rim of brown stylized flowers on long stems, green ground, early ship mark (repair to minor glaze flaking to rim) 2,860

Vase, 6 1/4" h., 5 1/4" d., flaring rim over a swollen flaring body, matte blue glaze, impressed mark (minor glaze scratches) 460

Unique and Rare Marblehead Vase

Vase, 6 3/4" h., 4" d., simple ovoid form w/a wide, flat mouth, decorated w/triple clusters of tall stylized flowers around the sides w/a lattice-like rim band, in shades of umber, black & cream on a speckled matte green ground, by Hannah Tutt, impressed mark & incised artist mark (ILLUS.) 120,750

Marblehead Vase with Trees & Berries

Vase, 7" h., gently swelled cylindrical form w/a wide flat rim, painted w/an Arts & Crafts band of tall stylized trees in dark green & brown w/dark red berries against a dark blue ground, impressed mark, original paper label, some minor glaze crawling (ILLUS.) 6,600

Fine Marblehead Sea Horse Vase

Vase, 7" h., slightly tapering cylindrical form w/a rounded bottom & wide flat rim, decorated around the top w/five delicately painted sea horses & seaweed in shades of blue against a grey ground, by Hanna Tutt, impressed mark (ILLUS.) 11,500

Vase, 7" h., tall cylindrical form, dark matte green glaze, impressed company cipher 518

Vase, 7 1/4" h., a wide flat mouth on a tapering swelled cylindrical body, decorated w/repeating stylized fruit trees in matte green & orange on a blue ground, marked, ca. 1915 4,888

Marblehead Vase with Tall Trees

Vase, 7 1/4" h., gently swelled cylindrical form w/a wide flat rim, decorated w/full-length bluish black stylized trees w/leafy branches w/white berries around the top & the trunks down the sides against a dark blue matte ground, impressed mark, tiny chip on edge of base (ILLUS.) **2,875**

Simple Cylindrical Marblehead Vase

Vase, 7 1/2" h., 3" d., plain cylindrical form, overall pink speckled matte glaze, stamped mark (ILLUS.)................................... **920**

Vase, 7 3/4" h., gently tapering rounded cylindrical body w/a short flared rim, dark blue matte glaze, impressed mark................ **805**

Marblehead Two-color Vase

Vase, 8" h., a wide flat mouth & wide low shoulder on a tapering cylindrical body, incised w/vertical panels of stylized floral & geometric designs in dark olive green on a lighter green ground, by Hannah Tutt, impressed mark & artist-initialed, ca. 1912 (ILLUS.)........................ **13,800**

Rare Marblehead Vase with Ducks

Vase, 8" h., 7" d., wide ovoid form w/a wide flattened shoulder to the closed rim, decorated around the shoulder w/a band of flying mallard ducks in shades of grey on a speckled matte grey ground, stamped & incised marks (ILLUS.)........................... **10,350**

Vase with Peacock Feathers

Vase, 8 1/2" h., 4" d., tapering cylindrical body w/molded rim, decorated in wax-resist w/stylized peacock feathers in brown on a mottled green ground, impressed ship mark & "W" (ILLUS.) **4,400**

Vase, 8 1/2" h., 8" d., heavy bell-form body w/closed rim, unusual frothy matte bluish green glaze, incised "M" w/sea gull (repair to small drilled bottom side hole)............ **990**

Vase, 8 3/4" h., 3 3/4" d., simple cylindrical form w/rounded edges on the flat base & a narrow rounded shoulder & closed rim, speckled blue matte glaze, ship mark........... **956**

Vase, 8 3/4" h., 4" d., simple cylindrical form w/rounded edges on the flat base & a narrow rounded shoulder & closed rim, greyish mauve speckled matte glaze, ship mark.. **844**

Simple Ovoid Marblehead Vase

Vase, 8 3/4" h., 5" d., simple ovoid body tapering to a wide flat mouth, overall smooth matte green glaze, impressed mark (ILLUS.).. **1,150**

Marblehead Vase with Quatrefoils

Vase, 9" h.., 3 3/4" d., tall cylindrical form w/rounded base edge & wide closed rim, incised around the rim w/a band of quatrefoils atop long bands down the sides, dark & lighter green mottled matte glaze, impressed & incised marks (ILLUS.).......... **9,200**

Rare Marblehead Vase with Poppies

Vase, 9" h., 5 1/2" d., cylindrical body rounded at the base & at the closed rim, decorated w/stylized upright poppies around the sides w/the arched leaves forming panels around the body, in three shades of matte olive green, two hairlines from rim, stamped mark (ILLUS.) **10,350**

Vase, 9 3/4" h., a rounded base edge on the tall gently tapering cylindrical body w/a flat rim, matte green ground incised & surface-painted w/a tapering stalk of stylized flowers in brown matte glaze, marked & artist-initialed, ca. 1912 .... **21,850**

Vase, 11 3/4" h., wide slightly tapering cylindrical form w/flat rim, blue matte glaze, impressed mark (tight line at rim).................. **660**

Marblehead Ringed Wall Pocket

Wall pocket, tapering conical form w/ringed design, flaring ruffled rim w/hanging hole, dark matte blue glaze, stilt pulls on rim, 4 1/4" w., 8 1/2" h. (ILLUS.) **173**

Wall pocket, widely flaring rounded trumpet form, brown speckled matte exterior glaze, smooth ivory interior glaze, paper label, 7" w., 6" h. (bruise at rim) **450**

Martin Brothers

Martin Brothers Mark

Martinware, the term used for this pottery, dates from 1873 and is the product of the Martin brothers—Robert, Wallace, Edwin, Walter and Charles—often considered the first British studio potters. From first to final stages, their hand-thrown pottery was completely the work of the team. The early wares may be simple and conventional, but the Martin brothers built up their reputation by producing ornately engraved, incised or carved designs as well as rather bizarre figural wares. The amusing face-jugs are considered some of their finest work. After 1910, the work of the pottery declined and can be considered finished by 1915, though some attempts were made to fire pottery as late as the 1920s.

Bowl-vase, footed wide squatty bulbous form tapering to a flat molded rim, faceted sides, covered in a fine red & green lustered crystalline glaze, incised "4-1900 - Martin Bro. - London and Southall," 1900, 7" d., 5" h. **$523**

Martin Brothers Gargoyle Dish

Dish, figural, the oblong form w/a crouching, grinning gargoyle at one end, the body forming the open dish composed of two tiered dishes, the neck & body w/fine incised lines to resemble hair, tan unglazed clay, very small edge nicks, signed "Martin Bros. - London & Southall - 4-1894," 5 1/2" l., 2 3/4" h. (ILLUS.) **1,870**

Martin Brothers Humidor

Humidor, cov., grotesque bird-shaped body on round base, the cover formed by the head, glazed in brown & black tones, both parts incised "R.W.Martin Bros. London & Southall - 1903," repair to tip of beak, 7 3/4" h., 3 1/4" d. (ILLUS.) **2,530**

Martin Brothers Bird Jar on Base

Jar, cov., figural, modeled as a large comical bird w/a rounded oversized head w/droopy beak & sleepy eyes, bulbous body & thick legs w/wide webbed feet, on a round platform base, dark brown, black & tan glazing, firing crack in body secured at factory w/beeswax, incised "R.W. Martin - London & Southall," 5 1/2" W., 11 1/2" h. (ILLUS.).............................. **10,450**

Martin Brothers Bird Jar

Jar, cov., modeled as a grotesque bird w/a bulbous oversized head w/large beak & sleepy expression, feathers in green, light blue & black, marked "Martin Bros - London + Southall - 6-1897," oval base mounted on oval ebonized wooden base, 1897, 10" h. (ILLUS.) **13,500**

Paperweight, figural flying lizard, glazed in black, green & beige, partially obscured mark "Martin Bros - London," 2 1/4 x 4" (restoration to small points)........................ **1,125**

Martin Brothers Decorated Pitcher

Pitcher, 9" h., salt-glazed stoneware, a footed ovoid body tapering to a high widely flaring & pinched neck, D-form strap handle, finely incised & decorated w/birds nestled amid branches, glazed in shades of brown, green & rust against a blue striped ground, marked "6-1-2 - 1-8-50 - Martin Bros London & Southall," 1902 (ILLUS.).................................... **1,500-2,000**

Pitcher, jug-type, 9 3/4" h., ovoid body w/swelled shoulder under D-form handle, short cylindrical neck w/slightly flared rim & small pinched spout, body incised w/sea reptiles in indigo & amber, mark partially obscured by paper label (fleck to rim).. **1,800**

Spoon warmer, stoneware, modeled as an open-mouthed caninesque face, glazed in green, brown & cobalt blue, applied loop handle, incised "R.W. Martin - London & Southall - 4-3-80," 5 1/2" h. **2,185**

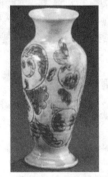

Martin Brothers Floral Vase

Vase, 4 1/4" h., 3 1/2" d., stoneware, flaring foot supporting a baluster-shaped body w/tall wide neck & flaring rim, incised rings near base & at shoulder, decorated overall w/plumes & blossoms in blue & brown on a greyish green ground, incised "R.W.Martin - 680" (ILLUS.) **220**

Vase, 9" h., 4" d., tall squared ovoid form tapering to short square neck w/molded rim, upturned loop handles at the shoulder, decorated in sgraffito w/a veined pattern on an amber ground, incised "N5-7-1903 - Martin Bros. - London & Southall" **1,100**

Vase, 9 1/4" h., 6 1/4" d., footed bulbous ovoid body tapering to a wide flaring neck, covered in vivid incised & modeled swirls, brown & black matte glaze, incised "1 - 1 - 1903 - Martin Bros. - London Southall" **1,870**

Vases, 9" h., simple ovoid body tapering to a slightly flaring cylindrical neck, decorated w/a large crab on one side & a lobster on the opposite side w/assorted sea creatures in brown against "1903," pr. **1,870**

Massier (Clement)

Clement-Massier
Sde Juan AM

Massier Mark

Clement Massier was a French artist potter who worked in the late 19th and early 20th centuries creating exquisite earthenware items with lustre decoration.

Massier Vase with Unusual Design

Vase, 3 7/8" h., simple ovoid form w/flat rim, clam & seaweed decoration in brilliant metallic glaze, marked "C.M. Golfe Juan A.M." (ILLUS.)... **$532**

Vase, 6 3/4" h., 2 1/2" d., bud-type, bottle-shaped, bulbous ovoid body tapering to a very tall slender 'stick' neck, decorated w/a design of mistletoe in a silky red, gold & green iridescent glaze, unmarked............. **220**

Vase, 8 3/4" h., baluster-shaped w/short flaring neck, glossy ruby glaze w/splotches of leaf-like designs, incised "J. Massier, Vallavris, France - 2008/6" (professional repair to rim) **179**

Merrimac Pottery

Merrimac Mark

The Merrimac Ceramic Company of Newburyport, Massachusetts, was initially organized in 1897 by Thomas S. Nickerson for the production of inexpensive garden pottery and decorated tile. Within the year, production was expanded to include decorative art pottery and this change was reflected in a new name, Merrimac Pottery Company, adopted in 1902. Early glazes were limited to primarily matte green and yellow but by 1903 a variety of hues, including iridescent and metallic lustres, were used. Marked only with a paper label until after 1901, it then bore an impressed mark incorporating a fish beneath "Merrimac." Fire destroyed the pottery in 1908 and this relatively short span of production makes the ware scarce and expensive.

Bowl-vase, wide flat-bottomed form w/low rounded sides w/a wide shoulder centering a short, wide cylindrical neck, fine matte green glaze, impressed mark, 9" d., 4" h. (minute fleck on rim) **$1,320**

Jar, cov., tapering cylindrical body w/a wide rounded shoulder centering a slightly domed cover w/knob finial, glossy speckled brown glaze, paper label, 3 1/4" d., 5 1/4" h. (stilt pulls inside rim of cover in the making) **495**

Pitcher, 6 3/4" h., 6 1/2" d., tapering cylindrical body w/a rolled rim, C-form handle, rich matte green mottled glaze, stamped mark (rim chip restoration) **330**

Large Merrimac Umbrella Stand

Umbrella stand, tall cylindrical form w/tooled & applied leaves under a leathery matte green glaze, crack to base crawls along the side, a few small chips to decoration & some glaze pooling, paper label, 8 1/2" d., 22 3/4" h. (ILLUS.) **4,125**

Vase, miniature, 4" h., 3 1/2" d., squatty bulbous baluster-form w/the wide shoulder centered by a widely flaring trumpet neck, feathered matte green & gunmetal glaze, mark partially obscured by glaze **495**

Vase, 7 1/2" h., 4 1/4" d., slightly swelled cylindrical form w/a small closed mouth, tooled & applied w/dogwood blossoms around the top on tall stems w/leaves around the base, rich leathery matte green glaze, impressed mark (opposing hairlines, one restored) **1,980**

Rare Merrimac Vase with Leaves

Vase, 7 3/4" h., 4 1/2" d., gently swelled cylindrical form w/a rounded shoulder to the closed rim, tooled & applied w/swirling leaves, fine feathered matte green glaze, carved "EB," several nicks to edges of leaves (ILLUS.) **4,219**

Vase, 10" h., globular base tapering to tall cylindrical neck w/flat rim, mottled rich green, gunmetal & mauve glaze **825**

Large Bottle-form Merrimac Vase

Vase, 10" h., 5" d., bulbous nearly spherical base tapering to a tall cylindrical neck, fine dark green & mirrored black mottled glaze, unmarked (ILLUS.) **1,650**

Tall Green Merrimac Vase

Vase, 10 1/2" h., tall ovoid body tapering to a flat molded mouth, overall matte green glaze, stilt pull & small chips on base (ILLUS.) **1,035**

Tall Simple Merrimac Vase

Vase, 11 1/2" h., tall slightly swelled cylindrical body w/a widely flaring rim, overall matte green glaze, impressed chip in rim, small glaze miss at base (ILLUS.) **690**

Vase, 11 1/2" h., 6" d., gently swelled cylindrical body w/a widely flared rim, applied stylized plant sprigs around the rim on tall thin stems w/a band of pointed leaves around the base, leathery semi-matte green glaze, stamped mark (restored chip at rim, hairline down body) **1,980**

Mettlach

Mettlach Mark

Ceramics with the name Mettlach were produced by Villeroy & Boch and other potteries in the Mettlach area of Germany. Villeroy and Boch's finest years of production are thought to be from about 1890 to 1910.

Mettlach Plaque with Cavalier & Maid

Plaque, pierced to hang, etched cavalier & barmaid, blue background, castle marked, dated 1900, No. 2322, 14 1/2"d. (ILLUS.) **$795**

Plaque, pierced to hang, round, blue-decorated village landscape on a white ground, titled on the back "Hannover," No. 5036, 17 3/8" d. **259**

Mettlach Plaque with Cavalier

Plaque, pierced to hang, round, etched in center w/scene of cavalier seated at table raising a glass of beer in one hand, browns & white on a blue ground w/brown border band, No. 2622, dated 1910, artist-initialed, 7 3/4" d. (ILLUS.) **235**

Mettlach Punch Bowl Set

Punch bowl, cover & undertray, bulbous urn-form footed body w/molded double-C scroll handles, flaring foot, low domed cover w/ladle hole & upright scrolled ring handle, printed under glaze w/a decoration of scenes of gnomes working at a wine press & drinking, No. 2339/1028, early 20th c., 7 1/2 liter, 16" h., the set (ILLUS.) **748**

Vase, 9 1/2" h., large ovoid body w/a short slightly tapering neck, the body in dark blue w/an overall latticework design, each diamond segment w/a small molded red dot or florette, the neck in brick red w/a gold zigzag band & white florettes, impressed marks **330**

Vase, 10" h., tall square tapering form swelled near the base, incised & painted w/a geometric design w/vertical bands down the sides connecting to a group of graduated squares all in dark green & red on a creamy ground, impressed marks......... **550**

Vase with Gargoyle Handles

Vase, 11 1/2" h., flared foot below wide bulbous body w/ringed cylindrical neck flanked by gargoyle handles, polychrome & gilt decoration on beige ground, impressed mark, No. 1409 (ILLUS.) **220**

Steins

Mettlach, No. 24, relief, figures on four separate panels, inlaid lid, 1 liter **300**

Mettlach, No. 485, relief, musicians & dancers on blue background, inlaid lid, 1 liter **350**

Mettlach, No. 954 (2176), PUG (printed-under-glaze), knight drinking, signed "Schlitt," pewter lid, 2 1/10 liters **600**

Mettlach Drinking Gnomes

Mettlach, No. 966 (2184), PUG, drinking gnomes, by Schlitt, inlaid lid, 1/2 liter (ILLUS.).. **300**

Mettlach, No. 1154, etched tour-panel scenes of hunters, inlaid lid, 1 liter................ **600**

Mettlach, No. 1527, etched, four men drinking, brown background, signed "Warth," inlaid lid, 1 liter **600**

Mettlach, No. 1566, etched, man on high-wheel bicycle, signed "Gorig," inlaid lid, 1/2 liter **1,000**

Mettlach, No. 1786, etched, lid w/relief scene of Munich, St. Floiran putting out fire, dragon handle, ceramic dragon's head thumblift, pewter lid, 1/2 liter **700**

Mettlach, No. 1818, etched, tavern scene, pewter lid, signed "Gorig," 6 1/5 liters **1,800**

Mettlach, No. 1821, relief, mucician w/guitar, inlaid lid, 3 1/5 liters.................................... **350**

Mettlach, No. 1909, colorful transfer-printed design of a man smoking a pipe while sitting at a tavern table w/stein, artist-signed, verse on reverse by B. Auerbach, inlaid pewter lid, 1/2 liter (chip beneath base of thumblift cover) **175**

Mettlach, No. 2001A, relief-molded in the form of hand-painted books of law, inlaid pewter lid, 1/2 liter **575**

Mettlach, No. 2024, etched 'Berlin' design w/shield of the city of Berlin, inlaid lid, 1/2 liter **550**

Mettlach, No. 2035, etched Bacchus carousing, inlaid lid, 1/2 liter.............................. **450**

Mettlach, No. 2038, decorated relief, town of Rodenstein, houses & towers on inlay, inlaid lid, 3 4/5 liters..................................... **3,800**

Mettlach, No. 2049, etched, chess stein, chessboard, inlaid lid, 1/2 liter **2,500**

Mettlach, No. 2090, etched club stein, man at table w/his club smoking pipe, signed "Schlitt," inlaid lid, 1/2 liter **550**

Mettlach, No. 2100, etched, Prosit stein, knight w/stein & man w/fur clothing, signed "Schlitt," inlaid lid, 1/2 liter **1,100**

Mettlach, No. 2106, decorated relief, monkeys in cage, monkey handle, inlaid lid, 1/2 liter **4,500**

Mettlach, No. 2126, etched symphonia stein, composers, signed "Schlitt," pewter lid, 5 1/2 liters **6,500**

Mettlach, No. 2136, etched, Anheuser Busch Brewery, inlaid lid, 1/2 liter.............. **2,500**

Mettlach, No. 2219, relief, dancing & musical scenes, three panels, inlaid lid, 3 1/10 liters **500**

Mettlach, No. 2235, etched scene of a barmaid holding steins, targets in the background, pewter lid, 1/2 liter............................ **460**

Mettlach, No. 2277, etched scene of Nurnberg, inlaid lid, 1/2 liter................................ **525**

Mettlach, No. 2401, etched decoration of Tannhauser titled "Tannhauser in the Venusberg," inlaid lid, 1 liter **345**

Mettlach, No. 2402, etched, the courting of Siegried, inlaid lid, 1/2 liter **900**

Mettlach, No. 2520, etched, student & barmaid, signed "Schlitt," inlaid lid, 1 liter.......... **700**

Mettlach, No. 2580, etched, Die Kannenburg stein, knight in castle, signed "Schlitt," conical inlaid lid, 1/2 liter................. **700**

Mettlach, No. 2722, etched, occupational, shoemaker, inlaid lid, 1/2 liter..................... **1,500**

Mettlach, No. 2782, Rookwood-style, h.p. bust portrait of a cavalier drinking, hinged pewter lid, 17 3/4" h, 4 1/2 liter...................... **489**

Mettlach, No. 3236, etched Art Nouveau design in blue & white, inlaid lid, 1/2 liter...... **575**

Mettlach, No. 3395, Cameo style, footed spherical body w/a cylindrical neck & rim spout w/mask, molded C-form handle, inlaid lid, the body w/a wide blue band decorated w/white relief peasant figures drinking, ten pin & vine design on blue neckband, 7" d., 12" h...................................... **385**

Mettlach, No. 5001, faience-type, PUG, coat of arms, pewter lid, 4.6 liters **850**

Moorcroft

Moorcroft Marks

William Moorcroft became a designer for James Macintyre & Co. in 1897 and was put in charge of their art pottery production. Moorcroft developed a number of popular designs, including Florian Ware while with Macintyre and continued with that firm until 1913 when they discontinued the production of art pottery.

After leaving Macintyre in 1913, Moorcroft set up his own pottery in Burslem and continued producing the art wares he had designed earlier as well as introducing new patterns. After William's death in 1945, the pottery was operated by his son, Walter.

Bowl, 4" d., Dawn Landscape patt., stylized design w/trees in matte blue glaze, artist-signed, impressed mark, ca. 1928.............. **$345**

Hibiscus Pattern Covered Bowl

Bowl, cov., 5 1/2" d., 3 1/2" h., bulbous body, button finial, Hibiscus patt., red & yellow blossoms on dark blue ground, incised "Made in England - Moorcroft" & stamped label "#222 By Appointment W. Moorcroft Potters to the Queen," artist-initialed (ILLUS.) **380**

Bowl, 8" d., Poppy patt., the interior tube-lined w/a garland of large & small blooms in tones of puce & purple, joined by scrolling green foliage, the exterior w/three spiraling stems, all reserved on a watery cobalt blue ground, impressed "MOORCROFT" & painted signature, ca. 1928 .... **747**

Large Moorcroft Pomegrante Bowl

Bowl, 8 1/4" d., 4" h., footed wide & deep rounded shape w/flat rim, Pomegranate patt., large red & orange fruits & greenish brown leaves w/purple & red berries in the background, stamped mark (ILLUS.)...... **805**

Bowl, 9" d., 4" h., footed wide rounded form w/flat rim, Waving Corn (wheat) patt., decorated in squeezebag w/large curved heads of wheat in green & maroon on a light celadon green ground, stamped Moorcroft & ink mark... **715**

Clematis Pattern Ginger Jar

Ginger jar, cov., Clematis patt., dark blue, rose & yellow flowers & green leaves on cobalt blue ground, incised stamp "Made in England," 6" h. (ILLUS.) **870**

Jar, cov., wide ovoid body w/a rounded shoulder to the short cylindrical neck fitted w/a domed cover, Eventide patt., decorated w/a landscape scene w/a band of large mushroom-shaped trees in brown, yellow & greenish brown against a shaded yellow & red sunset background w/brown mountains, ink artist-signature & die-stamped "Made in England - 760," 8 1/2" d., 11" h. **6,600**

Tall Moorcroft Floral Lamp Base

Lamp base, a metal round base supporting the slightly waisted cylindrical lamp decorated w/bold stylized flowers in red, green & yellow against a cream & cobalt blue ground, signed, replaced socket, minor crazing, 14" h. (ILLUS.) **546**

Lamp bases, Poppy patt., baluster-form, tube-lined w/a continuous band of flowers & foliage colored in tones of yellow, red, cobalt blue & green on a graduated mottled blue ground, all washed in a thin red flambé glaze, ca. 1950, 12 1/4" h., pr. ... **1,035**

Perfume bottle w/stopper, figural, round flattened sides molded as a large pansy blossom, painted in lavender & yellow on a cobalt blue ground, hallmarked silver cap, unsigned, 1 3/4" w., 2" h. **660**

Tea set: cov. teapot, open sugar & creamer; Pomegranate patt., large red & yellow fruits w/purple seeds w/yellowish green leaves, green mark, teapot 7 1/2" d., 8" h., the set (small chip & flat hairline in teapot, repair to spout & crack in handle of creamer) **2,860**

Vase, 1 3/4" h., 2" d., miniature, tiny spherical form w/a small flared neck, painted w/stylized roses & blue flowers on a white ground, stamped "MacIntyre Burslem" & script "WM" **935**

Vase, 3 1/2" h., miniature, tapering cylindrical body w/a rounded shoulder centering a short flaring neck, dark blue ground w/multicolored Orchid patt., original label **413**

Vase, 4 1/8" h., footed bulbous ovoid body tapering to rolled rim, Poppy patt., red blossom, green leaves on cobalt blue shading to green ground, cobalt blue in-

terior, incised "Made in England - Potters H.M. Queen" in blue **200**

Moorcroft Eventide Pattern Vase

Vase, 5" h., footed baluster-form, Eventide patt., large stylized trees in shades of brown against a light tan & deep rose ground (ILLUS.) **1,265**

Moorcroft Landscape Vase

Vase, 6" h., 5 1/4" d., Landscape patt., footed bulbous ovoid body w/flaring rim, scene of blue trees on a mottled blue & yellow ground, script mark (ILLUS.) **2,200**

Blackberry Pattern Vase

Vase, 6 1/8" h., footed baluster form w/flared rim, Blackberry patt., purple & red fruit & leaves on shaded dark & light blue & green ground, cobalt blue interior, incised "Made in England - Potter to the Queen" (ILLUS.) **340**

Vase, 6 1/4" h., 3 1/2" d., baluster-form w/widely flaring rim, Pansy patt., large red & purple blossoms & yellow leaves on a dark blue ground, fitted into a hammered pewter footed base marked "Made In England - Tudric - Moorcroft - 01516 - Made By Liberty & Co." **880**

Vase, 6 1/4" h., 4 1/2" d., Cornflower patt., ovoid body w/cylindrical molded rim, impressed "MOORCROFT - MADE IN EN-GLAND - 210" **1,320**

Vase, 6 1/2" h., footed baluster-form, large red six-petaled blossoms & green leaves on a shaded pale green to dark blue ground, impressed & painted marks **358**

Moorcroft Eventide Pattern Vase

Vase, 6 1/2" h., 3 1/2" d., baluster-form w/short flared neck, Eventide patt., squeezebag design of large stylized trees in shades of reddish orange & green flambé glaze, ca. 1925, signed (ILLUS.) **220**

Vase, 6 3/4" h., 3" d., Florian Ware, slightly waisted cylindrical form w/a rounded base rim & shoulder tapering to a short cylindrical neck, decorated in squeezebag w/blue stylized jonquils & green leaves on a blue ground, ink mark **1,980**

Vase, 6 3/4" h., 3" d., slender baluster-form w/short flared neck, decorated overall w/clusters of blue & pink flowers & green leaves on a white ground, Macintyre stamp, Moorcroft signature **1,980**

Moorcroft Clematis Pattern Vase

Vase, 7" h., footed ovoid body w/a wide flat mouth, "Clematis" patt., a large blossom & leaves in dark purplish red & orangish

red on a reddish orange ground, initials & impressed mark, paper label, mid-20th c., small glaze scratch (ILLUS.) **489**

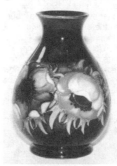

Poppy Pattern Vase

Vase, 7 1/4" h., footed bulbous ovoid body tapering to flared neck, Poppy patt., red & white blossoms & green leaves on dark blue ground, printed mark "Made in England," artist-initialed (ILLUS.) **700**

Moorcroft Claremont Vase

Vase, 8 1/2" h., Claremont patt., ovoid body decorated w/large mushrooms in red, green & yellow against a blue ground, impressed & painted marks (ILLUS.) **2,640**

Moorcroft Vase with Blue Berries

Vase, 9" h., 5 1/4" d., simple ovoid body tapering slightly to a short flaring rim, decorated in squeezebag w/a wide band of large blue berries & pale green leaves around the shoulder against a mottled green & dark blue ground, dark crazing lines around rim, ink signature & stamped mark (ILLUS.)................................. **1,150**

Vase, 9" h., 5 1/2" d., a wide disk foot supporting an ovoid body w/a wide flat mouth, decorated w/large red, garnet & orange fruits & leaves on a dark cobalt blue ground, paper label.............................. **2,138**

Vase, 10" h., Poppy patt., wide ovoid body w/slightly flaring rim, red & black ground, die-stamped mark & artist-signed **4,400**

Vase, 10 1/4" h., bulbous base tapering to a tall neck w/flared rim, decorated w/trailing rose blossoms in cobalt blue & mauve on a sage green lustre ground, signature mark, second quarter 20th c. **2,185**

Vase, 12" h., bottle-form, Eventide Landscape patt., the lower body tube-lined w/trees in an undulating landscape, glazed in watery tones of green, ochre & blue against a deep red sky, impressed "MOORCROFT - 156" & painted signature, ca. 1925 (hairline in upper rim) **862**

Tall Baluster-form Moorcroft Vase

Vase, 13" h., tall baluster-form body, Pomegranate patt., large deep red fruits w/moss green leaves against a dark blue ground, drill hole for lamp in base, signed (ILLUS.) **690**

Tall Moorcroft Claremont Vase

Vase, 14" h., tall baluster-form w/a short flared neck, Claremont patt., decorated in red, yellow & purple w/toadstools on a

mottled green & blue ground, Moorcroft signature & impressed "Moorcroft - Burslem - England M46," ca. 1916-18 (ILLUS.)... **5,100**

Large Moorcroft Spanish Pattern Vase

Vase, 16" h., 10 1/2" d., a round foot below the tall trumpet-form body, Spanish patt., overall bold scrolling blossoms & leaves in reds, pinks, greens & blues, two chips on base, green slip signature mark & stamped "Made for Liberty & Co.," 1903-13 (ILLUS.) **4,312**

Large Moorcroft Vase with Grapes

Vase, 17" h., "Grape and Leaf" patt., wide baluster-form w/a short flaring neck, decorated w/fruit & leaves in shades of orange, red, purple & mauve on a shaded rust & dark blue ground, glossy glaze, impressed mark, ca. 1930 (ILLUS.)............... **4,888**

Moorcroft Trumpet-Form Vase

Vase, 17 1/8" h., trumpet-form, gently flaring cylindrical body tube-lined w/Poppy patt., reserved on mottled blue & green ground, interior w/mottled dark cobalt blue glaze, impressed "Moorcroft," Co-bridge factory mark, W. Moorcroft signature in blue script, applied paper label "Potter to H.M. the Queen," ca. 1920, upper rim w/traces of restoration (ILLUS.) **2,070**

Newcomb College Pottery

Newcomb College Pottery Mark

This pottery was established in the art department of Newcomb College, New Orleans, Louisiana, in 1897. Each piece was hand-thrown and bore the potter's mark & decorator's monogram on the base. It was always a studio business and never operated as a factory and its pieces are therefore scarce, with the early wares being eagerly sought. The pottery closed in 1940.

Bowl, 4 1/2" d., 2 1/2" h., footed half-round form w/flat rim, carved around the rim w/a narrow band of pink buds on a green & blue ground, by Sadie Irvine, 1927, marked "NC - IS - PV71" **$1,238**

Bowl, 7" d., 2 1/2" h., footed wide squatty bulbous form w/a wide flat mouth, the shoulder decorated w/pairs of large pink blossoms w/yellow centers joined by slender green leaves all against a dark blue ground, matte glaze, impressed mark, "H. Bailey - #IZ31" **990**

Early Newcomb College Bowl

Bowl, 8 1/2" d., 3 1/4" h., low round body w/incurved sides & narrow flat rim, incised stylized white & yellow blossoms on a glossy cobalt & green ground, by Henrietta Bailey, 1904, two hairlines at rim, impressed "NC - HB - ZZ74" (ILLUS.) **4,950**

Bowl-vase, wide spherical form tapering to a wide flat rim, carved w/a continuous landscape of live oaks draped in Spanish moss w/a full moon behind, 1939, marked "NC - Y38 - FHF," 7" d., 5 1/2" h. (very tight short hairline at rim) **3,375**

Bowl-vase, footed squatty round bulbous body incised around top w/a band of white & yellow roses on a bluish green ground, by Henrietta Bailey, 1914, impressed "NC - HB - GT32 - JM - 256" 31/4 x 6 1/4" **1,870**

Newcomb Bowl-Vase with Crocus

Bowl-vase, decorated w/cobalt blue rim over incised band of repeating crocus above a band of leaves, cream, yellow, pale blue, blue & bluish green over light blue body, interior gloss glazed cream, by Marie H. LeBlanc, 1905, impressed "NC, W - JM - CB54" & artist's cipher, 5 1/2" d., 4 1/4" h. (ILLUS.) **4,025**

Bowl-vase, bulbous body w/deeply-colored landscape scene of a live oak w/Spanish moss w/full moon in background, by Sadie Irvine, ca. 1932, impressed "NC - SI - KS - UB46," 5 1/2" d., 3 3/4" h. **2,090**

Bowl-vase, squatty bulbous body w/short cylindrical neck, decorated w/light blue & yellow daffodils on a faded blue ground, by Sadie Irvine, ca. 1922, impressed "NC - SI - JM - MI38 - 212," 7" d., 4 1/4" h. **1,980**

Newcomb Glossy-glazed Charger

Charger, decorated overall w/large fig branches w/leaves & fruit in dark blue & bluish yellow on a pale blue ground, glossy glaze, by Irene Borden Keep, 1902, few tiny clay pimples, marked, 10 3/4" d. (ILLUS.) **10,350**

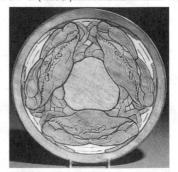

Large Newcomb Charger with Crabs

Charger, incised around the center w/three large blue crabs on a blue ground, by Sabrina Wells, 1904, marked "NC - M - S.E. Wells - YY64," short, tight line on back, 13" d. (ILLUS.)... **28,125**

Very Rare Newcomb College Jar

Jar, cov., large bulbous ovoid body w/a fitted domed cover, the upper half of the body carved w/a band of stylized sweet peas, the cover carved w/a central blossom surrounded w/a band reading "Here are sweet peas on tiptoe for a flight," by Mazie T. Ryan, 1903, signed "M.C. - M.T.R. - W - MR - SS - 64," 6" d., 8" h. (ILLUS.) **42,188**

Jardiniere, large bulbous ovoid form w/a wide flat closed rim, decorated w/large white lilies w/yellow centers raised on green stems against a cobalt blue ground, by Harriet Joor, 1903, marked "NC - JM - X97 - HJ," two rim repairs, 10 1/2" d., 8 3/4" h. (ILLUS. right with teapot & vase, below) **13,500**

Mug, slightly tapering waisted form w/loop handle, decorated w/a wide upper band of stylized landscape in bluish green above a wide blue-washed lower band, glossy glaze, painted by Desiree Roman & Marie Delavigne, 1901, impressed "NC - DR - MD - G73X - Q - JM," 5" w., 4" h. **3,575**

Pitcher, 5" h., 4 1/2" d., gently flaring cylindrical body w/a pinched rim spout & loop handle, decorated w/an upper band in the Espanol geometric patt., on a dark blue matte ground, impressed "207" **1,320**

Pitcher, cov., milk, 5 1/4" h., cylindrical body w/pinched spout, flat inset lid & button finial, large loop handle, the top decorated w/a band of incised stylized blossoms in orange, dark blue & bluish green against a light blue ground, orange spout, rim & narrow band on lid, decorated by Charlotte Payne, 1905, impressed "NC - CP - AT44" **3,850**

Pitcher, 8" h., 6" d., tall ovoid tapering to a short waisted neck w/angled handle from rim to shoulder, decorated around the neck w/a carved band of pink nasturium blossoms & green leaves on a matte dark blue ground, by Sadie Irvine, 1924, incised "NC - SI - 230 - OB65".................... **2,310**

Pitcher, 8" h., 6" d., tall ovoid tapering to a short waisted neck w/angled handle from rim to shoulder, decorated around the neck w/a carved band of pink morning glory blossoms & green leaves on a matte dark blue ground, by Sadie Irvine, 1924, incised "NC - SI - 230 - OB69" **3,850**

Newcomb Jardiniere, Teapot & Vase

Teapot, cov., footed conical body w/angled spout & handle, fitted low domed cover w/button finial, carved around the lower body w/a band of wild roses in light pink & yellow on a dark bluish green ground w/dark blue trim, by Alma Mason, 1911, marked "NC - EG44 - A.M. - B.," 5 1/2" d., 4 1/4" h. (ILLUS. front left with jardiniere & vase)... **3,375**

Newcomb College Tyge with Flowers

Tyge (three-handled mug), wide slightly tapering cylindrical body w/three squared tubular handles from the rim to the base, decorated around the rim w/a band of white flowers against bands of dark blue & white, pale blue lower body & white handles, old tight hairline in one handle, by Marie De Hoa LaBlanc, 1905, 5" d., 3 3/4" h. (ILLUS.) **4,600**

Vase, 3 " h., 3 3/4" d., miniature, bulbous ovoid form tapering to a short flat neck, decorated w/a vertical band of light blue bell-shaped flowers & green leaves around the sides on a cobalt blue ground, by Henrietta Bailey, 1929, marked "NC - HB3359 - JM"................................ **1,463**

Vase, 3 5/8" h., wide shoulder tapering toward the base, a short extended rim, decorated around the rim w/leafy vines & fruit in relief, bluish green matte glaze, impressed mark & artist's initials & "EM.55," early 20th c.. **920**

Vase, 3 1/2" h., wide bulbous ovoid body w/narrow cylindrical neck & closed rim, incised decoration of tall trees w/Spanish moss in shades of blue against a peach sunset background (ILLUS.)...................... **1,900**

Vase, 3 3/4" h., 3 1/4" d., miniature, simple ovoid body w/a flat mouth, painted w/a continuous upright band of strawberries & leaf clusters in dark blue on a pale blue ground, by Ester Elliott, 1902, marked "NC - JM - EHE - R19" (ILLUS. upper left with teapot & jardiniere).............................. **9,000**

Early Newcomb College Vase

Vase, 4 1/4" h., 4 1/2" d., footed squatty bulbous body, the wide shoulder tapering to cylindrical neck w/flat rim, decorated w/h.p. yellow sunflower petals & blue seeds, outlined in blue, on ivory ground, by S. Massegali, artist-signed & impressed "NC - P," stilt pull to base (ILLUS.) **4,950**

Vase, 4 1/2" h., 2 1/2" d., bud-type, waisted cylindrical form decorated up the sides w/sprigs of wide flowers & green long leaves on a bluish green ground, by Henrietta Bailey, 1915, impressed "NC - KB82 - HB - 212".. **1,870**

Vase, 5 1/4" h., bulbous ovoid form w/flat rim, incised w/yellow daisies on an ivory & light blue ground, by Desiree Roman, 1903, impressed "NC - D.R. - JM - Q - JJ79," (two tight hairlines to rim) **7,150**

Small Newcomb Vase

Newcomb Vase with Tall Pines

Vase, 5 1/4" h., 3 1/4" d., ovoid body w/a narrow shoulder tapering to a short, wide cylindrical neck, crisply carved w/a landscape of tall pines in bluish green on a washed blue ground, small stilt-pull chips, by Sadie Irvine, 1917, signed (ILLUS.) **3,450**

Vase, 5 1/2" h., bulbous ovoid body tapering to a short cylindrical neck, carved & painted around the shoulder w/a narrow band of pairs of small white blossoms & green leaves & vines against a dark blue matte ground, impressed mark, "#QP91 - A.F. Simpson"... **1,320**

Vase, 5 1/2" h., footed squatty bulbous body, shoulder tapering to wide cylindrical neck w/flat rim, decorated w/abstract floral pattern in blue, green & yellow on purple ground, ca. 1922, artist-signed & impressed "NC - JM - 121 - MQ40" **1,760**

Vase, 5 1/2" h., swelled cylindrical form tapering slightly to a wide flat mouth, carved & painted w/a continuous landscape of dark blue oaks hung w/green moss against a light blue sky w/a yellow moon, impressed mark, "J.M. - A.F. Simpson - #OQ81" **2,750**

Newcomb Scenic with Pink Sky

Vase, 5 1/2" h., 3" d., slender ovoid form tapering to a short cylindrical neck, decorated w/a landscape of large oak trees draped w/Spanish moss in shades of light & dark blue & green against a pink sky, by Anna Frances Simpson, 1929 (ILLUS.) **5,463**

Newcomb Vase with Flower Band

Vase, 5 3/4" h., 3" d., footed cylindrical form w/rounded bottom rim & shoulder centered by a short cylindrical neck, incised around the upper body w/a wide band of stylized flowers in yellow & green on a glossy washed blue ground, opposing hairlines in rim, stilt-pull chip, minute nick on base, by Marie De Hoa LeBlanc, 1903, signed (ILLUS.)................................... **4,600**

Newcomb College Vase w/Sailboats

Vase, 5 3/4" h., 5 3/4" d., wide expanding cylindrical body w/flat rim, carved & decorated w/a continuous band of blue sailboats w/clouds in background, glossy blue, white & green glaze, decorated by Desiree Roman, ca. 1903, impressed "NC - W - D.R. - X37 -JM" (ILLUS.) **13,750**

Vase, 6" h., bulbous body tapering to wide cylindrical neck w/closed rim, decorated w/light blue irises w/green leaves on faded blue ground, by C. Chalaron, ca. 1925, impressed "NC - JM - 26ON33 - CMC" **2,420**

Vase, 6" h., footed cylindrical body tapering above a shoulder to a flat molded rim, incised decoration of cotton plants in white on a light blue ground w/blue band around base & rim, by Mazie T. Ryan, 1904, impressed "NC - JM - MTRyan, 1904 - NN1".. **6,325**

Vase, 6" h., hand-thrown, a wide three-lobed lip on the wide cylindrical neck w/carved vertical fine ribs above the wide squatty bulbous lower body, brown clay body decorated w/pale blue interior & white thick drippy glaze down the sides, incised "NC - HB - M," by L. Nicholson **880**

Vase, 6" h., slightly swelled cylindrical form tapering slightly to a short cylindrical neck, carved & painted around the shoulder w/large light blue flowers w/ivory & green centers & green leaves against a dark blue matte ground, impressed mark, "#OY14 - #19 -Sadie Irvine"........................ **1,320**

Vase, 6" h., 3 1/4" d., simple ovoid form w/a tapering neck & flattened rim, crisply modeled w/a landscape of live oak trees & Spanish moss in shades of dark & light blue w/pale green, by Anna F. Simpson, 1930, matte glaze, impressed "NC - AFS - JH -78 - SG85" **4,400**

Vase, 6 1/4" h., pear-shaped body w/molded rim, modeled w/leaves at base & covered in mottled matte green glaze, incised "AVL" & "JM" **1,760**

Vase, 6 1/2" h., footed wide ovoid body w/a wide shoulder sloping to a small cylindrical neck, carved & painted around the shoulder w/large stylized pale lavender rose blossoms on pale green scrolled leafy stems down the sides against a streaky blue matte ground, impressed mark, "#GC26 - M. Robertson - A.F. Simpson" 4,675

Newcomb Vase with Jonquils

Vase, 6 1/2" h., large wide bulbous ovoid form tapering to a thin flat wide rim, carved & painted w/jonquils in white w/yellow centers on green stems w/green leaves against a dark blue ground, by A.F. Simpson, impressed mark (ILLUS.) 4,400

Vase, 6 1/2" h., simple ovoid form tapering to a short cylindrical neck, carved & painted w/tall pointed overlapping leaves, blue, green & ivory matte glaze, impressed marks, attributed to C. Chalaron, Joseph Meyer, marked "#MZ10 - 78" 1,650

Vase, 6 1/2" h., wide cylindrical base below bulbous body, narrow molded rim, sharply carved w/nighttime scene of live oak trees covered in Spanish moss, full moon, decorated by A.F. Simpson, ca. 1920, impressed "NC - LV31- JM - 183 - AFS" 4,950

Vase, 6 1/2" h., wide squatty bulbous base tapering to cylindrical sides w/a molded rim, decorated w/abstract organic forms up the sides in shades of blue against a green & blue streaky ground, glossy glaze, by Robert Beverly Kennon, impressed mark (ILLUS. left, top next column) 4,313

Vase, 6 1/2" h., 7 1/2" d., wide bulbous body tapering to a short cylindrical base, the rounded shoulder centered by a wide, short cylindrical neck, incised & painted around the shoulder w/narcissus in pink w/yellow centers & green leaves on a dark matte blue ground, impressed marks, "A.F. Simpson - J.M. - #PO70 - G1" 1,980

Vase, 7" h., 5" d., wide ovoid body w/a short cylindrical neck, decorated w/tooled stylized yellow flowers on tall stems & large pointed leaves in celadon green against an ivory ground, by Esther H. Elliott, stamped "NC - EHE - BB10 - Q - JM" 24,750

Short & Tall Newcomb Vases

Vase, 7 1/4" h., 3 1/4" d., cylindrical form w/rounded bottom & shoulder tapering to a short flat rim, carved around the upper half w/a wide band of stylized white primrose blossoms on blue leafy stems against a light blue ground over a dark blue lower band, by Mazie Ryan, 1904, marked "NC - SS12 - M. Tryan." 8,438

Rare Newcomb Vase with Pod Design

Vase, 7 1/4" h., 5 1/4" d., slightly tapering ovoid body w/a wide closed rim, incised around the shoulder w/large stylized seed pods on long stems in shades of blue & greenish blue, interior firing line at rim, by Marie Benson, 1905 (ILLUS.) 10,925

Vase, 7 1/4 x 7 1/4", footed wide spherical body tapering to closed rim, incised w/an Art Deco design under a matte blue green glaze, ca. 1930s, artist's cipher 1,540

Vase, 7 1/2" h., baluster-form body w/wide cylindrical neck & flat rim, incised lines under a semi-matte gold glaze, decorated by Juanita Gonzales, ca. 1931, artist's cipher & impressed "NC - G71 - TC47 - JH" 1,210

Vase, 7 1/2" h., footed wide expanding cylindrical ridged body by Kenneth Smith, covered in semi-matte turquoise glaze, impressed "NC - Kenneth Smith" **605**

Vase, 7 1/2" h., 4 1/2" d., simple ovoid body w/a small tapering neck, decorated around the upper two-thirds w/a paneled band of tall incised stylized birch seed pods in bluish green against an ivory ground, a blue-washed band around the lower section, by Henrietta Bailey, 1904, marked "NC - PP71 - HBailey - JM - Q"... **15,400**

Vase, 8" h., slender ovoid body w/narrow shoulder tapering to wide cylindrical neck, decorated w/scene of live oaks & Spanish moss w/full moon, green tones, by Sadie Irvine, ca. 1922, impressed "NC - SI - 250 - MW7M4".................................... **3,190**

Vase, 8" h., 6" d., tapering ovoid form w/the shoulder centering a wide low rolled neck flanked by upright angled loop handles, painted w/four different views of large white egrets among sea grass in blue, white & green on a cobalt blue ground, pre-1902, by Marie M. Ross, restoration to one handle, impressed mark (ILLUS.). **25,875**

Vase, 8 3/4" h., 4 3/4" d., gently tapering cylindrical form w/a rounded shoulder & short cylindrical rim, decorated w/light periwinkle blue wisteria blossoms on a cobalt blue & celadon ground, by Maude Robinson, 1904, restored rim hairline, marked "NC - JM - Maude Robinson - XX41" (ILLUS. below, left)......................... **13,500**

Early Newcomb Vase with Egrets

Floral Newcomb Vase

Three Early Newcomb College Vases

Vase, 9" h., ovoid body, the rounded shoulder centered by small cylindrical neck w/flared rim, decorated w/ivory & yellow blossoms & leaves outlined in blue, green ground, impressed "NC - JM - N or Z," firing lines & stilt pull under base (ILLUS. previous page) **6,600**

Vase, 9 1/2" h., bulbous w/tapering shoulder & closed rim, decorated w/incised band of stylized light blue flowers on a white ground over a dark blue band & glossy blue base, by Sabrina Wells, 1904, ink mark & "NC - S.E.WELL - SS38" (line inside rim, not through, from firing) **8,250**

Vase, 9 1/2" h., tall slender waisted cylindrical body, the upper half w/an incised & finely painted band of stylized slender upright leaves & spearpoint blossoms in ivory, green & blue above the lower body w/a streaked ivory, green & blue glossy glaze, "C. Payne - J.M. - #YY29" **6,050**

Rare Newcomb Vase with Flowers

Vase, 9 1/2" h., 4" d., footed cylindrical form w/rounded base & shoulder tapering to a short flat neck, decorated w/stylized yellow flowers & dark blue leaves on a pale denim ground, glossy glaze, four hairlines from rim, unknown artist, dated 1902 (ILLUS.) **27,600**

Fine Newcomb Landscape Vase

Vase, 10 1/4" h., 6 1/2" d., wide ovoid body tapering to a flat mouth, decorated w/a landscape of live oak trees & Spanish moss w/a full moon in the background, shades of dark & light blue & yellow, by Anna Frances Simpson, marked (ILLUS.) **17,250**

Vase, 10 1/2" h., inverted trumpet-form body w/slightly flared rim, decorated w/pink berries & long green leaves on faded blue ground, by Sadie Irvine, ca. 1920, impressed "NC - KZ21 - 83 - SI" **2,750**

Vase, 10 1/2" h., tall sharply tapering cylindrical form w/small flared mouth, carved & painted eucalyptus leaves & seed pods suspended from the rim, in light pink & green matte on a blue ground, by Sadle Irvine, impressed mark (ILLUS. right with abstract decorated vase) **4,485**

Vase, 11" h., 5" d., tall ovoid form, crisply carved & decorated w/a tall oak tree w/Spanish moss w/a full moon beyond, shades of dark & light blue w/a yellow moon, by A.F. Simpson, 1927, marked "NC - M - AFS - QC35" (ILLUS. center with wisteria vase) **16,313**

Exceptional Newcomb Landscape

Vase, 11" h., 6" d., slender ovoid form tapering to a short cylindrical neck, decorated w/a continuous landscape of live oak trees draped w/Spanish moss w/a full moon beyond, in shades of dark & light blue, greenish blue & white, exceptional, by Anna Frances Simpson, 1929 (ILLUS.) **17,250**

Tall Newcomb Vase with Trees

Vase, 11 1/4" h., 4 1/2" d., tall slender cylindrical form w/a widely flaring rim, finely carved w/a continuous band of tall cypress & pine trees in medium bluish green on a pale bluish green ground, by Leona Nicholson, 1907, restoration to a hairline, marked "NC - BP46 - M - LN" (ILLUS.) **8,625**

Very Rare Newcomb College Vase

Vase, 12" h., tall gently tapering cylindrical form w/a rounded shoulder centering a short rolled neck, carved & painted bamboo stalks in several tones of green against a blue ground, all covered in a glossy glaze, by Henrietta Bailey, ca. 1909 (ILLUS.) **46,750**

Vase, 12 1/4" h., tall ovoid body decorated w/moonlight scene of live oaks w/Spanish moss, by Sadie Irvine, ca. 1925, impressed "NC - SI - OX28 - JM - 117" **7,700**

Vase, 12 1/4" h., 7 1/2" d., large tapering ovoid form w/a closed rim, decorated w/tall pine trees in dark blue & green against a background of dark blue & pale & dark yellow, by Harriet Joor, 1902, restoration to line at shoulder, marked "NC - JM - HJ - U87 - Q" (ILLUS. right with wisteria vase) **21,375**

Rare Newcomb Roadrunner Vase

Vase, 12 1/2" h., 7 3/4" d., wide ovoid body tapering to a short cylindrical neck, decorated around the shoulder w/a wide band of racing roadrunner birds, the birds in bluish white on dark blue, the background in streaky cream & dark blue, glossy glaze, Marie De Hoa LeBlanc, 1902 (ILLUS.) **43,125**

Very Rare Newcomb Vase with Irises

Vase, 14 1/2" h., 9" d., simple tall ovoid form tapering to a flat mouth, carved overall w/tall blue & yellow irises on tall green leafy stems, glossy glaze, Henrietta Bailey, 1909 (ILLUS.) **46,000**

Rare Newcomb College Wall Pocket

Wall pocket, long slender conical form, carved around the upper body w/a band of stylized trees in cobalt blue & green, dark blue lower body, glossy glaze, by Leona Nicholson, ca. 1904, 4" d., 11" l. (ILLUS.) **9,350**

Niloak Pottery

Niloak Pottery Mark

This pottery was made in Benton, Arkansas, and featured hand-thrown varicolored swirled clay deco-

Niloak Bowl and Vases

ration in objects of classic forms. Designated Mission Ware, this line is the most desirable of Niloak's production which began early in this century. Less expensive to produce, the cast Hywood Line, finished with either high gloss or semi-matte glazes, was introduced during the economic depression of the 1930s. The pottery ceased operation about 1946.

Ashtray, Mission Ware, shallow round form w/curved sides & incurved rim, swirled tan & cream clays, 3 1/2" d. **$88**

Ashtray/match holder, Mission Ware, shallow round form w/rim rests centered by cylindrical match holder, swirled brown, orange & cream clays, paper label, 2 1/4 x 4 3/4" **440**

Bowl, 5" d., Mission Ware, squatty rounded base tapering slightly to the wide, flat rim, swirled red, brown, cream & blue clays, marked.. **176**

Bowl, 6 3/4" d., 3" h., Mission Ware, wide deep rounded form w/a flat mouth, swirled dark blue, light blue, dark brown, cream & reddish brown clays, impressed mark, paper label (ILLUS. left, above) **173**

Bowl-vase, Mission Ware, wide flat-bottomed form w/rounded bottom & tapering cylindrical sides to the wide flat mouth, dark brown, beige & dark terra cotta swirled clays, stamped mark, 8" d., 6" h. **440**

Box, cov., Mission Ware, squatty bulbous body & high squatty mushroom-shaped cover, swirled dark brown, reddish brown, tan & blue clays, impressed mark, 4" h.. **1,035**

Candlestick, Mission Ware, swirled colored clays, 10 1/4" h... **250**

Candlesticks, Mission Ware, widely flaring funnel base tapering to a molded cylindrical shaft topped by a wide cupped socket, swirled brown, blue, terra cotta & sand clays, stamped mark, 5" d., 8" h., pr. **330**

Chamber pot, child's, Mission Ware, footed squatty bulbous form w/wide flared rim & C-form handle, swirled cream & brown clays, 5 1/2" d. **550**

Chamberstick, Mission Ware, flaring base w/loop handle, swirled tan, brown, orange & cream clays, 4 1/2" h. **253**

Cigarette jar, cov., Mission Ware, cylindrical w/inset lid & bud finial, swirled blue, cream & brown clays, 4 3/4" h. **825**

Compote, open, Mission Ware, flared foot, shallow, round w/incurved sides & rim,

swirled grey, tan, orange & cream clays, 5" h., 10" d. **825**

Decanter w/original stopper, Mission Ware, swirled tan, orange, grey & cream clays, 10 1/2" h. (chips to top of decanter) **880**

Figurine, Southern Belle, Hywood Line, standing, wearing hat, pink & aqua matte glaze, 7" h. **110**

Flower bowl, Mission Ware, squatty bulbous body w/center opening & pierced rim, swirled brown, cream & orange clays, 3 x 5 1/2" (one line, probably in making).. **198**

Niloak Flower Frogs & Umbrella Stand

Flower frogs, Mission Ware, round, swirled multicolored clays, largest 4 1/2" w., set of 3 (ILLUS. front) **121**

Flowerpot w/undertray, Mission Ware, expanding cylindrical form w/flat rim, hole in bottom for drainage, swirled brown, tan, grey & cream clays, 9" d., 10" h. **1,045**

Humidor, cov., Mission Ware, wide waisted cylinder w/inset lid & large round flat finial, swirled cream, tan & light brown clays, 6 1/2" h. **1,430**

Jardiniere, Mission Ware, bulbous ovoid w/collared rim, swirled brown clays, 10" h. **1,210**

Jug, spherical body w/flat bottom, a pointed loop handle on the shoulder opposite a short, round spout, overall mottled golden tan & green matte glaze, ink mark, 6" h... **231**

Model of dog, bulldog w/collar, Hywood
Line, red matte glaze, 4" h. 110

Mug, Mission Ware, cylindrical w/C-form
handle, swirled multicolored clays, 5" h. 253

Mugs, Mission Ware, tapering cylindrical
form w/C-form handles, swirled light &
dark brown clays, patent pending mark,
4" h., set of 6 990

Necklace, Mission Ware, alternating small
& tiny stones suspending a pendant consisting of a group of long & round swirled
light clay stones, 18" l. 825

Pedestal base, Mission Ware, short wide
waisted cylindrical form, swirled cream,
tan, brown & grey clays, 7" h. (bruise to
bottom) 358

Pitcher, 9" h., Hywood Line, footed spherical body w/relief-molded circles, C-form
shoulder handle opposite collared rim
w/pointed spout, blue & mustard matte
glaze 99

Pitcher, 9" h., Mission Ware, bulbous ovoid
body w/flaring rim & C-form handle,
swirled grey, tan, brown, orange & cream
clays, paper label.. 1,045

Pitcher, tankard, 10 1/2" h., Mission Ware,
corseted form 495

Pitcher, 11" h., Mission Ware, tall slender
ovoid body w/rim spout & rim turned up
above large C-form handle, large swirls
of brown, tan, cream & grey clays............... 1,320

Powder bowl, cov., Mission Ware, footed
bulbous body, flat inset lid w/small button
finial, swirled grey, tan & cream clays,
6" w., 3 1/2" h. 523

Niloak Mission Ware Covered Jar

Puff box, cov., Mission Ware, footed wide
squatty bulbous body w/a low rim & flat
inset cover w/pointed finial, swirled dark
brown, tan & dark blue clays, 4" h.
(ILLUS.)... 575

Punch bowl, Mission Ware, pedestal foot,
deep rounded sides w/molded rim,
swirled cream, tan & brown clays, 13" d.,
9" h.. 2,640

Shot glasses, Mission Ware, tapering cylindrical form, swirled multicolored clays,
2 1/4" h., set of 6 (one chip)........................... 468

Tankard set: Mission Ware, cylindrical
10 1/2" h. tankard & twelve 2" h. cylindrical mugs; tan pitcher w/zig-zag swirls in
cream & brown, multicolored swirled
mugs, pitcher w/hairline, two mugs
w/flaws, the set... 1,760

Tray, Mission Ware, round w/straight sides,
swirled orange, cream, grey & brown
clays, 13" d. 1,045

Umbrella stand, Mission Ware, cylindrical
w/flared foot & rim, swirled cream, tan,
blue & brown clays, crack to base, 21" h.
(ILLUS. w/flower frogs) 1,650

Umbrella stand, Mission Ware, wide cylindrical body w/flared foot & rim, swirled
multicolored clays, 20" h. (firing crack in
base).. 2,310

Vase, 3" h., Mission Ware, heavy short cylindrical form w/closed rim, swirling
cream, brown, blue & red clays, im-
pressed mark.. 154

Large & Small Mission Ware Vases

Vase, 3 1/2" h., miniature, Mission Ware,
ovoid form tapering gently to a wide flat
mouth, swirled light & dark blue, tan &
light brown clays, minute flakes (ILLUS.
left) 242

Vase, 3 1/2" h., miniature, Mission Ware,
wide ovoid form tapering to a heavy
molded rim, swirled dark & light brown,
dark blue, cream & reddish brown clays,
impressed mark (ILLUS. right with bowl)...... 150

Vase, 4" d., Mission Ware, bulbous ovoid
body w/a thick molded rim, swirled grey,
tan, rust & blue clays, first art mark 69

Vase, 4 1/4" h., Mission Ware, waisted cylindrical form, swirled brown, cream, tan
& blue clays 52

Vase, 5" h., Mission Ware, simple slender
ovoid body tapering to a small neck
w/widely flaring flattened rim, swirled tan,
blue, rust, purple & brown clays 81

Vase, 5" h., 6" d., Mission Ware, flat-bottomed wide bulbous form curving to a
wide flat rim, swirled dark & light brown,
cream, reddish brown & blue clays, impressed mark (ILLUS. right with minia-
ture vase) 265

Vase, 5 1/2" h., Mission Ware, cylindrical,
swirled multicolored clays 132

Vase, 5 1/2" h., Mission Ware, simple cylindrical form, sharply contrasting swirled
cream, brown, tan & blue clays, first art
mark.. 104

Vase, 5 3/4" h., 7" d., Mission Ware, squatty
spherical form w/closed rim, swirled
brown, blue, terra cotta & sand clays,
stamped mark & paper label.......................... 248

Vase, 6" h., Mission Ware, bulbous lower
body tapering to a tall waisted neck,
swirled blue, brown & cream clays 92

Niloak Mission Ware Vase

Vase, 6" h., Mission Ware, simple baluster-form w/a wide closed rim, swirled red, cream & grey clays, impressed mark (ILLUS.).. **209**

Vase, 6" h., Mission Ware, wide cylindrical form rounded at the base & top rim, bold swirled bands of dark blue, reddish brown & dark & light brown clays, impressed mark (ILLUS. center with bowl)....... **403**

Vase, 7" h., Mission Ware, fan-type, swirled orange, grey, blue & cream clays **319**

Vase, bud, 7" h., Mission Ware, flared base tapering to slender cylinder w/flat rim, swirled multicolored clays............................... **154**

Two Cylindrical Niloak Vases

Vase, 7 1/4" h., Mission Ware, simple cylindrical form, fine swirls of dark blue, cream & dark brown clays, early impressed mark w/patent pending wording (ILLUS. left) **633**

Unusual Mission Ware Incised Vase

Vase, 8 1/4" h., Mission Ware, tall ovoid form tapering gently to flat rim, unusual decoration of overall incised squiggles in a tan matte glaze over a dark brown base, paper label (ILLUS.) **1,150**

Vase, 8 1/2" h., 4 1/2" d., Mission Ware, tall trumpet-form body on a flaring disk foot, swirled brown, blue & terra cotta clays, stamped mark **165**

Vase, 8 3/4" h., Mission Ware, large bulbous ovoid body tapering to a short slightly rolled neck, swirled dark & light brown clays, rare ink stamp mark............... **1,093**

Vase, 9 1/2" h., 5" d., Mission Ware, baluster-form w/short flared neck, banded swirls of brown, blue, terra cotta & sand clays, stamped mark **303**

Vase, 9 1/2" h., 5 1/2" d., Mission Ware, footed bulbous base tapering to a tall wide trumpet neck, swirled brown, blue, terra cotta & purple clays, stamped mark..... **358**

Vase, 9 3/4" h., 4 3/4" d., Mission Ware, footed elongated pear-form body tapering to a short cylindrical neck w/flattened flaring rim, swirled brown, blue, terra cotta & sand clays, stamped mark **385**

Vase, 10" h., Mission Ware, bulbous body tapering to a large wide trumpet neck, swirled blue, red, brown & cream glazes, impressed mark **275**

Vase, 10" h., Mission Ware, tall simple cylindrical form, bold swirls of medium blue, dark & light brown, cream & reddish brown clays, impressed mark (ILLUS. right with other cylindrical vase)................... **288**

Vase, 10" h., 4 1/2" d., Mission Ware, tall corseted form, brown, blue & terra cotta swirled clays, stamped mark........................ **220**

Vase, 10" h., 4 1/2" d., Mission Ware, tall cylindrical body w/flaring foot, swirled brown, blue & reddish terra cotta clays, stamped mark & paper label.......................... **385**

Vase, 11" h., Mission Ware, tall baluster-form w/widely flaring flattened neck, bold squiggly swirls of blue, cream, reddish brown, dark & light brown clays, impressed mark (ILLUS. center with miniature vase) **500**

Vase, 12" h., 7 1/2" d., Mission Ware, tall ovoid body tapering to a short flaring neck, finely swirled brown, ivory & terra cotta clays, stamped mark & paper label...... **495**

Vase, 12 1/4" h., footed bulbous body tapering to a tall flaring trumpet neck, overall dark matte blue glaze, impressed mark....... **748**

Vase, 12 1/4" d., 5 1/2" d., Mission Ware, tall slender corseted form, swirled brown, blue, terra cotta & purple clays, stamped mark.. **330**

Vase, 14" h., 7" d., Mission Ware, tall footed swelled cylindrical form w/a narrow shoulder tapering to a thick molded rim, finely swirled brown, blue, terra cotta & purple clays, stamped mark & paper label................ **880**

Wall pocket, Mission Ware, conical w/flat rim, swirled brown, orange, grey & cream clays, paper label, 7 1/2" l. **440**

Whiskey jug, Mission Ware, four-sided centered by cylindrical neck w/molded rim, wide shoulder w/loop handle, swirled blue, grey & cream clays, 6" h.................... **2,750**

North Dakota School of Mines

North Dakota School of Mines Mark

All pottery produced at the University of North Dakota School of Mines was made from North Dakota clay. In 1910, the University hired Margaret Kelly Cable to teach pottery making and she remained at the school until her retirement. Julia Mattson and Margaret Pachl were other instructors between 1923 and 1970. Designs and glazes varied through the years ranging from the Art Nouveau to modern styles. Pieces were marked "University of North Dakota - Grand Forks, N.D. - Made at School of Mines, N.D." within a circle and also signed by the students until 1963. Since that time, the pieces bear only the students' signatures. Items signed "Huck" are by the artist Flora Huckfield and were made between 1923 and 1949.

Small North Dakota Bowl

Bowl, 4 1/2" d., 2" h., low, flat-bottomed cylindrical form, incised continuous scrolling band, green matte glaze, signed (ILLUS.) **$201**

North Dakota School of Mines Bowl

Bowl, 6 1/2" d., 2" h., round straight sides decorated w/a h.p. & lightly tooled scene of oxen & covered wagons on the prairie against a blue sky, brown ground, decorated by Julia Mattson, circular ink mark & incised "JM#6 - 121 - Huck." (ILLUS.).... **1,045**

Bowl-Vase with Coyotes

Bowl-vase, squatty bulbous body decorated w/an embossed band of medium matte green coyotes silhouetted against a darker matte green ground, by Julia Mattson, 1925, ink-stamped circular mark & incised "JM25," stilt pull to base, 3" d., 4 1/4" h. (ILLUS.).................................. **660**

Bowl-vase, squatty bulbous body w/a narrow shoulder to a molded rim, carved band decoration of buffalo standing head to head & separated by three wide vertical bands, glossy medium blue carved to rich creamy white, stamped circular mark & incised "JM - 466," 4 1/2" d., 3 3/4" h. (ILLUS. front right, below) **1,913**

North Dakota Bowl-vases & Vase

Bowl-vase, round straight tapering sides w/a narrow shoulder & molded rim, decorated w/band of carved birds under a matte chartreuse glaze, ink stamp mark & incised "M. Cable - Meadowlark - 155," 5 1/2" d., 3 1/4" h. (ILLUS. front left, previous page) **675**

Bowl-vase, squatty bulbous body w/short incurved neck & flat mouth, Betonite clay w/a dark reddish color decorated in the Native American style w/a pattern of birds, stamped circular mark & incised "Armstrong - 1948," 4 3/4" d., 4 1/4" h. (ILLUS. top left, previous page **1,013**

Bowl-vase, wide bulbous body, the shoulder tapering to a short cylindrical neck w/flat mouth, embossed w/a band of oxen & covered wagons under a matte brown glaze, stamped circular mark & incised "MC - 186," 7 1/4" d., 6 1/2" h. (ILLUS. far right, previous page **1,463**

North Dakota Wheat Bowl-Vase

Bowl-vase, squatty bulbous form w/the shoulder tapering up to a flat mouth, carved around the middle w/a wide band showing shocks of wheat, in shades of dark & light brown, by Flora Huckfield, ink stamped "Hoffman - Huck - 1655 - No. Dakota Wheat," 7" d., 4 3/4" h. (ILLUS.).... **1,350**

North Dakota Round Box

Box, cov., low cylindrical form w/low domed fitted cover, the cover embossed w/the head of a Native American chief wearing a headdress, umber ground w/a mocha matte glaze on the cover, by Margaret Cable, stamped mark, incised "M. Cable - 156," 5" d., 2" h. (ILLUS.) **690**

Charger, decorated w/a large stylized five-petal blossom in yellow, white, deep red, blue & black cuerda seca, by Margaret Cable, 1949, ink stamped "M. Cable - 1949 - June Marks," 9 1/2" d. **534**

Charger, the center decorated w/a large stylized flower in polychrome cuerda seca, w/red flower petals at the dark border & centered between the five large flower petals, ink stamp & artist mark, 10" d. **770**

Figure of cowboy, bentonite, standing, wearing chaps & large hat, neckerchief & gun & holster, brown & black, by Julia Mattson, incised "JM 13 UND," 3 x 4 3/4" **605**

Model of a hawk, bentonite, wings & back decorated w/yellow & black stripes, rectangular base, by Julia Mattson, incised signature, 5" h., 3 3/4" l. **880**

North Dakota Pitcher

Pitcher, 5" h., 8 1/2" d., footed squatty bulbous body w/embossed frieze of "Red River Ox Carts" by M. Cable, glossy ivory glaze on buff clay body, die-stamped mark, embossed signature & title & "140" (ILLUS.) **990**

Pitcher, 5 1/2" h., bulbous body w/flaring neck, pinched spout & loop handle, incised decoration of children at play & stylized florals, polychrome matte glaze, decorated by Franc Freeman, ink stamp & incised signature, 1947 ...... **605**

North Dakota School of Mines Trivet

Trivet, round, decorated w/large stylized polychrome bird standing on long branch beneath a stylized flower, by Julia Mattson, ink mark & incised "JMattson," couple of small burst bubbles, 6" d. (ILLUS.) **440**

Vase, miniature, 3 1/4" h., squatty bulbous ovoid body w/green stripes on a mustard ground, by Julia Mattson, ink stamp & "M." **358**

Vase, 3 1/2" h., bentonite, bulbous body w/wide narrow rim, decorated w/a band of black wolves in silhouette on a brick red ground, ink stamp & "ML" **1,100**

Vase, 3 1/2" h., 3 1/2" d., wide bulbous body decorated overall w/painted white snowflakes on a dark blue ground, ink stamp **385**

Vase, 3 1/2" h., 5" d., wide conical form tapering to a small molded mouth, incised w/an overall pointed geometric design, matte green glaze, by M.J. Arnegard, 1932, ink stamped "M.J. Arnegard - 42132" **788**

Vase, 3 3/4" h., 3 1/4" d., miniature, simple ovoid form tapering to a closed rim, incised around the sides w/large upright stylized tulip-like flowers on leafy stems, celadon green semi-matte glaze, ink stamped "53H" **563**

Vase, 3 3/4" h., 4 3/4" d., wide squatty bulbous form tapering to a wide rolled rim, incised around the upper half w/a band of stylized blossoms & leaves, matte green mirocrystalline glaze, by Flora Huckfield, ink stamped "E. Ericson - Huck - 106" **506**

Vase, 4" h., 5 1/2" d., wide flat bottomed ovoid form w/a wide rounded shoulder centered by a short tapering wide mouth, the shoulder decorated w/a wide band of pink prairie roses & green leaves on a cream ground, pink background, by Flora Huckfield, ink stamped "Bridgeman - Huck - 4248" **788**

Vase, 5" h., 4 3/4" d., wide conical body tapering to molded rim, band around & below rim and at base in shades of blue, the center cream ground decorated w/a blue & green scene of a viking ship sailing on waves & flying birds, stamped circular mark & incised "J. Mattson - 149A - Viking Ship" (ILLUS. top, center, w/bowl-vases).. **1,688**

Vase, 5" h., 6" d., round sharply angled sides w/wide sloping shoulder tapering to short cylindrical neck w/flat rim, decorated w/a repeating incised frieze of bison in matte brown & green on dark brown ground w/dark brown band at mid-body & brown ground on lower body, carved by Margaret Cable, ink stamp & "M. Cable" ... **5,225**

Vase, 5 1/4" h., 6" d., wide bulbous ovoid form w/wide angled shoulder to flat mouth, molded around the shoulder w/rectangular panels each enclosing a bison in ochre on a brown ground, overall ochre background, by Margaret Cable, circular stamp mark & "Bison - 117A - M.Cable".. **1,980**

North Dakota School of Mines Vase

Vase, 5 1/2" h., ovoid body w/rolled rim, decorated w/polychrome horizontal stripes, by Julia Mattson, ink-stamped & incised mark (ILLUS.) **495**

Vase, 5 1/2" h., simple gently swelled cylindrical form w/a shoulder tapering slightly

to a short flaring neck, overall shaded brown & green matte glaze, stamp mark...... **253**

Vase, 5 1/2" h., slender ovoid w/ringed shoulder tapering to a short cylindrical neck w/closed rim, decorated w/incised cowboys w/lassos & "Why Not Minot" under a glossy blue glaze, by Julia Mattson, ink mark & incised mark **715**

Vase, 5 3/4" h., 2 3/4" d., gently swelled cylindrical form tapering to a ringed short neck, incised w/a design of a stylized cowboy w/his lariet spelling out "Why not Minot" around the shoulder, light periwinkle blue glaze, by Julia Mattson, ink stamped "JM - 175".. **422**

Vase, 5 3/4" h., 5 1/2" d., footed bulbous nearly spherical body w/wide raised mouth band, carved w/a band of Indian warriors on horseback under a dark brown matte glaze, originally sold w/or without a cover, by Flora Huckfield, titled "N.D. Sioux," ink stamp mark, title & incised "151".. **1,980**

Vase, 6" h., swelled cylindrical body tapering to wide flaring rim, decorated near the shoulder w/red & white daisies on long green stems, caramel ground, by Hildegarde Fried, 1924, ink stamp & "H.F." **3,300**

North Dakota Vase

Vase, 6 1/4" h., 7" d., spherical body w/wide shoulder band incised w/continuous scene of covered wagons pulled by oxen, shaded matte brown glaze, decorated by Margaret Cable, circular stamp & title "186, M. Cable" (ILLUS.) **2,530**

Vase, 7" h., shouldered slender ovoid body w/slightly flaring rim, decorated w/blue irises & green leaves on a shaded green ground, by Margaret Cable, ink mark & "MKC, 1916," **2,970**

North Dakota School of Mines Vase

Vase, 7 1/4" h., wide bulbous body tapering to short slightly flaring cylindrical neck, decorated w/large stylized purple flowers w/orange centers & green leaves on a brown ground, hand-carved by Julia Mattson, 1925, ink stamp & incised "M." (ILLUS.) **7,150**

Vase, 7 3/4" h., swelled cylindrical body w/narrow shoulder & wide molded rim, excised brown daffodils & leaves repeated around body on a dark brown ground, by Ruth Skyberg, 1949, ink stamp & incised signature **2,090**

Vase, 8 1/2" h., simple ovoid body tapering to a short cylindrical neck, deeply molded around the shoulder w/a stylized blossom band, the red clay covered w/a pale cream & lightly tinted blue matte glaze, stamped mark & incised "Cable" & "Prairie Rose" **605**

Vase, 8 3/4" h., ovoid body tapering to wide cylindrical neck, large stylized excised brown daffodils & leaves on a dark brown ground, by F. Cunningham, 1950, ink stamp & incised signature **1,870**

Vase, 9" h., tapering cylindrical body w/a rounded shoulder centering a short slightly flared neck, overall brownish green matte glaze, stamp mark & signed & numbered by J. Mattson (minor flake on bottom rim) **385**

Vase, 14" h., shouldered ovoid body tapering to a wide flaring neck, decorated w/large trees silhouetted against an orange sky, decorated by Margaret Cable, w/ink stamp mark & "M. Cable 1917" **9,350**

Ohr (George) Pottery

GEO. E. OHR
BILOXI, MISS.

Ohr Pottery Marks

George Ohr, the eccentric potter of Biloxi, Mississippi, worked from about 1883 to 1906. Some think him to be one of the most expert throwers the craft will ever see. The majority of his works were hand-thrown, exceedingly thin-walled items, some of which have a crushed or folded appearance. He considered himself the foremost potter in the world and declined to sell much of his production, instead accumulating a great horde to leave as a legacy to his children. In 1972 this collection was purchased for resale by an antiques dealer.

Bowl, 3 1/2 x 7 1/2", footed, bisque-fired free-form shape assymetrically pinched & folded, red & ivory marbleized clay, incised signature (one chip to edge) **$4,400**

Bowl, 4 1/2" d., 2 1/4" h., a wide flaring foot supports the squatty rounded body w/a flaring crimped rim, covered in a gunmetal volcanic glaze, die-stamped "G.E. OHR - Biloxi, Miss." **990**

Ohr Matte Glazed Small Bowl

Bowl, 4 3/4" d., 2 1/2" h., footed squatty bulbous form w/a wide rolled & inwardly folded labial rim w/two pulled-out spouts on the rim, rare green, brown & gunmetal dead-matte glaze, stamped "G.E. Ohr - Biloxi, Miss." (ILLUS.) **3,335**

Bowl, 4 3/4" d., 3 1/2" h., free-form collapsed body w/closed-in rim, covered in a speckled black & brown glaze, die-stamped "G.E. OHR - Biloxi, Miss." **2,530**

Bowl, 5" d., 3" h., footed irregular rounded sides in pinched & folded bisque red scroddled clay, incised script signature (minute nick on one fold) **2,310**

Ohr Bisque Clay Bowl-Vase

Bowl-vase, round foot below the compressed four-sided deeply indented & crumpled form w/an incurved pinched & twisted rim, oxidized beige bisque clay, minor kiln kiss, script signature, 5 3/4" w., 3 3/4" h. (ILLUS.) **3,738**

Bowl-vase, a short wide cylindrical neck above a squatty bulbous body w/a band of thumbprints around the sides, mottled brown glaze on red, impressed "GEO E OHR Biloxi, Miss.," 2 1/2" h. **1,150**

Bowl-vase, footed squatty bulbous form w/the top sides heavily dimpled & folded toward the center, overall aventurine glaze, impressed "G.E. OHR - Biloxi, Miss.," 4" d., 3" h. **2,310**

Bowl-vase, footed oblong upright sides w/deeply pinched & folded sides, bisque scroddled clay, incised script signature, 6" w., 4" h. **3,190**

Chamberstick, a round cushion base tapering to a short cylindrical stem w/a cupped socket, a low fanned handle on the base, mottled greenish brown glaze, impressed "GEO E OHR Biloxi," 3" h. **460**

Chamberstick, wide footed domed bulbous base w/a deep in-body twist, tapering to a cylindrical neck w/flared rim, applied angular handle from the neck to the base, gunmetal & green exterior glaze, matte ochre interior glaze, incised "G.E. OHR," 3 1/2" d., 4" h. **2,310**

Cup, footed deep gently flaring sides w/deep vertical dimples, small applied loop handle, glossy green & purple exterior glaze, matte red interior, original price tag on bottom, marked in black glaze "LG606," 4 3/4" d., 3" h. **2,860**

Cup, footed gently flaring rounded form w/dimpled sides & a crenolated rim, hand-built rounded loop handle, exterior w/a mottled mahogany glaze, interior in gunmetal, signed "Geo. E. Ohr - Biloxi - Miss." **1,463**

Unusual George Ohr Cup

Cup, small footring below a large nearly spherical body w/wide flat mouth, looped C-scroll handle, fine dripping gunmetal over mottled & speckled glossy green glaze, stamped mark, 6 3/4" d., 4 1/2" h. (ILLUS.) ....:......... **4,313**

George Ohr Ewer

Ewer, a short flaring pedestal foot supports a ringed spherical base tapering from the round shoulder to a tall cylindrical neck w/wide incurved rim w/small pinched spout, angled handle from below rim to shoulder, covered in a mottled umber & mirrored black glaze, impressed marks "G.E. OHR - Biloxi, Miss." 7 3/4" h., 4 1/2" d. (ILLUS.) **2,750**

Inkstand, a rectangular base w/serpentine front mounted w/a large mule head w/long pointed ears beside a low squatty bowl w/incurved sides, a small tree stump on the other side of the bowl, overall mottled green, brown & gunmetal glaze, stamped "G.E. Ohr - Biloxi," 4 3/4 x 7 1/4", 4" h. (touch-up to both ear tips) **4,500**

Model of a cabin on slats, pitch-roofed structure w/a diamond lattice roof design & a short round chimney, taupe-brown clay, signed "GEO. E OHR Biloxi, Miss.," 3" h. (in-the-making imperfections) **518**

George Ohr Pottery Hat

Model of a hat, tall tapering crown ripped at the top, crumpled sides & upturned brim, red, green & blue glossy glaze, restoration to small rim chip, marked "G.E. Ohr - Biloxi," 4 1/2" l., 4" h. (ILLUS.) **4,313**

Mug, footed bulbous angled ovoid body w/a squared tab handle pierced w/three openings, brown gunmetal glaze, impressed "G.E. OHR. - Biloxi, Miss.," 5 1/4" w., 3 1/2" h. **2,090**

Mug, Joe Jefferson-type, double-gourd form w/long pointed strap handle down the side, incised w/"Here's your good health...," overall speckled & mottled dark bluish green glaze, script signature & dated 1896, 5 3/4" d., 6 1/2" h. **2,363**

Mug, Joe Jefferson-type, cylindrical form w/pinched handle, covered in an unusual salmon pink & green glossy glaze, inscribed "Hers (sic) your good health and all your family's - may they all live long and prosper - J.Jefferson," die-stamped "G.E. OHR - Biloxi, Miss. - 8-18-1896," 4" h. **1,210**

Ohr Pinch-sided Pitcher

Pitcher, 2 1/2" h., 5" w., four pinched-in sides forming a diamond-shaped top opening, round foot, pointed angled loop handle, light mauve glaze on exterior, chartreuse green interior glaze, minute rim nick, signed "Geo. E. Ohr - Biloxi, Miss." **2,250**

Pitcher, 3" h., 5 1/2" d., footed squatty bulbous body w/a closed rim & small pinched upright rim spout, applied D-form handle, amber, green & gunmetal speckled glaze, signed "G.E. Ohr - Biloxi - Miss." **731**

George Ohr Pitcher

Pitcher, 3 1/2" h., 4 3/4" d., footed bulbous body w/flaring rim, pinched spout & C-scroll handle, covered in gunmetal volcanic glaze, die-stamped "G.E. OHR - Biloxi, Miss." (ILLUS.) **1,430**

Pitcher, 6 1/2" h., 4" d., footed bulbous base below a double-funnel form body w/tapering sides below the tall flaring neck w/pinched rim spout, applied looped strap handle, bright pink, green, red & white sponged matte glaze, impressed "G.E.OHR - Biloxi, Miss." **7,700**

Pitcher, puzzle-type, 6 1/2" h., 5 3/4" d., wide globular body incised w/a branch & medallion design, gently tapering shoulder above incised band, tall slender cylindrical neck w/flat rim, textured twig-shaped handle from center of neck to base, covered w/speckled glossy ocher & mahogany glazes, impressed "GEO. E. OHR - BILOXI. MISS." **2,530**

Large Ohr Pitcher

Pitcher, 10" h., 7" d., footed tapering ovoid dimpled body w/a folded side & single looped ribbon handle, red, pink, cobalt blue, green, yellow & white sponged glaze, one chip & several minor nicks at rim, one small base chip, impressed "G.E. Ohr - Biloxi, Miss." & script signature (ILLUS.) **44,000**

Puzzle mug, cylindrical w/large pierced holes around the molded rim above double bands of smaller holes, a pinched & twisted base band, stylized rabbit-form squared handle, mottled brown glaze, impressed "G. E. Ohr Biloxi, Miss.," 3 1/2" h. **1,150**

Rare George Ohr Teapot

Teapot, cov., footed w/a widely flaring flat-sided lower body below the angled shoulder band & domed top compressed down in the center w/a small cover, snake spout, C-scroll handle, cobalt blue glossy glaze, normal abrasion around rim, small nick on tip of spout, stamped "G.E. Ohr - Biloxi, Miss.," 8 3/4" l., 4" h. (ILLUS.) **11,250**

Vase, 2 1/2" h., 3 3/4" d., wide squatty bulbous base w/flared & ruffled rim, covered in a dark bottle green & gunmetal glaze w/melt fissures, die-stamped "G.E. OHR - Biloxi, Miss." **825**

Vase, 3" h., 4" d., footed squatty bulbous compressed base, the sides tapering sharply to a wide cylindrical neck w/flat rim, covered in indigo & green sponged pattern on a raspberry ground, overglazed in white, die-stamped "GEO. E. OHR - BILOXI, MISS." **1,870**

Vase, 3 1/2" h., 3 1/2" d., wide waisted cylindrical body w/torn & pinched rim, covered in dark olive green & black mottled glaze, die-stamped "G. E. OHR - Biloxi, Miss." (fleck to rim) **2,090**

Vase, 4" h., 2 3/4" d., footed tapering cylindrical body w/rounded base, molded rings at neck, covered in a fine & unusual sponged raspberry, red & black matte & glossy glaze, die-stamped " G.E. OHR - Biloxi, Miss" **2,090**

Vase, 4" h., 3 1/4" d., footed, bulbous base w/pinched & folded rim, covered in fine & unusual sponged cobalt, raspberry, ochre & green glossy glaze, die-stamped "G.E. OHR - Biloxi, Miss" (two glaze flecks to rim) **2,970**

Ohr Vase with Volcanic Glaze

Four George Ohr Vases

Vase, 4" h., 3 3/4" d., wide baluster-form w/flattened wide rim, fine cadnium yellow, lavender, green & pink volcanic glaze, stamped "G.E. Ohr - Biloxi, Miss." (ILLUS., previous page)............................... **3,038**

Vase, 4" h., 4 1/4" d., tapering cylindrical form w/flat flared rim w/an inset four-sided top w/pinched corners, covered in a marbleized brown & yellow glossy glaze, die-stamped "G.E. OHR - BILOXI, MISS.".. **2,970**

Vase, 4 1/4" h., round footring below the spherical body tapering to an upright pinched & folded cross-shaped rim, bisque scroddled clay, incised script signature.. **1,100**

Vase, 4 1/4" h., slightly waisted cylindrical body w/upright pinched & scalloped rim & ribbon handles, covered in a rare cobalt blue, green & raspberry mottled glaze, die-stamped "G. E. OHR - Biloxi, Miss.".... **4,675**

Vase, 4 1/4" h., 3" d., squatty low base w/sides tapering to short wide cylindrical neck, covered in speckled green, raspberry & ochre glaze, die-stamped "G.E. OHR - BILOXI".................................... **1,760**

Vase, 4 1/4" h., 4" d., a footring below a rounded dimpled base, gently tapering to an asymmetrically folded rim, covered in an ochre glaze w/overall green drip effect, die-stamped "G.E. OHR - Biloxi, Miss.".. **6,050**

Vase, 4 1/4" h., 4" d., ovoid body tapering toward the foot & w/a wide gently flared rim, the waist of the body deeply twisted, matte green & light blue exterior glaze, cobalt blue & green interior glaze, script signature... **4,125**

Vase, 4 1/4" h., 6" w., footed free-form folded & pinched upright sides w/flared & pinched rim, bisque-fired red & ivory marbleized clays, inscribed "XMAS FOR MASAbTLER - FROM EDNA - DEC 18/06," script signature (ILLUS.)................ **4,675**

Vase, 4 1/2" h., 2 1/2" d., footed bulbous spherical lower body tapering to an tall upright twisted, folded & pinched neck, dark speckled olive green glaze, neck in gunmetal glaze, marked "G.E. Ohr - Biloxi, Miss."... **2,588**

Vase, 4 1/2" h., 4" d., footed free-form shape w/collapsed body, dimpled top & torn rim, covered in green & ochre speckled glaze, die-stamped "G.E. OHR - BILOXI".. **8,250**

Vase, 4 1/2" h., 4 1/4" d., ringed tapering cylindrical form w/a collapsed & folded rim, covered in a speckled caramel & mahogany glossy glaze, die-stamped "G.E. OHR - Biloxi, Miss."................................... **3,850**

Vase, 4 1/2" h., 4 1/2" w., a footed wide swelled form w/a deeply folded rim & a collapsed side, overall speckled amber & gunmetal glaze, signed "G.E. OHR - Biloxi, Miss." (ILLUS. second from right, above).. **6,188**

Rare George Ohr Vase

Vase, 4 1/2" h., 4 1/2" w., round foot below the squatty bulbous four-sided body w/a deep in-body twist below the pinched,

Ohr Free-Form Bisque-Fired Vase

twisted & crumpled ragged rim, glossy indigo glaze w/red, amber & gunmetal, signed "G.E. Ohr - Biloxi, Miss." (ILLUS.).. **16,100**

Vase, 4 1/2" h., 5 1/4" d., footed squatty bulbous body w/large dimples around the middle, tapering to a short, wide cylindrical neck, fine mottled brown & gunmetal glossy glaze, stamped "G.E. Ohr - Biloxi" .. **3,150**

Vase, 4 1/2" h., 6" w., footed tilted free-form design w/heavily folded & pinched sides, bisque scroddled clay, incised script signature........... **3,575**

Vase, 4 3/4" h., a crimped rim on a cylindrical body w/thumbprints around the base, mottled black glaze, impressed "G.E. Ohr Biloxi, Miss." **1,380**

Vase, 4 3/4" h., squatty bulbous base w/upright dimpled neck & pinched & folded rim, covered in aventurine & black glaze, die-stamped "G.E. OHR - Biloxi, Miss." **2,750**

Vase, 4 3/4" h., 4 1/4" d., footed cylindrical two-tiered body w/the wide upper tier impressed w/large swirled dimples below the wide short cylindrical neck, overall speckled amber glaze, signed "G.E. Ohr - Biloxi".. **3,656**

Vase, 5" h., bulbous bottom tapering to a tall, wide cylindrical upper body w/long angled handles from the upper neck to the center base, gunmetal to brown glaze, impressed mark................................ **1,980**

Vase, 5" h., free-form bisque-fired pale clay, a footring below the squatty bulbous body, pierced & dimpled around the sides, a tall neck w/torn & folded rim, early price tag mounted w/new wire, script signature **2,310**

Vase, 5" h., 4" d., bulbous ovoid body below a twisted & crumpled shoulder & a wide upright neck w/ragged-edged torn rim, overall green, mahogany, gunmetal & ochre speckled glaze, impressed "G.E. OHR - Biloxi, Miss." **5,500**

George Ohr Spotted Vase

Vase, 5" h., 5 1/4" d., bulbous ovoid form w/wide, short cylindrical neck, one side pinched-in, the other side dimpled, large sponged maroon dots, spattered green & red glazes under a sheer semi-matte glaze, clay body showing through, restoration to rim hairline, signed (ILLUS.)......... **8,050**

Vase, 5" h., 5 1/4" d., footed squatty bulbous lower body below the tall flaring

neck pinched in the center to form two folded lobes, two incised lines around the shoulder, bisque scroddled clay, incised script signature (few minor flakes at rim)... **2,090**

Vase, 5 1/2" h., 3 1/2" d., ovoid body below a slightly flaring neck w/an exaggerated labial rim, green & gunmetal mottled glaze, unusual script signature w/"Biloxi" (restoration to stilt pulls at base)............... **1,650**

Vase, 6" h., bottle-shaped w/flaring rim, covered in an unusual sponged cobalt & green glaze on a pink & white matte glaze, die-stamped "G.E. OHR - Biloxi, Miss." **1,760**

Vase, 6" h., flared foot below bulbous base w/deep in-body twists at shoulder, tapering to wide cylindrical neck, covered in limpid mirrored mahogany speckled glaze, die-stamped "G.E. OHR - Biloxi, Miss" **2,090**

Vase, 6" h., 4" d., footed ovoid body tapering to a wide short cylindrical neck w/a tightly crimped upright rim, raspberry, green, blue & grey sponged glaze, stamped "G.E. OHR - Biloxi, Miss." (touch-ups to nick on two rim tips)............. **4,400**

Vase, 6 1/4" h., 5" d., footed ovoid pillow-style body w/a upright crimped rim folded down across the center, rare pink glaze w/a sponged-on green & gunmetal band, small kiln kiss on body, minor glaze nick & a few flakes inside rim, stamped "G.E. OHR - Biloxi, Miss." (ILLUS. far left with other vases).. **19,125**

Vase, 6 1/4" h., 5 1/2" d., footed wide bulbous body w/deep in-body twist near wide flaring rim, covered in a speckled gunmetal & khaki glaze, stamped "G.E. OHR - Biloxi, Miss." **1,980**

Ohr Pinched Neck Vase

Vase, 6 3/4" h., bulbous base w/tall upright tightly pinched neck, covered in a brown & caramel marbleized glossy glaze, die-stamped "G.E. OHR - Biloxi, Miss." (ILLUS.).. **2,200**

Vase, 7" h., 4" d., baluster-form body w/a medial raised band & a deep in-body twist at the neck below the closed rim, unusual green glaze around the lower body w/a drippy red & teal leathery matte glaze on the upper half, script signature (ILLUS. far right with other vases) **8,438**

George Ohr Vase with Applied Snake

Vase, 7 1/4" h., 3 3/4" d., flaring foot supporting a tall tapering ovoid body below a cupped neck w/a dimpled band below a plain slightly flared rim band, an applied snake looping around the lower neck & down the body, cobalt blue, amber & raspberry sponged glaze, restoration to base chip, some firing lines on snake, few minute rim nicks, stamped mark (ILLUS.) **10,688**

Vase, 9 1/2" h., 5" d., footed bulbous spherical lower body below a tall neck w/a band of dimples at the bottom below tall flutes to the crimped rim, mirrored cobalt blue & gunmetal glaze, restored rim chip, typical abrasion line in body, script signature & "M" (ILLUS. second from left with other vases) **9,563**

Rare George Ohr Whiskey Jug

Whiskey jug, flat-bottomed wide flaring cylindrical lower body below an angled twisted & pinched shoulder centered by a domed upper body w/a short molded spout, an S-scroll snake-like handle from side of neck to shoulder, mottled green & gunmetal lustered glaze, restoration to handle, two minute flecks inside rim, signed, 6" d., 6 1/2" h. (ILLUS.) **4,888**

Overbeck

The four Overbeck sisters, Margaret, Hannah B., Elizabeth G. and Mary F., established their pottery in their old family home in Cambridge City, Indiana

in 1911. Different areas of the house and yard were used for the varied production needs.

Their early production consisted mainly of artware before 1937 with most pieces being hand-thrown or hand-built in such forms as vase, bowls, candlesticks, flower frogs, tea sets and tiles. Pieces during this era were decorated generally either with glaze inlay or carving and several colors of subtle matte glazes were used first with brighter glazes added later.

After the death of Elizabeth G. in 1937 Mary F. became the driving force behind the pottery. The output became less varied, until mainly small molded figures of various sorts of humans, some humorous or grotesque, and animals and birds were the main products. Work was carried on alone by Mary F. until her death in 1955.

Marked pieces of Overbeck usually carry the "OBK" cipher and early wares may carry the initial or initials of the sister(s) who produced it.

Bowl, 5 7/8" d., 2 3/4" h., deep half-round form w/flat rim, red clay w/a glossy glazed interior in rust & maize, matte green drip glazed exterior w/whitish drips from rim, signed "Overbeck - 5 - 3," early 20th c. **$230**

Chalice, round stepped foot & short stem supporting a wide & deep thick rounded bowl, decorated w/a wide band of incised stylized camels & mountains in yellow & gunmetal on a raspberry ground, incised "OBK - E - F.," 5 1/4" d., 6" h. (tight rim crack) **1,688**

Figure group, ceramic tableau, "The Family," depicting a polychrome kitchen scene of stylized figures consisting of two children doing homework by lamp light at the dining table w/other family members sitting nearby, sewing & reading, a wood stove in the background, large rectangular tile floor base in red & blue, signed "Mary Overbeck " & impressed "OBK," base, 6 x 8 1/2", 12 pcs. **5,225**

Figurine, stylized figure of a postman in brown uniform & cap w/mail bag over one shoulder, marked "OBK," 5 1/2" h. **193**

Figurine, stylized portly bald gentleman standing, wearing blue striped trousers, a white shirt, pink bow tie & holding eyeglasses, marked "OBK," 5 3/4" h. (nick to foot) **660**

Model of a goose, a stylized large-footed bird, wings up & neck stretched forward, white w/black eyes, brown bill & feet, marked "OBK," 5" l. (roughness to feet) **880**

Overbeck Elephant

Model of an elephant, standing, head raised w/trunk curved down, white w/pink highlights & blue eyes, marked "OBK," glaze nick to tip of one tusk, 4 x 7" (ILLUS.) **1,430**

Tea set: cov. teapot, cov. sugar bowl, creamer, round trivet & four cups & saucers; all w/simple rounded forms, each decorated w/a panel of stylized white lily-of-the-valley in cuerda seca on a celadon matte ground, marked "OBK - E - H.," teapot 9 1/2" l., 5" h., the set (minor rim nick on creamer, small stilt pull chips on cups) **2,475**

Tumblers, cylindrical w/rounded bottom rim, embossed around the upper body w/a band of stylized green crickets on a beige ground, stamped "OBK - E - F.," 3" d., 3 3/4" h., set of 4................................. **1,463**

Vase, 3" h., 2 3/4" d., miniature, ovoid body decorated in the Japanese style w/three panels depicting a lady in matte pastel shades...................... **1,210**

Vase, 5" h., 6" d., flat-bottomed wide bulbous ovoid body tapering to a flat mouth flanked by heavy angled strap handles, carved & painted design of sixteen hummingbirds in brown & green matte amid delicately carved branches & blossoms, incised mark & initials "EF"........................... **6,050**

Vase, 5 3/8" h., tapering cylindrical body, green ground w/three panels decorated w/deeply carved & painted butterflies in green against a chocolate brown ground, by Elizabeth & Hannah Overbeck, marked w/Overbeck logo & initials "E" & "H," together w/copy of "The Chronicle of the Overbeck Pottery" (dark line at rim, not visible on outside) **1,210**

Vase, 5 x 5 1/2", wide bulbous base w/wide tapering cylindrical neck & flat rim, carved w/three panels of stylized birds in dusty pink against a mauve ground, incised "OBK -FM" **3,080**

Very Fine Carved Overbeck Vase

Vase, 7 3/8" h., a short cylindrical foot supporting a wide cylindrical body w/a stepped shoulder & short rounded neck, deeply carved & painted w/five sets of stylized lovebirds in rose red & bluish green against an elaborately carved background in red, blue & green, turquoise blue ground, semigloss glaze,

Overbeck logo & initials of Elizabeth & Mary Frances (ILLUS.) **8,800**

Overbeck Vase with Hostas

Vase, 14" h., slender ovoid body w/short cylindrical neck, decorated w/carved & painted hosta blossoms & large leaves, by Elizabeth G. & Mary F. Overbeck (ILLUS.)....................................... **22,000**

Owens

Owens Pottery Mark

Owens pottery was the product of the J.B. Owens Pottery Company, which operated in Ohio from 1890 to 1929. In 1891 it located in Zanesville and produced art pottery from 1896, introducing "Utopian" wares as its first art pottery. The company switched to tile after 1907. Efforts to rebuild after the factory burned in 1928 failed and the company closed in 1929.

Bowl, 3 3/4" h., Lotus line, footed spherical body, the wide shoulder tapering to narrow molded rim, decorated w/a dragonfly & a few grass stalks on shaded grey ground, impressed "Owens 202" & "L"........ **$495**

Bowl, 6 1/8" d., 1 5/8" h., Matt Green line, low round form w/incurved shoulder w/raised lines & flat rim, impressed "Owens 330".. **165**

Bowl, 3 1/2 x 11", Aborigine line, rounded sides w/flat rim, tan earthenware w/dark brown stripes & light & brown zigzag lines, interior w/dark brown glaze, incised "JBO" & mark No. 10...................................... **150**

Cruet, matt glaze in cream & grey, shape No. 1216, impressed "Owens 1216," 4 3/4" h. (fine overall crazing) **165**

Cruet, Lightweight line, footed bulbous ovoid body w/tri-point rim & C-form handle, wild rose decoration on shaded green to dark brown ground, by Cecil Excel, incised "CE" & "868," 3 1/4" h. 193

Cruet. Lightweight line, footed bell-shaped body w/upright petal-shaped spout & loop handle, yellow nasturtium w/green leaves decoration on dark brown ground, decorated by Harry Robinson, incised "HR" & "877" w/impressed "JBO" circular logo, 5 3/8" h. (slight roughness on spout tip) 220

Ewer, Metal Deposit line, three-footed bulbous body w/arched spout & large loop handle, electroplated copper, slip-decorated w/wild roses by Cecil Excel, marked "2 Owens 921," artist-initialed, 5 3/8" h. 385

Owens Ewer

Ewer, Utopian line, decorated w/yellow roses on a brown, green & amber ground, decorated by Sarah Timberlake, artist-initialed & impressed "Utopia, J.B. Owens, 181," minor crazing, 9 3/8" h. (ILLUS.) 303

Owens Alpine Line Humidor

Humidor, cov., Alpine line, squatty bulbous body, cover w/molded rim & large domed finial, decorated w/h.p. scene of pipe & bag of tobacco, shaded brown ground, mark No. 13, 5 7/8" h.(ILLUS.) 750

Jardiniere, footed cylindrical body w/scalloped rim, Majolica finish w/embossed flowers & birds in blue, white & green, marked w/raised J.B. Owens shield mark, 6 3/4' h. (small glaze flake off rim) 165

Owens Art Nouveau Jardiniere

Jardiniere, Art Nouveau line, footed, wide tapering cylindrical body w/flaring rim, under-glaze gold swirl decoration on dark brown ground, impressed "J.B. Owens" & "Art Nouveau," shape No. 1005, 7 1/2" h. 382

Jardiniere, Cyrano line, footed waisted cylindrical body, squeezebag applied filigree designs & beading at rim, dark brown glossy ground, unmarked, 8 1/4" h. 350

Jardiniere, Delft line, footed bulbous body w/slightly flaring rim, decorated w/typical Holland scene of a young girl & her mother standing near the water, a ship in the background, shaded blue ground, unmarked, 10 1/2" h. 750

Jug, Aborigine line, squatty bulbous base tapering to cylindrical neck & loop handle, tan & brown earthenware exterior, incised "JBO," shape No. 31, 5 1/8" h. 200

Corona Line Model of Dog

Model of a dog, Whippet or Greyhound, sitting, wearing collar, glass eyes, shaded grey, Corona line, unmarked (ILLUS.) 5,000

Model of a rabbit, sitting animal w/raised ears, glass eyes, shaded grey & tan, Corona line, marked "Corona," shape No. 8873, 13 x 15" 3,500

Mug, Matt Green line, tapering cylindrical body w/C-form handle, decorated w/impressed combed designs & impressed "Owens 46," 3 7/8" h. 220

Mug, Feroza line, cylindrical body w/C-form handle, molded uneven ground in iridescent deep red, shape No. 1108, 4 7/8" h. **450**

Paperweight, rectangular, Majolica Finish, green glossy ground w/embossed stag head & marked "Edmiston Horney Co. - Zanesville - Ohio" w/embossed scrolled border, "Made by the J.B. Owens Pottery Co." on reverse, 2 3/8 x 3 7/8" **83**

Pitcher, 3" h., Embossed Lotus line, tapering cylindrical form w/incurved rim, pinched spout & C-form handle, cream ground decorated w/embossed & slip-painted berries & leaves, marked "Lotus," shape No. X236, mark No. 10.......... **250**

Pitcher, 3 1/4" h., Embossed Lotus line, tapering cylindrical form w/incurved rim, pinched spout & C-form handle, grey ground decorated w/green & purple grape motif, impressed "Owens Lotus X 236" **248**

Owens Feroza Line Pitcher

Pitcher, tankard, 11 1/4" h., Feroza line, uneven molded ground w/mottled dark brownish iridescent finish, shape No. 1109 (ILLUS.) **850**

Tall Owens Decorated Pitcher

Pitcher, 12 1/4" h., tankard-form, flaring base below the tall slightly tapering cylindrical body w/a rim spout, arched long handle down the side, underglaze slip decoration of three tulips in yellow, rust & green on a shaded gold to brown ground, impressed mark, minor scratches, early 20th c. (ILLUS.) **345**

Pitcher, tankard, 17" h., Onyx line, tapering cylindrical form w/ringed base, long D-

form angled handle, shape No. 819, mark No. 8 .... **650**

Teapot cov., Lotus line, Aladdin-type, domed cover w/button finial, shaded green w/floral decoration in green, pink & white, marked "Owens" & "Denny," shape No. 1255, 3 1/4 x 7" **450**

Owens Nursery Rhyme Tile

Tile, square, color scene of "Little Bo Peep" w/rhyme in black & white in upper corner, in wide flat oak frame, minor edge roughness, 12" sq. (ILLUS.).................................. **2,645**

Tile, Arts & Crafts style, decoration w/acorns & oak leaves in grey, green & brown on tan ground, impressed "Owens," 5 3/8 x 5 7/8" **248**

Umbrella stand, Henri Deux line, baluster-form w/scalloped rim, portrait of woman w/tan, white & light blue floral decoration on blue ground, unmarked, 22 1/4" h. **850**

Vase, 2 1/2" h., Utopian line, squatty four-sided vase w/wild roses on dark brown glossy ground, by Sara Timberlake, marked "1 Owens Utopian 103," artist-initialed in slip on side.. **165**

Vase, 2 7/8" h., Lotus line, short wide tapering cylindrical form decorated w/a lotus blossom in white, yellow & green on dark brown ground, impressed "Owens 26".......... **303**

Vase, 3" h., Utopian line, footed bulbous base & loop handles from shoulder to rim, pansy decoration on dark brown glossy ground, marked "3 J.B Owens 866" & artist mark in slip on one handle **165**

Vase, 3 1/2" h., Utopian line, two-handled bulbous form w/wild rose decoration on shaded brown ground, most likely by Claude Leffler, marked "Utopian Owens 936" & artist-initialed **248**

Owens Aqua Verdi Vase

Vase, 3 7/8" h., Aqua Verdi line, short wide tapering cylindrical form w/three thick loop handles from rim to base, relief-molded lizard on textured variegated light to dark green ground (ILLUS.) 650

Vase, 3 7/8" h., Utopian line, square tapering body w/short cylindrical neck, red clover decoration on shaded brown ground, possibly the work of Virginia Adams, marked "Owens Utopian 2 8 111" w/artist's initials which appears to be a conjoined VA 138

Vase, 4" h., Soudaneze line, footed spherical body w/molded rim, decorated w/white pansies on glossy black ground, impressed "Owens 202" (minor glaze scratches & small bruise on rim) 330

Vase, 4 1/4" h., two-handled, squatty bulbous body w/narrow cylindrical neck, shaded brown ground w/wild rose decoration, most likely by Martha Gray, artist-initialed & marked "J.B. Owens Utopian 980" (small nick on rim & 1/2 x 1/2" kiln kiss on back side) 220

Vase, 4 3/8" h., Utopian line, twisted body w/floral decoration, marked "1 Owens Utopian 117" & obscure artist mark on side 165

Vase, 4 5/8" h., cylindrical w/bulbous base, raised repeating floral & leaf design, matte aqua glaze, impressed Owensart mark, ca. 1906 173

Vase, 4 3/4" h., Matt Utopian line, twisted body w/small cylindrical neck, pastel slip pansy decoration by Hattie Eberlein, impressed "Owens 102" & artist-initialed (some glaze discoloration & pinhead size glaze nick off base) 165

Owens Onyx Line Vase

Vase, 5" h., Onyx line, footed crescent-shaped body, mottled, striated brown, tan & cream ground, unmarked, shape No. 872 (ILLUS.) 250

Vase, 5" h., Utopian line, footed bulbous body w/wide shoulder tapering to short cylindrical neck w/wide flaring rim, decorated w/orange & green leaves on dark brown glossy ground, by Virginia Adams, marked "Utopian J.B. Owens 975" w/artist's initials on side in slip 193

Vase, 5 3/8" h., Aborigine line, bulbous shouldered body tapering to wide cylindrical neck w/flat rim, light tan earthenware w/rust band & geometric decora-

tion, chocolate brown rim & interior glaze, incised "JBO" & impressed "Owens 29" 165

Vase, 5 1/2" h., Feroza line, bulbous ovoid body w/tapering shoulder flanked by large loop handles, closed mouth, uneven molded ground in iridescent mottled brownish black, shape No. 1090 450

Vase, 5 1/2" h., Utopian line, bulbous ovoid body tapering to short cylindrical neck w/molded rim, decorated w/colorful Autumn leaves on dark brown glossy ground, marked "Owens Utopian 1048" (minor scratches & small glaze nick off high spot near base) 165

Vase, 5 5/8" h., Majolica finish, bulbous base tapering to cylindrical neck w/flat rim, shape No. 27, impressed "Owens 27" 83

Vase, 5 3/4" h., Art Vellum line, tapering square form w/small molded rim, yellow & orange floral decoration on brown ground, shape No. 112, mark No. 13 350

Vase, 5 3/4" h., Utopian line, twisted base tapering to square neck w/molded rim, wild rose decoration on shaded brown ground, impressed "2 Owens Utopian 115" 138

Vase, 5 7/8" h., Matt Green line, four buttressed feet support the spherical shouldered body tapering to short cylindrical neck w/molded rim, impressed "Owens 1155" (minor glaze nick off one foot) 275

Vase, 6" h., bulbous body w/molded rim, green Arts & Crafts style rectangular designs encircling body, impressed "Owens 218" 358

Vase, 6" h., Embossed Lotus line, wide ovoid body w/molded rim, dark brown ground w/cream band near rim decoration w/embossed & slip-painted berries & leaves, marked "Lotus," shape No. X218, mark No. 10 400

Owens Lotus Line Grey Vase

Vase, 6" h., Lotus line, simple wide ovoid shape tapering slightly to a wide molded rim, a wide shoulder band embossed w/small purple berries & grey leaves on a dark grey ground, a shaded grey to white background, impressed mark, some crazing (ILLUS.) 287

Vase, 6" h., Lotus line, waisted cylindrical body w/wide shoulder & flat mouth, decorated w/mushrooms painted by Frank Ferrell, shaded grey to cream ground, artist-initialed, impressed w/"Owensart" torch logo & shape No. 1236 (minor glaze nicks on bottom edge) 468

Owens Cyrano Line Vase

Vase, 6 1/4" h., Cyrano line, compressed base tapering to wide slightly waisted cylindrical body flanked by large loop handles, decorated w/squeezebag applied filigree lacy & floral design in white & tan w/beading at the base & rim, dark green glossy ground, unmarked, shape No. 357 (ILLUS.) **850**

Vase, 6 3/8" h., Oriental line, three-footed ovoid body, band of white lacy squeezebag design near top & small beads below rim, dark brown ground **300**

Vase, 6 3/8" h., Utopian Ware, flared rim on a tapered ovoid body, decorated w/rose blossoms & leaves in cream & brown on a shaded brown ground w/a glossy glaze, ornate silver overlay decoration, overlay impressed "Utopian J.B. Owens 923 - Phee F.N. Silver Co." (crazing, scratches, nicks) **288**

Vase, 6 1/2" h., footed spherical form w/incurved flat rim, shaded grey decorated near the rim w/three swimming fish, impressed "L" (minor glaze inconsistencies & discoloration) **280**

Vase, 6 3/4" h., Utopian line, waisted cylindrical form decorated w/detailed pansy blossoms, base impressed "Utopian J.B. Owens" **138**

Vase, 6 7/8" h., Art Nouveau line, slender baluster-form body, orange circular decoration on dark brown ground **150**

Vase, 6 7/8" h., Lightweight line, footed baluster-form body w/slightly flared rim, jonquil decoration by former Rookwood artist, Charles J. Dibowski, dark brown glossy glaze ground, incised artist's initials & "846," impressed "JBO" circular logo **358**

Vase, 8 1/2" h., Utopian line, bulbous ovoid base tapering slightly to wide cylindrical neck, nicely detailed ear of corn in yellow w/green husk done in heavy slip, impressed "Owens Utopian 223" (glaze scratches) **330**

Vase, 8 3/4" h., Henri Deux line, compressed bulbous base below tapering cylindrical neck w/closed rim, incised base & yellow floral decoration on dark brown ground, shape No. 1307, mark No. 10 .... **250**

Vase, 8 3/4" h., slightly swelled cylindrical body, Embossed Lotus line, dark brown ground decorated w/embossed & slip-painted berries & leaves, marked "Lotus," shape No. X220, mark No. 10 .... **600**

Vase, 9" h., Utopian line, footed tapering ovoid body w/flared rim, "First of Three Pharaoh's Horses," decorated by Hattie Eberlein, impressed Owens Utopian logo, artist's monogram in white slip on foot, shape No. 982, (some evidence of slightly cupped glaze) **358**

Vase, 9 7/8" h., Malachite Opalesce Inlaid line, footed bulbous ovoid body tapering to narrow cylindrical neck w/flared rim, Art Nouveau style metallic floral decoration (possibly a few missing beads at rim) .. **1,650**

Vase, 10" h., Opalesce line, footed bulbous ovoid body tapering to tall slender cylindrical neck w/flared rim, decorated w/Art Nouveau style metallic florals, marked "Owens," shape No. 1124 .... **850**

Vase, 10 1/4" h., Utopian Ware, bottle-shaped, coated w/gold & overlaid w/small coral-like beads, underglaze decoration of a rose branch in shades of green, rust & brown, impressed mark & No. 1010, ca. 1905 .... **345**

Vase, 10 3/4" h., Mission line, cylindrical body w/rounded shoulder to the tiny molded mouth, decorated w/a scene of a mission w/notation on side, "Bells of San Gabriel Mission California," & "312 F Mission Pottery" on base (minor paint loss) **523**

Vase, 10 3/4" h., 5 3/4" d., tall ovoid form w/three rings molded around the base, decorated overall in sgraffitto w/upright stylized iris-like flowers in orange & blue on a dark brown ground, by Henri Deux, pea-sized burst bubble on shoulder, unmarked **731**

Vase, 11" h., tall ovoid form tapering to a flat mouth, a black ground w/incised tall iris blossoms on leafy stems in shades of dark brown & blue outlined in cream, unsigned **1,380**

Owens Aborigine Line Vase

Vase, 8 3/4 x 11", Aborigine line, bulbous shouldered body tapering to wide cylindrical neck w/flat rim, light tan earthenware w/rust band & geometric decoration, chocolate brown rim & interior glaze, incised "JBO" (ILLUS.) **600**

Vase, 11 1/4" h., Oriental line, waisted cylindrical form w/rows of white & tan beading at rim & base & center band of lacy squeezebag design in white & tan, dark brown ground, unmarked, shape No. 863 ..... **350**

Vase, 12 1/4" h., Alpine line, footed bulbous ovoid body w/trumpet-form neck, shaded brown w/free-hand overglaze white slip floral decoration, matte finish, artist-initialed, shape No. 1122, mark No. 13 .... **1,000**

Vase, 13 1/2" h., Lotus line, ovoid body w/short wide cylindrical neck, decorated w/blue & white iris & green leaves on greyish green ground, by Walter Denny, impressed "Owens 1245" & "Denny" in light brown slip (minor color spots in flowers) **935**

Vase, 15 1/8" h., creamware, footed bulbous ovoid body tapering to slender cylindrical neck w/small bulbous top & flat rim, overall cream ground, shape No. 1126, mark No. 10 .... **650**

Vase, 16 1/2" h., Lotus line, compressed bulbous base tapering to tall cylindrical body w/slightly tapering neck & closed rim, decorated w/irises in rose, pink, purple & yellow w/green leaves against an ivory, grey & peach ground, artist-signed, impressed mark (harmless glaze flaws to top) **1,540**

Vase, Art Vellum line, footed bulbous body tapering to wide cylindrical neck, decorated w/scene of harbor w/boats, houses & trees, most likely by C. Minnie Terry, impressed w/Owens torch mark & shape No. 1039, artist-initialed in brown slip (base chip repaired) **1,045**

Wall pocket, Green Ware line, cornucopia-shaped w/scalloped rim, decorated w/relief-molded flowers & ribbon, marked "Owensart," 11" l. **400**

Paul Revere Pottery

S.E.G.

Paul Revere Marks

This pottery was established in Boston, Massachusetts, in 1906, by a group of philanthropists seeking to establish better conditions for underprivileged young girls of the area. Edith Brown served as supervisor of the small "Saturday Evening Girls Club" pottery operation which was moved, in 1912, to a house close to the Old North Church where Paul Revere's signal lanterns had been placed. The wares were mostly hand decorated in mineral colors and both sgraffito and molded decorations were employed. Although it became popular, it was never a profitable operation and always depended on financial contributions to operate. After the death of Edith Brown in 1932, the pottery foundered and finally closed in 1942.

Bowl, 4 1/2" d., 3 3/8" h., swollen form w/glossy green glaze & red-tinted rim, signed "S.E.G. 3.23 - SJM" **$173**

Bowl, 5 1/4" d., 2" h., wide flat bottom w/low rounded incurved sides, decorated w/a continuous landscape band w/clusters of trees done in cuerda seca, green, grey &

blue, 1915, ink mark "4-15 - S.E.G. - A.G." **935**

Bowl, 5 1/2" d., 2 1/2" h., squatty rounded sides w/a closed wide rim, the upper half decorated w/a continuous landscape scene w/brown trees outlined in black on a yellow ground & white sky, yellow on the lower half (repaired chips) **495**

Paul Revere Landscape Bowl

Bowl, 6" d., center medallion design of a stylized landscape scene in cuerda seca, w/brown tree outlined in black, against a blue sky, surrounded by dark blue band, light blue border (ILLUS.) **990**

Paul Revere/S.E.G. Large Bowl

Bowl, 7 1/4" d., 3 1/4" h., footed deep rounded & gently flaring sides w/rolled rim, decorated in cuerda seca w/an upper wide band w/white trefoil blossoms on a buff & light blue band against the dark blue background, S.E.G. mark (ILLUS.) **1,610**

Bowl, 8 1/4" d., wide flat bottom & low rounded incurved sides, decorated w/a stylized landscape w/clumps of trees in cuerda seca, in green, blue & grey, dark blue interior, ink mark "SEG - 7-20 - bvc" **1,650**

Center bowl, decorated w/white geese in cuerda seca against a band of yellow & brown, white interior w/matte green exterior, ca. 1912, ink mark, SACB paper label, SEG Bowl Shop label & ink mark, 4 1/2 x 11 3/4" (tight hairline from rim) **4,950**

Charger, round, a narrow rim band decorated w/green trees against a blue sky on an ivory ground, ivory center, signed "S.E.G. - E.T. - 5-17," 1917, 12 1/2" d. (minor inside footring chips) **660**

Paul Revere Plate and Vases

Creamer, decorated w/incised windmills in matte shades of green & cream, marked "SEG" & faint artist's initials, 3 1/4" h. (hairline) **403**

Creamer, short wide gently flaring cylindrical form w/a pointed rim spout & D-form handle, plain light blue rim band above alternating dark & light blue stripes, impressed mark, 2 1/4" h.................................... **121**

Inkwell, cov., square block-form, the cover decorated w/green trees in a dark blue landscape, base w/dark blue band over lighter blue bottom, inked S.E.G. mark & Bowl Shop paper label, 2 1/2 x 2 3/4", 2" h... **935**

Pitcher, 4 1/2" h., slightly flaring cylindrical body w/a small pinched rim spout & loop handle, decorated on the front under the spout w/an oval reserve showing a reclining white rabbit in green grass w/blue sky beyond, black banding on a light blue background, marked "Jane," impressed mark **468**

Paul Revere Plate w/Camel Border

Plate, decorated around the rim w/camel design, marked "S.E.G." (ILLUS.) **1,870**

Plate, 6 1/2" d., border decorated w/h.p. pine cones in brown & green, white matte ground, ink mark "SEG - 8.17"...................... **165**

Plate, 6 1/2" d., the border band w/a decoration of white hens & chicks spaced around the rim on a wide yellow band, white center, artist-signed, dated "9-13" **715**

Plate, 9 3/4" d., dinner, dark blue ground w/a wide white border band decorated in cuerda seca w/black wording "Give Us This Day Our Daily Bread," bruise to rim,

1921, ink stamp "S.E.G. 11-21 FL." (ILLUS. far right, top of page) **619**

Plates, 7 1/2" d., round w/wide flanged rim, overall light blue glaze, impressed mark, set of 3... **110**

Paul Revere Pottery Tea Set

Tea set: cov. teapot, cov. sugar & creamer; each of simple squatty, rounded form, overall greyish blue glaze, one ink-signed, two pieces stamped, 1927, minute glaze burst on rim of creamer, the set (ILLUS.) **288**

Tumbler, 3 1/4" d., tapering cylindrical form, decorated below rim w/h.p. frieze of squirrels in blue on white crackled ground, ca. 1912, ink mark "SEG - 91.7.12" (two nicks to rim)............................... **468**

Vase, 3 7/8" h., cylindrical w/flared rim, glossy cobalt blue glaze, impressed mark..... **144**

Vase, 4 1/2"h., 2 1/4" d., swelled & gently tapering cylindrical form w/flared rim, decorated in cuerda seca around the rim w/a band of Greek key design in brown & blue on a pale green ground, ink mark "S.E.G. - E.G. - 4-1-?"..................................... **825**

Vase, 4 1/2" h., 3 3/4" d., simple ovoid form w/a closed rim, dark bluish grey ground decorated around the top w/a wide cuerda seca band w/stylized white & blue lotus blossoms, 1914, ink mark "SEG - am - 11-14" (ILLUS. second from right with plate)... **1,238**

Vase, 5 1/4" h., 4 1/2" d., wide ovoid body w/a closed rim, a continuous abstract landscape of green trees against a frothy white sky & dark blue & grey ground, glossy glaze, 1922, signed "3-22 - S.E.G. - E.G.".. **1,540**

Vase, 5 3/4" h., 4 1/2" d., simple ovoid body w/a closed rim, matte light green ground decorated around the shoulder w/a wide band of stylized yellow tulips & greenish leaves on white w/black border bands,

Paul Revere stamp, illegible date (ILLUS. second from left with plate) **1,238**

Vase, 6 1/2" h., 5" d., ovoid body tapering to a thick, rolled rim, dark blue ground decorated around the shoulder w/a wide cuerda seca band w/yellow stylized tulips & dark blue leaves on a light blue ground, stamped mark (ILLUS. far left with plate) .. **1,463**

Vase, 7" h., wide tapering ovoid body w/a closed rim, mottled multi-toned turquoise blue glaze, ink mark, 1927 .... **231**

Vase, 7 1/2" h., wide bulbous ovoid body tapering sharply to a flat mouth w/closed-in rim, covered in mottled flowing medium green microcrystalline glaze, ink mark & paper label **385**

Paul Revere Vase with Daffodils

Vase, 10" h., slightly swelled tapering cylindrical body w/a wide mouth, decorated around the shoulder w/incised & painted daffodils in cream & yellow w/green stems & leaves, light blue sky beneath cream band at top, impressed mark, paper label, artist initialed & dated "4-24" (ILLUS.) **3,575**

Vase, 10" h., swelled cylindrical body w/wide flat mouth, medium blue semi-matte glaze, die-stamped mark & ink-marked "GM -7.25" **330**

Wall pocket, pocket-form w/slightly flared rim tapering to base, dark sage green glaze, marked "S.E.G." & Paul Revere Pottery paper label, 4" w., 6" l. **288**

Peters & Reed

Peters & Reed Mark

In 1897 John D. Peters and Adam Reed formed a partnership to produce flowerpots in Zanesville, Ohio. Formally incorporated as Peters and Reed in 1901, this type of production was the mainstay until after 1907 when they gradually expanded into the art pottery field. Frank Ferrell, a former designer at the Weller Pottery, developed the "Moss Aztec" line while associated with Peters and Reed and other art lines followed. Though unmarked, attribution is not difficult once familiar with the various lines. In

1921, Peters and Reed became Zane Pottery which continued in production until 1941.

Ewer, decorated w/lion's head w/grapevine, 11" h. **$160**

Moss Aztec Jardiniere

Jardiniere, Moss Aztec line, wide tapering ovoid form w/a wide flat mouth above a molded band of poppy blossoms & four wide buttress panels down the sides, minor chips & nicks, signed, 13" d., 9 3/4" h. (ILLUS.) **460**

Peters & Reed Cylindrical Jardiniere

Jardiniere, slightly tapering cylindrical form, molded around the sides w/high-relief rounded blossoms above a beaded base band, matte green glaze w/clay showing through, 5 1/2" d., 4" h. (ILLUS.) **115**

Pitcher, cavalier decoration **125**

Planter, hanging-type, Moss Aztec line, signed "Ferrell," 9 x 13" **325**

Vase, 6" h., tripod base, glossy brown glaze **160**

Vase, 8" h., Moss Aztec line **95**

Vase, 8 3/8" h., footed bulbous base tapering to slightly flared rim, decorated w/high glaze Chromal landscape scene in rich shades of blue, rust, cream, green & cobalt, unmarked **440**

Moss Aztec Vase & Wall Pocket

Vase, 9 3/4" h., Moss Aztec line, tapering cylindrical body decorated w/relief-molded pine cone decoration on matte brown ground w/green tinting, unmarked (ILLUS. right) **330**

Vase, 10" h., Moss Aztec line, tall slender waisted cylindrical form w/large heavily embossed triangular Art Nouveau-style blossoms around the top w/vines & leafy vines down the sides & around the bottom, greenish brown overall glaze **385**

Vase, 12" h., Landsun line, tall slender cylindrical body w/a flared base, streaky pale green, brown & blue banded glaze, ca. 1922, light crazing **115**

Large Peters & Reed Floor Vase

Vase, 18" h., floor-type, tall slightly waisted cylindrical form w/a flaring rim, molded around the top w/large stylized blossoms on slender stems slightly spiraling down the sides, dark green matte glaze w/clay showing through, unsigned (ILLUS.) **546**

Wall pocket, Egyptian line, matte green glaze **225**

Wall pocket, sprigged-on floral trim, glossy brown glaze **135**

Wall pocket, Moss Aztec line, conical, decorated at the top w/band of relief-molded Art Nouveau style poppies, matte brown ground w/green tinting, designed by Frank Ferrell & artist-signed, 9 1/4" h. (ILLUS. left, with pine cone vase) **138**

Pewabic

Pewabic Pottery Mark

Mary Chase Perry (Stratton) and Horace J. Caulkins were partners in this Detroit, Michigan pottery. Established in 1903, Pewabic Pottery evolved from their Revelation Pottery, "Pewabic" meaning "clay with copper color" in the language of Michigan's Chippewa Indians. Caulkins attended to the clay formulas and Mary Perry Stratton was artistic creator of forms & glaze formulas, eventually developing a wide range of colors for her finely textured glazes. The pottery's reputation for fine wares and

architectural tiles enabled it to survive the depression years of the 1930s. After Caulkins died in 1923, Mrs. Stratton continued to be active in the pottery until her death, at age ninety-four, in 1961. Her contributions to the art pottery field are numerous.

Bowl, 6 3/4" d., 3 3/4" h., hemispherical form w/a slightly flared rim, unusual gunmetal & turquoise dripping lustered glaze, circular stamp mark **$2,025**

Pewabic Footed Bowl

Bowl, 7 1/4" d., 4" h., a small footring below the squatty wide bulbous body tapering to a widely flaring rim, flowing matte brown exterior glaze, lavender & turquoise lustered interior glaze, stamped mark & paper label, small glaze nicks on foot (ILLUS.) **805**

Bowl, 8 1/2" d., 2 1/2" h., low canted sides w/incurved rim, the sides covered w/embossed lily pads, centered at the shoulder w/ring handles under a flowing matte green glaze, impressed mark **3,300**

Bowl, 3 3/4" d., 1 3/4" h., spherical w/incurved flat rim, iridescent dove grey lustre w/turquoise interior that flows out onto rim, outlined in brick red, the shoulder decorated w/an impressed pattern of rings, impressed mark **252**

Miniature Pewabic Bowl-Vase

Bowl-vase, miniature, a small footring supporting a wide squatty bulbous body w/a wide short cylindrical neck, mottled teal blue, green & gunmetal glossy glaze, circular mark, 3 3/4" d., 2 3/4" h. (ILLUS.) **460**

Pewabic Volcanic Glazed Bowl-Vase

Bowl-vase, footed wide half-round form w/a wide slightly rounded shoulder to a wide flat mouth, overall lustered volcanic cobalt blue & celadon greyish green glaze, mark covered by glaze, 9 1/4" d., 4 3/4" h. (ILLUS.) **5,344**

Box, cov., rectangular w/flat corners, center of lid w/relief-molded antelope, iridescent cream, yellow & green glaze, impressed "Pewabic Detroit," 4 3/4" w., 1 7/8" h............. **358**

Pewabic Eggplant-shaped Jar

Jar, cov., model of a large eggplant, the top & stem forming the cover, overall dark

matte purple flowing glaze, unmarked, 4 1/4" d., 6 3/4" h. (ILLUS.) **2,070**

Jardiniere, footed large, deep bulbous ovoid body w/a wide flat rim band, lustered cobalt blue glaze, stamped "Pewabic - Detroit," 9" d., 8" h. **2,475**

Plate, 10 3/4" d., flattened form w/wide flanged rim, painted w/a radiating design of dragonflies in blue slip on a white crackled ground, stamped mark, several glaze flakes & chips to footring, stamped mark (ILLUS. center, bottom of page)........ **1,100**

Miniature Vase with Test Glaze

Vase, 2" h., 2 1/2" d., miniature, test glaze, squatty bulbous body tapering to a short, wide flaring neck, dark Persian blue crackled glaze over a black-glazed lower body, circular stamp & "40B" (ILLUS.) **248**

Pewabic Miniature Vase

Vase, 2 1/4" h., 2 1/4" d., miniature, flat-bottomed ovoid form w/a closed rim, fine celadon green & lavender lustered glaze, no visible mark (ILLUS.) **385**

Pewabic Plate and Vases

Vase, 2 1/2" h., 2" d., miniature, cylindrical form slightly tapered at the base, fine turquoise, green & blue lustered dripping glaze, circular stamp mark (ILLUS. third from right with plate)... **468**

Two Small Pewabic Vases

Vase, 2 1/2" h., 2" d., miniature, flat-bottomed ovoid form, the rounded shoulder centered by a short cylindrical neck w/slightly flared rim, fine celadon & oxblood lustre glaze, stamped mark (ILLUS. left)... **385**

Vase, 2 1/2" h., 2 1/4" d., miniature ovoid body tapering to a small flat mouth, dripping pink crackled glaze on a blue lustered ground, stamped "PEWABIC - DETROIT" (some deep crazing lines, minute fleck at rim) **281**

Vase, 2 1/2" h., 2 3/4" d., miniature, simple wide ovoid form w/a closed rim, fine & thick pink, gold & blue lustered dripping glaze, circular stamp mark (ILLUS. second from left with plate) **1,320**

Vase, 2 1/2" h., 3 1/4" d., miniature, sharply tapering cylindrical sides below a wide shoulder tapering to a wide, flat mouth, fine gold, green & ivory lustered glaze, circular stamp mark & paper label (ILLUS. second from right with plate)........... **605**

Vase, 3 1/2" h., 2 1/4" d., miniature footed bottle-form, fine dripping turquoise & gold lustrered glaze, hand-incised "PEWABIC" (stilt pull chip on base).............................. **197**

Bulbous Miniature Pewabic Vase

Vase, 3 1/2" h., 3 3/4" d., miniature, footed bulbous body w/an angled shoulder to a low rolled rim, unusual white semi-matte glaze w/a lustered umber rim, stamped mark & paper label (ILLUS.) **575**

Vase, 3 1/2" h., 5 1/4" d., wide bulbous ovoid body w/a wide shoulder tapering to a wide flat molded rim, black, green & lavender lustred glaze, impressed circular mark **495**

Vase, 3 3/4" h., 2 1/2" d., miniature, ovoid base sharply tapering to wide cylindrical neck, iridescent cobalt glaze, impressed mark.. **385**

Large & Small Pewabic Vases

Vase, 3 3/4" h., 3 3/4" d., bulbous nearly spherical body w/a short cylindrical neck centered on the shoulder, fine thick & leathery cobalt blue & green lustered glaze, circular stamp mark (ILLUS. second from left, bottom previous page)............. **731**

Vase, 3 3/4" h., 3 3/4" d., miniature, simple ovoid form w/a wide shoulder tapering to a wide, flat mouth, fine dripping turquoise & purple lustered glaze, stamped circular mark.................. **660**

Vase, 3 3/4" h., 4" d., baluster-form body w/wide cylindrical neck covered in a lustered striated glaze in purple & green, unmarked.................. **825**

Vase, 4 3/4" h., 3 1/2" d., simple ovoid form w/a flat mouth, fine gold & mauve lustered glaze, circular stamp mark (ILLUS. far right with plate)............................. **715**

Vase, 4 3/4" h., 4" d., bulbous ovoid body w/a short cylindrical neck, fine mirrored gold glaze dripping over a glossy dark blue ground, circular stamp mark, small firing chip at base (ILLUS. far left with plate)................. **1,210**

Vase, 4 3/4" h., 4" d., bulbous wide body w/an angled shoulder tapering to a short flaring neck, lustered celadon green & purple glaze, stamped cylindrical mark, remnant of paper label..................... **550**

Vase, 5" h., 3 3/4" d., bottle-shaped, covered in a lustered celadon & blush glaze, circular die-stamped mark (ILLUS. right with miniature vase) **495**

Vase, 5" h., 4 1/2" d., footed w/angular ovoid sides, tapering shoulder w/flaring neck, covered w/an excellent red metallic luster glaze w/light green lowlights, unmarked.................. **550**

Vase, 5" h., 5" d., a cylindrical foot supporting a wide short flaring cylindrical body w/a wide shoulder tapering sharply to a short flared neck, overall purple mirror glaze, impressed circular mark..................... **770**

Vase, 5" h., 5" d., footed spherical ringed body tapering to a narrow mouth rim, overall orange matte glaze, circular stamp mark (restoration to small base chip)............... **450**

Vase, 5 1/2" h., 5 1/2" d., bulbous ovoid body w/a rounded shoulder tapering to a wide short flaring neck, overall streaky turquoise & taupe lustred glaze, impressed circular mark.................... **715**

Pewabic Baluster-form Vase

Vase, 6" h., wide baluster-form body w/flaring neck, dark greenish blue glaze, impressed mark, some crazing, small firing line in base, small glaze bubbles (ILLUS.)............... **345**

Vase, 6" h., 4 1/4" d., footed wide pear-shaped body tapering to a short flared neck, lustered dripping celadon green & purple glaze, circular stamp & paper label **844**

Vase, 6 1/2" h., 4 1/4" d., footed bulbous ovoid body w/a rounded shoulder to the wide, short cylindrical neck w/flaring rim covered in a mirrored purple, lavender & green glaze, circular die-stamped mark........ **880**

Pewabic Vase with Lustered Glaze

Vase, 7 1/2" h., 4" d., simple ovoid body w/a short, flared neck, lustered copper & gold mottled glaze, stamped mark (ILLUS.) **2,530**

Vase, 7 3/4" h., 5 1/2" d., footed wide bulbous ovoid body tapering to a short flared neck w/flattened rim, fine lustered blue & turquoise mottled glaze, stamped "PEWABIC - DETROIT"........................... **1,350**

Vase, 8" h., footed spherical lower body below a wide trumpet neck, metallic blue, green & gunmetal overall lustre glaze, impressed mark **605**

Large Pewabic Vase

Vase, 8" h., wide baluster-form body w/a wide flat rim, embossed w/large flowers & leaves under a flowing matte green glaze, impressed mark (ILLUS.)................. **6,325**

Vase, 8" h., 6" d., baluster-form w/the wide shoulder tapering to a short rolled neck, overall lustered dark blue glaze, impressed mark.................. **825**

Vase, 8" h., 7" d., the wide squatty base w/a knobby sharply angled shoulder tapering to a wide cylindrical neck molded w/light ribbing & knobby prunts around the wide flattened rim, smooth flowing matte green glaze, unmarked (firing lines around base prunts) **2,530**

Pewabic Vase with Unusual Glaze

Vase, 8 1/4" h., 6" d., flaring & swelled cylindrical sides below a wide angled shoulder centered by a small neck w/molded rim, unusual gunmetal brown, celadon & dripping turquoise mottled glaze, circular paster mark (ILLUS.).................................... **1,610**

Ovoid Pewabic Vase

Vase, 8 1/2" h., 4 1/2" d., bulbous ovoid body w/short molded rim, lustered burgundy & celadon glaze over a ridged body, circular die-stamped mark, paper label (ILLUS.) **1,650**
Vase, 9 3/4" h., 6 1/2" d., wide balusterform body w/a short flared neck, brilliant pulled cobalt blue & turquoise lustered glaze, stamped "Pewabic - Detroit" (ILLUS. second from right with other vases) **5,625**

Pewabic Vase with Modeled Leaves

Vase, 10" h., 5 3/4" d., ovoid form w/hand-modeled impressed arched leaves alternating w/raised wedged ribs continuing to curved shoulder, smooth matte green glaze, Pewabic stamp w/leaves, small glaze chips around base, T-lines in body (ILLUS.).. **4,600**
Vase, 10 1/2" h., 5" d., squatty bulbous base tapering to a tall ringed body w/a flared mouth, frothy, dripping celadon green & gold lustered glaze, drilled hole in bottom, stamped "PEWABIC - DETROIT" (ILLUS. far right with other vases) **2,363**
Vase, 10 1/2" h., 7" d., wide flaring cylindrical form w/horizontal band, ivory crackle glaze, incised "Pewabic - WBS - 1935"...... **1,125**
Vase, 11" h., 5 3/4" d., bulbous lobed body tapering to a tall slender cylindrical neck & flat rim, covered in a leathery cobalt matte glaze, stamped "Pewabic"................ **2,813**
Vase, 11" h., 8 1/2" d., large wide tapering cylindrical form w/a narrow angled shoulder to a wide flat mouth, embossed w/nubs around the shoulder, rare dripping matte mustard yellow glaze on a caramel ground, stamped "Pewabic" w/leaves (ILLUS. far left with other vases) **11,250**

Pisgah Forest Pottery

Pisgah Forest Marks

Walter Stephen experimented with making pottery shortly after 1900 with his parents in Tennessee. After their deaths in 1910, he eventually moved to the foot of Mt. Pisgah in North Carolina where he became a partner of C.P. Ryman. Together they built a kiln and a shop but this partnership was dissolved in 1916. During 1920 Stephen again began to experiment with pottery and by 1926 had his own pottery and equipment. Pieces are usually marked and may also be signed "W. Stephen" and dated. Walter Stephen died in 1961 but work at the pottery still continues, although on a part-time basis.

Bowl, 5 1/4" d., Cameo Ware, round, slightly curved sides, covered wagon scene in white on matte olive green ground, decorated by Walter Stephen, ca. 1953, marked "1953 Cameo Stephen Longpine Ardenne" on base & "Stephen" in white slip on side, 5 1/4" d., 2 1/4" h..................... **$138**
Bowl-vase, wide spherical body w/the wide round shoulder centered by a short cylindrical neck, amber glaze w/white & blue crystals, raised Stephen mark, dated 1947, 5 3/4" d., 5" h.. **385**
Bowl-vase, wide spherical form, the rounded shoulder centered by a short wide neck, amber flambé glaze w/celadon

crystals, raised Stephen mark & illegible date, 4 1/2" d., 3 3/4" h. **303**

Pisgah Forest Bowl-Vase

Bowl-vase, wide squatty bulbous body w/a wide shoulder tapering to a wide rolled rim, covered in white & umber glaze w/white & blue crystals, embossed mark & dated 1941, 6" d., 4 1/2" h. (ILLUS.) **440**

Creamer, Cameo Ware, bulbous shape w/small pinched spout & C-form handle, scene of covered wagon pulled by oxen on matte olive green ground, decorated by Walter Stephen, ca. 1953, Longpine Ardenne mark, artist's name in white slip, paper label from Allanstand Mountain Crafts, Asheville, N.C. on bottom, 3 1/8" h. **220**

Pisgah Forest Cameo Mug

Mug, Cameo Ware, white relief landscape scene of trees & a cabin in the mountains against a teal blue ground, ca. 1949, embossed "Stephen," 3 1/2 x 4" (ILLUS.) **303**

Teapot, cov., spherical form w/inset cover w/button finial, short cylindrical spout & D-form shoulder handle, fine Chinese blue glaze w/red, green & blue highlights, raised mark, 8" w. **231**

Teapot, cov., Cameo Ware, bulbous body w/inset lid w/button finial, short spout & C-form handle, pioneer family & cov. wagon scene in heavy white slip on medium blue ground, decorated by Walter Stephen, ca. 1953, Longpine Ardenne mark & date on bottom, artist's name on side, 5" h. **303**

Vase, 5" h., 4 3/4" d., wide squatty bulbous lower body tapering to a cylindrical neck w/rolled rim, white & amber glaze w/blue crystals, raised potter mark, dated 1940 .... **358**

Pisgah Forest Vase

Vase, 5 1/2" h., 5 1/2" d., wide bulbous body w/short cylindrical neck, celadon & pink glaze w/large blooming crystals, embossed mark, 1949 (ILLUS.) **990**

Vase, 6 1/4" h., trumpet-form body, grey & beige glaze w/densely-packed crystals, pink interior, embossed mark (some bubbles to glaze) **385**

Pisgah Forest Vases

Vase, 6 1/2" h., 4" d., simple baluster-form w/a short, wide flaring neck, fine amber glaze w/tightly packed white & dark blue crystals, raised potter mark, dated 1940 (ILLUS. left, bottom previous page) 660

Vase, 6 1/2" h., 4 1/2" d., tall deeply corseted form w/a wide flaring mouth, amber glaze w/grey crystals, raised potter mark & illegible date 413

Pisgah Forest Vase with Blue Crystals

Vase, 7" h., 4" d., ovoid body tapering to a cylindrical neck, brown & amber flambé glaze w/clusters of large blue crystals, grinding chip at base, embossed mark (ILLUS.) 605

Vase, 7 1/4" h., wide shoulder tapering to the base, extended neck, crystallized blue glaze over a mustard yellow ground, raised mark 546

Vase, 7 1/2" h., 4 3/4" d., baluster-form tapering to a short, wide rolled neck, amber flambé glaze w/a few blue crystals, raised Pisgah Forest mark & illegible date 523

Vase, 7 3/4" h., 4 3/4" d., wide baluster-form body tapering to a short, wide flaring neck, amber glaze w/white & blue large crystals around the lower half, raised Stephen mark, dated 1949 (ILLUS. right with two other vases) 770

Vase, 8" h., 5 1/4" d., wide bottle-form w/bulbous tapering body below a tall waisted cylindrical neck, overall white glaze w/white crystals, raised potter mark & dated 1941 (ILLUS. center with two other vases) 715

Vase, 8 3/4" h., 5 1/2" d., baluster-form w/short cylindrical neck & flaring rim, cream & celadon flambé glaze w/blue & white crystals near base, pink interior, shaved mark 715

Vase, 9" h., baluster-form w/short cylindrical neck & flaring rim, white, celadon & blue crystalline glaze, pink interior, embossed mark & dated 1949 1,100

Vase, 12 1/4" h., 8" d., wide bulbous ovoid base centered by a tall cylindrical neck, shaded ivory glaze w/blue & pearl scattered crystals, raised potter's mark & "Stephen - 1946" (firing lines around neck base) 788

Robineau (Adelaide)

Adelaide Alsop Robineau began her career as a china painter and teacher. After her marriage to Samuel Robineau in 1899 they founded the magazine, Keramic Studio, which was a practical guide to china painting.

After a few years she became frustrated with just simply decorating wares produced by others and she and her husband began production of earthenware and then later, porcelain.

Between 1904 and 1916 Adelaide Robineau produced a limited number of exquisite, detailed works which garnered her several awards at major international expositions.

After World War I their pottery ceased to operate independently and Mrs. Robineau joined the staff of Syracuse University in 1920 and worked there until her retirement in 1928. She died in 1929.

The Robineau Pottery was never a major commercial operation and reportedly sold only about 600 pieces over a twenty-five year period. Many examples were eventually purchased by museums so few examples of her work are offered for sale today.

Jar, cov., footed spherical form covered in mossy green flambé, the cover completely excised w/a geometric floral design under a bronze glaze, carved "AR - 44 - 1920," 4 1/2 x 4 1/2" (underglaze lines around rim from firing, grinding bruise to edge of base, also in manufacture) $14,625

Robineau Rabbit Tile

Tile, square, deeply carved w/the figure of a crouching stylized rabbit w/a matte celadon glaze, several minute edge nicks, very slight surface abrasion, carved "AR" mark, 4 3/4" w. (ILLUS.) 1,238

Vase, miniature, 2 x 2 1/2", ovoid body w/shoulder tapering to wide cylindrical neck w/closed rim, butterscotch flambé glaze, marked "AR - C - 4 - 11-111.," minor bruise to rim, 1904 (ILLUS. top left, next page) 2,363

Three Robineau Vases

Vase, miniature, 2 x 2 1/4", ovoid body tapering to short cylindrical neck w/flat rim, green & blue matte crystalline glaze, marked "AR - C - '04 - 11-111.," 1904 (ILLUS. top right, above) **1,913**

Vase, 3 3/4" h., 4 1/4" d., spherical form w/molded rim, cobalt blue crystalline glase, incised "AR" (ILLUS. bottom, above) **6,750**

Rookwood

Rookwood Mark

Considered America's foremost art pottery, the Rookwood Pottery Company was established in Cincinnati, Ohio in 1880, by Mrs. Maria Nichols Longworth Storer. To accurately record its development, each piece carried the Rookwood insignia, or mark, was dated, and, if individually decorated, was usually signed by the artist. The pottery remained in Cincinnati until 1959 when it was sold to Herschede Hall Clock Company and moved to Starkville, Mississippi, where it continued in operation until 1967.

A private company is now producing a limited variety of pieces using original Rookwood molds.

Basket, hanging-type, bulbous bullet-form, green Matte glaze, No. S1732, 1905, 10" d., 9" l. (minute flakes) **$440**

Basket, gondola-shaped w/curved & pointed ends, decorated w/slip-painted daisies in yellow on a shaded green ground, Standard glaze, No. 374, 1888, K. Shirayamadani, 15 1/2" l., 8" h. **660**

Book ends, figural, model of a squirrel seated on a log holding up & eating a nut, greyish green Matte glaze, No. 6025, 1928, Sallie Toohey, 4 1/4" h., pr. **748**

Book ends, figural, modeled as a blue jay, w/oak leaves & acorns, creamy Matte glaze, No. 2829, 1929, 5 3/8" h., pr. **316**

Book ends, figural, one w/Dutch girl dressed in blue & white, the other w/Dutch boy w/blue hat & lavender vest, leaning on dark brown stone wall behind a stand of pink tulips, Matte glaze, No. 6022, 1928, Sallie Toohey, 6" h., pr. **523**

Bowl, 4" d., slightly tapering upright flattened sides molded w/an Arts & Crafts design, brown & maroon Matte glaze, No. 1674, 1912 .... **275**

Bowl, 5" d., 4 1/2" h., '50th Anniversary' type, deep flaring rounded sides, the interior decorated w/a wide border band of polychrome blossoms & leaves on a mottled ivory ground, Wax Matte Glaze, No. 2253D, 1930, Elizabeth N. Lincoln **422**

Rookwood Bowl

Bowl, 6 1/2" d., porcelain, flared sides w/center decoration of six-pointed star design w/pink, white & red roses painted between star points, blue scroll design border w/gold trim, No. 2239, 1920, W.E. Hentschel (ILLUS.) **495**

Bowl, 6 1/2" d., wide low form w/incurved sides molded w/stylized florals below the closed wide rim, dark blue Matte Glaze, No. 1709, 1912 .... **209**

Bowl, 7" w., deep square, slightly rounded body w/indented corners on square foot, Limoges-style decoration w/two butterflies in brown tones soaring against a peach, green & white smeared ground w/gold highlights & black reeds, painted gold accents at rim, kiln mark, No. 166, 1883, N.J. Hirschfeld... **413**

Unusual Rookwood Bowl

Bowl, 12" l., oval w/incurved sides forming openings at each end, decorated w/detailed flowers in green & blue w/white centers against an ivory, light blue & medium blue ground, gold geometric & floral designs, No. 344B, 1887, Kataro Shirayamadani (ILLUS.) **1,540**

Bowl-vase, wide spherical body w/a wide flat rim, decorated around the rim w/a narrow band of red cherry blossoms on black branches on an ivory ground, the lower body in bluish grey shaded to rose, Vellum Glaze, No. 1375, 1920, E.T. Hurley, 9" d., 6 1/4" h.. **1,913**

Bowl-vase, bulbous body w/incurved rim, the upper body decorated w/pink flowers w/green centers on a light blue ground, the lower body darker blue w/scalloped edge, impressed "V" & signature, No. 214E, 1915, E.H. McDermott, 4 1/2" d......... **358**

Bowl-vase, molded production piece in a wide low squatty rounded form, the wide top reticulated & molded w/a design of pine cones & needles in light green & pink, No. 1214, Matte glaze, 1909, 7" d., 3" h.. **900**

Card holder, rectangular form on pedestal base, paneled design w/ribbed top, blue crystalline glaze, No. 2952, 1927, 3" w., 3 1/2" h. **220**

Unusual Rookwood Chalice

Chalice, cone-shaped body supported by three large loop handles from rim extending into feet w/relief-molded gargoyle heads, body decorated w/orange & yellow flowers & green foliage under a tiger eye glaze, early Standard glaze, No. 350, 1888, artist's signature illegible, 8" h. (ILLUS.).................... **605**

Clock, relief-molded panther on base, gunmetal glaze, No. 7039, 1950, 7 1/2" h. **286**

Compote, shallow oblong form w/crimped rim, floral medallion in center, pedestal base, glossy red glaze, No. S2205, 1955, marked w/Rookwood anniversary triangle, 6" d., 4 1/2" h. **231**

Cup & saucer, cylindrical w/D-form handle, painted & incised cherry blossoms on olive ground, saucer 5" d., cup 3" h., No. 208, 1886, Anna M. Bookprinter **275**

Standard Glaze Cup & Saucer

Cup & saucer, demitasse, the gold ground round saucer w/flared rim, the dark brown cylindrical cup w/D-form handle & gold interior, etched cherry blossom motif w/two blossoms in lighter glaze, the others in silhouette, Standard glaze, No. 208, 1886, Anna Bookprinter, remnants of salesroom label, 3" h., the set (ILLUS.)..... **476**

Standard Glaze Dresser Tray

Dresser tray, rectangular w/ruffled rim, decorated w/h.p. coral carnations on a shaded dark brown ground, Standard glaze, No. 591, 1894, Elizabeth Lincoln, few nicks & rough areas to edge, 7 x 10 3/4" (ILLUS.)... **392**

Ewer, squatty round ribbed melon-form base on small tab feet, the top centered by a tall slender neck w/a wide curled tricorner rim, a slender S-scoll handle from the rim to the shoulder, decorated around the neck w/Black-eyed Susans against a dark brown shaded to pale yellow ground, Standard glaze, No. 571C, 1894, H. Wilcox, 5 1/2" d., 8" h................................ **731**

Rookwood Silver Overlay Ewer

Ewer, footed, baluster-form w/a widely flaring rolled tricorner rim, slender S-scroll handle, decorated w/yellow blossoms on green leaves trimmed w/silver overlay flowering vines up the sides & beneath the handle w/a silver overlaid rim, handle & base, Standard glaze, No. 510, 1892, silver marked by Gorham Co., No. R198, Harriet R. Strafer, insignificant break in silver & fracture to base not visible from top or outside, 7" h. (ILLUS.) **3,850**

Ewer, flattened spherical body tapering to a slender tall neck w/a tricorner rim, a long C-form handle from rim to shoulder, decorated w/yellow flowers & green leaves on a dark brown to green ground, Standard glaze, No. 715D, No. X272X, 1898, Josephine Zettel, 7 1/2" h.............................. **660**

Rookwood Standard Glaze Ewer

Ewer, squatty bulbous base tapering to a tall slender cylindrical flaring neck w/a rolled tricorner rim, applied S-scroll handle from rim to top of body, the body decorated w/large yellow & orange mums w/green leaves & stems, Standard glaze, No. 495, 1893, A.B. Sprague, 8 1/2" h. (ILLUS.).. **715**

Ewer, squatty bulbous base on a narrow footring tapering to slender cylindrical neck w/flaring rim & pinched spout w/long arched handle, decorated w/yellow dogwood w/black centers on brown stems & green leaves on a dark brown, orange & green ground, Standard glaze, No. 495B, 1899, Mary Nourse, 9" h.............. **770**

Ewer, oviform w/an elongated neck & floriform spout, in a Standard glaze, decorated w/a mustard yellow & olive green branch of prunus, applied w/a C-scroll handle, No. 450 W, 1892, Albert R. Valentien, 17" h. **1,150**

Flower frog, figural satyr w/turtle, brown Matte glaze, No. 2336, 1921, 7" h. **468**

Inkwell, flat oval form w/flared rim, decorated w/feather among yellow & green clover, centered w/spherical well adorned w/silver overlay in elaborate scrolled design w/hammered silver top, Standard glaze, No. 586C, 1899, silver marked by Gorham Co., Constance Baker, 10" l. (minor flaws underneath base, probably in firing) **1,760**

Jar, cov., wide squatty compressed body raised on tiny peg feet, the wide shoulder centered by a low, wide domed cover, incised rectangular panels, fine dark red & dusty green Matte glaze, No. 1349, 1908, 6" d. (minor inner rim flake).............................. **413**

Rare Rookwood Jar

Jar, cov., bulbous ovoid body w/reticulated neck & domed cover, white ground decorated around the center w/brightly colored continuous scene depicting seven Chinese figures on horseback riding through rocky terrain w/one rider falling to the ground, by William Hentschel, interior of jar & lid in rich medium blue, artist-initialed, No. 2541, ca. 1921, 9 3/4" h. (ILLUS.)... **4,032**

Jug, floor-type, tall ovoid form w/the rounded shoulder centered by a flared molded neck, applied shoulder strap handle, small molded spout at the bottom front, overall glossy brown glaze, stamped "Rookwood - 1884," 16" d., 28" h. **1,069**

Silver-overlaid Rookwood Jug

Jug w/stopper, double-gourd bulbous form w/a short neck & shoulder handle, the handle, neck & round stopper w/silver overlay, the lower body lobe w/a silver overlay grapevine decoration, the upper lobe decorated w/a large ear of corn in yellow & green on a shaded brown ground, Standard glaze, No. S976, ca. 1890, illegible artist, 4 3/4" d., 8 1/2" h. (ILLUS.).. **2,300**

Unusual Rookwood Loving Cup

Loving cup, gently flaring cylindrical sides w/a wide flat rim flanked by two D-form angled handles, decorated w/a color bust portrait of a ragged African-American boy against a shaded light green & tan to brown ground, Standard glaze, No. 259, 1895, Bruce Horsfall, 9 1/2" w., 7" h. (ILLUS.) **4,600**

Model of an egret, head up & turned to the side, glossy black glaze, No. 6992, 1948, 8 1/2" h. **187**

Rookwood Mug with Indian Portrait

Mug, swelled bottom & tapering cylindrical sides w/a molded rim band, D-form handle, color bust portrait of Native American chief against a shaded deep gold & brown ground, Standard glaze, No. 656, 1896, Matt Daly, 5" w., 5" h. (ILLUS.) **1,380**

Mug, tall tapering cylindrical form w/a large D-form handle, Carved Matt design of stylized oak leaves & acorns in brown & butterfat green, No. 1014D, 1905, 4 1/4" d., 7" h. **478**

Native American Portrait Mug

Mug, ovoid body w/wide flat rim, C-form handle, decorated w/bust portrait of Native American brave w/one feather in head band & elaborate beadwork on chest, blue & yellow, Standard glaze, incised "Big Mane," No. 837, 1898, Sadie Markland, 5" h. (ILLUS.) **1,870**

Mug, tapering cylindrical body w/compressed base, decorated w/painted & molded clover in pink & green against a green to ivory ground, Vellum glaze, w/silver overlay C-form handle & rim, 1905, impressed signature & "Commercial Club of Cincinnati," Sara Sax, 5 1/2" h. **770**

Paperweight, figural seated female nude on rectangular base, ivory Matte glaze, impressed signature, No. 2868, 1928, 4" h. **330**

Pilgrim flask, spherical body w/narrow cylindrical neck, applied handle from neck to shoulder, Limoges-type, decorated w/scene of white geese in flight & white, orange & black water fowl wading in pool against smeared ground in olive green & white w/gold accents & black reeds, 1882, A.R. Valentien, 7" h. **880**

Pin tray, shallow oval form w/rolled rim, figural molded reclining nude female at one end, glossy green glaze, No. 2595, 1949, 4 1/2" w. **176**

Pitcher, 12" h., 5 3/4" d., tall slender ovoid form tapering to a gently flared rim w/pinched spout, applied C-form strap handle on the neck, decorated w/large cluster of gooseberry leaves in yellow, green & brown on a shaded light amber to green ground, Standard glaze, No. 567W, 1891, A.R. Valentien **1,800**

Plaque, rectangular, a scene depicting tall leafy birch trees by a lake at dusk in shades of blue & grey w/touches of pink & brown, Vellum glaze, 1921, Ed Diers, framed, 5 3/4 x 8" **2,415**

Plaque, rectangular, a wide landscape scene of trees along a riverbank, unusual red leaves on brown trunks w/green grass along light blue body of water, Vellum glaze, incised "V" & painted signature, 1915, original frame, E.T. Hurley, 5 1/2 x 9 1/2" **2,860**

Rare Sea Green Glazed Plaque

Plaque, unusual design of a songbird in flight near leafy stems on a shaded blue ground, unusual Sea Green glaze, A.R. Valentien, framed, 8 x 10" (ILLUS.) **19,550**

Rookwood Plaque with Ocean View

Plaque, rectangular, a landscape vista w/a tall lone pine tree in the foreground w/hills & the ocean in the distance, in shades of blue, green, tan & brown, titled "On the Bluffs," mounted in original gilt shadowbox frame, Vellum Glaze, 1916, Sara Sax, 8 1/2 x 10 3/4" (ILLUS.) **8,050**

Plaque, rectangular, a winter landscape depicting a wind-swept evergreen tree in the snow silhouetted against a pink sky,

Vellum glaze, 1915, E.F. McDermott, original wooden frame, 8 1/2 x 11" **4,675**

Plaque, rectangular, landscape scene of birch trees on river bank, blue, green & white, Vellum glaze, 1912, E.T. Hurley, wooden frame, plaque 9 x 11" (ILLUS. center, bottom of page) **7,088**

Plaque with Lake, Trees & Hills

Plaque, a landscape of a meadow leading down to tall slender leafy trees flanking a lake w/mountains in the distance below a pale blue cloudy sky, in shades of purple, blue, dark & light green, tan & brown, Vellum glaze, 1920, Lenore Asbury, framed, 10 x 11 3/4" (ILLUS.) **4,313**

Rookwood Plaque and Vases

Plaque, rectangular, large landscape of an autumn scene w/birch trees by a pond, Vellum glaze, original molded frame, 1940s, w/paper label & artist's initials, E.T. Hurley, 11 x 13" **11,000**

Mt. Ararat Vellum Plaque

Plaque, foreign landscape w/two distant pointed mountains w/a stream & scrubland in the foreground & tall trees in the front left, titled "Mt. Ararat in Armenia," Vellum glaze, 1914, Sara Sax, framed, 9 x 14 1/4" (ILLUS.) **5,750**

Large Rookwood Vellum Plaque

Plaque, rectangular, a tall unusual mountain & lake vista in shades of blue, green & mauve, mounted in original wide dark coved frame, Vellum glaze, 1912, Ed Diers, 11 1/4 x 16 1/2" (ILLUS.) **6,900**

Plaque, rectangular, cameo-style scene of relief-molded figures of men & women in Roman style, semi-gloss cream against a blue Matte glaze, in Arts & Crafts oak frame, 19" l., 8" h. (minor chips to edges) **550**

Plate, 6 1/2" d., Limoges-style decoration w/center scene of water bird in black w/black reeds & gold highlights, scal-loped rim w/gold trim, No. 87, 1882, N.J. Hirschfeld (minor flakes) **198**

Plate, 12" d., decorated w/daisies on a sienna ground, Cameo glaze, No. 520, 1890, Harriet E. Wilcox **575**

Scarce Rookwood Tankard with Imp

Tankard, cov., baluster-form w/low domed hinged cover & D-form handle, decorated w/a smiling imp-like character in shaded bright yellow swinging on bare brown branches against a shaded dark to light brown ground, copper overlay on cover, Standard glaze, 1899, Harriet Wilcox, 9" h. (ILLUS.) **9,200**

Rookwood Tea Set

Tea set: cov. 7 1/2" d., 5" h. teapot, 5" d. creamer & 6" d. cov. sugar bowl; each w/squatty bulbous bodies, decorated w/wild roses in salmon & white w/brown stems, thorns & leaves against a peach to ivory ground, Cameo glaze, the creamer w/C-form handle & pinched spout, the sugar bowl w/C-form handles & domed lip w/butterfly finial, the teapot w/swan's-neck spout, domed cover w/butterfly finial & rattan-wrapped swing bail handle, No. 404, 1891, H.E. Wilcox, teapot lid has crack & small flake to creamer, the set (ILLUS.) **660**

Rookwood Standard Glaze Teapot

Teapot, cov., cylindrical w/domed lid & knob finial, swan's-neck spout & C-scroll handle, decorated w/yellow & orange carnations w/green stems & buds on paneled body, Standard glaze, No. 552, 1894, L.N. Lincoln, 7 1/2" h. (ILLUS.) **770**

Tile, carved & painted stylized floral design in brown & green w/blue background, framed, 4" sq. **286**

Tile, geometric design of squares in tan, blue & purple, framed, 4" sq. **187**

Tile, deeply incised & painted decoration of windmill on hillside w/trees in green on a rose ground, framed, 6" sq. **231**

Tile, squeezebag technique decoration of white windmill, dark blue trees against a light blue sky, 1919, artist-signed, framed, 6" sq. **330**

Tray, molded design of a peacock feather, black & blue Matte glaze, No. 1668, 1922, 6 1/2" l. **165**

Rookwood Floral Decorated Urn

Urn, cov., porcelain, wide bulbous ovoid body w/high domed cover w/button finial, decorated w/elaborate overall floral design w/swirling blossoms & leaves in red, green, blue, yellow & brown against an ivory ground, decorated inner lid & decorated & pierced exterior top, No. 2448, 1921, Arthur Conant, harmless line in body, 14 1/2" h. (ILLUS.) **6,600**

Vase, 3" h., bulbous rounded body w/a four-sided wide neck incised w/a band of short pickets, shaded dark blue to moss green Matte glaze, No.1186, 1905 .... **440**

Vase, 4" h., 4" d., Jewel Porcelain, bulbous ovoid body tapering to a wide short flat mouth, a pale blue band of stylized cherry blossoms around the shoulder against an oxblood glazed ground, dark blue glazed interior, No. 8903, 1920, Sara Sax.. **1,800**

Vase, 4 3/4" h., 3" w., pentagonal, each panel w/embossed rook at base, embossed foliate design near rim, blue Matte glaze, production vase, No. 1795, 1927 .... **358**

Blossoms on Yellow Vellum Vase

Vase, 5" h., 3" h., gently tapering ovoid body w/a flat rim, a pale yellow ground decorated around the bottom w/a band of large & small pink blossoms & green leafy branches, Vellum glaze, 1924, Lenore Asbury (ILLUS.) **977**

Vase, 5" h., 3 3/4" d., wide simple ovoid form tapering slightly to a wide, flat mouth, decorated w/a continuous landscape scene w/groups of tall trees in a meadow w/hills in the distance, in shades of dark blue, light blue & cream, Vellum glaze, No. 942E, 1919, Ed Diers **1,463**

Vase, 5" h., 7" d., low wide squatty round form w/the wide top tapering up to a short trumpet neck, decorated w/a large cluster of orange & yellow poppies on a dark brown ground, Standard glaze, No. 671B, 1899 E. Lincoln **450**

Vase, 5 1/2" h., 4" d., wide baluster-form body tapering to a flaring trumpet neck, decorated w/stylized apple blossoms on a pink & ivory butterfat ground, Wax Matte glaze, No. 6148, 1937, Kataro Shirayamadani **1,125**

Rookwood Cherry Blossom Vase

Vase, 5 1/2" h., 5 1/2" d., bulbous footed ovoid body w/a wide, short rolled neck, light pink ground decorated around the shoulder w/a dark grey branch w/pink cherry blossoms, Vellum glaze, 1925, E.T. Hurley (ILLUS.) **862**

Vase, 5 1/2" h., 6" d., widely flaring trumpet-form body, decorated w/white dogwood blossoms & dark blue leaves against a sheer olive ground, purple interior, Black

Opal glaze, No. 2264E, 1925, Kataro Shirayamadani **2,925**

Vase, 5 3/4" h., short trumpet-form w/wide flaring rim, decorated w/cherry blossoms in white & pink under an orange to blue shaded ground w/yellow interior, Vellum glaze, No. 22643, 1925, Lenore Asbury **990**

Vase, 6" h., a gently tapering cylindrical form topped by a short cylindrical neck, the sides lightly molded w/tapering pointed panels resembling overlapping tall leaves, good green & rose Matte glaze, No. 1824, 1912 .... **495**

Vase, 6" h., ovoid body w/wide shoulder tapering to short cylindrical neck, painted stylized papyrus decoration in red, yellow & green on a grey ground, yellow leaf design outlined in blue on shoulder, Matte glaze, No. 1926, 1921, C.S. Todd **2,420**

Vase, 6" h., 3" d., slightly swelled cylindrical body tapering slightly to a flat mouth, decorated w/large pink & white clover blossoms on green arched leafy stems on a shaded creamy yellow to greyish green ground, Iris glaze, No. 951, 1905, Fred Rothenbusch (ILLUS. right, below) ... **1,380**

Vase, 6" h., 4 3/4" d., bulbous nearly spherical body tapering to a short flaring trumpet neck, decorated w/white hydrangea on an opalescent dark blue & green ground, Sea Green glaze, No. 402, 1902, Sara Sax **5,225**

Rookwood Iris Glaze Vases

Vase, 6" h., 5 1/2" d., Jewel Porcelain, wide bulbous body w/narrow rolled rim, decorated w/Art Deco flowers in pink, green & blue, No. 6180, 1930, Sara Sax **2,310**

Vase, 6 1/4" h., tapering ovoid form w/a wide flat mouth, molded around the shoulder w/a band of stylized flowers, Matte Green glaze, No. 2208, 1928 .... **489**

Vase, 6 1/2" h., bulbous ovoid w/closed rim, decorated w/carved & painted white & brown geese feeding at edge of pond, green grass in background shading from grey to yellow to green, Vellum glaze, No. 938D, incised signature & "V," 1907, Edith Noonan **2,420**

Pretty Rookwood Vase with Bayberries

Vase, 6 1/2" h., gently tapering cylindrical form w/a flat rim, decorated w/an elaborate overall design of pink bayberries w/green leaves & brown stems on a pale tan ground, Vellum glaze, No. 2102, 1923, Lorinda Epply (ILLUS.) **4,313**

Vase, 6 1/2" h., tapering cylindrical body w/slightly flared rim, band near bottom decorated w/scene of boats in cobalt blue against a cream sea & sky, cobalt blue Vellum glaze, incised initials, incised "GV," No. 1658F, 1912, Lenore Asbury **1,320**

Vase, 6 1/2" h., 3 1/2" d., simple ovoid form w/molded rim, scenic decoration of a snowy landscape in green, purple & ivory, Vellum glaze, No. 913E, 1918, Elizabeth McDermott **1,100**

Vase, 6 1/2" h., 4 1/2" d., tapering bulbous lower body w/a rounded wide shoulder centered by a tall trumpet neck, decorated w/a cluster of white clover blossoms & green leaves on a shaded dark blue to dark grey ground, Iris glaze, No. 754, 1901, Fred Rothenbusch **1,350**

Vase, 6 1/2" h., 5 1/2" d., bulbous ovoid form tapering to a low rolled mouth, decorated in squeezebag w/an abstract triangle & bar geometric design in dark brown on a coffee-colored ground, No. 6201d, 1931, Jens Jensen **1,069**

Vase, 6 3/4" h., 5 1/2" d., Jewel Porcelain, swelled & flaring cylindrical form w/a wide, flat mouth, decorated w/large stylized ivory magnolia blossoms w/ochre

trim on a teal blue ground, No. 2189, 1944, Jens Jensen **1,463**

Vase, 7" h., bulbous ovoid body tapering very slightly to wide closed rim, overall decoration of bushy green palms & a flock of birds on salmon ground, Vellum glaze, No. 942C, 1906, E.T. Hurley **1,760**

Unusual Matte Glaze Rookwood Vase

Vase, 7" h., bulbous ovoid form tapering to a wide flat rim, painted w/deep orangish red large blossoms on mottled dark green & orange leafy stems against a dark blue & orange ground, Matte glaze, 1902, Harriet Wilcox (ILLUS.) **8,625**

Vase, 7" h., tapering cylindrical body w/flat rim, scene of bluish green fish swimming against a pink shaded to green ground, Iris glaze, No. 1358E, 1911, Lenore Asbury **1,540**

Rookwood Scenic Vellum Vase

Vase, 7" h., wide cylindrical body w/rounded shoulder & short cylindrical neck, landscape scene of tall leafy trees by a lake w/forest in the background, in shades of light & dark green, blue & cream, Vellum glaze, No. 1873, 1922, Fred Rothenbusch (ILLUS.) **1,610**

Vase, 7 1/4" h., 3" d., swelled cylindrical body w/a narrow shoulder tapering to a short rolled neck, decorated w/a continuous marsh landscape in umber & brown surrounded by cobalt blue water, Green Vellum glaze, No. 904E, 1911, Sara Sax .. **5,063**

Vase, 7 1/4" h., 3 1/2" d., gently waisted cylindrical form w/a flat rim, decorated in the Japanese style w/a band of swimming fish around the lower third, shaded from creamy white to medium blue w/dark blue, green & cream fish, Vellum glaze, No. 1358, 1908, E.T. Hurley............. **2,363**

Vase, 7 1/2" h., tapering cylindrical body w/wide flat rim, decorated w/painted & carved mushrooms in peach & white outlined in black against a light lavender ground, Vellum glaze, No. 2066, 1916, impressed "V" & incised unknown artist signature **1,210**

Vase, 7 1/2" h., urn-form, swelled cylindrical lower body below the wide flattened shoulder centered by a wide cylindrical neck w/a wide, flattened rim, molded around the lower body w/a band of large pointed leaves alternating w/stylized blossoms on stems, light brown Matte glaze, No. 2413, 1928.................................... **468**

Vase, 7 1/2" h., 3 1/2" d., gently flaring trumpet-form body on a cushion base, continuous landscape of birch trees & hills in pale blues, green, violet & cream, Vellum glaze, No. 1357E, 1920, Fred Rothenbusch **1,913**

Vase, 7 1/2" h., 3 1/2" d., gently tapering cylindrical form, decorated around the top w/large stylized peacock feathers in blue & greens all on a shaded green & rose ground, Green Vellum glaze, No. 950E, 1910, Sara Sax **2,700**

Vase, 7 1/2" h., 3 3/4" d., slightly swelled cylindrical form w/a tapering shoulder to the molded rim, scenic design of tall slender trees in a misty landscape in shades of grey, blue & purple, Vellum glaze, No. 2001, 1914, C. J. McLaughlin (minor pitting) **935**

Vase, 7 3/4" h., 4 1/2" d., ovoid body tapering to rolled rim, decorated w/purple columbine on shaded blue to pink ground, No. 913D, 1931, Ed Diers (ILLUS. right, with plaque) **2,025**

Standard Glaze Vase with Blossoms

Vase, 8" h., footed ovoid body tapering to a short neck w/a widely flaring flattened rim, decorated w/large poppy-like blossoms on slender stems against a dark brown ground, Standard glaze, 1899, light crazing, signed (ILLUS.) **805**

Orchids on Matte Rookwood Vase

Vase, 8" h., gently swelled cylindrical form w/a tapering shoulder to a low, flattened rolled rim, decorated w/large purple orchids & dark green leaves & stems against a shaded lavender to pink ground, Matte glaze, No. 904D, 1942, Kataro Shirayamadani (ILLUS.) **4,025**

Wisteria Blooms on Rookwood Vase

Vase, 8" h., tall ovoid form w/a rounded shoulder to a short rolled neck, decorated w/large shaded blue wisteria blossoms & green leaves against a dark blue shaded to creamy white ground, Vellum glaze, No. 164E, 1928, E. T. Hurley (ILLUS.) **2,070**

Vase, 8" h., tall slender slightly waisted cylindrical body on four small tab feet, embossed around the lower half w/curling fern fronds, deep rose shaded to dusty

green Matte glaze, No. 1374, 1903, K.
Shirayamadani **495**

Vase, 8" h., 3 1/2" d., cylindrical form w/a
narrow tapering rim band to the wide flat
mouth, decorated w/a continuous landscape w/large leafy trees in the foreground & a lake beyond, in shades of
light & dark blue & green w/cream & pale
yellow, Vellum glaze, No. 952E, 1918, Ed
Diers...... .... **1,800**

Vase, 8" h., 3 1/2" d., tall slender ovoid body
tapering slightly to a short neck & flat rim,
decorated w/a cluster of tall Shasta daisies on green stems against a shaded
dark to light blue ground, Vellum glaze,
No. 901, 1913, M.H. McDonald **1,350**

Vase, 8" h., 4" d., tapering cylindrical form
w/flaring short neck, charcoal ground
decorated around the shoulder w/a wide
band of stylized pink blossoms & green
leaves, Matte glaze, No. 1655E, 1911,
O.G. Reed...................................... **1,463**

Vase, 8 1/4" h, gently flaring cylindrical body
w/flat rim, thickly enameled antelopes &
stylized foliage in white & brown under a
matte yellow Butterfat glaze, No. 6112,
1929, William Hentschel............................ **4,950**

Shirayamadani Vellum Blossom Vase

Vase, 8 1/4" h., 4" d., low flaring foot below
a bulbous flattened lower body below a
tall gently flaring trumpet neck, the upper
body decorated w/large pink cherry blossoms & green leaves on a pink ground
w/violet blue around the lower body & in
the interior, Vellum glaze, 1933, K.
Shirayamadani (ILLUS.) **1,437**

Vase, 8 1/4" h., 4 1/4" d., baluster-form,
decorated in squeezebag w/an overall
design of bands of alternating large dark
greenish brown triangles & blue circles
on a pale blue ground, No. 285, 1928,
William Hentschel **1,913**

Vase. 8 1/4" h., 5 1/2" d., six-paneled ovoid
body tapering to a cylindrical neck
w/flared rim, decorated w/large orange
maple leaves against a dark green shaded to mahogany brown ground, Standard
glaze, No. 850, 1903, Sallie Coyne **675**

Vase, 8 1/2" h., shouldered cylindrical body
tapering slightly to short neck w/molded
rim, decorated w/pink poppies on a shaded grey ground, Vellum glaze, No. 944D,
1907, Elizabeth Lincoln **523**

Vase, 8 1/2" h., 3" d., swelled cylindrical
form tapering to a short cylindrical neck,
decorated w/white arrowhead blossoms
& dark teal blue leaves & grasses on a
shaded pink ground, Vellum glaze, No.
932E, 1921, Kataro Shirayamadani........... **3,375**

Iris Glaze Vase with Rook Decoration

Vase, 8 1/2" h., 3 1/2" d., swelled cylindrical form tapering to a short rolled neck,
painted w/a spread-winged black rook
perched on a pine bough w/a full moon
beyond, in black, green, white & shaded
dark to light blue, Iris glaze, No. 904,
1908, Clara C. Lindeman (ILLUS.) **8,625**

Vase, 8 1/2" h., 4" d., gently swelled cylindrical body w/a short tapering neck w/a
rolled rim, decorated w/large white Shasta daisies w/yellow centers on tall dark
green leafy stems against a shaded pale
blue to cream to pink ground, Vellum
glaze, No. 614E, 1912, Elizabeth Lincoln.. **1,350**

Vase, 8 1/2" h., 4 1/2" d., ovoid body tapering to a short cylindrical neck, decorated
w/long stems of yellow & orange roses
against a very dark blue shaded to grey
ground, Iris glaze, No. 926C, 1903, Ed
Diers **2,138**

Vase, 8 3/4" h., 4" d., cylindrical w/incurved
rim, decorated w/a wide upper band
painted w/pale purple irises & green
leaves & stems on an ivory ground, lavender background, Iris glaze, No. 952,
1909, Lenore Asbury...................................... **1,980**

Vase, 8 3/4" h., 4 1/2" d., simple ovoid form
w/a rounded shoulder centered by a
short rolled neck, decorated w/a continuous sunset landscape scene w/tall birch
trees in the foreground by a lake, in
shades of dark blue, light blue, green &
grey, Vellum glaze, No. 614, 1914 C.J.
McLaughlin **2,363**

Vase, 8 3/4" h., 5" d., a short molded neck
on a bulbous deep shoulder tapering to a

cylindrical lower body, decorated w/large stems of purple thistles on a shaded pale yellow to grey ground, Iris glaze, No. 909C, 1906, Sara Sax.................................. **2,025**

Rookwood Vase with Landscape Band

Vase, 9" h., footed tapering cylindrical form w/a short angled shoulder & flat mouth, decorated around the upper body w/a wide winter landscape scene in white, grey, pink & dark blackish brown, on a dark moss green ground, Vellum glaze, 1912, Shirayamadani (ILLUS.).................... **2,415**

Vase, 9" h., footed trumpet-form w/handles at base, decorated w/molded design of two ladies & stars, glossy grey glaze, No. 6539, 1935.. **385**

Rookwood Animal Portrait Vase

Vase, 9" h., footed urn-form body w/narrow shoulder tapering to cylindrical neck w/wide flaring rim, decorated w/animal portrait of a growling leopard, Standard glaze, No. 410, 1893, overall crazing, Bruce Horsfall (ILLUS.).............................. **4,888**

Flower Band on Jewel Porcelain Vase

Vase, 9" h., Jewel Porcelain, bulbous lower body below tall tapering sides w/a rolled rim, painted around the upper body w/a wide band of stylized flowers in rose, blue & green on a yellow ground, lower body in dark greyish blue, turquoise interior, No. 975BT, 1918, Sara Sax (ILLUS.).. **4,313**

Rare Black Iris Vase

Vase, 9" h., slender ovoid body tapering to a short wide slightly rolled neck, decorated w/broad purple & pink irises w/yellow beards on green to blue stems w/green to blue leaves surrounding vase, two unopened buds in purple & yellow on a ground shading from peach, purple & light green to black, Black Iris glaze, No. 907E, 1907, Constance Baker (ILLUS.) **7,700**

Vase, 9" h., slender ovoid form decorated w/large red & white lotus blossoms w/yellow centers, brown stems & leaves on a shaded yellow ground, Wax Matte glaze, No. 951D, 1941, K. Shirayamadani............ **2,640**

Vase, 9" h., 4 1/2" d., baluster-form w/a swelled shoulder below the short cylindrical neck, decorated w/large white hydrangea & green leafy stems against a dark green to light grey shaded ground,

Iris glaze, No. 909C, 1902, Fred Rothen-busch (ILLUS. left with clover-decorated vase) **2,185**

Vase, 9" h., 5" d., tapering cylindrical body w/a narrow angled shoulder centering a short, wide cylindrical neck, decorated around the shoulder w/a band of stylized white cherry blossoms against a midnight blue ground, Vellum glaze, No. 918V, 1915, C.J. McLaughlin **1,688**

Vase, 9 1/8" h., tapered oviform w/raised rim, decorated w/a large iris blossom in dark blue & olive green on a mustard yellow & brown ground, Standard glaze, No. 94 DO, 1903, Sallie E. Coyne (crazing) **518**

Vase, 9 1/4" h., gently tapering cylindrical body w/flat rim, decorated w/green branches on a brown ground, Carved Matte glaze, No. 950C, 1905, Sallie Toohey **1,430**

Vase, 9 1/4" h., 3 3/4" d., tall slightly swelled cylindrical body tapering slightly to a short cylindrical neck, decorated w/large pale purple irises & dark green leaves & stems on a dark grey to white ground, Iris glaze, No. 907C, 1906, Sara Sax **4,125**

Vase, 9 1/2" h., 3 1/2" d., slender very slightly swelled cylindrical form w/a tapering shoulder & short cylindrical neck, decorated w/tall stems of white, grey & green Queen Anne's Lace on a shaded dark blue to white ground, Iris glaze, No. 941G, 1906, Sara Sax **2,700**

Vase, 9 1/2" h., 3 3/4" d., short wide ovoid body w/wide flat rim, decorated around the rim & down the sides w/three large cicada on twigs in blue, cream & tan on a pale blue ground, Carved Vellum glaze, No. 942D, 1905, Ed Diers **4,781**

Vase, 9 1/2" h., 4 3/4" d., Jewel Porcelain, swelled cylindrical body w/a thick molded rim, decorated w/stylized reclining nudes in ivory on a flowing brown & cobalt blue ground, No. 1121C, 1931, Jens Jensen **6,600**

Iris Glaze Vase with Poppies

Vase, 9 1/2" h., 5 1/4" d., large ovoid body tapering to a short cylindrical neck w/flared rim, decorated w/large white poppies on green stems against a shaded dark to light grey ground, Iris glaze, No. 849, 1903, Fred Rothenbusch (ILLUS.) **2,415**

Vase, 9 1/2" h., 6 1/4" d., Jewel Porcelain, bulbous ovoid body tapering to a wide narrow molded rim, decorated w/large pink & blue magnolia blossoms on a brown ground, drilled base, No. 5184, date obscured, K. Shirayamadani **2,310**

Vase, 9 3/4" h., 3 3/4 d., tall slightly swelled cyllindrical body tapering slightly to a short rolled rim, decorated w/large orange poppies & green leaves against a dark brown shaded to tan ground, Standard glaze, No. 904CC, 1903, Mary Nourse **1,125**

Vase, 9 3/4" h., 6" d., Jewel Porcelain, bulbous ovoid body w/a wide narrow molded rim, decorated w/a stylized bison in brown, black & bone, No. 6184C, 1944, Jens Jensen **2,860**

Vase, 10" h., 3 3/4" d., tall slender swelled cylindrical form tapering to a short cylindrical neck, decorated w/a pastel hillside landscape w/water & trees in background, in shades of light & dark green, dark blue, light blue & cream, No. 932D, 1917, Sallie Coyne (very small flat base nick) **1,575**

Vase, 10" h., 4 1/2" d., tall slightly swelled cylindrical form w/a short flared rim, continuous Venetian harbor scene in dark blue, pale green & lavender against a shaded blue to cream to blue ground, Vellum glaze, No. 1121C, 1925, Carl Schmidt **7,313**

Vase, 10" h., 4 3/4" d., tall ovoid form tapering to a short cylindrical neck w/flat rim, decorated w/a continuous landscape of large trees & bushes around a pond, in shades of dark & light blue, green, pale yellow & cream, Vellum glaze, No. 940D, 1921, E.T. Hurley **3,375**

Vase, 10" h., 6 1/2" d., footed bulbous ovoid body w/a rounded shoulder tapering to a short rolled neck, finely painted w/goldenrod on leafy green stalks against a shaded grey ground, Iris glaze, No. 814A, 1902, Rose Fescheimer **4,400**

Vase, 10" h., 9" d., large bulbous ovoid body w/a wide rounded shoulder centered by a short neck w/a widely flaring, flattened rim, decorated around the upper half w/large leafy branches of peaches on a shaded tan to dark green ground, Standard glaze, No. 488F, 1890, Matt Daly **1,800**

Vase, 10 1/4" h., 5 3/4" d., simple tall ovoid form w/short flared rim, decorated w/an autumnal landscape w/elm trees in yellow, brown & polychrome against cream & blue, Wax Matte glaze, No. 892C, 1938, Mary Helen McDonald **3,850**

Vase, 10 1/4" h., 7 1/4" d., simple ovoid form w/flat rim, decorated w/a continuous meadow landscape w/oak trees, green, blue & grey against cream ground, Vellum glaze, No. 604C, Ed Diers (ILLUS. left, with plaque) **4,219**

Jewel Glaze Vase in Shades of Pink

Vase, 10 1/2" h., 4" d., Jewel Porcelain, slightly swelled cylindrical form, a Japanese style scene of cherry blossoms & flying birds in shades of blue & pink under a glossy pink glaze, No. 951, 1922, Lorinda Epply (ILLUS.) **2,070**

Vase, 10 1/2" h., 4" d., tapering cylindrical body decorated w/purple lilacs against a grey to ivory ground, Iris glaze, No. S1771, 1904, Ed Diers (restoration to top) **550**

Vase, 10 1/2" h., 4 1/2" d., baluster-form, decorated w/a continuous lakeside landscape w/trees at sunset, in shades of dark blue, violet, green, pale yellow & cream, No. 1667, 1909, E.T. Hurley (small restoration at rim) **900**

Vase, 10 1/2" h., 5" d., simple ovoid form, decorated w/large stylized mushrooms in shades of blue, grey & tan against a shaded white to grey ground, Vellum glaze, No. 939B, 1905, Carl Schmidt **12,375**

Vase, 10 1/2" h., 5 1/2" d., gently swelled cylindrical form w/a short rolled rim, decorated w/a continuous landscape w/birch trees around a lake, in shades of pale blue, dark blue, greens, purples & cream, Vellum glaze, ungrazed, No. 892B, 1931, Ed Diers... **5,063**

Vase, 10 3/4" h., 5" d., tall ovoid body tapering to a short rolled neck, decorated w/large stylized pink waterlilies w/yellow centers & pale green stems & leaves on a butter yellow & blue butterfat ground, Wax Matte glaze, No. 614D, 1930, Sallie Coyne **2,250**

Vase, 11 3/4" h., 6 1/2" d., footed ovoid body tapering gently to a flaring neck, decorated w/large fleshy magnolias in lavender & white on a pale purple to blue ground, Vellum glaze, No. 827, 1927, Lenore Asbury **6,050**

Fine Rookwood Jewel Porcelain Vase

Vase, 12" h., 5" d., Jewel Porcelain, footed baluster-form w/a wide short cylindrical neck w/rolled rim, decorated in the Chinese style w/four panels of stylized flying bluebirds above tall stems of hollyhocks in blues & greens on an ivory butterfat ground, No. 2933, 1929, Lorinda Epply (ILLUS.).. **4,025**

Vase, 12" h., 12" d., large bulbous ovoid body w/a short, wide cylindrical neck, decorated w/large clusters of hydrangea on a shaded gold to dark green ground, Standard glaze, No. 531D, 1891, A.R. Valentien (lightly crazed, restored drill hole in base)... **3,150**

Vase, 12 1/4" h., 5" d., tall slightly tapering cylindrical form w/flat rim, dark violet ground decorated around the top w/a wide pale orange band painted w/ochre dogwood blossoms on violet stems, Matte glaze, No. 950B, 1906, H. Wilcox.... **4,219**

Rookwood Matte Dandelion Vase

Vase, 12 1/4" h., 5" d., gently flaring cylindrical form w/a shoulder & short tapering cylindrical neck, lightly carved decoration of upright dandelion leaves alternating w/white blossom heads, streaky dark grey to light green Matte glaze, No. 946, 1905, Rose Fescheimer (ILLUS.) **1,495**

Vase, 12 1/2" h., 5 1/2" d., slender swelled cylindrical form, decorated w/a continuous sunset landscape w/large tall dark trees in the foreground, in shades of dark blue, black & pale peach pink, Vellum glaze, No. 2032C, 1920, Sara Sax **13,500**

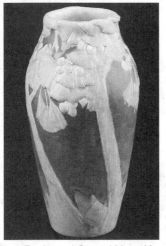

Rare Rookwood Carved Matte Vase

Vase, 12 1/2" h., 6" d., ovoid body tapering to a flat molded mouth, decorated w/crisply tooled gingko leaves & nuts in green on a brown ground, Matte glaze, No. 925B, 1901, tight 4" firing line in body, Kataro Shirayamadani (ILLUS.) **25,875**

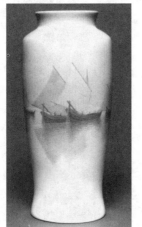

Rookwood Harbor Scene by Schmidt

Vase, 13" h., gently swelling cylindrical form w/an angled shoulder to a short, slightly flared neck, decorated w/a Venetian har-

bor scene, Glossy glaze, Carl Schmidt (ILLUS.) **13,200**

Vase, 13" h., 3" d., tall slender footed baluster-form w/a very slender trumpet neck, decorated w/a scene of a mother & young child playing amid waves on a beach, bisque finish w/Aerial Blue glaze, No. 242D, 1895, William McDonald.......... **12,375**

Vase, 13" h., 5" d., tall slender ovoid body tapering to a small trumpet neck, decorated w/a large cluster of blue irises on green leafy stems against a dark brown to amber ground, Standard glaze, No. 702A, 1898, A.R. Valentien (fine overall crazing).. **1,463**

Unusual Standard Glaze Vase

Vase, 14" h., a low stepped round foot supporting a tall slender trumpet body w/two long loop handles down one side, decorated w/yellow dogwood blossoms on branches down the sides against a shaded yellow, green, umbre & orange ground, Standard glaze, 1889, K. Shirayamadani (ILLUS.) **2,185**

Tall Scenic Vellum Vase with Trees

Vase, 14" h., baluster-form w/angled shoulder to a short rolled neck, painted w/a landscape w/a large leafy tree across a stream w/hills & mountains in the distance on one side & the stream leading to meadows w/trees on the other, Vellum glaze, No. 2251, 1926, Frred Rothenbusch (ILLUS.) **10,350**

Rookwood Vase with Swans

Vase, 14" h., tall slender gently swelled cylindrical form tapering to a short cylindrical neck, decorated w/a scene of a flock of white swans swimming on shaded blue water, Vellum glaze, 1915, Carl Schmidt (ILLUS.) **22,000**

Vase, 14" h., 5" d., tall slender very slightly swelled cylindrical form tapering to a short cylindrical neck, decorated around the shoulder w/large orange poppies on pale green leafy stems against a dark brown to green to light orange ground, Standard glaze, No. 907C, 1900, Mary Nourse **2,588**

Vase, 14" h., 5 1/2" d., tall slightly tapering swelled cylindrical form w/a flat rim, large abstract blue blossoms & green leaves on a mottled turquoise ground, Wax Matte glaze., No. 2441, 1925, Katherine Jones **1,688**

Fine Iris Glaze Vase with Irises

Vase, 14 1/2" h., tall slender ovoid form tapering to a flat rim w/a chased silver overlay narrow band, decorated w/large shaded blue irises on green leafy stems against a shaded blue to dark green ground, Iris glaze, No. 879C, 1904, Albert Valentien (ILLUS.)........................... **12,650**

Large Iris Glaze Vase with Mountains

Vase, 14 3/4" h., 7 1/2" d., slightly tapering cylindrical form w/a slightly indented wide flat rim, decorated w/a bold mountainous landscape w/ice-blue mountains & light & dark green fir trees in the foreground, shaded moss green to dark gold sky, Iris glaze, No. 1369B, 1911, Ed Diers, light overall crazing (ILLUS.)............................. **18,400**

Vase, 15" h., 7 1/2" d., gently flaring cylindrical form w/a wide flat rim, boldly decorated w/stylized blue iris & green leaves on a pink ground, Wax Matte glaze, No. 1369, 1925, Sallie Coyne............................. **3,575**

Vase, 16" h., 6 1/2" d., tall slightly tapering cylindrical form w/a thin flared rim, continuous misty landscape of birch trees around a lake at dusk in shades of pale cream, grey, blue & green, Vellum glaze, No. 1660A, 1912, E.T. Hurley..................... **7,313**

Standard Glaze Vase with Daylilies

Vase, 24 1/2" h., tall tapering cylindrical form, streak effect decoration of finely detailed daylilies & leaves, Standard glaze, No. 865, 1889, crazing, glaze bursts, firing cracks to base & body, Albert R. Valentien (ILLUS.) **1,725**

Vase, 26" h., 11" d., floor-type, tall ovoid body tapering to a flaring trumpet neck, a wide embossed stylized geometric band in yellow around the neck, overall frothy Matte green glaze, No. 306, 1916.............. **3,575**

Wall pocket, conical w/flared & scalloped rim, two loop handles near rim, blue Matte glaze, No. 2965, 1928, 6" h. **330**

Rookwood Cicada Wall Pocket

Wall pocket, model of a cicada, green Matte glaze, No. 1636, 1908, short glazed-over firing line, 4 1/2 x 9" (ILLUS.)... **3,080**

Wall sconce, rectangular plaque-form deeply embossed w/a pair of owls under a green & brown Matte glaze, candle socket at the bottom edge, No. 1688, 1910, 6 x 11 1/4" (minor restoration to candleholder & sides) **660**

Water jug, Turkish style, bulbous ovoid body tapering to closed flat mouth w/overhead loop handle, tapering cylindrical spout on one end w/short flaring cylindrical filling spout on the other, die impressed design at top, shoulder & base covered in gold w/gold trim on spouts & handle, body decorated w/two painted butterflies in tones of brown above black reeds & grasses on matte finish ground of cream & shaded blue, No. 41, 1886, Matt Daly, 9 1/2" h. **1,210**

Roseville

Roseville Mark

Roseville Pottery Company operated in Zanesville, Ohio, from 1898 to 1954 after having been in business for six years prior to that in Muskingum County, Ohio. Art wares similar to those of Owens and Weller Potteries were produced. Items listed here are by patterns or lines.

Apple Blossom (1948)
White apple blossoms in relief on blue, green or pink ground; brown tree branch handles.

Basket, hanging-type, blue ground, 8" **$190**
Basket, hanging-type, green ground, 8".......... **220**
Basket, hanging-type, pink ground, 8" **245**
Basket w/low overhead handle, blue ground, No. 310-10", 10" h. **280-285**
Basket w/low overhead handle, green ground, No. 310-10", 10" h. **300-350**

Apple Blossom Basket

Basket w/overhead handle, blue ground, No. 309-8", 8" h. (ILLUS.) **315**
Basket w/overhead handle, green ground, No. 309-8", 8" h. **150-200**
Basket w/overhead handle, pink ground, No. 309-8", 8" h. **140**
Book ends, green ground, No. 359, pr. **198**
Book ends, pink ground, No. 359, pr. **260**
Bowl, 6 1/2" d., 2 1/2" h., flat handles, green ground, No. 326-6"............................... **145**
Bowl, 8" d., blue ground, No. 328-8" **125**
Bowl, 8" d., green ground, No. 328-8"............... **83**
Candlesticks, pink ground, No. 351-2", 2" h., pr... **117**
Candlesticks, blue ground, No. 352-4 1/2", 4 1/2" h., pr. **350**
Console bowl, pink ground, No. 330-10", 10" l. **195**
Console bowl, blue ground, No. 331-12", 12" l. **158**
Console bowl, pink ground, No. 331-12", 12" l... **175**
Console bowl, green ground, No. 333-14", 14" l. **175-200**
Console bowl, pink ground, No. 333-14", 14" l... **175**
Console set, 8" l. bowl & pair of 2" h. candleholders, pink ground, No. 328-8" & No. 351-2", 3 pcs.. **500**
Cornucopia-vase, blue ground, No. 321-6", 6" h... **60**
Cornucopia-vase, green ground, No. 321-6", 6 " h.. **68**
Cornucopia-vase, pink ground, No. 321-6", 6 " h... **120**
Cornucopia-vase, blue ground, No. 323-8", 8" h. **150-175**

Cornucopia-vases, blue ground, No. 321-
6", 6 " h., pr. **165**
Cornucopia-vases, green ground, No.
321-6", 6 " h., pr. **280**
Ewer, ovoid, pink ground, No. 316-8", 8" h. **143**
Flowerpot & saucer, pink ground, No. 356-
5", 2 pcs. **170**
Jardiniere, blue ground, No. 300-4", 4" h. **130**
Jardiniere, green ground, No. 300-4", 4" h. **135**
Jardiniere, pink ground, No. 300-4", 4" h. **135**
Jardiniere, pink ground, No. 301-6", 6" h. **225**
Jardiniere & pedestal base, blue ground,
jardiniere, No. 302-8",8" h., pedestal, No.
305-8", 2 pcs. **880**
Jardiniere & pedestal base, pink ground,
No. 303-10", overall 31" h., 2 pcs. **1,250**
Tea set: cov. teapot, creamer & sugar bowl,
blue ground, No. 371-P, the set **440**
Tea set: cov. teapot, creamer & sugar bowl,
pink ground, No. 371-P, the set **303**
Teapot, cov., blue ground, No. 371-P **295**
Teapot, cov., pink ground, No. 371-P **260**
Vase, bud, 7" h., base handles, flaring rim,
pink ground, No. 379-7" **99**
Vase, 6" h., two-handled, squatty base, long
cylindrical neck, green ground, No. 381-
6" **70**
Vase, 6" h., two-handled, squatty base, long
cylindrical neck, pink ground, No. 381-6" **155**
Vase, 7" h., asymmetrical rim & handles,
blue ground, No. 373-7" **225**

Apple Blossom Vase

Vase, 7" h., asymmetrical rim & handles,
green ground, No. 373-7" (ILLUS.) **135**
Vase, 7" h., asymmetrical rim & handles,
pink ground, No. 373-7" **195**
Vase, bud, 7" h., base handles, flaring rim,
green ground, No. 379-7" **88**
Vase, 7" h., flaring foot w/tapering cylindri-
cal body, asymmetrical rim & handles,
pink ground, No. 382-7" **90-100**
Vase, 7" h., flaring foot w/tapering cylindrical body, asymmetrical rim & handles,
blue ground, No. 382-7" **130**
Vase, 8 1/4" h., flaring foot w/ovoid body &
wide flaring rim, pointed handles from
shoulder to middle of neck, green
ground, No. 385-8" **185**
Vase, 8 1/4" h., flaring foot w/ovoid body &
wide flaring rim, pointed handles from
shoulder to middle of neck, blue ground,
No. 385-8" **150-175**
Vase, 8 1/4" h., flaring foot w/ovoid body &
wide flaring rim, pointed handles from

shoulder to middle of neck, pink ground,
No. 385-8" **185**
Vase, 9 1/2" h., 5" d., asymmetrical han-
dles, cylindrical w/disc base, green
ground, No. 387-9" **213**
Vase, 10" h., wide flaring foot w/base han-
dles, trumpet-form body, blue ground,
No. 388-10" **275**
Vase, 10" h., wide flaring foot w/base han-
dles, trumpet-form body, green ground,
No. 388-10" **297**
Vase, 10" h., wide flaring foot w/base han-
dles, trumpet-form body, pink ground,
No. 388-10" **306**
Vase, 10" h., swelled cylindrical body
w/shaped rim, base handles, blue
ground, No. 389-10" **350**
Vase, 10" h., swelled cylindrical body
w/shaped rim, base handles, green
ground, No. 389-10" **187**
Vase, 10" h., swelled cylindrical body
w/shaped rim, base handles, pink
ground, No. 389-10" **185**

Apple Blossom Vase

Vase, 12 1/2" h., base handles, pink
ground, No. 390-12" (ILLUS.) **295**
Vase, 15" h., floor-type, double base handles, short globular base, long cylindrical
neck, green ground, No. 392-15" **445**
Vase, 15" h., floor-type, double base handles, short globular base, long cylindrical
neck, pink ground, No. 392-15" **512**

Apple Blossom Floor Vase

Vase, 15" h., floor-type, double base handles, short globular base, long cylindrical
neck, blue ground, No. 392-15" (ILLUS.) **776**

Vase, 18" h., floor-type, slender ovoid body w/wide cylindrical neck, blue ground, No. 393-18" (two chips & one bruise to base, hairline to rim) **358**

Vases, 6" h., two-handled, squatty base, long cylindrical neck, blue ground, No. 381-6" **200**

Apple Blossom Wall Pocket

Wall pocket, conical w/overhead handle, blue ground, No. 366-8", 8" h. (ILLUS.) **288**

Wall pocket, conical w/overhead handle, brown ground, No. 366-8", 8" h. **190**

Wall pocket, conical w/overhead handle, green ground, No. 366-8", 8" h. **200-225**

Window box, end handles, blue ground, No. 368-8", 2 1/2 x 10 1/2" **153**

Window box, end handles, pink ground, No. 368-8", 2 1/2 x 10 1/2" **50**

Window box, rectangular, blue ground, No. 369-12", 12" l. **180**

Window box, rectangular, green ground, No. 369-12", 12" l. **160**

Aztec (1915)

Muted earthy tones of beige, grey, brown, teal, olive, azure blue or soft white with slip-trailed geometric decoration in contrasting colors.

Aztec Pitcher

Pitcher, 5" h., footed w/round curved sides tapering to wide flaring rim, grey & white design on blue ground (ILLUS.) **193**

Vase, 6 3/8" h., tapering cylindrical body w/bulbous top, slip decoration of stylized mushrooms in white & orange w/blue ribbon bands above & below, on a bluish grey ground, artist-initialed "E" & old oval paper la (base & rim chips) **138**

Vase, 8" h., tapering cylinder swelling slightly at top, squeezebag decoration of lacy

loops & swags in white & yellow against a blue ground, artist-initialed **495**

Vase, 8" h., tapering cylinder swelling slightly at top, squeezebag decoration of white trillium on orange stems against a blue/grey ground, unmarked (lentil-size chip to base & 1" hairline to rim) **523**

Aztec Vase

Vase, 10" h., flared foot w/expanding cylindrical body & flared rim, white & tan decoration against a blue ground, artist-signed (ILLUS.) **248**

Baneda (1933)

Band of embossed pods, blossoms and leaves on green or raspberry pink ground.

Bowl, 6" d., raspberry pink ground, No. 232-6" **385**

Candleholders, raspberry pink ground, No. 1088-4", 4 1/2" h., pr. **575**

Candlesticks, raspberry pink ground, No. 1087-5", 5" h., pr. **750**

Console bowl, raspberry pink ground, No. 233-8", 10" l. **395**

Console bowl, six-sided, w/handles from base to rim, green ground, No. 234-10", 11" l. **523**

Jardiniere, two-handled, green ground, 4" h., No. 626-4" **385**

Jardiniere, two-handled, green ground, No. 626-7", 7" h. **413**

Jardiniere, two-handled, green ground, No. 626-7", 7" h. **1,540**

Jardiniere, two-handled, raspberry pink ground, No. 626-10", 10" h. **1,800**

Jardiniere & pedestal base, raspberry pink ground, No. 626-8", 8" h., 2 pcs. **1,870**

Jardiniere & pedestal base, green ground, No. 626-10", jardiniere marked "1 spot" & "9," pedestal unmarked, overall 28" h., 2 pcs. (two tight, short lines at rim of jardiniere) **4,290**

Urn, small rim handles, bulbous, green ground, No. 235-5", 5" h. **517**

Urn, small rim handles, footed bulbous body w/flat rim, raspberry pink ground, No. 606-7", 7" h. **770**

Various Baneda Vases

Vase, 4" h., footed bulbous body w/incurved flat rim, flat shoulder handles, raspberry pink ground, No. 587-4" **220**

Vase, 4" h., footed bulbous body w/incurved flat rim, flat shoulder handles, green ground, No. 587-4" **368**

Vase, 4" h., footed, wide squatty bulbous base tapering sharply to small molded mouth, tiny rim handles, raspberry pink ground, No. 603-4" (ILLUS. lower left, above).. **495**

Vase, 5" h., footed, pear-shaped w/small loop handles near rim, green ground, No. 601-5" **422**

Vase, 5" h., footed, pear-shaped w/small loop handles near rim, raspberry pink ground, No. 601-5" **400**

Vase, 6" h., two-handled, footed, bulbous base w/wide cylindrical neck, raspberry pink ground, No. 589-6" (ILLUS. bottom right, with group below) **427**

Vase, 6" h., two-handled, footed, bulbous base w/wide cylindrical neck, green ground, No. 589-6" **605**

Vase, 6" h., bulbous body w/short slightly flaring rim, small loop shoulder handles, raspberry pink ground, No. 591-6" (ILLUS. bottom left with group below) **550**

Vase, 6" h., bulbous body w/slightly flaring rim, small loop shoulder handles, green ground, No. 591-6" (ILLUS. top row, far right with group below).................................... **660**

Group of Roseville Baneda Vases

Fig. 1

Fig. 1 From left: A pair of Cowan Chinese-style pillow-form vases each with a reclining molded phoenix bird at the base, 11¼" h., pr. $1,350

A bulbous ovoid Cowan vase decorated with small stylized fish, seaweed & bubbles in sgraffito, 6¼" h. $1,069

Cowan "Colonial Head" bust with an overall peach crackled glaze; designed by Waylande Gregory, 14" h. $3,656

Fig. 2 Miniature Arequipa vase decorated in squeezebag with a band of holly leaves & red berries on a mottled greenish-blue ground, 3½" h. $6,325

Fig. 3 This Dedham-marked vase features an experimental lustered oxblood glaze by Hugh Robertson, 7½" h. $4,313

Fig. 4 A Chelsea Keramics Art Works pilgrim flask-form covered jar molded on the oval sides with scenes of a girl feeding geese, 10½" w., 9¼" h. $1,840

Fig. 5 The Chelsea Keramic Art Works pilgrim flask-form vase features a decoration of incised pine boughs & flowers by George Ferrety, 7½" h. $1,495

All courtesy of David Rago Auctions, Lambertville, NJ.

Fig. 2

Fig. 3

Fig. 4

Fig. 5

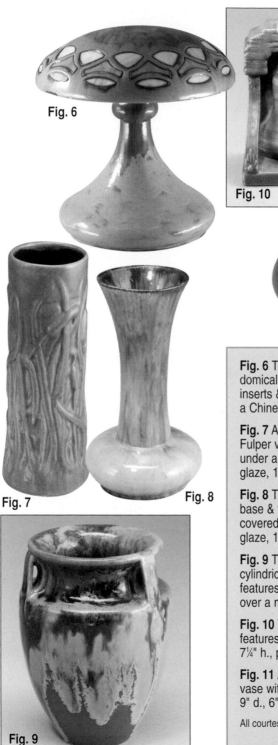

Fig. 6

Fig. 10

Fig. 11

Fig. 7

Fig. 8

Fig. 9

Fig. 6 This Fulper table lamp features a domical pottery shade with slag glass inserts & a matching pottery base all with a Chinese blue flambé glaze, 18" h. . . $10,350

Fig. 7 A tall slightly waisted cylindrical Fulper vase with molded tall cattails under a Cucumber Matte crystalline glaze, 13" h. $5,750

Fig. 8 This Fulper vase features a low bulbous base & tall trumpet neck and is covered in a Cat's-Eye blue flambé glaze, 13" h. $1,955

Fig. 9 This Fulper vase with a swelled cylindrical body & short buttress handles features a lustered frothy turquoise glaze over a matte blue ground, 4½" d., 7" h. . . . $978

Fig. 10 This pair of Fulper book ends features a model of the Liberty Bell, 7¼" h., pr. $690

Fig. 11 A wide squatty bulbous Fulper vase with a frothy Wisteria Matte glaze, 9" d., 6" h. $863

All courtesy of David Rago Auctions, Lambertville, NJ.

Fig. 12

Fig. 13

Fig. 14

Fig. 15

Fig. 16

Fig. 17

Fig. 12 Two Hampshire Pottery vases.
Left: This vase has a bulbous base tapering to a tall cylindrical neck flanked by long angled & pierced handles all highlighted by geometric bands & a green matte glaze, 15" h. . . $2,070
Right: This vase features an ovoid body decorated with broad overlapping & slightly swirled leaves under an unusual blue & green suspended matte glaze, 8" h. . . . $1,495
Courtesy of Treadway Gallery, Cincinnati, OH.

Fig. 13 This Grueby bowl-shaped vase features a tooled & applied decoration of papyrus under a fine oatmealed matte green glaze & was done by Wilhelmina Post, 10" d., 5" h. $10,925

Fig. 14 This tall gently-waisted cylindrical Grueby vase features tall rounded leaves alternating with stems & yellow blossoms & an overall frothy matte green glaze, 9½" h. $6,900

Fig. 15 A Grueby wall pocket with a bulbous pointed form decorated with broad ribbed leaves under a leathery matte green glaze, 5¾" w., 7" h. $1,840

Fig. 16 This small Grueby vase with a squatty bulbous body features tooled & applied wide arched & pointed leaves around the lower body with stems & yellow blossoms around the top, 5½" d., 5" h. $12,650

Fig. 17 A square Grueby tile decorated in cuenca with a turtle in shades of brown & ivory below a green bough of leaves on an ochre matte ground, 6" w. $7,450
All courtesy of David Rago Auctions, Lambertville, NJ.

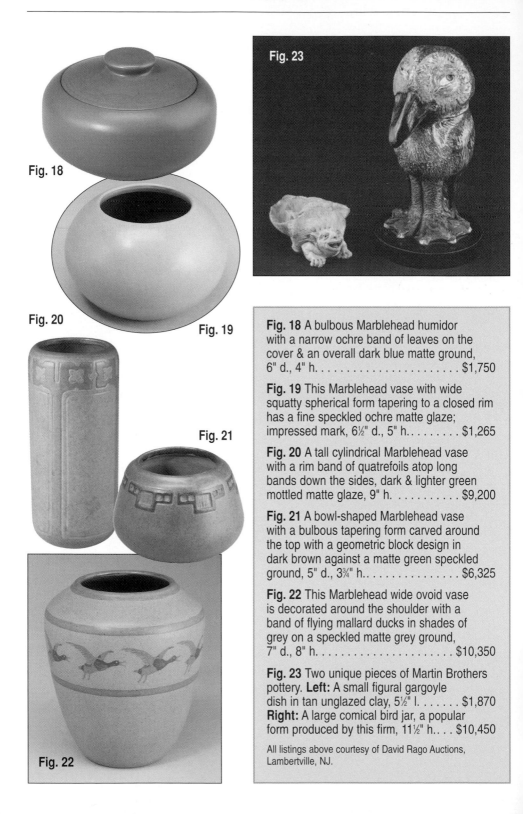

Fig. 23

Fig. 18

Fig. 20

Fig. 19

Fig. 21

Fig. 22

Fig. 18 A bulbous Marblehead humidor with a narrow ochre band of leaves on the cover & an overall dark blue matte ground, 6" d., 4" h. $1,750

Fig. 19 This Marblehead vase with wide squatty spherical form tapering to a closed rim has a fine speckled ochre matte glaze; impressed mark, 6½" d., 5" h. $1,265

Fig. 20 A tall cylindrical Marblehead vase with a rim band of quatrefoils atop long bands down the sides, dark & lighter green mottled matte glaze, 9" h. $9,200

Fig. 21 A bowl-shaped Marblehead vase with a bulbous tapering form carved around the top with a geometric block design in dark brown against a matte green speckled ground, 5" d., 3¾" h. $6,325

Fig. 22 This Marblehead wide ovoid vase is decorated around the shoulder with a band of flying mallard ducks in shades of grey on a speckled matte grey ground, 7" d., 8" h. $10,350

Fig. 23 Two unique pieces of Martin Brothers pottery. **Left:** A small figural gargoyle dish in tan unglazed clay, 5½" l. . . . . . . $1,870 **Right:** A large comical bird jar, a popular form produced by this firm, 11½" h. $10,450

All listings above courtesy of David Rago Auctions, Lambertville, NJ.

Fig. 24

Fig. 25

Fig. 26

Fig. 24 This baluster-form Moorcroft vase in the Eventide pattern features a reddish orange & green flambé glaze, 6½" h.. . . . $220

Fig. 25 This unusual Newcomb College handled vase features a design of large white egrets among sea grass & pre-dates 1902. Even with restoration to one handle is sold for. $25,875

Fig. 26 A Moorcroft tea set in the Pomegranate pattern: teapot, open sugar & creamer, teapot 8" h., the set with some slight damages $2,860

All courtesy of David Rago Auctions, Lambertville, NJ.

Fig. 27 A tall slender cylindrical Newcomb College vase with a finely-carved continuous band of tall cypress & pine trees by Leona Nicholson, 1907, 4½" d., 11¼" h.. . . . . $8,625

Fig. 28 A truly exceptional Newcomb College tall vase carved overall with tall blue & yellow irises under a glossy glaze. The decorator was Henrietta Bailey in 1909, 9" d., 14½" h. $46,000

Fig. 29 A tall slender ovoid Newcomb College vase with live oaks draped with Spanish moss under a full moon was decorated by Anna Frances Simpson in 1929, 6" d., 11" h.. . . . . $17,250

All courtesy of David Rago Auctions, Lambertville, NJ.

Fig. 30 A tall ovoid Niloak Mission Ware vase with an unusual design of incised squiggles, 8¼" h. $1,150

Courtesy of Treadway Gallery, Cincinnati, OH.

Fig. 27

Fig. 28

Fig. 29

Fig. 30

Fig. 31

Fig. 33

Fig. 34

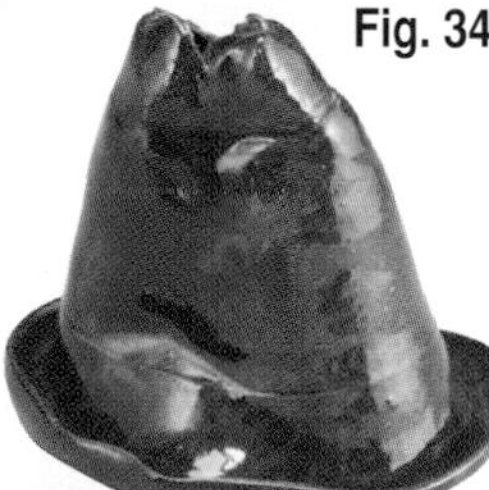

Fig. 32

Fig. 36

Fig. 35

Fig. 37

Fig. 31 A group of Niloak Mission Ware.
From left: Bowl, 6¾" d. $173
Cylindrical vase, 6" h. $403
Miniature vase, 3½" h. $150
A boldly patterned vase, 11" h. $500
Puff box, 4" h. $575
Niloak vase, 5" h. $265
A miniature Niloak vase with some
minute flakes $242
Courtesy of Treadway Gallery, Cincinnati, OH.

Fig. 32 This tall ovoid Owens vase
features tall iris blossoms & stems
on a black background, 11" h. $1,380
Courtesy of Treadway Gallery, Cincinnati, OH.

Fig. 33 An unusual North Dakota School
of Mines covered box with a Native
American chief portrait on the cover was
done by Margaret Cable $690

Fig. 34 A unique George Ohr pottery
model of a hat with a red, green &
blue glossy glaze, 4" h. $4,313

Fig. 35 The Ohr boat-shaped pitcher
with an umber glaze speckled with
gunmetal is 6" l., 3" h. $2,185

Fig. 36 This George Ohr vase in a
typical contorted form is 4½" w. & 4¼" h.,
with a glossy indigo glaze with red,
amber & gunmetal $16,100
All courtesy of David Rago Auctions, Lambertville, NJ.

Fig. 37 A colorful cylindrical vase by
the Overbeck sisters is decorated with
stylized lovebirds against an ornately
carved ground, 7⅜" h. $8,800
Courtesy of Cincinnati Art Galleries, Cincinnati, OH.

Fig. 38

Fig. 39

Fig. 40

Fig. 41

Fig. 42

Fig. 38 This rectangular Owens tile is decorated in cuenda with a landscape of large trees, mounted in a narrow wood frame, 8½ x 11½"............. $1,320
Courtesy of David Rago Auctions, Lambertville, NJ.

Fig. 39 This square Owens tile has a colorful scene of Little Bo Peep & is mounted in a wide flat oak frame, 12" w. $2,645
Courtesy of Treadway Gallery, Cincinnati, OH.

Fig. 40 A large Pewabic ovoid vase hand-modeled with impressed arched leaves alternating with wedged ribs under a smooth matte green glaze, 5¾" d., 10" h..................... $1,600

Fig. 41 This unusual Pewabic jar is modeled as a large eggplant with stem forming the cover, 4¼" d., 6¾" h...... $2,070

Fig. 42 A Pewabic footed bowl with a bulbous body decorated with a flowing matte brown exterior glaze & lavender & turquoise lustered interior glaze, 4" h., 7¼" d. $805

Fig. 43 A foreign landscape is featured on this Rookwood tile. It is titled "Mt. Ararat in Armenia" & is covered in a Vellum glaze, 1914, Sara Sax, 9 x 14¼"...... $5,750
All courtesy of David Rago Auctions, Lambertville, NJ.

Fig. 44 This rare Rookwood plaque features a songbird in flight near leafy stems covered in a Sea Green glaze, by A.R. Valentien, 8 x 10"......... $19,500
Courtesy of Treadway Gallery, Cincinnati, OH.

Fig. 43

Fig. 44

Fig. 45

Fig. 45 A grouping of Paul Revere Pottery pieces.
From left: A 6½" h. vase with a dark blue ground decorated around the shoulder with a wide cuerda seca band of stylized yellow tulips with dark blue leaves on a light blue ground $1,463
    A 5¾" h. vase with a light matte green ground decorated around the shoulder with wide band of stylized yellow tulips & green leaves, Paul Revere stamp $1,238
    A 4½" h. vase in dark bluish-grey decorated with stylized white & blue lotus blossoms, 1914 . . . . $1,238
    A 9¾" d. plate decorated in cuerda seca with black wording "Give Us This Day Our Daily Bread," Saturday Evening Girls stamp, 1921. . . . . $619
Courtesy of David Rago Auctions, Lambertville, NJ.

Fig. 47

Fig. 46

Fig. 48

Fig. 49

Fig. 46 An unusual Rookwood covered tankard decorated with an imp-like character among bare branches all under a Standard glaze, 1899, Harriet Wilcox, 9" h. $9,200
Courtesy of Treadway Gallery, Cincinnati, OH.

Fig. 47 A bulbous ovoid 7" h. Rookwood vase with large red blossoms on mottled dark green & orange leafy stems on a dark blue & orange ground, Matte glaze, 1902, Harriet Wilcox $8,625

Fig. 48 This Rookwood loving cup features a charming portrait of a ragged African-American boy under a glossy Standard glaze, 1895, Bruce Horsfall, 9½" w., 7" h. $4,600

Fig. 49 A Rookwood mug painted with a Native American chief against a shaded ground & a Standard glaze, 1896, Matt Daly, 5" w., 5" h. $1,380
All courtesy of David Rago Auctions, Lambertville, NJ.

Fig. 51

Fig. 50

Fig. 52

Fig. 50 This Rookwood Jewel Porcelain vase stands 9" h. and is decorated with a band of stylized flowers on the upper body, 1918, Sara Sax. $4,313

Fig. 51 This gently-tapering cylindrical 6½" h. Rookwood vase has an overall decoration of pink bayberries & green leaves on a pale tan ground all under a Vellum glaze, 1923, Lorinda Epply $4,313

Fig. 52 A tall slender ovoid 14½" h. Rookwood vase decorated with large shaded blue irises on green leafy stems against a shaded blue to dark green ground & trimmed with a narrow silver overlay rim band, Iris glaze, 1904, Albert Valentien $12,650

Fig. 53 This Rookwood 10½" h. vase in Jewel Porcelain is decorated with Japanese-style cherry blossoms & flying birds in shades of blue & pink under a glossy pink glaze, 1922, Lorinda Epply. $2,070

Fig. 54 Famous Rookwood decorator Kataro Shirayamadani decorated this 8" h. vase with large purple orchids & dark green leaves on a shaded lavender to pink ground, Matte glaze, 1942 . . . . $4,025

Fig. 55 A handsome 14" h. baluster-form Rookwood vase painted with a landscape of leafy trees near a stream under a Vellum glaze, 1926, Fred Rothenbusch $10,350

Fig. 56 This swelled cylindrical 8½" h. vase is decorated with a black rook perched on a pine bough below a full moon, Iris glaze, 1908, Clara C. Lindeman. $8,625

All courtesy of Treadway Gallery, Cincinnati, OH.

Fig. 53

Fig. 54

Fig. 55

Fig. 56

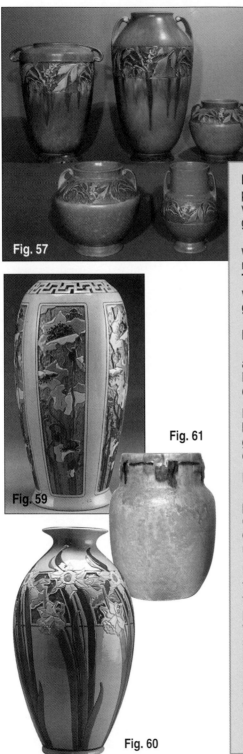

Fig. 57

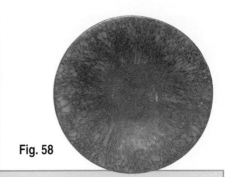

Fig. 58

Fig. 61

Fig. 59

Fig. 60

Fig. 57 A large grouping of Roseville Baneda pattern vases. **Front row:** A 6" h. bulbous vase with small loop handles, raspberry ground, No. 591-6"................$550

A 6" h. two-handled footed vase with a bulbous base & cylindrical neck, raspberry ground, No. 589-6"........$427

Top row: A 12" h. expanding cylindrical vase with small rim handles, green ground, No. 599-12"...............$1,540

A 15" h. floor vase with shoulder handles, green ground, No. 600-15"... $4,400

A 6" h. vase with a bulbous body and small loop handles, green ground, No. 591-6".......................$660

Courtesy of Cincinnati Art Galleries, Cincinnati, OH.

Fig. 58 A Roseville Carnelian II 12½" d. bowl, deeply mottled dark rose & tan glaze, original foil label.............$1,150

Courtesy of Treadway Gallery, Cincinnati, OH.

Fig. 59 A rare Roseville Della Robbia 17½" h. ovoid vase with a reticulated rim & panels decorated in seven colors with excised poppies on a mint green ground, discreet restoration & short hairline, unmarked $18,400

Fig. 60 A 21" h. Roseville Della Robbia floor vase decorated in seven colors with tall daffodils & leaves, probably an exhibition piece, some professional restoration to rim, wafer mark & original paper price tag, signed by H. Smith...............$37,350

Both courtesy of David Rago Auctions, Lambertville, NJ.

Fig. 61 An 8¼" h. Roseville Imperial II vase with a mottled orange & green glaze with tan, green, dark brown & blue around the neck..................$2,415

Courtesy of Treadway Gallery, Cincinnati, OH.

Fig. 63

Fig. 64

Fig. 62

Fig. 62 A variety of Roseville Futura items.
Front row: A 4½" h., 6½" w. vase with straight handles rising from a sharply canted low base to the rim, the upper portion with square cut corners & canted sides, No. 85-4" $289
  A 5" h. squared footed bowl with a tan, green & blue glaze, No. 198-5" $812
Back row: a 7" h., 5½" d. vase of high domed & stepped beehive form below a wide flaring neck & short strap handles, No. 403-7" $880
  A 14" h., 5½" d. vase with two large handles at the lower half & a squat stacked base & faceted squared neck, No. 411-14" $3,190
  A 6" d., 5" h. bowl raised on squared feet & with slightly canted sides, No. 197-6" . . $660
  A 8¼" h., 4¼" w. tall triangular form tapering slightly to a stepped
triangular foot, No. 383-8" $935
  A 8" w., 4" h. five-sided bowl on a square base, No. 188-8" $537
Courtesy of Cincinnati Art Gallery, Cincinnati, OH.

Fig. 63 Roseville Futura vases. **Left:** A 12" h. vase with a wide ovoid body &
a neck composed of tapering bands, No. 394-12" $920
Right: A 10" h. vase with a compressed globular body supporting a long
squared neck, No. 392-10", black paper label $752

Fig. 64 Two Roseville Pauleo vases. **Left:** A 16½" h. vase with a pearl grey to orange
lustre glaze decorated with yellow & red fruit & pale green leaves, impressed mark $690
Right: An 18½" h. footed bulbous vase tapering to a tall cylindrical neck,
shaded red glaze, base drilled. $403
Both courtesy of Treadway Galleries, Cincinnati, OH.

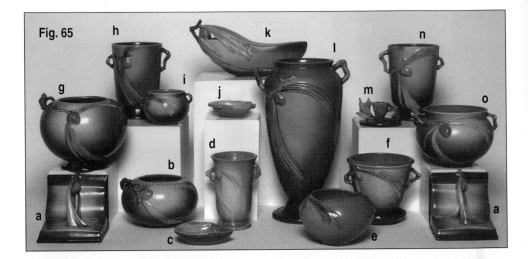

Fig. 65 Roseville Pine Cone pieces.

a. Book ends, blue ground, No. 1, pr. $288

b. Bowl, 4" d. bulbous spherical body, blue ground, No. 278-4" $150-250

c. Ashtray, blue ground, No. 499, 4½" l. $225

d. Vase, 6" h., wide cylindrical body with flaring rim, asymmetrical handles,
green ground, No. 838-6". $150

e. Bowl, 4" d., bulbous with incurved irregular rim, brown ground, No. 441-4" $325

f. Flowerpot & saucer, blue ground, No. 633-5", 5" h. $288

g. Bowl, 6½" d., 3¾" h., spherical foot form with small twig handle, blue ground,
No. 426-6" $256

h. Urn-vase, pedestal foot below a tall slightly flaring cylindrical body with
two small twig handles, brown ground, No. 907-7", 7" h. $114

i. Jardiniere, spherical with two twig handles, blue ground, No. 632-3", 3" h. $214

j. Ashtray, brown ground, No. 499, 4½" l. $200-225

k. Bowl, boat-shaped, 10" l., green ground, No. 429-10" $275-325

l. Vase, floor-type, 14" h., footed tall ovoid form with small angled twig
handles at shoulder, brown ground, No. 850-14". $805

m. Candleholders, flat disk base supporting candle nozzle in the form of a
pine cone, brown ground, No. 112-3", 3" h., pr., illustration of one $240

n. Urn-vase, pedestal foot below a tall slightly flaring cylindrical body with two
small twig handles, blue ground, No. 907-7", 7" h. $230

o. Jardiniere, spherical with two twig handles, blue ground, No. 632-5", 5" h. $288

Courtesy of Treadway Galleries, Cincinnati, OH.

Fig. 66 Roseville Miscellaneous Items.
a. Clematis hanging basket, brown ground, No. 470-5"...........................$175
b. Jonquil bowl, 3" h., No. 523-3"...$200-250
c. Ming Tree vase, 8" h., blue ground, No. 582-8".............................$299
d. Magnolia basket with overhead handle, green ground, No. 384-8"..............$173
e. Vista floor vase, 15" h., No. 121-15"...............................$650-1,100
f. Magnolia vase, 6" h., tan ground, No. 88-6"..........................$75-150
g. Freesia ewer, green ground, No. 19-6"...................................$151
h. Fuchsia two-handled jardiniere, terra cotta ground, No. 645-4".............$190
i. Cherry Blossom 12" h. cylindrical vase, pink ground, No. 627-12"...........$546
j. Sunflower bowl, 5" d., wide squatty form, No. 208-5"......................$748
k. Futura jardiniere, No. 616-6", terra cotta ground.....................$250-275
l. Peony basket, pink ground, No. 377-8"...................................$115
m. Water Lily vase, 9" h., footed bulbous ovoid body with a large trumpet neck
    & angled handles, pink shaded to green ground, No. 79-9"...................$207
Courtesy of Treadway Gallery, Cincinnati, OH.

Fig. 67 A group of Teco vases.
From left: 7¼" h., 4¼" d., conical body tapering to a flared neck with a thick rim band issuing four heavy squared buttress handles to the base, smooth medium green matte glaze, short abrasion to rim $4,025

7¼" h., 4¼" d., ovoid body tapering to a flaring cylindrical neck flanked by heavy square buttress handles down the sides, mottled matte green glaze, some glaze curdling at base, No. 435........... $3,220

7½" h., 4¼" d., same design on left with a smooth matte brown glaze..... $3,450
Courtesy of David Rago Auctions, Lambertville, NJ.

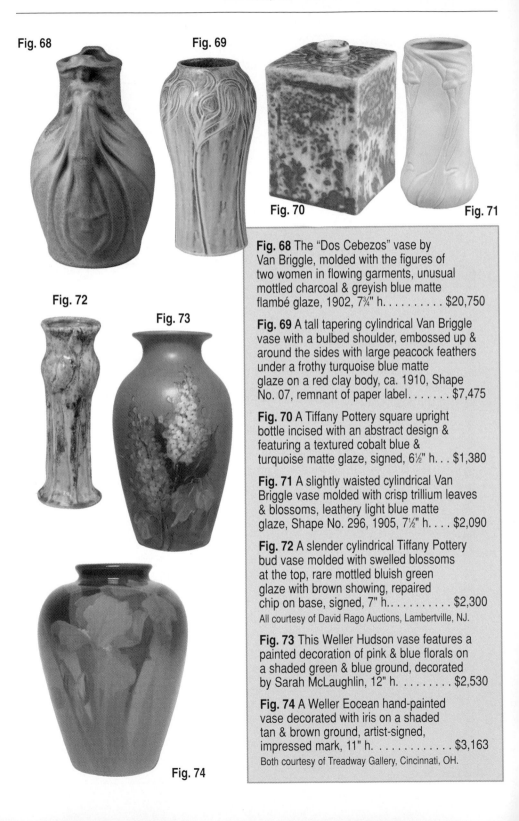

Fig. 68

Fig. 69

Fig. 70

Fig. 71

Fig. 72

Fig. 73

Fig. 74

Fig. 68 The "Dos Cebezos" vase by Van Briggle, molded with the figures of two women in flowing garments, unusual mottled charcoal & greyish blue matte flambé glaze, 1902, 7¾" h. $20,750

Fig. 69 A tall tapering cylindrical Van Briggle vase with a bulbed shoulder, embossed up & around the sides with large peacock feathers under a frothy turquoise blue matte glaze on a red clay body, ca. 1910, Shape No. 07, remnant of paper label. $7,475

Fig. 70 A Tiffany Pottery square upright bottle incised with an abstract design & featuring a textured cobalt blue & turquoise matte glaze, signed, 6½" h. . . $1,380

Fig. 71 A slightly waisted cylindrical Van Briggle vase molded with crisp trillium leaves & blossoms, leathery light blue matte glaze, Shape No. 296, 1905, 7½" h. . . . $2,090

Fig. 72 A slender cylindrical Tiffany Pottery bud vase molded with swelled blossoms at the top, rare mottled bluish green glaze with brown showing, repaired chip on base, signed, 7" h. $2,300
All courtesy of David Rago Auctions, Lambertville, NJ.

Fig. 73 This Weller Hudson vase features a painted decoration of pink & blue florals on a shaded green & blue ground, decorated by Sarah McLaughlin, 12" h. $2,530

Fig. 74 A Weller Eocean hand-painted vase decorated with iris on a shaded tan & brown ground, artist-signed, impressed mark, 11" h. $3,163
Both courtesy of Treadway Gallery, Cincinnati, OH.

Fig. 75

Fig. 76

Fig. 77

Fig. 78

Fig. 79

Fig. 75 A group of Weller Sicardo vases. **From left:** A gourd-shaped body decorated with chrysanthemum blossoms in iridescent green & purple, glaze drips from rim, 4¾" h. $605
   A bulbous cylindrical form decorated with berries & leaves in iridescent green & bronze glaze, 6" h. $990
   A bulbous four-sided form with square molded rim, decorated with flowers in green & red iridescence, 4½" h. $880
   A corseted cylindrical form with lobed base & flared rim, decorated in an Art Nouveau design in iridescent green & purple, a few surface scratches, 8¾" h. . . $990
Courtesy of David Rago Auctions, Lambertville, NJ.

Fig. 76 A rare tall Weller Muskota garden ornament of a Fishing Boy standing on a round base, 20⅝" h. $6,325
Courtesy of Cincinnati Art Galleries, Cincinnati, OH.

Fig. 77 A tall cylindrical Jap Birdimal Weller umbrella stand decorated with a landscape scene, impressed mark, minor chips, 20" h. $1,035

Fig. 78 A Weller Louwelsa vase decorated with white stylized roses on a red ground, minor chip on lip, 10½" h. $3,450
Both courtesy of Treadway Gallery, Cincinnati, OH.

Fig. 79 A Geode pattern vase by Weller, decorated with white stars & comets on a dark blue ground, glaze chip on base, 6" h. $748
Courtesy of David Rago Auctions, Lambertville, NJ.

Fig. 80 A large grouping of Weller Coppertone pieces.

a. Console bowl in a shallow oblong form with a frog seated near a
water lily at one end, 11" l. $805
b. A very tall 15¼" h. vase with a footed trumpet-form body $1,144
c. A model of a frog, 2½" h. $322
d. An 8½" h. footed trumpet-form vase $403
e. A bowl with original flower holder, low form with flaring sides & down-curved rim,
marked "Weller Hand Made," 11" d. $173
f. A 6" h. ovoid vase with flat closed rim. $345
g. A 6" h. vase with a wide tapering cylindrical form & molded rim $334
h. Another 6" h. vase with a wide tapering cylindrical form & molded rim. $161
i. An 11" h. vase with a footed bulbous base & wide cylindrical neck,
large loop handles from rim to shoulder $431
j. An 8" h. footed vase with a two-handled spherical base & wide flaring rim $265
k. Two 6½" h. footed vases with tapering cylindrical bodies,
marked "Weller Hand Made," each $115
l. A footed 11" h. vase with a bulbous base & wide trumpet-form neck, heavy
strap handles, marked "Weller Hand Made" $575
Courtesy of Treadway Gallery, Cincinnati, OH.

Fig. 81

Fig. 82

Fig. 81 A large Wheatley vase based on a
Teco Pottery form with a bulbous bottom
tapering slightly to a wide cylindrical body
with a four-scallop ring issuing four vine-like
handles down the sides, frothy matte green
glaze, incised "WP - 615," 14¼" h. $2,875

Fig. 82 A Wheatley Pottery vase in a wide
baluster form below a wide cushion neck, in
the style of Grueby's "Kendrick" vase,
molded with wide leaves, fine frothy matte
light brown glaze, small chip to edge of
neck, remnants of paints, 12½" h. $3,450
Both courtesy of David Rago Auctions, Lambertville, NJ

Vase, 6" h., footed, slender ovoid body w/short collared neck, loop handles from shoulder to rim, raspberry pink ground, No. 602-6"... **400-450**

Vase, 6" h., footed, slender ovoid body w/short collared neck, loop handles from shoulder to rim, green ground, No. 602-6", original black paper label.......................... **650**

Vase, 6" h., green ground, No. 605-6", original label.. **518**

Vase, 6" h., raspberry pink ground, No. 605-6", original label................................... **520**

Vase, 7" h., footed wide cylindrical body w/wide collared rim, small loop handles from shoulder to rim, raspberry pink ground, No. 610-7" **500**

Vase, 7" h., footed swelled cylindrical body tapering to a short, wide cylindrical neck flanked by small down-curved loop handles, raspberry pink ground, No. 590-7" (ILLUS. lower center with 4" squatty vase).. **443**

Vase, 7" h., footed swelled cylindrical body tapering to a short, wide cylindrical neck flanked by small down-curved loop handles, green ground, No. 590-7" **525**

Vase, 7" h., footed wide cylindrical body tapering to short wide cylindrical neck, small loop handles, raspberry pink ground, No. 592-7" (ILLUS. lower right with 4" squatty vase) **479**

Vase, 7" h., footed wide cylindrical body tapering to short wide cylindrical neck, small loop handles, green ground, No. 592-7" **1,100**

Vase, 7" h., trumpet-shaped w/handles from base to mid-section, green ground, No. 604-7".. **350-400**

Vase, 7" h., trumpet-shaped w/handles from base to mid-section, raspberry pink ground, No. 604-7" **700**

Vase, 7" h., footed wide cylindrical body w/wide collared rim, small loop handles from shoulder to rim, green ground, No. 610-7" **660**

Vase, 8" h., footed, globular w/shoulder handles, raspberry pink ground, No. 595-8" **880**

Vase, 9" h., cylindrical w/short collared neck, handles rising from shoulder to beneath rim, raspberry pink ground, No. 594-9" **649**

Vase, 9" h., cylindrical w/short collared neck, handles rising from shoulder to beneath rim, green ground, No. 594-9" (ILLUS. top right with 4" squatty vase)......... **990**

Vase, 9" h., bulbous body tapering to short wide cylindrical rim, handles from mid-base to below rim, raspberry pink ground, small chip to base, No. 596-9" (LLUS. top left with 4" squatty vase) **729**

Vase, 9" h., bulbous body tapering to short wide cylindrical rim, handles from mid-base to below rim, green ground, No. 596-9" **853**

Vase, 10" h., footed bulbous body tapering to closed rim, two handles rising from shoulder to beneath rim, raspberry pink ground, No. 597-10" **995**

Baneda Vase

Vase, 12" h., trumpet-form on flaring foot, base handles, green ground, No. 598-12" (ILLUS.).. **880**

Vase, 12" h., expanding cylinder w/small rim handles, green ground, No. 599-12" (ILLUS. top row, left with Baneda group)... **1,540**

Vase, 12" h., expanding cylinder w/small rim handles, raspberry pink ground, No. 599-12" (repairs to rim, handles & base)...... **770**

Vase, 15" h., floor-type, bulbous ovoid body w/flat rim, shoulder handles, green ground, No. 600-15" (ILLUS. center top row, with Baneda group) **4,400**

Wall pocket, flaring sides, green ground, No. 1269-8", gold foil label, 8" h. (small chip to hole in back) **2,645**

Bittersweet (1940)
Orange bittersweet pods and green leaves on a grey blending to rose, yellow with terra cotta, rose with green or solid green bark-textured ground; brown branch handles.

Basket, hanging-type, green ground **244**

Basket, low overhead handle, shaped rim, green ground, No. 810-10", 10" h. **193**

Basket w/overhead handle, green ground, No. 809-8", 8" h. **242**

Bowl, 7" d., green ground, No. 842-7" **225**

Candleholders, handles rising from conical base to midsection of nozzle, green ground, No. 851-3", 3" h., pr. **125**

Cornucopia-vase, green ground, No. 882-8", 8" h. **185**

Creamer, yellow ground, No. 871-C **100**

Jardiniere, green ground, 4" h., No. 400-4" **130**

Jardiniere, pink ground, No. 842-7", 7" h. **165**

Jardiniere & pedestal base, yellow ground, No. 802-8", 8" h., 2 pcs. (chip to bottom ring of jardiniere) **880**

Jardiniere & pedestal base, green ground, overall 24" h., 2 pcs. **1,295**

Planter, curved shaped sides, grey ground, No. 828-10", 10 1/2" l................................. **110**

Bittersweet Planter

Planter w/undertray, grey ground, No. 856-5", slight interior discoloration from usage & small bruise to one of rim points, 5 1/2" h. (ILLUS.) 67
Planter w/undertray, green ground, No. 856-5", 5 1/2" h. (minor crazing).................... 143
Teapot, cov., yellow ground, No. 871-P 225
Urn, green ground, No. 842-7", 7" h. 150
Vase, double bud, 6" h., green ground, No. 873-6" 235
Vase, 7" h., base handles, squared form w/flaring rim, yellow ground, No. 874-7" 138
Vase, 7" h., green ground, No. 879-7" 83

Bittersweet Vases

Vase, 7" h., yellow ground, No. 879-7", embossed "Roseville U.S.A. 879-7" (ILLUS. right) 138
Vase, 8" h., asymmetrical handles, bulging cylindrical form, grey ground, No. 883-8" 135
Vase, 10" h., handles at midsection, scalloped rim, green ground, No. 885-10" 165
Vase, 10" h., handles at midsection, scalloped rim, grey ground, No. 885-10" (ILLUS. left)...................................... 193
Wall pocket, curving conical form w/overhead handle continuing to one side, grey ground, No. 866-7", 7 1/2" h. 316

Blackberry (1933)
Band of relief clusters of blackberies with vines and ivory leaves accented in green and terra cotta on a green textured ground.

Basket, hanging-type, 6 1/2" (two flakes to berries) 633
Bowl, 6" d., No. 226-6" 300
Console bowl, rectangular w/small handles, No. 228-10", 3 1/2 x 13"...................... 432
Jardiniere, two-handled, No. 623-4", 4" h. 290
Jardiniere, two-handled, No. 623-5", 5" h. 358
Jardiniere, two-handled, No. 623-6", 6" h. 495
Jardiniere, two-handled, 8" h........................... 1,045
Jardiniere, two-handled, No. 623-9", 9" h. 1,010
Jardiniere & pedestal base, 28" h., 2 pcs.... 3,400
Planter, hanging-type, No. 348-5", 5" h. (one rim hanging hole only partially pierced) 800

Planter, six-sided, gold foil label, 3 3/4 x 10"..... 460
Vase, 4" h., two-handled, bulbous, No. 567-4" 355
Vase, 4" h., 6" d., squatty bulbous form w/small angled shoulder handles, No. 568-4" 460

Blackberry Vase

Vase, 5" h., tiny rim handles, canted sides, No. 565-5" (ILLUS.)................................... 539
Vase, 5" h., loop handles at midsection, bulbous base tapering to wide cylindrical neck, No. 570-5" 482
Vase, 6" h., bulbous ovoid w/wide rim, small shoulder handles, No. 571-6" 550-600
Vase, 6" h., No. 572-6" 554
Vase, 6" h., two handles at midsection, No. 573-6".. 595

Blackberry Vase

Vase, 6" h., globular w/tiny rim handles, No. 574-6" (ILLUS.)................................... 660
Vase, 8" h., handles at mid-section, slightly globular base & wide neck, No. 575-8"......... 940
Vase, 10" h., bulbous base w/wide cylindrical neck, handles at mid-section, No. 577-10 1,648
Vase, 12 1/2" h., ovoid w/loop handles from shoulder to rim, No. 578-12" (minor chip to bottom).................................... 1,320
Wall pocket, basket-shaped w/narrow base & flaring rim, No. 1267-8" 6 3/4" w. at rim, 8 1/2" h. 883

Bleeding Heart (1938)
Pink blossoms and green leaves on shaded blue, green or pink ground.

Basket, pink ground, No. 359-8", 8" h. 325
Basket, hanging-type, two-handled, blue ground, No. 362-5", 8" d. 288
Basket, hanging-type, two-handled, green ground, No. 362-5", 8" d.............................. 242
Basket, hanging-type, two-handled, pink ground, No. 362-5", 8" w. 225

Basket w/circular handle, blue ground,
No. 360-10", 10" h. **250**
Basket w/circular handle, brown ground,
No. 360-10", 10" h. **403**

Bleeding Heart Basket

Basket w/circular handle, pink ground,
360-10", 10" h., w/gold foil label (ILLUS.) **331**
Basket w/overhead handle, pink ground,
No. 359-8", 7 1/2" h. **200**
Basket w/pointed overhead handle,
w/flower frog, pink ground, No. 361-12",
12" h., 2 pcs. **300**
Basket w/pointed overhead handle,
w/flower frog, green ground, No. 361-12",
12" h., 2 pcs. **358**
Book ends, book-shaped, pink ground, No.
6, pr. **385**
Bowl, 8" w., hexagonal, pink ground, No.
380-8" **110**
Candleholders, pink ground, No. 1140-2",
pr. **165**
Candlesticks, pink ground, 1139-4 1/2",
4 1/2" h., pr. **165**
Console bowl, blue ground, No. 382-10",
10" l. **295**
Console bowl, pink ground, No. 382-10",
10" l. **250**
Console bowl, pink ground, No. 383-14",
14" l. **450**
Cornucopia-vase, pink ground, No. 141-6",
6" h. **165**
Ewer, green ground, No. 963-6", 6" h. **200-225**
Ewer, pink ground, No. 972-10", 10" h. **275**

Bleeding Heart Flower Frog

Flower frog, round base, scalloped edge,
overhead handle, pink ground, No. 40,
3 1/2" h. (ILLUS.) **110**
Flower frog, round base, scalloped edge,
overhead handle, blue ground, No. 40,
3 1/2" h. **220**

Jardiniere, small pointed shoulder handles,
blue ground, No. 651-3", 3" h. **100**
Jardiniere, small pointed shoulder handles,
green ground, No. 651-3", 3" h. **110**
Jardiniere, small pointed shoulder handles,
pink ground, No. 651-3", 3" h. **118**
Jardiniere, blue ground, No. 651-5", 5" h. **413**
Jardiniere, green ground, No. 651-6", 6" h.
(small glaze chip to handle) **248**
Jardiniere & pedestal base, pink ground,
jardiniere 8" h., No. 651-8", 2 pcs. **1,045**
Jardiniere & pedestal base, blue ground,
jardiniere 10" h., No. 651-10", 2 pcs. **3,500**

Bleeding Heart Pitcher

Pitcher, 8" h., asymmetrical w/high arched
handle, pink ground, No. 1323 (ILLUS.) **399**
Plate, 10 1/2" w., hexagonal, pink ground,
No. 381-10" **110**
Urn-vase, pink ground, No. 377-4", 4" h. **118**
Vase, 5" h., blue ground, No. 962-5" **115**
Vase, 6 1/2" h., base handles, blue ground,
No. 964-6" **175**
Vase, 6 1/2" h., base handles, pink ground,
No. 964-6" **185**
Vase, 8" h., green ground, No. 139-8" **325**

Bleeding Heart Vase

Vase, 8" h., pillow-type, pink ground, No.
968-8" (ILLUS.) **275**
Vase, 9" h., pillow-type, blue ground, No.
970-9" **300**
Vase, 12" h., expanding cylinder w/small
handles at shoulder, blue ground, No.
974-12" **660**
Vase, 12" h., expanding cylinder w/small
handles at shoulder, green ground, No.
974-12" (tiny glaze nick off one handle) **468**

Vase, 12" h., expanding cylinder w/small handles at shoulder, pink ground, No. 974-12" (tiny glaze nick off one handle) **385**

Vase, 15" h., two-handled, flaring hexagonal mouth, pink ground, No. 976-15" **775**

Vase, 18" h., floor-type, blue ground, No. 977-18" **1,200**

Wall pocket, conical w/pointed overhead handle, blue ground, No. 1287-8", 8 1/2" h. (minor crazing) **619**

Burmese (1950s)

Oriental faces featured on pieces such as wall plaques, book ends, candleholders and console bowls. Some plain pieces also included. Comes in green, black and white.

Book ends, green ground, pr. **250**

Book ends, black, No. 71-B, pr., 6 1/2" h. **150**

Candleholders-book end combination, black glaze, No. 80-B, 7 1/2" h., pr. **248**

Candleholders-book end combination, woman & man, green glaze, Nos. 80-B & 70-B, pr. **350**

Candleholders-book end combination, woman & man, white glaze, Nos. 80-B & 70-B, pr. **138**

Planter, green ground, No. 908-10", 10" **100**

Burmese Wall Pocket

Wall pocket, bust of a woman, white glaze, No. 72-B, 7 1/2" h. (ILLUS.) **165**

Bushberry (1948)

Berries and leaves on blue, green or russet bark-textured ground; brown or green branch handles.

Ashtray, blue ground, No. 26 .... **195**

Basket, hanging-type w/original chains, blue ground, No. 465-5", 7" **346**

Basket, hanging-type w/original chains, green ground, No. 465-5", 7" **275**

Basket, hanging-type w/original chains, russet ground, No. 465-5", 7" **425**

Basket, blue ground, No. 370-8", 8" h. **265**

Basket w/asymmetrical overhead handle, blue ground, No. 369-6 1/2", 6 1/2" h. **195**

Basket w/asymmetrical overhead handle, green ground, No. 369-6 1/2", 6 1/2" h. **250**

Basket w/asymmetrical overhead handle, ivory ground, No. 369-6 1/2", 6 1/2" h. **112**

Basket w/asymmetrical overhead handle, russet ground, No. 369-6 1/2", 6 1/2" h. **180**

Basket w/asymmetrical overhead handle, green ground, No. 370-8", 8" h. **275**

Basket w/asymmetrical overhead handle, blue ground, No. 371-10", 10" h. **353**

Basket w/low overhead handle, russet ground, No. 357-10", 10" h. **280**

Basket w/low overhead handle, asymmetric rim, blue ground, No. 372-12", 12 h. **420**

Beverage set: 8 3/4" h. pitcher w/ice lip & six 3 1/2" h. mugs; blue ground, pitcher No. 1325, mugs No. 1-3 1/2", 7 pcs. **1,500**

Beverage set: 8 3/4" h. pitcher w/ice lip & six 3 1/2" h. mugs; russet ground, pitcher No. 1325, mugs No. 1-3 1/2", 7 pcs. **1,100**

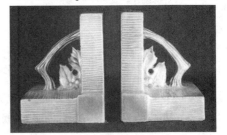

Bushberry Book Ends

Book ends, green ground, No. 9, pr. (ILLUS.) **300**

Bowl, 3" h., small side handles, globular, green ground, No. 657-3" **120**

Bowl, 4" d., two-handled, russet ground, No. 411-4" **123**

Bowl, 6" d., russet ground, No. 412-6" **195**

Bowl, 10" d., russet ground, No. 1-10" **195**

Console bowl, two-handled, blue ground, No. 414-10", 10" d. **180**

Console bowl, end handles, blue ground, No. 385-10", 13" l. **154**

Cornucopia-vase, single handle, green ground, No. 153-6", 6" h. **135**

Cornucopia-vase, double, green ground, No. 155-8", 6" h. **100**

Bushberry Cornucopia-vase

Cornucopia-vase, double, russet ground, No. 155-8", 6" h. (ILLUS.) **175**

Cornucopia-vase, double, blue ground, No. 155-8" **163**

Ewer, green ground, No. 1-6, 6" h. **150**

Ewer, russet ground, No. 1-6, 6" h. **185**

Ewer, blue ground, No. 2-10", 10" h. **300**

Ewer, green ground, No. 2-10", 10" h. **275**

Flower frog, blue ground, No. 45 .... **160**

Jardiniere, 3" h., small side handles, globular, russet ground, No. 657-3" **50**

Jardiniere, two-handled, russet ground, No. 657-4", 4" h. **100**

Jardiniere, two-handled, blue ground, No. 657-4", 4" h. **165**

Jardiniere, russet ground, No. 657-5", 5" h. **170**

Jardiniere & pedestal base, two-handled, green ground, No. 657-10", 2 pcs. (chip to rim, sm. chip to base & one handle of pedestal) **1,045**

Jardiniere & pedestal base, two-handled, russet ground, No. 657-8", 2 pcs. **850**

Jardiniere & pedestal base, two-handled, blue ground, No. 657-8", overall 24" h., 2 pcs. **798**

Mug, green ground, No. 1-3 1/2", 3 1/2" h. **135**

Pitcher, 8 3/4" h., blue w/green branch handle, No. 1325 .... **427**

Pitcher, 8 3/4" h., russet w/green branch handle, No. 1325 .... **300**

Sand jar, green ground, No. 778-14", 14" h. ... **1,400**

Tea set: cov. teapot, creamer & sugar bowl; blue ground, No. 2, No. 2C, No. 2S, 3 pcs. **550-575**

Tea set: cov. teapot, open creamer & sugar; russet ground, No. 2, No. 2C & No. 2S, 3 pcs. **650**

Umbrella stand, double handles, blue ground, No. 779-20", 20 1/2" h. **985**

Urn, two-handled, green ground, No. 411-6", 6" h. (couple of very minor nicks to horizontal ridges) **112**

Vase, 3" h., conical w/tiny rim handles, russet ground, No. 283" **30**

Vase, 4" h., conical w/tiny rim handles, russet ground, No. 28-4" **135**

Bushberry Double Bud Vase

Vase, double bud, 4 1/2" h., gate-form, russet ground, No. 158-4 1/2" (ILLUS.) **185**

Vase, 6" h., asymmetrical side handles, cylindrical w/low foot, russet ground, No. 29-6" **145**

Vase, 6" h., two-handled, green ground, No. 30-6" **90-100**

Vase, 6" h., two-handled, russet ground, No. 30-6" **70**

Vase, 6" h., angular side handles, low foot, globular w/wide neck, blue ground, No. 156-6" **165**

Vase, 6" h., angular side handles, low foot, globular w/wide neck, green ground, No. 156-6" **138**

Vase, 6" h., angular side handles, low foot, globular w/wide neck, russet ground, No. 156-6" **165**

Vase, 7" h., footed cylindrical body w/asymmetrical handles, blue ground, No. 32-7" **235**

Vase, bud, 7" h., asymmetrical base handles, cylindrical body, blue ground, No. 152-7" **160**

Vase, bud, 7 1/2" h., asymmetrical base handles, cylindrical body, russet ground, No. 152-7" **145**

Bushberry Vase

Vase, 8" h., footed tapering squared body w/flaring rim flanked by down-turned forked branch handles, green ground, No. 33-8" (ILLUS.) **295**

Vase, 9" h., two-handled, ovoid, blue ground, No. 35-9" **205**

Vase, 9" h., two-handled, ovoid, green ground, No. 35-9" **175**

Vase, 9" h., two-handled, ovoid, russet ground, No. 35-9" **200-225**

Vase, 9" h., footed cylindrical body w/small angled handles near rim, green ground, No. 36-9" **225**

Vase, 10" h., two-handled, russet ground, No. 37-10" **265**

Vase, 12 1/2" h., large asymmetrical side handles, bulging cylinder w/flaring foot, green ground, No. 38-12" **225**

Vase, 12 1/2" h., large asymmetrical side handles, bulging cylinder w/flaring foot, russet ground, No. 38-12" **345**

Vase, 12 1/2" h., large asymmetrical side handles, bulging cylinder w/flaring foot, blue ground, No. 38-12" **375**

Vase, 14 1/2" h., blue ground, No. 39-14" **605**

Vase, 18" h., floor-type, blue ground, No. 41-18" (short tight line to rim, restoration to one handle) **550**

Vase, 18" h., floor-type, green ground, No. 41-18" (grinding chips to base) **880**

Wall pocket, high-low handles, russet ground, No. 1291-8", 8" h. (glazed over bruise to back) **259**

Carnelian I (1910-15)

Matte glaze with a combination of two colors or two shades of the same color with the darker dripping over the lighter tone or heavy and textured glaze with intermingled colors and some running.

Bowl, 6 1/2" d., 3" h., two-handled, canted sides, pink & grey **231**

Bowl, 8" d., 3" h., deep green & light green, No. 163-8" **88**

Bowl, 9 1/2" d., wide squatty bulbous sides tapering sharply to a wide molded rim, deep green & light green **69**

Candleholder, green ground, No. 1059-2 1/2", 2 1/2" h. **70**

Candleholders, simple disk base w/incised rings at base of candle nozzle, deep green & light green, No. 1063-3", 2 1/2" h., pr. **110**

Console bowl, footed low oval form w/canted sides & ornate scrolled end handles, light & dark green, No. 152-8", 10 3/4" l., 4" h. **165**

Console bowl, hexagonal, blue & green, No. 170-14", 14" l., 4" h. **83**

Console bowl, footed shallow oval form w/angled end handles, light & dark green, No. 157-14", 16" l., 2 3/4" h. **248**

Carnelian I Console Set

Console set: 9 1/2" l. 3 1/2" h. octagonal bowl & pair of 3" h. candleholders; pink & blue, Nos. 164-3" & 1064-3", 3 pcs. (ILLUS.) **103**

Ewer, footed wide compressed globular body w/wide shoulder to the pointed & arched spout, scrolled C-form handle from the neck to lower base, dark & light blue, No. 1314-8", 8" h. **220**

Flower frog, blue & grey ground, 6 1/4" w., 2 1/2" h. **120**

Flower frog, green ground, 4 1/2" h. **170**

Vase, pillow-type, green & turquoise **160**

Carnelian I Double Bud Vase

Vase, double bud, 5" h., gate-form, olive green & mustard yellow, No. 56-5" (ILLUS.) **83**

Vase, 5" h., flat pierced handles, rectangular w/slightly bulging sides, rose w/deep purple drip, unmarked, No. 65-2-5 .... **275**

Vase, 5" h., two-handled, squatty bulbous form, shades of green, No. 357-5" **110**

Vase, 5" h., blue & grey ground, No. 642-5" **175**

Vase, 6" h., pillow-type, light blue & dark blue **75-100**

Vase, 6" h., footed fan-shaped body, mustard yellow over light green, No. 52-6" **83**

Vase, 7" h., footed wide ovoid base w/wide shoulder to short collared neck, ornate

handles from mid-section to rim, light & dark blue, No. 271-7" **110**

Vase, 7" h., double gourd-form w/wide neck & flaring rim, ornate pointed & scrolled handles from mid-section of base to below rim, light & dark green, No. 310-7" **138**

Vase, 7" h., bulbous base w/wide collared neck, ornate handles from shoulder to beneath rim, light & dark green, No. 311-7" **110**

Vase, 7" h., footed bulbous ovoid w/shoulder tapering to wide molded rim, handles from shoulder to rim, light & dark blue, No. 331-7" **183**

Vase, 7" h., footed bulbous ovoid w/shoulder tapering to wide molded rim, handles from shoulder to rim, green ground, No. 331-7" **235**

Vase, 7" h., footed bulbous ovoid w/shoulder tapering to wide molded rim, handles from shoulder to rim, rose & grey ground, No. 331-7" **358**

Vase, 8" h., base handles, fan-shaped, aqua **95**

Vase, 8" h., two-handled, ovoid base & ringed neck, turquoise blue & aqua, No. 317-8" **110**

Vase, 8" h., footed wide compressed bulbous body w/wide collared neck, ornate scroll handles from center of base to rim, light & dark green & mustard yellow, No. 318-8" **138**

Vase, 9" h., cylindrical w/wide collared neck, dark blue & light blue, No. 313-9" **250**

Vase, 9" h., wide ovoid w/collared neck & rolled rim, mustard yellow over light green, No. 314-9" **110**

Vase, 10" h., semi-ovoid base & long wide neck w/rolled rim, ornate handles, dark blue & light blue, No. 337-10" **125-175**

Vase, 10" h., semi-ovoid base & long wide neck w/rolled rim, ornate handles, grey & mauve, black label, No. 337-10" **413**

Vase, 12" h., bulbous ovoid body w/wide cylindrical neck, scrolled shoulder handles, grey & mauve, No. 338-12" **440**

Wall pocket, ornate side handles, flaring rim, turquoise blue & aqua, 8" h. **375**

Wall pocket, conical w/ornate side handles, flaring rim, blue & grey, No. 1251-8" (very minor chips around hanging hole) **242**

Wall pocket, ornate side handles, flaring rim, mustard over light green, No. 1249-9", 9" h. **267**

Carnelian II (1915)
Intermingled colors, some with a drip effect.

Bowl, 10" d., low faceted body, mottled pink & green glaze **495**

Bowl, 10 1/2 x 3 1/2", footed w/curved end handles, semi-matte drip glazes in purple & green intermingled w/maroon **468**

Bowl, 12 1/2" d. footed wide shallow round form, deeply mottled dark rose & tan glaze, foil label **1,150**

Bowl, 14" d., short pedestal foot below compressed round body w/incurved sides & wide flaring rim, scrolled handles, mottled pink & green glaze **550**

Bowl, footed, six-sided, w/drip glaze in shades of rose, grey, green & tan, small separation at the rim, 4 x 15".......................... **330**

Candleholders, aqua & lilac glaze, No. 1059-2 1/2", 2 1/2" h., pr. **150**

Console bowl, stepped base, flaring octagonal shape, mottled mauve, grey, cream & black glaze, 9 5/8" l., 3 5/8" h...................... **220**

Console set: 9 3/4" d., bowl & pair of 3 5/8" h. candleholders; shades of green over blue textured glaze, the set................... **413**

Ewer, pink, mauve, green & black mottled matte glaze, 15" h............................... **1,760**

Lamp base, footed spherical body w/wide cylindrical neck & scrolling angled handles, raspberry & green mottled matte glaze, metal fittings, 8" h. (bruise to one handle).. **330**

Urn, squatty bulbous body w/wide flaring rim, scrolled handles, 5" h. **303**

Urn, globular body tapering to flaring rim, scrolled shoulder handles, rose, green & grey ground, 6" h. **660**

Urn, globular body tapering to flaring rim, scrolled shoulder handles, light & dark blue ground, No. 333-6", 6" h. **413**

Urn, footed, compressed globular form w/short molded neck, ornate scrolled handles, mottled pink, yellow & green glaze, 7" h. **358**

Urn, bulbous body w/wide cylindrical neck & slightly flaring rim, scrolled shoulder handles, mottled pink & green glaze, 7 1/4" h. **330**

Urn, globular body w/tapering wide cylindrical neck & molded rim, scrolled angular handles from shoulder to rim, mottled pink, yellow & green glaze, 8" h. **935**

Urn, ornate handles, compressed globular form, purple & rose, 9" d., 8" h. **825**

Urn, bulbous body w/wide cylindrical neck, ornate scrolled handles from shoulder to rim, mottled pink, yellow & green glaze, 9 3/4" h. **770**

Carnelian II Vase

Vase, 5" h., fan-shaped body on round disk foot, scrolled handles from base to midsection, intermingled green & pink glaze (ILLUS.).. **138**

Vase, 5" h., footed, fan-shaped body w/shaped rim, small handles base handles, mottled grey, green & pink glaze, No. 351-5 .... **110**

Vase, bud, 6" h., footed trumpet-form w/ornate handles from base to mid-section, blue ground, No. 341-6" **90**

Vase, bud, 6" h., footed trumpet-form w/ornate handles from base to mid-section, turquoise ground, No. 341-6".................. **99**

Vase, bud, 6" h., footed trumpet-form w/ornate handles from base to mid-section, intermingled shades of raspberry pink, No. 341-6".. **135**

Vase, 7" h., compressed globular base w/short wide neck, large handles, purple & rose **238**

Vase, 7" h., footed baluster-form w/small low loop handles from shoulder to rim, shades of green **240**

Vase, 7" h., footed, bulbous base tapering to wide cylindrical neck w/rolled rim, ornate handles from shoulder to below rim, mottled rose, grey & green glaze (customary grinding chips to base & tight line to one handle) **239**

Vase, 7" h., footed, wide cylindrical body tapering slightly to rolled rim, gloopy pink, mauve, green, black & cream matte glaze (small base chip professionally repaired) **165**

Vase, 8" h., intermingled shades of blue **185**

Vase, 8" h., tapering cylindrical body w/short cylindrical neck, mottled pink & green glaze **250-300**

Vase, 8 1/4" h., squattly bulbous body tapering to flared rim, angled scrolled handles, mottled matte mauve drip glaze, partial paper label.................................. **423**

Vase, 9" h., bulbous ovoid body w/short collared mouth, angled shoulder handles, mottled pink, yellow & green glaze **715**

Vase, 9" h., ovoid body tapering to cylindrical neck w/molded rim, mottled pink & green glaze.. **440**

Vase, 9" h., ovoid w/short collared mouth, intermingled shades of pink, purple, green & tan, unmarked **399**

Vase, 10" h., compressed globular base w/trumpet form neck, ornate handles from base to midsection, mottled pink, amber & green glaze.. **605**

Vase, 10" h., compressed globular form w/angled handles from mid-section to rim, intermingled blue & green glaze (small glaze flake off one handle) **193**

Vase, 10" h., compressed globular form w/angled handles from mid-section to rim, mottled rose & green glaze **1,100**

Vase, 10" h., footed tapering cylindrical body w/wide slightly flaring neck, mottled green glaze.. **259**

Vase, 10" h., footed wide tapering cylindrical body w/wide slightly flaring neck, mottled pink & green glaze **523**

Vase, 12" h., bulbous ovoid body w/wide flaring rim flanked by buttressed handles, rose, mauve & green mottled glaze, No. 445-12" (restoration to drill hole at base)... **1,650**

Vase, 12" h., flaring foot below wide bulbous body w/shoulder tapering to wide flaring cylindrical neck, rose, yellow, blue, violet & green mottled matte glaze, No. 446-12".. **2,860**

Vase, 13 1/2" h., ovoid body w/slightly flaring rim, mottled pink & green glaze (bruise to base) 990

Carnelian II Floor Vase

Vase, 15" h., floor-type, footed baluster-form w/angled handles from shoulder to below rim, mottled grey, blue & green matte glaze (ILLUS.) **1,540**
Vase, 18" h., floor-type, tall ovoid body w/ringed base and flaring foot, molded rim & scrolled shoulder handles, mottled pink & green glaze **1,815**
Vase, large bulbous handled form, pink & purple ground 550
Wall pocket, slender fanned body flanked by double-scroll handles, intermingled shades of pink & blue, 8" h. 345
Wall pocket, slender fanned body flanked by double-scroll handles, shaded green ground, 8" h. 283
Wall pocket, slender fanned body flanked by double-scroll handles, shaded brown ground, 8" h. 460

Cherry Blossom (1933)

Sprigs of cherry blossoms, green leaves and twigs with pink fence against a combed blue-green ground or creamy ivory fence against a terra cotta ground shading to dark brown.

Basket, hanging-type, brown ground, 8" 546
Bowl, 4" h., two-handled, canted sides, terra cotta ground 275
Candlesticks, brown ground, pr. 400
Jardiniere, squatty bulbous body, two-handled, blue-green ground, No. 627-4", 4" h. (overall crazing w/discoloration at base) 325
Jardiniere, squatty bulbous body, two-handled, terra cotta ground, No. 627-4", 4" h. 450
Jardiniere, shoulder handles, terra cotta ground, 6" h., No. 627-6" (ILLUS. top, below) 358
Jardiniere, shoulder handles, terra cotta ground, No. 627-7", 7" h. 550
Lamp base, footed globular base tapering to short cylindrical neck flanked by small loop handles, terra cotta ground, shape No. 625-8", overall 9" h. 770

Cherry Blossom Long Planter

Planter, rectangular w/two small handles, terra-cotta ground, No. 240-8", 3 x 11", 7" l. (ILLUS.) 303
Urn, two-handled, terra cotta ground, No. 350-5", 5" h. 420

A Variety of Cherry Blossom Pieces

Vase, ball-shaped, blue-green ground 535

Vase, 4" h., compressed squatty bulbous body w/a short slightly flared neck flanked by small loop handles, blue-green ground, No. 617-3 1/2" 468

Vase, 4" h., compressed squatty bulbous body w/a short slightly flared neck flanked by small loop handles, terra cotta ground, No. 617-3 1/2" (ILLUS. lower right with jardiniere) 337

Vase, 5" h., two-handled, slightly ovoid, terra cotta ground, No. 619-5" (ILLUS. lower left with jardiniere) 275

Vase, 5" h., two-handled, globular w/wide mouth, blue-green ground, No. 627-5" 310

Vase, 5" h., two-handled, globular w/wide mouth, terra cotta ground, No. 627-5" 275

Vase, 6" h., bulbous body, shoulder tapering to wide molded mouth, small loop shoulder handles, terra cotta ground, No. 621-6 354

Vase, 6" h., bulbous body, shoulder tapering to wide molded mouth, small loop shoulder handles, blue-green ground, No. 621-6 605

Vase, 7" h., terra cotta ground, No. 622-7" 525

Vase, 7" h., ovoid body w/tiny shoulder handles, No. 623-7" 596

Vase, 7 1/2" h., two-handled, footed cylindrical body, terra cotta ground, No. 620-7" 359

Vase, 8" h., handles at midsection, terra cotta ground, No. 624-8" 468

Cherry Blossom Vase

Vase, 8" h., two-handled, globular, terra cotta ground, No. 625-8" (ILLUS.) **600-700**

Vase, 10" h., slender ovoid body w/wide cylindrical neck, loop handles from shoulder to middle of neck, terra cotta ground, No. 626-10" 800

Vase, 10" h., slender ovoid body w/wide cylindrical neck, loop handles from shoulder to middle of neck, blue-green ground, No. 626-10" 1,430

Vase, 12" h., tall swelled cylindrical form tapering to a short flaring neck flanked by small loop handles, pink ground, No. 627-12" 546

Vase, 15" h., floor-type, bulbous ovoid w/wide molded mouth, small loop shoulder handles, blue-green ground, No. 628-15" (few minute flecks to decoration, glazed-over chip to branch & few minor chips to base) 3,575

Wall pocket, brown ground, No. 1270-8", gold foil label, 8" h. (short tight line to rim) 863

Chloron (1907)

Molded in high-relief in the manner of early Roman and Greek artifacts. Solid matte green glaze, sometimes combined with ivory. Very similar in form to Egypto.

Vase, 6 1/2" h., two-handled, expanding cylinder, green ground, No. 750-6" 300

Vase, 9" h., squatty bulbous body tapering to a wide flat mouth, small loop handle on shoulder w/molded double curved branch handle on opposite side rising from base to neck, molded flower decoration, signed 525

Vase, 12" h., three heavy feet rising to form base for tapering body w/flared rim, green matte finish 990

Wall pocket, No. 326, unmarked (small chip off back edge on left side, small glaze zit on front) 660

Clematis (1944)

Clematis blossoms and heart-shaped green leaves against a vertically textured ground — white blossoms on blue, rose-pink blossoms on green and ivory blossoms on golden brown.

Basket, hanging-type, blue ground, No. 470-5", 5" h. 225

Clematis Hanging-Type Basket

Basket, hanging-type, brown ground, No. 470-5", 5" h. (ILLUS.) 175

Basket, hanging-type, green ground, No. 470-5", 5" h. 162

Basket, waisted cylindrical body, green ground, No. 387-7" 134

Basket, blue ground, No. 388-8" 160

Basket w/ornate circular handle, waisted cylindrical body, brown ground, No. 387-7", 7" h. 183

Basket w/overhead handle, pedestal base, blue ground, No. 389-10", 10" h. 195

Basket w/overhead handle, pedestal base, green ground, No. 389-10", 10" h. **175-200**

Bowl, 10" d., green ground, No. 6-10" 250

Candleholders, bulbous w/tiny pointed handles, brown ground, No. 1158-2", 2" h., pr. 98

Candleholders, bulbous w/tiny pointed handles, green ground, No. 1158-2", 2" h., pr. 165

Console bowl, two-handled, green ground, No. 460-12", 12" l. 140

Console bowl, blue ground, No. 461-14", 14" l. 200

Console bowl, green ground, No. 461-14",
14" l. (fleck to one petal) 110
Console bowl, brown ground, end handles,
17 1/2" l. 132
Cookie jar, cov., blue ground, No. 3-8",
8" h. 400
Cookie jar, cov., brown ground, No. 3-8",
8" h. 427
Cookie jar, cov., green ground, No. 3-8",
8" h. 550
Cornucopia-vase, blue ground, No. 193-
6", 6" h. 85
Creamer, blue ground, No. 5C 80
Creamer, green ground, No. 5C 75
Creamer & open sugar bowl, green
ground, No. 5S & 5C, pr. 155
Ewer, green ground, No. 16-6", 6" h. 145
Ewer, blue ground, No. 17-10", 10" h. 173
Ewer, green ground, No. 17-10", 10" h. 245
Ewer, blue ground, No. 18-15", 15" h. 365
Ewer, brown ground, No. 18-15", 15" h. 290
Flower frog, green ground, No. 50,
4 1/2" h. 28
Flower frog, green ground, No. 192-5",
5" h. 115
Flowerpot w/saucer, blue ground, No. 668-
5", 5 1/2" h. 120-140
Jardiniere, blue ground, No. 667-8", 8" h. 322
Tea set: cov. teapot, creamer & open sugar
bowl, green ground, No. 5, 3 pcs. 325
Teapot, cov., green ground, No. 5 200
Vase, 6" h., two-handled, green ground, No.
102-6" 55
Vase, 6" h., two-handled, blue ground, No.
103-6" 110
Vase, 6" h., two-handled, brown ground,
No. 103-6" 85
Vase, 6" h., two-handled, urn-form, blue
ground, No. 188-6" 95
Vase, 6" h., two-handled, urn-form, brown
ground, No. 188-6" 105

Clematis Vase

Vase, 7" h., blue ground, No. 105-7"
(ILLUS.) 110
Vase, 7" h., brown ground, No. 105-7" 125
Vase, bud, 7" h., angular handles rising
from flared base to slender neck, green
ground, No. 187-7" 150
Vase, 8" h., two-handled, blue ground, No.
107-8" 103

Vase, 8" h., two-handled, globular base
w/high collared neck, green ground, No.
108-8" 90
Vase, 8" h., footed baluster-form w/flaring
mouth & angled shoulder handles, blue
ground, No. 122-8" 185
Vase, 9" h., blue ground, No. 109-9" 225
Vase, 10" h., two-handled, brown ground,
No. 111-10" 210
Vase, 15" h., brown ground, No. 114-15" 275
Vase, 15" h., green ground, No. 114-15" 765
Wall pocket, angular side handles, brown
ground, No. 1295-8", 8 1/2" h. 124
Wall pocket, angular side handles, green
ground, No. 1295-8", 8 1/2" h. 150

Columbine (1940s)
*Columbine blossoms and foliage on shaded
ground — yellow blossoms on blue, pink blossoms
on pink shaded to green and blue blossoms on tan
shaded to green.*

Basket, elaborate handle rising from mid-
section, blue ground, No. 365-7", 7" h. 250
Basket, elaborate handle rising from mid-
section, pink ground, No. 365-7", 7" h. 220
Basket, hanging-type, pink ground, 8" h. 220
Basket, blue ground, No. 366-8", 8" h. 225
Basket, asymmetrical overhead handle, tan
ground, No. 367-10", 10" h. 230
Basket, blue ground, No. 367-10", 10" h. 220
Basket, pointed handle rising from flat
base, ovoid w/boat-shaped top w/shaped
rim, pink ground, No. 368-12", 12" h. 335
Basket, pointed handle rising from flat
base, ovoid w/boat-shaped top w/shaped
rim, blue ground, No. 368-12", 12" h. 450
Basket w/overhead handle, footed, bul-
bous ovoid body w/irregular rim, brown
ground, 610-12", 12" h. (small chip to
base) 275
Book end planters, blue ground, No. 8,
5" h., pr. 295
Bowl, 6" d., two-handled, squatty bulbous
body w/small angled shoulder handles,
tan ground, No. 400-6" 168

Columbine Bowl

Bowl, 6" d., two-handled, squatty bulbous
body w/small angled shoulder handles,
blue ground, No. 400-6" (ILLUS.) 220
Bowl, 8" d., tan ground, No. 402-8" 125
Candleholders, tan ground, No. 1145-
2 1/2", 2 1/2" h., pr. 60

Candlesticks, flat disk base w/handles rising to nozzle, tan ground, No. 1146-4 1/2", 5" h., pr. **224**
Console bowl, stepped handles rising from rim, tan ground, No. 404-10" **135**
Console bowl, pink shading to green ground, No. 404-10", 10" l. **150**
Ewer, sharply angled handle, pink ground, No. 18-7", 7" h. **190**
Jardiniere, squatty w/small handles at shoulder, blue ground, No. 655-3", 3" h. **120**
Jardiniere, squatty w/small handles at shoulder, pink ground, No. 655-3", 3" h. **140-150**
Jardiniere, squatty w/small handles at shoulder, tan ground, No. 655-3", 3" h. **90**
Jardiniere, two-handled, pink ground, No. 655-6", 6" h. **138**
Jardiniere, two-handled, tan ground, No. 655-6", 6" h. (restoration to rim chip) **99**
Jardiniere, two-handled, blue ground, No. 655-10" 10" h. **413**
Jardiniere & pedestal base, two-handled, tan ground, No. 655-10", 10" h., 2 pcs. **1,800**
Rose bowl, bulbous body flanked by angled handles, wide slightly flared & shaped rim, pink ground, No. 399-4", 4" h. **150**
Urn-vase, pink ground, No. 150-6", 6" h. **155**
Urn-vase, tan ground, No. 150-6", 6" h. **165**
Urn-vase, pink ground, No. 151-8", 8" h. **140**
Vase, 6" h., pink shaded to green ground, No. 13-6" **125**
Vase, 4" h., ovoid body w/wide flared & shaped rim flanked by small angled handles, pink ground, No. 12-4" **135**
Vase, 4" h., blue ground, No. 657-4" **250**
Vase, 6" h., blue ground, No. 13-6" **110**
Vase, 6" h., tan ground, No. 13-6" **135**
Vase, 6" h., pink ground, No. 14-6" **132**
Vase, 7" h., blue ground, No. 16-7" **108**
Vase, 7" h., tan ground, No. 16-7" **133**

Columbine Vase

Vase, 7 1/2" h., two-handled, ovoid w/slightly flaring mouth, pink ground, small chip to handle, No. 17-7" (ILLUS.) **88**
Vase, 7" h., blue ground, No. 18-7" **225**
Vase, 8" h., handles rising from base, blue ground, No. 19-8" **125**

Vase, 8" h., handles rising from base, tan ground, No. 19-8" **195**
Vase, 9" h., two-handled, blue ground, No. 21-9" **220**
Vase, 10" h., ovoid body w/angular handles rising from base to midsection, tan ground, No. 24-10" **273**
Vase, 10" h., ovoid body w/angular handles rising from base to midsection, blue ground, No. 24-10" **285**

Columbine Vase

Vase, 12" h., swelled ovoid body w/flaring rim, angular handles at midsection, flat disk base, pink ground, No. 25-12 (ILLUS.) **384**
Vase, 14" h., floor-type, slender ovoid body tapering to a flared & shaped rim, pointed angular handles at midsection, flat disk base, tan ground, No. 26-14" **463**
Vase, 16" h., floor-type, footed slender ovoid body tapering to a slightly flared & shaped rim, pointed angular shoulder handles, blue ground, No. 27-16" **585**
Wall pocket, squared flaring mouth, conical body w/curled tip, blue ground, No. 1290-8" **625**
Wall pocket, squared flaring mouth, conical body w/curled tip, brown ground, No. 1290-8" **518**

Corinthian (1923)
Deeply fluted ivory and green body below a continuous band of molded grapevine, fruit, foliage and florals in naturalistic colors, narrow ivory and green molded border at the rim.

Basket, hanging-type w/chains, 8" d. **260**
Bowl, 5" h., No. 121-5" **60**
Bowl, 7" d. **75**
Candlestick, No. 1048-10", 10" h. **110**
Flower frog, No. 14-3 1/2", 3 1/2" h. **50**
Jardiniere, 8" h., No. 601-8" **325**
Jardiniere, 9" h., No. 601-9" **185**
Vase, double bud, 4 1/2" h., 7" w., gate-form, No. 37-7" **138**
Vase, 6" h., semi-ovoid **193**
Vase, bud, 6 1/4" h. **195**

Corinthian Vase

Vase, 7" h., footed, baluster-form tapering to wide cylindrical neck, No. 215-7" (ILLUS.) **138**
Vase, 7" h., waisted cylindrical body, No. 235-7 .... **138**
Vase, 8 1/2" h. **90**
Vase, 12" h., cylindrical w/flared rim, No. 235-12" (1/8" glaze flake off one vertical rib) **110**
Wall pocket, No. 1232-8", 8" h. **275**
Wall pocket, conical base tapering to wide neck w/flaring rim, No. 1228-10", 10" h. (few glaze bubbles to front) **173**
Wall pocket, No. 1229-12", 12" h. **250**

Cosmos (1940)

Embossed blossoms against a wavy horizontal ridged band on a textured ground — ivory band with yellow and orchid blossoms on blue, blue band with white and orchid blossoms on green or tan.

Basket, hanging-type, handles rising from midsection to rim, blue ground, No. 361-5", 7" h. **295**
Basket, hanging-type, handles rising from midsection to rim, brown ground, No. 361-5", 7" h. **230**
Basket, blue ground, No. 357-10", 10" h. **363**
Basket w/overhead handle, green ground, No. 357-10", 10" h. **250**
Basket w/pointed overhead handle, pedestal base, blue ground, No. 358-12", 12" h. **485**
Bowl, 4" d., blue ground, No. 375-4" **185**
Bowl, 4" d., tan ground, No. 375-4" **165**
Bowl, 6" d., two-handled, shaped rim, tan ground, No. 369-6" **60**
Bowl, 6" d., No. 376-6" **225**
Bowl, 8" d., blue ground, No. 370-8" **195**
Bowl, 8" d., tan ground, No. 370-8" **110**

Cosmos Candleholder

Candleholders, loop handles above flat disk base, slender candle nozzle, blue ground, No. 1136-2", 2 1/2" h., pr. (ILLUS. of one) **179**
Candlesticks, loop handles rising from disk base, slightly tapering candle nozzle, green ground, No. 1137-4 1/2", 4 1/2" h., pr. **303**
Console bowl, green ground, No. 370-8", 8" l. **163**
Console bowl, blue ground, No. 371-10", 10" l. **160**
Console bowl, footed oblong boat-shape w/an undulating & double-notched rim, blue groung, No. 374-14", 15 1/2" l. **193**
Flower frog, pierced globular body w/asymmetrical overhead handle, blue ground, No. 39, 3 1/2" h. **145**
Flower frog, pierced globular body w/asymmetrical overhead handle, tan shaded to green ground, No. 39, 3 1/2" h. **110**
Flower frogs, pierced globular body w/asymmetrical overhead handle, blue ground, No. 39, 3 1/2" h., pr. **248**
Jardiniere, two-handled, blue ground, No. 649-3" **100**
Jardiniere, two-handled, green ground, No. 649-3" **145**
Jardiniere, two-handled, tan ground, No. 649-4", 4" h. **100-125**
Jardiniere, two-handled, blue ground, No. 649-6", 6" h. **150-225**
Jardiniere & pedestal base, blue ground, No. 649-10", overall 30" h., 2 pcs. **2,600**
Planter, rectangular w/shaped rim, blue ground, No. 381-9", 9" l. **320**
Rose bowl, two-handled, blue ground, No. 375-4", 4" h. **175**
Rose bowl, two-handled, green ground, No. 375-4", 4" h. **135**
Urn-vase, blue ground, No. 135-8", 8" h. **275**
Urn-vase, green ground, No. 135-8", 8" h. **250**
Vase, 4" h., double bud, gate-form, tan ground, No. 133-4" **110**
Vase, 4" h., two-handled, globular base & wide neck, green ground, No. 944-4" **135**
Vase, 4" h., two-handled, globular base & wide neck, tan ground, No. 944-4" **99**
Vase, 6" h., green ground, No. 947-6" **175**
Vase, 7" h., globular base w/long slender neck w/cut-out rim, large loop handles rising from midsection of base to middle of neck, green ground, No. 948-7" **193**
Vase, 7" h., handles at base, trumpet-form body, green ground, No. 949-7" (small chip off bottom of rim) **83**
Vase, bud, 7" h., slender, slightly tapering cylinder w/large loop handles at base, green ground, No. 959-7" **248**
Vase, 8" h., footed bulbous base w/wide cylindrical neck w/scalloped rim, large loop handles, No. 135-8" **248**
Vase, 8" h., two-handled, cut-out top edge, tan ground, No. 950-8" **260**
Vase, 9" h., handles rising from midsection of ovoid body to neck, green ground, No. 952-9" **500**
Vase, 9" h., handles rising from midsection of ovoid body to neck, tan ground, No. 952-9" **175**

Vase, 9" h., tapering cylinder w/shaped flaring mouth, curved handles at midsection, green ground, No. 953-9" **250**

Vase, 10" h., trumpet-shaped w/slender curved handles from base to midsection, tan ground, No. 954-10" **245**

Vase, 10" h., trumpet-shaped w/slender curved handles from base to midsection, green ground, No. 954-10" **375**

Cosmos Vase

Vase, 12 1/2" h., ovoid w/large loop handles, tan ground, No. 956-12" (ILLUS.)......... **300**

Wall pocket, fanned conical shape w/high arched handle across the top, blue ground, No. 1285-6", 6 1/2" h. **518**

Wall pocket, fanned conical shape w/high arched handle across the top, tan ground, No. 1285-6", 6 1/2" h. **259**

Wall pocket, double, tan ground, No. 1286-8", 8 1/2" h. **345**

Window box, tan ground, No. 381-9 x 3 x 3 1/2", 9" l. **242**

Cremona (1927)
Relief-molded floral motifs including a tall stem with small blossoms and arrowhead leaves, wreathed with leaves similar to Velmoss or a web of delicate vines against a background of light green mottled with pale blue or pink with creamy ivory.

Console bowl w/flower frog, green ground, No. 178-8", 8" l. **225**

Vase, 4" h., rectangular mouth w/pointed ends, slightly canted sides, stepped foot, pink ground, No. 72-4" **95**

Vase, 4" h., squatty w/narrow flared mouth, pink ground, No. 351-4"................................. **230**

Vase, 5" h., fan-shaped, green ground, No. 73-5" **83**

Vase, 5" h., bulbous ovoid w/flaring mouth, green ground, No. 352-5" **110**

Vase, 7" h., round foot below squared flaring baluster-form body w/a wide rolled square rim, No. 354-7" **141**

Cremona Vase

Vase, 8" h., footed, wide cylindrical body tapering to wide flat mouth, No. 355-8", black paper label (ILLUS.)............................. **220**

Vase, 10" h., footed square tapering body, No. 358-10"... **220**

Vase, 10" h., baluster-form body w/flaring foot & rim, green ground, No. 350-10" (fleck to tip of one leaf) **193**

Vase, 12" h., footed, slender baluster-form body w/narrow shoulder to the cylindrical neck w/flaring rim, green ground, No. 361-12" **385**

Dahlrose (1924-28)
Band of ivory daisy-like blossoms and green leaves against a mottled tan ground.

Basket, hanging-type w/original chain, No. 343-6", 7 1/2" d. **243**

Bowl, 8" d., footed squatty bulbous body tapering to a wide flared rim, angular end handles from rim to shoulder, No. 180-8"..... **210**

Bowl, 10" l., oval, footed sharply canted sides w/a low molded rim w/angular end handles from rim to shoulder, No. 179-8"..... **148**

Bowl, 10" d., 3 1/2" h., spherical w/incurved sides & molded rim, unmarked..................... **275**

Candleholders, angular handles rising from low slightly domed base, No. 1069-3", 3" h., pr. **135**

Candleholders, angular handles rising from low slightly domed base, 3 1/2" h., pr. **95**

Console set: 8" console bowl & pair of candleholders; No. 180-8" & 1069-3", bowl & one candleholder w/black label, the set....... **375**

Jardiniere, No. 614-4", 4" h. **110**

Jardiniere, tiny rim handles, No. 614-7", 7" d., 4" h. **122**

Jardiniere, squatty bulbous form w/tiny rim handles, No. 614-6", 6" h. **110**

Jardiniere, tiny rim handles, No. 614-8", 8" h. **400**

Jardiniere & pedestal base, No. 614-10", 10" h., 2 pcs. (re-glued base chip to jardiniere)... **935**

Dahlrose Pedestal Base

Pedestal base, flaring foot, tapering cylindrical form w/flaring rim, small chips to bottom, glaze chips & one small chip to rim, 16" h. (ILLUS.) **604**

Dahlrose Triple Bud Vase

Vase, triple bud, 6" h., a domed round base w/a swelled cylindrical central shaft joined by floral panels to outcurved squared side holders, No. 76-6" (ILLUS.) **256**

Vase, double bud, 6" h., gate-form, No. 79-6", black paper label **145-175**

Vase, 6" h., cylindrical w/small pointed handles at the shoulder, No. 363-6" **146**

Vase, 6" h., squatty bulbous body tapering to wide rolled rim, tiny angled handles from shoulder to rim, No. 364-6" **259**

Dahlrose Bud Vase

Vase, bud, 7" h., a ringed oblong domed base supports at one side a slender swelled cylindrical vase w/a flaring rim, a long, high arched handle runs from one side of vase down to a forked juncture w/the base, a smaller down-curved angular handle joins the two sides, No. 77-7 (ILLUS.) **275**

Vase, bud, 8" h., slender swelled body w/flaring base & rolled rim, angled buttress side handles w/blossoms, No. 78-8" **235**

Dahlrose Vase

Vase, 8" h., footed bulbous ovoid, No. 365-8" (ILLUS.) **413**

Vase, 8" h., footed ovoid body w/flared rim, angled handles from shoulder to rim, No. 366-8" **250**

Vase, 10" h., footed tapering square form, paper label **329**

Vase, 10" h., two-handled, ovoid w/wide flaring rim, No. 369-10" **380**

Vase, 12" h., footed wide ovoid w/wide flaring rim, angled handles from shoulder to rim, No. 370-12" **523**

Wall pocket, conical w/molded rim, tiny rim handles, No. 1258-8", 8" h. **550**

Wall pocket, a pointed bullet-form body below a swelled neck w/a molded rim, long angled handles from rim to sides of body, 1258-10", 10" h. **316**

Dawn (1937)

Incised spidery flowers on green ground with blue-violet tinted blossoms, pink or yellow ground with blue-green blossoms, all with yellow centers.

Dawn Console Bowl

Console bowl, long angular foot supporting a deep boat-shaped bowl w/high stepped end panels, green ground, No. 317-10", 10" l. (ILLUS.) **440**

Dawn Vase

Vase, 6" h., cylindrical w/tab handles below rim, square foot, green ground, No. 826-6" (ILLUS.) **110**

Vase, 6" h., tab handles at rim, semi-ovoid, square foot, green ground, No. 827-6" **185**

Vase, 8" h., angled squatty base tapering to a tall cylindrical neck w/small tab handles, raised on a square foot, yellow ground, No. 829-8" **175-250**

Dawn Vase

Vase, 9" h., tapering conical form on square base, buttressed base handles, green ground, small chip on corner of base, light crazing, No. 831-9" (ILLUS.) **230**

Vase, 10" h., bulbous ovoid body on square foot, buttressed shoulder handles, yellow ground, No. 832-10" (glaze flakes to base & handle) **358**

Della Robbia, Rozane (1906)

Naturalistic or stylized designs executed by hand using the sgraffito method.

Della Robbia Vase with Flower Band

Vase, 9 1/2" h., footed wide ovoid body tapering to a short cylindrical neck, incised decoration of stylized flowers in large teardrops w/bands of spade-shaped leaves around the top & base, in six colors including white, blue, yellow & dark green, signed, minor chip repairs (ILLUS.) **6,325**

Unusual Della Robbia Vase

Vase, 10 1/2" h., flaring foot below compressed round base, tall cylindrical body w/flaring rim, deeply carved & cut-back fish decoration under a multi-tone green glaze, partial wafer mark, restored, minor chip to top (ILLUS.) **2,400**

Large Della Robbia Vase

Vase, 10 1/2" h., large spherical body w/short cylindrical neck, flaring rim, cutback & incised floral design in shades of blue, aqua & olive green, brown & yellow, restoration to top & bottom (ILLUS.)........... **8,800**

Large Della Robbia Vase with Poppies

Vase, 17 1/2" h., 9 1/2" d., tall ovoid body w/the rim reticulated in a Greek key design above five tall rectangular panels decorated in seven colors w/excised poppies in ivory & taupe on a mint green ground, discreet restoration around rim & to short hairline, unmarked (ILLUS.)......... **18,400**

Rare Della Robbia Floor Vase

Vase, 21" h., 10 1/2" d., floor-type, large ovoid form tapering to a small flattened & flared neck, excised, incised & enameled in seven colors w/yellow daffodils & shiny leaves in shades of green on a mint green & indigo blue ground, probably an exhibition piece, professional restoration to rim, several underglaze chips on base, invisible touch-ups to glaze nicks, wafer mark & original paper price tag marked $50, signed by H. Smith (ILLUS.) **37,375**

Dogwood I (1916-18)
White dogwood blossoms and brown branches against a textured green ground.

Basket w/overhead handle, 8" h. **440**
Bowl, 5" d., No. 150-5".. **100**

Dogwood I Vase

Vase, 6" h., bulbous ovoid body, No. 300-6"
    (ILLUS.)... **222**
Vase, 9" h., ovoid body w/flaring rim, No.
    303-9"... **385**
Wall pocket, cone-shaped, green ground,
    No. 1245-9", 9 1/2" h.. **334**

Dogwood II (1928)
White dogwood blossoms & black branches against a smooth green ground.

Basket, hanging-type **238**

Dogwood II Basket

Basket, 8" h. (ILLUS.) **179**
Jardiniere, No. 590-7", 7" h. **210**
Jardiniere, No. 590-8", 8" h. **254**
Jardiniere, No. 490-10", 10" h. **575**
Jardiniere & pedestal base, No. 590-12",
    12" h., 2 pcs.. **1,700**

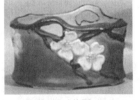

Dogwood II Planter

Planter, tub-shaped w/rim handles, 7" d.,
    4" h. (ILLUS.)... **123**
Vase, bud, 8" h., tusk-form w/single handle
    rising from base to midsection **135**
Vase, 8" h., ovoid body tapering to wide cylindrical neck, No. 135-8" (couple of burst bubbles to neck & body)................................ **115**

Wall pocket, double, 9" h. **423**
Wall pocket, two handles in the form of
blossoming branches, No. 1218-10",
10" h. (rim repair) **173**

Donatello (1915)
Deeply fluted ivory and green body with wide tan band embossed with cherubs at various pursuits in pastoral settings.

Basket, hanging-type, No. 327-6", 7" d.,
5" h. **201**
Basket w/tall pointed overhead handle,
cylindrical body, No. 304-12", 12" h. **358**

Donatello Candlesticks

Candlesticks, flaring base & rim w/tall slen-
der cylindrical stem, No. 1022-10",
10" h., pr. (ILLUS.) **303**
Flower frog, No. 14-2 1/2", 2 1/2" d. **70**
Jardiniere, No. 575-4", 4" h. **95**
Jardiniere, No. 575-6", 7" d., 6" h. **150**
Jardiniere, No. 579-8", 8" h. **250**
Jardiniere, No. 579-10", 10" h. **395**
Jardiniere & pedestal base, 12" h. jardi-
niere, No. 579-12", overall 34" h., 2 pcs. ... **1,300**
Planter, No. 238-7" (pinhead nicks on in-
side rim) **56**
Powder jar, cov., lid decorated w/scene of
cherubs playing musical instruments,
5" d., 2" h. **330**
Umbrella stand, cylindrical, No. 753-10",
10" h. (three glaze nicks to rim, a couple
of tight lines to relief band, not through) **413**

Donatello Double Bud Vase

Vase, double bud, gate-form, No. 8 (ILLUS.) **70**
Vase, bud, 10" h., bottle-form, No. 115-10" **255**
Wall pocket, ovoid, No. 1212-9", 9" h. **275-300**
Wall pocket, No. 1202-10", 10" h. **190**
Wall pocket, No. 1219-10", 10" h. **226**
Window box, rectangular, No. 60-12",
6 x 12" l. **295**

Earlam (1930)
Mottled glaze on various simple shapes. The line includes many crocus or strawberry pots.

Bowl, 4" h., canted sides w/scroll handles,
bluish green glaze on exterior & salmon
interior, unmarked, No. 217-4" **248**
Bowl, 4" d., blue ground, No. 515-4" **188**
Planter, rectangular w/shaped rim, blue
ground, No. 88-6 x 10" **295**
Planter, two-handled, rectangular
w/shaped rim, curved end handles, mot-
tled green glaze, No. 89-8", 5 x 10 1/2" **275**
Strawberry pot w/saucer, four pockets,
mottled green glaze, No. 91-8", 8" h. **1,045**
Urn-vase, two-handled, mottled blue-green,
No. 521-7", 7" h. **440**
Vase, 6" h., two-handled, semi-ovoid, mot-
tled blue-green glaze, No. 518-6" **220**
Vase, 7" h., bulbous ovoid w/large loop handles, orange, green & blue matte glaze,
No. 519-7" (minute burst bubble ar rim &
small flat chip inside bottom ring) **413**
Vase, 7" h., globular w/handles at shoulder,
mottled blue & green glaze, No. 521-7" **375**
Wall pocket, No. 1263, 7 1/2" h. (small nick
to back of hole) **805**

Early Embossed Pitchers (pre-1916)
High gloss, utility line of pitchers with various embossed scenes.

Boy w/horn **550**

Goldenrod Pitcher

Goldenrod, 9 1/2" h., minor bruise to rim &
touch-ups around base (ILLUS.) **303**

Landscape Pitcher

Landscape, 7 1/2" h. (ILLUS.) **95-100**
The Bridge, 6" h. **258**
The Cow, 6 1/2" h. **399**
The Owl, 6 1/2" h. **599**

Wild Rose Pitcher

Wild Rose, 9 1/2" h., small spout chip
(ILLUS.) **125**

Falline (1933)
Curving panels topped by a semi-scallop sepa-
rated by vertical peapod decorations; blended
backgrounds of tan shading to green and blue or
tan shading to darker brown.

Console bowl, shallow w/end loop handles,
tan ground, No. 244-8", 8" l. **394**
Console bowl, shallow w/end handles, tan
shading to brown, 11" d. **275**
Vase, 6" h., footed cylindrical body w/large
loop handles from midsection to rim, tan
shading to blue & green, No. 642-6" **990**

Falline Vase

Vase, 6" h., footed cylindrical w/large loop
handles from midsection to rim, tan shad-
ing to brown, No. 642-6" (ILLUS.) **280**
Vase, 6" h., two-handled, ovoid, tan shading
to blue & green, No. 643-6" **935**
Vase, 6" h., two-handled, ovoid, tan shading
to brown, No. 643-6" **392**
Vase, 6" h., globular body w/a narrow
swelled shoulder below the wide short
cylindrical neck, C-scroll handles from
the neck to the top of the body, green
"pods" on a light shaded to dark brown
ground, No. 644-6", gold foil label **798**
Vase, two-handled, tan shading to darker
brown, 6" h., No. 650-6" **503**
Vase, 6 1/2" h., bulbous ovoid w/large loop
handles, tan shading to darker brown
ground, No. 645-6 1/2" **660**

Vase, 7" h., globular body tapering to
stepped shoulder & wide cylindrical neck
w/shoulder loop handles, shaded brown
body, No. 648-7" **1,045**
Vase, 7 1/2" h., two-handled, slightly round-
ed cylinder, tan shading to blue & green,
restoration to handles, No. 647-7" **750-800**
Vase, 7 1/2" h., two-handled, slightly rounded cylinder, tan shading to brown, No.
647-7" **715**
Vase, 8 1/4" h., 6" d., footed trumpet-form
w/a widely flaring rim, low arched handles from under the rim to mid-body, tan
shading to green & blue (7" l. Y-shaped
line from rim) **495**

Ribbed Falline Vase

Vase, 9" h., two large handles rising from
midsection to neck, horizontally ribbed
lower section, shaded brown, No. 652-9"
(ILLUS.) **963**

Ferella (1931)
Impressed shell design alternating with small
cut-outs at top and base; mottled brown or tur-
quoise and red glaze.

Ferella Bowl

Bowl, 12" d., canted sides, low foot, mottled
brown glaze, No. 212-12" (ILLUS.) **523**

Ferella Candlesticks

Candleholders, chalice-form w/a low pedestal base supporting a wide deep
pierced rounded cup centered by a cylindrical candle socket, mottled brown
glaze, No. 1078-4", professional repair to
one, 4 1/2" h., pr. (ILLUS.) **413**

Console bowl w/attached flower frog,
deep flaring sides, mottled brown glaze,
No. 87-8", 8" d. **473**

Urn-vase, compressed globular form w/tiny
handles at midsection, reticulated foot &
rim, turquoise & red glaze, No. 505-6",
6" h. **468**

Vase, 4" h., angular handles, short narrow
neck, mottled brown glaze, No. 497-4" **429**

Vase, 4" h., angular handles, bulbous, turquoise & red glaze, No. 498-4" **300-350**

Vase, 5" h., footed wide ovoid form w/flaring
rim, long side handles, turquoise & red
glaze, No. 500-5" **523**

Vase, 5" h., two-handled, turquoise & red
glaze, No. 500-5" **640**

Vase, 5" h., two-handled, flaring rim, mottled brown glaze, No. 503-5" **400**

Vase, 6" h., large semi-circular handles, turquoise & red glaze, No. 499-6" **575**

Vase, 6" h., tapering cylinder w/angular side
handles, turquoise & red glaze, No. 501-
6" **950**

Ferella Vase

Vase, 6" h., handles rising from shoulder of
compressed globular base to beneath
the rim of the long tapering neck, mottled
brown glaze, No. 502-6" (ILLUS.) **650**

Vase, 6" h., bulbous base w/canted shoulder flanked by small angular handles,
wide cylindrical neck, & turquoise & red
glaze, No. 505-6" **700**

Vase, 8" h., slightly ovoid, turquoise & red
glaze, No. 508-8" **1,093**

Vase, 8" h., spherical body on low foot
w/wide slightly flared cylindrical neck,
arched handles from mid-section to
shoulder, mottled brown ground, No.
509-8" **550**

Vase, 8" h., spherical body on low foot
w/wide slightly flared cylindrical neck,
arched handles from mid-section to
shoulder, turquoise & red glaze, No. 509-
8" **850**

Vase, 9 1/4" h., 5 1/4" d., footed slender
ovoid body tapering to a short flaring
neck, low arched handles down the
sides, stylized green & yellow blossoms
on reticulated bands, mottled brown
glaze, No. 507-9" **667**

Vase, 9 1/4" h., 5 1/4" d., footed slender
ovoid body tapering to a short flaring
neck, low arched handles down the
sides, stylized green & yellow blossoms
on reticulated bands, turquoise & red
glaze, No. 507-9" **1,223**

Vase, 10" h., 6" 1/4" d., ovoid body on flaring foot & tapering to a widely flaring
mouth, low angular handles down the
sides, the foot pierced w/a band of small
squares, the mouth pierced w/two bands
of small rectangles, brown glaze, No.
511-10" **935**

Vase, 10" h., 6" 1/4" d., ovoid body on flaring foot & tapering to a widely flaring
mouth, low angular handles down the
sides, the foot pierced w/a band of small
squares, the mouth pierced w/two bands
of small rectangles, turquoise & red
glaze, No. 511-10" **1,650**

Wall   pocket, half-round   basket-form
w/widely flaring rim & high shaped &
arched backplate w/hanging hole, turquoise & red glaze, No. 1266-6 1/2",
6 1/2" h. **2,300**

Florane I (1920s)

*Terra cotta shading to either dark brown or deep
olive green on simple shapes, often from the Rose-
craft line.*

Florane Basket

Basket, footed, ovoid body w/flaring rim,
overhead handle, terra cotta shading to
olive green, 8 1/4" h. (ILLUS. far right) **358**

Bowl, 6" d., dark brown, No. 60-6" **110**

Bowl, 8" d., low, dark brown **110**

Bowl, 8" d., rounded w/upright sides &
slightly scalloped rim, No. 62-8" **50**

Vase, double-bud, 5" h., gate-form **125**

Vase, 5 5/8" h., footed swelled cylindrical
body w/short collared neck, terra cotta
shading to olive green **110**

**Vase,   6"   h.,   cylindrical   body   w/short
squared shoulder handles, terra cotta
shading to olive green **165**

Vase, 6 5/8" h., footed, wide ovoid body
w/flat flared rim, terra cotta shading to ol-
ive green **193**

Vase, 8" h., footed, cylindrical body w/wide
flaring rim, squared handles, terra cotta
shading to olive green.................................... **165**

Vase, bud, 8" h., dark brown................................ **80**

Vase, 12" h., slender ovoid form, terra cotta
shading to olive green ground, No. 64-12" **100**

Wall pocket, two-handled, ovoid w/fan-
shaped top, terra cotta shading to olive
green, 9 3/4" h... **330**

Florentine (1924-28)

*Bark-textured panels alternating with embossed
garlands of cascading fruit and florals; ivory with
tan and green, beige with brown and green or
brown with beige and green glaze.*

Ashtray, brown ground, No. 17-3", 3" **165**

Bowl, 5 1/4" d., beige ground **140**

Bowl, 7 1/2" d., brown ground............................. **99**

Bowl, 7" d., No. 125-7".. **40**

Candlesticks, flaring base, expanding cylindrical stem, No. 1049-8", 8" h., pr. **125**

Candlesticks, flaring base, expanding cylindrical stem, brown, No. 1050-10",
10" h., pr... **358**

Compote, 4" d., brown ground, No. 6-4" **195**

Jardiniere, brown, No. 130-4", 7" d., 4" h. **165**

Jardiniere, bulbous footed body w/a wide
molded mouth flanked by tiny angled rim
handles, pastel decoration on a pink
ground, early mark, No. 602-7", 9 1/2" d.,
7" h. **61**

Jardiniere, brown, No. 602-8", 8" h. **495**

Jardiniere & pedestal base, 2 pcs. **1,350**

Sand jar, green ground, 15 x 17"...................... **440**

Urn, brown ground, 4 1/2" h................................ **125**

Vase, 8" h., squared handles rising above
rim, ovoid w/collared neck, ivory, No.
255-8" **155**

Vase, 8 1/2" h., squared handles at rim,
ovoid, brown, No. 231-8" **219**

Wall pocket, conical, No. 1239-7", 7" h. **229**

Wall pocket, overhead handle, brown
ground, No. 1238-8", 8 1/2" h. **173**

Florentine Wall Pocket

Wall pocket, brown ground, 9 1/2" h.
(ILLUS.)... **325**

Wall pocket, conical, No. 1231-12", 12" h. **251**

Florentine II (after 1937)

*Similar to the ivory Florentine, but with lighter
backgrounds, less decoration and without cascades on the dividing panels.*

Basket, hanging-type, No. 337-7", 7" h. **172**

Florentine II Basket and Vase

Basket w/pointed overhead handle, footed, bulbous body w/flared rim, No. 321-
7", 7" h. (ILLUS. right)................................... **138**

Vase, 12" h., ovoid body tapering to wide
cylindrical neck w/flaring rim, angled handles from shoulder to rim, No. 234-12"
(ILLUS. left) **303**

Foxglove (1940s)

*Sprays of pink and white blossoms embossed
against a shaded matte-finish ground.*

Basket, hanging-type, blue ground, No.
466-5", 6 1/2" h. **300-350**

Basket, hanging-type, green ground, No.
466-5", 6 1/2" h. **250-300**

Basket, hanging-type, blue ground, No.
466-5", 10" **201**

Basket w/circular overhead handle, conical body w/asymmetric & shaped rim on
round disk base, No. 373-8", 8" h. **213**

Basket w/circular overhead handle, footed conical body w/widely flaring rim,
green ground, No. 374-10", 10" h. **495**

Basket w/circular overhead handle, footed conical body w/widely flaring rim, pink
ground, No. 374-10", 10" h. **220**

Basket w/circular overhead handle, footed fan-shape w/shaped rim, green
ground, No. 375-12", 12" h. **275**

Basket w/circular overhead handle, footed fan-shape w/shaped rim, pink ground,
No. 375-12", 12" h. **330**

Book ends, blue ground, No. 10, pr. **250**

Foxglove Book Ends

Foxglove Conch Shell

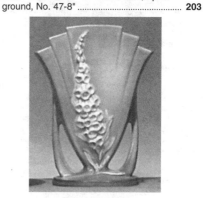

Foxglove Vase

Vase, 18" h., floor-type, two-handled, footed baluster-form w/narrow flared rim, pink ground, artist-initialed, No. 56-18" **715**

Wall pocket, conical w/flaring rim, loop handles, blue ground, No. 1292-8", 8" h. **335**

Wall pocket, conical w/flaring rim, loop handles, green ground, No. 1292-8", 8" h. **400**

Freesia (1945)

Trumpet-shaped blossoms and long slender green leaves against wavy impressed lines — white and lavender blossoms on blended green; white and yellow blossoms on shaded blue or terra cotta and brown.

Basket, hanging-type, blue ground, No. 471-5" **300**

Basket, hanging-type, terra cotta ground, No. 471-5" **259**

Basket, green ground, No. 390-7", 7" h. **220**

Basket, terra cotta ground, No. 390-7", 7" h. **167**

Basket, terra cotta ground, No. 392-10", 10" h. **231**

Basket w/low overhead handle, green ground, No. 310-10", 10" h. **250**

Basket w/overhead handle, terra-cotta ground, No. 391-8", 8" h. **154**

Book ends, blue ground, No. 15, 5 1/4" h., pr. **248**

Bowl, 6" d., green ground, No. 464-6" **135**

Bowl 6" d., terra cotta ground, No. 464-6" **155**

Bowl, 11" d., two-handled, terra cotta ground, No. 465-8" **135**

Candleholders, tiny pointed handles, domed base, blue ground, No. 1160-2", 2" h., pr. **88**

Candleholders, tiny pointed handles, domed base, green ground, No. 1160-2", 2" h., pr. **90**

Candleholders, tiny pointed handles, domed base, terra cotta ground, No. 1160-2", 2" h., pr. **118**

Candlestick, disk base, cylindrical w/low handles, green ground, No. 1161-4 1/2", 4 1/2" h. **75**

Candlesticks, disk base, cylindrical w/low handles, blue ground, No. 1161-4 1/2", 4 1/2" h., pr. **150**

Candlesticks, disk base, cylindrical w/low handles, green ground, No. 1161-4 1/2", 4 1/2" h., pr. **125**

Candlesticks, disk base, cylindrical w/low handles, terra cotta ground, No. 1161-4 1/2", 4 1/2" h., pr. **120-130**

Console bowl, oval w/angled end handles, green ground, No. 7-10", 10" **250**

Console bowl, low, round, green ground, No. 465-8", 8" d. **175**

Console bowl, terra cotta ground, No. 466-10", 10" l. **143**

Console bowl, oval w/shaped flaring rim & angled end handles, green ground, No. 469-14", 16 1/2" l. **208**

Console bowl, oval w/shaped flaring rim & angled end handles, terra cotta ground, No. 469-14", 16 1/2" l. **135**

Console set: 12" l., 4 1/2" h. console bowl & pr. of candlesticks; blue ground, No. 468-12", 3 pcs. **88**

Cookie jar, cov., bulbous ovoid body w/angled shoulder handles, slightly domed lid w/knob finial, green ground, No. 4-8", 8" h. **350**

Cookie jar, cov., bulbous ovoid body w/angled shoulder handles, slightly domed lid w/knob finial, terra cotta ground, No. 4-8", 8" h. **438**

Cookie jar, cov., bulbous ovoid body w/angled shoulder handles, slightly domed lid w/knob finial, blue ground, No. 4-8", 8" h. **550**

Cornucopia-vase, terra cotta ground, No. 198-8", 8" h. **165**

Cornucopia-vases, terra cotta ground, No. 197-6", 6" h., pr. **121**

Creamer, green ground, No. 6C **100**

Ewer, blue ground, No. 19-6", 6" h. **149**

Freesia Ewer

Ewer, green ground, No. 19-6", 6" h. (ILLUS.) **112**

Ewer, terra cotta ground, No. 19-6", 6" h. **151**

Ewer, blue ground, No. 20-10", 10" h. **300**

Ewer, terra cotta ground, No. 20-10", 10" h. **325**

Ewer, blue ground, No. 21-15", 15" h. **299**

Ewer, terra cotta ground, No. 21-15", 15" h. **500**

Jardiniere, tiny rim handles, terra cotta ground, No. 669-4", 4" h. **125**

Jardiniere, rim handles, blue ground, No. 669-8", 8" h. **425**

Jardiniere & pedestal base, green ground, No. 669-8", 2 pcs. **805**

Jardiniere & pedestal base, terra cotta ground, No. 669-8", 2 pcs. **1,125**

Lamp, blue ground, No. 145 .... **468**

Pitcher, 10" h., tankard, footed slender ovoid body w/wide spout & pointed arched handle, terra cotta ground, No. 20-10" **150-200**

Pitcher, 10" h., tankard, footed slender ovoid body w/wide spout & pointed arched handle, green ground, No. 20-10" **450**

Freesia Teapot

Tea set: cov. teapot, creamer & open sugar bowl; blue ground, Nos. 6, 6C & 6S, 3 pcs. (ILLUS. of teapot) **605**

Tea set: cov. teapot, creamer & open sugar bowl; Nos. 6, 6C & 6S, terra cotta ground, 3 pcs. **450**

Teapot, cov., terra cotta ground, No. 6 .... **200**

Urn-vase, two-handled, green ground, No. 463-5", 5" h. **220**

Urn-vase, two-handled, bulbous body tapering to wide cylindrical neck, green ground, No. 196-8", 8" h. **209**

Urn-vase, two-handled, bulbous body tapering to wide cylindrical neck, terra cotta ground, No. 196-8", 8" h. **225**

Vase, bud, 7" h., handles rising from compressed globular base, long slender tapering neck, terra cotta ground, No. 195-7" **86**

Vase, 6" h., terra cotta ground, No. 117-6" **165**

Vase, 6" h., footed squatty bulbous base w/wide cylindrical neck, large angled handles, terra cotta ground, No. 118-6" **105**

Vase, 6" h., two-handled, wide fan-shaped body, terra cotta ground, No. 199-6" **165**

Vase, 7" h., base handles, long cylindrical neck, terra cotta ground, No. 119-7" **75-125**

Vase, 7" h., two-handled, slightly expanding cylinder, blue ground, No. 120-7" **140**

Vase, 7" h., two-handled, slightly expanding cylinder, green ground, No. 120-7" **161**

Vase, bud, 7" h., handles rising from compressed globular base, long slender tapering neck, green ground, No. 195-7" **95-100**

Vase, 7" h., two-handled, fan shaped, blue ground, No. 200-7" **150**

Vase 7" h., two-handled, fan-shaped, terra cotta, No. 200-7" **165**

Vase, 8" h., footed ovoid body flanked by D-form handles, blue ground, No. 121-8" **149**

Vase, 8" h., footed ovoid body flanked by D-form handles, terra cotta ground, No. 121-8" **150**

Vase, 8" h., globular base & flaring rim, handles at midsection, blue ground, No. 122-8" **125-150**

Vase, 8" h., globular base & flaring rim, handles at midsection, terra cotta ground, No. 122-8" **148**

Vase, 9" h., two angular handles at base, cylindrical top w/flaring rim, terra cotta ground, No. 124-9" **124**

Vase, 9" h., two angular handles at base, cylindrical top w/flaring rim, blue ground, No. 124-9" **178**

Vase, 9 1/2" h., a short ringed pedestal base supporting a flaring half-round base w/an angled shoulder tapering slightly to a tall, wide cylindrical neck, down-curved angled loop handles from center of neck to rim of lower shoulder, blue ground, No. 123-9" **149**

Vase, 9 1/2" h., a short ringed pedestal base supporting a flaring half-round base w/an angled shoulder tapering slightly to a tall, wide cylindrical neck, down-curved angled loop handles from center of neck to rim of lower shoulder, terra cotta ground, No. 123-9" **195**

Vase, 10" h., two-handled, spherical base w/wide cylindrical neck & flat rim, terra cotta ground, No. 126-10" (ILLUS.) **165**

Freesia Vase

Vase, 10" h., two-handled, spherical base w/wide cylindrical neck & flat rim, blue ground, No. 126-10" **230**

Vase, 10 1/2" h., two-handled, trumpet-form body, blue ground, No. 125-10" **165**

Vase, 10 1/2" h., two-handled, trumpet-form body, green ground, No. 125-10" (professional repair) **175**

Vase, 15" h., tall slender ovoid body tapering to narrow cylindrical neck w/wide flaring rim, pointed shoulder handles, terra cotta ground, No. 128-15" **275**

Vase, 15" h., tall slender ovoid body tapering to narrow cylindrical neck w/wide flaring rim, pointed shoulder handles, blue ground, No. 128-15" **660**

Vase, 18" h., floor-type, tall slender ovoid body w/slightly flared rim, angled shoulder handles, green ground, No. 129-18" **550**

Vase, 18" h., floor-type, tall slender ovoid body w/slightly flared rim, angled shoulder handles, blue ground, No. 129-18" **495**

Wall pocket, waisted long body w/small angled side handles, green ground, No. 1296-8", 8 1/2" h. **237**

Wall pocket, waisted long body w/small angled side handles, terra cotta ground, No. 1296-8", 8 1/2" h. **213**

Window box, two-handled, green ground, No. 1392-8", 10 1/2" l. **150**

Window box, two-handled, terra cotta ground, No. 1392-8", 10 1/2" l. **125**

Fuchsia (1939)

Coral pink fuchsia blossoms and green leaves against a background of blue shading to yellow, green shading to terra cotta or terra cotta shading to gold.

Basket, hanging-type, green ground, No. 359-5", 5" h. **350-450**

Basket, hanging-type, terra cotta ground, No. 359-5", 5" h. **375-450**

Basket, hanging-type, terra cotta ground, No. 359-5", 7" h. **201**

Basket, a short pedestal foot supports a wide squatty half-round body w/small half-round tabs on two sides of the incurved rim, a high round handle joins the two other edges, terra cotta ground, No. 350-8", 8" h. **358**

Basket, a short pedestal foot supports a wide squatty half-round body w/small half-round tabs on two sides of the incurved rim, a high round handle joins the two other edges, green ground, No. 350-8", 8" h. **560**

Basket, w/overhead handle, blue ground, No. 351-10", 10" h. **248**

Basket, w/overhead handle, terra cotta ground, No. 351-10", 10" h. **220**

Basket w/flower frog, a short pedestal foot supports a wide squatty half-round body w/small half-round tabs on two sides of the incurved rim, a high round handle joins the two other edges, blue ground, No. 350-8", 8" h. **457**

Bowl, urn-form, two-handled, blue ground, No. 346-4", 4" h. **253**

Bowl, urn-form, two-handled, green ground, No. 346-4" **140**

Bowl, 5" d., two-handled, squatty bulbous body w/incurved rim, blue ground, No. 348-5" **150**

Bowl, 5" d., two-handled, squatty bulbous body w/incurved rim, green ground, No. 348-5" **101**

Bowl, 6" d., footed bulbous body w/wide flat rim, loop shoulder handles, blue ground, No. 347-6", w/sticker **275**

Bowl, 6" d., footed bulbous body w/wide flat rim, loop shoulder handles, terra cotta ground, No. 347-6" **275**

Bowl, 6" d., footed bulbous body w/wide flat rim, loop shoulder handles, green ground, No. 347-6" **280**

Bowl, 8" d., two-handled, blue ground, No. 349-8" **216**

Candleholders, two handles rising from disk base, green ground, No. 1132-2", 2" h., pr. **193**

Candlesticks, conical body supported by two handles rising from domed base, terra cotta ground, No. 1133-5", 5" h., pr. **275**

Console bowl, footed oval w/shaped rim & small loop end handles, blue ground, No. 352-12", 12" l. **335**

Console bowl, two-handled oval w/shaped rim, green ground, No. 351-10", 12 1/2" l., 3 1/2" h. **195**

Fuchsia Console Bowl

Console bowl, two-handled oval w/shaped rim, terra cotta ground, No. 351-10", 12 1/2" h. (ILLUS.) **193**

Console bowl, footed low oblong boat-shaped w/under-rim end loop handles, blue ground, No. 353-14", 15 1/2" l. **220**

Console bowl, footed low oblong boat-shaped w/under-rim end loop handles, terra cotta ground, No. 353-14", 15 1/2" l. **375**

Console set: 10" bowl & pair of 5" h. candleholders, blue ground, Nos. 351-10" & 1133-5", the set **750**

Cornucopia-vase, blue ground, No. 129-6", 6" h. **150**

Cornucopia-vase, green ground, No. 129-6", 6" h. **175**

Cornucopia-vase, terra cotta ground, No. 129-6", 6" h. **200**

Ewer, terra cotta ground, No. 902-10", 10" h. **300**

Flower frog, green ground, No. 37 .... **225**

Flower frog, terra cotta ground, No. 37 .... **125**

Flowerpot, blue ground, No. 646-5", 5" h. **303**

Flowerpot, terra cotta ground, No. 646-5", 5" h. **155**

Jardiniere, two-handled, blue ground, No. 645-3", 3" h. **140**

Jardiniere, two-handled, green ground, No. 645-3", 3" h. **189**

Jardiniere, two-handled, blue ground, No. 645-4" 4" h. **253**

Jardiniere, two-handled, green ground, No. 645-4", 4" h. **135**

Jardiniere, two-handled, terra cotta ground, No. 645-4" 4" h. **190**

Jardiniere, two-handled, blue ground, No. 645-5" 5" h. **225**

Jardiniere, two-handled, green ground, No. 645-6", 6" h. **193**

Fuchsia Jardiniere

Jardiniere, two-handled, blue ground, No. 645-8", 8" h. (ILLUS.) **715**

Jardiniere & pedestal, green ground, No. 645-10", 2 pcs. **2,400**

Fuchsia Pitcher

Pitcher w/ice lip, 8" h., blue ground, No. 1322-8" (ILLUS.) **420**

Pitcher w/ice lip, 8" h., green ground, No. 1322-8" **395**

Pitcher w/ice lip, 8" h., terra cotta ground, No. 1322-8" **358**

Vase, 6" h., footed spherical body w/a ringed cylindrical neck w/a flaring rim, long C-form handles from center of the neck to the center of the body, blue ground, No. 891-6" 250

Vase, 6" h., footed spherical body w/a ringed cylindrical neck w/a flaring rim, long C-form handles from center of the neck to the center of the body, terra cotta ground, No. 891-6" 253

Vase, 6" h., ovoid w/handles rising from shoulder to rim, blue ground, No. 892-6"...... 173

Vase, 6" h., ovoid w/handles rising from shoulder to rim, green ground, No. 892-6".. 200

Vase, 6" h., ovoid w/handles rising from shoulder to rim, terra cotta ground, No. 892-6".. 130

Vase, 6" h., footed swelled cylindrical body w/long loop handles, blue ground, No. 893-6".. 248

Vase, 6" h., footed swelled cylindrical body w/long loop handles, terra cotta ground, No. 893-6".. 180

Vase, 7" h., ovoid body w/cut-out rim & large loop handles, blue ground, No. 894-7" 250

Vase, 7" h., ovoid body w/cut-out rim & large loop handles, terra cotta ground, No. 894-7".. 193

Fuchsia Vase

Vase, 7" h., bulbous base tapering to flaring rim, large loop handles from shoulder to below rim, terra cotta ground, No. 895-7" (ILLUS.)... 190

Vase, 7" h., bulbous base tapering to flaring rim, large loop handles from shoulder to below rim, green ground, No. 895-7"............ 220

Vase, 7" h., bulbous base tapering to flaring rim, large loop handles from shoulder to below rim, blue ground, No. 895-7" 275

Vase, 8" h., wide ovoid body w/handles rising from flat base to shoulder, terra cotta ground, No. 897-8"...................................... 225

Vase, 8" h., wide ovoid body w/handles rising from flat base to shoulder, green ground, No. 897-8".. 259

Vase, 8" h., wide ovoid body w/handles rising from flat base to shoulder, blue ground, No. 897-8" 385

Vase, 8" h., footed bulbous body tapering slightly to a wide gently tapering cylindrical neck w/a rolled rim, long curved han-

dles from just under the rim to the mid-body, blue ground, No. 898-8"................ **350-400**

Vase, 8 1/2" h., pillow-type w/handles rising from base to midsection, blue ground, No. 896-8" 425

Vase, 9" h., footed ovoid body w/flared rim & large C-form handles, blue ground, No. 899-9"... 495

Vase, 9" h., footed ovoid body w/flared rim & large C-form handles, green ground, No. 899-9"... 285

Vase, 9" h., footed ovoid body w/flared rim & large C-form handles, terra cotta ground, No. 899-9"...................................... 179

Vase, 9" h., footed cylindrical w/wide flaring rim & large C-form handles, blue ground, No. 900-9".. 350

Vase, 10" h., footed swelled ovoid body w/wide shaped rim & large C-form handles, terra cotta ground, No. 901-10" 302

Vase, 10" h., footed swelled ovoid body w/wide shaped rim & large C-form handles, blue ground, No. 901-10"...................... 485

Vase, 12" h., cylindrical body w/slightly flared neck, two handles rising from above base to neck, terra cotta ground, No. 903-12"... 400

Vase, 12" h., cylindrical body w/slightly flared neck, two handles rising from above base to neck, blue ground, No. 903-12" 431

Vase, 12" h., cylindrical body w/slightly flared neck, two handles rising from above base to neck, green ground, No. 903-12" 627

Vase, 15" h., slender ovoid body w/wide cylindrical neck & large C-form handles, blue ground, No. 904-15" **650-700**

Vase, 15" h., slender ovoid body w/wide cylindrical neck & large C-form handles, terra cotta ground, No. 904-15"............. **550-600**

Vase, 15" h., slender ovoid body w/wide cylindrical neck & large C-form handles, green ground, No. 904-15"............................ 840

Vase, 18" h., 10" d., floor-type, a disk foot supports a tall baluster-form body w/long low C-form handles down the sides, green ground, No. 905-18"......................... 1,500

Vase, 18" h., 10" d., floor-type, a disk foot supports a tall baluster-form body w/long low C-form handles down the sides, blue ground, No. 905-18"..................................... 1,650

Vase, 18" h., 10" d., floor-type, a disk foot supports a tall baluster-form body w/long low C-form handles down the sides, terra cotta ground, No. 905-18".......................... 1,200

Wall pocket, green ground................................ 850

Wall pocket, two-handled, blue ground, No. 1282-8", 8 1/2" h. (minute nick to hanging hole & minor glaze scaling to corner of rim) 575

Wall pocket, two-handled, green ground, No. 1282-8", 8 1/2" h....................................... 475

Fudji (1904)

Same technique as Rozane Woodland. Sometimes trimmed w/dots & studs & wavy lines. Matte-finished ground. Detailed decorations are in high gloss.Kovel-See Rozane Woodland--when the dots were omitted, it was called Fujiyama or Rozane Fudji.

Fudji Vase

Vase, 8 1/2" h., footed baluster-form decorated w/enamel-like Art Nouveau design in blue & brown on beige ground, marked w/Rozane Ware wafer seal & incised w/the numbers "1" & "20", pin head size glaze nick near base (ILLUS.) **935**

Rare Roseville Fudji Vase

Vase, 10" h., 3 3/4" w., slender tall square twisted body, decorated in squeezebag w/stylized bands of flowers in cobalt blue,

green & ochre on a cream ground, Rozane wafer seal & "20," small surface abrasion on one base corner (ILLUS.) **2,925**

Vase, 10" h, waisted cylindrical body, Art Nouveau squeezebag decoration design in cobalt, teal & gold, artist-signed, (several hairlines to interior) **1,495**

Futura (1928)

Varied line with shapes ranging from Art Deco geometrics to futuristic. Matte glaze is typical although an occasional piece may be high gloss.

Futura Basket

Basket, hanging-type, wide sloping shoulders, sharply canted sides, terra cotta & brown w/embossed stylized pastel foliage, No. 344-5", 5" h. (ILLUS.)...................... **248**

Basket, hanging-type, wide sloping shoulders, sharply canted sides, terra cotta & brown w/embossed stylized pastel foliage, No. 344-5", 7 1/2" h. (bruise to rim) **288**

Basket, hanging-type, wide sloping shoulders, sharply canted sides, brown w/embossed stylized pastel foliage, 9" h. **230**

Bowl, 5" h., square w/flared rim, raised on four feet, tan, green & blue glaze, No. 198-5" (ILLUS. bottom right, below) **812**

Bowl, 6" d., 5" h., raised on squared feet, slightly canted sides, yellow & green glaze, No. 197-6" (ILLUS. top center, below) **660**

Bowl, 8" w., 4" h., five flaring sides on square base, orange & green glaze, No. 188-8" (ILLUS. top, far right, below) **537**

A Variety of Futura Items

Bowl w/flower frog, 8" d., collared base, shaped flaring sides w/relief decoration, orange glaze w/polychrome geometric design, Nos. 187-8" & 15-3 1/2", 2 pcs. (professional repair to rim) 330

Bowl w/flower frog, 8" d., collared base, shaped flaring sides w/relief decoration, rose glaze, Nos. 187-8" & 15-3 1/2", 2 pcs. (small glaze nick & burst bubble to flower frog).. 276

Bowl-planter, 5 1/2" h., square w/flared rim, raised on four feet, grey & green glaze, No. 190-3 1/2 - 6"................................ 286

Bowl-planter, 5 1/2" h., square w/flared rim, raised on four feet, mottled green glaze, No. 190-3 1/2 - 6"................................ 303

Candleholders, conical base w/square handles, widely flaring shallow socket, green & orange glaze, No. 1072-4", 4" h., black paper label on one, pr. 711

Candleholders, shaped square base rising to square candle nozzle, relief-molded stylized green vine & foliage on sandy beige ground, No. 1073-4", 4" h., pr............. 385

Candleholders, stepped tapering cylindrical base w/wide flaring foot & flaring shallow socket, mottled green glaze, No. 1075-4", 4" h., black paper label on one, pr. (professional repair to one) 990

Console bowl w/flower frog, footed shallow flaring form, shaded green glaze, No. 195-10", 10" d., 2 1/2" h., 2 pcs.................. 1,045

Console bowl w/flower frog, cut-out base, sharply canted sides w/embossed stylized design, No. 196, 3 1/2 x 5 x 12"............. 317

Jardiniere, angular handles rising from wide sloping shoulders to rim, sharply canted sides, terra cotta ground w/green & orange florals, No. 616-6", 6" h. **250-275**

Jardiniere, angular handles rising from wide sloping shoulders to rim, sharply canted sides, aqua & green w/pink leaves, No. 616-6", 6" h.................................. 275

Jardiniere, angular handles rising from wide sloping shoulders to rim, sharply canted sides, pink & grey ground, No. 616-6", 6" h.. 299

Jardiniere, angular handles rising from wide sloping shoulders to rim, sharply canted sides, terra cotta ground, No. 616-7", unmarked, 7" h...................... 413

Jardiniere, angular handles rising from wide sloping shoulders to rim, sharply canted sides, terra cotta ground, No. 616-8", 8" h.. 468

Jardiniere, angular handles rising from wide sloping shoulders to rim, sharply canted sides, grey ground, No. 616-8", 8" h. 495

Jardiniere, angular handles rising from wide sloping shoulders to rim, sharply canted sides, pink & purple heart-shaped leaves on a greyish-purple ground, No. 616-9", 9" h. (three hairlines to base & up side, 3" & less) 275

Jardiniere, angular handles rising from wide sloping shoulders to rim, sharply canted sides, terra cotta ground, No. 616-9", 9" h. 358

Jardiniere, flaring flat sides below the narrow angled shoulder molded w/stylized leaves & a short cylindrical neck, small squared shoulder handles, pink & lavender leaves on the grey ground, 9" d., 6" h. 408

Jardiniere, angular handles rising from wide sloping shoulders to rim, sharply canted sides, terra cotta ground, No. 616-14", 14" h. 440

Jardiniere & pedestal base, angular handles rising from wide sloping shoulders to rim, sharply canted sides, brown ground, No. 616-10", 10" h., unmarked, 2 pcs. 1,100

Planter, square w/low flat base, sides decorated w/relief stylized tree w/sparse foliage, cream w/green highlights, No. 191-8", 7" sq. 330

Vase, 4" h., square mounted cone-shaped body w/four vertical supports extending down from mid-point of sides to corners of square disk base, striated blue, green & yellow, No. 430-9"................................. **450-500**

Vase, 4 1/2" h., 6 1/2" w., straight handles rising from sharply canted low base to rim, upper portion square w/cut corners & canted sides, low-relief curving design on sides & base, terra cotta, No. 85-4" (ILLUS. bottom left, with group) 289

Vase, 5" h., flaring squared footed & slightly flaring squared sides, embossed green leaf decoration on foot, shaded brown & gold, No. 421-5".. 303

Vase, 5" h., 5" w., 1 1/2" d., stepped base, incised fan effect, light & darker blue glaze, No. 81-5", ... 293

Vase, 5" h., flat flaring body in a mottled blue over orange glaze w/a green geometric pattern on the shoulders, low rectangular mouth, No. 82-6", unmarked 366

Vase, 6" h., footed, wide bulbous form, brown & blue ground, No. 137-6"................... 660

Vase, 6" h., stepped shoulders, square body w/canted sides, grey w/green & blue elongated triangles, No. 380-6" 429

Vase, 6" h., 3 1/2" d., cylindrical body swelling to wider bands at the top & base, long pierced angled handles down the sides, apricot w/green bands & handles, one w/paper label, No. 381-6".......................... 409

Vase, 6" h., octagonal cone-shaped body on a conforming low base, bluish green semi-crystalline glaze, No. 397-6" 376

Vase, bud, 6" h., widely flaring conical foot tapering to a slender tall slightly flaring cylindrical body flanked by slender straight handles from near the rim to the foot, stylized floral design in blue & green on a tan shaded to cream ground, No. 422-6" 413

Vase, 6" h., squared buttressed form, terra cotta & gold, No. 423-6", unmarked 366

Vase, 6 1/2" h., a tall squared & gently twisted slightly tapering form w/molded stylized foliage in yellow & green, No. 398-6 1/2"... 385

Vase, 7" h., sharply canted base, handles rising from shoulder to below rim of long cylindrical stepped neck, grey-green & tan, No. 382-7" **425-450**

Vase, 7" h., spherical top w/large pointed dark blue & green leaves curving up the sides, resting on a gently sloped rectangular foot, shaded blue & green blue ground, No. 387-7" **1,185**

Vase, 7" h., square shape tapering to round foot w/green trim, green "V" design on pink ground, No. 399-7" (professional repair to base).. **289**

Vase, 7" h., egg-shaped body supported by small tabbed feet on a square flaring base, mottled tan & green, No. 400-7"......... **303**

Vase, 7" h., 5 1/2" d., high domed & stepped beehive-form body below a wide & flaring neck joined by two short strap handles to the shoulder, shaded cream to blue body w/green leaves around the body, unmarked, No. 403-7" (ILLUS. top, far left, with group).. **880**

Vase, 7" h. ringed ovoid body w/closed rim flanked by four stepped buttresses, light & dark blue glaze, No. 405-7" **807**

Vase, 7" h., footed ringed-ovoid body w/short flaring wide mouth, yellow, green & blue glaze, No. 424-7" (professional repair of small glaze nicks off foot)................... **385**

Vase, 8" h., footed, wide ovoid body w/short collared neck, buttressed sides, embossed design of thistles on front & back, green, lavender & brown (minor bruise to base).. **358**

Vase, 8" h., spherical body on polyhedron base, tiny cylindrical neck, blue ground w/green design (restored base)..................... **495**

Vase, 8" h., bottle-shaped w/stepped back bands, green & pink, No. 384-8" **465**

Vase, 8" h., bottle-shaped w/stepped back bands, grey-blue & pink, No. 384-8"............. **495**

Vase, 8" h., upright rectangular form on rectangular foot, stepped neck, long square handles, grey & pink ground, No. 386-8", unmarked **550-650**

Vase, 8" h., square buttressed body flaring slightly at neck, orange, green & taupe glaze, No. 402-8" **899**

Vase, 8" h., squared form w/angled buttress corners & flared rim, shaded green, No. 402-8" **550-600**

Vase, 8" h., cylindrical base expanding to bulbous ringed top, four green & blue Art Deco design feet, blue matte ground w/green shoulder design, No. 405-7 1/2" **935**

Vase, 8" h., high domed & stepped beehive-form, shaded tan w/green leaves around the body, unmarked, No. 406-8" **825**

Vase, 8" h., square, slightly tapering body twisting toward the rim, pink ground, No. 425-8".. **537**

Vase, 8" h., semi-ovoid, flaring foot, flat closed handles from midsection to neck, molded trailing florals on side, purple & mauve, No. 427-8" (professional repair to small chips).. **340**

Vase, 8" h., globular w/low canted foot & short collared neck, brown shading to tan, embossed cluster of small flowers & leaves at shoulder & three rings around middle, No. 428-8" **440**

Vase, 8" h., globular w/low canted foot & short collared neck, pink-beige shading to sand white, embossed cluster of small

flowers & leaves at shoulder & three rings around middle, No. 428-8" **262**

Vase, 8" h., 3 3/4" d., star-shaped slender tapering body on stepped circular base, pink & grey ground, No. 385-8", unmarked **392**

Vase, 8" h., 5 3/4" d., a high pyramidal foot w/four straight pierced legs supporting the spherical body w/a small conical mouth, decorated w/white, light blue, green & yellow circles on blue ground, No. 404-8"... **1,400-1,500**

Futura "Globe on Legs" Vase

Vase, 8" h., 5 3/4" d., a high pyramidal foot w/four straight pierced legs supporting the spherical body w/a small conical mouth, green ground decorated w/purple, yellow & orange circles, No. 404-8" (ILLUS.)... **1,054**

Vase, 8 1/4" h., 4 1/4" w., tall triangular body tapering slightly to a stepped triangular foot, the body w/wide light blue triangles flanked by slender dark blue triangles, dark & light blue base, unmarked, No. 383-8" (ILLUS. top, second from right, with group)... **935**

Vase, 8 1/4" h., 5" d., conical body on flat disk base, buttressed sides, orange w/green buttresses & blue base, No. 401-8"... **506**

Vase, 9" h., triangular shaped body tapering to stepped round base, leafy branch design, light & dark blue, No. 388-9" **732**

Vase, 9" h., "Emerald Urn," angular handles rising from bulbous base to rim, sharply stepped neck shaded dark to light green high gloss glaze, No. 389-9", unmarked....... **961**

Futura Vase

Vase, 9" h., footed bulbous base w/canted sides to wide sloping shoulder w/tapering stepped cylindrical neck, angled handles from shoulder to neck, green ribbed leaf design on shaded tan to brown ground, No. 409-9" (ILLUS.) **998**

Vase, 9 1/2" h., stepped sloping rectangular foot supporting a body w/flat multi-faceted flat sides on lower half & contrasting panels on upper half tapering to small rectangular neck, shaded yellow & green, No. 412-9" **5,060**

Vase, 9" h., a wide low domed foot below four short, narrow side buttresses flanking the tall gently flaring trumpet-form body decorated w/crocuses, purple, No. 429-9" **875**

Vase, bud, 10" h., stacked conical form w/gold, green & purple scattered design against a cobalt blue ground, No. 390-10" **880**

Futura "Christmas Tree" Vase

Vase, bud, 10" h., stacked conical form w/ivory, green & lavender scattered design against an orange ground, No. 390-10" (ILLUS.) **605**

Vase, 10" h., wide nearly spherical body raised on a small cylindrical foot, the steeply stepped round neck w/narrow mouth, swirled black flame-like design around the lower half, green, No. 391-10" **853**

Vase, 10" h., compressed globular base supporting long flaring squared neck, elongated triangular design on each side, blue & green, No. 392-10", black paper label **752**

Vase, 10" h., cylindrical, embossed stylized sea gulls decoration, charcoal shading to terra cotta, No. 408-10" (some staining from use) **798**

Vase, 10" h., four flat vertical handles at flaring collared neck, cylindrical body, brown & yellow, No. 432-10" **880**

Vase, 10" h., 6" d., a narrow flaring foot below the wide ovoid body tapering to a wide, deep flaring neck flanked by small straight handles down to the shoulder, small molded brown pine cones & dark green pine sprigs on the neck & shoulder on the mottled green crystalline glaze, No. 433-10" **1,000-1,200**

Vase, 10" h., squatty bulbous base w/molded ring mid-section, wide cylindrical neck

w/flaring rim, No. 435-10" (professional repair of minor rim chips) **715**

Vase, 10" h., 8 1/2" d., narrow base flaring to wide shoulder, graduated ringed neck, orange & green, No. 395-10" **660**

Vase, 10" h., large spherical body on a small footring, the neck composed of stepped bands, flame-form molded design around the lower half, No. 391-10" **900**

Vase, 10 1/4" h., 5 1/4" d., small buttressed handles at disk base, slightly swollen cylindrical lower portion flaring to a wide mouth, decorated w/blue flowers on green stems against a shaded orange body, No. 431-10", unmarked **1,073**

Vase, 12" h., wide ovoid body on a footring, the neck composed of tapering bands, smooth sides, multi-toned deep green overall glaze, No. 394-12" **920**

Vase, 12" h., wide ovoid body on a footring, the neck composed of tapering bands, smooth sides, turquoise glaze w/gunmetal shading, No. 394-12" **807**

Vase, 12" h., stepped domed base, expanding cylindrical body flanked by buttressed handles, chevron pattern in green on orange ground, No. 410-12" (1/4" chip to rim, very short & tight line opposing) **1,045**

Vase, 12" h., slightly tapering tall cylindrical body w/flat flared rim, flanked by long tapering buttress handles, No. 437-12" **1,288**

Vase, 12 1/4" h., 5 1/2" d., tall flaring column rising from four spheres & resting on a square base, grey & peach, No. 393-12" **1,320**

Vase, 14" h., 5 1/2" d., two large handles at lower half, squat stacked base & faceted squared neck, matte glaze in three shades of brown, No. 411-14" (ILLUS. top, second from left, with group) **3,190**

Vase, 15" h., footed tapering cylindrical body w/wide flaring neck, long slender handles, thistle decoration in green on terra cotta & gold ground, No. 438-15" (professional repair of base chip) **1,155**

Wall pocket, canted sides, angular rim handles, geometric design in blue, yellow, green & lavender on brown ground, No. 1261-8", 6" w., 8 1/4" h. **494**

Window box, rectangular, Art Deco-type shaped rectangular strapwork on sides & ends, grey-blue shading to tan, No. 376-15, 15 1/2" x 5" (small flat base chip) **825**

Gardenia (1940s)

Large white gardenia blossoms and green leaves over a textured impressed band on a shaded green, grey or tan ground.

Gardenia Hanging Basket

Basket, hanging-type, green ground, 8"
(ILLUS.) 220
Basket w/circular handle, grey ground,
No. 609-10", 10" h. 193
Basket w/circular handle, green ground,
No. 609-10", 10" h. 180
Book ends, brown ground, No. 659,
5 1/2" h., pr. 275

Gardenia Book End

Book ends, green ground, No. 659,
5 1/2" h., pr. (ILLUS. of one) 250
Bowl, 10" d., grey ground, No. 628-10" 120
Candleholders, grey ground, No. 651-2",
2" h., pr. 75
Candleholders, grey ground, No. 652-4",
4 1/2" h., pr. 115
Console set: 11" l. footed oblong boat-
shaped bowl & a pair of 2" h. candlehold-
ers; green ground, No. 374-11 & 651-2,
the set 165
Cornucopia-vase, tan ground, No. 621-6",
6" h. 80
Cornucopia-vase, double, green ground,
No. 622-8", 8" h. 70
Cornucopia-vase, double, grey ground,
No. 622-8", 8 3/4" 60
Ewer, ovoid base, green ground, No. 617-
10", 10" h. 180
Ewer, ovoid base, grey ground, No. 617-
10", 10" h. 150
Ewer, tan ground, No. 618-15", 15" h. (pro-
fessional repair to base) 225
Jardiniere, grey ground, No. 603-10" (two
small petal nicks) 350
Jardiniere, footed wide bulbous body ta-
pering to a scalloped rim flanked by two
small shoulder handles, No. 641-5",
5" h. 92
Spooner, green ground, No. 656-3", 3" h. 125
Vase, 8" h., handles rising from base to midsection, cylindrical body, tan ground, No.
683-8" 125
Vase, 8" h., handles rising from base to mid-
section, cylindrical body, grey ground,
No. 683-8" 165
Vase, 8" h., green ground, No. 684-8" 195
Vase, 8" h., tan ground, No. 684-8" 165

Gardenia Vase

Vase, 10" h., tall ovoid body w/fanned rim,
base handles, grey ground, No. 685-10"
(ILLUS.) 275
Vase, 10" h., two-handled, tan ground, No.
924-9" 325
Vase, 10 1/2" h., large handles rising from
base to shoulder, ornate rim, green
ground, No. 686-10" 130
Vase, 10 1/2" h., large handles rising from
base to shoulder, ornate rim, tan ground,
No. 686-10" 198
Vase, 12" h., handles rising from low base
to midsection, tan ground, No. 687-12"
(glaze flakes to bottom) 138
Vase, 14 1/2" h., floral-type, two handles
rising from midsection to below rim, tan
ground, No. 689-14" 375
Wall pocket, brown ground, No. 662-8",
8" h. 263
Wall pocket, large handles, green ground,
No. 666-8", 9 1/2" h. 231
Wall pocket, large handles, tan ground, No.
666-8", 9 1/2" h. 225
Window box, green ground, No. 668-8",
8" l. 95
Window box, green ground, No. 669-12",
14" l. 150
Window box, grey ground, No. 669-12",
14" l. 115

Good Night Candleholder

Good Night Candleholder

Good Night candleholder, closed back, chamberstick-type, unmarked, 7" h. (ILLUS.) 715

Imperial I (1916)
Pretzel-twisted vine & stylized grape leaves decorate rough-textured background in green and brown. Style of modeling is rather crude.

Basket, tall tapering cylindrical form w/circular overhead handle, 12 1/2" h., unmarked 495
Basket w/overhead handle, rounded sides, 6" h. 190
Bowl, 7" d., No. 71-7" 85
Bowl, 8" d., No. 71-8" 125
Bowl, 8" d., No. 71-8" 95
Bowl, 9" d., two-handled 80
Jardiniere & pedestal, 2 pcs. 1,300
Planter, open-handled, 3 1/4 x 8", No. 251, unmarked 80
Vase, 8" h., bulbous w/pierced handles at shoulder 145
Vase, triple bud, 8" h., No. 25-8" 145

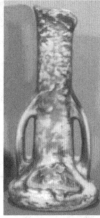

Imperial I Bud Vase

Vase, bud, 9" h., cylindrical w/flaring base, long pierced side handles, No. 31-9" (ILLUS.) 165

Imperial I Wall Pocket

Wall pocket, double, the two openings joined by slender bridge, No. 1222-9", 10" h. (ILLUS.) 289

Imperial II (1924)
Much variation within the line. There is no common characteristic, although many pieces are heavily glazed, and colors tend to run and blend.

Bowl, 4 1/2" d., ivory ground 75
Bowl, 8" d., 5 1/2" h, squatty gourd-shape, mottled green glaze over smooth sky blue base, No. 203-5" 660

Imperial II Vase

Vase, 4 1/2" h., hemispherical w/flat shoulders & short neck, mauve & turquoise glaze, No. 200-4 1/2", w/black paper label (ILLUS.) 413
Vase, 5" h., wide squatty bulbous body w/a wide shoulder to the short rolled neck, embossed designs around the rim, blue flambé ground, marked w/gold foil label & incised "9" 220
Vase, 5" h., tapering ovoid ringed body, tan shading to green, No. 467-5" 200-225
Vase, 5" h., tapering ovoid ringed body, yellow ground, No. 467-5" 275
Vase, 5 1/2" h., tapering cylinder w/horizontal ribbing above base, mottled green ground, No. 468-5" 185-200
Vase, 5 1/2" h., two-handled, bulbous body tapering slightly to short cylindrical neck, blue ground w/glossy mottled ivory glaze on interior which spills over the rim in one area, laced w/tawny yellow, No. 517 150
Vase, 6" h., purple & yellow ground, No. 469-6" 419
Vase, 7" h., globular w/horizontal ribbing at neck, mottled rose glaze, No. 471-7" 650-750
Vase, 7" h., No. 472-7" 192
Vase, 7" h., hemispherical w/sloping shoulder & short collared neck, No. 474-7" 425
Vase, 7" h., 8" d., turquoise & yellow 425
Vase, 8" h., fan-shaped, two handles from base to midsection, intermingled shades of blue & green 150
Vase, 8" h., barrel-shape w/horizontal ribbing around upper portion, wide shoulder & small molded rim, mottled cobalt & turquoise glaze, No. 473-7 1/2" 715
Vase, 8 1/4" h., wide ovoid form slightly tapering to a wide, short cylindrical neck, mottled orange & green w/tan glaze w/green, dark brown & blue around the neck 2,415
Vase, 10" h., baluster form w/short wide cylindrical neck, cobalt blue ground, No. 477-9 1/2" 1,320
Vase, 11" h., tapering ovoid body with short wide rim, blue ground 795
Wall pocket, mottled pink & green glaze, No. 1263 403

Wall pocket, rounded form, relief-molded wavy horizontal lines, red over grey glaze, No. 1262, 6 1/2" h. **575**

Iris (1938)
White or yellow blossoms and green leaves on rose blending with green, light blue deepening to a darker blue or tan shading to green or brown.

Basket, hanging-type, brown ground, 305-5", 8 1/2" h. (glaze flake to all three flowers) **259**
Basket, tan ground, 10" d., 8 1/2" h. **263**
Basket w/pointed overhead handle, compressed ball form, blue ground, No. 354-8", 8" h. **303**

Iris Basket

Basket w/pointed overhead handle, compressed ball form, rose ground, No. 354-8", 8" h. (ILLUS.) **112**

Roseville Iris Basket

Basket w/semicircular overhead handle, rose ground, No. 355-10", 9 1/2" h. (ILLUS.) **468**
Book ends, rose ground, No. 5, pr. **425**
Bowl, 5" d., two-handled, footed, tan ground, No. 359-5" **165**

Iris Bowl-vase

Bowl-vase squatty bulbous body w/stepped shoulder handles, blue ground, No. 357-4", 4" h. (ILLUS.) **110**
Bowl-vase squatty bulbous body w/stepped shoulder handles, rose ground, No. 357-4", 4" h. **105**

Iris Candleholders

Candlesticks, flat disk base, cylindrical nozzle flanked by elongated open handles, rose ground, No. 1135-4 1/2", 4 1/2" h., pr. (ILLUS.) **180**
Console bowl, 8" d., tan ground, No. 361-8" **150**
Console bowl, pink ground, No. 362-10", 10" l. **80**
Cornucopia-vase, blue ground, No. 130-4", 4" h. **75**
Cornucopia-vase, rose ground, No. 131-6", 6" h., silver foil label **138**
Cornucopia-vase, blue ground, No. 132-8", 8" h. **90**
Ewer, bulbous body, cut-out rim, blue ground, No. 926-10", gold foil label, 10" h. **304**
Ewer, bulbous body, cut-out rim, rose ground, No. 926-10", 10" h. **225-275**
Flower frog, blue ground, No. 38...................... **125**
Flower frog, rose ground, No. 38...................... **130**
Flowerpot, brown ground, No. 648-5" **90**
Jardiniere, two-handled, rose ground, No. 647-3", 3" h. **70**
Jardiniere, two-handled, rose ground, No. 647-4", 4" h. **154**
Jardiniere, two-handled, tan ground, No. 647-4", 4" h. **67**
Jardiniere, two-handled, pink ground, No. 647-5", 5" h. (shallow spider-line at base, not through) **380**
Pedestal base, rose blending w/green ground, unmarked, 16" h. **715**
Rose bowl, rose ground, No. 356-6", 6" h. **185**
Vase, 4" h., base handles, rose ground, No. 914-4" **99**
Vase, 4" h., base handles, tan ground, No. 914-4" **110**
Vase, 5" h., ovoid body on flat circular base, rim handles, blue ground, No. 915-5" **101**
Vase, 6 1/2" h., two handles rising from shoulder of globular base to midsection of wide neck, tan ground, No. 917-6" **165**
Vase, 6 1/2" h., two handles rising from shoulder of globular base to midsection of wide neck, rose ground, No. 917-6" .. **150-175**

Vase, 6 1/2" h., two handles rising from shoulder of globular base to midsection of wide neck, blue ground, No. 917-6" **152**

Vase, 6 1/2" h., two handles rising from shoulder of globular base to midsection of wide neck, tan shading to brown ground, No. 917-6" **225**

Vase, bud, 7" h., two-handled, blue ground, No. 918-7" **231**

Vase, 7" h., blue ground, No. 919-7" **175**

Vase, 8" h., bulbous base w/short shoulder tapering to wide cylindrical neck & flat rim, handles from shoulder to middle of neck, tan shading to brown ground, No. 921-8" **175**

Vase, 8" h., urn-form w/pedestal base, tan ground, No. 923-8" **225**

Vase, 10" h., two-handled, rose ground, No. 924-9" **344**

Vase, 10" h., rose ground, No. 927-10" **475**

Vase, 12 1/2" h., semi-ovoid base w/two handles rising from shoulder to beneath rim of short, wide mouth, brown ground, No. 928-12" **350**

Vase, floor-type, 15" h., two large handles rising from shoulder to rim, blue ground, No. 929-15" **950**

Vase, floor-type, 15" h., two large handles rising from shoulder to rim, pink ground, No. 929-15" **475**

Wall shelf, rose ground, No. 2, 8" h. **450**

Ivory II (1937)

White matte-glazed shapes from earlier lines such as Orian, Velmoss, Donatello and others. Also included are figurines of a draped mule and a sleeping dog.

Vase, 8" h., matte white ground **150**

Ivory II Vase

Vase, 18" h., floor-type, footed ovoid w/angled handles, No. 837-14" (ILLUS.) **193**

Ixia (1930s)

Embossed spray of tiny bell-shaped flowers and slender leaves — white blossoms on pink ground; lavender blossoms on green or yellow ground.

Bowl, 4" d., pointed closed handles at rim, pink ground, No. 326-4" **113**

Bowl, 6" d., pink ground, No. 387-6" **225**

Bowl, 6" d., yellow ground, No. 387-6" **125**

Candleholders, double, pink ground, No. 1127, 3" h., pr. **138**

Console bowl, pink ground, No. 330-9", 9" l. **140**

Console bowl, pink ground, No. 331-9", unmarked, 9" l. **80**

Console bowl, green ground, No. 330-7", 10 1/2" l., 3 1/2" h. **135**

Console bowl, pink ground, No. 332-12", 12" l. **300**

Console set: 9" l. console bowl, & pr. of 3" h. double candleholders; green ground, Nos. 330-9" & 1127-3", the set **303**

Jardiniere, green ground, No. 640-4", 4" h. **60**

Jardiniere, yellow ground, No. 640-4", 4" h. **95**

Jardiniere, green ground, No. 640-6", 6" h. **80**

Jardiniere, green ground, No. 640-7", 7" h. **300**

Jardiniere, pink ground, No. 640-7", 7" h. (tight 1" crack to rim) **220**

Vase, 6" h., elongated closed handles at shoulders, ovoid body, pink ground, No. 853-6" **98**

Vase, 6" h., elongated closed handles at shoulders, ovoid body, yellow ground, No. 853-6" **133**

Vase, 7" h., closed handles rising from midsection to rim, expanding cylindrical body, pink ground, No. 854-7" **160**

Ixia Vase

Vase, 7" h., footed ovoid body w/small tab handles flanking the short neck, pink ground, No. 855-7" (ILLUS.) **138**

Vase, 7" h., footed ovoid body w/small tab handles flanking the short neck, green ground, No. 855-7" **150**

Vase, 8" h., cylindrical shape tapering slightly to disk foot, buttressed handles from base to midsection, yellow ground, No. 856-8" **220**

Vase, 8" h., pillow-form, green ground, No. 858-8" **265**

Ixia Vase

Vase, 8 1/2" h., closed handles at midsection, globular w/long wide neck, green ground, No. 857-8" (ILLUS.) 165
Vase, 10" h., green ground, No. 863-10" 231
Vase, 12" h., closed handles, cylindrical, pink ground, No. 864-12"................................ 385
Vase, 12" h., closed handles, cylindrical, yellow ground, No. 864-12"............................ 350

Jonquil (1931)

White jonquil blossoms and green leaves in relief against textured tan ground; green lining.

Basket, hanging-type, 7 1/4" 345
Bowl, 3" h., large down-turned handles, No. 523-3" **200-250**
Bowl, 4 x 12" 145
Bowl-vase, bulbous nearly spherical body w/downward looped shoulder handles, No. 524-4", 4" h.. 177
Candleholders, No. 1082-4", 4" h., pr.............. 400
Console bowl, oval, No. 220-10", 10" l., unmarked, black sticker 225

Jonquil Crocus Pot

Crocus pot, No. 93-4 1/2", 4 1/2" h. (ILLUS.)... 413
Crocus pot w/attached saucer, No. 96-7", 7" h.. 475
Jardiniere, No. 621-4", 4" h. 220

Jonquil Jardiniere

Jardiniere, No. 621-5", 5" h. (ILLUS.) 112
Jardiniere, two-handled, No. 621-8", 8" h. 445
Jardiniere, No. 621-10", 10" h. 1,200
Strawberry jar, No. 95-6 1/2", 6 1/2" h. 495
Vase, 4" h., bulbous spherical form, loop handles from mid-section to rim 165
Vase, 4 1/2" h., two-handled, No. 539-4"............. 89
Vase, 5" h., No. 525-5" 231
Vase, 5 1/2" h., No. 542-5 1/2"........................... 150

Jonquil Vase

Vase, 6 1/2" h., wide bulbous body tapering to flat rim, C-form handles, No. 543-6 1/2" (ILLUS.) 341
Vase, 7" h., bulbous base tapering slightly to flat mouth, No. 527-7"................................ 413
Vase, 7 1/5" h., two-handled, trumpet form, handles from foot to mid-section, No. 541-7" 3,385
Vase, 8" h., tapering cylinder w/elongated side handles, No. 528-8" 440
Vase, 8" h., ovoid body tapering to short cylindrical neck, turned-down shoulder handles, No. 529-8".. 325
Vase, 8" h., bulbous ovoid body w/short collared neck, closed handles from shoulder to rim, terra cotta ground, No. 672-8"........... 413
Vase, 9 1/2" h., bulbous base tapering slightly to wide cylindrical neck, loop handles at midsection, No. 544-9"...................... 550
Vase, 10" h., compressed bulbous base tapering to wide tapering cylindrical neck w/flat rim, loop handles from mid-section to rim, No. 530-10" 303
Vase, 10 1/2" h., cylindrical w/narrow shoulder, asymmetrical, branch handles, white ground, No. 583-10"...................................... 225

Juvenile (1916 on)

Transfer-printed and painted on creamware with nursery rhyme characters, cute animals and other motifs appealing to children.

Cup & saucer, Sunbonnet Girl, cup 2" h., saucer 3" d., pr.. 125
Feeding dish w/rolled edge, "Baby's Plate" around rim, five chicks around interior, 7" d. 195

Juvenile Feeding Dish

Juvenile Mugs & Pitcher

Feeding dish w/rolled edge, "Baby's Plate" around rim, four rabbits around interior, 7" d. (ILLUS.) **195**

Feeding dish w/rolled edge, sitting rabbits, 7" d. **145**

Feeding dish w/rolled edge, "Baby's Plate," nursery rhyme, "Higgledy Piggledy......." 7 1/2" d., stamped in red on rolled rim "From G.A. Stower's Furniture Co.," unmarked **190**

Feeding dish w/rolled edge, chicks decoration, 8" d.. **121**

Feeding dish w/rolled edge, dogs, 8" d........... **187**

Feeding dish w/rolled edge, nursery rhyme, "Bye Baby Bunting," w/cat, 8" d. **110**

Feeding dish w/rolled edge, nursery rhyme, "Hickory, Dickory Dock," 8" d............ **120**

Feeding dish w/rolled edge, nursery rhyme, "Little Bo Peep," 8" d......................... **193**

Feeding dish w/rolled edge, nursery rhyme, "Tom, The Piper's Son," 8" d. (slight wear to design).................................... **100**

Feeding dish w/rolled edge, Santa Claus, 8" d... **750**

Feeding dish w/rolled edge, Sunbonnet girl, 8" d. **165**

Feeding dish w/rolled edge, three ducks, 8" d... **238**

Mug, sitting puppy, 2 3/4" h. (ILLUS. above. far left) **213**

Mug, chicks, 3 1/2" h. (ILLUS. above, second from left) **149**

Mug, duck w/hat, 3" h. **150**

Mug, standing rabbit, 3" h. **75-175**

Mug, two-handled, rabbits, 3" h. **195**

Pitcher, 3" h., chicks.................................... **115**

Pitcher, 3" h. rabbits (ILLUS. above, far right).. **214**

Pitcher, 3 1/2" h., chicks (ILLUS. above, second from right)...................................... **233**

Pitcher, 3 1/2" h., duck w/hat **145**

Pitcher, 3 1/2" h., fat puppy........................ **85**

Pitcher, 3 1/2" h., side pour, chicks **140**

Pitcher, 3 1/2" h., side pour, rabbits............. **145**

Pitcher, rabbit design, 3 1/2" h. **413**

Plate, divided, 9 1/2" d., well worn dressed-up pig, duckling wearing high top boots & hat & very worn kitten under an umbrella, chick & running rabbit wearing a jacket, color worn on border, stamped "Rv-9"......... **168**

Plate, 8" d., chicks...................................... **185**

Plate, 8" d., Sunbonnet girl **200**

Laurel (1934)

Laurel branch and berries in low relief with reeded panels at the sides. Glazed in deep yellow, green shading to cream or terra cotta.

Bowl, 6" d., squatty bulbous body w/incurved rim & angled shoulder handles, yellow ground, No. 250-6 1/4" **248**

Laurel Bowl

Bowl, 6" d., 3 1/2" h., green ground (ILLUS.).. **193**

Bowl, 7" d., shallow, green ground **121**

Candlestick, green ground, 4 1/2" h. **895**

Laurel Urn

Urn, bulbous base w/ringed neck, closed shoulder handles, green ground, No. 250-6 1/4", 6 1/2" h. (ILLUS.) **468**

Urn, deep yellow, No. 250-6 1/2", 6 1/2" h....... **265**

Vase, 6" h., No. 239-6"................................. **130**

Vase, 6" h., tapering cylinder w/wide mouth, closed angular handles at shoulder, deep yellow, No. 667-6" **231**

Vase, 6" h., angular shoulder handles, green ground, No. 668-6"............................... **358**

Vase, 6 1/4" h., green ground, No. 250-6 1/4" **450**

Vase, 6 1/2" h., green, No. 669-6 1/2" **185**

Vase, 7" h., green ground **350**

Vase, 7 1/4" h., green, No. 670-7 1/4" **358**

Vase, 7 1/2" h., tapering cylinder w/pierced angular handles at midsection, terra cotta, No. 671-7 1/4"....................................... **267**

Vase, 8" h., bulbous ovoid body w/short collared neck, closed handles from shoulder to rim, yellow ground, No. 672-8"................. **342**

Vase, 8" h., deep yellow & black, No. 673-8" (minor chip repair to base) **163**

Vase, 9" h., short cylindrical bottom w/wide slightly flaring neck, closed handles at midsection, deep yellow, No. 675-9" 343

Vase, 9" h., short cylindrical bottom w/wide slightly flaring neck, closed handles at midsection, terra cotta, No. 675-9" 358

Vase, 9 1/4" h., angular side handles, globular base w'wide stepped mouth, terra cotta, No. 674-9 1/4" (repaired chips) 110

Vase, 9 1/4" h., angular side handles, globular base w/wide mouth, green ground, No. 674-9 1/4" 475

Vase, 9 1/4" h., angular side handles, globular base w/wide stepped mouth, deep yellow, No. 674-9 1/4"................................ 358

Vasc, 10" h., footed trumpet-form body w/tapering tab handles, green, No. 676-10" (minor losses on base) 330

Vase, 14 1/2" h., base handles rising from stepped disk base to midsection of slightly flaring cylindrical body, green ground, No. 678-14 1/2" (chip to rim).......................... 880

Lotus (1952)

Pointed spires of stylized leaves surround each piece. High-gloss glaze in combinations of maroon with beige, brown with beige, and turquoise with beige.

Bowl, 3 1/2 x 11", 3" h., blue & white high-gloss finish, No. L7-10"................................... 330

Vase, 10" h., cylindrical, yellow & blue high-gloss finish, No. L3-10"................................ 275

Vase, 10" h., cylindrical, blue & grey, No. L3-10, embossed "Lotus L3-10" & bottom impressed w/"U-323 Paint" & "G-484" in black slip, possibly experimental.................... 600

Vase, pillow-type, 10 1/2" h., blue & ivory, No. L4-10"... 253

Wall pocket, green, No. L8-7", 7" h. (very short inner firing line)....................................... 575

Wall pocket, yellow & brown, No. L8-7", 7" h. (underglaze line from rim to pierced hole) 170

Luffa (1934)

Relief-molded ivy leaves and blossoms on shaded brown or green wavy horizontal ridges.

Bowl, 7" d., bulbous w/small pointed rim handles, green ground, No. 257-7"............... 220

Luffa Bowl-vase

Bowl-vase, bulbous body tapering to wide closed mouth, small angled shoulder handles, green ground, No. 255-6", 6" h. (ILLUS.)... 264

Luffa Candlesticks

Candlesticks, two-handled, bell-shaped base, brown ground, No. 1097-4 1/2", 4 1/2" h., pr. (ILLUS.)..................................... 330

Console bowl, green ground, 13" l................... 345

Jardiniere, green ground, No. 631-4", 4" h. 440

Jardiniere & pedestal base, brown ground, overall 24" h., 2 pcs. 2,600

Lamp base, 9" h., bulbous body tapering to wide flat rim flanked by small angled handles, brown & blue ground w/metal fixture, No. 690-9"... 715

Lamp base, 9" h., bulbous body tapering to wide flat rim flanked by small angled handles, brown ground w/metal fixture, No. 690-9" 605

Vase, 6" h., two-handled, cylindrical, green ground 145

Vase, 6" h., tapering cylindrical body w/angled handles from shoulder to rim, brown ground, No. 683-6".. 211

Vase, 6" h., two-handled, cylindrical body, brown ground, No. 684-6" 187

Vase, 6" h., two-handled, cylindrical body, green ground, No. 684-6" 180

Vase, 7" h., brown ground.................................. 300

Luffa Vase

Vase, 7" h., ovoid body w/small angled handles from shoulder to rim, green ground, No. 685-7" (ILLUS.)... 220

Vase, 7" h., brown ground, No. 686-7" 250-300

Vase, 8" h., shaded brown ground, No. 688-8", original label 296

Vase, 9" h., bulbous body tapering to wide flat rim flanked by small angled handles, brown ground, No. 690-9".............................. 422

Vase, 12" h., footed slender baluster-form w/a widely flaring mouth flanked by angular handles to the shoulder, brown ground, No. 691-12".. 628

Wall pocket, No. 1272-8", 8" h.......................... 863

Magnolia (1943)

Large white blossoms with rose centers and black stems in relief against a blue, green or tan textured ground.

Magnolia Ashtray

Ashtray, two-handled, low bowl form, green ground, No. 28, 7" d., 2" h. (ILLUS.)............... **83**

Basket, hanging-type, green ground, No. 469-5"... **144**

Basket, hanging-type, tan ground, No. 469-5"... **149**

Basket, blue ground, No. 385-10", 10" h. **278**

Basket w/ornate overhead handle, blue ground, No. 383-7".. **132**

Basket w/ornate overhead handle, blue ground, No. 384-7", 7" h. **83**

Basket w/ornate overhead handle, footed ovoid body w/long angled overhead handle, green ground, No. 384-8", 8" h. **173**

Book ends, green ground, No. 13, 5 1/2" h., pr. **180**

Book ends, tan ground, No. 13, 5 1/2" h., pr. **198**

Bowl, 8" d., two-handled, No. 448-8"................... **73**

Bowl, 10" l., two-handled, blue ground, No. 450-10"... **425**

Bowl, 10" l., two-handled, tan ground, No. 450-10"... **175**

Bowl, tan ground, No. 452-14", 14" l.. .... **70**

Candlesticks, angular handles rising from flat base to midsection of stem, green ground, No. 1157-4 1/2", 5" h., pr. **165**

Console bowl, round w/angular side handles, green ground, No. 5-10", 10" d............ **245**

Cookie jar, cov., shoulder handles, tan ground, No. 2-8, overall 10" h........................ **450**

Cookie jar, cov., shoulder handles, blue ground, No. 2-8", overall 10" h. **425**

Cookie jar, cov., shoulder handles, green ground, No. 2-8, overall 10" h........................ **429**

Cornucopia-vase, tan ground, No. 184-6", 6" h.. **30**

Creamer & sugar bowl, blue ground, Nos. 4C & 4S, pr. **150**

Ewer, green ground, No. 13-6", 6" h. **145**

Magnolia Ewer

Ewer, blue ground, No. 14-10", 10" h. (ILLUS.)... **165**

Ewer, brown ground, No. 15-15", 15" h. **540**

Jardiniere, two-handled, tan ground, No. 665-4", 4" h.. **60**

Jardiniere, two-handled, tan ground, No. 665-5", 5" h... **132**

Jardiniere & pedestal base, blue ground, No. 665-8", 2 pcs...................................... **950**

Model of a conch shell, green ground, No. 453-7", 6 1/2" w. **187**

Pitcher, blue ground, No. 1327........................... **335**

Pitcher, cider, 7" h., green ground, No. 132-7".. **313**

Pitcher, cider, 7" h., tan ground, No. 132-7"..... **200**

Planter, shell-shaped w/angular base handles, green ground, No. 183-6", 6" l................. **125**

Planter, shell-shaped w/angular base handles, tan ground, No. 183-6", 6" l.................... **60**

Planter, angular end handles, tan ground, No. 388-6", 8 1/2" l. **125**

Tea set: cov. teapot, creamer & open sugar bowl; green ground, No. 4, 3 pcs.................. **473**

Tea set: cov. teapot, creamer & sugar bowl; blue ground, Nos. 4, 4C & 4S, 3 pcs. (very shallow & small chip to bottom of lid, minor bruise to base of creamer & petal on sugar bowl)... **220**

Teapot, cov., green ground, No. 4 .... **330**

Vase, double bud, 4" h., green ground, No. 186-4 1/2" (very minor grinding nicks on one base)... **90**

Vase, 5" h., blue ground, No. 182-5"................. **121**

Vase, 6" h., two-handled, blue ground, No. 87-6" **165**

Vase, 6" h., angular pointed handles from base to midsection, tan ground, No. 88-6" **75-150**

Vase, 7" h., bud, green ground, No. 179-7" **155**

Vase, 8" h., globular w/large angular handles, green ground, No. 91-8" **263**

Vase, 8" h., blue ground, No. 92-8" **165**

Vase, 9" h., two-handled, tan ground, No. 93-9" (chipped)... **110**

Vase, 9" h., green ground, No. 94-9" **110**

Magnolia Vase

Vase, 14" h., green ground, repaired base chip, No. 97-14" (ILLUS.) **431**

Vase, floor-type, 15" h., green ground, No. 98-15"... **333**

Wall pocket, overhead handle w/pointed ends, blue ground, No. 1294-8 1/2", 8 1/2" h. **375**

Wall pocket, overhead handle w/pointed
ends, brown ground, No., 1294-8 1/2",
8 1/2" h. **223**
Wall pocket, overhead handle w/pointed
ends, green ground, No. 1294-8 1/2",
8 1/2" h. **225**

Ming Tree (1949)
*High gloss glaze in mint green, turquoise, or
white is decorated with ming branch: handles are
formed from gnarled branches.*

Basket, hanging-type, green ground, 6" **234**
Basket, hanging-type, blue ground, No.
505-8", 8" h. **220**
Basket, overhead branch handle, rounded
body w/shaped rim, blue ground, No.
508-8", 8" h. **125**
Basket w/overhead branch handle, ruffled
rim, blue ground, No. 509-12", 13" h. **150**
Candleholders, squat melon-ribbed body
w/angular branch handles at shoulder,
blue ground, No. 551, pr. **98**
Candleholders, squat melon-ribbed body
w/angular branch handles at shoulder,
white, No. 551, pr. **50**
Console bowl, blue ground, No. 528-10",
10" l. **165**
Console bowl, green ground, No. 528-10",
10" l. **110**
Console set: 10" l. bowl, No. 528-10" & pair
of candleholders, No. 551; green ground,
3 pcs. **225**

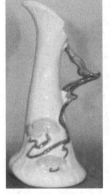

Ming Tree Ewer

Ewer, white ground, No. 516-10", very
minor grinding nicks off base, 10" h.
(ILLUS.) **220**

Ming Tree Conch Shell

Model of a conch shell, white ground, No.
563-7, minor crazing, 8 1/2" w. (ILLUS.) **138**
Vase, 8" h., asymmetrical branch handles,
blue ground, No. 582-8" **299**
Wall pocket, overhead branch handle,
green ground, No. 566-8", 8 1/2" h. **240**
Wall pocket, overhead branch handle,
white ground, No. 566-8", 8 1/2" h. **275**

Moderne (1930s)
*Art Deco-style rounded and angular shapes
trimmed with an embossed panel of vertical lines
and modified swirls and circles, white trimmed with
terra cotta, medium blue with white and turquoise
with a burnished antique gold.*

Moderne Bowl

Bowl, 7 x 11", 4" h., pleated body, tur-
quoise, No. 301-10" (ILLUS.) **178**
Bowl, 7 x 11", 4" h., pleated body, white,
No. 301-10". **259**
Bowl-vase, low foot, compressed ball-form,
blue ground, No. 299-6", 6 1/2" **173**
Candleholder, triple, turquoise ground, No.
1112-5 1/2", 5 1/2" h. (small nick in base
under foot, not visible from side) **202**
Candleholder, triple, white, No. 1112-
5 1/2", 6" h. **170**
Candleholders, triple, blue ground, No.
1112-5 1/2", 5 1/2" h., pr. (fleck to rim of
one) **440**
Compote, 5" h., open stem, white & tan,
No. 295-6 .... **177**
Compote, 6" h., blue ground, No. 297-6" **440**
Console bowl, blue ground, No. 302-14",
14" l. **450**

Moderne Vase

Vase, 6" h., a round foot tapering to a narrow short stem supporting a tall conical
body, two small curved handles from foot
to lower body, white ground, No. 788-6"
(ILLUS.) **164**

Vase, 6" h., a round foot tapering to a narrow short stem supporting a tall conical body, two small curved handles from foot to lower body, blue ground, No. 788-6"......... **345**

Vase, 6" h., a round foot tapering to a narrow short stem supporting a tall conical body, two small curved handles from foot to lower body, turquoise & gold ground, No. 788-6".. **385**

Moderne Triple Bud Vase

Vase, triple bud, 7" h., medium blue, No. 792-7" (ILLUS.).. **392**

Vase, bud, 8" h., cone-shaped on low foot, asymmetrical handles rising from base, turquoise, No. 791-8"....................................... **388**

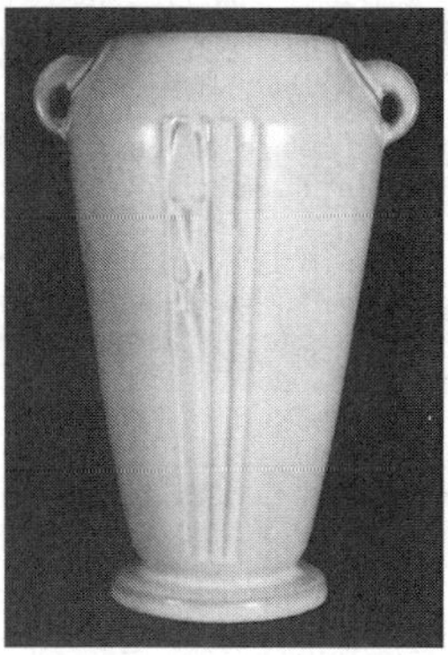

Moderne Vase

Vase, 8" h., expanding cylinder, small loop handles at shoulder, white ground, No. 797-8" (ILLUS.).. **193**

Vase, 9 1/2" h., white ground, No. 799-9" (1/8 x 1" repair on inside edge of rim)........... **225**

Montacello (1931)

White stylized trumpet flowers with black accents on a terra cotta band, light terra cotta mottled in blue, or light green mottled and blended with blue backgrounds.

Basket, bulbous base w/wide neck & flaring rim, a long curved upright handle from shoulder to shoulder coming to a point above the neck, green ground, No. 333-6", 6" h. (handle repaired).............................. **358**

Basket w/pointed overhead handle, tall collared neck, green ground, No. 332-6", 6 1/2"... **605**

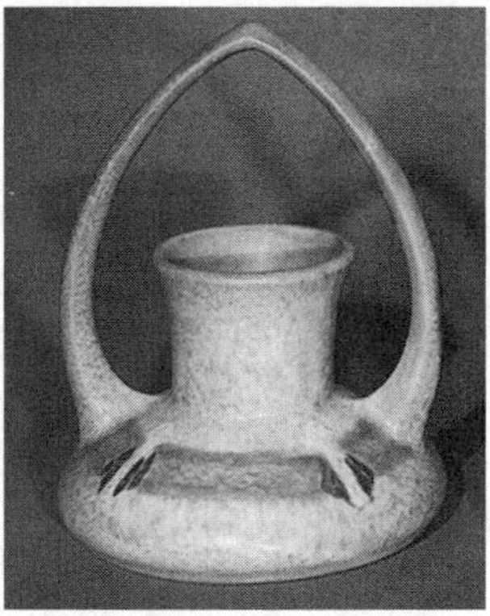

Montacello Basket

Basket w/pointed overhead handle, tall collared neck, terra cotta ground, No. 332-6", 6 1/2" h. (ILLUS.)................................ **728**

Console bowl, low squatty bulbous oblong form w/flat rim & small round end handles, blue ground, No. 225-9", 13" l., 3" h...... **385**

Console bowl, low squatty bulbous oblong form w/flat rim & small round end handles, terra cotta ground, No. 225-9", 13" l., 3" h. **422**

Jardiniere, two-handled, terra cotta ground, No. 559-5", 5" h. **537**

Vase, 4" h., two-handled, terra cotta ground, black paper label, No. 555-4" (rough drill hole in bottom)............................ **235**

Vase, 5" h., two-handled, conical, terra cotta, black paper label.. **413**

Vase, 5" h., two handles at mid-section, blue ground, No. 556-5" (small chip to bottom ring)... **303**

Vase, 5" h., two handles at mid-section, terra cotta ground, No. 556-5"........................... **358**

Vase, 5" h., ovoid w/shoulder handles, blue ground, No. 557-5"... **413**

Vase, 5" h., ovoid w/shoulder handles, terra cotta ground, No. 557-5"............................... **388**

Vase, 5 1/4" h., raised rim on an ovoid body w/two handles, decorated w/stylized fleur-de-lis design in cream within a brown band, dark blue ovals on a streaked light green & tan ground................. **431**

Vase, 6" h., ovoid w/large ring shoulder handles, terra cotta ground, No. 560-6"........ **413**

Vase, 7" h., two-handled, slightly ovoid, wide mouth, blue ground, No. 561-7", very minor glaze flaws (ILLUS. right, top next page)... **413**

Vase, 7" h., spherical base tapering to wide collared neck w/flat rim, loop handles from shoulder to mid-neck, terra cotta ground, No. 562-7" (ILLUS. center, top next page).. **550-700**

Vase, 8 1/2" h., small loop handles at shoulder, cylindrical w/flared lip, terra cotta ground, No. 563-8"... **495**

Vase, 9" h., bulbous ovoid w/flat rim, loop handles, blue ground, No. 564-9" (ILLUS. left, top next page)... **880**

Vase, 10" h., footed trumpet-form w/base handles, terra cotta ground, No. 565-10"... **1,760**

Three Roseville Montacello Vases

Morning Glory (1935)
Delicately colored blossoms and twining vines in white or green with blue.

Morning Glory Basket

Basket, w/high pointed overhead handle, globular body, green ground, No. 340-10", restored handle, 10 1/2" h. (ILLUS.)...... **385**

Basket, w/high pointed overhead handle, globular body, white ground, No. 340-10", 10 1/2" h... **638**

Bowl, 4" d., squatty bulbous body w/tiny angled shoulder handles, green ground, No. 268-4" (restoration to nick at rim) **468**

Console bowl, small pointed end handles, white, 4 1/2 x 11 1/2"...................................... **330**

Urn-vase, two-handled, green ground, No. 269-6, 6" h. (glaze nick to rim, light bubbling to glaze on one side) **440**

Urn-vase, two-handled, white ground, No. 269-6, 6" h. **550**

Vase, 5" h., footed, flaring sides w/small angled handles at midsection, white ground, No. 723-5".. **303**

Vase, 7" d., squatty bulbous body w/small angular handles at the shoulder, white ground **358**

Vase, 7" h., tapering sides, base handles, white ground... **525**

Vase, 7" h., tapering sides, base handles, green ground, No. 725-7" (small chips to base)... **303**

Vase, 8" h., bulbous ovoid body w/flat mouth, angled shoulder handles, white ground, No. 727-8" (small chip & in-the-making bruise to base) **424**

Vase, 9" h., squatty bulbous ovoid body w/angled handles from mid-section to rim, green ground, No. 728-9" (small glaze chip to rim) **660**

Vase, 9" h., squatty bulbous ovoid body w/angled handles from mid-section to rim, green ground, No. 729-9" (small chip to handle, three glaze nicks to rim)............... **523**

Vase, 10" h., bulbous base tapering to wide molded rim, two-handled, white ground, No. 730-10"... **675**

Vase, 12" h., footed flaring cylindrical body w/a wide closed rim flanked by small pointed loop handles, white ground, No. 731-12", ... **880**

Wall pocket, No. 1275-8", 8" h. (tight line to interior) **1,150**

Wall pocket, white ground, No. 1275-8", 8" h. (crack to handle & one corner, one small chip)... **460**

Moss (1930s)
Green moss hanging over brown branch with green leaves; backgrounds are pink, ivory or tan shading to blue.

Basket, hanging-type, blue ground, No. 353-5", unmarked (small abrasion to tip & next to handle) **230**

Bowl, 6" d., footed w/rounded sides, small angled side handles, pink ground, No. 291-6"... **165**

Bowl, 7" d., footed w/rounded sides & small angled side handles, pink ground, No. 291-7" **143**

Bowl, 8" d., footed, round sides & small angled handles, pink shading to blue, No. 291-8"... **143**

Bowl, 8" d., blue ground, No. 292-8" (nick to handle) **275**

Bowl, 8" d., pink & green, No. 292-8"............... **170**

Bowl, 10" l., oblong w/end handles, No. 293-10"... **210**

Bowls, 5" d., footed, round sides & small angled handles, pink shading to blue, No. 291-5", pr. **358**

Candleholders, flat disk base, ball-shaped, pink ground, No. 1109-2", 2" h., pr. **220**

Moss Console Bowl

Console bowl, oval w/shaped rim & angled end handles, tan shading to blue ground, No. 293-10", 10 1/2" l., 3" h. (ILLUS.)............ **193**

Jardiniere & pedestal base pink ground, No. 635-10", 10" h., 2 pcs. (two small chips to decoration of jardiniere) **2,420**

Rose bowl, footed spherical body w/angled side handles, pink shading to blue ground, No. 289-4", 4" h. **182**

Urn, small angular handles rising from base to mid-section, globular, pink ground, No. 290-6", 6" h. **200**

Vase, 6" h., footed, expanding cylinder w/angled handles, pink shading to blue, No. 775-6" (restored small chip to bottom ring) **220**

Vase, 6" h., angular handles, pink ground, No. 776-6" **175**

Vase, 7" h., stepped bulbous base tapering to slightly flaring cylindrical neck, angular side handles, pink ground, No. 777-7" **275**

Vase, 7" h., pink ground, No. 778-7" **353**

Vase, triple bud, 7" h., pink ground, No. 1108 .... **358**

Vase, 8" h., ovoid w/slightly flaring rim, ornate angular side handles, blue ground, No. 780-8" (pinhead size glaze nick on one handle) **273**

Vase, 8" h., ovoid w/slightly flaring rim, ornate angular side handles, pink ground, No. 780-8" **330**

Moss Pillow-type Vase

Vase, 8" h., pillow-type w/small angular handles rising from midsection to rim, tan shading to blue ground, light crazing, minor glaze bubbles, No. 781-8" (ILLUS.) **288**

Vase, 8 1/2" h., flared foot, bulbous body w/wide flaring rim, blue ground, No. 779-8" **220**

Vase, 8 1/2" h., flared foot, bulbous body w/wide flaring rim, tan & green, No. 779-8" **358**

Vase, 10" h., two-handled, footed ovoid body w/flaring rim, tan shading to blue, No. 784-10"... **660**

Vase, 12" h., ivory ground, ... **750**

Vase, 12" h., pink ground, No. 785-12" (minor bruises)... **523**

Moss Wall Pocket

Wall pocket, elongated side handles, flaring rim, blue ground, No. 1278-8", 8 1/2" h. (ILLUS.).. **660**

Wall pocket, bucket-shaped, pink ground, No. 1279-10", 10" h... **431**

Mostique (1915)

Indian designs of stylized flowers and arrowhead leaves, slip decorated on bisque, glazed interiors. Occasional bowl glazed on outside as well.

Basket, hanging-type, heart-shaped leaves & geometric designs, grey ground, No. 334-6", 6" h.. **450**

Basket, hanging-type, heart-shaped leaves & geometric designs, tan ground, 8 1/4" h. (small burst bubbles & nicks to rim).. **403**

Basket, hanging-type, heart-shaped leaves & geometric designs, grey ground, 7 1/4" h. **230**

Mostique Bowl

Bowl, 7" d., stylized flowers, grey ground, No. 131-7" (ILLUS.).. **134**

Bowl, 7 1/2" d., floral design, sandy beige ground, No. 73 .... **60**

Jardiniere, geometric design, grey ground, 6" h.. **150**

Jardiniere, geometric floral design w/arrowhead leaves, tan ground, No. 606-6", 6" h. **250**

Jardiniere, bulbous nearly spherical body w/a wide flat mouth flanked by small arched loop handles, a terra cotta ground decorated w/large geometric white & gold blossoms on tall brown stems w/white & blue angular leaves down the sides, triple dark brown bands under the blossoms near the rim, 8" h. **1,430**

Jardiniere, floral design, tan ground, 8" h. **303**

Jardiniere, green, blue, yellow & brown geometric design on grey ground, No. 622-8", 8" h. **441**

Mostique Jardiniere

Jardiniere, bulbous form w/molded rim, tan ground w/stylized floral design, small chips to rim & enamel, 9" h. (ILLUS.) **397**

Mostique Geometric Design Jardiniere

Jardiniere, geometric floral design w/arrowhead leaves, tan ground, 10" h., small glaze chip minor firing lines on handles (ILLUS.) **319**

Jardiniere, grey ground, 10" h., unmarked (minor chips to rim, chips to base) **330**

Umbrella stand, tall slightly waisted cylindrical form w/large incised squared fourpetal white blossoms above forked & spearpoint dark green stylized leaves around the rim, light green incised rim & base bands, all on a light terra cotta ground, marked, 21" h. (harmless tight line in top) **1,045**

Vase, 6" h., arrowhead leaves design **176**

Vase, 6" h., two-handled, brown ground **185**

Vase, 6" h., tapering cylinder, geometric floral design, tan ground, No. 164-6" **132**

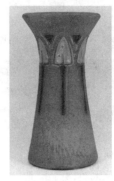

Mostique Vase

Vase, 10" h., slightly waisted cylinder w/flaring mouth, arrowhead designs, grey ground, No. 164-10" (ILLUS.) **193**

Vase, 15" h., floor-type, arrowhead design, grey ground, No. 164-15" **643**

Vase, 15" h., 8" w., floral & geometric design, grey ground **770**

Wall pocket **395**

Wall pocket, conical, pointed end, floral decoration on grey ground, No. 1224-12", 12" h. (chip to hole) **259**

Orian (1935)

Characterized by handles formed on blade-like leaves with suggestion of berries at base of handle, high-gloss glaze; blue or tan with darker drip glaze forming delicate band around rim, or in plain yellow with no over drip.

Bowl, 11" d., flared foot, sharply canted sides w/wide flared rim, turquoise, No. 272-10" **143**

Console bowl, pedestal footed, tan & blue ground, No. 275-5", 5" l. **275**

Urn, two handled, footed spherical body w/closed rim, shaded red glossy exterior & green interior glaze, unmarked, No. 274-6", 6" h. **220**

Vase, 6" h., flared foot below a cylindrical body w/a spherical top & short cylindrical neck, long & low loop handles down the sides, white ground, No. 733-6" **250**

Orian Vase

Vase, 6" h., flared foot below a cylindrical body w/a spherical top & short cylindrical neck, long & low loop handles down the sides, turquoise, No. 733-6" (ILLUS.) **252**

Vase, 7" h., slender handles rising from shoulder of squatty ringed base to rim of short wide neck, glossy tan w/turquoise lining, No. 735-7" 165

Vase, 9" h., slender handles rising from compressed ringed base to middle of long wide neck, turquoise w/beige interior, No. 739-9" 231

Vase, 9" h., slender handles rising from compressed ringed base to middle of long wide neck, rose/magenta ground, No. 739-9" 275

Vase, 10" h., footed, two-handled, cylindrical form, turquoise w/tan interior, gold foil label, No. 741-10" (very minor grinding chips on base) 275

Orian Vase

Vase, 10 1/2" h., baluster form w/slender handles rising from low foot to shoulder, glossy turquoise blue w/orange lining, No. 740-10", gold foil label (ILLUS.) 199

Vase, 14 1/2" h. 475

Wall pocket, double, two cylindrical tubes, one slightly longer & wider than the other, joined by two swirls, turquoise blue, No. 1276-8", 8" h. 1,495

Panel (Rosecraft Panel 1920)

Background colors are dark green or dark brown; decorations embossed within the recessed panels are of natural or stylized floral arrangements or female nudes.

Bowl, 8" d., 2 3/8" h., shallow round form w/rolled rim, orange floral decoration on brown ground 138

Candleholders, decorated w/purple flowers on dark green ground, 2" h., pr. 165

Jar, cov., dark brown ground w/embossed dandelion decoration, No. 295-9, 9" h. 523

Panel Vase

Vase, 6" h., cylindrical, decorated w/purple flowers on dark green ground (ILLUS.) 248

Vase, 6" h., fan-shaped body w/wide disk foot, brown ground w/nude decoration in orange on either side, unmarked (very minor glaze inconsistencies) 551

Vase, 6" h., fan-shaped, female nudes, dark green ground 825

Vase, 6" h., pillow-shaped, dark brown ground 358

Vase, 7" h., footed ovoid body w/short cylindrical neck, embossed flowers & leaves on dark green ground 358

Vase, 8" h., fan-shaped, nude in panel, dark green ground 605

Vase, 8" h., fan-shaped w/nudes decoration in orange, brown ground 1,100

Panel Vase

Vase, 8" h., footed, wide, slightly expanding cylindrical body w/short rolled rim, floral panels, dark green ground, No. 191-8" (ILLUS.) 413

Vase, 8" h., two small rim handles, expanding cylinder, stylized florals, dark brown ground, No. 292-8 374

Vase, 8" h., wide bulbous body w/a round shoulder to the molded neck, decorated w/vines, leaves & fruit in orange on brown ground, No. 293-8" 358

Vase, 8 1/4" h., 5 1/4" w., flattened fan-shaped bowl on a short knob pedestal on flaring round foot, light green on dark green 715

Panel Vase

Vase, 9" h., baluster-form body w/trumpet-form neck, orange floral decoration on dark brown ground, No. 294-8" (ILLUS.) 248

Vase, 10 1/4" h., 4 1/4" d., tall ovoid body w/widely flaring rim, female nudes, dark green ground, No. 296-10" (small glaze chip to base, possibly in making) 1,430

Vase, 11" h., footed conical form. nude in panel, dark brown ground, No. 298-11" (drill hole to bottom).. **605**

Vase, 11" h., footed conical form, nude in panel, dark green ground, No. 298-11"...... **1,870**

Vase, 12" h., embossed flowers & leaves on dark green ground, No. 299-12 .... **1,045**

Wall pocket, conical form w/ruffled rim flanked by cut-out panels, nude decoration in orange, dark brown ground, 7" h........ **729**

Wall pocket, conical form, curved backplate w/pointed center w/hanging hole, nude, green ground, 9" h............................... **297**

Wall pocket, conical form, curved backplate w/pointed center w/hanging hole, floral, green ground, 9" h. **417**

Wall pocket, conical form, curved backplate w/pointed center w/hanging hole, nude, brown ground, 9" h. **675**

Wall pocket, cylindrical w/rounded end, curved asymmetrical rim, 9" h. **316**

Wall pocket, wide conical shape w/rounded end, leaves in panel, brown ground, 9" h. **326**

Pauleo (1914)

Prestige line of 222 color combinations and two glaze types, lustre or marbleized.

Pauleo Vases

Vase, floor type, 19" h., footed baluster form w/narrow shoulder tapering to cylindrical neck w/slightly flaring rim, dark brown glaze (chip repair to base, drilled)................. **322**

Pauleo Covered Jar

Jar, cov., hexagonal, red, blue, purple & black glaze, marked w/impressed "B" & "322" in black slip, 6 3/4" h. (ILLUS.).......... **1,320**

Lamp, tall ovoid body tapering to a short, wide cylindrical neck w/flared rim, semimatte blue glaze, original electric lamp fittings, 19" h.. **440**

Vase, 16 1/2" h., pearl grey to orange lustre glaze w/yellow & red fruit w/pale green leaves decoration bordered by green bands around shoulder, impressed mark (ILLUS. left)... **690**

Vase, 17 3/8" h., slightly swelled cylindrical tapering to wide neck w/flaring rim, decorated w/evenly spaced black streaks descending from the rim, mottled bluegreen lustre glaze (ILLUS. bottom, next column)... **1,760**

Vase, 18 1/2" h., footed, bulbous base tapering to tall cylindrical neck w/flat rim, shaded red glaze, drilled (ILLUS. right) **403**

Large Pauleo Vase

Peony (1942)

Floral arrangement with green leaves on textured, shaded backgrounds in yellow with brown, pink with blue, and green.

Ashtray, gold ground, No. 27............................. **155**

Basket, fan-shaped w/high overhead handle, green ground, No. 377-8", 8" h. **185**

Basket, fan-shaped w/high overhead handle, pink ground, No. 377-8", 8" h. **115**

Basket w/angular overhead handle, shaped rim, disk foot, gold ground, No. 379-12", 11" h. (chip & bruise to base) **130**

Basket w/overhead handle, hanging-type, green ground, No. 467-5"................................ **225**

Basket w/overhead handle, hanging-type, green ground, No. 376-7", 7" h. **187**

Basket w/overhead handle, hanging-type, pink ground, No. 376-7", 7" h. **185**

Basket w/overhead handle, gold ground, No. 378-10", 10" h. **185**

Peony Book End & Jardiniere

Book ends, pink ground, No. 11, 5 1/2" h.,
pr. (ILLUS. of one) **260**
Bowl, 10" l., two-handled, irregular rim,
green ground, No. 430-10" **125**
Bowl, 10" l., two-handled, irregular rim, pink
ground, No. 430-10" **150**
Cornucopia-vase, double, pink ground,
No. 172 .... **110**
Ewer, green ground, No. 7-6", 6" h. **112**
Ewer, pink ground, No. 8-10", 10" h. **225**
Ewer, pink ground, No. 9-15", 15" h. **600**
Flower frog, gold ground, No. 47-4", 4" h. **40**
Jardiniere, tiny rim handles, green ground,
No. 661-3", 3" h. **100**
Jardiniere, green ground, No. 661-4", 4" h
(ILLUS. top w/book end) **58**
Jardiniere & pedestal, green & gold,
30" h., 2 pcs. **950**
Jardiniere & pedestal base, gold ground,
No. 661-8", 8" h., overall, 24 1/2" h., 2
pcs. (two hairlines & small firing fleck to
rim, small chip to one leaf of jardiniere &
couple of minute flecks to pedestal) **440**
Jardiniere & pedestal base, pink ground,
No. 661-8", 8" h., 2 pcs. (shallow glaze
scaling 1/2" to shoulder, probably from
firing) **715**
Model of a conch shell, gold ground, No.
436, 9 1/2" w. **198**
Tea set: cov. teapot, creamer & open sugar;
green ground, No. 3, 3 pcs. **300**
Vase, double bud, 4" h., gold & green
ground, No. 167-4 1/2" **99**
Vase, 6 " h., two-handled, green ground,
No. 58-6" **90**
Vase, bud, 6" h., pink ground, No. 173-6" **125**
Vase, 7" h., pink ground, No 61-7" **145**
Vase, 15" h., floor-type, gold ground, No.
69-15" **440**
Vase, 15" h., floor-type, pink ground, No.
69-15" **470**
Vase, 18" h., floor-type, gold ground, No.
70-18" **465**
Vase, 18" h., floor-type, green ground, No.
70-18" **523**
Wall pocket, gold ground **325**
Wall pocket, two-handled, brown ground,
No. 1293-8", 8" **259**
Wall pocket, two-handled, green ground,
No. 1293-8", 8" **225**

Pine Cone (1931)

*Realistic embossed brown pine cones and green
pine needles on shaded blue, brown or green
ground. (Pink is extremely rare.)*

Ashtray, blue ground, No. 499, 4 1/2" l. **225**
Ashtray, brown ground, No. 499, 4 1/2" l... **200-225**
Ashtray, green ground, No. 499, 4 1/2" l. **116**
Basket, hanging-type, squatty bulbous
body tapering slightly toward the base,
w/a short wide cylindrical neck flanked by
tiny branch hanging handles, brown
ground, No. 352-5", 7" d., 5 1/2" h. **450**
Basket, w/overhead branch handle, asymmetrical body, brown ground, No. 408-6",
6" h. **347**
Basket, w/overhead branch handle, disk
base, flaring rim, blue ground, No. 338-
10", 10" h. **550-650**
Basket, w/overhead branch handle, disk
base, flaring rim, green ground, No. 338-
10", 10" h. **379**

Pine Cone Basket

Basket, w/overhead branch handle, boat-
shaped, blue ground, No. 410-10", 10" h.
(ILLUS.) **398**
Basket, brown ground, No. 353-11", 11" h. **475**
Book ends, blue ground, No. 1, pr. **288**
Bowl, 4" d., bulbous spherical body
w/incurved rim, blue ground, No.
278-4" **150-250**
Bowl, 4" d., bulbous spherical body w/in-
curved rim, brown ground, No. 278-4"
(pin prick glaze nick at mid-body) **138**
Bowl, 4" d., brown ground, bulbous w/in-
curved irregular rim, No. 441-4" **325**
Bowl, 6" d., blue ground, No. 261-6" (tight
hairline) **176**
Bowl, 6 1/2" d., 3 1/4" h., spherical footed
form w/small twig handle, blue ground,
No. 426-6" **256**
Bowl, boat-shaped, 8" l., brown ground, No.
427-8" **325**
Bowl, 8", blue ground, No. 428-8" **325**
Bowl, 9" d., 4" h., two-handled, footed with
rounded sides & pleated & shaped rim,
brown ground, No. 355-8" (small repair to
rim) **330**
Bowl, boat-shaped, 10" l., brown ground,
No. 429-10" **500**
Bowl, boat-shaped, 10" l., green ground,
No. 429-10" **275-325**
Bowl-vase, two handles, green ground, No.
400-4" **176**
Candleholders, flat disk base supporting
candle nozzle in the form of a pine cone

Pine Cone Fan Vase

Poppy (1930s)

Shaded backgrounds of blue or pink with decoration of poppy flower and green leaves.

small flat chip to bottom ring, hairline to
edge of pedestal) 440
Urn, green handled, 6" h. 200
Vase, 6" h., footed trumpet-form w/base
handles, green ground, No. 866-6" 132

Poppy Vase

Vase, 8" h., footed, wide cylindrical form
w/C-form handles, green ground, No.
871-8" (ILLUS.) 165
Vase, 9" h., two-handled, ovoid w/wide
mouth, green ground, No. 872-9" 303
Vase, 9" h., bulbous base w/wide cylindrical
neck, small scrolled handles, pink
ground, No. 873-9" 300
Vase, 9" h., bulbous base w/wide cylindrical
neck, small scrolled handles, green
ground, No. 873-9" 303
Vase, 10" h., cylindrical w/base handles,
pink ground, No. 874-10" 475
Wall pocket, triple, tapering center section
flanked by small tapering cylinders,
green ground, No. 1281-8", 8 1/2" h. 748

Primrose (1932)
*Cluster of single blossoms on tall stems, low
pad-like leaves; backgrounds are blue, tan, or pink.*

Basket, hanging-type, pink ground, No.
354-6", 6" h. 275
Cornucopia-vase, pink ground, No. 125-6",
6" h. 168

Primrose Jardiniere

Jardiniere, blue ground, No. 634-5", 5" d.
(ILLUS.) 193
Jardiniere, blue ground, No. 634-6", 6" d. 225

Rose bowl, blue ground, No. 284-4", 4" d.
(tiny bruise to one flower, splash of yellow in blue background near base of one
plant) 78
Rose bowl, pink ground, No. 284-4", 4" d. 121
Umbrella stand, tan ground, No. 773-21",
21" h. 1,320
Vase, 6 1/2" h., ovoid body w/angled han-
dles, blue ground, No. 761-6" 128
Vase, 6 1/2" h., ovoid body w/angled handles, tan ground, No. 761-6" 90
Vase, 7" h., two-handled, blue ground, No.
762-7" 143
Vase, 7 1/2" h., tan ground, No. 763-7"
(minute flake to handle) 165
Vase, 8" h., fan-shaped, pink ground, No.
765-8" 209
Wall pocket, angular side handles, blue
ground, No. 1277-8", 8 1/2" 863
Wall pocket, angular side handles, pink
ground, No. 1277-8", 8 1/2" h. 480
Wall pocket, angular side handles, tan
ground, No. 1277-8", 8 1/2" 660
Window box, tan ground, No. 381-10",
12 1/2" l., 6 1/2" h. 440

Russco (1930s)
*Octagonal rim openings, stacked handles, nar-
row perpendicular panel front and back. One type
glaze is solid matte color; another is matte color
with lustrous crystalline over glaze, some of which
shows actual grown crystals.*

Urn-vase, angular handles, blue, No. 108-
6, 7" h. 128
Urn-vase, angular handles, crystalline
green to gold glaze, No. 108-6, 7" h. 220
Urn-vase, angular handles, orange, No.
108-6, 7" h. 225
Urn-vase, footed, bulbous base w/small
buttressed handles, wide tapering cylindrical neck w/slightly flaring rim, gold
crystalline glaze, partial paper label, No.
109-8", 8 1/2" h. 187
Vase, 6" h., two-handled, footed globular
body w/wide shoulder tapering to flared
rim, turquoise glaze, No. 259-6", silver
foil label 83

Russco Snowflake Crystalline Vase

Vase, 6" h., two-handled, footed globular
body w/wide shoulder tapering to flared
rim, snowflake crystalline yellow over
green glaze, No. 259-6", silver foil label
(ILLUS.) 220

Vase, 8" h., green w/crystalline overglaze......... **193**
Vase, double bud, 8" h., No. 107-8"................. **200**
Vase, 8" h., rust ground, No. 696-8".................. **220**
Vase, 8 1/2" h., maroon... **95**
Vase, 8 1/2" h., flared foot, slender trumpet
  form w/curved base handles, cream
  w/green crystalline overglaze, No. 695-8"..... **242**
Vase, bud, 9" h., rust ground, No. 695-9"......... **245**
Vase, 10" h., footed baluster form w/flaring
  rim & slender scrolled handles, orange
  glaze, No. 700-10".. **263**

Silhouette (1952)

Recessed area silhouettes nature study or female nudes. Colors are rose, turquoise, tan and white with turquoise.

Silhouette Basket

Basket, flaring cylinder w/pointed overhead
  handle, florals, turquoise blue, No. 708-
  6", 6" h. (ILLUS.).. **82**
Basket, florals, rose ground, No. 708-6",
  6" h.. **258**
Basket, curved rim & asymmetrical handle,
  florals, rose ground, No. 710-10", 10" h....... **183**
Basket w/overhead handle, tan, No. 708-
  6", 6" h... **113**
Bowl, 6", white, No. 726-6"................................. **70**
Bowl, 8" d., florals, tan ground, No. 727-8"........ **70**
Candleholders, florals, tan ground, No.
  751-3", 3" h., pr.. **50**
Cornucopia-vase, rose ground, No. 722-
  6", 6" h.. **178**
Ewer, bulging base, florals, rose, No. 716-
  6", 6" h.. **80**
Ewer, bulging base, florals, white, No. 716-
  6", 6" h... **105**
Jardiniere, footed wide nearly spherical
  body w/an incurved wide irregular rim,
  small pointed angular shoulder handles,
  female nudes, blue ground, No. 742-6",
  6" h. (tight line to rim, small chip to base,
  spider lines to base **303**
Planter, florals, rose ground, No. 769-9",
  9" l.. **210**
Planter, florals, turquoise ground, footed
  long rectangular form, No. 756-5", 5" h.......... **75**
Planter, rose ground, No. 768-8", 8" l.............. **200**
Rose bowl, female nudes, turquoise blue
  ground, No. 742-6", 6" h. (repair to base)..... **264**
Rose bowl, female nudes, rose ground, No.
  742-6", 6" h.. **293**

Silhouette Urn

Urn, four wing-shaped feet on disk base, re-
  clining female nudes, turquoise ground,
  No. 763-8", 8" h. (ILLUS.) **420**
Urn, four wing-shaped feet on disk base, re-
  clining female nudes, white ground, No.
  763-8", 8" h.. **358**
Vase, 5" h., florals, turquoise blue ground,
  No. 779-5"... **135**
Vase, 5" h., florals, white ground, No. 779-
  5".. **125**
Vase, 7" h., florals, double wing-shaped
  handles above low footed base, cylindrical w/asymmetrical rim, rose, No. 782-7"....... **78**
Vase, 7" h., fan-shaped, nude lady, rose
  ground, No. 783-7" (small rim chip pro-
  fessionally repaired) **383**
Vase, 8" h., urn-form, tapering ovoid body
  raised on four angled feet on a round disk
  base, wide slightly flaring mouth, female
  nude, rose ground, No. 763-8" **374**
Vase, 8" h., rose ground, No. 784-8" **245**
Vase, 8" h., white ground, No. 784-8" **60**
Vase, 9" h., double, base w/canted sides
  supporting two square vases w/sloping
  rims, joined by a stylized branch-form
  center post, florals, orange shading to
  brown ground, No. 757-9" **165**
Vase, 9" h., double, base w/canted sides
  supporting two square vases w/sloping
  rims, joined by a stylized branch-form
  center post, florals, rose ground, No.
  757-9"... **245**
Vase, 10" h., small open handles between
  square base & waisted cylindrical body,
  shaped rim, female nudes, white ground
  No. 787-10"... **248**
Vase, 10" h., small open handles between
  square base & waisted cylindrical body,
  shaped rim, female nudes, rose ground,
  No. 787-10" (one corner of base profes-
  sionally repaired) **330**
Vase, 12" h., florals, rose ground, No. 788-
  12".. **253**
Vase, 12" h., florals, white ground, No. 788-
  12".. **99**

Vase, 14" h., globular base w/expanding cylindrical neck w/fluted rim, foliage, rose ground, No. 789-14", each **460**

Wall pocket, bullet-shaped w/angular pierced handles, florals, rose ground, No. 766-8", 8" h. **431**

Snowberry (1946)
Brown branch with small white berries and green leaves embossed over spider-web design in various background colors (blue, green and rose).

Ashtray, round dished form, shaded green ground, 5 1/4" d. **80**

Basket, footed fan-shaped body w/wide looped & pointed handle, shaded green ground, No. 1BK-7", 7" h. **193**

Basket, footed fan-shaped body w/wide looped & pointed handle, shaded rose ground, No. 1BK-7", 7" h. **168**

Basket, w/asymmetrical overhead handle, shaded blue ground, No. 1BK-8", 8" h. **130**

Basket, w/asymmetrical overhead handle, shaded green ground, No. 1BK-8", 8" h. **165**

Basket, w/asymmetrical overhead handle, shaded rose ground, No. 1BK-8", 8" h. **138**

Basket w/curved overhead handle, disk base, shaded green ground, No. 1BK-10", 10" h. **227**

Basket w/curved overhead handle, disk base, shaded green ground, No. 1BK-12", 12" h. **209**

Book ends, shaded blue ground, 1BE, pr. **275**

Book ends, shaded green ground, No. 1BE, pr. **231**

Snowberry Low Bowl

Bowl, 6" d., two-handled, rose ground, small chip at corner of handle, light crazing, No. 1BL1-6" (ILLUS.) **144**

Bowl, 10" d., footed, shaded green ground, No. 1FB-10" **182**

Candleholders, squatty w/angular handles at shoulder, shaded rose ground, No. 1CS1-2", 2" h., pr. **115**

Candleholders, squatty w/angular handles at shoulder, shaded green ground, No. 1CS1-2", 2" h., pr. **88**

Console bowl, pointed end handles, shaded green ground, No. 1BL1-10", 10" l. **99**

Console bowl, shaded rose ground, No. 1BL1-10", 10" l. **125**

Console bowl, shaded green ground, No. 1BL-8", 11" l. **88**

Console bowl, shaded rose ground, No. 1BL-8", 11" l. **115**

Console bowl, boat-shaped, pointed end handles, shaded rose ground, No. 1BL2-12", 15" l. **145**

Cornucopia-vase, shaded green ground, No. 1CC-8", 8" h. **132**

Snowberry Ewer

Ewer, shaded green ground, No. 1TK-6", 6" h. (ILLUS.) **119**

Ewer, shaded rose ground, No. 1TK-6", 6" h. **127**

Ewer, sharply compressed base w/long conical neck, shaded green ground, No. 1TK-10, 10" h. **240**

Ewer, flaring base, oval body, shaded rose ground, No. 1TK-15", 16" h. **319**

Jardiniere, two-handled, shaded green ground, No. 1J-4", 4" h. **122**

Jardiniere, two-handled, shaded rose ground, No. 1J-4", 4" h. **104**

Jardiniere & pedestal, shaded blue ground, No. 1J-8", 2 pcs. **1,350**

Jardiniere & pedestal base, shaded green ground, No. IJ-8", overall 25" h., 2 pcs. **750**

Pedestal base, rose ground, 16" h. **168**

Rose bowl, two handled, shaded blue ground, No. 1RB-5", 5" d. **130**

Rose bowl, two-handled, shaded green, No. 1RB-5", 5" h. **165**

Tea set: cov. teapot, open sugar bowl & creamer; shaded green ground, Nos. 1TP, 1S & 1C, 3 pcs. **360**

Tea set: cov. teapot, open sugar bowl & creamer; shaded blue ground, Nos. 1TP, 1S & 1C, the set **303**

Tray, long leaf-shaped, shaded rose ground, No. 1BL1-12", 14" l. **104**

Tray long leaf-shaped, shaded green ground, No. 1BL1-12", 14" l. **200**

Urn-vase, two-handled, shaded green ground, No. 1UR-8", 8 1/2" h. **200**

Vase, 6 1/2" h., pillow-type, shaded blue ground, No. 1FH-6" **110**

Vase, 6 1/2" h., pillow-type, shaded green ground, No. 1FH-6" **159**

Vase, 7" h., two-handled, shaded blue ground, No. 1V1-7" **145**

Vase, 7" h., two-handled, shaded rose ground, No. 1V1-7" **95**

Snowberry Vase

Vase, 8" h., ovoid w/flat shoulder & flaring rim, small pointed shoulder handles, shaded green ground, No. 1V2-8" (ILLUS.) **176**

Vase, 9" h., shaded blue ground, No. 1V2-9" **175**

Vase, 9" h., shaded green ground, No. 1V2-9" **185**

Vase, 9" h., shaded rose ground, No. 1V2-9" **200**

Vase, 10" h., shaded green ground, No. 1V2-10" **231**

Vase, 10" h., shaded rose ground, No. 1V2-10" **209**

Vase, 15" h., floor-type, shaded green ground, 1V1-15" **450**

Vase, 15" h., floor-type, shaded rose ground, 1V1-15" **750**

Vase, 18" h., shaded blue ground, No. 1V-18 .... **475**

Vase, 18" h., shaded rose ground, No. 1V-18" **440**

Snowberry Wall Pocket

Wall pocket, wide half-round form tapering to a pointed base, low angled handles along the lower sides, shaded green ground, No. 1WP-8", 8" w., 5 1/2" h. (ILLUS.) **144**

Wall pocket, wide half-round form tapering to a pointed base, low angled handles along the lower sides, shaded blue ground, No. 1WP-8", 8" w., 5 1/2" h. **250-300**

Wall pocket, wide half-round form tapering to a pointed base, low angled handles along the lower sides, shaded rose ground, No. 1WP-8", 8" w., 5 1/2" h. **243**

Window box, rectangular, shaded blue ground, No. 1WX-8", 8" l. **155**

Window box, shaded green ground, No. 1WX-8", 8" l. **289**

Sunflower (1930)

Tall stems support yellow sunflowers whose blooms form a repetitive band. Textured background shades from tan to dark green at base.

Basket, hanging-type, 8" d., 5" h. **985**

Basket, hanging-type, 6 3/4" (exterior spider lines & horizontal line to rim) **460**

Bowl, 3 5/8" h., flaring sides, slender loop handles **750**

Bowl, 5" d., wide squatty form w/wide flat rim, No. 208-5" **748**

Jardiniere, No. 619-4", 4" h. **616**

Jardiniere, No. 619-6", 6 1/4" h. **1,955**

Jardiniere, No. 619-8", 8" h., unmarked (two hairlines from rim, straight 1" & T-shaped 1/1/2") **880**

Jardiniere, No. 619-10", unmarked (restoration to opposing hairlines, small chip to edge of leaf) **1,045**

Jardiniere, No. 619-12" (minor scrape inside rim, stress fracture to base) **2,530**

Planter, wide tapering cylindrical body w/incurved rim, 5 x 6 1/4" **1,265**

Umbrella stand, footed cylindrical form, No. 770-20", unmarked, 20" h. **7,425**

Urn-vase, nearly spherical w/tiny rim handles, 4" h. **506**

Urn-vase, nearly spherical w/short wide neck, No. 489-7", 7" h. **1,540**

Vase, 5" h., swelled cylindrical body w/long side handles & closed rim **498**

Vase, 5" h., No. 486-5", unmarked (ILLUS. second from right, below) **560**

Vase, 5 1/2" h., 5 1/4" d., bulbous ovoid body tapering to a wide flat mouth, small loop handles at the shoulder **515**

Vase, 6" h., swelled cylindrical body w/short cylindrical neck flanked by small loop handles, No. 485-6" (ILLUS. far right, below) **669**

Vase, 6" h., squatty bulbous body, wide shoulder w/short cylindrical neck, No. 488-6" (bruise to rim, abrasion to one flower) **770**

Vase, 7" h., bulbous base below expanding cylindrical neck w/wide flaring flat rim (crack from rim) **413**

Vase, 7" h., waisted cylindrical form w/wide flaring mouth, No. 487-7" **990**

Sunflower Vases & Wall Pocket

Sunflower Vase

Vase, 8" h., bulbous base, wide tapering cylindrical neck, No. 490-8" (ILLUS.).............. **1,115**
Vase, 8" h., two-handled, ovoid w/flaring rim, No. 491-8" **1,460**
Vase, 9" h., bulbous base w/wide cylindrical neck, small loop handles, No. 493-9" (ILLUS. second from left, previous page).... **1,161**
Vase, 10" h., tall swelled cylindrical body tapering slightly to a wide flat mouth flanked by tiny loop handles, No. 494-10" (nearly invisible flat chip off base)............... **1,375**
Wall pocket, No. 1265-7", minute glaze nick to front of pierced back brace, glazed over chip to back corner, 7" h. (ILLUS. far left, previous page) **1,427**
Window box, 3 1/2 x 11" **1,500**

Teasel (1936)

Embossed decorations of long-stems gracefully curving with delicate spider-like pods. Colors and glaze treatments vary from monochrome matte to crystalline. Colors are beige to tan, medium blue highlighted with gold, pale blue and deep rose (possibly others).

Bowl, 4" d., pale blue ground, No. 342-4" **187**
Bowl, 8" d., blue ground, No. 344-8" **175**
Candleholders, shaded blue ground, No. 1131, 2" h., pr... **165**
Jardiniere, footed squatty bulbous body w/a wide cylindrical neck, small angled shoulder handles, rust ground w/green flowers, No. 644-4", 4" h. (small glaze flake off one handle).. **83**
Jardiniere, footed squatty bulbous body w/a wide cylindrical neck, small angled shoulder handles, brown ground, No. 644-4", 4" h. **150**
Jardiniere, footed squatty bulbous body w/a wide cylindrical neck, small angled shoulder handles, peach matte ground, No. 644-4", 4" h. **165**
Jardiniere, footed spherical body w/a wide closed rim & small tab shoulder handles, blue ground, No. 343-6", 6" h. **178**
Rose bowl, footed spherical body w/a wide closed rim & small tab shoulder handles, beige shading to tan ground, No. 343-6", 6" h. **132**

Vase, 6" h., closed handles at midsection, cut-out rim, beige shading to tan ground, No. 881-6"... **150**
Vase, 6" h., closed handles at midsection, cut-out rim, mottled blue ground, No. 881-6" **165**
Vase, 6" h., closed handles at rim, beige shading to tan ground, No. 882-6"................. **176**
Vase, 6" h., closed handles at rim, deep rose, No. 882-6"... **138**

Teasel Vase

Vase, 8" h., closed handles at shoulder, low foot, blue ground, No. 884-8" (ILLUS.) **193**
Vase, 8" h., blue ground, rectangular foot below flaring rectangular body w/stepped rim ends, shaped low buttress side handles, No. 885-8" **190**

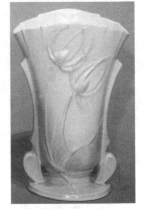

Teasel Vase

Vase, 9" h., closed handles at base, flaring mouth, beige shading to tan, No. 886-9" (ILLUS.)... **330**
Vase, 9" h., closed handles at base, flaring mouth, deep rose, No. 886-9" **110**
Vase, 9" h., closed handles at base, flaring mouth, shaded blue, No. 886-9" **195**

Thorn Apple (1930s)

White trumpet flower with leaves reverses to thorny pod with leaves. Colors are shaded blue, brown and pink.

Basket, hanging-type, shaded blue ground, No. 355-5", 5" h., 7" d. **288**

Book ends, shaded brown ground, No. 3,
pr. 308
Book ends, shaded blue ground, No. 3, pr. 140
Bowl, 8" d., pointed handles, shaded pink
ground, No. 309-8" 275

Thorn Apple Centerpiece

Centerpiece, shaded blue ground, No. 313-
11", 11" l. (ILLUS.) 134
Centerpiece, shaded brown ground, No.
313-11", 11" l. 358
Ewer, shaded pink & green ground, No.
816-8", 8" h. 265

Thorn Apple Ewer

Ewer, shaded pink & green ground, No.
825-15", small bruise & flat chip to base,
15" h. (ILLUS.) 770
Flowerpot, shaded blue ground, No. 639-
5", 5" h. (spider line to base of pot does
not go through) 220
Jardiniere, shaded brown ground, No. 638-
4", 4" h. 100
Jardiniere, spherical form w/three openings
& buttressed handles, shaded brown
ground, No. 305-6" (minor nick to one
corner, short tight line to rim) 165
Urn, stepped handles, disk foot, shaded
brown ground, No. 304-4" 80
Urn, stepped handles, disk foot, shaded
pink ground, No. 304-4" 95
Urn, stepped handles, disk foot, shaded
blue ground, No. 305-6", 6" h. 160
Urn, footed spherical body flanked by
stepped, angled handles, shaded brown
ground, No. 305-6", 6 1/2" h. 78
Vase, 4" h., squatty body w/short narrow
neck, angular pierced handles rising from

midsection, shaded blue ground, No.
308-4" 138
Vase, 4" h., jug-form, shaded pink ground,
No. 808-4" 138
Vase, 6" h., shaded blue ground, No. 810-6" 165
Vase, 6" h., shaded brown ground, No. 810-
6" 175

Thorn Apple Vase

Vase, 6" h., bulbous ovoid body w/sharply
angled shoulder handles, short cylindrical neck, shaded pink ground, No. 811-6"
(ILLUS.) 193
Vase, 6" h., shaded brown ground, No. 811-
6" 132
Vase, bud, 7" h., shaded brown ground, No.
813-7" 150-200
Vase, bud, 7" h., shaded pink ground, No.
813-7" 145
Vase, 10" h., footed, bulbous body tapering
to flaring rim, angled shoulder handles,
shaded brown ground, No. 821-10" 275
Vase, 10 1/2" h., angular handles rising
from shoulder to middle of wide neck,
footed, shaded brown ground, No. 822-
10" 138
Vase, 10 1/2" h., angular handles rising
from shoulder to middle of wide neck,
footed, shaded pink ground, No. 822-10" 225
Vase, 12" h., footed, bulbous base w/small
tab handles, horizontal rings below large
wide trumpet-form neck, shaded brown
ground, No. 774-8 x 12 (restoration to
two small rim chips & two small base
chips) 413
Vase, 15" h., shaded pink & green ground,
No. 824-15" 525
Wall pocket, brown ground, No. 356-4",
4" h. (minute nick to back of hole) 978
Wall pocket, triple, shaded brown ground,
No. 1280-8", 8" h. (small stilt pull chips) 500

Topeo (1934)

Simple forms decorated with four vertical evenly spaced cascades of leaves in high relief at their ori-gin, tapering downward to a point. A light green crystalline glaze shades to a mottled medium blue, with cascades in alternating green and pink. A sec-ond type is done completely in a high-gloss dark red.

Bowl, 6" d., shaded blue ground, No. 245-6" 300
Bowl, 9" d., sharply canted sides, red
ground, silver label, No. 246-3" 231
Console bowl, glossy dark red glaze, paper
label, 11 1/2" l., 3" h. 255

Vase, 6 1/2" h., ovoid w/flaring mouth, shaded blue glaze, No. 656-6" (ILLUS.) **201**

Topeo Vase

Vase, 6 1/2" h., ovoid w/flaring mouth, glossy deep red glaze, No. 656-6" (ILLUS.)... **193**

Vase, 6 3/4" h., ovoid body w/short wide cylindrical neck w/flat rim, red ground, No. 657-6 3/4"... **220**

Vase, 6 3/4" h., ovoid body w/short wide cylindrical neck w/flat rim, green crystalline shading to blue, No. 657-6 3/4".................... **278**

Vase, 7" h., compressed globular base & flaring mouth, green crystalline glaze shading to blue, No. 658-7 1/4"................... **403**

Vase, 8" h., blue ground, No. 659-8"................. **633**

Vase, 8 1/4" h., footed ovoid body w/short flaring rim, shaded blue ground, No. 660-8 1/4".. **500**

Vase, 12 1/4" h., ovoid tapering sides, green crystalline glaze shading to blue, No. 664-12 1/4"....................................... **863**

Tourmaline (1933)

Although the semi-gloss medium blue, highlighted around the rim with lighter high gloss and gold effect, seems to be accepted as the standard Tourmaline glaze, the catalogue definitely shows this and two other types as well. One is a mottled overall turquoise, the other a mottled salmon that appears to be lined in the high gloss but with no overrun to the outside.

Bowl, 7" d., shallow w/sharply canted sides, intermingled blue crystalline matte glaze, No. 152-7 .... **495**

Bowl, 7" d., shallow w/sharply canted sides, mottled blue semi-gloss glaze, No. 152-7 ..... **111**

Bowl, 7" d., mottled blue ground, No. A-152-7"... **130**

Bowl, 8" d., low incurved sides, mottled turquoise glaze **88**

Candlesticks, flared ribbed base, flaring nozzle, mottled blue ground, gold labels, No. 1089-4 1/2", 4 1/2" h., pr. **165**

Urn-vase, compressed globular base w/short collared neck, mottled blue, No. A-200-4", 4 1/2" h. **253**

Vase, 5 1/2" h., globular w/loop handles rising from midsection to rim, glossy glaze over matte blue, unmarked, A-517-6" **134**

Vase, 5 1/2" h., globular w/loop handles rising from midsection to rim, mottled turquoise blue, gold foil label, No. A-517-6" d... **124**

Vase, 6" h., pillow-type, mottled blue glaze **75**

Vase, 6" h., mottled blue ground, No. A517-6".. **175**

Vase, 7" h., cylindrical w/low flaring foot, slightly flared rim, mottled blue, No. 308-7".. **121**

Vase, 7" h., shaded orange glaze, No. 318-7".. **150**

Tourmaline Vase

Vase, 8" h., hexagonal twisted form, mottled pink & green semi-gloss glaze, large gold foil label (ILLUS.) **220**

Vase, 8" h., twisted paneled effect, mottled blue, No. A-425-8" **385**

Vase, 8" h., twisted paneled effect, pink, No. A-425-8" **210**

Vase, 9" h., flared foot below buttressed base, trumpet-form body, mottled turquoise glaze, No. A-429-9" **413**

Tourmaline Vase

Vase, 10" h., squatty bulbous base w/wide cylindrical neck w/horizontally ribbed lower half & slightly flaring rim, mottled blue matte over blue-yellow glossy glaze, gold foil label, No. 435-10" (ILLUS.) **468**

Vase, 10" h., squatty bulbous base w/wide cylindrical neck w/horizontally ribbed lower half & slightly flaring rim, mottled pink to blue glaze, No. 435-10" **690**

Tuscany (1927)

Marble-like finish most often found in a shiny pink, sometimes in matte grey, more rarely in a dull turquoise. Suggestion of leaves and berries, usually at the base of handles, are the only decorations.

Console bowl, rectangular w/rounded
ends, mottled pink, unmarked, 11" l. 225
Console bowl, rectangular w/rounded
ends, No. 174-12", 12" l................................. 250
Flower frog, mottled pink, small 65
Urn-vase, mottled pink, 4" h. 200
Vase, 5" h., 7" d., mottled turquoise, No. 70-
5" 88
Vase, 5" h., 7" d., mottled pink, No. 70-5" 130
Vase, 5 1/2" h., fan-shaped, mottled pink
ground 95

Tuscany Vase

Vase, 7" h., tri-shaped, two-handled, grey,
w/original sticker, No. 343-7" (ILLUS.) 202
Vase, 8" h., mottled pink ground, No. 344-8" 275
Vase, 9" h., two-handled, globular base,
short wide neck, mottled grey glaze 150
Vase, 10" h., shoulder handles, bulbous
body, mottled pink ground, No. 347-10" 395
Vase, 10" h., shoulder handles, bulbous,
mottled pink glaze, No. 348-10" 257
Wall pocket, long open handles, rounded
rim, grey glaze, No. 1255-8", 8" h. 288

Velmoss (1935)

*Characterized by three horizontal wavy lines
around the top from which long, blade-like leaves
extend downward. Colors are green, blue, tan and
pink.*

Jardiniere, footed spherical body w/short
wide neck & pointed shoulder handles,
mottled blue glaze, No. 264-5", 5" h. 207
Urn-vase, angular pointed side handles,
mottled pink, No. 265-6", 6" h. 132

Velmoss Vase

Vase, 6" h., swelled cylindrical body
w/pointed shoulder handles, mottled
raspberry red glaze, No. 714-6", gold foil
label (ILLUS.) 255

Vase, 6" h., swelled cylindrical body
w/pointed shoulder handles, mottled tan
& green crystalline glaze, No. 714-6",
gold foil label 358
Vase, bud, 7" h., rose ground, No. 115-7" 154

Velmoss Bud Vase

Vase, double bud, 8" h., triangular base
w/tall conical form joined to shorter cylindrical form by figural leaf cluster, mottled
blue, No. 116-8" (ILLUS.) 223
Vase, 9 1/2" h., ovoid body w/pointed shoul-
der handles, mottled blue glaze, No. 719-
9" 500
Vase, 12" h., ovoid body tapering to wide
cylindrical neck w/wide flat rim, angled
handles, mottled raspberry red, No. 721-
12", gold foil label 468
Vase, 14 1/2" h., tall trumpet-form body
w/low foot, angular pointed handles, mot-
tled rose glaze, No. 722-14" 616
Wall pocket, double, mottled green crystal-
line glaze, No. 1274-8", 8 1/2" h. 3,190

Vista (1920s)

*Embossed green coconut palm trees & lavender
blue pool against grey ground.*

Basket, hanging-type, wide low-sided cylindrical form w/three low strap handles
along the sides, 8" d., 4" h. (abrasion to
bottom, glaze scaling to edge & rim,
tough-up to a couple of points) 385
Basket w/pointed overhead handle, ta-
pering square form w/pointed side rim,
5 1/2 x 6 1/2" 454
Bowl, 7" d., 3 1/2" h., deep, few minor
flakes 300

Vista Bowl

Bowl, 8 3/8" d., 4" h., cylindrical form w/flat
rim, unmarked (ILLUS.) 220
Jardiniere, 9" h. 465
Jardiniere & pedestal base, 12" h., jardi-
niere, overall 36" h., 2 pcs. (two glaze
flakes to rim & "T"-shaped hairline to

base of jardiniere which crawls up side & spreads 4".. **2,200**

Planter, rectangular w/curved sides & end handles, 4 1/2 x 11 1/2", 6" h. (bruise to corner of base, shallow line to bottom that does not go through, small chip to inner rim, minor glaze scaling)........................ **715**

Vista Vase

Vase, 9 3/4" h., cylindrical body tapering to flared base, round shoulder w/flat molded mouth, unmarked (ILLUS.) **660**

Vase, 10" h., bulbous base tapering to cylindrical neck flanked by buttressed handles (restoration to rim chip) **523**

Vase, 10" h., tapering cylindrical body w/flaring base **660**

Vase, 12" h., ovoid body tapering to round base **660**

Vase, 12" h., wide cylindrical form expanding slightly at top flanked by buttressed handles **823**

Vase, 12" h., 4 3/4" d., footed, bulbous base tapering to tall wide cylindrical neck w/flat rim **715**

Vase, floor-type, 14" h., footed tapering cylindrical form **1,045**

Vase, floor-type, 15" h., tall tapering cylindrical body w/flared foot & molded rim band, No. 121-15"................................. **650-1,100**

Water Lily (1940s)

Water lily and pad in various color combinations: tan to brown with yellow lily, blue with white lily, pink to green with pink lily.

Basket, hanging-type, shaded blue ground, No. 468-5", 9" h.. **110**

Basket, conch shell-shaped w/high arched handle, gold shading to brown ground, No. 381-10", 10" h. **235**

Basket, w/asymmetrical overhead handle, curved & sharply scalloped rim, shaded blue ground, No. 382-12", 12" h. **160**

Basket, w/asymmetrical overhead handle, curved & sharply scalloped rim, pink shading to green ground, No. 382-12", 12" h.. **275**

Basket w/pointed asymmetrical overhead handle & pleated rim, pink shading to green ground, No. 381-10", 10" h. **100**

Basket w/pointed overhead handle, cylindrical w/flaring rim, pink shading to green ground, No. 380-8", 8" h. **150**

Basket w/pointed overhead handle, cylindrical w/flaring rim, shaded blue ground, No. 380-8", 8" h. **140**

Cookie jar, cov., angular handles, blended blue ground, No. 1-8", 8" h......................... **358**

Cookie jar, cov., angular handles, gold shading to brown ground, No. 1-8", 8" h....... **459**

Cornucopia-vase, gold shading to brown ground, No. 176-6", 6" h................................ **176**

Cornucopia-vase, blue ground, No. 178-8", 8" h. **195**

Cornucopia-vases, pink ground, No. 177-6", 6" h., pr.. **295**

Ewer, flared bottom, blended blue ground, No. 10-6", 6" h.. **70**

Ewer, blue ground, No. 12-15", 15" h. **450**

Flower holder, two-handled, fan-shaped body, gold shading to brown ground, No. 48, 4 1/2" h. **90**

Flower holder, two-handled, fan-shaped body, pink shading to green ground, No. 48, 4 1/2" h. **121**

Water Lily Flowerpot

Flowerpot w/saucer, gold shading to brown ground, No. 664-5, clay fold on inner rim of pot, 5" h. (ILLUS.).......................... **101**

Jardiniere, blended blue ground, No. 663-8", minute flake to petal, 9" d., 8" h. **248**

Jardiniere & pedestal base, blended blue ground, overall 24" h. **448**

Model of a conch shell, blended blue ground, No. 438-8", 8" h.................................. **172**

Model of a conch shell, pink shading to green ground, No. 438-8", 8" h. **175**

Rose bowl, two-handled, gold shading to brown ground, No. 437-6", 6" d..................... **176**

Vase, 4" h., gold shading to brown ground, No. 71-4"... **55**

Vase, 6" h., shaded blue ground, No. 174-6"....... **95**

Vase, 8" h., footed w/squatty bulbous bottom section below a wide cylindrical body flanked by long arched handles, blue ground, No. 76-8".. **104**

Vase, 8" h., two-handled, gold shading to brown, No. 77-8".. **245**

Vase, 9" h., footed bulbous ovoid body w/a large trumpet neck flanked by angled handles, gold shading to brown ground, No. 79-9"... **160**

Vase, 9" h., footed bulbous ovoid body w/a large trumpet neck flanked by angled handles, pink shaded to green ground, No. 79-9"... **207**

Vase, 14" h., angular side handles, blended blue ground, No. 82-14" **303**

Vase, 14" h., angular side handles, gold shading to brown ground, No. 82-14"........... **324**

Vase, 14" h., angular side handles, pink shading to green ground, No. 82-14" (small chip to bottom ring) 264

Vase, 15" h., pink shading to green ground, No. 83-15" 459

Vase, 15" h., two-handled, gold shading to brown ground, No. 83-15" 413

Vase, 18" h., floor-type, tall baluster-form w/pointed shoulder handles, gold shading to brown ground, No. 85-18" 425

Large Water Lily Vase

Vase, 18" h., floor-type, tall baluster-form w/pointed shoulder handles, pink shading to green ground, No. 85-18" (ILLUS.) 523

White Rose (1940s)

White roses and green leaves against a vertically combed ground of blended blue, brown shading to green or pink shading to green.

Basket, hanging-type, blended blue ground, No. 463-5" 244

Basket, hanging-type, pink shading to green ground, No. 463-5", 5" h....................... 325

Basket, oblong flaring bowl w/high heart-form pointed overhead handle, brown shading to green ground, No. 362-8", 8" h. 175

Basket w/pointed circular handle, pink shading to green ground, No. 363-10", 10" h.. 303

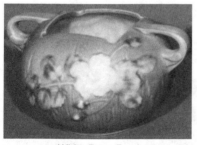

White Rose Bowl

Bowl, spherical body, two-handled, blended blue ground, No. 387-4", 4" d. (ILLUS.) 110

Candleholders, two-handled, low, blended blue ground, No. 1141-2", 2" h., pr. 95

Console bowl, blended blue ground, No. 391-10", 10" l.. 185

Console bowl, pink shading to green ground, No. 391-10", 10" l............................ 175

Console bowl, pink shading to green ground, No. 394-14", 14" l. 225

Cornucopia-vase, brown shading to green ground, No. 144-8", 8" h. 190

Cornucopia-vase, double, brown shading to green ground, No. 145-8", 8" h. (flat 1/8" chip to rim of one horn)..................... 90

Ewer, semi-ovoid w/high pointed handle at shoulder, blended blue ground, No. 990-10", 10" h. 295

Flower frog, basket-shaped w/overhead handle, pink shading to green ground, No. 41... 110

Jardiniere, spherical w/small shoulder loop handles, blended blue ground, No. 653-5", 5" h. 150

Jardiniere & pedestal base, blended blue ground, No. 653-8", 8" h., 2 pcs. 770

Tea set: cov. teapot, sugar bowl & creamer; brown shading to green ground, Nos. 1T, 1S, 1C, 3 pcs. 385

Urn-vase, handles rising from base to rim, footed, pink shading to green ground, No. 146-6", 6" h. 150

Urn-vase, spherical body on footring w/small loop handles flanking the flat mouth, blended blue ground, No. 388-7", 7" h... 395

Urn-vase, pink & blue ground, No. 147-8", 8" h. 175

Vase, 4" h., footed ovoid body w/lobed rim, pink shading to green ground, No. 978-4"....... 95

Vase, double bud, 4 1/2" h., two cylinders joined by an arched bridge, brown shading to green ground, No. 148...................... 160

Vase, 5" h., footed trumpet-form body w/notched rim & asymmetrical base loop handles, brown shading to green ground, 980-6" 120

Vase, 5" h., footed trumpet-form body w/notched rim & asymmetrical base loop handles, pink shading to green ground, 980-6" 147

Vase, 5" h., footed trumpet-form body w/notched rim & asymmetrical base loop handles, blended blue ground, 980-6" 160

Vase, 6" h., footed swelled cylindrical body w/a short notched neck flanked by pointed angled handles, pink shading to green ground, No. 979-6" 130

Vase, 7" h., blended blue ground, No. 983-7" 185

Vase, 7" h., pink shading to green ground, No. 983-7".. 165

Vase, 8" h., flattened ovoid body on a rectangular foot, small pointed shoulder handles, brown shading to green ground, No. 984-8" 248

Vase, 8" h., flattened ovoid body on a rectangular foot, small pointed shoulder handles, blended blue ground, No. 984-8"......... 265

Vase, 9" h., footed, wide tapering cylindrical body w/large handles from foot to shoulder, notched rim, pink shading to green ground, No. 986-9" 300

Vase, 12 1/2" h., ovoid, angular handles at
rim, blended blue ground, No. 991-12" **595**
Vase, 15 1/2" h., footed baluster-form
w/flaring split rim, long low side handles,
blended blue ground, No. 992-15" **388**

Large White Rose Vase

Vase, 18" h., floor-type, two-handled,
blended blue ground, No. 994-18"
(ILLUS.) **440**
Wall pocket, swirled handle, flaring rim,
pink shading to blue ground, No. 1288-
6", 6 1/2" h. **345**
Wall pocket, conical w/flaring rim w/over-
head handle continuing to one side, pink
shading to green ground, No. 1289-8",
8 1/2" h. **345**

Wincraft (1948)

*Revived shapes from older lines such as Pine
Cone, Bushberry, Cremona, Primrose and others.
Vases with animal motifs, contemporary shapes in
high gloss of blue, tan, lime and green.*

Ashtray, glossy turquoise blue ground, No.
240-T **60**
Basket, hanging-type, blue ground, No.
261-6", 6" h. **201**
Basket, hanging-type, tan ground, No. 261-
6", 6" h. **230**
Basket, hanging-type, lime green ground,
8" h. **175**
Basket, hanging-type, tan ground, 8" h. **165**
Basket, footed half-round form w/arched
rim & angled overhead handle, lime
green ground, No. 208-8", 8" h. **190**
Basket, footed half-round form w/arched
rim & angled overhead handle, tan
ground, No. 208-8", 8" h. **154**
Bowl, 8" d., glossy blue ground, No. 226-8" **132**
Cigarette box, cov., rectangular, glossy
chartreuse, No. 240, 4 1/2" l. **165**
Cigarette box, cov., shaded blue ground,
No. 240, 4 1/2" l. **121**
Coffeepot, cov., glossy tan, No. 250-P,
9 1/2" h. **140**
Console bowl, rectangular foot supporting
a long, low serpentine bowl w/pointed
ends, green ground, No. 227-10",
13 1/2" l., 4" h., ... **49**

Console bowl, brown ground, No. 233-14",
14" l. (small glaze chip to interior, col-
ored-in chip to both rim & base) **173**
Cornucopia-vase, florals in relief on shad-
ed green ground, No. 222-8", 8" h. **95**
Ewer, bell-form body below a tall neck w/up-
right tall spout & angled shoulder handle,
chartreuse ground, No. 216-8", 8" h. **115**
Flowerpot, blue ground, No. 265-5", 5" h. **80**
Jardiniere, pink ground, No. 635-6", 6" h. **330**
Planter, blue, No. 256-5", 5" h. **80**
Teapot, cov., brown & yellow ground, No.
271-P **265**
Vase, 6" h., blue ground, No. 241-6" **154**
Vase, 6" h., asymmetrical fan shape, pine
cones & needles in relief on lime ground,
No. 272-6" **115**
Vase, 8" h., blue ground w/arrow leaf de-
sign, No. 273-8" **125**
Vase, 8" h., flowing lily form w/asymmetrical
side handles, tulip & foliage in relief on
shaded blue ground, No. 282-8" **121**
Vase, 8" h., flowing lily form w/asymmetrical
side handles, tulip & foliage in relief on
glossy green & yellow ground, No. 282-8" **150**
Vase, 8" h., brown ground, No. 283-8" **165**
Vase, 10" h., ovoid base & long cylindrical
neck w/wedge-shaped closed handle on
one side & long closed column-form handle on the other, glossy mottled blue, No.
284-10" **165**
Vase, 10" h., ovoid base & long cylindrical
neck w/wedge-shaped closed handle on
one side & long closed column-form handle on the other, shaded green ground,
No. 284-10" **176**
Vase, 10" h., wide disk foot below the tall
cylindrical body joined to the foot w/a
leaf-form handle, blue ground, No. 285-
10" **230**

Wincraft Vase

Vase, 10" h., cylindrical, tab handles, black
panther & green palm trees in relief on
glossy shaded tan ground, 1/4" dark line
at rim, No. 290-10" (ILLUS.) **550**
Vase, 10" h., cylindrical, tab handles, black
panther & green palm trees in relief on
blue ground, No. 290-10" **703**

Wincraft Vase

Vase, 12" h., yellow, No. 275-12" (ILLUS.) **605**
Vase, 12" h., fan-shaped, glossy gold
ground, No. 287-12" **99**
Wall pocket, glossy tan ground, No. 267-5" **248**
Wall pocket, rectangular box-like holders
w/horizontal ribbing & ivy leaves as rim
handle, brown ground, No. 266-4",
8 1/2" h. **226**

Windsor (1931)
*Brown or blue mottled glaze, some with leaves,
vines and ferns, some with a repetitive band
arrangement of small squares and rectangles in
yellow and green.*

Windsor Bowl

Bowl, 10 5/8" l., 3 1/2" h., angular end handles, slightly canted sides, geometric design against mottled terra cotta ground
(ILLUS.) **413**
Vase, 5" h., No. 545-5" **535**
Vase, 6" h., canted sides, handles rising
from shoulder to rim, geometric design
against mottled terra cotta ground, No.
546-6" **440**
Vase, 6" h., canted sides, handles rising
from shoulder to rim, geometric design
against mottled blue ground, No. 546-6" **440**
Vase, 7" h., large handles, globular base,
stylized ferns against mottled terra cotta
ground, No. 548-7" (restoration to base
chip) **330**
Vase, 7" h., large handles, globular base,
stylized ferns against mottled blue
ground, No. 548-7" **715**
Vase, 7" h., trumpet-shaped w/long loop
handles from rim to midsection, green
leaves on terra cotta ground, No. 550-7" **495**
Vase, 7 1/2" h., 10" widest d., two handles
rising from shoulder of compressed globular base to rim of short wide mouth, stylized ferns against mottled terra cotta
ground **900**

Windsor Vase

Vase, 8" h., two-handled cylindrical body,
decorated w/floral sprays in green on
terra cotta ground, No. 552-8", black
paper label & old sales room label
w/price (ILLUS.) **660**

Wisteria (1933)
*Lavender wisteria blossoms and green vines
against a roughly textured brown shading to deep
blue ground, rarely found in only brown.*

Basket, hanging-type, brown ground,
7 1/2" h. **633**
Bowl-vase, squatty bulbous form tapering
sharply to a flat mouth flanked by small
loop handles, brown ground, No. 242-4",
4" h. **446**
Bowl-vase, squatty bulbous form tapering
sharply to a flat mouth flanked by small
loop handles, blue ground, No. 242-4",
4" h. **585**
Urn, blue ground, No. 632-5", 5" h. **683**

Wisteria Urn

Urn, bulbous body w/wide flat mouth, small
loop shoulder handles, brown ground,
6" h. (ILLUS.) **518**
Urn, bulbous body w/wide flat mouth, small
loop shoulder handles, brown ground,
8" h. **880**
Urn-vase, small rim handles, straight sides,
brown ground, No. 632-5", 5" h. **540**
Urn-vase, small rim handles, straight sides,
No. 632-5", 5" h. (glaze scrape to base,
few minor flecks to decoration) **330**
Vase, 4" h., squatty, angular handles on
sharply canted shoulder, blue ground,
No. 629-4", silver foil label **512**

Various Wisteria Vases

Vase, 4" h., squatty, angular handles on sharply canted shoulder, brown ground, No. 629-4", silver foil label.............................. 315

Vase, 6" h., ovoid body tapering to short cylindrical neck flanked by small loop handles, brown ground, No. 631-6"..................... 480

Vase, 6" h., ovoid body tapering to short cylindrical neck flanked by small loop handles, blue ground, No. 631-6" 581

Vase, 6 1/2" h., 4" d., bulbous ovoid body w/a wide shoulder tapering up to a small mouth, small angled shoulder handles, mottled blue & blue ground, No. 630-6"........ 523

Vase, 6 1/2" h., globular w/angular rim handles, blue ground, No. 637-6 1/2" 650

Vase, 6 1/2" h., globular w/angular rim handles, brown ground, No. 637-6 1/2" 768

Vase, 6 1/2" h., 4" d., bulbous ovoid body w/a wide shoulder tapering up to a small mouth, small angled shoulder handles, mottled blue & brown ground, No. 630-6" (ILLUS. far right, above) 605

Vase, 7" h., bulbous waisted ovoid body w/small pointed shoulder handles, brown ground, No. 634-7" 648

Vase, 8" h., pear-shaped body w/short cylindrical neck & tiny angled shoulder handles, blue ground, No. 636-8" 1,018

Vase, 8" h., 6 1/2" d., wide tapering cylindrical body w/small angled handles flanking the flat rim, brown ground, No. 633-8" (ILLUS. second from right, above)..... 661

Vase, 8" h., 6 1/2" d., wide tapering cylindrical body w/small angled handles flanking the flat rim, blue ground, No. 633-8", gold foil label & orange crayon notation "633"...... 728

Vase, 8 1/2" h., bulbous ovoid body tapering to a short cylindrical neck w/a wide flat rim, pointed angled handles from the neck to the shoulder, blue ground (ILLUS. center, above) 2,090

Vase, 8 1/2" h., slender base handles, conical body bulging slightly below rim, brown ground, No. 635-8" (ILLUS. far left, above) 509

Vase, 8 1/2" h., slender base handles, conical body bulging slightly below rim, blue ground, No. 635-8" 964

Vase, 9 1/2" h., cylindrical ovoid body w/angular handles rising from shoulder to midsection of slender cylindrical neck, brown ground, No. 638-9", partial paper label 523

Vase, 10" h., corseted form w/flaring rim, angled mid-section handles, brown ground (hairline & small chip to rim, one chip per handle & one to base) 385

Vase, 10" h., cylindrical body w/closed rim, angled shoulder handles, brown ground, No. 639-10" 605

Vase, 10" h., cylindrical body w/closed rim, angled shoulder handles, blue ground, No. 639-10" 2,143

Vase, 12" h., two-handled, expanding cylinder w/flaring rim, brown ground, No. 640-12" (ILLUS. second from left, above) 1,650

Vase, 15" h., bottle-shaped w/angular handles at shoulder, blue ground, No. 641-15" (restoration to rim & handles, small flakes to a few petals) 1,705

Wall pocket, fan-shaped, blue ground, 8" h... 2,070

Zephyr Lily (1946)
Tall lilies and slender leaves adorn swirl-textured backgrounds of Bermuda Blue, Evergreen and Sienna Tan.

Basket, footed half-round body w/curled-in rim tabs & high arched handle, terra cotta ground, No. 393-7", 7" h................................. 225

Basket, hanging-type, green ground, No. 472-5", 7 1/2" w. 188

Basket, w/low wide overhead handle, disk foot, cylindrical body flaring slightly to an ornate cut rim, terra cotta ground, No. 395-10", 10" h. 220

Book ends, green ground, No. 16, 5 1/2" h., pr. 178

Book ends, terra cotta ground, No. 16, 5 1/2" h., pr. 231

Bowl, 6" d., terra cotta ground, No. 472-6" 95

Zephyr Lily Candlesticks

Candlesticks, blue ground, No. 1163-
4 1/2" h., pr. (ILLUS.) **225**
Console bowl, low oblong form w/curved
end tab handles, blue ground, No. 474-
8", 8" l. **110**
Console bowl, end handles, terra cotta
ground, No. 479-14", 16 1/2" l. **99**
Cookie jar, cov., blue ground, No. 5-8",
10" h. **358**
Cornucopia-vase, terra cotta ground, No.
203-6", 6" h. **135**
Ewer, blue ground, No. 22-6", 6" h. **120**
Ewer, footed flaring lower body w/angled
shoulder tapering to a tall forked neck
w/upright tall spout, long low arched han-
dle, green ground, No. 23-10", 10" h. **135**
Ewer, footed flaring lower body w/angled
shoulder tapering to a tall forked neck
w/upright tall spout, long low arched han-
dle, blue ground, No. 23-10", 10" h. **148**
Flowerpot w/saucer, blue ground, No. 672-
5", 5" h. **225**
Flowerpot w/saucer, terra cotta ground,
No. 672-5", 5" h. **150**
Jardiniere, terra cotta ground, No. 671-8",
8" h. **193**
Jardiniere, two-handled, green ground, No.
679-9", 9" h. **385**
Jardiniere & pedestal base, green ground,
No. 671-8", overall 25" h., 2 pcs. **748**
Rose bowl, terra cotta ground, No. 471-6",
6" h. **180**
Tea set: cov. teapot, creamer & open sugar
bowl; terra cotta ground, 3 pcs. **413**
Vase, 6" h., two-handled, terra cotta, No.
130-6" **165**
Vase, 7" h., blue ground, No. 132-7" **160**
Vase, 7" h., terra cotta ground, No. 132-7" **109**
Vase, 8" h., two-handled, terra cotta ground..... **195**
Vase, 8 1/2" h., a disk foot & short pedestal
support a tall slightly swelled cylindrical
body w/a thin-rolled rim, low curved handles from mid-body to the base of the
pedestal, green ground, No. 133-8".............. **143**
Vase, 9" h., conical w/flaring buttressed
base, blue ground, No. 136-9"...................... **110**

Zephyr Lily Vase

Vase, 12 1/2" h., handles rising from
shoulder of compressed globular base to

middle of slender neck w/flaring mouth,
blended blue ground, No. 140-12"
(ILLUS.)... **207**
Vase, 12 1/2" h., handles rising from shoul-
der of compressed globular base to middle of slender neck w/flaring mouth,
green ground, No. 140-12"............................. **295**
Wall pocket, pointed conical form w/base
handles, green ground, No. 1297-8",
8" h. **250**
Wall pocket, pointed conical form w/base
handles, terra cotta ground, No. 1297-8",
8" h. **202**

Royal Dux

Royal Dux Marks

*This factory in Bohemia was noted for the figural
porcelain wares in the Art Nouveau style which
were exported around the turn of the century. Other
notable figural pieces were produced through the
1930s and the factory was nationalized after World
War II.*

Two Royal Dux Female Busts

Bust of lady, ornately dressed in late
Victorian costume, a large pierced lacy
hat w/ribbons & a high & widely flaring
ruffled lacy collar w/ribbons, decorated
in pale pink, green & yellow w/the hat in
pink, molded rectangular pad mark
impressed "452 - A," applied pink
triangle impressed "Royal Dux
Bohemia," early 20th c., some
restoration, 21 3/4" h. (ILLUS. left)......... **$1,800**
Bust of water nymph, shown emerging
from foaming blue waves amid pink orchids & green leaves, her skin & face
w/naturalistic coloring, molded rectangular pad mark w/"507," applied pink triangle mark w/"Royal Dux Bohemia," early
20th c., part of one orchid petal missing,
small chips to leaves & other petals,
21 1/4" h. (ILLUS. right with bust of lady) .. **4,800**

Ornate Royal Dux Figural Centerpiece

Centerpiece, figural, a large shaped ornately scalloped & pierced bowl atop a pierced curved flowering vine pedestal w/a full-length Art Nouveau maiden in a swirled gown also supporting the bowl, on a scalloped & swirled rounded base, natural colors, ca. 1900, 16" h. (ILLUS.)....... **900**

Centerpiece, figural, modeled in high-relief as branches & foliage in a buff glaze, the heads of four maidens incorporated into the upwardly flowing form ending in large leaves forming a bowl, marked "Royal Dux Bohemia" & w/a large "E" in a triangle, impressed "333 13," 18 1/2" h. (restoration) **748**

Figure group, a young boy w/a Setter dog, enameled & gilt-trimmed, Czechoslovakia mark, early 20th c., 13 1/4" h.................. **288**

Detailed Royal Dux Figure Groups

Figure groups, one w/a shepherd playing pipes w/sheep around his feet & standing next to an Ionic column, the other w/a shepherdess w/a staff standing w/goats at her feet, also beside an Ionic column, fine enameled decoration, late 19th - early 20th c., 16 1/2" h., pr. (ILLUS.).................. **748**

Serving dish, figural, a maiden & a pair of lovebirds on an open shell dish, ca. 1900, 8 1/2" h. **230**

Vases, 19" h., Art Nouveau design w/an ivory ground decorated w/stylized leaves & berries in relief, raised "Czechoslovakia" mark, early 20th c., pr. **978**

Large Figural Royal Dux Vase

Vases, 37 1/4" h., figural, a tall flaring cluster of banana tree leaves & fruit behind the standing figure of an Arab girl leaning on a tall jug, other one w/man beneath the tree playing a lute, heavy gold trim on white w/pink trim, marked "Royal Dux - Made in Czechoslovakia," ca. 1920s, pr. (ILLUS. of one).. **1,210**

Sascha Brastoff

Sascha Brastoff

Sascha B.

Brastoff Marks

Sascha Brastoff dedicated his life to creating works with a flair all his own. He was a costume designer for major movie studios, a dancer, a window dresser and a talented painter. The creator in Sascha put him on the path to ceramics early in life when he was awarded a scholarship to the Cleveland Art School; however, he also worked with watercolors, charcoals, pastels, resin, fabrics, ceramics, metal sculptures, and enamels. Nelson Rockefeller, Brastoff's friend, understood the uniqueness of his talents and, in 1953, he built a complex in Los Angeles, California to house the many creations Sascha was able to produce.

A full line of hand-painted china with names such as Allegro, La Jolla, Roman Coin and Night Song was created. Surf Ballet was a popular dinnerware line and was achieved by dipping pieces of blue, pink or yellow into real gold or platinum. Also highly popular was Sascha's line of enamels on copper. Many collectors do not know that Sascha dabbled in textiles. A yard of cloth in good condition might command several hundred dollars on today's market. His artware items included patterns such

as Star Steed, a leaping-fantasy horse and Rooftops, a series of houses where the roofs somehow
seemed to be the prominent feature. Even then, as
well as today, these pieces were and are, two of the
most highly collectible Sascha artware patterns.

Sascha Brastoff also created a line of Alaskan-
motif items. Many collectors confuse Matthew
Adams pieces with those of Sascha. Even though
Adams worked for Brastoff for a period of time, his
pieces are not nearly as sought after as those that
Sascha created.

Brastoff's crystal ball served him well during his
lifetime. In the late 1940s and early 1950s he created a series of Western motif cachepots which
excites any collector when found today. Almost a
decade before the poodle craze in the 1950s,
Sascha created a line of poodle products. In the
1950s, cigarette smoking was at an all-time high
and Sascha was there with smoking accessories.

From 1947-1952 pieces were signed "Sascha
B." or with the full signature, "Sasha Brastoff." After
1953 and before 1962, during the years of his fac-
tory-studio, pieces done by his employees showed
"Sascha B." and more often than not, also included
the chanticleer back stamp. Caution should be
taken to understand that the chanticleer with the full
name "Sascha Brastoff" below it is not the "full signature" mark that elevates pieces to substantial
prices. The chanticleer mark is usually in gold and
will incorporate Sascha's work name in the same
color. Sascha's personal full signauture is the one
commanding the high prices.

Health problems forced Sascha to leave his
company in 1963. After 1962 pieces were marked
"Sascha B." and also included the 'R' in a circle
trademark. Ten years later the business closed.

Sascha Brastoff died on Feburary 4, 1993. The
passing of this flamboyant artist, whose special
character was well reflected in his work, means that
similar creations will probably never be achieved
again.

Ashtray, floral decoration, No. 110AC............. $45
Ashtray, round, leaf decoration, full signa-
ture, large.. 350
Ashtray, Western scene w/covered wagon,
rare promotional piece, 14" w. 175
Bowl, 8" d., footed, abstract design..................... 38
Box, cov., Jewel Bird decoration, No. 020 70
Candleholder, resin, green or blue, 6" h.,
each 65
Cigarette box, cov., Rooftops patt., No.
021, 8" l. 70
Cigarette box, cov., "Star Steed" decora-
tion 145
Compote, polar bear decoration, No. 085 65
Dish, horse decoration on green ground,
6 1/2" sq. 30
Dish, three-footed, fish-shaped (flounder),
house decoration, 8 1/4 x 8 1/2"..................... 90
Lamp base, mosaic tile, 27" h........................... 210
Model of polar bear, blue resin, 10" h. 400
Model of rooster, mosaic design, 15" h. 515
Plate, square, vegetable decoration, full sig-
nature.. 275
Plate, 9" d., Merbaby patt..................................... 65

Sascha Brastoff Horse Salt Shaker

Salt shaker, model of a horse, white, pro-
duced in 1947-1948, 5 1/4" l, 3 1/4" h.
(ILLUS.)... 85
Tray, floral decoration, marked "Sample"
under glaze, 7" sq.. 95
Vase, 5" h., Provincial Rooster patt., No.
F20 400
Wall pocket, Rooftops patt., No. 031, 20" h. 415

Teco Pottery

Teco Mark

Teco Pottery was actually the line of art pottery
introduced by the American Terra Cotta and
Ceramic Company of Terra Cotta (Crystal Lake),
Illinois in 1902. Founded by William D. Gates in
1881, American Terra Cotta originally produced
only bricks and drain tile. Because of superior facili-
ties for experimentation, including a chemical labo-
ratory, the company was able to develop an art
pottery line, favoring a matte green glaze in the earlier years but eventually achieving a wide range of
colors including a metallic lustre glaze and a crystalline glaze. Though some hand-thrown pottery
was made, Gates favored a molded ware because
it was less expensive to produce. By 1923, Teco
Pottery was no longer being made and in 1930
American Terra Cotta and Ceramic Company was
sold. A book on the topic is Teco: Art Pottery of the
Prairie School, by Sharon S. Darling (Erie Art
Museum, 1990).

Bowl, 4 1/2" d., wide flat bottom w/low incurved sides, green matte glaze, im-
pressed marks, No. 350 .... $286
Bowl, 4 1/2" d., 2 1/2" h., low squatty wide
bulbous sides w/throwing ridges, a wide
shoulder curving up to a closed rim, deep
raspberry matte finish, impressed mark
(short hairline) 220
Bowl, 8 1/2" d., 2 1/2" h., a wide flat-bot-
tomed squatty bulbous lower body curving upward to a wide flat mouth, upper
portion w/a green matte glaze shading
into a heavy charcoal glaze, impressed
mark.. 385
Bowl, 9" d., 2" h., wide flat bottom w/shal-
low rounded sides & closed molded wide
mouth, overall green matte glaze, im-
pressed marks.. 605

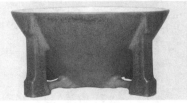

Fine Teco Bowl-Vase

Bowl-vase, wide sharply tapering round bowl supported by four heavy squared pierced buttress legs around the rim, design by Holmes Smith, fine green matte glaze w/charcoal highlights, impressed marks, minor crazing on interior, 12" d. (ILLUS.) **5,500**

Box, cov., squatty rounded rectangular form sharply incurved to the rectangular base, w/a flat fitted rectangular cover, smooth matte green glaze w/charcoaling, stamped mark, 2 1/2 x 3 1/2", 2 1/4" h. (bruise on base) **788**

Chamberstick, a wide round dished base w/a tapering short center shaft w/a thick molded socket rim & an open squared handle from the rim to the base rim, good ivory matte glaze, impressed marks, paper label, 5" d. (flaw in glaze on handle in making) **523**

Chamberstick, a wide round dished base w/a tapering short center shaft w/a thick molded socket rim & an open squared handle from the rim to the base rim, good green matte glaze, impressed marks, paper label, 5" d. **605**

Chamberstick, wide cushion foot centered by a tall slender waisted cylindrical shaft molded w/stylized leaves & flowers, a long loop handle from the upper side to the base of the shaft, smooth matte green glaze, paper label, 5" d., 10 3/4" h. **900**

Ewer, bulbous tapering ovoid body w/the wide shoulder centered by a short small neck w/a deeply folded tricorner rim & loop handle from rim to shoulder, unusual matte brown glaze, 4" h. (stilt chips) **154**

Jardiniere, wide ovoid body tapering to a short flaring neck, molded around the lower body w/eight lily lily pads below a row of water lily blossoms alternating w/pointed arrowhead leaf buttress-form open handles attaching to the neck rim, smooth matte green glaze, stamped mark, 9 3/4 x 10" (some restoration) **12,100**

Jardiniere, round bulbous body w/heavily molded wide shoulder band around the wide flat mouth supported on four buttressed legs, smooth matte green glaze, stamped "TECO," 11" d., 7" h. **6,750**

Pitcher, 8 1/2" h., 5" d., tall slender waisted body w/a wide rim w/pinched spout & integral pinched & forked loop handle reaching down nearly to the bottom, mottled matte green & charcoal glaze, stamped mark **844**

Pitcher, 9" h., 3 1/2" d., corseted form w/an organic wishbone handle & an undulating

rim, smooth matte green glaze, stamped "TECO," (small firing flaw to handle) **1,125**

Vase, 3" h., 1 1/4" d., miniature, simple ovoid form w/two tiny buttress handles at the rim, smooth matte green glaze, original paper label **956**

Vase, 3 3/4" h., 3 1/4" d., footed ovoid body w/dimpled sides, wide molded rim, dark speckled matte green & charcoal glaze, incised "Teco/519" (ILLUS. second from right with group of Teco vases) **619**

Vase, 4" h., bulbous nearly spherical form tapering slightly to a wide short flared neck, dark matte green glaze, impressed mark & incised number **440**

Vase, 4" h., slightly tapering cylindrical form w/four deep oval indentations up the sides below the short flared neck, green matte glaze, No. 356 .... **605**

Vase, 4" h., 4" d., squatty bulbous ovoid body tapering to a small flared neck, smooth matte green glaze, stamped mark **2,640**

Vase, 4 1/2" h., bulbous rounded base w/a deep indentation on each side & tapering to a wide squared neck, good matte green glaze, impressed mark **660**

Vase, 4 1/2" h., gently flaring wide cylindrical body w/an angled shoulder tapering to a flat mouth, green matte glaze, impressed marks, paper label **770**

Vase, 4 3/4" h., compressed bulbous base w/wide horizontally ribbed cylindrical neck & flat rim, green matte glaze, marked twice on base **495**

Vase, 4 3/4" h., gently tapering cylindrical body w/slightly flared flat rim, molded w/thin rings up the sides, green matte glaze, impressed mark **495**

Vase, 5" h., footed squatty bulbous lower body tapering to a waisted neck w/a four-ruffle flared rim, good green matte glaze, impressed marks **715**

Vase, 5 1/2" h., simple ovoid body w/short flared neck flanked by square pierced buttress handles extending halfway down the sides, overall dark matte green glaze (repaired chips) **385**

Vase, 5 1/2" h., 2 3/4" d., cylindrical body tapering slightly at the top to a molded rim, thin square buttress handles down the sides, smooth deep blue matte glaze, impressed mark **825**

Vase, 6" h., 9 1/2" d., squatty bulbous body, the wide shoulder tapering to a slightly flared rim w/four curled leaves, smooth matte green glaze, restoration to two rim chips, stamped "Teco/272" (ILLUS. bottom left with group of Teco vases) **2,700**

Bulbous Teco Vase

Vase, 6 1/4" h., 5" d., bulbous ovoid body, the rounded shoulder tapering to a short cylindrical neck w/slightly flaring rim, matte green glaze, tight hairline from rim, stamped mark (ILLUS.)..................................... **303**

Vase, 6 1/4" h., 6 1/2" d., a wide cylindrical finely ringed body w/three long squared handles from the rim to the base, each handle w/ribbing down the front, smooth matte green glaze, fine charcoaling, stamped mark (bruise to rim)....................... **1,238**

Unusual Pierced Teco Vase

Vase, 6 1/2" h., bulbous ovoid four-sided form tapering to four short pierced buttress shoulder handles attaching to the flattened pierced rim & mouth, molded leaf design at the bottom center of each side, green matte glaze w/light charcoaling, designed by Fritz Albert, impressed marks (ILLUS.).. **3,850**

Vase, 6 1/2" h., large mug-form, the wide cylindrical body w/thin narrow rings & molded looped scrolls at the front, a long low angled open handle down the side, dark matte green glaze, impressed mark **550**

Vase, 6 1/2" h., 2 1/4" d., slender cylindrical body tapering to a flaring rim, buttressed handles down the sides, rich yellow matte finish, impressed mark...................... **1,045**

Vase, 6 3/4" h., simple ovoid body tapering to a short flared neck, green matte glaze, impressed marks **523**

Double-gourd Teco Handled Vase

Vase, 7" h., 6" d., bulbous double-gourd form body w/four heavy curved buttress handles from the rim to the base, fine leathery matte green glaze, small long bruise at rim, stamped mark (ILLUS.) **2,990**

Vase, 7 1/4" h., tall tapering cylindrical form w/flared & molded rim, four squared buttress handles from the rim to the edge of the base, seafoam green glaze, impressed twice w/mark, ca. 1910................. **1,840**

Vase, 7 1/4" h., 4 1/4" d., conical body tapering to a flared neck w/a thick rim band issuing four heavy squared buttress handles from the rim to the base, smooth medium green matte glaze, short abrasion to rim, stamped mark (ILLUS. left with buttress-handled vase, below) **4,025**

Three Teco Buttress-handled Vases

Vase, 7 1/4" h., 4 1/4" d., ovoid body tapering to a flaring cylindrical neck flanked by heavy square buttress handles going down the sides, mottled matte green glaze, some glaze curdling to base, No. 435, stamped mark (ILLUS. center) **3,220**

Vase, 7 1/2" h., a bulbous spherical base tapering to a tall slender tapering neck topped by a squatty cupped & closed rim, green matte glaze, impressed mark **715**

Vase, 7 1/2" h., 4 1/4" d., conical body tapering to a flared neck w/a thick rim band issuing four heavy squared buttress handles from the rim to the base, smooth matte brown glaze, mark obscured by glaze (ILLUS. right with buttress-handled vase, above) **3,450**

Vase, 8" h., ovoid body tapering to tall wide slightly flaring cylindrical neck, matte green finish, impressed mark **440**

Vase, 8 3/4" h., 4" d., a tall bullet-shaped body w/a rounded shoulder & small molded mouth, supported by four tall V-form buttresses around the base, smooth medium matte green glaze, stamped mark (ILLUS. far left, with group of vases).......... **4,219**

Vase, 9" h., tall slightly tapering cylindrical body w/flaring rim, two small closed buttress handles at shoulder, covered in a matte green glaze w/heavy charcoaling, impressed mark **1,650**

Vase, 9" h., tall swelled cylindrical body tapering slightly to the widely flaring neck, small squared shoulder handles, overall dark green matte glaze w/heavy charcoaling, impressed mark................................. **770**

Vase, 9" h., 4" d., 'rocketship' style, long tapering ovoid body w/a small molded mouth, wide molded V-shaped fins at the base, unusual mauve matte glaze, stamped "Teco" **7,875**

restoration to a few chips, base & mark, marked (ILLUS.) **2,185**

Vase, 11" h., tall slender swelled cylindrical body tapering at the shoulder to a slender flaring trumpet neck, overall terra cotta-colored matte glaze, impressed mark **495**

Vase, 11 1/4" h., footed bulbous base tapering to a tall cylindrical neck w/flared rim, four whiplash handles from base to below rim, matte green glaze (restoration to small chip at base & on two handles)......... **1,870**

Tall Teco Vase with Buttresses

Vase, 10 1/4" h., 5 3/4" d., tapering cylindrical body w/a wide flattened rim, four low square buttress handles down the sides, green & charcoal mottled glaze w/a splotch of yellow under the rim, invisible

Tall Buttress-handled Teco Vase

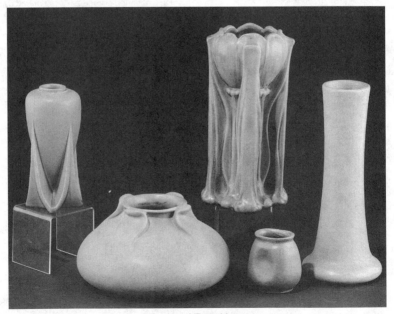

Group of Teco Vases

Vase, 11 1/4" h., 3 3/4" d., tall slender swelled cylindrical body tapering to a slightly flaring neck flanked by squared short buttress handles continuing down the sides to the base, smooth matte green glaze, stamped mark (ILLUS.) **5,175**

Teco Vase with Entwined Handles

Vase, 11 1/2" h., 9" d., large ovoid body w/a narrow shoulder tapering to a wide short cylindrical neck w/a thick flattened rim, pairs of entwined loop handles on each side from rim to shoulder, smooth matte green glaze, stamped mark & remnant of paper label (ILLUS.) **5,175**

Vase, 11 3/4" h., a large cupped tulip blossom framed by four heavy buttress leaf-molded supports forming the squared body, matte green glaze, designed by Fernand Moreau, stamped "Teco" (invisible repair to small chip at rim) **4,125**

Tall Teco Vase w/Leaves

Vase, 11 3/4" h., footed wide cylindrical body w/trumpet-form neck, body covered w/relief-molded narrow leaves forming handles, smooth matte green glaze, stamped "TECO" (ILLUS.) **16,500**

Vase, 12 1/4" h., 5" d., a large cupped tulip blossom framed by four heavy buttress leaf-molded supports forming the squared body, matte green glaze, stamped "Teco," (ILLUS. top right with group of Teco vases) **5,063**

Unusual Tall Teco Bud Vase

Vase, 12 1/2" h., 5 1/2" d., bud-type, an unusual organic form w/two upturned & two downturned handles projecting from the rim above the slender two-lobed stem above forked short leaves above the multi-petaled foot, heavily charcoaled matte green glaze, three tiny chips to base, No. 153, stamped mark (ILLUS.) **2,415**

Vase, 13" h., 6 1/4" d., footed swelled cylindrical body w/a narrow shoulder to the short flaring neck, smooth matte green glaze, impressed mark................................ **1,100**

Vase, 13 1/4" h., 5 1/4" d., tall slender tapering cylindrical body w/cushion foot, smooth matte grey glaze, stamped "Teco" (ILLUS. far right with group of Teco vases)... **1,688**

Tall Organic-form Teco Vase

Vase, 13 3/4" h., 8 1/4" d., tall cylindrical organic form w/pinched four-petaled scalloped & gently flared rim, long bulbed buttresses down the sides forming feet, smooth green matte glaze, flat chip to one rim petal, bruise to another, stamped mark (ILLUS.)... **2,300**

Rare Tall Paneled Teco Vase

Vase, 14 3/4" h., tall tapering four-sided form w/long panels to small open buttresses around the small flat mouth, fine green matte charcoaled glaze, designed by Fritz Albert, No. 181A, marked (ILLUS.).. **33,350**

Vase, 16 1/2" h., 8" d., footed wide squatty bulbous lower body w/a wide shoulder tapering to a very tall slender lobed neck w/flared rim, smooth matte green glaze, stamped mark (restored rim section)......... **1,688**

Rare Teco Vase

Vase, 17 1/2" h., 6 1/2" d., tall lobed body w/tapering cylindrical neck & molded rim, embossed calla lily between each lobe & extending to rim, light green matte glaze, restoration to small drill hole on side at base, small nick on leaf point, (one of two known), stamped "TECO" (ILLUS.)........... **28,125**

Large Plain Teco Floor Vase

Vase, 20 1/4" h., 10 3/4" d., floor-type, tapering cylindrical body below a wide shoulder tapering to a wide cylindrical neck w/rolled rim, leathery matte green glaze, stamped mark, several small base chips (ILLUS.) **4,313**

Large Teco Floor Vase

Vase, 22" h., 8 1/2" w., floor-type, a flared stepped foot on the swelled squared body w/molded buttress corners at the closed mouth, molded on each side w/tall slender leaves, microcrystalline matte green glaze, stamped "Teco 343," restoration to base chip, four hairlines at rim (ILLUS.)... **6,188**

Teplitz - Amphora

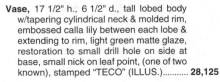

Teplitz-Amphora Marks

In the late 19th and early 20th centuries numerous potteries operated in the vicinity of Teplitz in the Bohemian region of what was Austria but is now the Czech Republic. They included Amphora, RStK, Stellmacher, Ernst Wahliss, Paul Dachsel, Imperial and lesser-known potteries such as Johanne Maresh, Julius Dressler, Bernard Bloch and Heliosine.

The number of collectors in this category is growing while availability of better or rarer pieces is shrinking. Consequently, prices for all pieces are appreciating, while those for better and/or rarer pieces, including restored rare pieces, are soaring.

The price ranges presented here are retail. They presume mint or near mint condition or, in the case of very rare damaged pieces, proper restoration. They reflect such variables as rarity, design, quality of glaze, size and the intangible "in-vogue factor." They are the prices that knowledgeable sellers will charge and knowledgeable collectors will pay.

Bowl, 10 1/4" w., 5 1/4" h., consisting of two wonderfully detailed high-glazed fish swimming around the perimeter, each executed in the Art Nouveau style w/flowing fins & tails, tentacles drip from their mouths, high-relief w/gold & reddish highlights, rare theme, impressed in ovals "Amphora" & "Austria" w/a crown **$3,500-4,000**

Bowl, 14 1/2" w., 4 3/8" h., an exotic Paul Dachsel design of calla lilies growing out of stems which originate at the bottom & gracefully extend around the sides to fully developed calla lilies at each end, in the center on each side are several 'jewels' w/abstract leaves of high-glazed green w/gold overtones, mottled texture w/'jeweled' greenish gold embellishments, stamped over glaze w/intertwined "PD - Turn-Teplitz," handwritten over glaze "0/45" **4,500-5,500**

Bust of a Sultry Princess

Bust of a woman, perhaps Sarah Bernhardt in the role of a sultry princess, magnificently finished w/plentiful gold &

bronze glazes without excessive fussiness, mounted on a base featuring a maiden on a horse in a forest setting, the bust seemingly supported by stag horns protruding from each side, impressed "Amphora" & "Austria" in a lozenge w/a crown, 1431 & "A" in blue, 13 1/2" w., 18 1/4" h. (ILLUS.) **3,000-4,000**

Bust of a young woman, a very young Art Nouveau maiden w/long flowing hair, elegant in her simplicity & beautiful, a 'clean' presentation without the excessive fussiness of many Teplitz busts, manufactured in varying tones, the most desirable being of the soft muted type, semi-rare, impressed "Amphora" in an oval, red "RStK Austria" stamp over the glaze, impressed illegible numbers & "246 - D202" printed in blue over the glaze, 15 1/4" h. **2,000-2,500**

Bust of Richard Wagner

Bust of Richard Wagner, the somber looking composer mounted on a pedestal emblazoned "Wagner" on the front, the head w/a beautiful soft flesh-toned Amphora glaze, the pedestal w/a shriveled tan & white glaze w/shades of olive green highlights, one of a rare series of composers, impressed "Amphora" & "Austria" in ovals w/a crown, a circle w/"Imperial Amphora" & "250 -1," 19 3/4" h. (ILLUS.) **2,000-2,500**

Candlestick, rare Amphora piece w/many of their special characteristics including jewels, spider webs, butterflies & wonderful soft muted Amphora glazes w/reds, blues & gold, a large handle extends from near the top of the socket, four smaller handles extend up & outward from the base, eleven jewels of various sizes & colors, impressed "Amphora" in an oval & a crown & "28," 14" h. **3,500-4,000**

Centerpiece, an expansive bowl w/a 'jeweled' effect along the rim, supported by two seated male lions w/fine details, a round base w/a 'jeweled' effect, the underside of the bowl suggests a tropical jungle, a better example of a design featuring animals supporting a bowl, multicolored 'jewels,' lion in a natural brownish glaze, stamped "Amphora - Made in Czecho-slovakia" in an oval, "734 - 261" in black ink, 12" w., 9 5/8" h. **1,000-1,500**

Centerpiece, figural, a long low oblong wave-molded bowl base centered by the large standing figure of an Art Nouveau maiden rising from the waves, wearing a diaphanous gown w/one arm on her hip & enclosing a cluster of blossoms, the other arm above her head supporting an oversized tulip or poppy blossom, pastel coloring, marked "Turn - Teplitz - Bohemia - E. Stellmacher," early 20th c., 28" h. (glaze repair in base) **1,238**

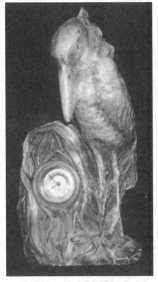

Fantasy Stork Clock

Clock, table model, a fantasy stork, similar to Martin Bros. birds, stands next to a clock dial framed by Art Nouveau-style leaves, fine detailing, soft brownish tan glaze, rare, raised rectangle w/factory logo & "AK-Turn," impressed "319," 13" h. (ILLUS.).................................... **3,500-4,000**

Ewer, a bulbous Austrian form tapering to a narrow top w/a handle extending vertically several inches & then horizontally across the ewer to the spout, cascades of more than 150 pearl-like 'jewels' adorn the sides, handle, spout & top, finished in a mottled soft grey & soft tan w/undertones of gold, impressed "Amphora" in an oval & crown, & "3969 - 51- 5," also impressed circle w/factory logo "Amphora - Faience," 11 1/4" h. **1,500-2,000**

Ewer, an Art Nouveau design w/extraordinary detail combining a reticulated handle suggesting Paul Dachsel & varied circles on the body suggesting Gustav Klimt, a reticulated top, many 'jewels' of different colors & sizes randomly located

over the body suggesting a spectrum of stars in the milky way, unusual gold bud spout, high-glazed blue garlands randomly draped about the body, heavy gold trim on the upper part of the handle, top & spout, a subdued gold trim extends down the handle to & around the bottom where there is an abstract tree design, very difficult to produce, rare, impressed "Amphora" in a circle & "40 - 537," 14" h. **4,000-5,000**

Ewer, gilt-trimmed ivory ground w/enamel-decorated birds in the paneled sides, Teplitz mark, Czechoslovakia, early 20th c., 10 5/8" h. **345**

Figure group, a small fine scenic figural group w/a rooster & hen perched side by side overlooking a pond, a small gold frog climbing into the pond, gives a barnyard feeling, soft muted shades of tan w/highlights of gold, a realistic theme & valuable because of the small size, impressed "Amphora" in an oval & illegible numbers, 6 1/2" w., 7 3/4" h. **750-1,000**

Elephant & Tigers Amphora Group

Figure group, model of a bull elephant being attacked by two male tigers, natural tones of browns, cream, tan & green w/gilt trim on rockwork base, printed & impressed Amphora marks, ca. 1920, 26" h. (ILLUS.) **920**

Unique Figural Humidor

Humidor, cov., figural, a fantasy piece featuring a large globe representing the world being shot from a tiny cannon & caught by a jester lying on his back, the jester reputedly represents a prime minister of the time, a hat at the top of the globe forms the handles, soft muted grey Amphora glaze, rare, impressed "Amphora" in an oval & "4216," 14" w., 9" h. (ILLUS.) **3,000-4,000**

Humidor, cov., figural, a massive Native American theme composed of three Indian heads w/high-glazed pink & green feathered headdresses, 'jeweled' & draping beaded necklaces on two, a draping necklace of animal teeth on the third, high-glaze green & cobalt blue finial handle on a decorative mixed glazed top, basic color of Campina brown w/much contrasting high-glaze in green, pink, brown & blue, rare, impressed ovals w/"Amphora" & "Austria," a crown & "Imperial - Amphora - Turn" in a circle & "S-1633-46," 10 1/2" h. **2,000-3,000**

Humidor, cov., figural, an authentic looking Native American teepee w/an Indian in green feathered headdress peering out of the bottom, finished in flat Campina brown w/contrasting highlights of high-glaze brown, light blue & cobalt blue, rare, impressed ovals w/"Amphora" & "Austria" & a crown, "Imperial Amphora Turn" in a circle & "S-1738-44," 10 1/2" h. **2,000-2,500**

Ornate Amphora Jardiniere

Jardiniere, bulbous squatty form w/wide flat mouth, molded around the lower body w/large horse chestnut leaf clusters & nuts, the wide shoulder molded w/threaded rings centered by jewels, shades of light & dark brown & dark green & greenish gold w/gilt highlights, impressed "Amphora - 02050 - D.," ca. 1900, 19" d., 14 3/4" h. (ILLUS.) **4,025**

Model of a bull, proudly standing & of large stature, realistic colors, on a rocky slope w/his tail extending in an enclosed arch, realistic folds in his skin, prices vary depending on realism of the colors, the more realistic the better, impressed "Amphora" & "Austria" in ovals w/a crown, 18 1/2" l., 15" h. **1,500-3,000**

Amphora Fish Pitcher

Pitcher, 12" h., cov., footed, modeled as a stylized fish, ribbed body decorated w/gilt outlined yellow flowers, fish scale texture near rim, spout & lid form mouth w/splashes of water at top of lid, stamped "R S + K, Turn-Teplitz, made in Austria" (ILLUS.) **316**

Plaque, a large oval shape centered by an Art Nouveau lady in high-relief attired in a luminescent pink dress blowing a double-horned musical instrument. She is seated on a rocky ledge. The border of the plaque consists of garlands of flowers & leaves in high-relief, especially the buds, basic color of seafoam green, the surrounding florals in greens & tans, impressed "Ernst Wahliss," 17 x 19 1/2" **1,400-1,800**

Plaque, terra cotta rectangular form depicting a very stylized beautifully coiffed Art Nouveau lady in profile in high-relief, her unique elegance suggesting a lady of high social stature, the borders are garlanded leaves & buds in high-relief, organic mossy shades of green, soft purples, tans & warm browns, impressed marks "Ernst Wahliss - Made in Austria - Turn - Wien - 157," 11 3/4 x 17" **1,200-1,500**

Tray, a desk piece consisting of a ferocious eagle w/wings spread & beak open, staring at a snake draped over the inside & outside of the tray edge, finished in a soft bronzy cast w/contrasting deep brown, unusual theme, impressed signature of artist Klimt, also "BB" in a half circle w/dot in center & "N - 6244," stamped over glaze in black "Crownoakware - Teplitz - Austria," 15" l. overall w/eagle figure 5 1/2" h. **1,200-1,500**

Vase, 5 1/2" h., 3 3/4" d., bottle-form w/a footed squatty wide ovoid body tapering sharply to a slender cylindrical neck w/a wide bulbed rim, painted w/a bust portrait of an Art Nouveau maiden w/long hair trimmed w/blue enameled flowers, cream background, impressed "Amphora 492" **440**

Vase, 5 3/4" h., figural, elegantly executed Paul Dachsel creation w/a greenish cast & numerous vertical ribs extending up from the base, four intertwined gold-bodied dragonflies form a reticulated top, immediately below a series of smaller dragonflies encircle the vase, two multi-layered handles within handles complete the design, stamped over glaze w/intertwined "PD - Turn - Teplitz," impressed "104".. **2,000-2,500**

Vase, 6 3/8" h., spherical base tapering to tall slender cylindrical neck, shoulder loop handles, decorated w/bright yellow & orange irises & green leaves on a chocolate brown ground, by Stellmacher, impressed Stellmacher Teplitz mark, "2820," & "17" w/"2220" in brown slip on base **110**

Vase, 6 1/2" h., simple ovoid body tapering to a small, flat mouth, painted w/the bust portrait of a young woman in a voluminous hood surmounted by a Byzantine crown surrounded by an aura, above a border of roses, the crown & roses w/applied glass bosses, glazed in shades of bronze, green, pink & black, printed mark "Turn - Teplitz - Bohemian - R. St. - Made in Austria" & impressed "Amphora 2037," ca. 1920 .... **1,840**

Vase, 7 1/2" h., a playful expression of Amphora w/a pink snake draped around the body of the bulbous vase & extending to the top where its delicate tongue protrudes, a subtle leaf design extends around the bottom, the pink color of the snake distinguishes this piece from more drab versions, impressed in ovals "Amphora" & "Austria," & "4114 - 52"..... **1,500-1,800**

Vase, 7 3/4" h., round bulbous shape, decorated w/a profile of a young girl w/long flowing brownish hair full of numerous multicolored high-glazed flowers w/gold touches, all surrounded by a brownish tan forest scene, finely executed, impressed "Amphora - 663," overglaze red mark "RStK - Turn - Teplitz - Made in Austria" **1,700-2,200**

Vase, 8" h., two-handled form almost literally a golden jewel because of the overall gold high-glazed finish w/just a touch of red on one handle & a portion of the bottom, randomly covered w/a multitude of 'jewels' varying in size & color, jewel upon jewel, impressed ovals w/"Amphora" & "Austria" w/a crown, illegible numbers **2,200-2,700**

Vase, 8 1/2" h., portrait-type, flat shape w/narrow base, a front facing Mucha-style Art Nouveau portrait of a lady w/golden brown hair full of white flowers against a brownish white forest scene, lovely but lacks some of the elaborate gold decorations, multi-colors & 'jewels' of higher quality pieces, impressed "576" & "Amphora - Turn" enclosed in a large heart, red "RStK" stamp & artist mark "HH" in gold over glaze **900-1,300**

Vase, 8 3/4" h., a restrained Edda piece exhibiting the wonderful 'drip' design characteristic of Edda without appliques of leaves & fruit, etc., which can mar the fabulous designs, a green metallic glaze w/twelve open "portholes" around the bottom, free-form shape, marked w/a raised "Edda" & swastika in a raised triangle, impressed in oval "Amphora," & "3622 - 1C," ink over glaze "22" **1,200-1,500**

Vase, 8 3/4" h., figural, fantasy octopus piece w/head forming the top & mouth & the tentacles extending down around the sides, a dimpled bulbous form, finished in various glazes, the most desirable being a gold-finished octopus contrasting w/a matte background of various colors, impressed "Amphora" in an oval, a crown & "Imperial - Amphora - Turn" in a medallion & "4547 - 32" **2,000-2,500**

Vase, 8 3/4" h., four-paneled high-shouldered squared form w/a front-faced Mucha-style Art Nouveau princess portrait, elaborate gold enameling against a landscape decorated w/blue & purple trees w/gold highlights above a base decorated w/Paul Dachsel-style abstract red flowers in a green base, impressed "Amphora" in oval & "579-40," red "RStK Austria" overglaze mark, artist mark "Fr" in gold overglaze............................... **3,000-3,500**

Vase, 9" h., a bulbous Paul Dachsel forest scene w/reticulated gold top & varied reddish mushrooms in high-relief encircling the bottom, a production mold but hand-painted to produce a uniquely different forest scene, stamped over the glaze w/intertwined "PD - Turn - Teplitz," impressed "1106 -2," blue overglaze "094" **3,000-4,000**

Vase, 9" h., three-legged triangular-shaped piece consisting of an indented top composed of three leaves w/Art Nouveau stems extending down the sides & then away from the body to form legs, the stems divide the body into panels which contain abstract Art Nouveau-Art Deco designs from the rim to base, greenish metallic glaze, Heliosine Ware, a line growing in popularity, marked "Heliosine Ware - Made in Austria - 21048 - 1 - PP" **500-1,000**

Rare Amphora Cat Head Vase

Vase, 9" h., wide bulbous tapering form, rare form suggesting an inverted Tiffany lamp shade, four large Persian cat heads molded in full relief & projecting from the sides w/a forest of abstract trees w/160-170 opal-like translucent 'jewels' symbolizing fruits, the jewels in various sizes & shades of opal blue mounted in gold surrounds, heavy gold rim, the tree branches extending to the jewels on a background of Klimt-like subtle gold circles, holes behind the jewels permit candlelight or an electric bulb to illuminate the jewels, cat heads finished in a soft pinkish gold w/traces of green & gold highlights on the ears, impressed "Amphora - Austria" in a lozenge, a crown & "8183 - 28" (ILLUS.) **12,000-14,000**

Vase, 9 3/4" h., an organic piece consisting of a large frog perched on the top & side of the body w/one leg partially extended, his main body 4" l. w/his partially extended leg reaching over 7" l., finely detailed w/a realistic appearance, natural-looking bluish green & tan colors, rare form, impressed "Amphora" & "Turn" in oval, illegible numbers **2,000-2,500**

Vase, 9 7/8" h., a Paul Dachsel abstract design w/a reticulated geometric top & a reticulated handle within a reticulated handle sweeping in an arc from the top to the bottom w/abstract tendrils extending around the bottom of the body & back of the handles, several high-glazed green pods resembling teardrops of various sizes hang from the abstract handle, vines & a center funnel, the top rim & top of handle finished in gold, rare, stamped over glaze w/intertwined "PD - Turn - Teplitz" **3,500-4,000**

Vase, 10" h., a Paul Dachsel abstract architectural style w/a geometric design consisting of a rounded bottom from which four handles begin flush & extend to the top of the rim where they flare open, each handle suggests an abstract candelabrum w/charcoal flames rising from each, finished in iridescent gunmetal grey w/charcoal black sheen touches, gold wash on top, modern in all respects even though produced in the 1904-10 period, rare form, stamped over glaze w/intertwined "PD - Turn - Teplitz," impressed "1049" **4,500-5,500**

Amphora Vase with Birds & Branch

Vase, 10" h., tapering ovoid form w/indented teardrops around the sides, molded & applied w/a pair of bluebirds at the top w/a twig & leaf handle from the rim down

the front, green mottled ground, blue, rust & brown trim, Riessner - Amphora mark, ca. 1930 (ILLUS.) **220**

Vase, 10 1/2" h., Imperial Ware, wide semi-ovoid form w/flat rim, decorated w/two exotic birds in bright blues, pink, green & brown enamels on a soft brown matte ground, dark blue loop handles & rim w/lighter blue dots around rim & stylized reddish brown leaves & green flowers in a continuous band around the base, impressed marks & "Amphora" & "Austria" in ovals w/"Campina" inside a rectangle & the numbers "11614" & "64" **275**

Vase, 10 1/2" h., wonderful Teplitz Art Nouveau form by Bernard Bloch featuring a large ocean wave finished in sea green tossing a scantily clad finely detailed flesh-toned mermaid w/two finned legs instead of a tail & a large brown-shelled sea turtle, designed by Schwarz, increasingly sought by Amphora collectors who consider it an early form of Amphora-Teplitz, value increasing, impressed "Schwarz - BB" & dot in a half-circle & "M - 7099" **1,500-2,000**

Vase, 10 5/8" h., figural, in the form of a prancing male lion, snarling open mouth, standing on a broad base narrowing at the top, numerous concentric circles form bands around the top & bottom, lion reflects an iridescent gold, green & rose combination of color, body of base in metallic green w/undertones of blues & splotches of reds, impressed "Amphora" & "Austria" in oval, a crown & "500-52," handwritten in black ink over glaze "CB - 613417," estimated value without jewels, $1,500 to 2,000, value w/jewels **2,500-3,500**

Vase, 10 3/4" h., exquisitely executed form consisting of several variously colored thistles in high-relief, realistic detail w/the body in a soft mottled blue w/tinges of soft greens, yellow, pinks & washed w/gold overtones, two gold handles, impressed "Amphora" & "Austria" in ovals, a crown & "2213 - 64 - G" **2,000-2,500**

Amphora Vase with Goat in Landscape

Vase, 10 3/4" h., simple ovoid form tapering to a low flat neck, the upper portion decorated w/a painted pastoral scene w/a goat reclining by trees in a field in blue tones on a cream ground, the lower portion w/raised repeating scallops, circle & columns in glossy glazed black, the columns in mottled iridescent colors, gilt trim, impressed Amphora lozenge mark & "32 59,"early 20th c. (ILLUS.)...................... **920**

Vase, 11" h., four gold Persian cat heads adorn a center-pillared body w/four surrounding gold 'jeweled' arms extending from each cat head to the base, metallic blue w/a gold wash, cobalt blue 'jewels,' rare design, more common versions have cabochons inside animal heads, marked "Amphora" & "Austria" in ovals, a crown & impressed "Imperial" circle mark & "11677 - 51" **2,000-3,000**

Vase, 11 1/8" h., large pear-shaped body tapering to a short cylindrical neck, wide curved integral side handles pierced w/three openings, mottled matte green & brown glaze, inscribed cipher & mark of Riessner & Kessel (crazing, base chip) **1,035**

Vase, 11 1/4" h., figural, a rare Bernard Bloch Austrian Teplitz design consisting of a boy, half-human & half creature of the sea w/scaled fishtail & webbed hands emerging from the water, very expressive face, three beautifully detailed fish in semi-relief swimming about the body of the vase, designed by Schwarz w/name on the side, soft sea green & golden highlights, impressed "BB" & dot in a circle & "P - 3776"... **1,500-2,000**

Vase, 11 1/4" h., figural, an open-mouthed fish w/well-defined teeth swimming around the chimney of the base w/a finely executed tail fin extending up & beyond the vase, a realistic representation produced in various color tones which will determine the price, one w/brighter colors brings more, semi-rare, impressed "Amphora" in an oval, & "4112 - 10" **2,000-3,000**

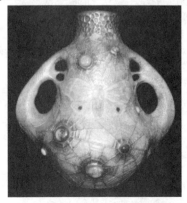

Ornate Jeweled Art Nouveau Vase

Vase, 11 1/4" h., tapering lobed ovoid form of exceptional Art Nouveau design w/numerous 'jewels,' spider webs & two butterflies w/heavy pierced extended handles suggesting a larger butterfly, 17 'jewels' in varying sizes & colors, red abstract circles drape from the gold-edged top, soft muted tan, red, blue & green glazes w/gold iridescence, impressed "Amphora" & "Austria" in ovals, a crown & "8551 -42," red "RStK Austria" overglaze mark (ILLUS.).................................... **4,000-5,000**

Vase, 11 1/2" h., wicker basket-form w/round loop handles extending up from the rim, large relief-molded iridescent white blossoms, rose leaves & green buds on front w/rose band at rim & base, shaded tan ground w/touches of fired-on gold, impressed marks & "Austria Amphora - 115 - 37" **550**

Vase, 12" h., figural, three standing cockatoos, fully feathered, extend around the body of the vase, their plumes rising over the rim, very detailed w/glossy glaze, subtle color mix of blues, greens & tans w/brown streaks, semi-rare, impressed "Amphora" & "Austria" in ovals, a crown & Imperial circle & "11986 - 56" **1,500-2,000**

Vase, 12 3/4" h., elegant form consisting of four beautifully veined tall leaves forming the funnel of the vase w/the stem of each leaf forming a handle extending into the bottom, each stem issues an additional flat leaf extending across the bottom, leaves finished in a mottled orange w/touches of greens & yellows w/gold overtones, although marked by Ernst Wahliss the design indicates the work of Paul Dachsel who worked at various Amphora factories, rare, stamped over glaze "EW" red mark, impressed "9491," "9786a - 10" in ink over the glaze **3,000-3,500**

Vase, 13" h., figural, an exceptional form w/three cherubic children in great detail playing around the basket-like body, the child at the top reaching down in, another child reaching up to the top w/one hand & the third child moving in the direction of the reaching child, w/their arms extended the children reach from the base to the rim & in good proportion, unlike most similar vases there are no added florals or fruits, impressed "Amphora" & "Austria" in oval, a crown & "1397 - 41"........... **1,200-1,500**

Dachsel "Enchanted Forest" Vase

Vase, 13" h., wide-shouldered tapering cylindrical body, a fantasy design by Paul Dachsel worthy of the description "enchanted forest," the design consists of slender molded abstract trees extending from the narrow base to the bulbous top, lovely heart-shaped leaves extend in clusters from the various branches, trees in muted green, the leaves in pearlized off-white w/gold framing, the symbolic sky in rich red extending between the trees from the bottom to the top, rare, intertwined "PD" mark rubbed off (ILLUS.).......... **5,500-6,500**

Vase, 13 1/8" h., a special creation by Paul Dachsel, perhaps a one-of-a-kind, it may be a commemorative piece honoring an early 20th c. polar expedition, a h.p. polar bear shown standing on a snowy surface, his body outlined by puffy clouds in a blue sky, a soft lustre to the sky, snow & bear w/subtle pink iridescence, below the snow a ring of blue Dachsel circles w/gold inserts extends around the body, a similar design above the sky w/a reddish gold metallic glaze, value hard to estimate to the ultimate Paul Dachsel collectors, stamped over glaze w/intertwined "PD - Turn Teplitz"............. **6,000+**

Vase, 13 1/2" h., an Amphora creation of Julius Dressler, Arts & Crafts style, matte green w/majolica highlights, four panels w/the same geometric pattern in each, this type increasing in interest to collectors, marked w/a raised "JBK" & impressed "Austria - 1194".................. **1,000-1,500**

Vase, 14" h., figural, a fantasy dragon featuring two flaring wings, one extending practically from the top to the bottom of the body, the other well above & beyond the rim, creature w/a convoluted tail, spine & teeth, the head w/open mouth positioned at top of the vase, bluish green gold iridescence, glazes vary from a flat tan to a variety of very iridescent colors, made in 14" & 17" size, impressed "Amphora" in oval, illegible numbers, large size w/better glazes, $6,500, 14" size w/drab glazes.. **3,000**

Vase, 14" h., figural, three curious mice, two at the top & one at the bottom, mischievously explore a forbidden environment, bluish green w/splotches of red & goldish leaves, iridescent glaze, a rare design, impressed "Amphora" & "Austria" in ovals, a crown & "4522-52" **3,000-3,500**

Vase, 14 1/4" h., elegant center-pillared piece surrounded by four supporting arms extending from the underside of the bowl-form top to the bottom, a flowing design decorated w/block-outlined painted floral designs, mottled green & tan w/gold luster, similar pieces designed by Paul Dachsel in his own factory so may have designed this piece, impressed "Amphora" & "Austria" in ovals, a crown & "3899 - 42"... **1,200-1,500**

Vase, 14 5/8" h., a figural fantasy piece, a different variety of dragon vase but not highly glazed, the dragon is mostly brown but it features a well-defined head, body, clawed feet & tail, a snake tongue drapes from the mouth, hideously beautiful, the body contrasts nicely w/the metallic greenish blue iridescence of the mottled background, found in various glazes, impressed "Amphora" & "Austria" in oval, a crown & "C 4543"............................... **3,000-4,000**

Vase, 15 1/2" h., cascades of golden grapes stream down on all sides between four funnel necks, the central funnel projecting skyward, this funnel design suggests Paul Dachsel, especially desirable because the piece is viewable from any angle, metallic purplish glaze w/metallic gold highlights containing numerous little gold circles, marked "Amphora" & "Austria" in ovals, a crown & "3680".. **1,500-2,000**

Vase, 15 3/4" h., an Egyptian theme consisting of a vertical mummy case, probably representing King Tut's, surrounded by kneeling slaves, a blue bulbous bottom & narrow slender neck, geometric decorations around top & base, a semi-rare Czech piece, marked in blue stamped underglaze "Amphora - Made in Czecho-slovakia" in an oval, illegible marks w/one in a blue circle w/a logo & another in a red circle **1,000-1,500**

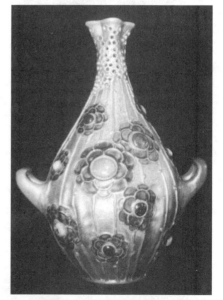

Rare Jeweled Amphora Vase

Vase, 16" h., bulbous ovoid body tapering to a slender flaring lobed reticulated neck, outswept loop handles at the lower sides, shimmering burnished gold ground w/red touches, adorned randomly w/twenty large variously colored 'jewels,' one handle in red, the other in gold, overall molded vertical ribbing, rare form, impressed "Amphora" in an oval, crown, old "RStK" mark & "3349" (ILLUS.) **7,500-8,000**

Amphora Vase with Judaica Decor

Vase, 16" h., Judaica decoration, double cylindrical necks w/gently scalloped rims
continuing into a tubular oval body raised
on a flaring oblong foot, decorated
around the necks & body w/raised Star-
of-David designs & applied domed 'jewels,' glossy teal blue & brown glazes &
opalescent glazed 'jewels,' textured gilt
ground, impressed Amphora marks, ear-
ly 20th c. (ILLUS.) **690**

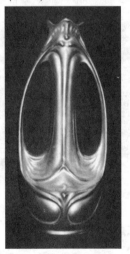

Tall Heliosine Ware Art Nouveau Vase

Vase, 16" h., tall elegant Heliosine ware
piece w/a striking Art Nouveau design,
two curved slender handles swoop
gracefully from the top rim to the bottom
w/a slender central shaft, a wide array of
iridescent metallic glazes, an
increasingly popular line, marked
"Heliosine Ware - Austria" & impressed
"21020 -D" (ILLUS.) **1,000-1,500**
Vase, 16 1/4" h., finely executed dragon design by Johanne Maresh, the dragon's
body swirls around the base from the
broad bottom to the top of the neck &
down to the middle of the vase where the
head is well defined, detailed feet grip the
front & back, the main body of the piece

suggests ocean waves, the dragon finished in soft mustard tan shades w/or-
angy highlights, the waves in lighter mustard tan, the neck in dark gunmetal
green, increasingly sought-after & values
rising, impressed "JM - 1614," handwrit-
ten over glaze "716.20" **1,200-1,800**

Rare Amphora Octopus Vase

Vase, 16 1/2" h., a massive fantasy piece
w/a large golden iridescent octopus
around the bottom, its tentacles extending around the sides & up to the top
where they grab a large swimming sea
horse, a particularly rare style of octopus
w/only one known at present, impressed
"Amphora" & "Austria" in ovals, a crown &
"4597 - 50" (ILLUS.) **6,000-7,000**
Vase, 16 1/2" h., fine Paul Dachsel creation
in an undulating free-form design consisting of several abstract trees extending from the bottom to the top where a
branch wraps around the top & then
down dividing into other branches w/a
series of red-glazed leaves, numerous
white 'jewels' suggesting seeds & seed
pods attached to the branches & trunks,
red leaves w/gold-tinged ends, very rare
form, stamped over the glaze w/inter-
twined "PD - Turn - Teplitz," impressed
"1115" **5,000-6,000**
Vase, 16 1/2" h., tall bulbous pot-form divid-
ed into four panels by raised free-form
gold-finished lines extending from the
bottom to the top & ending in a series of
concentric circular forms, each panel
contains a spider web, one panel w/a
larger spider web w/an entrapped dragonfly, tan to cream w/a gold-finished top
& base, exudes a sense of reality & age,
rare w/many hand-finished details, impressed "Amphora" & "Austria" in ovals,
red "RStK Austria" mark over the glaze,
impressed hand-etched heart-shaped
artist mark, "9029" in ink over the
glaze **5,000-7,000**

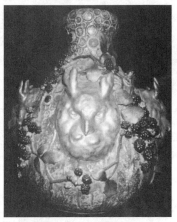

Rare Owl Head Vase

Vase, 17" h., massive bulbous bottle-form w/four finely detailed gold-finished owl heads projecting from the sides surrounded by brambles, leaves & many clusters of berries & numerous 'jewels' of various sizes & colors interspersed among the brambles, unusual & complicated design, some similar pieces w/other animal heads exist but few survive intact, rare, impressed "Amphora" in oval, a crown & "8160" (ILLUS.) **8,500-9,500**

Vase, 17 1/8" h., tall Art Nouveau form gradually tapering to a narrower top, the bottom w/seven delicate female heads w/long flowing hair emerging from a swirling ocean, tan w/highlights of gold & green, a similar example found in a Berlin museum, marks include a raised Art Nouveau girl's head & "Amphora" in a raised rectangle, red "RStK Austria" mark over the glaze, impressed illegible numbers, handwritten "1081 - L - 372" over the glaze... **2,000-3,000**

Rare Reticulated Amphora Vase

Vase, 17 1/2" h., an important reticulated piece composed of a basket-like vase within a vase elaborately entwined w/swooping gold handles joined in the middle, numerous varied colored 'jewels' around the sides, viewed through the reticulation a high-glazed blue swirly design w/gold highlights is seen, the exterior w/a metallic bluish green w/gold wash & gold highlights, high-glazed gold rim, only one known so far, impressed "Amphora" & "Austria" in ovals, a crown & "3791 -45" (ILLUS.) **12,000-14,000**

Vase, 17 3/4" h., figural, an Art Nouveau woman finished in gold w/soft rose highlights & draped around the bottom portion of the tall form w/a flowing leaf growing out of the bottom & extending to the top, mottled greens, blues, creams w/a gold wash, impressed "Amphora" & "Austria" in ovals, Imperial circle mark & "824 - 30," later Czechoslovakian versions w/lesser glazes bring about half the value.............. **3,000-4,000**

Vase, 18 1/4" h., a fantasy piece w/a coiling beast not really a dragon, snake nor octopus but w/characteristics of each, finished in a golden color w/gold highlights, the head extends above the top, the body entwines down around the sides, mottled metallic purplish blue background, impressed "Amphora" & "Austria" in ovals, a crown & "4539 -50," values vary w/the glaze **3,500-4,500**

Vase, 18 1/2" h., slightly flaring cylindrical body w/a bulbous shoulder tapering to a mouth mounted w/a gilt-bronze leaf-cast neck & issuing slender serpentine handles attached to the sides, fitted on a gilt-bronze ring foot w/four flared leaves, the body covered in a light blue, green & ivory crystalline glaze dripping down the buff-colored ground, partial impressed mark "Borsi - Teplitz," base drilled, ca. 1900... **1,150**

Vase, 19 3/4" h., figural, a lively form w/two squirrels, one at the base & one at the top, each eagerly pursuing the other w/ears raised in excitement, various finishes, a rare form, impressed & raised "EST" monogram, "Stellmacher - Teplitz" stamped in red, an impressed heart **3,500-4,500**

Amphora Dragon Vase

Vase, 20" h., footed tall wide cylindrical body w/squatty bulbous base & closed-in rim, mottled mauve glaze w/relief-molded dragon figure in yellow, tan & gilt glaze conforming entirely around body & rim, minor restorations to chips, impressed "AMPHORA" in a lozenge, a crown & "4548 50" (ILLUS.) **5,750**

Vase, 20" h., tall slightly tapering cylindrical form w/a widely flared base, boldly molded pine cones hang around the top section from symbolic green trees divided by red indented vertical panels, a Paul Dachsel Secessionist design, rare, stamped over the glaze w/intertwined "PD - Turn - Teplitz" & impressed "2038 - 6" **7,000-8,000**

Vase, 20 1/4" h., elegant tall form featuring two sunbursts, front & back, two gold handles, reticulated gold circles at the top & several elongated gold 'jewels' rising from the sunbursts, a subtle bluish white w/soft gold tones reflecting the sunbursts, free-form lines in soft green highlighted w/gold extending from the bottom to the top & suggests a randomly built stone wall, rare form, impressed "Amphora" & "Austria" in ovals, a crown, "Imperial" in a circle & "12081 -47" **3,000-4,000**

Vase, 20 1/4" h., squatty bulbous base tapering to cylindrical neck w/flat rim, relief-molded mermaid clinging to side along w/clusters of blackberries & blackberry vines, glaze on body & mermaid give the impression of a gold doré finish on bronze, impressed "Amphora" inside an oval on bottom (restoration to several leaves & vines & also to one of the mermaid's arms & end of tail)............................ **3,080**

Vase, 20 3/4" h., a massive form consisting of two golden pterodactyls who have mated & produced hundreds of eggs clustered at the top of the body, numerous tendrils of bluish flowers stream down from the top & are joined randomly by an abundance of golden spider webs, the body finished in soft glowing luster, very elegant, rare, impressed "Amphora" & "Austria" in ovals, a crown & "2059 - 41 - B" **8,000-10,000**

Massive Amphora Mermaid Vase

Vase, 21" h., 18" w., figural, a wide squatty bulbous base centered by a tall neck, Art Nouveau style w/a mermaid clinging to the top rim, her well-defined body extends down along the side, applied berries, vines & leaves complete the decoration, finished in a matte tan w/gold wash & highlights, bluish berries, red stems, greenish red leaves & a high-glazed gold rim, important & very rare, would be rare even without the applied foliage, impressed "Amphora" in oval & "07 - 7 - 3" (ILLUS.)... **8,000-10,000**

Vase, 21 1/2" h., portrait-type, a very large profiled Sarah Bernhardt portrait inspired by Gustav Klimt featuring a majestic bird headdress w/eleven 'jewels' of various sizes & colors, the figure w/long flowing hair streaming from under the headdress to her shoulders, below her neck is a jeweled butterfly, on one side a golden sun rises from the ocean emitting numerous golden rays, bluish green metallic background w/heavy gold detail, impressed "Amphora" & "Austria" in a lozenge, a crown & "02047 - 28" **14,000-16,000**

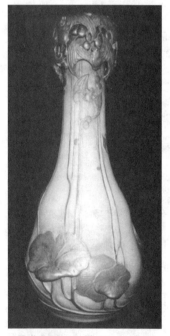

Tall Amphora Vase with Bats

Vase, 21 1/2" h., tall bottle-form w/swarms of gold bats feeding on golden fruits around the reticulated top, they are about to be joined by other bats flying up the sides, tall graceful form w/the rounded base encircled by golden lily pad leaves w/the stems extending up the sides on an eggshell off-white ground, impressed "Amphora" in oval, red "Austria RStK" mark over glaze, impressed "41 - 668" & "750 - 1029" in ink (ILLUS.) **7,000-9,000**

Somber, Eerie Dragon Vase

Vase, 22" h., figural, a somber swampy-green dragon encircles the tall body several times, his wings spread like a cobra's hood, leering down hungrily at a frog restrained by his tail at the base, this piece can be found finished in other colors including red & tan, this eerie somber look compensates for what the glaze may lack, impressed "Amphora" & "Austria" in ovals, a crown & "4536 - 6" (ILLUS.) **4,000-5,000**

Amphora Sea Serpent & Crab Vase

Vase, 22 1/4" h., figural, a bulbous base tapering to a tall slender cylindrical body a large relief-molded sea serpent wrapped down the sides w/a molded crab grasping the lower body, shaded ivory & brown glaze on an iridescent blue, green & gilt ground, impressed Amphora, Austria

mark w/crown, early 20th c., minor gilt wear at rim (ILLUS.) **5,750**

Vase, 22 1/2" h., figural, an extraordinary dragon w/bat-like wings entwines around the body, numerous golden drops dripping from its open fanged mouth, Art Nouveau stems rise from the bottom to form pink button blossoms, the dragon shows a glitter of silver & gold, impressed "Amphora" in an oval & "8762 - 52" **9,000-9,500**

Vases, 10 1/2" h., footed bulbous ovoid body tapering to a slender cylindrical neck w/a flattened disk rim, painted in shades of purple, pink, green, blue, black & gilt w/the bust of a young maiden wearing a voluminous hood surmounted by a Byzantine crown surrounded by a gilt aura, a lower border of roses, the crown & roses w/applied bosses, one printed w/mark "Turn - Teplitz - Bohemia - R. St. - Made in Austria," the other impressed "Amphora," each impressed "2014 -28," pr. **6,900**

Amphora Sea Life Vases

Vases, 19 1/2" h., tapering cylindrical form w/cushion foot & spiky rim, applied w/a realistically modeled octopus capturing a crab, covered in a sponged blue, white & yellow glaze, the creatures in beige & burnt orange, printed in blue "AMPHORA - Made in Czecho-Slovakia" & impressed numbers, pr. (ILLUS.) **2,875**

Tiffany Pottery

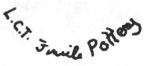

Tiffany Pottery Mark

In 1902 Louis C. Tiffany expanded Tiffany Studios to include ceramics, enamels, gold, silver and gemstones. Tiffany pottery was usually molded rather than wheel-thrown, but it was carefully finished by hand. A limited amount was produced until about 1914. It is scarce.

Tiffany Pottery Square Bottle

Bottle, square upright form w/a small round neck centered on the flat top, incised abstract design around the sides, textured cobalt blue & turquoise matte glaze, incised "LCT," 4" w., 6 1/2" h. (ILLUS.) **$1,380**

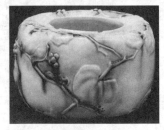

Tiffany Pottery Vase with Vines

Bowl-vase, wide short cylindrical form w/flattened rounded base & top rim w/closed mouth, molded w/a bold design of vines, leaves & berries under an Old Ivory glaze, incised "LCT" & etched "Favrile Pottery - P22Y Tiffany," three chips, tight line at rim, nick on branch on top, 7 1/2" d., 5" h. (ILLUS.) **4,500**

Tiffany Bowl-Vase

Bowl-vase, footed wide bulbous body w/wide molded rim, decorated w/low relief-molded flowers & vines, matte tan glaze, inscribed on base "LCT," 9 1/4" h. (ILLUS.) **863**

Rare Tiffany Pottery Box and Ewer

Box, cov., flat-bottomed w/deep gently rounded flaring sides molded w/a berry & twig design, the domed cover w/a matching design, deep yellow & orange berries on a dark green ground, marked "LCT - 7," 5 1/2" d., 4" h. (ILLUS. right) **9,600**

Ewer, flat-bottomed conical form w/a deep cupped neck w/long pinched spout, long tapering handle from edge of neck to base, lightly molded overall w/a design of a stylized parrot, mottled light green & black glaze, marked "L.C.T. - P 159," 8 3/4" h. (ILLUS. left with box) **5,100**

Tiffany Vase with Reticulated Shoulder

Vase, 5 1/2" h., wide baluster-form body w/the shoulder reticulated w/a wide band of cherry blossoms on stems, tan bisque finish (ILLUS.) **1,725**

Tiffany Pottery Vase

Vase, 6" h., bulbous base w/shoulder tapering to short wide cylindrical neck w/flat rim, molded w/stylized leaves & berries, covered in a mottled sea green & cobalt glaze, ca. 1910, unsigned (ILLUS.) **3,450**

Vase, 6 5/8" h., wide gently waisted cylindrical form, molded up the sides w/long pointed leaves w/three leaf stems forming arched loop handles down the sides, streaky light & dark blue glaze, signed "LCT - Tiffany Favrile Pottery - P 412" (chip to rim) **4,800**

Tiffany Pottery Bud Vase

Vase, 7" h., bud-type, slender cylindrical form w/ribbed stems up the sides to swelled molded blossoms at the top just below the flaring rim, rare mottled bluish green glaze w/brown showing through, incised "LCT - 65D - EL," repaired chip on base (ILLUS.) **2,300**

Cylindrical Tiffany Pottery Vase

Vase, 8 3/4" h., cylindrical body w/flared foot & slightly swelled top, decorated w/molded & reticulated arrowhead plants under blue & green lustered glaze, irregular rim formed by leaftips & blossoms, three very short, very tight hairlines from

rim, incised "LCT - acid-etched L.C. Tiffany - Favrile Pottery" (ILLUS.) **15,400**

Rare Tiffany Organic Vase

Vase, 9 1/2" h., base w/an Art Nouveau design consisting of four long relief-molded lobes, the body swelling slightly at the top w/an undulating rim, covered in an unusual glossy metallic black & green finish, incised "LCT" (ILLUS.) **7,700**

Vase, 10" h., tall cylindrical form w/scalloped rim, glossy pale green glaze on white clay w/a molded organic design of fiddleback fern heads around the top above full-length stems, center base inscribed w/"LCT" monogram (glaze crazing, some interior water stain) **2,875**

Very Rare Tiffany Pottery Fern Vase

Vase, 11 1/8" h., molded stylized fern design, the body formed by a cluster of molded fern fronds which extend down to form short legs, a cluster of tall slender fronds extend up from the rim & arch together to form open handles, streaky green & dark gold glaze on a creamy body, signed "Tiffany - Pottery - H 9 A - Coll - 49B," firing crack around base (ILLUS.) **21,450**

Vase, 12" h., tall slender cylindrical form flaring slightly at base, decorated w/embossed jonquil & carved leaves & stems under a shellac & moss satin matte finish, incised "LCT" **5,500**

Tiffany Vase with Narcissus

Vase, 14 1/2" h., stepped disk foot supporting a bulbous ovoid body tapering to a
wide cylindrical neck w/flat rim, decorated w/raised narcissus & leaves swirling
around the body under a fading brown,
dark blue & khaki matte glaze, chip on
base, inscribed "LCT" (ILLUS.).................... **1,380**

Tiles

American Encaustic Tiles

American Encaustic Tiling Company,
Zanesville, Ohio, rectangular, molded figure of a Colonial gentleman holding a
cane & gloves under a glossy brown
glaze, impressed "American Encaustic
Tiling Co. Limited New York Works
Zanesville, O.," minor flaws, 5 7/8 x 18"
(ILLUS. right) **$330**
American Encaustic Tiling Company,
Zanesville, Ohio, rectangular, molded figure of a young Colonial woman holding a
fan under a glossy brown glaze, impressed "American Encaustic Tiling Co.
Limited New York Works Zanesville, O.,"
minor flaws, 5 7/8 x 18" (ILLUS. left) **330**

American Encaustic Stove Tile

American Encaustic Tiling Company,
Zanesville, Ohio, rectangular stove tile
depicting a seated Roman soldier w/one

arm resting across the shoulder of a bear
standing beside him, blue high glaze, unmarked, small glaze nicks to edges,
4 1/4 x 7 3/8" (ILLUS.) **280**

Franklin Pottery Faience Tile

Franklin Pottery, Lansdale, Pennsylvania,
rectangular, faience tile w/colorful parrot
perched on a branch, gloss & matte glazes of blues, green, pink, black & yellow,
back die-impressed "Franklin Pottery
Faience," ca. 1936, very minor chips to
back edges, accompanied by photocopy
of Franklin Tile catalog, tile 8 7/8 x 8 3/4"
(ILLUS.).. **605**
Grueby Faience & Tile Company, Boston,
Massachusetts, square, decorated in
cuenca w/a stylized yellow stag w/brown
antlers under a green leafy tree w/green
grass & pale blue sky, in a new wide flat
oak Arts & Crafts frame, unmarked, tile
4" w... **1,069**
Grueby Faience & Tile Company, Boston,
Massachusetts, decorated in cuenca w/a
large pale yellow seated rabbit in a cab-
bage patch w/light bluish green foliage
against a dark green ground, artist-initialed, in a new wide flat oak Arts & Crafts
frame, tile 6" w. (some surface abrasion) .. **3,375**

Rare Grueby Turtle Tile

Grueby Faience & Tile Company, Boston,
Massachusetts, square, decorated in
cuenca w/a turtle in shades of brown &
ivory below a bough of green leaves all
on an ochre matte ground, stamped mark
& paper label, 6" w. (ILLUS.) **7,450**

Grueby Faience & Tile Company, Boston, Massachusetts, rectangular, decorated in cuenca w/a yellow chamberstick & candle against a green ground below molded wording "Grueby Tile," artist-initialed, in a new wide flat Arts & Crafts oak frame, tile 4 1/2 x 6" **4,500**

Grueby Tile with Horses

Grueby Faience & Tile Company, Boston, Massachusetts, square, decorated w/a row of prancing white horses in cuenca on a blue & green ground, unmarked, restoration to edge chip, 6 1/4" w. (ILLUS.) **3,450**

Grueby Tile in Tiffany Brass Frame

Grueby Faience & Tile Company, Boston, Massachusetts, square, decorated in cuenca w/a yellow tulip blossom flanked by pairs of large arched leaves on a green ground, mounted in a brass Tiffany Studios frame w/squared floral-form feet, 7" w. (ILLUS.) **5,750**

Grueby Tile with Sailing Galleon

Grueby Faience & Tile Company, Boston, Massachusetts, square, a galleon under full sail, in cream & brown on a dark green ground, unsigned, 8" w. (ILLUS.)..... **2,013**

Grueby Faience & Tile Company, Boston, Massachusetts, seven-tile frieze designed by Addison Le Boutillier, titled "The Pines," decorated in cuenca w/pine trees in a valley, green, blue, brown & cobalt matte oatmealy glazes, ca. 1902, small chip to corner of one tile, 6 x 42" (ILLUS. below) **42,188**

Hamilton Tile Works Company, Hamilton, Ohio, rectangular, a woodland scene of deer, brown & tan, back embossed "The Hamilton Tile Works Co Hamilton Ohio," last quarter 19th c., 6 x 12 1/8" (glaze scratches & minor edge chips) **275**

Marblehead Pottery, Marblehead, Massachusetts, square, a matte-painted stylized landscape silhouetted against an evening sky, in shades of blues & yellows, ship mark, 5 3/4" sq. (several small edge nicks) **1,913**

Fine Marblehead Framed Tile

Marblehead Pottery, Marblehead, Massachusetts, square, painted w/a stylized floral design of blue delphiniums & green leaves on a white ground, in a wide flat oak frame, paper label, 6" w. (ILLUS.) **1,100**

Exceptional Grueby Seven-tile Frieze

Marblehead Pottery, Marblehead, Massachusetts, square, decorated w/a scene of a house in a landscape, the house in colors of transparent rust & blue bordered by green grass, flanked by trees in matte blue & brown, the whole on a matte grey ground, marked, ca. 1908, 6 1/4" w. (few minor edge chips) **1,150**

Marblehead Pottery, Marblehead, Massachusetts, square, embossed w/a large stylized spreading oak tree in a forest, fine dark green crystalline matte glaze, mounted in a fine flat wide oak framed w/rounded corners in the style of Greene & Greene, tile w/stamped ship mark & paper label, 6 1/4" sq. **3,656**

Unusual Muresque Pottery Tile

Muresque Pottery, Oakland, California, square, a molded Southwestern landscape w/palm tree & adobe home, in cream, tan, green & blue, impressed "Muresque - Oakland," early 20th c., framed, 6" w. (ILLUS.) **460**

Newcomb College Tile with Galleon

Newcomb College Pottery, New Orleans, Louisiana, square, molded design depicting a galleon under full sail w/dolphins along side, Persian blue crackled glaze, by Leona Nicholson, marked, 5 1/4" w. (ILLUS.) **805**

Norweta Tile with Minstrels

Norweta (Northwestern Terra Cotta Company), Chicago, Illinois, rectangular, colorful scene of six performing minstrels dancing & playing musical instruments against a cream matte glaze, surface embossed "Norweta," two cast holes in top edge for hanging, professional repair of vertical crack across center, 4 1/2 x 14 1/2" (ILLUS.) **935**

Large Owens Framed Tile

Owens Floor & Wall Tile Company (Empire), Zanesville, Ohio, rectangular, decorated in cuenda w/a landscape of large trees in green, brown & blue, mounted in a narrow wood frame, no visible mark, small chips in two corners, firing bubbles, 8 1/2 x 11 1/2" (ILLUS.) **1,320**

Pardee Tile with Sailing Ship

Pardee, C. Works, Perth Amboy, New Jersey, square, depicts a large brown & white sailing ship at sea, shaded blue sky & shaded green sea, rich matte glaze, embossed on back "The C. Pardee Works" & "- O," two small nicks of edges, 4 1/4" sq. (ILLUS.) **330**

Pardee, C. Works, Perth Amboy, New Jersey, square, yellow & green tulip on pale blue matte glaze ground, artist-initialed in blue slip "PS," the back embossed "The C. Pardee Work," 4 1/4" sq. **220**

Rare Rookwood Tile Frieze

Rookwood Pottery, Cincinnati, Ohio, four-tile frieze, decorated in cuenca & forming a continuous landscape w/large green & brown trees & green grass & bushes in the foreground, a long blue lake in the center ground & a series of mountains in green in the background, previously mounted w/remnants of mounting mortar, one reglued corner, minor corner chips, impressed mark, 12 x 48" (ILLUS. above) **23,000**

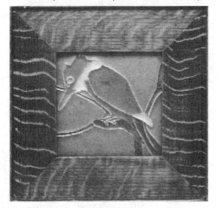

Rare Framed Van Briggle Tile

Van Briggle Pottery, Colorado Springs, Colorado, square, a kingfisher perched on a branch, in polychrome glazes including brown, white, green & blue, minute glaze flecks, unmarked, in wide flat oak period frame, 6" w. (ILLUS.) **4,600**

Torquay Pottery

Torquay Pottery Marks

In the second half of the 19th century several art potteries were established in the South Devon region of England to take advantage of a belt of fine red clay. The coastal town of Torquay gives its name to this range of wares which often featured incised sgraffito decoration or colorful country-style decoration with mottos.

The most notable potteries operating in the Torquay area were the Watcombe Pottery, The Torquay Terra-cotta Company and the Aller Vale Art Pottery, which merged with Watcombe Pottery in 1901 and continued production until 1962. Other firms whose wares are collectible include Longpark Pottery and The Devonmoor Art Pottery.

Early wares feature unglazed terra cotta items in the Victorian taste including classical busts, statuary and vases and some painted and glazed wares including examples with a celeste blue interior or highlights. In addition to sgraffito designs other decorations included flowers, Barbotine glazes, Devon pixies framed in leafy scrolls and grotesque figures of cats, dogs and other fanciful animals produced in the 1890s.

The dozen or so potteries flourishing in the region at the turn of the 20th century introduced their most popular product, motto wares, which became the bread and butter line of the local industry. The most popular patterns in this line included Cottage, Black and Colored Cockerels and Scandy, based on Scandinavian rosemaling designs. Most of the mottoes were written in English with a few in Welsh. On early examples the sayings were often in Devonian dialect. These motto wares were sold for years at area seaside resorts and other tourist areas with some pieces exported to Australia, Canada and, to a lesser extent, the U.S.A. In addition to standard size teawares and novelties some miniatures and even oversized pieces were offered.

Production at the potteries stopped during World War II and some of the plants were destroyed in enemy raids. The Watcombe Pottery became Royal Watcombe after the war and Longpark also started up again, but produced simpler patterns. The Dartmouth Pottery started in 1947 and produced cottages similar to those made at Watcombe and also developed a line of figural animals, banks and novelty jugs. The Babbacombe Pottery (1950-59) and St. Marychurch Pottery (ca. 1962-69) were the last two firms to turn out motto wares but these later designs were painted on and the pieces were lighter in color with less detailing.

Many books on the various potteries are available and information can be obtained from the products manager of the North American Torquay Society.

Miniature Motto Ware Pieces

Ashtray, Motto Ware, Colored Cockerel patt., "A place for ashes," Longpark, 1910, 3 1/2" d. **$56**

Ashtray, Motto Ware, Cottage patt., "Who burnt the Tablecloth," Royal Watcombe, 3" d. **35**

Torquay Motto Ware Ashtray

Ashtray, rectangular, Motto Ware, Cottage patt., "Better to Smoke Here Than Hereafter - Paignton," 3 1/4 x 5 1/4" (ILLUS.)......... **45**

Bank, figural, model of an owl in brown, nice detailing, Dartmouth, 1960s, 8" h. **63**

Basket, B2 Scroll patt., colored scrolls on green, painted by H.M. Exeter, 1930, 3 1/2" h. **113**

Basket, hanging-type, Persian patt., decorated overall & on the base, Aller Vale white clay, rare, ca. 1890s, unmarked, 2 5/8" h.(small restoration) **167**

Basket, Motto Ware, Colored Cockerel patt., twisted handle, "No life can be dreary when work's a delight," Watcombe, ca. 1901-20 mark, 3 1/4" h. **129**

Bowl, 4 3/8" d., two-handled, Ladybird (Bug) patt., ladybugs in a cream band on a blue ground, Watcombe, ca. 1901-20 mark **129**

Bowl, 4 3/8" h., four-handled, Motto Ware, Windmill patt., "Despise school and remain a fool," Crown Dorset Pottery, ca. 1910 .... **126**

Bowl, 8" d., advertising-type, Kingfisher patt., "National Association of Master Bakers, Confectioners & Caterers Conference - Torquay 1931" on blue, Watcombe **239**

Butter tub, two-handled, Motto Ware, Cottage patt., "Du'ee 'ave zum butter," Watcombe, ca. 1925-35, 4 3/4" w. **90**

Candlestick, miniature, Motto Ware, Scandy patt., "The night is long that never finds a day," Longpark, ca. 1910, expert restoration, 2 1/2" h. (ILLUS. left above)....... **110**

Candlestick, Motto Ware, Colored Cockerel patt., "He who would thrive must rise at five," Longpark Torquay, ca. 1903-09, 8" h. **156**

Candy bowl, cov., advertising-type, "The Stationers Association Conference - Torquay 1930," decoration of an inkwell & quill pen in white on blue, Longpark, 6 1/2" h. **222**

Cauldron pot, Motto Ware, Scandy patt., "Well paid, well satisfied," Watcomb, 2 1/2" h. **64**

Chamberstick, Motto Ware, Cottage patt., "Many are called but few get up," Watcombe Torquay impressed mark, ca. 1910-27, 2 3/4" h. **115**

Torquay Pottery Chamberstick

Chamberstick, Motto Ware, Sailboat patt., round dished base w/a cylindrical standard w/side handle below the wide cupped socket, "Guid Nicht an Joy Be Wi Ye," 3 1/2" d., 4 1/4" h. (ILLUS.)...................... **85**

Chamberstick, Motto Ware, Scandy patt., "'Tis the mind that makes the body rich - Shakespeare, Taming of the Shrew," Aller Vale, ca. 1915, 5 1/4" h.................... **123**

Cheese dish, cov., Motto Ware, Cottage patt., "Don't worry and get wrinkles - Smile and have dimples," also "Cheese," Watcombe, ca. 1930, 6 1/2" d. base, 3 3/4" h. **150**

Coaster, advertising-type, "Camwal Table Waters," Watcombe, 1920, 3 7/8" d. **116**

Coffeepot, cov., Motto Ware, Cottage patt., "Sow a character, reap a destiny," Watcombe, 8 3/4" h.. **218**

Coffeepot, cov., Motto Ware, Sailboat patt., "Time and tide for no man bide," Longpark, 6 1/4" h. **89**

Scandy Motto Ware Coffeepot

Coffeepot, cov., Motto Ware, Scandy patt., "Gude things be scarce, take care of me," Watcombe, 7" h. (ILLUS.) **156**

Condiment pot, side handle, Motto Ware, Cottage patt., "Better tae sit still than rise tae fall," Aller Vale, ca. 1902-24, 2 1/4" h. **89**

Condiment pot, side-handled, Motto Ware, Cottage patt., "Waste not, Want not," Longpark Torquay England mark, ca. 1930s, 2 1/4" h. **65**

Condiment set: salt & pepper shakers, cov. mustard pot & center-handled holder; Motto Ware, Cottage patt., mottos on all pieces except the holder, Watcombe, ca. 1920, the set.. **167**

Isle of Wight Torquay Souvenir Cream

Creamer, Motto Ware, Cottage patt., bulbous base tapering slightly to wide cylindrical sides w/slightly flared rim & pinched spout, C-scroll handle, "Help yourself to Milk - Isle of Wight," 3 1/2" d., 3 3/4" h. (ILLUS.) **65**

Torquay Bulbous Creamer with Motto

Creamer, Motto Ware, Cottage patt., bulbous ovoid body w/a wide flat rim &

pinched spout, C-scroll handle, "Take A Little Milk - Mevrgissey," 3 1/4" d., 3" h. (ILLUS.).. **55**

Creamer, Motto Ware, Cottage patt., "Hasty climbers have sudden falls," Watcombe, 2 1/4" h.. **45**

Creamer, Motto Ware, Cottage patt., "There's a time for all things," Watcombe, 2 1/2" h.. **39**

Creamer, souvenir, Heather patt., "Hastings," white heather on mauve ground, 3 1/4" h.. **62**

Crocus vase, Motto Ware, Cottage patt., spherical body, "Gather the roses while ye may" & "Old time is still a flying," 3" d., 3 3/4" h. **95**

Torquay Cup & Saucer

Cup & saucer, Motto Ware, Cottage patt., footed flaring cylindrical cup, inscribed "Have another cup full," saucer 5 3/8" d., cup 3 3/8" d., 3" h. (ILLUS.) **75**

Dish, figural fish, Motto Ware, Colored Cockerel patt., "A pla(i)ce for ashes," Longpark Torquay, ca. 1904-18, 3 3/4 x 5 3/4" **95**

Dish, figural fish, Motto Ware, Cottage patt., "A pla(i)ce for ashes," Longpark, ca. 1930s, 3 3/4 x 5 1/2" **98**

Dish, figural fish, Motto Ware, Sailboat patt., "Time and tide for no man bide," 3 1/2 x 5 1/2" **72**

Dish, figural fish, two-eyed, Motto Ware, Black Cockerel patt., "A pla(i)ce for ashes," Watcombe, ca. 1920, 3 1/4 x 5 1/4"........ **87**

Dresser tray, Motto Ware, Colored Cockerel patt., "A place for everything," Longpark Torquay, ca. 1903-09, uncommon, 7 1/2 x 10 3/4" **360**

Dresser tray, Motto Ware, Cottage patt., Devon dialect, "Dinna lie in yer bed an lippen tae yer neebor," Watcombe, 1920s, 7 1/2 x 10 3/4" (restored)................................ **210**

Dresser tray, Motto Ware, Scandy patt., "A place for Everything," Watcombe Torquay, ca. 1920s, 7 3/8 x 10 1/2".............. **234**

Torquay Egg Cup

Egg cup, Motto Ware, Black Cockerel patt., "Fresh today" Longpark Tormohun ware, ca. 1910.. 67

Egg cup, Motto Ware, Black Cockerel patt., inscribed "Just laid," 1 1/2" d., 1 3/4" h. (ILLUS.)... 45

Egg cup, Motto Ware, Cottage patt., "Fresh today," Longpark Torquay, ca. 1930, 2 1/2" h. 53

Egg cup, Motto Ware, Cottage patt., "New laid," Royal Watcombe, ca. 1950, 2 3/4" h. 42

Egg cup, Motto Ware, Cottage patt., "Waste not - Want not," Watcombe, ca. 1950, 2 3/4" h. 45

Torquay Footed Egg Cup

Egg cup, footed, Motto Ware, Cottage patt., "Laid to day," 3 1/4" h., 3 1/2" d. (ILLUS.) 45

Ewer, cov., Floral patt., white floral spray on front & reverse on a tan ground, silver plated cover w/"J.A.R." silversmith's mark, Watcombe, ca. 1890s, 8 1/2" h. 310

Ewer, Floral patt., fuschia on cream ground, celeste blue trim, early Watcombe porcelain mark, ca. 1884-1901, 4 1/2" h. 156

Scandy Pattern Hatpin Holder

Hatpin holder, footed dished base centered by hourglass-shaped holder, Motto Ware, Scandy patt., "A present from Arnside," Longpark Torquay, ca. 1910-20, 4 5/8" h. (ILLUS.) 133

Cottage Pattern Hot Water Pot

Hot water or coffeepot, cov., bulbous ovoid body tapering to a flaring neck w/rim spout, inset cover w/knob finial, Motto Ware, Cottage patt., "Never put off till tomorrow what can be done today - Newquay," Watcombe, 1925-35 mark, 6" h. (ILLUS.)... 137

Hot water or coffeepot, cov., Motto Ware, "Life is mostly froth and bubble...," scarce motto, Watcombe, ca. 1925-35 mark, 7 3/4" h. 202

Hot water pot, cov., Motto Ware, Colored Cockerel patt., "Two men look through prison bars - One sees the mud and the other the stars," Longpark, ca. 1910-20, 5 1/2" h. 169

Hot water pot, cov., Motto Ware, Scandy patt., "To err is human, to forgive divine," Watcombe Torquay, ca. 1910-27 mark, 6" h. 127

Inkwell, Motto Ware, Shamrock patt., "The chosen leaf of Bard and Chief," Aller Vale, ca. 1902-10 mark, 3" h. 105

Torquay Motto Ware Jam Jar

Jam jar, cov., Motto Ware, Cottage patt., cylindrical w/a low pyramidal cover w/knob finial & spoon notch at rim, "Go Asy Wi It Now," 3 1/4" d., 4 1/4" h. (ILLUS.)... 65

Jardiniere, B2 Scroll patt., colored scrolls on a green ground, H.M. Exeter Pottery, ca. 1910, 5 1/2" h............................ 285

Jardiniere, faience, Lantern patt., a lantern in branches on blue ground, Barton Pottery mark, ca. 1920s, small, 3 1/2" h. 84

Jardiniere, Motto Ware, Passion Flower patt., flowers on a blue ground, motto in cream, "For every evil under the sun...," unmarked, Exeter, ca. 1925, 6 1/4" h. **385**

Model of a frying pan, Motto Ware, Black Cockerel patt., "I cum frum Totnes - Waste not, want not," Torquay Pottery Co., ca. 1918-24, 4 1/8" l. plus handle **69**

Mug, child's, Motto Ware, Cottage patt., "Mary had a little lamb," St. Marychurch, 1960s, 3" h. **68**

Mug, child's, Motto Ware, Scandy patt., "Hold me tight and don't be clumsy or you'll break this mug from Romsey," Watcombe, ca. 1902-15, 2 1/4" h. **80**

Mustard pot, cov., Motto Ware, Cottage patt., w/"Lands End" on front & "I improve everything" on back, 2 1/4" d., 2 3/4" h. **55**

Torquay Cottage Pattern Mustard Pot

Mustard pot, cov., Motto Ware, Cottage patt., "Soft words win hard hearts," 2 1/2" d., 3" h. (ILLUS.) **55**

Pin tray, Motto Ware, Cottage patt., "Don't Grouse - Work like Helen B. Merry - Ilfracombe," Watcombe, ca. 1901-10 mark, 3 1/4" sq. **52**

Pin tray, Motto Ware, Scandy patt., "Tell truth and shame the Devil - Port Arthur Canada," Watcombe, ca. 1910-27, 3 1/4 x 5" **56**

Pitcher, 1 3/4" h., miniature, Motto Ware, Cottage patt., "Little and good - Brixham," Royal Watcombe **55**

Pitcher, 1 3/4" h., miniature, Motto Ware, Cottage patt., "Little Jack Horner - Runswick Bay" (ILLUS. right w/candlestick) **65**

Pitcher, 2" h., miniature, Motto Ware, Cottage patt., "For my Dolly," Royal Watcombe **62**

Pitcher, 2" h., miniature, Motto Ware, Scandy patt., "Thumbs Up," Royal Watcombe........ **55**

Pitcher, 2 1/2" h., miniature, Motto Ware, Scandy patt., "Demsher Craim tak an try it," Aller Vale **60**

Pitcher, 2 7/8" h., front pouring spout, Motto Ware, Scandy patt., "The red kine bathing in the stream," Aller Vale H.H. & Co., ca. 1897-1902 mark..... **80**

Pitcher, 3 5/8" h., advertising-type, Cottage patt., "The Oldest Chemist Shoppe in England - Knaresborough," Royal Watcombe, ca. 1950 ..... **50**

Pitcher, 3 3/4" h., Motto Ware, Cottage patt., "Fresh from the cow," Watcombe, ca. 1930 ..... **45**

Pitcher, 4 1/8" h., Motto Ware, Colored Cockerel patt., "Success comes not by wishing but hard work bravely done," Aller Vale, ca. 1891-1901..... **133**

Pitcher, 4 1/8" h., Shakespeare's House patt., faience, rendering of Shakespeare's House w/green sprayed borders, Watcombe, ca. 1910-20 ..... **96**

Pitcher, 4 1/2" h., Sgraffito patt., band of leafy scrolls & flowers on glazed terra cotta, Q1 pattern code, Aller Vale, 1890s....... **88**

Torquay Cottage Pattern Pitcher

Pitcher, 5" h., 4" d., Motto Ware, Cottage patt., bulbous body w/tall cylindrical neck, "If you can't be aisy Be as aisy as you can" (ILLUS.) **110**

Torquay Motto Ware Pitcher

Pitcher, 5 1/4" h., 4 1/2" d., Motto Ware, Cottage patt., spherical base tapering slightly to wide cylindrical neck, "Help yourself when you be shy" (ILLUS.) **100**

Pitcher, 5 1/2" h., pierced rim, handle passes through, Motto Ware, Scandy patt., "If it be so so it is you know...," Aller Vale, ca. 1900 ..... **185**

Pitcher, 5 3/4" h., Motto Ware, Forget-me-not patt., "From Launceston," white script on dark blue, light blue forget-me-nots on white band w/trellis, Exeter, 1920 ..... **123**

Pitcher, 6" h., Motto Ware, Black Cockerel patt., "It's an ill wind that blows nobody good," Longpark, ca. 1918-30 ..... **142**

Pitcher, 6" h., Motto Ware, Scandy patt., "There's a saying old and musty - yet it is ever new...," Aller Vale, ca. 1891-1910........ **116**

Pitcher, 6" h., slim shape, Scroll patt., colored scrolls on a green ground, Watcombe **72**

Pitcher, 6 1/4" h., artware, Sailboats patt., boats on aqua blue water, Watcombe, ca. 1920s..... **123**

Pitcher, 6 1/2" h., Motto Ware, Cottage patt., "Little duties still put off may end in never done," Watcombe, ca. 1930................. **142**

Scandy Pattern Motto Ware Pitcher

Pitcher, 7 3/4" h., Motto Ware, Scandy patt., "Little duties still put off may end in never done...," Aller Vale, ca. 1891-1910 (ILLUS.) **199**

Plate, 4 1/4" d., miniature doll size, Motto Ware, Scandy patt., "Gude folks be scarce take care of me," colored border, Longpark, ca. 1920 .... **75**

Plate, 4 3/8" d., miniature doll size, Motto Ware, Cottage patt., "A rolling stone gathers no moss," Royal Watcombe, ca. 1950 .... **65**

Plate, 4 3/8" d., miniature doll size, Motto Ware, Cottage patt., "Good examples are the best sermons," Royal Watcombe, ca. 1950 .... **65**

Plate, 5" d., Motto Ware, Scandy patt., "Do not burden today's strength...," Aller Vale **68**

Black Cockerel Motto Plate

Plate, 6" d., Motto Ware, Black Cockerel patt., "Good morning," Aller Vale, 1891-1910 (ILLUS.) **125**

Plate, 6 1/4" d., Motto Ware, Cottage patt., "Enough's as good as a feast," Royal Watcombe **60**

Plate, 6 1/2" d., Motto Ware, Sailboat patt., "Gather the roses while ye may...," Watcombe **69**

Plate, 7 1/4" d., Motto Ware, Cottage patt., "Be a little deaf and blind, Happiness you'll always find," Watcombe DMW mark, ca. 1918-27 .... **80**

Plate, 7 1/4" d., Motto Ware, Scandy patt., "A fellow feeling makes us wondrous kind...," Aller Vale, ca. 1891-1902 mark **120**

Plate, 8 1/8" d., Motto Ware, Scandy patt., "As I was going to St. Ives - I met a man with seven wives...," long motto, Watcombe, ca. 1925-35 .... **235**

Plate, 8 1/2" d., Motto Ware, Cottage patt., "Some hae meat and canna eat...," Scottish prayer motto, Watcombe DMW mark, ca. 1918-27 .... **96**

Motto Ware Puzzle Jug

Puzzle jug, Motto Ware, Colored Cockerel patt., "May you find that all life's troubles after all are only bubbles," Longpark Tormohun ware, ca. 1910, 4" h. (ILLUS.) **182**

Puzzle jug, Motto Ware, Scandy patt., "Within this jug there is good liquor...," Aller Vale, ca. 1910, 4 1/2" h. **175**

Salt & pepper shakers, Motto Ware, Cottage patt., "Waste not, want not" & "A necessity of life," Watcombe, 1920s, 2 3/4" h., pr. **55**

Scent bottle, Devon Violets patt., unmarked Longpark, ca. 1930, 2 1/4" h. (ILLUS. left, below) **32**

Torquay Scent Bottles

Scent bottle, handled, Devon Violets patt., white clay, motto painted on, marked "Made in Great Britain," 1960s, 2 3/4" h. **30**

Scent bottle, marked "Genuine Devon Lavender," small silver paper label under name, Watcombe - Made in England mark, ca. 1930 (ILLUS. right, previous page).. **62**

Scent bottle, Somerset Violets patt., inkwell-shaped, Longpark, ca. 1930, 2"h. **54**

Scent bottle w/old brass crown stopper, Devon Violets patt., "Torquay" under green band, Longpark, ca. 1930, 4 1/2" h. (ILLUS. center, previous page)........ **98**

Sugar bowl, cov., Motto Ware, Ivy patt., "Sweeten for yourself," Aller Vale, ca. 1910, 3 1/4" h. **62**

Small Torquay Sugar Bowl

Sugar bowl, open, round tapering sides, Mottto Ware, Black Cockerel patt., "Be aisy with tha sugar," 3 1/4" d., 1 3/4" h. (ILLUS.) **65**

Torquay Sugar Bowl

Sugar bowl, open, pedestal base, Motto Ware, Black Cockerel patt., "Be aisy with tha sugar," 5 1/4" d., 4 1/4" h. (ILLUS.) **85**

Supper dish, three-part w/handle, Cottage patt., marked "Butter - Cheese - Biscuits," Watcombe Torquay, ca. 1930, 8 x 8 1/2" **165**

Supper dish, three-part w/handle, Scandy patt., marked "Jam - Butter - Cream," Watcombe Torquay, ca. 1901-20, 8 x 9" **139**

Tankard, Motto Ware, Cottage patt., "I have a good reason for drinking...," Royal Watcombe, ca. 1950, 3 1/2" h. **68**

Tankard, Motto Ware, Cottage patt., "To thine own self be true," Dartmouth Pottery, 5" h. **69**

Tankard, Motto Ware, Scandy patt., "Every blade of grass...," Aller Vale, ca. 1910, 4" h. **78**

Teapot, cov., bulbous body, Motto Ware, Cottage patt., "From Torquay" on front & "Du'ee Drink a cup a tay," 4 1/2" d., 3 3/4" h. **110**

Teapot, cov., miniature, Motto Ware, Scandy patt., "Droon yer sorrows in a cup a Tay," Longpark Torquay, ca. 1918-30, 2 3/4" h. (ILLUS. center w/candlestick) **124**

Teapot, cov., miniature, nursery rhyme & souvenir, Cottage patt., "Mary had a little lamb..." & "Kents Cavern," Royal Watcombe, 3 3/8" h. **153**

Molded Cottage Teapot

Teapot, cov., Molded Cottage patt., cottage-shaped, inscribed "Old Uncle - Tom Cobley's - Cottage - Widdecombe," Torquay Pottery Co., ca. 1920, 4 7/8" h. (ILLUS.)... **139**

Teapot, cov., Motto Ware, Black Cockerel patt., "Du'ee drink a cup a Tay," Longpark, ca. 1918-30, overall 7 1/2" l., 4 5/8" h. **124**

Cottage Pattern Motto Teapot

Teapot, cov., Motto Ware, Cottage patt., "Fair is he that comes but fairer he that brings," Made in England - Watcombe mark, ca. 1930s, overall 7 1/4" l., 4 1/4" h. (ILLUS.)................................. **89**

Toast rack, Motto Ware, Cottage patt., center handle, three tines, "Take a little toast," Watcombe, ca. 1920, 3 1/2" h. **129**

Trivet, round, Motto Ware, Cottage patt., "Except the kettle boiling B Filling the tpot spoils the T" & "Mablethorpe," 5 1/2" d. **55**

Vase, 1 7/8" h., miniature, Motto Ware, Scandy patt., "Niver say die - Up man and try," Longpark **65**

Vase, 2" h., miniature, tri-corner pinched top, blue flower on white clay ground, Aller Vale, ca. 1900... **80**

Vase, 2 1/4" h., miniature, Motto Ware, Scandy patt., "Du'ee think tis yer dooty? Then du et," Longpark, ca. 1910 .... **109**

Vase, 2 3/4" h., Motto Ware, Rose patt., "It's a good horse that never stumbles," ca. 1930 .... **67**

Vase, 3 5/8" h., Motto Ware, Colored Cockerel patt., "We're not the only pebbles on the beach," Longpark Torquay, ca. 1910-24 .... **109**

Vase, 4 1/2" h., D1 Scroll patt., colored scrolls on a blue ground, Aller Vale, rare...... **164**

Vase, 4 1/2" h., faience, Tintern Abbey patt., abbey ruins in a landscape, cloud-filled sky, Longpark, ca. 1910 .... **149**

Stork Pattern Vase

Vase, 4 5/8" h., faience, waisted shape w/bulbed top pierced w/holes, Stork patt., white & black stork against green ground w/reeds, Crown Dorset, ca. 1910 (ILLUS.) **219**

Vase, 5 7/8" h., Butterflies patt., spherical body w/four flared necks at top, two butterflies on a streaky mauve ground, Longpark, ca. 1904-18 .... **142**

Vase, 7 1/2" h., two-handled, Motto Ware, Scandy patt., "Take fortune as you find her...," H.M. Exeter, ca. 1920 (professional restoration) **154**

Longpark Scroll Pattern Vase

Vase, 7 3/4" h., footed tapering cylindrical form, B2 Scroll patt., colored scrolls on a dark green ground, Longpark, ca. 1909 (ILLUS.) **143**

Vase, 8" h., artware, Wild Rose patt., roses on a black lattice, cream ground, Watcombe Pottery, ca. 1901-20 mark................ **194**

Van Briggle

Early Van Briggle Pottery Mark

The Van Briggle Pottery was established by Artus Van Briggle, who formerly worked for Rookwood Pottery, in Colorado Springs, Colorado at the turn of the century. He died in 1904 but the pottery was carried on by his widow and others. From 1900 until 1920, the pieces were dated. It remains in production today, specializing in Art Pottery.

Bowl, 5 1/2" d., 2" h., squatty bulbous body w/a wide tapering shoulder to the wide flat mouth, embossed w/holly under a fine speckled matte green glaze, the brown clay showing through, ca. 1906, incised "AA - Van Briggle - Colo Spgs. - 1906" **$880**

Bowl, 6" d., 3" h., wide flat-bottomed squatty bulbous form w/the sharply tapering top centered w/a wide, flat molded mouth, light turquoise matte glaze, Shape No. 50B, 1905........................ **900**

Fine Early Van Briggle Bowl-Vase

Bowl-vase, a wide squatty bulbous form tapering to a wide, flat mouth, molded around the sides w/stylized undulating & looping floral designs, dark brown clay shows through the fine suspended blue matte glaze, dated 1907, 5" d. (ILLUS.)..... **4,675**

Van Briggle Bowl-Vase with Leaves

Bowl-vase, large squatty bulbous ovoid form tapering to a wide flat mouth, molded around the shoulder w/a band on pointed leaves atop long curved stems, matte brown glaze, 1916, 7" d., 4 3/4" h. (ILLUS.)... 920

Bowl-vase, squatty bulbous deep vessel w/a wide shoulder & molded flat mouth, good matte green glaze, ca. 1905, 5 1/2" h.. 880

Bowl-vase, wide rounded squatty lower body below a wide angled & sloping shoulder to the wide flat mouth, molded w/large, wide pointed leaves around the sides, overall maroon & blue matte glaze, post-1920s, 9 1/2" d., 5" h............................... 330

Bowl-vase, very wide squatty bulbous form w/the upper sides tapering to a flat mouth, embossed around the mouth w/a wide band of mistletoe berries & leaves down the sides, sheer mottled mauve glaze, Shape No. 387, dated 1905, incised mark, 11" d., 5" h................................. **4,125**

Bowl-vase, wide bulbous body w/molded rim, covered in a fine matte green glaze, incised "AA - VAN BRIGGLE - Colo. Spgs. - 1910," 1910, 4 x 5 1/2"...................... 440

Bowl-vase, squatty bulbous body w/shoulder tapering sharply to incurved rim, molded w/triangular leaves under a matte light green glaze, ca. 1906, incised "AA - Van Briggle - 1906 - 428 - 3," 4 x 7" .. **2,200**

Bowl-vase, wide rounded squatty lower body below a wide angled & sloping shoulder to the wide flat mouth, molded arrowhead leaves around shoulder, turquoise blue matte glaze, ca. 1918, incised marks, 9 3/4" d., 4 3/4" h. (minor bubbles in glaze)... 495

Van Briggle Mermaid Chalice

Chalice, a round foot & slender stem supporting a squatty bulbous cup tapering to a flat rim, molded around the cup w/the figure of a mermaid, swirled light green & dark blue matte glaze, signed, small glaze miss, paint flecks, 10 1/2" h. (ILLUS.)...................................... **6,325**

Mug, ovoid form w/thick C-form handle from rim to base, matte green glaze, incised "AA - COLO SPRINGS - 1907 - 28B," 4 1/2" d., 5" h.............................. 358

Paperweight, figural horned toad in matte green on an oval mustard base, marked "AA - 1913," ca. 1913, 1 1/2 x 4 3/4" (firing line to base)............................... **1,463**

Paperweight, figural, modeled as a horned toad on a thin oval base, the toad in a yellowish amber glaze on a matte green base, unmarked, ca. 1914, 3 1/4 x 4 1/2"..... 990

Plate, 8 1/4" d., molded w/a cluster of purple grapes & large leaves against a textured turquoise ground, incised mark, 1907-11 605

Van Briggle Plate with Poppies

Plate, 8 1/2" d., crisply incised w/poppies & covered in a bright green glaze, incised "AA - Van Briggle - 1902 - III" (ILLUS.) **1,540**

Plate, 8 1/2" d., heavily embossed w/large grapes & leaves under a deep burgundy & blue matte glaze, incised marks ca. 1907-12 231

Vase, 2 1/2" h., 3" d., small bulbous form w/a closed rim, three spread-winged finely carved dragonflies around the rim, overall mustard yellow matte glaze, ca. 1907-12 880

Vase, miniature, 3" h., 3" d., wide cylindrical base w/shoulder tapering to closed rim, embossed w/trefoils & covered in fine curdled brown glaze, marked "AA - Van Briggle - Colo. Spgs.," ca. 1907-11 563

Vase, 3 3/4" h., 4 1/2" h., flat-bottomed spherical form w/a flat molded mouth, pale turquoise matte glaze, dated 1903 (ILLUS. bottom row, center, with group) 900

Vase, 3 3/4" h., 5" d., flat-bottomed squatty bulbous body w/the wide shoulder centered by a short, wide cylindrical neck, embossed around the sides w/butterflies, green & pale red matte glaze, Shape No. 626, 1908-11 (overfired, restoration to rim chip)... 506

Large Grouping of Van Briggle Vases

Vase, 4" h., a small footring supporting a bulbous nearly spherical body tapering slightly to a wide, flat molded rim, molded down the sides w/swirled florals, unusual purple, grey & green matte glaze, ca. 1907-12 .... **715**

Vase, 4 x 4", footed bulbous ovoid body w/shoulder tapering to wide short cylindrical neck, embossed w/stylized floral pattern under a matte green & speckled mustard ground, ca. 1915-20, incised "AA - Van Briggle - 20" **523**

Vase, 4 x 4 1/4", wide cylindrical base tapering to rounded shoulder & flat mouth, molded poppies under a fine speckled matte green glaze, the brown clay showing through, ca. 1903, incised "AA - Van Briggle - 1903 - 204 - III" **2,200**

Vase, 4 x 4 3/4", copper-clad bulbous ovoid body w/shoulder tapering to wide flat neck, embossed w/stylized leaves, original dark patina, ca. 1908-11, incised "AA - Van Briggle - Colo. Spgs. - 151" **3,938**

Vase, 4 1/4" h., squatty bulbous form, sharply canted sides to flat rim, decorated w/stylized relief-molded flowers & stems, mulberry & blue glaze, incised marks & "U.S.A." & "NP" in rectangle, ca. 1922-26 .... **523**

Vase, 4 1/2" h., wide heavy slightly tapering cylindrical form w/deeply carved upright flowers on stems flanked by pairs of pointed leaves, overall dark green & purple matte glaze, incised marks, ca. 1905...... **880**

Vase, 4 1/2 x 5", spherical body w/slightly rolled lip, molded stylized design under a matte green glaze, ca. 1904, incised "AA - Van Briggle - 1904 - V - 148" (restored lines to body) **413**

Vase, 4 1/2" h., 5 3/4" d., footed compressed spherical body, the wide shoulder tapering to a small cylindrical neck w/molded rim, light robin's-egg blue matte glaze, incised "AA - VAN BRIGGLE - 1905" 1905 .... **358**

Vase, 4 3/4" h., 3 3/4" d., squatty bulbous lower body tapering to a tall cylindrical neck w/a molded rim, the lower body molded w/swirled pointed leaves, bluish green matte glaze, Shape No. 730, 1908-11 .... **534**

Vase, 5" h., waisted cylindrical body slightly swelled near the top then tapering to a wide flat mouth, decorated w/embossed iris blossoms on swirling vertical stems & leaves under a matte raspberry pink glaze, Shape No. 26, 1907-11 .... **660**

Vase, 5" h., 3 1/2" d., wide squatty base & tapering cylindrical sides to a small flat mouth, embossed w/swirled yucca leaves up the sides, overall curdled brown glaze, incised mark, Shape No. 162, 1907-11 .... **990**

Vase, 5" h., 6" d., footed bulbous body w/wide molded rim, curdled matte bluish green glaze, Shape No. 240C, 1907........... **330**

Vase, 5 1/4" h., 3 1/2" d., simple ovoid form w/small molded mouth, embossed w/large stylized crocus blossoms around the shoulder w/stems down the sides, green & pink matte glaze, Shape No. 823, ca. 1910 (ILLUS. front row, second from left, above)............................... **506**

Vase, 5 1/2" h., ovoid body molded w/four large leaves, matte green glaze on brown ground, ca. 1910............................... **259**

Vase, 5 3/4" h., 3 3/4" d., wide low rounded base below a sharply tapering cylindrical body w/flat rim, matte mustard yellow glaze, Shape No. 825, 1908-11 (ILLUS. front row, second from right, above)............. **534**

Van Briggle Trefoil Vase

Vase, 6" h., simple ovoid body tapering to a small mouth flanked by relief-molded blue trefoils & small in-body handles, light matte green ground, Shape No. 165 (ILLUS.) **1,623**

Vase, 6" h., slightly tapering swelled cylindrical body w/a tiny flat neck, molded w/small stylized upright buds on stems spaced around the sides, dark brown matte glaze, imcised mark, ca. 1915 .... **440**

Vase, 6" h., 4" d., wide low rounded base below a sharply tapering cylindrical body w/flat rim, embossed around the lower body & up the sides w/medallions of wheat sheaves, fine leathery matte green glaze, Shape No. 347, 1905 (ILLUS. front row, far left, with group) **2,138**

Small Van Briggle Vase with Flowers

Vase, 6" h., 4 1/4" d., wide squatty bulbous base tapering sharply to a cylindrical neck, molded around the lower body w/five-petal blossoms & leaves w/stems & leaves up the sides, chartreuse matte mottled glaze, Shape No. 188, 1903 (ILLUS.) **2,415**

Vase, 6 1/2" h., slightly flaring cylindrical body w/a bulbed top w/closed mouth, molded around the top w/tulip blossoms, the stems down the sides, ivory w/light green matte glaze, incised marks, ca. 1905 (tight line at top) **358**

Bottle-form Van Briggle Vase

Vase, 6 1/2" h., 3 3/4" d., footed bulbous bottle-form body tapering to a thick closed rim, embossed down the sides w/stylized flowers & long tiered rows of leaves, feathered dark matte green glaze, 1908-11 (ILLUS.) **1,035**

Vase, 6 1/2" h., 4 1/2" d., footed baluster form w/recticulated shoulder & flat rim, embossed from base to rim w/papyrus plants & covered in green & rose matte glaze, marked "AA - 1916," ca. 1916 (small glaze chip to base) **2,138**

Vase, 7" h., bottle-form, a thin footring below the bulbous ovoid body tapering sharply to a tall 'stick' neck, fine green & charcoal matte glaze, incised mark, Shape No. 338, ca. 1905................................. **275**

Vase, 7" h., cylindrical body w/small loop handles & relief-molded design at base, leathery green matte glaze, Shape No. 535, incised marks & partially obscured date, 1907 (grinding chips off base) **715**

Vase, 7" h., cylindrical form w/swelled shoulder & short molded rim, relief-molded poppy pod decoration covered w/maroon matte glaze w/green highlights, incised marks & "Colo. Spgs.,"K" & "7," Shape No. 694, 1907-12 (nearly invisible glaze skip on base) **1,210**

Vase, 7" h., slender cylindrical lower body w/a swelled shoulder tapering slightly to a flat mouth, molded around the shoulder w/dragonflies extending down the sides, dark blue to deep red matte glaze, post-1920s... **319**

Vase, 7" h., slender ovoid body w/trumpet neck, overall maroon matte glaze, incised marks & dated "1914"........................... **330**

Vase, 7" h., wide ovoid base, sharply tapering sloping shoulder w/wide cylindrical neck & flat rim, matte green glaze, Shape No. 415, 1906.. **523**

Vase, 7" h., 3 1/2" d., slender cylindrical form w/a swelled shoulder & short tapering neck, embossed around the top w/jonquils on tall stems, dark purple dead-matte glaze, incised mark & dated 1902.. **2,750**

Vase, 7" h., 6 1/2" d., wide bulbous ovoid body w/a wide short rolled rim, embossed around the sides w/large butterflies, cobalt & turquoise matte glaze, 1916... **513**

Vase, 7 1/4" h., 3 1/2" d., swelled cylindrical form w/a narrow shoulder centered by a short cylindrical neck, embossed around the neck w/poppy pods w/the slender vines curving down the sides, purple matte glaze, Shape No. 830, 1915 (ILLUS. back row, far left, with group)........ **1,125**

Vase, 7 1/4" h., 4" d., gently swelled ovoid body tapering to a short neck w/thick molded rim, embossed around the neck w/stylized flower blossoms on slender stems down the sides, fine leathery dark blue glaze, Shape No. 287, 1905 (ILLUS. back row, far right, with group) **3,150**

Van Briggle Vase

Vase, 7 1/2" h., bulbous ovoid body w/a narrow cylindrical neck & flat rim, embossed w/wide triangular ribbed leaves w/ruffled edges & flowers, the leaves covered in an unusual brown matte glaze against a robin's-egg blue ground, Shape No. 797, 1907-11 (ILLUS.) **1,430**

Vase, 7 1/2" h., slender swelled cylindrical body tapering to a small, flat molded mouth, molded around the shoulder w/large tulip blossoms atop long leafy stems, multi-toned blue matte glaze, ca. 1915-20 .... **523**

Van Briggle Vase with Trilliums

Vase, 7 1/2" h., 3 1/2" d., slightly waisted cylindrical form, molded w/crips trillium leaves & blossoms swirling up around the sides & rim, leathery light blue matte glaze, 1905, Shape No. 296 (ILLUS.) **2,090**

Vase, 7 1/2" h., 3 3/4" d., tall waisted double-gourd form, embossed around the top w/crocus blossoms on tall slender stems w/pointed leaves around the bottom, matte dark green glaze, Shape No. 692, impressed mark, 1907-11 (chip to base, probably in the making) **770**

Van Briggle Vase with Papyrus Leaves

Vase, 7 3/4" h., bulbous base tapering to long slender cylindrical neck w/flaring rim, embossed around base w/papyrus leaves under a matte robin's-egg blue glaze, Shape No. 734, 1907-11 (ILLUS.) **770**

Vase, 7 3/4" h., bulbous paneled base tapering to a wide cylindrical neck, embossed w/stylized blossoms on four long stems, deep mustard yellow matte glaze, 1916... **990**

Rare Van Briggle "Dos Cebezos" Vase

Vase, 7 3/4" h., 4 3/4" d., "Dos Cebezos,"
ovoid body tapering to a cylindrical neck,
closed shoulder handles molded as two
women in flowing garments, unusual
mottled charcoal & greyish blue matte
flambé glaze, 1902 (ILLUS.) **20,750**

Vase, 7 3/4" h., 5" d., slightly lobed gourd-
form body w/a flat mouth, embossed
w/stylized flowers around the top, fine
teal blue glaze, Shape No. 864, 1912
(tight hairline in rim) **731**

Vase, 8" h., bulbous w/tapering cylindrical
neck & flat rim, embossed w/leaves &
covered in a fine mauve glaze w/clay
showing through, ca. 1908-11, incised
"AA - Van Briggle - Colo. Spgs. - 742" **1,320**

Vase, 8" h., cylindrical body w/gently
swelled shoulder curving in to a closed-in
mouth, matte purple glaze, Shape No.
343, 1905 .... **880**

Vase, 8" h., footed spherical body tapering
to tall cylindrical neck w/flat rim, base embossed w/wide triangular leaves against
a burgundy ground, incised "AA -19??,"
dating to the teens **715**

Vase, 8" h., ovoid body tapering to base,
decorated w/four large molded leaves,
matte yellowish green glaze, dated 1902 .. **2,415**

Vase, 8" h., 5 1/2" d., wide simple ovoid
body tapering to a short cylindrical neck,
overall turquoise matte glaze, Shape No.
269, 1906 (ILLUS. front row, far right,
with group) **1,069**

Baluster-form Van Briggle Blue Vase

Vase, 8 1/4" h., 4 1/2" d., baluster-form w/a
rounded shoulder to a short cylindrical
neck, embossed around the shoulder
w/stylized blossoms, the stems down the
sides, sheer robin's-egg blue glaze
w/clay showing through, 1906 (ILLUS.) **1,840**

Vase, 8 1/2" h., 3 1/2" d., slender baluster-
form w/a short neck, lavender matte
glaze, Shape No. 343C, 1905 .... **1,013**

Vase, 8 1/2" h., 7" d., bulbous ovoid body
tapering to a flat-rimmed neck, embossed around the neck & shoulder
w/green-washed leaves & red berries
w/an overall rich matte raspberry glaze,
incised mark, Shape No. 164, dated
1904 .... **3,300**

Vase, 8 3/4" h., slender ovoid body tapering
to a cupped rim w/small D-form handles

from rim to sides, molded around the
base w/large pointed & veined upright
leaves, mulberry glaze w/blue overspray,
marked, ca. 1920s **288**

Vase, 9" h., bulbous base tapering to a tall
cylindrical neck, molded around the neck
w/flower blossoms on tall stems down
the neck & wide pointed leaves around
the bottom, two-tone blue shaded to dark
green matte glaze, incised marks, ca.
1907-12 .... **770**

Vase, 9" h., wide bulbous ovoid body
w/short incurved cylindrical neck, decorated w/large relief-molded daisies &
leaves & covered w/rich mulberry & blue
glaze, incised mark, ca. 1918 (1/4" glaze
nick off rim) **468**

Vase, 9" h., 4" d., tall waisted form w/the
swelled top below a wide molded rim,
embossed around the shoulder w/large
daffodil blossoms on tall leafy stems
swirled down the sides, bluish green
matte glaze, two small flat base chips,
small bruise on rim, bottom dirty, Shape
No. 120, 1920s (ILLUS. back row, center,
with group) **619**

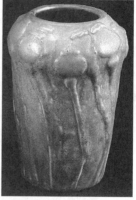

Early Rare Van Briggle Vase

Vase, 9" h., 6" d., wide tapering cylindrical
body w/a bulbous swelled shoulder tapering slightly to an incurved rim, decorated around the shoulder w/embossed
poppy pods & leaves on long stems, covered in a mottled red, blue & mauve
matte glaze w/the brown clay body showing through, incised "AA VAN BRIGGLE
- 1902 - III" (ILLUS.) **15,600**

Vase, 9" h., 6 1/4" d., wide gently flaring cylindrical body w/swelled shoulder &
closed rim, embossed around the top
w/large poppy pods on sinewy stems
curving down the sides, overall rich dead
matte burgundy & green glaze, incised
mark, dated 1902 .... **12,100**

Vase, 9 1/4" h., 4 1/4" d., trumpet form embossed w/jonquils under a fine leathery
pink matte glaze, marked "AA - Van Briggle - 1906 - 367," ca. 1906 (drill hole un-
der base) **2,363**

Vase, 9 1/2" h., tapering cylindrical body
gently swelled at the top w/a closed rim,

loop handles, decorated w/embossed daffodils on swirling stems & leaves, covered in a superior curdled brown matte glaze w/the brown clay showing through, incised "AA VAN BRIGGLE - Colo. Sprgs. 1906," 1906 .... **2,970**

Vase, 9 1/2" h., trumpet-form, the sides molded w/a horizontal vine w/large & small pointed leaves up & down around the sides, turquoise blue ground w/blue overspray, ca. 1930s...................................... **230**

Van Briggle Cylindrical Vase

Vase, 10" h., tall cylindrical form w/swelled closed rim, embossed near top & on rim w/blossoms & leaves on long stems, burgundy glaze, incised "AA - VAN BRIGGLE - 1903 - III," 1903 (ILLUS.) **2,750**

Vase, 10" h., 8" d., wide ovoid body tapering to a cylindrical neck flanked by small loop shoulder handles, molded w/stylized desert flowers & leaves, dark matte green & burgundy glaze, incised mark, dated 1904 .... **2,475**

Vase, 10 1/2" h., "Lorelei," figural mermaid wrapped around the tall swelled body, black matte glaze, post-1930s........................ **825**

Van Briggle Vase with Leaves & Stems

Vase, 10 1/2" h., 4" d., tall cylidnrical form w/swelled shoulder & tapering neck, embossed around the neck w/large curled leaves on long stems swirled down the sides, matte green & tobacco brown

feathered glaze, 1906, Shape No. 289 (ILLUS.)... **4,888**

Vase, 10 1/2" h., 4 1/4" d., tapering cylindrical form w/small loop handles, molded rim, covered in unusual veined green & burgundy matte glaze w/melt fissures, marked "AA - Van Briggle - 224 - 1904 - V," ca. 1904 .... **2,475**

Vase, 10 3/4" h., tall cylindrical body w/low buttress-type handles flanking the flat mouth, molded w/morning glories under a rare matte yellow glaze, ca. 1903, incised "AA Van Briggle - 1903 - 228" (repair to small base chip) **4,400**

Vase, 11" h., footed tall slender cylindrical body gently swelled at the top w/a closed rim, embossed w/leaves atop long vertical stems under a thick, curdled matte green glaze, incised "AA - VAN BRIGGLE - COLO. SPGS." 1907-11 (kiln kiss to shoulder)... **1,320**

Vase, 11" h., 9 1/2" w., "Lady of the Lily" figural design, a large nude Art Nouveau maiden arched back & leaning against the side of a large, widely flaring lily-form vase, brown & green mottled matte glaze, 1930s (dirty bottom, few deep crazing lines in base) **2,138**

Lady of the Lily Van Briggle Vase

Vase, 11 1/2" h., 9 1/2" w., "Lady of the Lily," figural w/nude maiden rising from waves & curving back to lean against a large lily-form vase, Persian Rose matte glaze, 1920s, dirt on base (ILLUS.)............ **1,955**

Vase, 11 3/4" h., 4 1/2" d., tall ovoid bottle form w/short cylindrical neck, embossed w/morning glory vines under a frothy chartreuse matte glaze, marked "AA - Van Briggle - 1904 - 108," ca. 1904........... **2,250**

Vase, 12 3/4" h., 4 14" d., tall cylindrical form w/swelled closed rim, embossed near top & on rim w/peacock feathers under an olive green & purple glaze, incised "AA - Van Briggle - 1905 - VV - 12," **3,375**

Vase, 13" h., tapering cylindrical body w/rounded base, closed mouth, embossed w/daffodils under a matte turquoise & blue glaze, ca. 1920s, incised "AA - VAN BRIGGLE - COLO SPGS" **770**

Vase, 14" h., slightly waisted cylindrical body gently swelled at the top w/a closed rim, embossed w/a design of stylized lilies & leaves atop wide stems, matte dark purple glaze, incised "AA - VAN BRIG-GLE - 1903 - III- 3," 1903 (minor grind at base from in-fire stilt pull) **5,225**

Van Briggle Peacock Feather Vase

Vase, 16 1/2" h., 8 1/2" d., tapering cylindrical form w/a bulbed shoulder & flat rim, embossed up & around the sides w/large peacock feathers under a frothy turquoise matte glaze on a red clay body, ca. 1910, Shape No. 07, remnant of paper price tag (ILLUS.)........................... **7,475**

Weller

Weller Marks

This pottery was made from 1872 to 1945 at a pottery established originally by Samuel A. Weller at Fultonham, Ohio, and moved in 1882 to Zanesville. Numerous lines were produced and listings below are by the pattern or lines.

Reference books on Weller include The Collectors Encyclopedia of Weller Pottery by Sharon & Bob Huxford (Collector Books, 1979) and All About Weller by Ann Gilbert McDonald (Antique Publications, 1989). ALSO SEE Antique Trader Books Pottery and Porcelain - Ceramics Price Guide, 3rd Edition.

Ardsley (1928)
Various shapes molded as cattails among rushes with water lilies at the bottom. Matte glaze.

Bulb bowl, lobed blossom form base w/leaf-form openwork top, half kiln ink stamp logo, 4 7/8" h. **$110**
Candleholders, lily pad & blossom disk base centered by a flaring blossom-form socket, half kiln ink stamp logo & old sales tag, one w/original "Weller Ardsley Ware" paper label, 2 3/4" h., pr. (minor glaze inconsistencies)...................................... **138**

Planter, pillow-form, overall incised leaves w/irregular rim formed by leaf tips & irises, 7 x 7".. **358**
Vase, 7 1/2" h., bud-type, gently flaring cylindrical form w/molded green & brown cattails w/white blossoms around the bottom **138**

Ardsley Vase

Vase, double, 9 1/2" h., connected by a pointed branch handle, marked w/half kiln ink stamp logo (ILLUS.)........................... **138**
Vase, 11" h., tall slightly flaring cylindrical form w/flaring base molded w/large blossoms **121**
Vase, 19" h., floor-type, compressed domed base w/lotus blossom & tall trumpet-form body embossed w/cattails & leaves, marked w/full circle kiln ink stamp logo **1,210**
Wall pocket, double, conical sections embossed w/cattails & leaves & joined by figural water lily blossom, 9 1/2 x 11 1/2" **468**

Aurelian (1898-1910)
Similar to Louwelsa line but brighter colors and a glossy glaze. With bright yellow/orange brushapplied background along with brown and yellow transparent glaze.

Lamp, oil, bell-shaped body on small knob feet, decorated w/two medallions of ivory roses, by C. Mitchell, complete w/oil font, artist-signed & stamped "K116," 10 1/2 x 11".. **605**
Lamp, kerosene table-type, a wide baluster-form body on small knob feet, the deep shoulder w/a wide short molded neck supporting a collar w/a kerosene burner & glass globe shade, the body decorated w/bold grape clusters & leaves on a fiery gold, green & mahogany ground, decorated by Eugene Roberts, incised "Aurelian" on the base, electrified, base only 9 1/2" d., 11" h............... **600-660**
Mug, tapering cylindrical body w/C-form handle, cherry decoration by Charles Chilcote, ca. 1900, impressed w/circular "Aurelian Weller" logo & incised shape number "435" w/"Chil" painted on side near bottom of handle, 6 1/8" h. **275**
Plaque, rectangular, decorated w/life-sized red apples hanging on leafy branches against a streaky brown, orange & yellow background, decorated by Frank Ferrell, ca. 1898, w/old metal framework & hanging chain, 10 7/8 x 16 1/2" (several glaze scratches, small patch of glaze loss, some bubbles in glaze) **935**

Aurelian Umbrella Stand

Umbrella stand, decorated w/bright yellow irises, late 19th c., unmarked, removable galvanized sheet metal insert, 23 7/8" h. (ILLUS.) **1,650**

Vase, 6" d., 4" h., compressed spherical form painted w/yellow roses on a black & mahogany ground (minimal crazing) **358**

Vase, 5 1/2" h., 5 3/4" d., spherical w/pinched neck, decorated w/yellow, brown & green roses on a fiery yellow & brown ground **375-450**

Vase, 7" h., bulbous ovoid body tapering to a trumpet neck, decorated w/yellow & orange rose blossoms & green leaves against a dark brown ground, the neck & rim mounted w/a foliate-case sterling silver mount, decorated by Hattie Mitchell, artist-initials & impressed "WELLER - 838 - 6," silver impressed "STERLING - 634" w/hallmark, ca. 1900-10 .... **2,000-2,500**

Vase, 9" h., 8" d., very bulbous body w/tiny cylindrical rim, decorated w/red carnations on shaded brown & yellow ground, artist-initialed **880**

Baldin (about 1915-20)
Rustic designs with relief-molded apples and leaves on branches wrapped around each piece.

Bowl, 4" d., brown ground (unusual high gloss) **170**

Lamp base, footed metal base w/squatty bulbous body tapering to wide closed rim, decorated w/red & yellow apples, green leaves, brown branches on blue ground, metal fittings, 12 1/2" h. **880**

Pedestal base, twisted tapering cylindrical base w/curved branch handles, decorated w/red apples & green leaves on brown & green ground, 28 1/2" h. **286**

Baldin Vase

Vase, 5 1/2" h., spherical body tapering to slightly flared rim, impressed "Weller" in large block letters (ILLUS.) **275**

Vase, 7 1/4" h., extended flared rim w/wide shoulder tapering to the base, branching red & yellow apples & green leaves on a tan & green ground, impressed mark ca. 1917 (small glaze nick near base) **169**

Vase, 9 1/2" h., wide cylindrical body flaring at base & rim, apple decoration in rose & yellow, green & yellow ground, marked "Weller" in large block letters **248**

Vase, 10" h., wide bulbous base tapering slightly to flat rim (firing line to bottom) **578**

Baldin Vase

Vase, 10 5/8" h., bulbous base w/slightly tapering wide cylindrical neck & flat rim, unmarked (ILLUS.) **303**

Wall pocket, unmarked, 11 1/4" l. **440**

Blue & Decorated Hudson (1919)
Hand-painted lifelike sprays of fruit blossoms and flowers in shades of pink and blue on a rich dark blue ground.

Vase, 7 3/4" h., bulbous ovoid body decorated w/a band of flowers & leaves (stilt-pulls to base) **385**

Vase, 9 1/8" h., ovoid body w/rolled rim, decorated near top w/bright orange & yellow flowers painted by Hester Pillsbury, unmarked, artist-initialed among flowers (4" crack descending from rim) **193**

Vase, 9 3/4" h., bulbous ovoid w/closed rim, decorated w/band of flowering cherry branches, artist's mark & impressed "Weller" **440**

Vase, 10" h., bulbous base tapering to wide cylindrical neck w/flat rim, light & dark pink band w/multicolored flowers around base, dark blue ground, impressed mark **286**

Vase, 10" h., slender cylindrical body flaring at base & tapering to small flat rim, center of body decorated w/a band of brightly colored flowers & impressed "Weller" in large block letters **248**

Vase, 10 3/4" h., waisted cylinder w/flared foot & widely flaring rim, decorated w/a band of cherry branches **330**

Blue & Decorated Weller Vase

Vase, 11 1/2" h., decorated w/two large sprays of blue & white lilacs, impressed "Weller" in large block letters & probably original Weller sales room label, small burst glaze bubble on rim (ILLUS.) **660**

Rare Blue & Decorated Vase

Vase, 11 5/8" h., deeply incised h.p. grape cluster decoration in shades of pink & blue, green leaves & brown vine, signed "McLaughlin" on side & impressed "Weller" in large block letters, w/probably original Weller paper showroom label (ILLUS.) **2,090**

Six-sided Blue & Decorated Vase

Vase, 11 7/8" h., hexagonal, decorated w/yellow & pink nasturtiums, unmarked (ILLUS.) **504**

Blue Louwelsa (ca. 1905)

A high-gloss line shading from medium blue to cobalt blue with underglaze slip decorations of fruits & florals and sometimes portraits. Decorated in shades of white, cobalt and light blue slip. Since few pieces were made, they are rare and sought after today.

Pitcher, tankard, 12" h., decorated w/white grape cluster & leaves on blue ground, artist-signed "C. Leffler," impressed marks (restoration) **770**

Vase, 5 3/8" h., pillow-form w/nasturtium decoration, unmarked (1/4" chip off left edge of rim) **523**

Vase, 6 1/2" h., tapering cylindrical body decorated w/delicate crocus blossoms in cream & blue w/dark & light blue leaves against a shaded blue ground, impressed mark... **1,210**

Vase, 7" h., bottle-shaped, decorated w/honeysuckle blossoms & leaves on shaded cobalt ground **825**

Blue Louwelsa Vase with Crocuses

Vase, 10 1/2" h., cylindrical body w/short rolled rim, unusual decoration of white crocuses against a shaded blue ground, impressed mark (ILLUS.) **1,980**

Vase, 10 1/2" h., tall slender ovoid body tapering to a very slender neck w/flared rim, decorated w/dark & light blue florals under a shaded light to dark blue overall glaze, incised "X 431" & "A 59" **1,150**

Tall Louwelsa Blue Vase with Berries

Vase, 10 7/8" h., tall slender ovoid body tapering to a very slender neck w/flared rim, decorated w/dark & light blue blackberries & vines under a shaded light to dark blue overall glaze, incised "X 431" & "A 59," very minor glaze scratch (ILLUS.) .. **1,760**

Blue Ware (before 1920)
Classical relief-molded white or cream figures on a dark blue ground.

Bowl-vase, squatty bulbous body decorated w/relief-molded dragonflies, 3 1/4" h........ **715**

Blue Ware Jardiniere

Jardiniere, footed, semi-ovoid form w/slightly flared rim, relief-molded winged figures & garlands, unmarked, glaze chip to one foot, 8 1/2 x 10 1/4" (ILLUS.) **303**

Blue Ware Vase

Vase, 11" h., cylindrical body w/closed-in rim, decorated w/scene of dancing maidens, trees & birds, narrow floral band at base & below rim (ILLUS.) **413**

Bonito (1927-33)
Hand-painted florals and foliage in soft tones on cream ground. Quality of artwork greatly affects price.

Bowl, 8 1/2" d... **60-70**
Vase, 4" h., large pansy decoration by Naomi Walch, artist-signed "N" **138**

Bonita Vase

Vase, 5 1/2" h., ovoid body tapering to a low fanned mouth flanked by small C-scroll handles, a band of delicate blossoms around the center on the ivory ground by Hester Pillsbury, marked "Weller Pottery" in script, artist-signed in brown slip (ILLUS.).. **138**
Vase, 5 1/2" h., ovoid body tapering to a low fanned mouth flanked by small C-scroll handles, a band of delicate blossoms around the center on the ivory ground, marked **144**
Vase, 6" h., footed widely flaring bulbous ovoid body w/a squared diamond-shaped wide mouth flanked by two small tab rim handles, painted w/a leafy swag centered by blossoms, signed in script **144**
Vase, 6" h., slightly flaring cylindrical body on short flaring foot, artist-signed............... **80-90**
Vase, 7" h., handled, decorated w/red flowers & leaves on front & back, artist-signed "L"... **135**

Bonito Vase

Vase, 11" h., footed ovoid body w/slightly flaring rim, shoulder handles, decorated w/orange & lavender flower & bud & green leaves, incised "Weller Pottery" & "N" in brown slip, dark craze line at rim (ILLUS.)... **165**
Vase, 11" h., footed wide ovoid body w/round shoulder & short wide cylindrical neck, small ornate shoulder handles, decorated w/stylized floral spray tied w/a ribbon bow & green lines around foot & neck, marked & initialed "N. Walsch" **358**
Vase, urn shape decorated overall w/red roses & buds, artist-signed "C"...................... **125**

Brighton (1915)
Various bird or butterfly figurals colorfully decorated and with glossy glazes.

Flower frog, model of a flamingo standing in rushes, head turned facing backward, marked, 6" h. **288**

Brighton Woodpecker Flower Frog

Flower frog, model of a blue, red & grey woodpecker w/black beak on branch, marked "X" in black slip, 5 5/8" h. (ILLUS.) **303**
Flower frog, model of a kingfisher, perched on open arched twig, 6 1/2" h. **173**
Flower frog, model of a kingfisher, 9" h. **440**

Brighton Bird of Paradise

Model of bird of paradise, rose, black, yellow, green, grey, orange, teal & brown on green & brown stand, impressed "Weller" in large block letters, 10 3/8" h. (ILLUS.) .. **2,310**
Model of kingfisher, blue, brown, black & white on green & brown stand, impressed "Weller" in large block letters, 8 1/2" h. (bubble on bird's back) **248**
Model of "Mad Parrot," blue, lavender, red & yellow on green & brown stand, impressed "Weller" in large block letters, 8" h. **715**
Model of parakeet, on tapering cylindrical pedestal perch, bird in polychrome colors of pink, yellow & blue, on a green perch, 5 3/4" d., 7 1/2" h., unmarked **1,000-1,200**
Model of parakeets, perched on a curving branch, birds brightly colored in red, yellow & blue, brown perch, glossy finish, unmarked, 5 3/4 x 9" **1,100-1,400**
Model of parrot, bright raspberry red & blue, yellow & green, on a tall swirled

brown upright perch, die-stamped mark, 9" w., 14" h. **1,400-1,600**
Model of woodpecker, perched on a base of entwined branches, blue & orange bird on a green perch, glossy glaze, unmarked, 3 1/2" d., 6 1/4" h. **150-185**
Name card holder w/figural butterfly & attached bud vase **395**

Burnt Wood (1910)
Molded designs on an unglazed light tan ground with dark brown trim. Similar to Claywood but no vertical bands.

Plate, 9" d., decorated w/birds on branch & flowers, cream cork-like finish, dark brown border (minor flakes to back) **187**
Vase, 6 1/2" h., decorated w/scene of children at play (minor flakes) **495**

Burnt Wood Vase with Pine Cones

Vase, 8 1/4" h., slender ovoid body w/pine cone decoration (ILLUS.) **83**
Vase, 9" h., 4" d., decorated w/three mockingbirds **299**
Vase, 10 1/2" h., large ovoid body w/a short cylindrical neck, neck & base band in dark brown, the body in cream w/a speckled brown ground & etched vertical bands of large stylized blossoms alternating w/bands of leafy branches, impressed mark **173**
Vase, 11" h., birds decoration **135**

Chase (late 1920s)
White relief fox hunt scenes usually on a deep blue ground.

Vase, 7 5/8" h., footed baluster-form w/rolled rim, dark blue ground w/white hunt scene, incised "Weller Pottery" on bottom **248**

Chase Hunting Scene Vase

Vase, 8" h., footed bulbous ovoid body w/flaring rim, blue ground (ILLUS.) **275**

Chase Vase with Silver Overlay

Vase, 8 7/8" h., ovoid form w/flat rim, mottled blue matte ground decorated w/applied silver overlay hunt scene, marked "Sterling" & impressed "Weller Pottery" in script (ILLUS.) **358**

Vase, 9" h., footed, flattened, rounded pillow-form body w/three slightly flaring cylindrical necks at the top, a larger central one flanked by two smaller angled ones, matte blue ground, marked **288**

Vase, 12" h., footed baluster-form w/flat rim, mottled green ground decorated w/sterling silver deposit hunt scene, marked on base **288**

Claywood (ca. 1910)
Etched designs against a light tan ground, divided by dark brown bands. Matte glaze.

Bowl, 6 1/4" d., wide flat-bottomed form w/low gently rounded sides, paneled design of stylized florals in dark brown & creamy tan **52**

Flower frog, cov., a wide squatty bowl w/slightly tapering sides fitted w/a pierced disk cover, a dark brown band around the top & bottom rims, the sides of the base in cream etched in dark brown w/a continuous band of large stylized blossoms, the cover w/similar blossoms w/their centers pierced to form the frog, 5" d. **115**

Humidor, cov., etched floral panels **165**

Claywood Jardiniere

Jardiniere, bulbous ovoid body divided into panels by dark brown bands, the creamy panels w/floral decoration outlined in brown, unmarked, 3 1/2" h. (ILLUS.).............. **28**

Vase, 7" h., bulbous ovoid body embossed w/a scene of children at play under stylized trees, matte umber ground (minor glaze flaking at rim, spider lines to body) **220**

Claywood Vase

Vase, 8" h., tapering cylindrical body w/compressed base, the sides divided into tall panels by dark brown bands, each panel etched w/a grape cluster on leafy vines in creamy white outlined in brown (ILLUS.).. **55**

Vase, 8 1/2" h., slender ovoid body w/short cylindrical rim, pine cone decoration **187**

Vase, 10" h., tall cylindrical body w/a wide flattened rim, the sides divided into tall panels by dark brown bands, each panel etched w/a grape cluster on leafy vines in creamy white outlined in brown **98**

Vase, 10" h., tall cylindrical form w/a wide flattened rim, Egyptian design divided by tall panels, etched border around top (minor flakes) **413**

Coppertone (late 1920s)
Various shapes with an overall mottled bright green glaze on a "copper" glaze base. Some pieces with figural frog or fish handles. Models of frogs also included.

Bowl, 9" d., 3 3/4" h., two raised open square handles on flat rim, mottled green & brown matte glaze (two pinhead glaze nicks to rim) **100-125**

Bowl, 9 3/4" l., 5 1/2" h., deep rounded sides w/an undulating oblong molded rim molded at one side w/a frog, each side embossed w/a carp, rich mottled green & brown glaze, ink kiln mark "191-G" **1,210**

Bowl, 3 1/2 x 12", flaring sides w/down-curved rim, incised "Weller Handmade" **605**

Bowl w/original flower holder, 11" d., low form w/flaring sides & down-curved rim, incised "Weller Hand Made" (ILLUS. bottom row, second from right, top next page)... **173**

A Variety of Coppertone Items

Coppertone Turtle Candleholder

Candleholders, model of a turtle beside a
water lily blossom, 3" h., pr. (ILLUS. of
one).. **660**

Card tray, in the form of a lily pad leaf
w/shallow dished sides, molded at one
side w/a crouching frog on the rim, ink
kiln mark, 6" l., 2 1/4" h. **250-285**

Center bowl, deep w/irregular rim, frog
perched on one edge, mottled green &
brown glaze, 10 1/2" w., 5 1/2" h., ... **525-650**

Coppertone Center Bowl & Frog

Center bowl & flower frog, shallow form
w/flaring sides, embossed w/lily pads &
buds, flower frog in the form of a cluster
of leaves centered by an upright water lily
blossom, bowl 12" d., 3" h., 2 pcs.
(ILLUS.)... **650-850**

Center bowl & flower frog, shallow leaf-
shaped w/figural frog perched on edge of

rim next to water lily blossom, bowl
4 x 15 1/2", 2 pcs.. **743**

Cigarette or match holder, model of a lily
pad bloom w/seated frog, 5 1/2" w.,
4 1/2" h... **330**

Cigarette stand, model of a frog, 5" h....... **250-275**

Console bowl w/figural lily pad & frog
flower frog, oblong bowl, 8 x 10 1/2", 2
pcs. **900-1,100**

Console bowl, shallow oblong form w/frog
seated near water lily on one end, 11" l.
(ILLUS. bottom row, left, above) **805**

Console bowl, long narrow oblong form
w/undulating rim, molded at one end w/a
small figural frog & at the opposite end
w/a water lily & leaves, ink kiln mark,
15 1/2" l., 3 1/2" h. **990**

Flower frog, model of lily pad bloom w/seat-
ed frog, 3 7/8" h. (small chip inside edge
of one petal)... **168**

Fountain, tall boy holding fishing pole
standing on pedestal surrounded by
four upright fish on flared base, rich
mottled green & brown semi-gloss finish
glaze, boy & fish are fitted w/water
nozzles... **5,000**

Fountain, figural frog, 5 1/2 x 6 1/2" **715**

Jardiniere, large nearly spherical body w/a
closed rim, large arched eared shoulder
handles, covered w/a fine green & rust
mottled matte glaze, incised signature,
8 1/2" d., 7" h... **660**

Model of a frog, 2" h., incised "Weller Pot-
tery" **224**

Model of a frog, green, tan, brown & black
matte glaze, 2 1/2" h. (ILLUS. bottom
row, third from left, above) **322**

Model of a frog, incised "Weller Pottery -
12" 4" h.. **330**

Model of a frog, large animal w/a hole in its
mouth to accommodate a sprinkler, dark
mottled green & brown w/ivory chest,
10 1/4" l., 8 1/2" h. **2,800-3,500**

Model of a turtle, incised "Weller Pottery,"
1 1/4 x 4 1/4" **303**

Rare Weller Coppertone Fish Pitcher

Pitcher, 7 5/8" h., bulbous ovoid body
w/arched spout, figural fish handle,
marked w/half kiln ink stamp logo, couple
of burst bubbles inside mouth (ILLUS.) **1,760**

Planter, miniature, figural frog holding a water lily blossom, incised "Weller Pottery,"
4 x 4" **303**

Vase, 5 3/4" h., wide tapering cylindrical
body w/rolled rim, marked in script
"Weller Hand Made" **358**

Vase, 6" h., tapering ovoid body w/a wide
closed flat rim, overall vivid mottled green
over dark brown glaze, unmarked
(ILLUS. bottom row, far right, with bowl
and flower holder)... **633**

Vase, 6" h., wide tapering cylindrical form
(ILLUS. top row, far right with bowl and
flower holder).. **334**

Vase, 6" h., wide tapering cylindrical form
w/molded rim (ILLUS. top row, far left
with bowl and flower holder) **161**

Vase, 6 1/2" h., footed slender gently flaring
cylindrical body, mottled heavy green
over a blackish brown ground, incised
mark (ILLUS. top row, fourth from right
with bowl and flower holder) **297**

Vase, 6 1/2" h., footed tapering cylindrical
form, incised "Weller Hand Made"
(ILLUS. top row, third from right with bowl
and flower holder)... **115**

Weller Coppertone Spherical Vase

Vase, 7" h., large spherical form tapering to
a wide flaring neck flanked by heavy D-
form handles, signed (ILLUS.)......................... **374**

Vase, 7" h., 9" d., spherical body w/closed
handles.. **425**

Vase, 8" h., bulbous ovoid body w/molded
rim, figural frog shoulder handles, ink kiln
mark (short tight line to rim) **1,540**

Vase, 8" h., footed, bulbous base w/wide
flaring neck, large C-form handles from
mid-base to just below rim, mottled dark
green glaze, marked w/incised "M".............. **385**

Vase, 8" h., footed, two-handled spherical
base w/wide flaring rim (ILLUS. top row,
third from left with bowl and flower hold-
erf)... **265**

Coppertone Vase

Vase, 8 1/4" h., 9" w., fan-shaped top molded w/reeds above a low squatty bulbous
base composed of lily pads & molded w/a
pair of figural frogs on the shoulder,
stamp mark & artist-initialed (ILLUS.) **1,045**

Vase, 8 3/8" h., bulbous base w/trumpet-
form neck, scrolled handles from base to
below rim, incised "Weller Hand Made"
on bottom (three small burst bubbles on
back side of vase)... **220**

Vase, 8 1/2" h., footed wide trumpet form
(ILLUS. bottom row, third from right with
bowl and flower holder) **403**

Vase, bud, 9" h., 3 1/4" d., slender body
w/flaring irregular rim, frog crawling up
the side, mottled green & brown glaze.......... **467**

Vase, 9 1/8" h., round foot & trumpet-
shaped body molded around the scalloped rim w/lily pads & buds, matte olive
green shading to tan, black round stamp **374**

Vase, 10" h., trumpet-shaped w/molded lily
pads **325**

Vase, 11" h., footed bulbous base w/wide
cylindrical neck w/slightly flared rim,
large loop handles from shoulder to rim
(ILLUS. top row, second from left, with
bowl and flower holder) **431**

Vase, 11" h., footed bulbous base w/wide
trumpet-form neck, heavy strap handles,
incised "Weller Hand Made" (ILLUS. top
row, second from right, with bowl and
flower holder) **575**

Vase, 12 1/2" h., waisted cylinder w/flaring
rim, mottled green & brown glaze, in-
scribed "Weller Handmade"............................ **604**

Vase, 15 1/4" h., footed trumpet-form body
(ILLUS. bottom row, second from left,
with bowl and flower holder) **1,144**

Vase, 19" h., floor-type **750**

Dickensware 1st Line (1897-98)
*Underglaze slip-decorated designs on a brown,
green or blue ground. Glossy glaze.*

Jardiniere & pedestal, the squatty bulbous
jardiniere w/a wide, rolled rim & tapering
to a flared foot, the sides in black decorated w/a flock of walking yellow geese,

the tall cylindrical pedestal flared at the rim & base & decorated w/a scene of a little girl feeding geese all against a black ground, glossy glaze, signed, ca. 1907, 41 1/2" h., 2 pcs. **2,500-3,500**

Jug, footed spherical body w/overhead handle & small cylindrical spout, decorated w/African-American face on dark blue ground, 6 1/4" h. (reglued chips to spout) **385**

Lamp base, kerosene-type, lily of the valley decoration on dark green ground, artist-signed, 12" h... **450-600**

Mug, h.p. deer head, tall, artist-signed **125-150**

Dickensware Mug

Mug, h.p. Virginia creeper decoration by Sarah Reid McLaughlin, monogrammed in brown slip on side, impressed "Dickens Ware Weller" & "327," w/semicircular logo, 6 3/4" h. (ILLUS.) **248**

Mug, decorated w/floral design, impressed mark, 7" h.. **99**

Vase, 12 1/4" h., cylindrical body decorated w/yellow & orange chrysanthemums on shaded brown ground, decorated by Eugene Roberts, artist-initialed **605**

Vase, 17" h., baluster form w/monk decoration in orange & yellow on shaded green ground, impressed mark (restoration) **468**

Dickensware 2nd Line (early 1900s)

Various incised "sgraffito" designs usually with a matte glaze. Quality of the artwork greatly affects price.

Ewer, tall slender cylindrical body w/flaring ringed foot, C-form handle, decorated w/a bust profile portrait of "Chief Hollowhorn Bear," shaded tan to dark green ground, 16" **750-1,250**

Humidor, cov., figural, model of a Chinese man's head, realistic coloring, 5 1/2" h. **518**

Jug, footed spherical body w/overhead handle & small cylindrical spout, scene w/trees & bridge, incised "The Mt. Vernon Bridge Co. Mt. Vernon, O.," 6" h. (glaze flake to handle, pin-sized fleck to spout).. **440**

Mug, depicts detailed image of deer **175-250**

Mug, footed, waisted cylindrical body w/C-form handle, decorated w/incised & embossed fish on shaded green & turquoise ground, 5" h. **275**

Mug, tapering cylinder w/C-form handle, incised w/bust of an Indian brave on a

shaded brown & green ground by Anthony Dunlavy, artist-signed, 5 1/4" h. **413**

Mug, 5 1/2" h., decorated w/scene of monk drinking from mug, green ground.................. **385**

Mug, bust portrait of American Indian "Tame Wolf," artist-signed, 6 1/4" h....... **625-750**

Pitcher, 10 1/2" h., portrait of monk, blue & white, marked "X" **625-750**

Pitcher, tankard, 12" h., portrait of monk, orange ground (repaired) **275**

Vase, 5 1/4" h., 5 1/4" w., pocket-form, flattened bulbous ovoid sides tapering to a short flaring rim pinched together at the center, sgraffito marsh scene w/a duck & reeds by a lake in shades of brown & green, die-stamped "Dickensware - Weller - X352".. **220-250**

Vase, 6 1/2" h., footed, bulbous body w/flaring rim, incised decoration of monk in profile (two minute glaze flecks to base....... **330**

Dickensware Vase

Vase, 6 3/4" h., footed three-sided form w/three tiny loop shoulder handles, scene of fish in water on green ground (ILLUS.).. **495**

Vase, 7" h., 7 1/4" d., four-footed pillow-form body w/curved rim, by Anthony Dunalavy, decorated w/incised scene of deer leaping through woods, artist-signed (restoration to one foot & spider lines to base crawl up sides)......................... **413**

Vase, 7 3/4" h., shouldered ovoid body tapering to wide molded rim, incised w/figure of a monk on shaded brown & green ground, decorated by Anthony Dunlavy, artist-signed...................................... **275**

Vase, 8 3/4" h., 5" d., gourd-shaped body w/narrow shoulder & short flaring rim, landscape scene w/children playing, highlighted w/various colors, shaded tan & green ground, ca. 1903............................. **575**

Vase, 8 7/8" h., ovoid body w/short wide flaring neck, shows scene of a young woman wearing blue gown, sitting in a crescent moon playing a long-necked mandolin, green & yellow, decorated by Anthony Dunlavy, impressed "Dickensware - Weller" & "X31" w/"M" incised on base, artist-initialed (glaze nicks on rim)....... **385**

Vase, 9 1/4" h., slightly expanding cylindrical body w/wide flaring rim, golfing scene featuring a golfer & caddy, trees & a fence, brown, gold & blue, marked "Dick-

ensware - Weller" & impressed "X 169,"
"12" & "KVV" **2,200**

Vase, 9 1/2" h., baluster-form body
w/closed rim, scene of two Spanish galleons on stormy seas, polychrome glaze,
decorated by Carl Weigelt **1,540**

Dickensware Scenic Vase

Vase, 9 3/4" h., ovoid body decorated w/for-
est scene of semi-nude woman holding a
bunch of flowers, green trees, dark
brown glossy ground, impressed
w/"Dickens Ware Weller" semi-circular
logo & what appears to be "578" (ILLUS.) **330**

Vase, 10" h., bottle-shaped form w/scene of
man playing golf, polychrome matte
glaze on a shaded brown & green
ground, artist-initialed.................................. **1,430**

Vase, 10" h., cylindrical, decorated w/in-
cised portrait of Native American, "Chief
White Man," by L.J. Burgess........................ **1,100**

Vase, 10" h., squatty bulbous base tapering
to cylindrical body w/slightly flared rim,
scene of woman playing golf in polychrome matte glaze on shaded brown &
green ground, artist-initialed **1,760**

Vase, 11 7/8" h., tall waisted cylindrical
body w/narrow shoulder & short flaring
neck, depicts an intricately carved & colorfully painted scene of Colonial life
w/seven people, three horses & two stat-
ues in a densely wooded area, all in 18th
c. costume, brown, green, grey & black
glossy glaze, rim chip has been professionally repaired, impressed marks
"Dickensware - Weller" & "X 48," "8" &
"W" **1,540**

Vase, 12 3/8" h., slender waisted cylindrical
form w/short cylindrical neck & flaring
rim, decorated w/scene of a nude woman
& an angel w/flowers & flowering trees,
impressed "Dickens Ware Weller" (pro-
fession repair of rim chip) **896**

Vase, 12 1/2" h., tall cylindrical body w/a
narrow shoulder to the short rolled rim,
continuous landscape scene of white
mounted knights in deep woods, blue sky
above, glossy glaze.......................... **3,100-3,750**

Vase, 14" h., tall slender ovoid body w/short
narrow flared neck, decorated w/an outdoor scene showing a young mother
walking through a wooded area w/her
two daughters, all dressed in white,
shaded brown ground w/green trees in

background, artist-initialed, small chip on
rim, die-stamped "Dickensware - Weller
X 290 0".. **990**

Vase, 15" h., baluster form w/sgrafitto decoration of man w/staff between two trees,
impressed mark (restored chips) **468**

Vase, 16" h., etched scene w/hunting
dogs... **1,400-2,500**

Two Scenic Dickensware Vases

Vase, 17" h., slender cylindrical form w/in-
cised Venetian scene by C.A. Dusen-
bery, impressed mark (ILLUS. right) **1,150**

Vase, 17 1/2" h., 5 1/2" d., tall slender ovoid
form w/incised decoration of a man holding a bird saying "A Bird in the Hand is
Worth Two in the Bush," brown, blue,
pink, yellow & white, decorated by Edwin
L. Pickens, incised "Dickens, Weller, E.L.
Pickens" (minute glaze nicks to inside
rim).. **805**

Vase, 17 7/8" h., very tall slender cylindrical
body w/a narrow rounded shoulder to the
short rolled neck, decorated w/a standing
monk tasting wine, in browns & yellow
against a shaded brown to gold ground,
glossy glaze, decorated by Mary
Gellier, ca. 1900, marked & artist-signed .. **1,650**

Vase, 20" h., baluster-form w/wide cylindrical neck w/flared rim, decorated w/in-
cised & painted scene of marching sol-
diers, impressed mark, restoration
(ILLUS. left) **575**

Eocean and Eocean Rose (1898-1925)

*Early art line with various hand-painted flowers
on shaded grounds, usually with a clear glossy
glaze. Quality of artwork varies greatly.*

Candlesticks, widely flaring domed foot
supporting a swelled tapering slender
standard below the tall socket w/a wide
flattened rim, large pink & yellow blossoms around the center of the standard
w/dark charcoal above & light lavender
below, 10 1/2" h., pr. **316**

Jardiniere, h.p. red roses, leaves & branches decoration on green/grey to white
ground, 9" d., 7 1/2" h. **253**

Eocean Mug

Mug, tapering cylindrical body w/C-form handle, wild rose decoration on shaded green ground, 4 7/8" h. (ILLUS.) **138**

Pitcher, 8" h., bulbous ovoid body w/figural fish handle (firing lines) **1,980**

Vase, 4 7/8" h., pillow-form, wild rose decoration on shaded green ground, unmarked (glaze on four stubby feet a bit gritty in the making) **193**

Vase, 5" h., bulbous base tapering to flat rim, decorated w/pink & white floral spray on shaded green ground (minor scratches) **413**

Vase, 5" h., short wide cylinder w/round shoulder tapering to wide neck w/flat rim, h.p. mushroom decoration in burgundy, lavender & white on grey ground, incised & painted mark **1,210**

Vase, 5 1/8" h., squared shape, pink, white & blue flowers on slate blue ground, ca. 1910 .... **165**

Vase, 5 1/8" h., squatty bulbous body on a narrow footring, tapering to a cylindrical neck w/rolled rim, decorated around the shoulder w/large maroon & grey Virginia creeper leaves & berries, against a grey/green to pale green ground, decorated by Claude Leffler, incised "Eocean Rose Weller" & stamped "9056" artist-initialed (professionally repaired small glaze nicks on rim & foot) **303**

Vase, bud, 5 1/2" h., slip-painted florals on shaded pale blue to grey ground..................... **75**

Vase, 5 3/4" h., corseted form w/pink nasturtium on shaded grey ground, decorated by Mary Pierce, incised "Eocean-Weller 890 6" & artist-signed "MP"............... **303**

Vase, 6" h., 5" d., swelled cylindrical body w/a wide flat shoulder to the short cylindrical neck, decorated w/wild roses in ivory & red on shaded grey ground, incised "Eocean-Rose Weller 9061" **358**

Vase, 6" h., 5" d., swelled cylindrical body w/a wide flat shoulder to the short cylindrical neck, decorated w/dogwood branches in white & purple against a shaded dark blue to ivory ground, glossy glaze, marked, Eocean Rose.......................... **330**

Vase, 6 1/2" h., bulbous body tapering to cylindrical neck w/flat rim, white clover on bluish grey ground... **330**

Vase, 6 1/2" h., simple cylindrical body, decorated w/wild mushrooms on a shaded grey ground.. **770**

Vase, 6 1/2" h., 3" d., simple cylindrical body, decorated w/a large polychrome stork standing on one leg against a shaded dark grey to white ground, incised "Eocean - Weller" (crazed).................. **900-1,100**

Vase, bud, 6 5/8" h., decorated w/daisies, impressed "Weller" in large block letters **193**

Vase, 7" h., bulbous ovoid body tapering to closed rim, decorated by Frank Ferrell w/blue grapes, lavender & celadon leaves on a shaded green ground, artist-signed.. **1,430**

Vase, 7" h., swelled cylindrical body w/flat shoulder tapering to wide incurved rim, pink rose on shaded lavender ground (glaze drips from shoulder) **330**

Vase, 7" h., swelled cylindrical body w/flat shoulder tapering to wide incurved rim, white dogwood decoration on shaded lavender ground, artist-signed...................... **523**

Vase, 8" h., 2 1/2" d., slender cylindrical body w/a narrow round shoulder & short rolled neck, decorated w/purple & green lily-of-the-valley against a shaded black to light green ground, die-stamped circle mark... **400-425**

Vase, 8" h., 7 1/4" d., footed bell-shaped body centered by collared neck, four slender handles from rim to shoulder, decorated w/berries & leaves by Tot Steele **1,100**

Vase, 8 1/4" h., baluster-form body decorated w/pink cherry blossoms on a brown to grey shaded ground, stamped & incised marks... **358**

Vase, 8 1/4" h., bulbous ovoid body w/closed rim, purple gooseberries & celadon leaves on a shaded green to pink ground... **440**

Vase, 8 1/2" h., slender ovoid body decorated w/Virginia creeper against a shaded dark green to cream ground, by William Stemm, incised "Eocean Weller" "F." artist-initialed on side below leaves **660**

Vase, 8 1/2" h., waisted cylindrical form decorated w/pink flowers on green to ivory ground... **413**

Vase, 10" h., slender ovoid body decorated w/h.p. white wild roses on shaded black to grey ground... **385**

Vase, 10" h., slender ovoid body, pink thistle decoration on shaded bone to grey ground **935**

Vase, 10 3/8" h., gently tapering cylindrical body w/a swelled shoulder tapering to a short cylindrical rim, decorated w/pink wild roses on shaded green glossy ground, decorated by Levi J. Burgess, artist-signed, stamped "Weller" & incised "Eocean," "X" & "50" **935**

Vase, 10 1/2" h., slender ovoid body w/burgundy & pink flowers on celadon leaves, shaded green ground..................................... **523**

Vase, 10 1/2" h., squared shape w/pink thistle decoration on dark green shaded to cream ground, incised "Eocean Rose Weller" & "S" on bottom & impressed "447" & "4" (pinhead glaze nick on top of rim) **440**

Vase, 10 5/8" h., wide slightly tapering cylindrical body w/a wide shoulder to the compressed incurved short neck, decorated w/a band of swimming green fish against a shaded dark green to cream ground, signed, ca. 1905, Eocean Rose **2,500-2,800**

Vase, 11" h., bulbous ovoid body w/short shoulder tapering to incurved rim, decorated around upper body w/pink & lavender roses, shaded grey, white & pink ground **1,045**

Eocean Vase with Iris Decoration

Vase, 11" h., bulbous ovoid form, painted iris decoration on shaded tan & brown ground, impressed mark, artist-signed (ILLUS.) **3,163**

Vase, 11" h., ovoid shouldered body w/cylindrical neck & molded rim, red poppies on shaded green ground, unmarked **495**

Vase, 11" h., slender ovoid body decorated w/pink & purple irises on shaded grey ground (underglaze flaw) **770**

Eocean Vase with Egrets

Vase, 11" h., wide tapering cylinder decorated w/two finely detailed fluffy egrets in white, lavender, orange & red on green, cream & lavender ground, incised signature, impressed mark (ILLUS.) **2,750**

Vase, 11 1/2" h., bulbous ovoid body w/cupped rim, decorated w/snapdragons in red & celadon on shaded grey ground (overglaze slightly overfired causing minute bubbles) **880**

Vase, 12" h., tall tapering cylindrical form decorated w/yellow narcissus on celadon & lavender leaves, shaded grey ground, stamped "Weller" **1,100**

Vase, 12" h., tapering cylindrical form w/rolled rim, berry decoration in pink & red on green ground, impressed mark.......... **935**

Vase, 12 1/4" h., slender ovoid body decorated w/pears in lavender & celadon on shaded lavender ground, incised "Eocean Weller"... **880**

Eocean Vase with Blossoms

Vase, 12 1/2" h., expanding cylindrical body w/six open handles rising from narrow shoulder to flared rim, decorated pink & burgundy flowers w/yellow & green leaves, buds & stems against a glossy pale blue to green ground (ILLUS.) **1,650**

Vase, 12 1/2" h., footed tapering cylindrical body w/flaring rim, pastel daisies on black to lavender ground, unmarked............ **900**

Vase, 12 1/2" h., tall ovoid body tapering to molded rim, decorated w/branches of raspberries w/blossoms & fruit in purples & celadons on shaded ground.................... **1,100**

Vase, 12 3/4" h., tall ovoid form w/wide rolled rim, decorated w/red & white tulips & green leaves on glossy white ground, incised "Eocean - Weller," "F" & impressed "X 467," artist-signed **1,320**

Vase, 12 3/4" h., 4 3/4" d., slender tapering body w/six open handles rising from narrow shoulder to flared rim, decorated w/large green & violet leaves against a shaded pale pink & dark green ground **900-1,400**

Vase, 12 7/8" h., slender ovoid body w/wide flat mouth, wisteria decoration on shaded brown to yellow ground, glossy glaze, marked & incised "X," artist-initialed (tight 2" hairline from rim) **468**

Vase, 13" h., bulbous base tapering to tall cylindrical neck, red poppies on shaded green ground, unmarked................................ **358**

Vase, 14 1/8" h., tall cylindrical body w/the narrow flat shoulder tapering to a short rolled neck, decorated w/two finely detailed fish swimming among lily pads & flowers, dark greyish green to pale green ground, decorated by Eugene Roberts, incised "Eocean Rose Weller" & impressed with shape number 579, artist-signed.. **3,850**

Vase, 14 3/4" h., baluster-form body w/six loop shoulder handles, decorated w/lavender & grey dogwood blossoms on a shaded purple ground **2,200**

Vase, 15 1/4" h., tall slender cylindrical body w/six S-form rim handles, blue & grey hollyhocks on shaded green ground, incised "Weller Eocean" **1,320**

Vase, 16" h., cylindrical body w/six loop rim handles, decorated w/h.p. red cherries & green leaves, incised "Weller" in block letters **935**

Vase, 18" h., footed slender ovoid body w/flared rim, berries & leaves in pastel tones on shaded black to lavender ground, stamped "Weller" (shallow glaze flake to rim) **990**

Rare Large Weller Eocean Vase

Vase, 24" h., 12" h., large ovoid body tapering to a short widely flaring neck, decorated w/large white tea roses & pale green leafy stems on a dark blue shaded to creamy white ground, by Mae Timberlake, incised mark & artist-signed, couple of minor flakes on base (ILLUS.) **7,313**

Vase, bulbous ovoid tapering to rolled rim, decorated a/portrait of a spaniel w/brown eyes, shaded grey ground, incised "Eocean Weller S" & impressed "2" **1,540**

Ethel (about 1915)
Profile of Ethel Weller, in a circle, sniffing a rose. Cream color. Matt finish.

Vase, 6 1/4" h., footed fan shape w/reticulated rim & applied ring handles, floral decoration **110**

Vase, 11 1/4" h., disk foot w/tapering cylindrical body, applied ring handles & reticulated rim w/profile of young woman on each side, incised "Weller" **330**

Etna (1906)
Colors similar to Early Eocean line but designs are molded in low relief and colored.

Jardiniere, bulbous body w/shoulder tapering to flat rim, embossed w/red pansies on a shaded grey ground, impressed "Weller Etna," 5 x 6" **165**

Jardiniere, wide bulbous body w/flat rim, decorated w/embossed red thistle & green leaves on shaded green & purple ground, impressed "Eocean," 8 x 10" **193**

Jardiniere, bulbous ovoid body w/slightly flared rim, embossed w/light blue irises on a shaded green ground, stamped "Weller," 7 1/2 x 9" **193**

Lemonade set: a 14" h. tankard pitcher & two cylindrical mugs; each w/an angled handle decorated w/a large cluster of deep reddish purple grapes & green leaves at the top against a shaded grey to pink ground, signed, 3 pcs. (hairline in one mug) **400-450**

Etna Vase

Vase, 5" h., footed squatty bulbous body tapering to wide cylindrical neck w/molded rim, decorated w/purple & mauve nasturtiums, impressed "Etna" on bottom & "Weller" on side & bottom (ILLUS.) **168**

Etna Floral Vase

Vase, 5" h., 9" d., wide squatty lower body w/entwined vine handles tapering to wide flared neck, embossed floral decoration in pink & yellow w/green leaves, shaded tan to cream ground, impressed "Weller" in small block letters (ILLUS.) **165**

Vase, 5 1/2" h., simple cylindrical form, decorated w/two long-stemmed blossoms on a dark shaded to light grey ground, signed **144**

Vase, 6 1/2" h., footed angular bulbous body tapering to a wide cylindrical neck w/slightly flaring rim, slip-painted floral design **125**

Vase, 7" h., cylindrical, decorated w/yellow dandelions on grey ground **165**

Vase, 7 1/2" h., wide conical lower body tapering to a wide cylindrical neck, dark shaded to light grey ground slip-decorated w/a tall cluster of pink & red carnations on green leafy stems, impressed mark **173**

Vase, 8 3/8" h., gently flaring cylindrical body tapering to a short wide neck, decorated w/embossed flowers in pink & yellow on a shaded grey to pink ground **220**

Vase, 8 1/2" h., cylindrical body tapering to short slightly flared rim, decorated w/embossed pink thistles & green leaves on grey shaded to cream ground, marked "Weller" on side & on bottom in small block letters **248**

Vase, 10" h., cylindrical base tapering to bulbous neck w/slightly flaring rim, decorated w/embossed red & pink poppies, green leaves, bud & stem on shaded brown ground, incised "Weller" **358**

Vase, 10 1/4" h., ovoid body tapering to a wide cupped rim, dark charcoal shaded to grey ground decorated w/swags of jewel around the shoulder w/an oval reserve w/a white bust profile of a pope, unmarked.............. **316**

Vase, 10 1/2" h., tapering cylindrical body w/flat rim, dark charcoal shaded to grey, decorated at the neck & base w/lavender nasturium blooms, base impressed "Weller" & "Etna," body incised "Weller" in body near lower blooms (moderate crazing) **190**

Vase, 10 7/8" h., tall gently flaring cylindrical body w/flat shoulder tapering to a short rolled rim, embossed pink carnation decoration on dark blue shaded to pink ground **220**

Vase, 11" h., tall ovoid body w/bulbous short neck w/closed rim flanked by short twisted strap handles, low-relief floral bouquet in rosey red & pale green leafy stems against a shaded grey ground **300**

Vase, 13 3/8" h., gently swelled cylindrical body tapering to a short cylindrical neck, decorated w/embossed pink roses, grey to ivory ground **550**

Vase, 15" h., baluster-form body w/shoulder tapering to closed mouth, decorated w/embossed grape vines in blues & reds on a shaded green to grey ground, stamped "Weller" **605**

Flemish (mid-teens to 1928)
Clusters of pink roses and green leaves, often against a molded light brown basketweave ground. Some pieces molded with fruit or small figural birds. Matte glaze.

Flemish Jardiniere & Pedestal Base

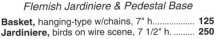

Basket, hanging-type w/chains, 7" h................. **125**
Jardiniere, birds on wire scene, 7 1/2" h. **250**

Jardiniere, wide slightly flaring cylindrical body raised on three small peg feet, molded around the bottom rim w/large lily pad leaves & pink blossoms, marked, 8" d........ **69**

Jardiniere, wide slightly swelled cylindrical body, pink floral decoration on cream ground, 8 1/2" h. **175**

Jardiniere, decorated w/four lion heads & garlands, 13" d., 10" h. **250**

Jardiniere & pedestal base, decorated w/bright blue birds, overall 32" h., firing line, 2 pcs (ILLUS.)............. **1,763**

Pedestal base, decorated w/bright blue cockatoo, 21 5/8" h. (5 1/2" portion of upper rim chipped off & reglued) **336**

Planter, figural log, 4 1/2" h.................. **35**

Tub, basket-shaped w/rim handles, rose swag on front, 8 1/2" d., 5 1/2" h............. **165**

Flemish Cylindrical Vase

Vase, 8 1/2" h., footed cylindrical body w/embossed rose tied w/yellow bow, impressed "Weller" in large block letters (ILLUS.)............. **193**

Flemish Ovoid Vase

Vase, 12 1/4" h., ovoid form w/flaring cylindrical neck, decorated w/red flowers on green vines, brown matte glaze, minor chip,impressed mark (ILLUS.)....... **748**

Fleron (late '20s)
Green glaze, made to look hand turned (called Ansonia if blue or grey). Middle period.

Fleron Jar

Jar, wide, flat-bottomed ovoid body tapering to a four-lobed widely rolled mouth, molded rope handles at the shoulder, shaded green exterior & pink interior, incised "Weller Ware Hand Made," 6 3/8" h. (ILLUS.) **193**

Forest (mid-teens to 1928)
Realistically molded and painted forest scene.

Basket, footed, flaring conical shape w/overhead handle, unmarked, 7 x 10"......... **234**
Jardiniere, 3 1/4" h., unmarked........................... **55**
Planter, tub-shaped w/rim handles, 6 1/2" d., 4 1/4" h. **83**

Cylindrical Weller Forest Vase

Vase, 8" h., cylindrical w/slightly flared rim (ILLUS.) **124**

Forest Vase

Vase, 8" h., waisted cylinder w/flaring rim, marked "H-" in black slip (ILLUS.).................. **165**

Vase, 8" h., waisted cylinder w/flaring rim (minute flake to foot) **132**

Tall Flaring Weller Forest Vase

Vase, 12" h., tall footed expanding cylindrical body w/flaring rim (ILLUS.) **250-350**
Wall pocket, w/copper liner, conical w/owl peering out of tree trunk, die-stamped "Weller," 5 1/2 x 11" (mold firing line, small chip to hanging hole, couple of minor nicks to high points)................................. **303**

Geode (1934)
A line of simple forms decorated with blue stars and comets on a white background or white stars and comets on a medium blue background.

Scarce Weller Geode Vase

Vase, 6" h., a small footring below the broad bulbous squatty ovoid body tapering to a small flared neck, blue ground w/white stars & comets, small glaze miss, glaze chip in base (ILLUS.) **748**

Glendale (early to late 1920s)
Various relief-molded birds in their natural habitats, lifelike coloring.

Candleholders, flared base tapering to cupped socket, chickadees among flowering cherry branches, 2 1/2" h., pr. (restoration to base of one)................................... **275**

Console bowl, decorated w/molded sea gulls in yellow, blue, brown & green, 15" d. **413**

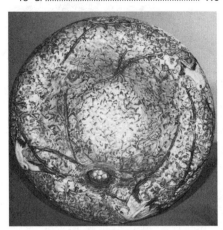

Glendale Bowl

Console bowl w/flower frog, round w/wide flared rim, decorated w/nesting birds w/eggs, 15 1/2" d. bowl marked "Weller" in black slip, frog impressed "Weller" in large block letters (ILLUS. of bowl)............... **770**

Console set: 16" d. bowl w/flower frog & pr. of 5 1/2" d. candleholders; embossed w/flying chickadees among flowering cherry branches, the set (opposing hairlines to base of frog)... **880**

Vase, 4 1/2" h., bulbous body, wooded scene of wren in nest, unmarked **220**

Vase, 6" h., cylindrical, large standing marsh bird.. **400**

Vase, 6 1/2" h., footed bulbous ovoid w/flared rim, embossed w/polychrome marsh scene of rook & nest (firing line to base).. **715**

Vase, 6 1/2" h., ovoid body w/slightly tapering neck & a flat rim, decorated w/outdoor scene of a bird in flight............................ **365**

Vase, 7" h., baluster-form body w/gently flaring rim, decorated w/a brown bird standing beside its ground nest w/eggs, green grass & white & yellow daisies under a blue sky in background.......................... **450**

Vase, double-bud, 7" h., gate-form, tree trunk-form vases flank a panel embossed w/a bird & nest w/four eggs, original label **326**

Vase, double-bud, 4 3/4 x 8", gate-form, square shape, wren & grapevine decoration **303**

Vase, 8 1/2" h., ovoid body, decorated w/bridge scene & wrens in a nest, polychrome glazes.. **880**

Vase, 9" h., flaring cylindrical body w/narrow angled shoulder to the flat mouth, molded w/two love birds in color on a leafy tree branch, stamped mark.................... **776**

Vase, 10" h., slender ovoid w/short rolled rim, decorated w/red & blue flowers & berries & a blue & yellow bird w/nest in tree, molded McLaughlin signature on reverse, impressed mark **523**

Glendale Vase

Vase, 11 3/8" h., bulbous base tapering to cylindrical neck & flat rim, decorated w/long-legged plover guarding a nest of speckled eggs surrounded by cattails & a patch of wild berries in red & deep blue, ink stamped "Weller Ware" (ILLUS.) **1,568**

Vase, 11 1/2" h., bulbous base tapering to cylindrical neck & flat rim, embossed polychrome glaze decoration of a quail & nest in gladed thicket (fleck to manufacturing defect at base) **825**

Vase, 11 7/8" h., baluster-form tapering to flaring rim, decorated scene of a goldfinch on a nest, yellow & orange butterflies, thistles & daisies, ink stamped "Weller Ware," no artist signature **1,904**

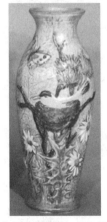

Artist-signed Glendale Vase

Vase, 11 7/8" h., baluster-form w/trumpet neck, decorated w/h.p. scene of a goldfinch on a nest, butterflies, thistles & daisies, artist-signed "Dorothy England" & marked w/the circular "Weller Ware" ink stamp logo (ILLUS.) **1,210**

Vase, 12 7/8" h., ovoid body w/short cylindrical neck, w/scene of nesting bird w/eggs in a swampy, cattail-filled area, impressed "Weller" in large block letters.... **1,925**

Wall pocket, half round bulbous form w/sharply pointed backplate w/hanging hole, two chickadees on a flowering cherry blossom branch, 7 x 7 1/4" **468**

Glendale Wall Pocket

Wall pocket, gate-form, center oval form w/chickadee in nest, pointed backplate w/hanging hole, flanked by cylindrical slender tree trunk-form bud vases, unmarked, 7 1/4 x 7 1/2" (ILLUS.) **523**

Wall pocket, conical, polychrome decoration w/wrens on a branch, unmarked, 5 x 8 3/4" (firing line to rim) **358**

Wall pocket, cornucopia-form w/curved tall, arched & scalloped backplate pierced w/a hanging hole, the base molded w/a wren & its young on a flowering cherry blossom branch, unmarked, 6 1/2 x 12 1/2" **523**

Greenbriar (early 1930s)
Hand-made shapes with green underglaze covered with flowing pink overglaze marbleized with maroon striping.

Greenbriar Vase

Vase, 4 5/8" h., bulbous twist-form body w/wide tapering cylindrical neck, unmarked (ILLUS.) **83**

Vase, 7 1/2" h., compressed bulbous base w/ovoid body & flared rim, one Art Deco design handle at base on one side w/another at the shoulder on the opposite side **110**

Vase, 8 1/2" h., an ovoid lower half below a wide trumpet-form upper half, mottled & streaked shades of green on a lavender ground **69**

Vase, 8 3/4" h., bulbous ovoid body tapering to wide cylindrical neck w/flared rim, greenish purple drip glaze **154**

Vase, 15 1/2" h., handled **525**

Greora (early 1930s)
Various shapes with a bicolor orange shaded to green glaze splashed overall with brighter green. Semigloss glaze.

Strawberry pot, ovoid body w/openings around the upper half, 5" h. **165**

Greora Vase

Vase, 7 1/4" h., footed, bulbous ovoid w/round shoulder tapering to short cylindrical neck, small shoulder handles, incised "E" (ILLUS.) **220**

Vase, 8 3/4" h., cylindrical, incised "Weller Pottery" in script & marked "1B" in black slip on bottom **193**

Vase, 9" h., wide cylindrical body w/flat rim **297**

Greora Wall Pocket

Wall pocket, arrowhead shape w/pointed overhead handle, marked w/the letter "X" painted in black slip on the back, 10 3/8" h. (ILLUS.) **358**

Hudson (1917-34)
Underglaze slip-painted decoration, "parchment-vellum" transparent glaze.

Candlestick, cylindrical w/flaring base & cupped socket w/floral decoration by Mae Timberlake, pink & shaded grey ground, artist-initialed in black slip among the flowers, 8 5/8" h. **303**

Lamp base, footed, spherical base w/tall square-form body, molded pink pansy at top of each panel, white & grey ground, 13" h. (restored original lamp base) **319**

Hudson Winter Scenic Vase

Vase, 6 3/8" h., bulbous base on narrow foot ring, wide cylindrical neck w/slightly flaring rim, decorated w/detailed scene of a two-story house in a pine forest, nestled in deep snow, snow-covered trees blow in the wind, artist-signed "Timberlake" on side in black slip, base is incised w/"31" & "Weller Pottery" (ILLUS.) **6,325**

Vase, 6 7/8" h., ovoid body w/wide flat rim, blue pansy decoration by Edith Hood, pink shaded to green ground, marked w/full kiln "Weller Pottery" ink stamp logo (tight line at rim) **220**

Hudson Lake Scenic Vase

Vase, 7" h., bulbous ovoid w/narrow footring & flaring rim, decorated by Hester Pillsbury w/a scene of trees near a lake & a blue cloud-filled sky, shades of blue, green & white (ILLUS.) **3,100**

Vase, 7" h., swelled cylindrical body w/a flaring base & widely flaring rim, decorated around the top w/a pink, yellow & blue blossom against a group of pale green leaves all against a shaded white to pale green ground, decorated by Sara Timberlake, ca. 1920, marked.............. **250-275**

Vase, 7" h., 3 1/2" d., ovoid, decorated w/white & pink dogwood blossoms against a blue shading to cream to pink ground, artist-signed **300-350**

Vase, 7 1/2" h., octagonal ovoid body w/flat rim, pastel orange & yellow wild rose decoration around top, grey shading to light green ground, faintly impressed "Weller" in small block letters (some dirty crazing especially on interior) **303**

Vase, 7 7/8" h., ovoid body w/flat rim, decorated w/white & yellow wild roses, artist-signed, silver foil half kiln label over a half kiln ink stamp logo **448**

Hudson Winter Landscape Vase

Vase, 8" h., bulbous ovoid body w/rolled rim, decorated w/a colorful winter landscape scene w/a fox standing beside a blue stream & near nicely detailed snow-covered conifers & deciduous trees, by Hester Pillsbury w/"Pillsbury" in black slip, incised "43" & "Weller Pottery" (ILLUS.) **7,425**

Vase, 8" h., footed bulbous ovoid body tapering to a short wide cylindrical neck w/molded rim, loop handles from shoulder to rim, decorated w/branches of flowering cherry blossoms in white on a shaded brown ground, by Mae Timberlake, ink-stamped "Weller Ware".................. **770**

Hudson Floral Vase

Vase, 8" h., footed bulbous spherical body w/flaring rim, loop shoulder handles, white flowers & large green leaves on green to blue ground, decorated by Hester Pillsbury & marked w/half kiln "Weller Pottery" ink stamp logo & "Pillsbury" on side in black slip, w/original paper label (ILLUS.).. **880**

Vase, 8" h., 5" d., footed bulbous spherical body w/flaring rim, loop shoulder handles, decorated w/blossoming branches in pink tones against a shaded ground, by Mae Timberlake, artist-initialed, kiln mark... **990**

Vase, 8 1/4" h., baluster-form w/flaring rim, decorated w/blue flowers & green leaves on green shaded to pink ground, by Naomi Walch, marked w/half kiln ink stamp logo & artist-signed............................. **715**

Vase, 8 1/4" h., 3" d., cylindrical, decorated w/large blue & yellow iris on a pale yellow to pale sage green ground, matte glaze, artist-signed.. **495**

Vase, 8 1/4" h., 3 1/2" d., baluster-form, decorated w/slip-painted trefoil blossoms in dark & light blue w/green leaves on a blue to cream ground, die-stamped "WELLER"... **350-400**

Vase, 8 1/2" h., cylindrical form decorated w/several sailboats plying quiet blue sea while sea gulls fly overhead, shaded pink ground, decorated by Sarah Reid McLaughlin, artist-signed on side w/"A" in black slip on base **3,850**

Vase, 8 5/8" h., decorated w/a Spanish caravel under full sail moving over blue sea w/white-capped waves, two other crafts behind, flying sea gulls accompany the boats, shaded blue to pink ground w/red & yellow designs on sails, decorated by Hester Pillsbury, artist-signed on side, the base marked w/the letter "A" in black slip... **4,510**

Vase, 8 3/4" h., trumpet-form, decorated w/multicolored daisies & leaves by Dorothy England, shaded green to pink ground, half kiln ink stamp Weller logo & artist-signed "D. England" in black slip.......... **550**

Vase, 8 7/8" h., swelled cylindrical body w/a short molded mouth, decorated w/large white jonquils on pale green leafy stems against a green to pale cream ground, stamped "Weller" in block letters............ **450-500**

Hudson Vase with Lily of the Valley

Vase, 9" h., ovoid body w/elaborate decoration of lily of the valley in cream w/green leaves on a blue to green ground, signed "Hood," stamp mark (ILLUS.)...................... **1,045**

Vase, 9 1/4" h., 4 3/4" d., wide ovoid body w/flaring rim, purple & blue irises on periwinkle blue ground, decorated by H. Pillsbury, artist-signed, ink stamp (stilt-pull chip to base).. **2,970**

Hudson Vase with Iris Decoration

Vase, 9 3/8" h., footed cylindrical body w/flat rim, decorated w/blue & yellow irises in very heavy slip by Mae Timberlake, shaded green to yellow ground, professional repair of two cracks at rim, artist-signed (ILLUS.)... **605**

Vase, 9 3/8" h., swelled cylindrical shouldered body w/a short rounded neck w/flat rim, decorated around the top half w/large creamy white nasturtium blossoms & green leaves & vines against a shaded blue to pale green ground, decorated by Sarah McLaughlin, ca. 1920, artist-signed & marked............................ **500-550**

Vase, 9 1/2" h., bulbous base w/wide cylindrical neck & flat rim, decorated w/water lilies & leaves on shaded grey ground, stamped "Weller"... **385**

Vase, 9 1/2" h., footed cylinder w/h.p. blue & white iris w/green leaves, decorated by Mae Timberlake, artist-signed & incised "Weller Pottery"... **1,760**

Vase, 9 1/2" h., 5" d., swelling cylindrical body w/a wide shoulder tapering to a short wide mouth, decorated around the upper half w/large white & blue morning glories & green leaves against a shaded blue to green ground, decorated by Hester Pillsbury, artist's initials on side, black kiln mark on base **600-650**

Vase, 9 3/4 x 9 3/4", footed spherical body w/flared rim, loop shoulder handles, pink trumpet vines on shaded blue ground, decorated by H. Pillsbury, artist-signed, incised "Weller Pottery" **1,430**

Vase, 10 1/4" h., footed bulbous base tapering to cylindrical neck w/flat rim, white dogwood decoration by Hester Pillsbury, grey shading to pink ground, impressed "Weller" in script & artist-initialed **770**

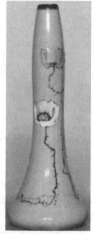

Unusual Hudson Bud Vase

Vase, bud, 10 1/4" h., slender waisted cylinder w/flaring base, decorated w/pink & white poppies on trailing stems in stylish Art Nouveau manner, glossy tan ground w/dark band at rim, impressed "Weller" in large block letters (ILLUS.) **770**

Vase, 10 1/2" h., footed, bulbous base tapering to wide cylindrical neck w/molded rim, yellow daisies on shaded green ground, decorated by Mae Timberlake, artist-initialed & stamped "Weller" **825**

Vase, 10 5/8" h., cylindrical body w/short slightly flared rim, blackberry decoration in pastel colors on light grey shading to yellow ground, impressed "Weller" in small block letters **440**

Vase, 11" h., 'Hudson Light,' tall slender ovoid body tapering to a molded rim, decorated w/large pastel pink & white iris blossoms w/pale green leaves & stems against a shaded dark to light green ground, signed (few small glaze imperfections in the making) **385**

Large Hudson Vase with Roses

Vase, 12" h., ovoid body w/cylindrical neck & slightly flaring rim, front decorated w/large rose blossoms w/a bee & roses on the obverse, by Hester Pillsbury, minor flake to base, incised mark (ILLUS.).... **2,530**

Vase, 12 1/8" h., ovoid body tapering to flaring rim, red & blue hollyhocks on a medium blue ground, decorated by Mae Timberlake, artist-signed on side in dark blue slip, impressed "Weller" (professional repair to rim chip) **770**

Vase, 12 1/4" h., bulbous ovoid body tapering to a cylindrical neck w/flaring rim, decorated w/a scene depicting a distant city across a bay, tall bamboo shoots & leaves tower over sea gulls flying toward wood pilings in the bay, impressed "Weller" (a 1/2" drill hole in bottom professionally repaired) **2,200**

Vase, 13 1/2" h., urn-form, the wide ovoid body tapering to a short cylindrical neck w/rolled rim, wide strap handles from neck to shoulder, decorated w/a scenic design of a large peacock resting near a large wrought-iron gate & stone fence in shades of blue, white, yellow, green & black against a mottled blue-green to tan ground, attributed to Mae Timberlake, the base marked w/a letter "A" in black slip **4,500-6,000**

Vase, 15 1/4" h., 6 1/2" d., ovoid, white & blue iris & green leaves on shaded blue & pale pink matte ground, decorated by Sarah McLaughlin, artist-signed & incised "Weller" (glaze flake at base, minor glaze scrape to shoulder) **1,100**

Vase, 15 1/2" h., ovoid body w/wide flaring rim, h.p. large yellow, pink & purple irises on shaded blue ground, decorated by Mae Timberlake, drilled base, artist-signed & stamped "Weller" **2,310**

Wall pocket, conical, decorated w/pink & white wild roses on a shaded blue matte ground, die-stamped "Weller" 7 1/4 x 2 1/2" (minor nick to back) **550**

Hunter (before 1910)

Brown with under-the-glaze slip decoration of ducks, butterflies and probably other outdoor subjects. Signed only "HUNTER." High gloss glaze. Usually incised decoration.

Vase, 4 1/4" h., 6" w., a squatty bulbous body formed as six incurved panels, the wide top centered by a short flaring neck, sgraffito decoration on three panels w/a fish under water in brown & greens, glossy glaze, by Upjohn, incised "UJ" on the side, die-stamped "N36-2" on the base **500**

Hunter Vase

Vase, 5" h., pillow form w/incised & painted scene w/duck in browns & green, glossy glaze, impressed mark (ILLUS.) **403**

Vase, 6" h., flattened tapering three-sided body w/rounded corners below an incurvate round rim, three applied strap handles, decorated w/swimming fish in bluish water against a shaded green ground, incised "Hunter" & stamped "356 - 3 -X," artist-initialed **385**

Vase, 7" h., footed bulbous body w/wide shoulder tapering to small cylindrical neck w/molded rim, decorated w/flying duck, shaded brown & green ground, glossy glaze **431**

Ivory (1910 to late 1920s)

Ivory-colored body with various shallow embossed designs with rubbed-on brown highlights.

Ivory Jardiniere

Jardiniere, round squatty bulbous sides w/incurved closed mouth, decorated w/Eskimo & moose designs, unmarked, 11 1/2" d., 7 3/4" h. (ILLUS.) **413**

Jardiniere & pedestal, tapering jardiniere bowl on scrolled feet w/molded Art Nouveau women & scrolling on sides, on matching pedestal, 2 pcs............................ **2,090**

Planter, rose trellis design, 5 1/2 x 7 1/2", 7 1/2" h. **195**

Vase, 10" h., waisted cylindrical form w/floral & fruit design around the top & ornate design of alternating openings & ram heads around base, unmarked...................... **176**

Vase, 11" h., decorated w/molded peacocks design.. **80**

Vase, 12" h., decorated w/peacocks **110**

Wall pocket, figural stag's head, 6 1/2 x 8 3/4" (glaze scaling & a few chips to several edges, hairline from hole) **248**

Window box, embossed Victorian nudes, 7 x 13".. **275-350**

Window box, w/relief-molded classic scenes of cherubs, putti, griffins & horses, "Weller" impressed in large block letters, repair to small chips at high points & to one handle, 20 3/8" l, 8" h........................... **550**

Jap Birdimal (1904)

Stylized Japanese-inspired figural bird or animal designs on various solid colored grounds.

Jap Birdimal Umbrella Stand

Hair receiver, decorated w/four Norse sailing ships, dark blue ground, artist's initials "VH," 4" w., 2" h. **209**

Jardiniere, bulbous body w/wide flat rim, decorated landscape scene of blue trees, yellow moon, grey ground, 8" h. (hairline crack)... **275**

Umbrella stand, wide cylindrical form w/narrow shoulder & slightly flaring rim, landscape decoration w/large blue trees, impressed mark, minor chips, 20" h. (ILLUS.).. **1,035**

Vase, 4 1/2" h., spherical body on three outswept knob feet, tricorner rounded rim, bluish grey ground decorated w/two white geese in flight.. **265**

Vase, bud, 5 1/2" h., cylinder w/bulbous top, decorated w/stylized peacock feathers on a dark green ground **990**

Vase, 6" h., bulbous body w/wide shoulder & short molded rim, decorated w/a scene of a Japanese maiden under a stylized tree, green ground, (glazed stilt-pull to base)... **605**

Vase, 6" h., shouldered ovoid body w/molded rim, decorated in squeezebag w/swimming blue carp on a green ground, unmarked **1,100**

Jap Birdimal Vase with Geisha

Vase, 7" h., ovoid shouldered body tapering to flat mouth, decorated w/geisha girl w/stringed musical instrument, gold, cream, brown, black & green, outlined by slip trailing w/green & yellow leaf decoration around shoulder & green stems around base, small line in base, possibly in the making, impressed "804" & "5" & incised artist's initials "C.M.M." (ILLUS.).... **1,320**

Vase, 7 1/2" h., decorated w/black cat, back & tail raised, lime green ground **935**

Vase, 10 1/2" h., footed waisted cylindrical body w/tapering shoulder & short slightly flared neck, geisha girl in multicolored robe holding umbrella, trees in background, incised "Weller Rhead Faience," artist-initialed "L.S." **1,980**

Vase, 11 3/4" h., ovoid body w/tapering shoulder, short neck w/flaring rim, squeezebag decoration w/geisha playing shamisen under stylized trees, tan, blue & red on brown ground, incised "Weller - Rhead Faience" (couple of shallow scratches to body, two glazed-over glaze flecks to rim, stilt-pull chip to base) **1,045**

Rare Jap Birdimal Weller Vase

Vase, 12 7/8" h., very tall slender & slightly waisted cylindrical form w/an angled shoulder tapering to a short wide trumpet neck, decorated w/a full-length geisha girl & stylized trees in slip-trail outline, glossy glazed in shades of olive green, yellow, rust, brown & blue on a black ground, incised "Weller Faience - Rhead," ca. 1904 (ILLUS.) **1,955**

Vase, 14" h., simple ovoid form decorated in squeezebag w/landscape scene w/trees, grey ground (glaze misses to base, short lines & restored rim flakes).............................. **385**

Jewell & Cameo Jewell (about 1910-15)

Similar to the Etna line but most pieces molded with a band of raised oval 'jewels' or jewels and cameo portraits in color against a light or dark shaded ground.

Vase, 7 1/2" h., ovoid body, decorated front & back w/incised design of fern fronds w/swirling blue jewels on a blue, green & light pink ground, impressed mark................ **770**

Jewell Vase

Vase, 11" h., ovoid, decorated w/relief-molded vine & leaf design w/red flowers & jewels, impressed mark (ILLUS.) **978**

Knifewood (late teens)

Pieces feature deeply molded designs of dogs, swans, and other birds and animals or flowers in white or cream against dark brown grounds.

Jardiniere, w/swan decoration, impressed "Weller" in large block letters (two dark lines at rim mostly visible from inside, one a tight crack) **193**

Tobacco jar, cov., barrel-shaped w/low domed cover w/button finial, the sides molded in relief w/a continuous scene of a hunting dog & wild fowl in shades of dark & light brown, impressed mark, 6 1/2" h. **920**

Knifewood Vase

Vase, 5" h., squatty bulbous body w/wide flat rim, decorated w/molded goldfinches on branches of wisteria, impressed "Weller" in large block letters (ILLUS.) **770**

Vase, 6" h., squatty bulbous body w/wide flat rim, decorated w/molded blue & yellow birds sitting on branches w/cherries, impressed "Weller" in large block letters....... **495**

Vase, 7 1/4" h., ovoid body embossed w/daisies & butterflies on a textured ground, unmarked **275**

Vase, 11 1/2" h., waisted cylindrical body, peacock among trees & roses in pale polychrome on a green ground, unmarked **660**

L'Art Nouveau (1903-04)

Various figural and floral-embossed Art Nouveau designs.

Cane stand, bamboo stalk-shaped, embossed w/climbing sunflowers, matte green & yellow, unmarked, 34 1/2" h. (several glaze flakes & one large chip to base)... **1,430**

L'Art Nouveau Powder Box

Powder jar, cov., footed round body w/cabochons, restored, 4 1/2" d. (ILLUS.) **275**

Vase, bud, 7 1/4" h., flaring base w/two figural birds holding a lily bud (short tight line to body, touch-up to nick at rim) **495**

Unusual L'Art Nouveau Vase

Vase, 8" h., slender four-sided body w/molded florals at the top, decorated on one side w/embossed figure of young woman & floral decoration on the other side, semi-gloss glaze of rose to blue to cream, marked "Weller" in small block letters, unobtrusive stilt pulls on bottom (ILLUS.) **248**

L'Art Nouveau Four-sided Vase

Vase, 10 1/4" h., slender four-sided body w/embossed panels of flowers & Art Nouveau woman, impressed "Weller" in small block letters (ILLUS.)...................................... **358**
Vase, 11" h., two-handled, footed pillow-form body w/flared scalloped rim, embossed w/flowers **385**

Large L'Art Nouveau Vase

Vase, 11 1/4" h., waisted cylindrical body w/four-lobed base & molded florals at top, very minor glaze rubs on one side at bottom, impressed "Weller" in small block letters (ILLUS.)... **440**
Vase, 12" h., tall cylindrical body swelled at the top & tapering to a closed rim, molded at the top w/large peach & brown irises against a shaded green & tan ground, matte glaze, impressed mark **825**
Vase, 12" h., tapering four-sided body w/scalloped rim & shaped base, embossed flowers near rim **220**
Vase, 12 3/4" h., four-sided tapering vase embossed w/fruits & flowers, scalloped rim (minor glaze scaling to rim, nick to leaf, burst blemish) **440**

Lasa (1920-25)

Various landscapes on a banded reddish and gold iridescent ground. Lack of scratches and abrasions important.

Lasa Stylized Floral Vase

Vase, 3 1/2" h., bulbous body w/short rolled rim, decorated w/stylized green flowers & geometric designs on reddish & gold iridescent ground, unmarked (ILLUS.) **275**
Vase, 3 5/8" h., wide bulbous body w/short rolled rim, decorated w/h.p. yellow flowers w/green leaves & stems on gold iridescent ground w/reddish rim **248**
Vase, 4" h., lakeside scene w/three pines, lake & mountains, iridescent glaze **350**

Lasa Vase

Vase, 6" h., footed wide ovoid body decorated w/a frieze of foliage & berries, gold, green & magenta glaze, unmarked (ILLUS.)... **660**
Vase, 6 1/4" h., footed, tapering cylindrical body decorated w/landscape scene

w/oak trees on iridescent ground (two very small glaze flakes, light wear) **165**

Vase, 6 1/4" h., scenic decoration w/mountains, ocean, palm trees **423**

Vase, 6 1/2" h., ovoid body tapering to rolled rim, decorated w/scene of mountain lake sunset, iridescent glaze, signed "Weller - Lasa" **393**

Vase, 7 1/4" h., wide disk foot supporting a slender trumpet-form body, decorated w/a landscape of bare trees (small nick on base) **138**

Vase, 7 5/8" h., slender trumpet-shaped body w/widely flaring foot, decorated w/landscape done in gold, reddish & green gold, iridescent metallic glaze **325-400**

Vase, 10" h., footed, wide ovoid body tapering to a flat mouth, decorated w/scene of pine trees & water, gold iridescent ground **468**

Vase, 12" h., wide flaring foot tapering to slender cylindrical body & flat rim, decorated w/a scene of twisted trees on shoreline, red, green & gold, artist-signed (worn glaze) **198**

Vase, 16" h., ovoid body tapering to cylindrical neck w/slightly flaring rim, decorated w/water scene, two palm trees in the foreground, on an iridescent ground **2,070**

Louwelsa (1896-1924)

Hand-painted underglaze slip decoration on dark brown shading to yellow ground; glossy yellow glaze.

Candlestick, squatty bulbous base w/narrow cylindrical neck, spout-shaped candle cup & ornate D-form handle, floral decoration, artist-initialed, impressed mark, 6" h. **286**

Candlestick, decorated w/pansies, 10" h. **225**

Clock, curvilinear stylized five-point star-shaped case decorated w/chrysanthemum blossoms in orange & yellow on standard glaze brown ground, artist-initialed "ER" on side, round white enamel clock face w/black Roman numerals, impressed "Louwelsa Weller," early 20th c., 10" h. (minor foot chip) **863**

Clock, mantel-type, scalloped case w/orange nasturtiums, Gilbert clock works, stamped "Louwelsa Weller 706," 4 x 10 1/2 x 12 1/2" (colored-in chip to side & a few glaze flakes & chip to base) **523**

Louwelsa Table Clock

Clock, table model, scalloped case decorated w/yellow daffodils, tiny base repair, artist-signed (ILLUS.) **650-700**

Cruet, bulbous body decorated w/palm fronds, by Mary Gillie, impressed "Louwelsa Weller," artist-initialed, 4 3/8" h. **83**

Ewer, squatty bulbous body decorated w/cherry blossoms, impressed "Louwelsa Weller," 6 1/2" h. **165**

Louwelsa Humidor

Humidor, cov., bulbous body decorated w/h.p. matches & pipes, decorated by Lizabeth Blake, artist-initialed & impressed "Louwelsa Weller" & "X 176 6," lid chips repaired, tiny glaze nicks off rim, 6 1/2" h. (ILLUS.) **550**

Jardiniere, wide flaring waisted cylindrical body w/a wide molded rim, decorated w/a large yellow iris among green leaves on a shaded brown & ochre ground, glossy glaze, impressed mark, 9" h. (glaze scratches) **288**

Lamp base, wide squatty baluster-form body on scrolled tab feet, decorated w/large yellow iris & green leaves on a shaded dark brown to yellow ground, early 20th c., original oil font & burner adapted for electricity, marked on the base, 10 7/8" h. **880**

Louwelsa Banquet Lamp

Lamp base, banquet-type, trumpet-shaped body w/narrow flat shoulder & short rolled neck, lily decoration done by Minnie Mitchell, artist's name on side & impressed "Louwelsa Weller," "K 617" & half circle logo inside base, metal sleeve for oil font fits inside rim, early 1900s, 26 5/8" h. (ILLUS.) **3,300**

Mug, slightly tapering cylindrical body w/a thick D-form handle, decorated w/the bust portrait of a smiling monk in dark brown, rust & blue against a dark brown ground, decorated by Levi J. Burgess, ca. 1898, marked, 5 7/8" h. (very minor glaze scratches) **250-300**

Pitcher, 4 1/8" h., tapering cylindrical body w/pinched spout & C-form handle, decorated w/palm fronds, by William F. Hall, impressed "Louwelsa Weller" & "X 215 11" (small rim chips) **83**

Pitcher, 12" h., tankard-type, cavalier decoration, artist-signed (repaired) **385**

Pitcher, 16 3/4" h., tankard-type, a flaring ringed base below the tall slender & slightly tapering body w/a rim spout & a C-form handle halfway down the side, decorated w/dark yellowish brown clusters of grapes on leafy vines against a dark shaded ground, artist-signed & marked on base **518**

Planter, cylindrical tree trunk form w/three small foxes peeking out at side, 4 1/2" h. **330**

Vase, 'Green Louwelsa,' tall very slender cylindrical body w/a slightly flaring foot, the narrow shoulder tapering to a short flaring neck, decorated w/a long swirled school of grey & white fish down the sides against a shaded black to dark green to pale yellowish green ground **4,000**

Vase, 3 1/2" h., jug-shaped, bright yellow floral decoration on dark brown ground **175**

Vase, 5" h., pillow-form, decorated w/wild roses, impressed "Louwelsa Weller" on bottom (minor scratches).................................. **83**

Vase, 5 1/2" h., globular body w/stick neck, decorated w/wild rose, artist-signed **250**

Vase, 6 1/2" h., slightly tapering cylindrical body, carnation decoration, impressed "Louwelsa Weller 525 K"........................... **165**

Vase, 6 5/8" h., 'Blue Louwelsa,' plain cylindrical body decorated in shades of dark blue w/large poppies, base stamped "Louwelsa Weller" & "X 516" & incised "7," ca. 1900 .... **600-650**

Unusual Louwelsa Pillow Vase

Vase, 7" h., pillow-form, decorated w/scene of a small house at end of a dirt path w/scruffy plants in foreground & cloudy sky in background, impressed "Louwelsa Weller 41 0" (ILLUS.) **1,100**

Vase, 9" h., tapering cylindrical form w/wild rose decoration, unmarked, (very minor scratches & glaze inconsistencies) **193**

Vase, 9 1/4" h., bottle-shaped body w/flaring ruffled neck, decorated w/yellow nasturtiums, stamped mark (small bruise & nick to rim) **303**

Vase, 9 1/2" h., pillow-form, footed, hollyhock decoration, artist-initialed, impressed mark (minor scratches).................... **358**

Rare Red Louwelsa Vase

Vase, 10 1/2" h., cylindrical form decorated w/white stylized rose design on red ground, minor chip to lip (ILLUS.) **3,450**

Vase, 10 1/2" h., ovoid form w/flaring rim, decorated w/wild roses, incised artist's initials on side (professional repair to rim, area of loose glaze on shoulder)................... **193**

Vase, 10 1/2" h., wide cylindrical body decorated w/bright red wild roses, possibly by Albert Haubich, impressed on bottom, "Louwelsa Weller 602 5" & artist initialed "A.H." on side (glaze scratches) **358**

Vase, 12" h., tall slender ovoid w/loop handles from shoulder to rim, green leaf & berry decoration (minor scratches to rim)..... **385**

Vase, 13 1/2" h., tall slender cylindrical body w/a narrow flat shoulder to a short rolled neck, h.p. bust portrait of a Cavalier in brown, black, tan & cream against a black shaded to green shaded to brown ground **3,300**

Vase, 15" h., 11" d., wide bulbous body tapering to short cylindrical neck w/flared rim, large h.p. roses on shaded brown ground, decorated by Hester Pillsbury....... **3,080**

Vase, 18 1/2" h., slightly tapering cylindrical shouldered body w/small flaring neck, decorated w/lifelike red & purple grapes hanging from finely detailed vine, by Frank Ferrell, impressed "Louwelsa Weller" logo & "200" & "55" (professional repair of small base chip) **1,540**

Vase, 19 3/4" h., squatty bulbous base w/trumpet-form neck, wild rose decoration, base impressed "Weller Louwelsa, 9, 8, X 271," decorated by Sarah Reid McLaughlin & artist-signed just below flower (scuff marks & glaze flakes off rim) **468**

Vase, 24" h., 8 3/4" d., floor-type, baluster-shaped body w/a tall flaring neck, decorated w/yellow & orange carnations w/green foliage, on a shaded brown ground, decorated by Eugene Roberts, artist's initials...................................... **1,500-2,000**

Mammy Line (1935)

Figural black mammy pieces or pieces with figural black children as handles.

Batter bowl, large **995**
Cookie jar, cov., 11" **2,161**
Creamer, little black boy figural handle,
3 1/2" h. **500-650**
Creamer & cov. sugar bowl, pr. **1,450**
Sugar bowl, cov., 3 1/2" h. **1,150**
Syrup pitcher, cov., 6" h. **700-775**
Teapot, cov. **800-1,100**

Marbleized (Bo Marblo, 1915)

Simple shapes with swirled "marbleized" clays, usually in browns and blues.

Bowl, cov., 7" d., 3 1/2" h., wide bulbous shape w/eared handles, knob finial on lid, swirled green & cream high glaze **176**
Compote, 8" h., 5" d., flaring foot tapering to tall cylindrical stand supporting shallow round bowl w/flattened rim, swirled brown & cream, impressed mark **88**
Console bowl, swirled brown, 10" d. **55**
Vase, 7" h., slightly flaring cylindrical sides below a slightly tapering wide neck, swirled colors of dark brown, tan & blue, impressed mark on base **138**
Vase, 9 1/2" h., swelled cylindrical body tapering slightly to a wide flat rim, swirled colors of cream, green & brown, impressed mark **176**

Two Marbleized Vases

Vase, 11 1/4" h., square slightly flared base tapering to flat rim, swirled colors of brown, rust, cream & black, very minor glaze nicks on underside of base, impressed "Weller" in small block letters & incised "Weller" directly over impressed mark (ILLUS. right) **110**
Vase, 12 1/2" h., waisted cylindrical body w/swirled colors of tan, brown, maroon, black & grey, 1/4" chip edge of base, impressed "Weller" in small block letters (ILLUS. left) **110**

Matt Green (ca. 1904)

Various shapes with slightly shaded dark green matte glaze and molded with leaves and other natural forms.

Ewer, spherical body molded w/a lizard around the sides below a cylindrical neck w/pinched spout & long angled handle,
rich mottled matte greenish blue glaze, die-stamped "WELLER," 3 1/4" d., 5" h. **600-750**
Jardiniere, six-footed round body w/tapering sides, embossed w/stylized leaves, unmarked, 7 3/4" d., 6 1/4" h. **413**

Matt Green Jardiniere

Jardiniere, bulbous ovoid body w/a wide molded mouth flanked by four small ribbon handles, molded around the shoulder w/stylized florals, unmarked, 7 1/4" h. (ILLUS.) **500-575**
Jardiniere, decorated w/embossed hosta leaves, impressed "Weller" in small block letters & incised "Matt," 8" h. **284**
Jardiniere, wide, cylindrical body w/molded rim flanked by four small loop handles, four wide ribs down the sides to the rounded bottom edge, embossed w/a wide center band of repeating herringbone, unmarked, 11" d., 8 1/4" h. **350-425**
Jardiniere, round body w/relief-molded lines around base & top, buttressed handles, unmarked, 7 x 10 1/2" (minute glaze fleck to rim) **523**

Matte Green Lamp Base

Lamp base, wide bulbous multi-lobed gourd-form body tapering sharply to a slender cylindrical neck w/a molded rim, embossed on each side of the base w/grotesque 'devil' heads, raised on a narrow flaring base w/four 'knob' feet, smooth matte green glaze, complete w/original gas fittings, unmarked, 8 1/2" d., 14 1/2" h. (ILLUS.) **440-600**

Planter, footed cylindrical w/flared rim & side handles, embossed w/stylized roses, unmarked, 7 1/4" d., 5 3/4" h. **358**

Matt Green Planter

Planter, attribution, footed, decorated w/molded landscape w/sheep & flowers, dark green glaze, 6 1/2 x 10 1/2" (ILLUS.) **413**

Vase, 5" h., 3 3/4" d., bulbous base w/cylindrical four-sided twisted neck, unmarked **495**

Vase, 11" h., 10" d., compressed globular lower section on a low foot, broad stovepipe neck, covered in a leathery green to terra cotta matte glaze **375-425**

Vase, 13" h., bulbous ovoid body w/wide molded rim & four twisted handles, embossed w/swirling pattern **990**

Muskota (1915 - late 1920s)
Figural pieces with human figures, birds, animals or frogs. Matte glaze.

Bowl, 5 1/2 x 10", shallow round form w/leaf-shaped rim & center branch handle, figural squirrel w/nut on one end, die-stamped "Weller" **413**

Centerbowl w/attached flower frog, figural turtle w/water lily flower frog, stamped "Weller," 4 3/4 x 10" (restoration to small chip on edge of lily pad & to two feet) **413**

Centerpiece, disk base w/two figural baby chicks on grassy mound, unmarked, 5" h. (repair to beaks of both birds)....................... **165**

Muskota Flower Frog

Flower frog, figural frog emerging from a lotus blossom, unmarked, 4 1/2" h. (ILLUS.) **220**

Flower frog, Fishing Boy, boy seated on rockwork w/original "Weller Muskota Ware" paper label, 6 7/8" h. **330**

Flower frog, figural geese on round footed base, 7" h. x 7" d.. **350**

Muskota Figural Garden Ornament

Garden ornament, Fishing Boy, boy standing on round base, brown pants w/one leg rolled up to knee, light blue shirt & black hat, marked w/half-kiln ink stamp logo, two unobtrusive glazed over chips on base, 20 5/8" h. ((ILLUS.)....................... **6,325**

Model of split rail fence, green & charcoal matte glaze, unmarked, 5" h.......................... **220**

Vase, 7" h., 5 1/2" d., bulbous ovoid body tapering to wide slightly flared rim, decorated w/relief-molded frog & water lily on shaded green matte glaze, stamped "Weller" **880**

Patra (late 1920s-'30s)
Rough orange-peel-like finish with stylized design at the bottom. Matte finish. Middle period.

Patra Jardiniere

Jardiniere, bulbous body, marked "Weller Pottery" in script & "3X" in brown slip, 8 1/2" h. (ILLUS.) **275**

Vase, 4 7/8" h., cylindrical lower body below a rounded flaring upper body w/a narrow molded rim & three-leaf molded designs at the rim, the base tapering to three short pointed feet, polychrome glaze **50**

Patricia (early 1930s)
Glossy pale cream glaze, sometimes tinted, with leaf decoration, swan handles.

Planter, figural swan, white, 6" l., 4" h. **50**

Patricia Vase

Vase, 7" h., 4" d., footed bulbous body w/short wide rolled neck, figural swan neck handles, slightly crystalline green glaze w/lustre effect, marked "Weller Pottery" in script (ILLUS.) 107

Vase, 11 5/8" h., squatty bulbous base w/trumpet neck, relief-molded duck's head on each side at base w/embossed leaves at base & neck, gold, tan & green crystalline glaze 770

Perfecto (early 1900s)
Predominantly sea green, blending into a delicate pink matte finish unglazed painted decoration.

Vase, 7 5/8" h., slender ovoid body w/flat rim, embossed scene of nude sitting on a rock, sea gulls overhead, impressed "Weller" in large block letters & signed "Timberlake" on side near base (tight short line at rim) **2,750**

Bird-decorated Perfecto Vase

Vase, 9 1/2" h., footed cylindrical body tapering to short wide rim, rare carved scene depicting small brown bird perched in a tree of ripe cherries, the background cut back to resemble weathered wood, by Sarah Reid McLaughlin, impressed "Weller" in large block letters & signed "SMcL" on side in black slip (ILLUS.) **3,300**

Roma (1912-late '20s)
Cream-colored ground decorated with embossed floral swags, bands or fruit clusters.

Compote, open, an oblong bowl w/shaped rim & scroll end handles raised on a low pedestal, decorated w/garlands of leaves & small plaques on each side w/bright yellow birds & flowers, unmarked, 11" l., 4 7/8" h. 220

Humidor, cov., octagonal, inset cover w/large knob finial, marked, 7" h. 109

Vase, 6 7/8" h., footed tapering cylinder w/molded ring rim, floral decoration, impressed "Weller" in large block letters 55

Vase, 7" h., cylindrical body w/panels of pine cone decoration in brown & green **143**

Roma Vase

Vase, 9" h., tapering cylinder w/molded ring rim, floral decoration, marked "Weller" in large block letters (ILLUS.) 110

Vase, 10" h., slightly swelled cylindrical body w/a wide flattened rim, a paneled decoration of carved leaves, twisting stems & berries in pale pink & pale green against a bone white ground, marked ... **140-170**

Roma Vase

Vase, 10" h., tapering cylindrical body w/a wide flattened rim, embossed rings around lower body w/paneled decoration of pink dogwood blossoms & leaves, unmarked (ILLUS.) 110

Roma Vase

Vase, 12 3/8" h., tapering cylindrical body
w/four panels of stylized roses, un-
marked (ILLUS.)... **248**
Wall pocket, conical, decorated w/flowers
on a trellis w/bumble bee near rim, cream
ground, stamped "WELLER," on back,
5 5/8" h. **303**
Wall pocket, conical, incised vertical lines &
decorated w/roses & grape cluster near
top, green leaves w/yellow center at
base, cream ground, marked "28" in blue
slip on back, 8 1/4" h. (very minor staining from use & small bruise on one hori-
zontal band at mid body) **165**

Sabrinian (late '20s)
Seashell body with sea horse handle. Pastel col-
ors. Matte finish. Middle period.

Sabrinian Covered Box

Box, cov., square seashell-form sides & lid
w/tall sea horse finial & sea horses on
corners, lid & box marked w/half kiln ink
stamp logo, very minor edge chips to in-
side lip of lid, 8 1/4" h. (ILLUS.)...................... **770**
Console bowl, 2 1/2 x 9"..................................... **195**
Wall pocket, stamp in label **725**

Selma (ca. 1923)
Knifewood line with a high-gloss glaze. Occa-
sionally with peacocks, butterflies, and daisies.
Middle period.

Selma Vase

Vase, 4" h., squatty bulbous body w/wide
flat rim, decorated w/molded daisies &
butterflies, marked "Weller" in large block
letters & "F" in black slip (ILLUS.) **193**
Vase, 5" h., bulbous body w/flat rim, decorated w/goldfinches among wisteria blossoms, impressed "Weller " in large block
letters & "C" painted in brown slip................. **248**
Vase, 5" h., cylindrical w/flat rim, decorated
w/white & yellow daisies................................. **110**

Sicardo (1902-07)
Various shapes with iridescent glaze of metallic
shadings in greens, blues, crimson, purple or cop-
pertone decorated with vines, flowers, stars or free-
form geometric lines.

Candlestick, sharply tapering conical base
below the wide conical socket, small loop
handles from base of socket to sides,
socket w/electric fitting & a small domed
reverse-painted shade, signed **385**
Jardiniere, very wide bulbous body raised
on short arcaded feet, the sides boldly
embossed w/large Moorish arabesques,
tapering to a wide short flaring scalloped
neck, iridescent purple, gold & green
glaze, painted "Weller SICARD" on the
side, 14 1/2" d., 12 1/2" h. **1,500-2,000**
Vase, miniature, 1 7/8" h., squatty bulbous
form w/wide shoulders tapering to closed
rim, in-body loop handles from shoulder
to rim, deep purple ground, impressed
"15"... **330**
Vase, 3 1/4" h., 5 3/4" d., footed wide & low
cushion-form body centered by a short
widely flaring trefoil neck, bright satiny
decoration of gold arabesques against a
lustred green & burgundy ground, signed
on the side **700-800**
Vase, 3 1/2 x 5 3/4", squatty bulbous body
w/wide shoulder tapering to short wide
cylindrical neck, iridescent gold abstract
flowers & leaves, green & purple ground...... **770**

Sicardo Lobed Vase

Vase, 4" h., three-lobe form, signed "Sicard," impressed mark (ILLUS.)................. **1,100**

Vase, 4 1/2" h., bell-shaped body decorated w/leaves & berries against a bronze, blue, green, rose & purple iridescent ground, signed "Sicard Weller".................... **1,380**

Vase, 4 1/2" h., bulbous four-sided body w/square molded rim, decorated w/flowers in green & red iridescent glaze (ILLUS. second from right, below) **880**

Vase, 4 3/4" h., gourd-shaped body, decorated w/chrysanthemum blossoms in iridescent green & purple glaze, glaze drips from rim (ILLUS. far left, below)............ **605**

Vase, 4 3/4" h., ovoid body tapering to a short thick rim, embossed ears of corn on iridescent ground of purple & gold, decorated by Jacques Sicard, signed "Weller Sicard" on the side... **770**

Vase, 5" h., baluster-form, a multicolored iridescent glaze decorated w/mistletoe branches, signed **400-450**

Sicardo Vase

Vase, 5" h., bulbous base below gently tapering conical sides, floral decoration in green & gold iridescent glaze, artist-signed (ILLUS.) **413**

Vase, 5" h., tapering four-sided form, floral decoration in iridescent highlights of gold, purple & rose, signed "Weller Sicard" **550**

Vase, 5 1/2" h., waisted cylindrical body w/swelled shoulder tapering to small flat rim, cloud-like decoration, iridescent blue, green & burgundy glaze, unmarked **605**

Vase, 6" h., bulbous cylindrical body w/swelled shoulder tapering to closed rim, decorated w/berries & leaves in iridescent green & bronze glaze (ILLUS. second from left, below) **990**

Vase, 6 1/4 x 9 1/2", pillow-form, wide rectangular body w/scalloped rim & side ribbon handles, decorated w/arabesques & curlicues, iridescent green ground............. **2,090**

Vase, 6 1/2" h., 4 1/4" d., tapering ovoid body w/a bulbous compressed & closed neck flanked by small loop handles, iridescent gold flowers on a deep purple ground, unmarked **850-1,100**

Vase, 7" h., tall tri-lobed upright undulating body, floral designs on sides, covered in iridescent glaze in shades of green & gold **1,150-1,300**

Vase, 7 1/2" h., tapering cylindrical body w/wide neck & flat rim, decorated w/elaborate iridescent scrollwork, purple & green ground... **633**

Vase, 8 1/2" h., 5 3/4" d., ovoid gourd-form w/wide shoulder & bulbed tapering neck, decorated w/swirling poppies & leaves w/a lustrous gold, blue, green & purple glaze, signed... **2,925**

Vase, 8 5/8" h., wide bulbous ovoid body tapering sharply to a molded flat mouth, incurved loop handles on the sides, decorated w/several snails amid leafy vegetation, base cut "36," glaze flaw from bottom up side 1/2", signed "Weller Sicard," ca. 1905................................... **950-1,100**

Vase, 8 3/4" h., corseted cylindrical body w/lobed base & flared rim, decorated in an Art Nouveau motif, iridescent green & purple glaze, few surface scratches, unmarked (ILLUS. far right, below) **990**

Vase, 9" h., wide ovoid shouldered body tapering to a short rounded neck w/flat rim, decorated w/flowing chrysanthemums & buds against a background of scattered dots, ca. 1904..................................... **2,200-2,600**

Four Sicardo Vases

Vase, 9 1/4" h., expanding cylinder w/rounded shoulders & rolled rim, decorated w/wild violets, iridescent gold, burgundy & green glaze, signed "Weller Sicard" & impressed "6" **935**

Vase, 9 1/2" h., expanding cylinder w/rounded shoulders & rolled rim, a profusion of daisies encircle the body, iridescent gold, blue, burgundy & green glaze, decorated by Jacques Sicard, signed "Sicard Weller" on side (pinhead size glaze flake off rim) **1,650**

Vase, 10 1/8" h., slender, slightly swelled cylindrical body w/short flaring rim, decorated overall w/stylized arrowroot decoration, iridescent glaze, signed "Weller Sicard" on side & bears older paper label which reads "Whitlow Collection," stamped numbers on base are not legible **770**

Vase, 10 1/2" h., tapering ovoid body w/flaring rim, iridescent floral decoration of gold mums w/green highlights against a purple, blue & red ground, signed "Weller Sicard" **1,870**

Vase, 12" h., twisted-form tapering ovoid body w/flat rim, floral decoration in gold, green & blue w/gold, blue & purple iridescent highlights, signed "Weller Sicard" **2,090**

Tall Sicardo Vase

Vase, 13" h., 5 3/4" d., bulbous top w/closed small mouth above tapering cylindrical sides, embossed w/large, tall irises, rich burgundy & gold lustre glaze, unmarked (ILLUS.) **7,700-8,500**

Vase, 14 1/2" h., footed four lobed ovoid body w/twisted cylindrical neck & floriform rim, painted w/daisies in gold on a lustered purple & green ground (restoration to rim) **2,530**

Vase, 14 1/2" h., 7" d., tall ovoid form w/a rounded shoulder centering a short rolled neck, decorated overall w/poppies & vining leaves in celadon & gold on a purple iridescent ground, marked, restored drill hole in base **2,925**

Vase, 15 1/2" h., wide ovoid body tapering to short narrow cylindrical neck w/flared rim, decorated w/iridescent sunflowers & clusters of small circles in green, blue & purple on iridescent red ground (restoration to drill hole at base & rim, glaze flake to interior neck) **2,090**

Vase, 19 1/2" h., 13" d., Art Nouveau style, ovoid body on scroll-molded feet, the sides tapering to a bulbous, pierced rim molded w/whiplash swirls above large pendent blossoms above the relief-molded figures of two swirling Art Nouveau maidens flanked by long scrolls, the body flanked by large, long pierced scrolling handles continuing down to the scrolled feet, gold, green, blue & purple iridescent glaze, signed "Weller - Sicard" **7,700-9,500**

Vase, floor-type, 21 3/4" h., wide ovoid body w/a molded mouth, decorated w/large Art Nouveau stylized poppies against a streaked ground, ca. 1905, signed **12,100**

Silvertone (1928)

Various flowers, fruits or butterflies molded on a pale purple-blue matte pebbled ground.

Silvertone Basket

Basket, fan-shaped w/overhead gnarled branch handle, decorated w/cranberry colored flowers & green leaves, marked w/half kiln ink stamp logo & "3" in black slip, 8 1/2" h. (ILLUS.) **303**

Silvertone Vase

Vase, 6" h., footed squatty bulbous body w/wide flaring rim, decorated w/embossed pink roses & green leaves against a purple ground, ink mark (ILLUS.) **330**

Vase, 6 3/8" h., footed bulbous ovoid body w/wide flaring rim & small loop handles at shoulder, decorated w/relief-molded grape clusters & leaves, full kiln ink stamp (slight roughness to high points) **224**

Vase, 6 1/2" h., footed squatty bulbous body w/wide flaring rim, decorated w/pink & lavender poppies & green leaves against a purple ground, ink mark **413**

Vase, 7" h., gently tapering cylindrical sides w/D-form handles from rim to center of the sides, molded flowers, marked **320**

Vase, 7 1/2" h., footed ovoid fan-shaped w/widely flaring rim, swirled clusters of flowers **345**

Vase, 8 1/4" h., 7 3/4" d., footed, spherical body w/scalloped rim, C-form shoulder handles, embossed w/pink poppies on lavender "hammered" ground **275**

Vase, 10" h., bulbous base w/wide cylindrical neck w/molded rim, D-form handles rising from base to rim, decorated w/red & white embossed flowers on a purple, pink & white ground, original labels **550**

Vase, 11 3/4" h., slender trumpet-form, calla lily decoration in white w/green leaves, pale purple ground, marked & paper label **605**

Wall pocket, conical w/molded floral decoration on multicolored ground, stamp mark, 10" h. (minute bruise to top) **385**

Souevo (1907-10)

Unglazed redware bodies with glossy black interiors. The exterior decorated with black & white American Indian geometric designs.

Basket, hanging-type, w/original chains, 9 1/2" h. **198**

Pitcher, tankard, tall tapering cylindrical body w/a flaring cylindrical neck & rim spout, long D-form handle, decorated down the sides w/stripes of graduated triangles **285**

Souevo Vase

Vase, 7" h., bulbous ovoid body w/short cylindrical neck, decorated w/Native American designs under a cranberry glaze, impressed "Weller" in large block letters (ILLUS.) **413**

Velvetone (late 1920s)

Blended colors of green, pink, yellow, brown, green, matte glaze.

Velvetone Vase

Vase, 11" h., baluster form w/wide slightly flaring cylindrical neck, loop handles, green, orange & yellow mottled matte glaze (ILLUS.) **690**

Warwick (1929)

Modeled rustic background with trees and fruit. Matte finish. Middle period.

Bowl, 3 1/2 x 8 1/2", shallow round form w/end handles **77**

Planter, log-shaped w/twisted branches forming end handles, stamp mark, 12" l. (minor flake to base) **88**

Warwick Planter

Planter & frog cover, bulbous body w/vine handles, half kiln ink stamp logo & artist initialed, 5 1/4" h. (ILLUS.) **358**

Warwick Vase

Vase, 4 1/2" h., two-handled, footed ovoid body tapering to a flared rim flanked by loop handles, half kiln ink stamp logo & "XII" in black slip (ILLUS.) **55**

Wall pocket, 11 1/2" l., half kiln mark **385**

White & Decorated Hudson (1917-34)

A version of the Hudson line usually with dark colored floral designs against a creamy white ground.

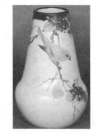

White & Decorated Hudson Vase

Vase, 6" h., inverted pear-shaped body w/narrow cylindrical rim, center decorated w/blue band w/lion & lioness **1,870**

Vase, 6 5/8" h., squatty bulbous base w/tapering cylindrical neck & flat rim, decorated w/multicolored prunus blossoms & a beautifully detailed gold finch on cream ground, impressed "Weller" in large block letters (ILLUS.) **1,100**

Vase, 7" h., fruit blossoms decoration on cream ground **275**

Vase, 8" h., ovoid body w/wide closed rim, black & pale green slip decoration of grapes, grape leaves & vines, cream ground, stamped "Weller" in large block letters **358**

Vase, 8 1/4" h., tapering cylindrical body w/closed rim, hand-thrown w/horizontal lines & decorated w/repeating floral sprays of heavy slip-painted stylized blue flowers, green leaves & narrow green band around rim, cream ground, unmarked **468**

Vase, 8 1/2" h., tapering cylindrical body, heavy slip decoration of multicolored berries & leaves, impressed "Weller" in large block letters... **440**

Vase, 8 5/8" h., cylindrical, decorated w/yellow jonquils & green stems, stamped "Weller" in small block letters.......................... **330**

Vase, 9 3/8" h., bulbous base tapering to wide cylindrical neck, decorated w/mauve & blue Virginia creeper leaves, vines & berries & narrow band near rim & wide band at top portion of base, cream ground, unmarked **523**

Vase, 9 1/2" h., ovoid, decorated w/rose & pink irises w/yellow centers, yellow to grey ground... **264**

White & Decorated Hudson Vase

Vase, 9 1/2" h., ovoid w/short round shoulder tapering to flat neck, blue band at shoulder w/multicolored floral decoration, black band around neck, impressed mark (ILLUS.) **330**

Vase, 10" h., overall floral decoration on white ground **550**

Vase, bud, 10" h., slender waisted cylinder w/flaring base, decorated w/trailing blossoms on grey to glossy pink ground.............. **325**

Vase, 10" h., 5 1/4" d., octagonal, decorated w/stylized blossoms in black, burgundy & grey in slip relief on a cream ground, die-stamped "WELLER".......................... **275-350**

Vase, 11 1/8" h., hexagonal w/Oriental prunus blossoms decoration in red, yellow, green & black on cream ground, impressed "Weller" in large block letters.......... **344**

Vase, 13" h., footed, tall tapering cylindrical body decorated w/two sparrows perched on a branch, floral band around top (several chips to base, partly in making) **1,210**

Wall pocket, conical, decorated w/h.p. pink cherry blossom, die-stamped "Weller," 4 x 9"... **605**

Wall pocket, decorated w/roses, 10" h. **450-500**

Woodcraft (1917)

Rustic designs simulating the appearance of stumps, logs and tree trunks. Some pieces are adorned with owls, squirrels, dogs and other animals. Matte finish.

Basket, hanging-type, unmarked, 9" d., 4" h... **220**

Woodcraft Basket

Basket, figural acorn w/overhead branch handle, marked "Weller" in large block letters, 9 1/2" h. (ILLUS.)............................... **358**

Bowl, 6 1/4" d., 3" h., footed, deep gently flaring form w/scalloped rim, relief-molded squirrel decoration, marked in black slip "29".. **101**

Bowl, 4 1/2" h., shallow bulbous form w/oak leaves & acorns around the rim & figural squirrel seated on rim eating a nut, unmarked (repair to oak leaves on rim opposite squirrel)... **193**

Bowl, 5 7/8" h., 2 7/8" h., footed round body w/flared sides & scalloped rim, decorated w/embossed squirrels & trees, unmarked **140**

Woodcraft Bowl With Squirrel

Bowl, 5 1/2 x 7", shallow bulbous form w/oak leaves & acorns around the rim & figural squirrel seated on rim eating a nut, ink stamp mark "Weller Ware," full kiln logo & "H" in black slip, two small chips to oak leaves (ILLUS.)....................................... **220**

Candlelamps, footed tree trunk-form w/red berry decoration, branch handles & molded leaves around top, brown & green ground, original candlelamp holder & old bulbs, overall 17" h., pr. (one w/tiny chip to leaf) **825**

Candlestick, double, modeled as an owl perched at the top of an apple tree between candle nozzles, 8" w., 13 1/2" h.. **325-350**

Compote, deep rounded & flaring sides supported by figural branches on tree trunk-form pedestal, molded leaves around rim, earth tones w/red berries, impressed mark, 10" h. **468**

Flower frog, figural lobster **120-170**

Woodcraft Figural Flower Frog

Flower frog, figural crab, small nick on left hind leg, 5" l., 1 3/8" h. (ILLUS.) **110**

Woodcraft Jardiniere

Jardiniere, log form w/woodpecker on side, impressed "Weller" in large block letters on bottom, short tight line at rim, 6" h. (ILLUS.) **358**

Lamp, table-type, w/double branched tree trunk & two electric lights w/lamp shades, owl sitting in center of branched fixtures, 15" h. **499**

Lawn ornament, figural, model of a large squirrel seated & holding an acorn, mottled brown & green, stamped "WELLER POTTERY," 11 1/2" w., 11 3/4" h. (restoration to ears, tight hairline in tail) ... **2,000-2,500**

Model of dogs, two brown to yellow hunting dogs in grasses, base in earth tones & green, impressed block mark, 11" l., 7" h. **715**

Mug, cylindrical tree trunk form w/three small molded foxes peeking out of trunk opening, double loop branch handle, large loop above smaller loop, small flake off nose of one fox, 6" h. **193**

Planter, log-form w/three embossed foxes on front, crossed branch handles across top, impressed "Weller" in large block letters, 5 3/4" h. **220**

Planter, log-form w/molded leaf & narrow strap handle at top center, 11" l., 4 1/4" h. **75-100**

Vase, 12" h., smooth tree trunk form w/molded leafy branch around rim & down sides w/hanging purple plums...... **175-225**

Woodcraft Double Bud Vase

Vase, bud, 8" h., cylindrical tree trunk-forms connected by an arch of branches & molded red berries & green leaves (ILLUS.) **152**

Vase, 9" h., chalice shape w/three branch handles rising from base, impressed mark **187**

Vase, bud, 10 1/4" h., cylindrical tree trunk form, hollow branch opening in front, flared base & molded apples, branches & leaves, impressed "Weller" in large block letters... **124**

Vase, 13" h., waisted cylindrical tree trunk form w/relief-molded branch, apple & leaves down the front............................... **250-300**

Wall hanging, model of a large climbing squirrel, matte brown & green glaze, black ink kiln mark, 4 3/4" w., 13 1/2" h. **1,200-1,500**

Woodcraft Squirrel Wall Pocket

Wall pocket, conical w/applied figural squirrel, 9 1/2" h. (ILLUS.) **316**

Wall pocket, relief-molded log w/flowers & berries, marked "Weller" in large block letters on back, 9" h. (minor glaze flakes)..... **193**

Woodcraft Wall Pocket

Wall pocket, relief-molded purple plums & green leaves against cylindrical tree branch body, openings at ends of branches, 9" l. (ILLUS.) **495**

Zona (about 1920)

Red apples and green leaves on brown branches all on a cream-colored ground; some pieces with molded florals or birds with various glazes. A line of children's dishes was also produced featuring hand-painted or molded animals. This is referred to as the "Zona Baby Line."

Pitcher, 8" h., wide cylindrical form w/flat rim & high arched spout, squared handle, Kingfisher decoration, blue & grey................ **344**

Plate, 8 7/8" d., Apple patt., pairs of red apples & green leaves around the border on brown branches against the ivory ground **44**

Umbrella stand, tapering cylindrical body w/embossed figures of ladies holding flower garlands, unmarked, 10 " d., 20" h. (three small chips to base & some glaze misses & glazed over chips) **1,540**

Wheatley Pottery

Wheatley Marks

Thomas J. Wheatley was one of the original founders of the art pottery movement in Cincinnati, Ohio in the early 1880s. In 1879 the Cincinnati Art Pottery was formed and after some legal problems it operated under the name T.J. Wheatley & Company. Their production featured Limoges-style hand-painted decorations and most pieces were carefully marked and often dated.

In 1882 Wheatley disassociated himself from the Cincinnati Art Pottery and opened another pottery which was destroyed by fire in 1884. Around 1900 Wheatley finally resumed making art pottery in Cincinnati and in 1903 he founded the Wheatley Pottery Company with a new partner, Isaac Kahn.

The new pottery from this company featured colored matte glazes over relief work designs and green, yellow and blue were the most often used colors. There were imitations of the well-known Grueby Pottery wares as well as artware, garden pottery and architectural pieces. Artwork was apparently not made much after 1907. This plant was destroyed by fire in 1910 but was rebuilt and run by Wheatley until his death in 1917. Wheatley artware was generally unmarked except for a paper label.

Bowl, 6" d., 2 1/2" h., low upright corseted sides w/a wide incurved rim, embossed around the sides w/a band of short upright pointed wide leaves, thick matte green glaze, illegible mark **$165**

Chamberstick, wide round dished base w/heavy molded leaves tapering up the center short shaft molded w/buds under the rolled socket rim, a scrolled loop handle at one side of the base, overall dark green matte glaze, 6" d., 3 1/2" h. (small repaired rim chip) **605**

Teco-style Wheatley Jardiniere

Jardiniere, wide thick ovoid body w/a thick squared rim band joining four heavy squared buttresses down the sides, feathered matte green glaze, in the style of Teco, small chip on edge of foot, 9" d., 7" h. (ILLUS.) **920**

Jardiniere, wide bulbous base tapering to tall wide cylindrical neck w/incurved-rim, four buttressed handles from rim to base, covered in a leathery matte green glaze, 7 3/4" d., 7" h. (nearly invisible restoration to drilled base hole) **3,080**

Wheatley Lamp with Buttresses

Lamp base, thick slightly tapering cylindrical body w/a wide squared rim band issuing four thick squared buttresses down the side, a copper tube running through the lower buttresses, fine feathered matte green glaze, unmarked, 8 1/2" d., 11" h. (ILLUS.) **575**

Lamp base, wide tapering double gourd-form body w/four heavy squared buttress handles from the top rim to the base, leathery matte green glaze, w/original oil font insert, several burst bubbles, incised "WP - 672," 10 1/2" d., 11 1/2" h. (ILLUS. back left, top next page) **2,813**

Lamp base, wide round flaring base tapering to a slender baluster-form standard, embossed oblong leaves around the foot w/the stems continuing up the standard, fine leathery matte green glaze, unmarked, 10" d., 16 1/4" h. **1,575**

Wheatley Octagonal Planter

Planter, octagonal, sharply canted sides to rolled rim, each panel decorated w/relief-molded woven design in a buff terra cotta, impressed mark, minor chips, 24" d., 14" h. (ILLUS.) **770**

Vase, 5 1/2" h., 7" d., wide bulbous form w/a wide rounded shoulder centered by a wide flat molded mouth, deeply embossed w/a band of wide ribbed upright leaves alternating w/small buds, thick & frothy matte green glaze, incised "W-685" **1,320**

Wheatly Lamp Base and Vases

Vase, 6" h., 5" d., wide ovoid body tapering slightly to a wide flat mouth, embossed w/large upright arrowhead leaves around the sides, matte green glaze, incised "WP," several burst bubbles (ILLUS. front left with lamp base) **788**

Vase, 6 5/8" h., 4" w., rectangular form decorated w/a Limoges-style branch of white apple blossoms on a glossy dark blue ground, incised marks including "T J W Co, Pat. Sep 28," ca. 1880 (minor scratches) **144**

Vase, 7 1/4" h., 7 1/4" d., squatty bulbous body molded around the lower half w/a band of overlapping rounded, pointed leaves, the sides tapering to a cylindrical neck w/narrow molded rings, frothy light green & amber glaze, signed "WP" (several burst glaze bubbles) **900**

Vase, 7 1/4" h., 9" d., a deep thick rounded form w/a thick squared flat rim band issuing four heavy squared buttresses down the sides, flower dead-matte green glaze, marked "61" (ILLUS. front right with lamp base) **1,800**

Large & Small Wheatley Vases

Vase, 6 3/4" h., 5" d., ovoid shouldered form w/a short, wide neck & flat rim, molded w/a continuous vertical band of wide tapering ribbed leaves, mottled matte green glaze, several clay pimples, mark partially obscured (ILLUS. center) **956**

Wheatly Vase with Upright Leaves

Vase, 8 1/2" h., slightly ovoid body tapering to a wide flat mouth, the sides molded w/alternating upright pointed & rounded leaves, matte green glaze, several small chips on leaf edges (ILLUS.) **978**

Wheatley Vase with Tendril Handles

Vase, 10 1/4" h., 5" d., footed baluster-form body w/the shoulder issuing four long scrolled tendril-like handles to the rim, matte green glaze, marked (ILLUS.) **1,035**

Wheatley Vase with Buttress Feet

Vase, 10 1/2" h., four heavy square buttress feet tapering up the wide slightly tapering cylindrical sides, wide molded mouth, overall matte green glaze, illegible mark, several small glaze chips on feet (ILLUS.) **1,438**

Wheatley Vase with Incised Design

Vase, 11 1/2" h., slightly swelled cylindrical form w/a wide bulbed ring around the middle, wide flat rim, mottled matte green glaze w/incised geometric design, un-marked (ILLUS.) **978**

Large Tapering Wheatley Vase

Vase, 11 1/2" h., 9 1/4" d., small rectangular feet supporting the wide tapering cylindrical body w/a wide, thick molded rim w/four projecting blocks above buttresses, pulled matte green glaze, base pierced w/ five drainage holes in the making, some minor glaze flecks, chips to feet, signed (ILLUS.)................................. **2,070**

Vase, 12" h., 7 1/2" d., large slightly tapering cylindrical form w/a thick rolled rim above a recessed neck band w/four small buttress handles, embossed around the sides w/large, rounded veined leaves alternating w/buds on the rim, curdled medium matte green glaze, couple of burst bubbles, marked "WP - C13" (ILLUS. back right with lamp base)... **2,700**

Vase, 12 1/2" h., 6" d., simple ovoid body tapering to a short cylindrical neck, the sides molded w/tall arrowroot leaves, medium matte green glaze, mark obscured (several clay pimples & burst bubbles) **1,800**

Wheatley Grueby-style Vase

Vase, 12 1/2" h., 9" d., wide baluster-form w/wide cushion neck, in the style of Grueby's Kendrick vase, molded around the sides & neck w/wide leaves, fine frothy matte light brown glaze, small chip to edge of neck, remnants of paint (ILLUS.) **3,450**

Wheatley "Kendrick" Vase

Vase, 13" h., 9" d., large ovoid body w/a wide squatty bulbed neck w/incurved rim, molded around the sides w/wide tapering ribbed leaves w/matching shorter leaves around the neck, leathery green matte glaze, two small chips on side decoration, marked, after a model by G.P. Kendrick (ILLUS.) **3,938**

Teco-form Wheatley Vase

Vase, 14 1/4" h., 8" d., based on a Teco form, a bulbous bottom tapering slightly to wide cylindrical body w/a four-scallop ring issuing four vine-like handles down the sides, frothy matte green glaze, incised "WP - 615" (ILLUS.) **2,875**

Vase, 14 1/4" h., 8" d., footed bulbous base narrowing slightly to a tall, wide cylindrical neck flanked by four arched & webbed handles from the rim to the shoulder, leathery matte green glaze, incised "WP" (several burst bubbles, few glaze chips at rim, grinding chips to base) .. **3,150**

Large Wheatley Vase with Cubes

Vase, 14 1/2" h., 9 1/4" h., footed tapering slightly ovoid body molded w/tall ribbed & pointed leaves up the sides alternating w/shorter leaves topped by projecting blocks embossed on the front w/small swastikas, frothy matte green glaze, several burst bubbles, touch-ups to two corners of cubes & tip of one leaf, no visible mark (ILLUS.) **1,610**

Vase, 18 1/2" h., 10 1/2" d., tall paneled ovoid form w/a short rolled neck, each panel molded w/a tall serrated & veined leaf alternating w/a stem topped by a three-petal blossom, leathery matte green glaze, two glaze chips on ribs, incised "WP" (ILLUS. right with small vase) .. **3,938**

Vase, 20" h., 10" d., the tall swelled cylindrical body tapering to a slightly bulbed cylindrical neck flanked by pointed tall buttress handles down the side, each w/a half-round cut-out, the body molded w/tall ribbed & pointed leaves alternating w/stylized blossom buds around the neck, dark leathery matte green glaze, mark obscured, long grinding chip on base (ILLUS. left with small vase) **4,500**

Wall pocket, half-round body composed of three wide, tapering leaf-form panels curled in at the top & alternating w/buds, a low arched backplate w/hanging hole, curdled medium matte green glaze, unmarked, 9 1/4" w., 8" h. **675**

Zsolnay

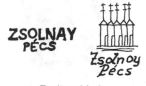

Zsolnay Marks

This pottery was made in Pecs, Hungary, in a factory founded in 1862 by Vilmos Zsolnay. Utilitarian earthenware was originally produced but by the turn of the century ornamental Art Nouveau style wares with bright colors and lustre decoration were produced and these wares are especially sought today. Currently Zsolnay pieces are being made in a new factory.

Basket, egg-shaped, reticulated, yellow, blue & pink, 6 1/2 x 8 1/2" **$795**

Bowl-vase, round footring below the squatty rounded body w/incurved sides pinched in at the rim on one side & molded in relief w/a large moth in iridescent green, gold, purple & blue on a deep red glossy ground, molded factory mark & "6383 - M" on the base, ca. 1901, 3" h....... **1,610**

Center bowl, long oblong boat-shaped form, the top of one end w/a standing figural polar bear peering into water that forms the walls of the piece, waves & fish in relief, iridescent purple, blue & amber glaze w/matte lustre, convex round trademark stamp, early 20th c., chips on base, minor wear, 6 1/2 x 19", 9" h. (ILLUS., below) **690**

Pitcher, cov., the pierced body enamel-decorated & molded in relief w/flowers & leaves, early 20th c., 12 1/4" h. **403**

Rare Zsolnay Umbrella Stand

Umbrella stand, tall slightly waisted cylindrical form w/rolled rim, the sides decorated w/dark golden iridescent fish swimming in iridescent swirls of dark blue, purple & gold, impressed "Zsolnay - Pecs - 4036 - 21," ca. 1900, 26 3/4" h. (ILLUS.).. **14,400**

Vase, 10" h., 5" d., tall slender ovoid body tapering to a flat rim, decorated w/ruby red pomegranate design against a nacreous "Eocin" ground, die-stamped & wax-resist mark **1,760**

Vase, 10 1/4" h., Art Nouveau style, elongated ovoid form w/extended neck & handle, the surface in brilliant orangish red, fiery purples & gold w/floral & leaf designs & a sunset over a tree-lined landscape, raised round stamp trademark, impressed "5572 M 23," ca. 1900.... **1,610**

Zsolnay Iridescent Vase

Vase, 11" h., slightly swelled cylindrical lower body below a bulbed upper body & angled shoulder to the short flared neck, iridescent gold glaze w/purple & blue marbleized striations, impressed "Zsolnay - 7595" & gilt stamp mark, early 20th c. (ILLUS.)` **460**

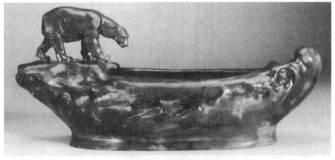

Zsolnay Center Bowl with Polar Bear

GLOSSARY OF SELECTED ART POTTERY TERMS

Bas relief—Literally "low relief," referring to lightly molded decorations on ceramic pieces.

Bisquit—Unglazed pottery or porcelain left undecorated or sometimes trimmed with colors. Also known as bisque.

Bowl-vase—A deep bulbous bowl-form vase, often with a fairly small rim opening.

Buttress—A heavy angular handle that forms a thick supporting rib down the sides of a piece. Named for the 'flying buttresses' used in early Gothic architecture.

Closed rim—A rim on a vase or bowl which curves in or downward.

Crackled glaze—A glaze with an intentional network of fine lines produced by uneven contracting of the glaze during firing. First popular on Chinese wares.

Crazing—The fine network of cracks in a glaze produced by uneven contracting of the glaze during firing or later reheating of a piece during usage. An unintentional defect usually found on earthenwares.

Crystalline glaze—A glaze containing fine crystals resulting form the presence of mineral salts in the mixture. It was a popular glaze on American art pottery of the late 19th and early 20th century.

Flambé glaze—A special type of glaze featuring splashed or streaked deep reds and purples, often dripping over another base color. Popular with some American art pottery makers but also used on porcelain wares.

Glaze—The general term for a vitreous (glass-like) coating fired on to pottery and porcelain to produce an impervious surface and protect underglaze decoration.

Jardiniere—A French term for a planter, usually a wide or deep bulbous shape.

Mission Ware—A decorative line of pottery developed by the Niloak Pottery of Benton, Arkansas. It featured variously colored clays swirled together and was used to produce such decorative pieces as vases and candlesticks.

Mouth—The top rim of a ceramic piece.

Pilgrim flask vase—A vase in the form of an ancient pilgrim flask, a flattened round body with a short neck and small loop handles at the shoulder. Sometimes called a moon flask since it resembles a full moon.

Pillow vase—A form of vase designed to resemble a flattened round or oblong pillow. Generally an upright form with flattened sides. A similar form to a pilgrim flask vase.

Porcelain—The general category of translucent, vitrified ceramics first developed by the Chinese and later widely produced in Europe and America. Hard-paste is 'true' porcelain, white soft-paste is an artificial version developed to imitate hard-paste using other ingredients. Soft-paste was only produced on a limited scale in the late 18th century.

Pottery—The very broad category of ceramics produced from various types of clay. It includes redware, yellowware, stoneware and various earthenwares. It is generally fired at a much lower temperature than porcelain.

Sang-de-boeuf—A French term literally meaning 'ox blood,' it refers to a deep red glaze produced with copper oxide. It was first produced by the Chinese and imitated by European and American potters in the late 19th and early 20th century.

Sgrafitto—An Italian-inspired term for decorative designs scratched or cut through a layer of clay slip before firing. Gener-ally used on earthenware forms and especially with the Pennsylvania-German potters of America.

Slip—The liquid form of clay, often used to decorate earthenware pieces in a process known as slip-trailing or slip-quilling.

Standard glaze—The most common form of glazing used on Rookwood Pottery pieces. It is a clear, shiny glaze usually on pieces decorated with florals or portraits against a dark shaded background.

Stoneware—A class of hard, high-fired pottery usually made from a dense grey clay and most often decorated with a salt glaze. American 19th century stoneware was often decorated with slip-quilled or hand-brushed cobalt blue decorations.

Vellum glaze—A Rookwood glaze with a satiny matte finish, often used on pieces with landscape scenes.

APPENDIX I

COLLECTOR GROUPS

American Ceramic Circle
520 – 16th St.
Brooklyn, NY 11215

American Art Pottery Association
P.O. Box 834
Westport, MA 02790-0697

Amphora Collectors Club
129 Bathurst St.
Toronto, Ontario, CANADA M5V
   2R2

National Association of Arkansas
   Pottery Collectors
2006 Beckenham Cove
Little Rock, AR 72212

Clarice Cliff Collector's Club
Fantasque House
Tennis Drive, The Park
Nottingham, NG1 1AE ENGLAND

Dedham Pottery Collectors Society
248 Highland St.
Dedham, MA 02026-5833

Delfware Collectors Assoc. (Gouda)
P.O. Box 670673
Marietta, GA 30066

Frankoma Family Collectors Assoc.
P.O. Box 32571
Oklahoma City, OK 73123-0771

Stangl/Fulper Collectors Club
P.O. Box 538
Flemington, NJ 08822

Minnesota Art Pottery Association
10120 – 23rd Ave.
Minneapolis, MN 55441

Moorcroft Collectors Club
Sandback Road
Burslem, Stoke-on-Trent,
   ENGLAND ST6 2DG

North Dakota Pottery Collectors
   Society
P.O. Box 14
Beach, ND 58621-0014

North American Torquay Society
214 N. Ronda Rd.
McHenry, IL 60050

Pewabic Pottery
10125 E. Jefferson Ave.
Detroit, MI 48214

Pottery Lovers Reunion
4969 Hudson Dr.
Stow, OH 44224

San Francisco Ceramic Circle
P.O. Box 15163
San Francisco, CA 94115

Van Briggle Collectors Society
600 S. 21st St.
Colorado Springs, CO 80901

APPENDIX II

MUSEUMS & LIBRARIES WITH ART POTTERY COLLECTIONS

Cincinnati Art Museum
Eden Park
Cincinnati, OH 45202

(Clewell) Jesse Besser Museum
491 Johnson St.
Alpena, MI 49707

Cowan Pottery Museum
Rocky River Public Library
1600 Hampton Rd.
Rocky River, OH 44116-2699

Dedham Historical Society
612 High St.
Dedham, MA 02027-0215

Everson Museum of Art
401 Harrison St.
Syracuse, NY 13202-3019

Jones Museum of Glass & Ceramics
35 Douglas Mountain Road
East Sebago, ME 04029

Newcomb Art Gallery
1229 Broadway
New Orleans, LA 70118

Ohio Ceramic Center
The Ohio Historical Society
P.O. Box 200
Crooksville, OH 43731

Ohr/O'Keefe Museum of Art
136 G. E. Ohr. St.
Biloxi, MS 39530

Museum of Overbeck Art Pottery
33 W. Main St.
Cambridge City, IN 47327

Roseville Historical Society
91 Main St.
Roseville, OH 43777

Zanesville Art Center
620 Military Rd.
Zanesville, OH 43701

GENERAL COLLECTIONS

The Bayou Bend Collection
#1 Wescott
Houston, TX

Greenfield Village and The Henry Ford
Museum
Oakwood Blvd.
Dearborn, MI 48121

The Margaret Woodbury Strong
Museum
700 Allen Creek Rd.
Rochester, NY 14618

APPENDIX III

SPECIALIZED ART POTTERY AUCTIONEERS AND SHOWS

Auctioneers Specializing in Art Pottery

Cincinnati Art Galleries
225 E. Sixth St.
Cincinnati, OH 45202
(513) 381-2128
e-mail: info@cincinnatiartgalleries.com
www.cincinnatiartgalleries.com

David Rago Arts & Crafts
9 So Main St.
Lambertville, NJ 08530
(609) 397-9374
www.ragoarts.com

Treadway Gallery
2029 Madison Road
Cincinnati, OH 45208
(513) 321-6742
e-mail: treadway2029@earthlink.net
www.treadwaygallery.com

*General Auctions
offering some Art Pottery*

Christie's
502 Park Ave.
New York, NY 10022
(212) 546-1000

Jackson's Auctioneers & Appraisers
P.O. Box 50613
Cedar Falls, IA 50613
(319) 277-2256

Skinner, Inc
357 Main St.
Bolton, MA 01740
(508) 779-6241

Sotheby's
1334 York Ave.
New York, NY 10021
(212) 606-7000

Art Pottery Shows

American Art Pottery Association Convention
    & Show - April
Patti Bourgeois, AAPA Secretary
P.O. Box 834

Westport, MO 20790-0697
www.AmArtPot.org.

American Pottery, Earthenware & China
    Show
Norm Haas, Manager
264 Clizbe Road
Quincy, MI 49082
(517) 639-8537
Illinois Bldg., State Fairgrounds
Springfield, IL - September

Pottery Lovers Reunion Pottery Show
Jen Stofft, Manager
45 - 12th St.
Tell City, IN 47586
(812) 547-5707
Zanesville, OH area - July

Pottery Show - California
Penelope Cloutier, Manager
Glendale Civic Auditorium
1401 No. Verdugo Rd.
Glendale, CA
(707) 865-1576
October each year

Bay Area Pottery Show
Martha & Steve Sanford, Managers
Santa Clara County Fairgrounds
344 Tully Rd.
San Jose, CA 95111
(408) 978-8408
February each year

Los Angeles Pottery Show
Ken Stalcup, Manager
The Pasadena Center Conference Bldg.
300 E. Green St.
Pasadena, CA
(909) 864-1304
February each year

Pottery Fest
Don Gill - Patti Bourgeois, Managers
Maitland Civic Center
Near Orlando, FL
(508) 679-5910
February

ART POTTERY SELECT BIBLIOGRAPHY

General References

Eidelberg, Martin, editor. *From Our Native Clay – Art Pottery From The Collections of The American Ceramic Arts Society.* New York, New York: The American Ceramic Arts Society, 1987.

Evans, Paul. *Art Pottery of the United States.* New York, New York: Feingold & Lewis Publishing Group, 1987.

Henzke, Lucile. *American Art Pottery.* New York, New York: Thomas Nelson, Inc. 1970.

Henzke, Lucile. *Art Pottery of America.* Exton, Pennsylvania: Schiffer Publishing, Ltd., 1982.

Kovel, Ralph and Terry. *The Kovels' Collector's Guide to American Art Pottery.* New York, New York: Crown Publishers, 1974.

Cowan

Saloff, Tim and Jamie. *The Collector's Encyclopedia of Cowan Pottery.* Paducah, Kentucky: Collector Books, 1994.

Fulper

Hibel, John and Carole Goldman Hibel and Robert DeFalco and Dave Rago. *The Fulper Book.* Lambertville, New Jersey: Dave Rago, undated.

Hampshire

Pappas, Joan and A. Harold Kendall. *Hampshire Pottery manufactured by J. S. Taft & Company, Keene, New Hampshire.* Manchester, Vermont: Forward's Color Productions, Inc., 1971.

Hampshire Ware – A Portfolio of Pottery. Catalog reprint. Keene, New Hampshire: Towar Arnold, 1971.

Newcomb College

Poesch, Jessie. *Newcomb Pottery: An Enterprise for Southern Women.* Exton, Pennsylvania: Schiffer Publishing, Ltd., 1984.

Niloak

Gifford, David Edwin. *The Collector's Encyclopedia of Niloak.* Paducah, Kentucky: Collector Books, 1993.

Niloak Pottery Catalog (reprint). Dumas, Arkansas: Kenneth Mauney, 1971.

North Dakota School of Mines

Barr, Margaret Libby and Robert Barr and Donald Miller. *University of North Dakota Pottery – The Cable Years.* Grand Forks, North Dakota: self-published, 1977.

Rookwood

Cummins, Virginia Raymond. *Rookwood Pottery Potpourri.* Silver Spring, Maryland: Nothing New, 1980

Ellis, Anita J. *The Collectors Series – Rookwood Pottery* – Video program adapted from "Rookwood Pottery – The Glorious Gamble." Sarasota, Florida: Award Video and Film Distributors.

Peck, Herbert. *The Book of Rookwood Pottery.* New York, New York: Bonanza Books, 1968.

Peck, Herbert. *The Second Book of Rookwood Pottery.* Tucson, Arizona: self-published, 1985.

Roseville

Bassett, Mark. *Introducing Roseville Pottery.* Atglen, Pennsylvania: Schiffer Publishing, Ltd., 2001.

Bomm, Jack and Nancy. *Roseville In All Its Splendor.* Gas City, Indiana: L-W Book Sales, 1998.

Huxford, Sharon and Bob. *The Collectors Encyclopedia of Roseville Pottery, First Series.* Paducah, Kentucky: Collector Books, 1980.

Huxford, Sharon and Bob. *The Collectors Encyclopedia of Roseville Pottery, Second Series.* Paducah, Kentucky: Collector Books, 1980.

Teco

Darling, Sharon S. *Chicago Ceramics and Glass, An Illustrated History From 1871 to 1933.* Chicago, Illinois: The Chicago Historical Society, 1980.

Darling, Sharon S. *Teco – Art Pottery of The Prairie School.* Erie, Pennsylvania: Erie Art Museum, 1989.

Van Briggle

Bogue, Dorothy McGraw. *The Van Briggle Story.* Colorado Springs, Colorado: self-published, 1976.

Carlton, Carol and Jim. *Collector's Encyclopedia of Colorado Pottery.* Paducah, Kentucky: Collector Books, 1994.

Nelson, Scott H. and Lois K. Crouch, Euphemia B. Demmin and Robert Wyman Newton. *A Collector's Guide to Van Briggle Pottery.*

Sasicki, Richard and Josie Fania. *The Collector's Encyclopedia of Van Briggle Art Pottery.* Paducah, Kentucky: Collector Books, 1993.

Weller

Huxford, Sharon and Bob. *The Collectors Encyclopedia of Weller Pottery.* Paducah, Kentucky: Collector Books, 1979.

McDonald, Ann Gilbert. *All About Weller, A History and Collector's Guide to Weller Pottery, Zanesville, Ohio.* Marietta, Ohio: Antique Publications, 1989.

English and European Art Pottery

Bartlett, John A. *British Ceramic Art, 1870-1940.* Atglen, Pennsylvania: Schiffer Publishing, Ltd., 1993.

Bergesen, Victoria. *Encyclopedia of British Art Pottery, 1870-1920.* London, England: Barrie & Jenkins, 1991.

Coysh, A. W. *British Art Pottery.* Rutland, Vermont: Charles E. Tuttle Company, 1976.

Godden, Geoffrey A. *British Pottery, An Illustrated Guide.* New York, New York: Clarkson N. Potter, Inc., 1975.

Schwartzman, Paulette. *A Collector's Guide to European and American Art Pottery.* Paducah, Kentucky: Collector Books, 1978.

Watson, Howard and Pat. *Collecting Clarice Cliff.* London, England: Kevin Francis Publishing, Ltd., 1991.

Watson, Howard and Pat. *The Colourful World of Clarice Cliff.* London, England: Kevin Francis Publishing, Ltd., 1992.

AMERICAN & EUROPEAN ART POTTERY INDEX